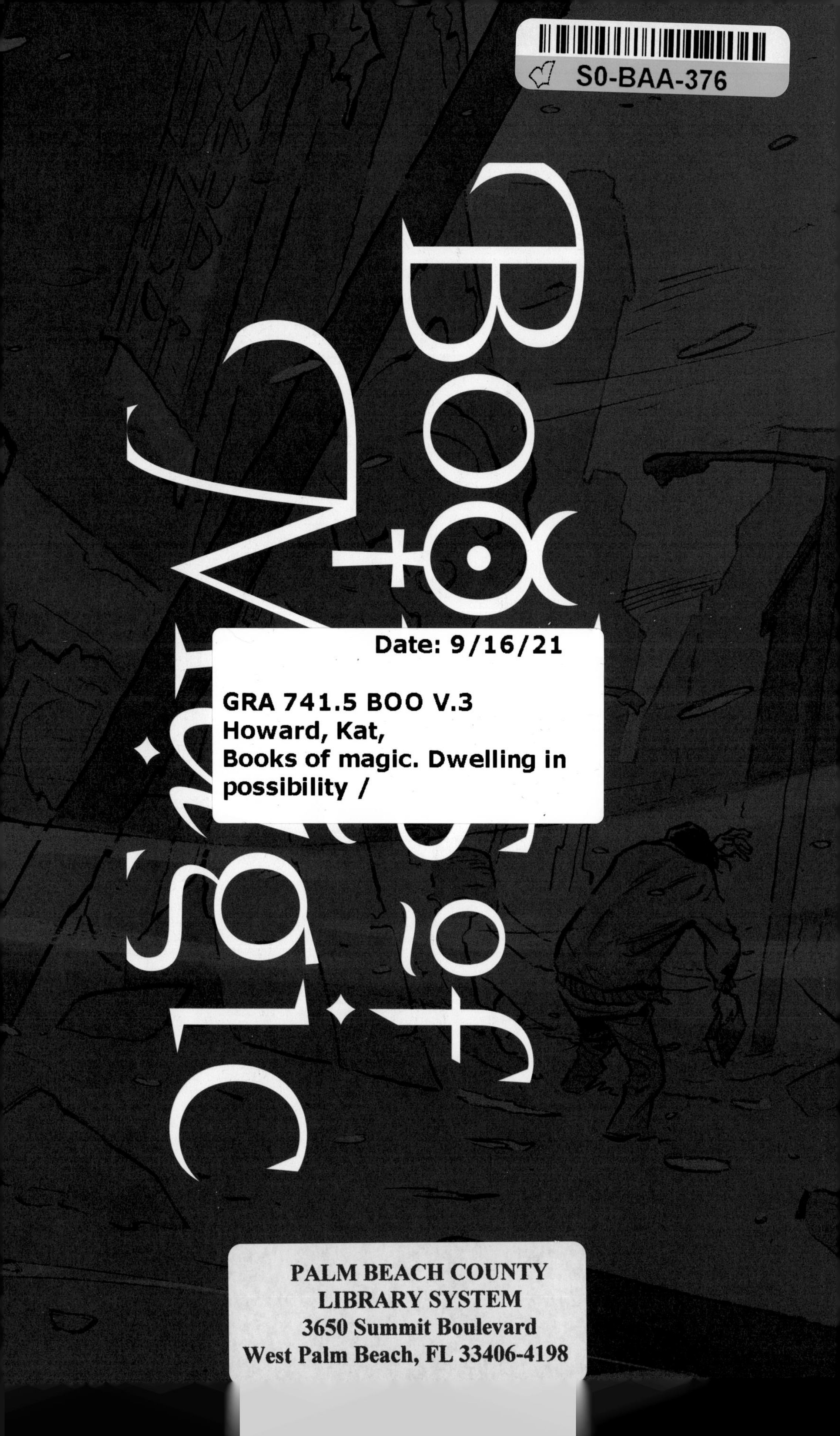
Books of Magic

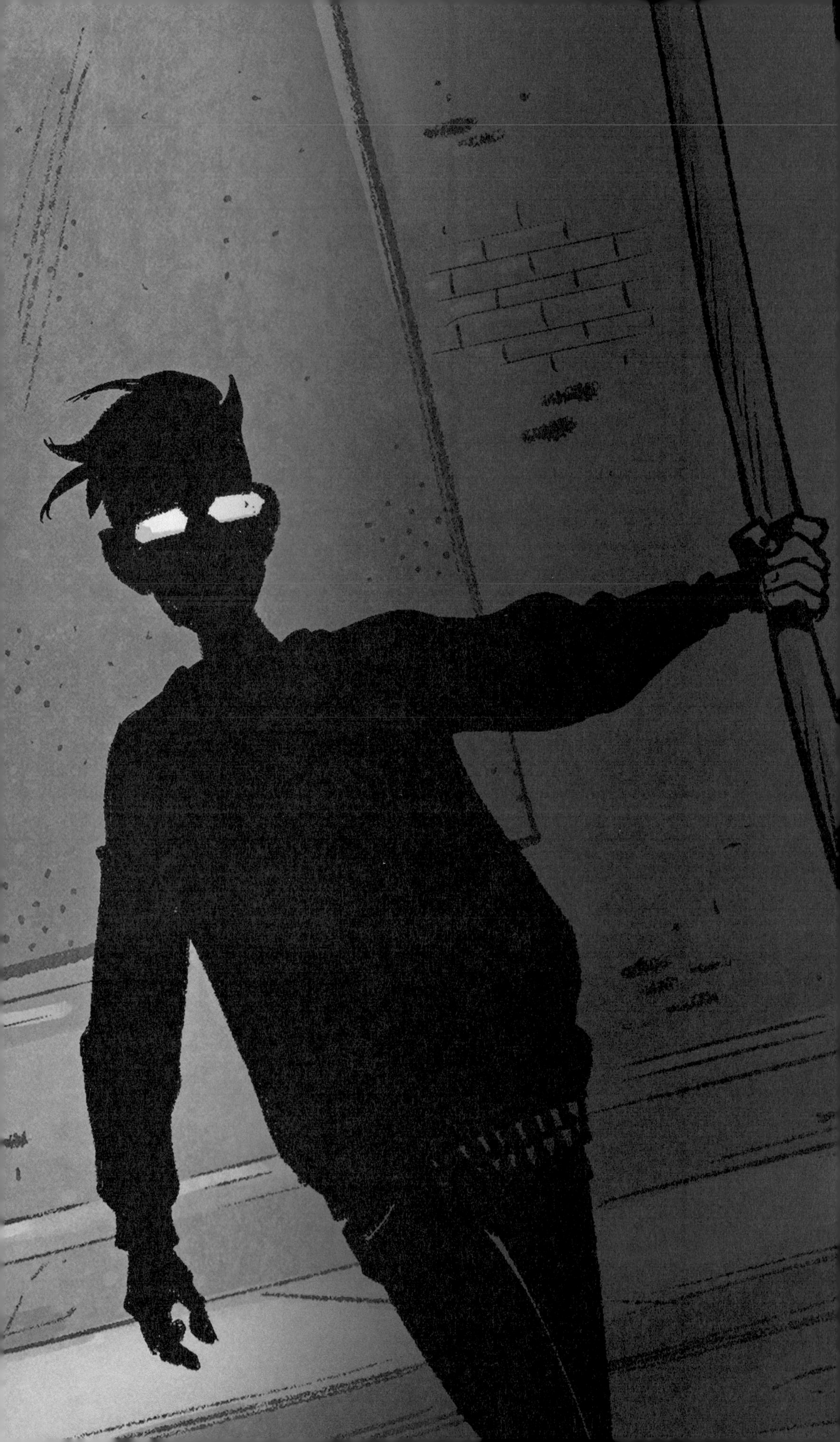

Books of Magic

VOLUME THREE

Dwelling in Possibility

WRITTEN BY
Kat Howard
David Barnett
Simon Spurrier

ART BY
Tom Fowler
Craig Taillefer

COLORS BY
Jordan Boyd
Marissa Louise
Brian Reber

LETTERS BY
Todd Klein

COLLECTION COVER ART AND ORIGINAL SERIES COVERS BY
Kai Carpenter

Timothy Hunter and the Books of Magic created by Neil Gaiman and John Bolton

John Constantine created by Alan Moore, Steve Bissette, John Totleben, and Jamie Delano & John Ridgway

The Sandman Universe curated by Neil Gaiman

CHRIS CONROY — *Editor – Original Series*
AMEDEO TURTURRO
MAGGIE HOWELL — *Associate Editors – Original Series*
JEB WOODARD — *Group Editor – Collected Editions*
SCOTT NYBAKKEN — *Editor – Collected Edition*
STEVE COOK — *Design Director – Books and Publication Design*
ERIN VANOVER — *Publication Production*

BOB HARRAS — *Senior VP – Editor-in-Chief, DC Comics*
MARK DOYLE — *Executive Editor, DC Black Label*

DANIEL CHERRY III — *Senior VP – General Manager*
JIM LEE — *Publisher & Chief Creative Officer*
BOBBIE CHASE — *VP – Global Publishing Initiatives & Digital Strategy*
DON FALLETTI — *VP – Manufacturing Operations & Workflow Management*
LAWRENCE GANEM — *VP – Talent Services*
ALISON GILL — *Senior VP – Manufacturing & Operations*
HANK KANALZ — *Senior VP – Publishing Strategy & Support Services*
DAN MIRON — *VP – Publishing Operations*
NICK J. NAPOLITANO — *VP – Manufacturing Administration & Design*
NANCY SPEARS — *VP – Sales*
JONAH WEILAND — *VP – Marketing & Creative Services*
MICHELE R. WELLS — *VP & Executive Editor, Young Reader*

BOOKS OF MAGIC VOL. 3: DWELLING IN POSSIBILITY

Published by DC Comics. Compilation Copyright © 2021 DC Comics. All Rights Reserved.

Originally published in single magazine form as *Books of Magic* 14-23. Copyright © 2019, 2020 DC Comics. All Rights Reserved. All characters, their distinctive likenesses, and related elements featured in this publication are trademarks of DC Comics. The stories, characters, and incidents featured in this publication are entirely fictional. DC Comics does not read or accept unsolicited submissions of ideas, stories, or artwork. DC – a WarnerMedia Company.

DC Comics, 2900 West Alameda Ave., Burbank, CA 91505
Printed by LSC Communications, Owensville, MO, USA. 1/8/21. First Printing.
ISBN: 978-1-77950-300-8

Library of Congress Cataloging-in-Publication Data is available.

PEFC Certified

This product is from sustainably managed forests and controlled sources

PEFC/29-31-337   www.pefc.org

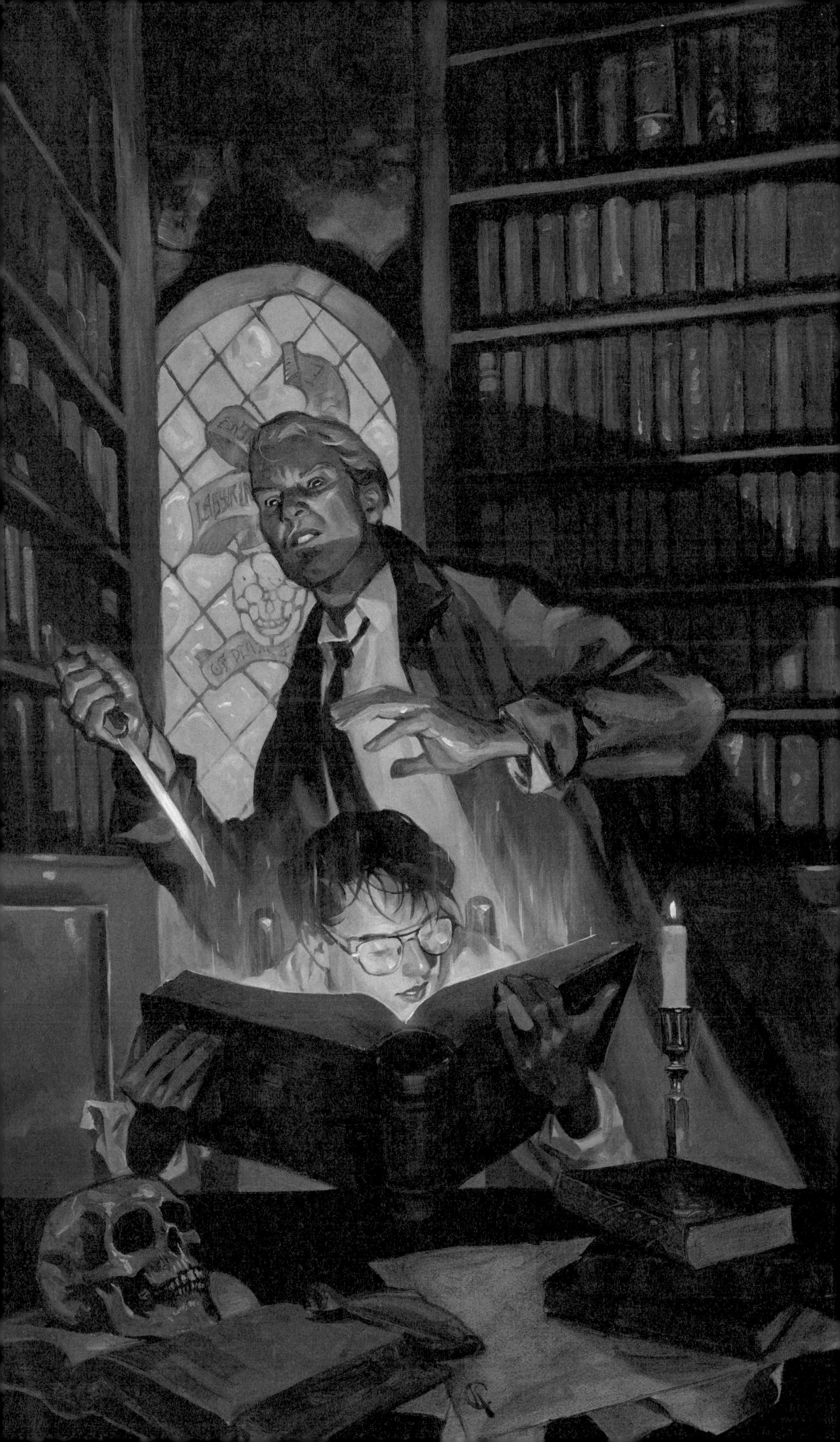

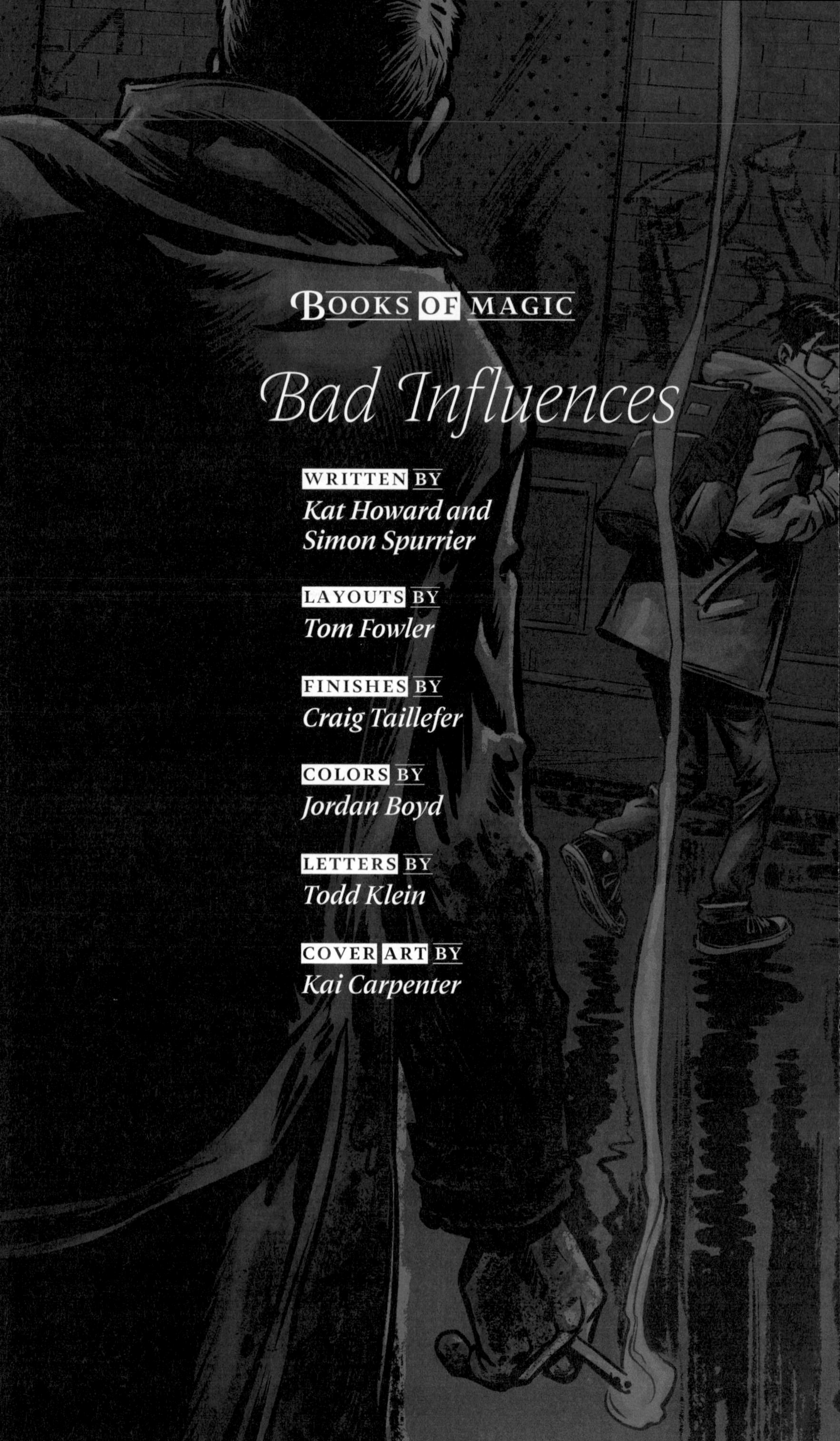

BOOKS OF MAGIC

Bad Influences

WRITTEN BY
Kat Howard and Simon Spurrier

LAYOUTS BY
Tom Fowler

FINISHES BY
Craig Taillefer

COLORS BY
Jordan Boyd

LETTERS BY
Todd Klein

COVER ART BY
Kai Carpenter

I was surprised to hear from him. I'd thought we were done, and now he says he has a book for me.

No idea what kind of book, or why I have to meet him at the Fox and Owl, which isn't even open anymore. Still, it won't be the weirdest thing I've done.

Guess we'll see.

FOOTSTEPS. *KNEW* HE COULDN'T RESIST.

TIM HUNTER. FATED TO BE THE MOST POWERFUL SORCERER EVER, BUT HE DON'T KNOW *BETTER* THAN TAKING *GIFTS* OFF DODGY OLD BLOKES IN ALLEYS.

NEVER MET A *WAND-BOTHERER* YET WHO WOULDN'T DROP HIS KNICKERS FOR A SHINY SPELLBOOK.

METAPHORICALLY SPEAKING.

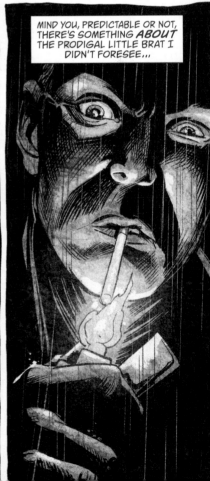

MIND YOU, PREDICTABLE OR NOT, THERE'S SOMETHING *ABOUT* THE PRODIGAL LITTLE BRAT I DIDN'T FORESEE...

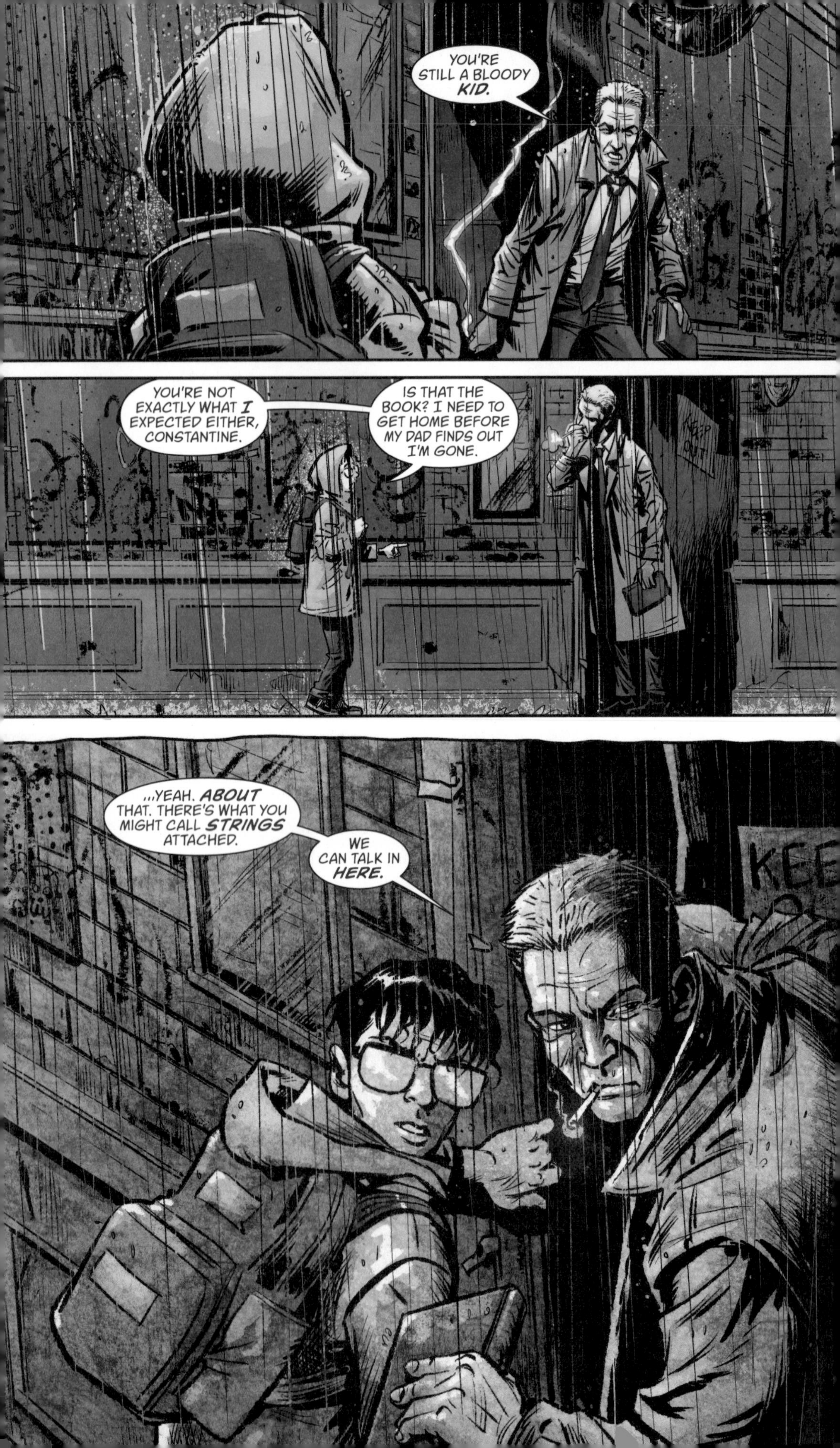
YOU'RE STILL A BLOODY KID.
YOU'RE NOT EXACTLY WHAT I EXPECTED EITHER, CONSTANTINE.
IS THAT THE BOOK? I NEED TO GET HOME BEFORE MY DAD FINDS OUT I'M GONE.
KEEP OUT!
...YEAH. ABOUT THAT. THERE'S WHAT YOU MIGHT CALL STRINGS ATTACHED.
WE CAN TALK IN HERE.
KEE

THIS USED TO BE A NICE BOOZER, ONCE-- SHADY TYPES UP TO NO GOOD. SAME OLD, SAME OLD.

He's staring at me like I have spinach in my teeth.

He nods at the book, tells me to open it. That I'll understand when I do.

Just once I'd like a normal book.

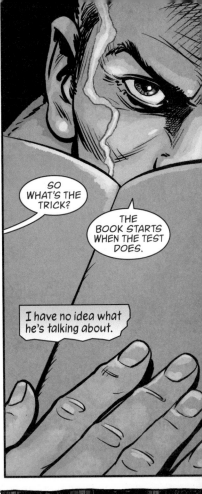

SO WHAT'S THE TRICK?

THE BOOK STARTS WHEN THE TEST DOES.

I have no idea what he's talking about.

I GIVE HIM THE SPIEL. CLASSIC BLOODY TEENAGER--ALL ROLLED EYES AND IMPATIENCE. HOW IS HE SO YOUNG?

PLACE I CAME FROM, IT'S BEEN YEARS SINCE HE LOOKED LIKE THIS. YEARS SINCE HE WAS ANYTHING BUT ROTTEN FROM ARSE TO ELBOW.

SOMEONE'S BEEN PLAYING SILLY BUGGERS WITH TIME-- AND FOR ALL I KNOW IT'S HIM.

JUST ANOTHER REASON TO GET THIS DONE.

THE BOOK STARTS WHEN THE TEST DOES. YOU GOT SOME DOUBTS TO DISPEL, TWINKLE-TOES.

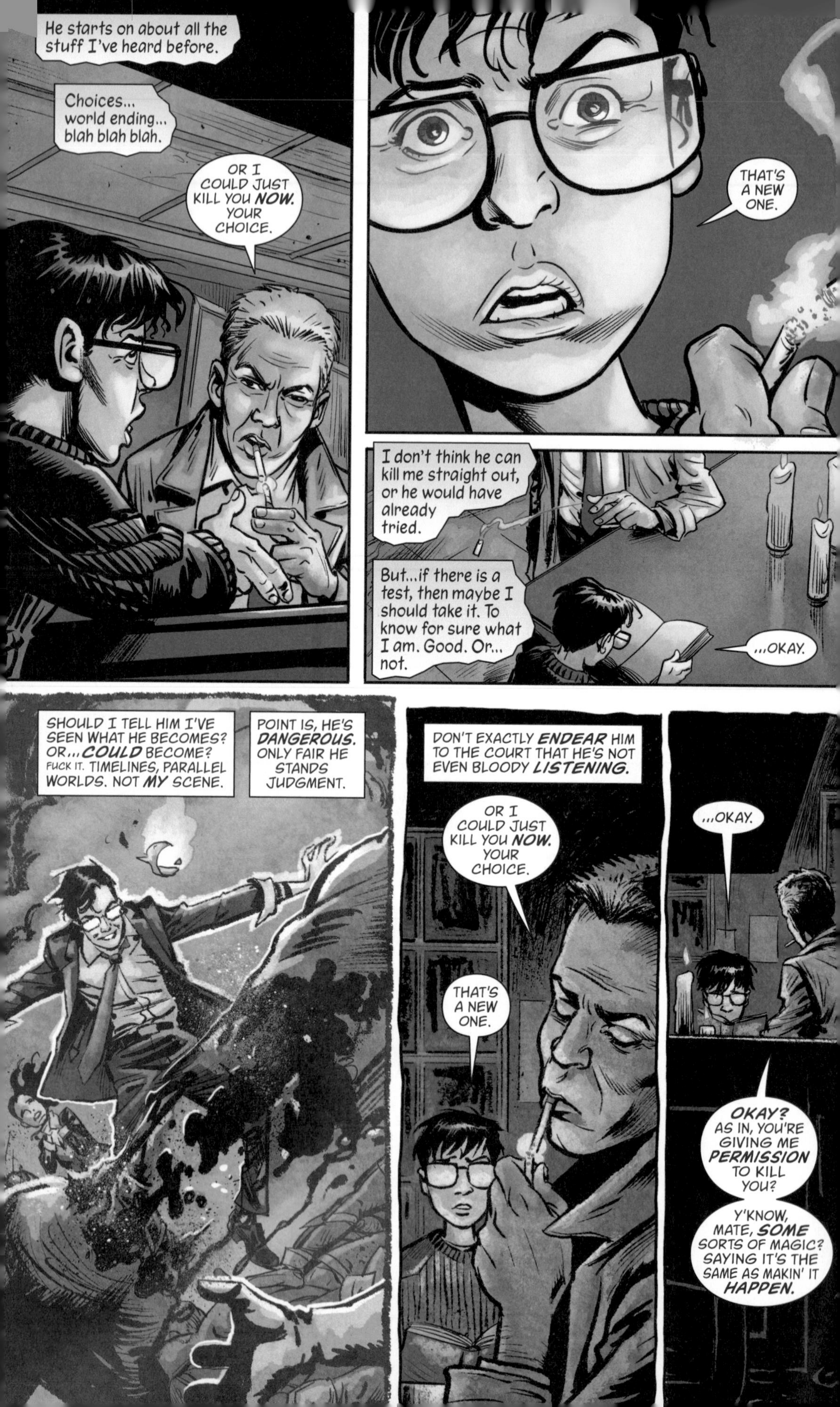
He starts on about all the stuff I've heard before.
Choices... world ending... blah blah blah.
OR I COULD JUST KILL YOU NOW. YOUR CHOICE.
THAT'S A NEW ONE.
I don't think he can kill me straight out, or he would have already tried.
But...if there is a test, then maybe I should take it. To know for sure what I am. Good. Or... not.
...OKAY.
SHOULD I TELL HIM I'VE SEEN WHAT HE BECOMES? OR...COULD BECOME? FUCK IT. TIMELINES, PARALLEL WORLDS. NOT MY SCENE.
POINT IS, HE'S DANGEROUS. ONLY FAIR HE STANDS JUDGMENT.
DON'T EXACTLY ENDEAR HIM TO THE COURT THAT HE'S NOT EVEN BLOODY LISTENING.
OR I COULD JUST KILL YOU NOW. YOUR CHOICE.
THAT'S A NEW ONE.
...OKAY.
OKAY? AS IN, YOU'RE GIVING ME PERMISSION TO KILL YOU?
Y'KNOW, MATE, SOME SORTS OF MAGIC? SAYING IT'S THE SAME AS MAKIN' IT HAPPEN.

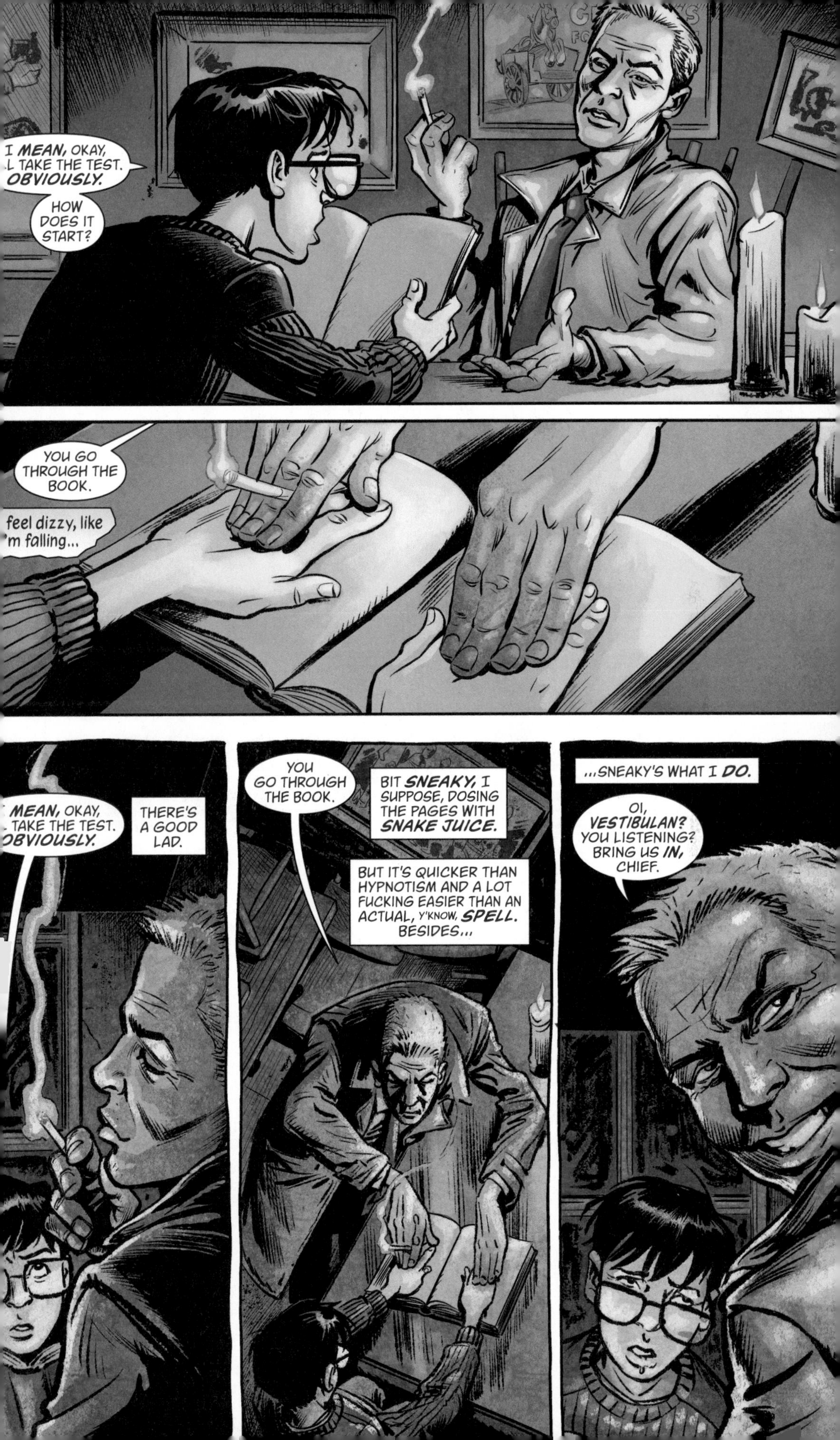
I MEAN, OKAY, I'LL TAKE THE TEST. OBVIOUSLY.
HOW DOES IT START?
YOU GO THROUGH THE BOOK.
feel dizzy, like 'm falling...
MEAN, OKAY, TAKE THE TEST. OBVIOUSLY.
THERE'S A GOOD LAD.
YOU GO THROUGH THE BOOK.
BIT SNEAKY, I SUPPOSE, DOSING THE PAGES WITH SNAKE JUICE.
BUT IT'S QUICKER THAN HYPNOTISM AND A LOT FUCKING EASIER THAN AN ACTUAL, Y'KNOW, SPELL. BESIDES...
...SNEAKY'S WHAT I DO.
OI, VESTIBULAN? YOU LISTENING? BRING US IN, CHIEF.

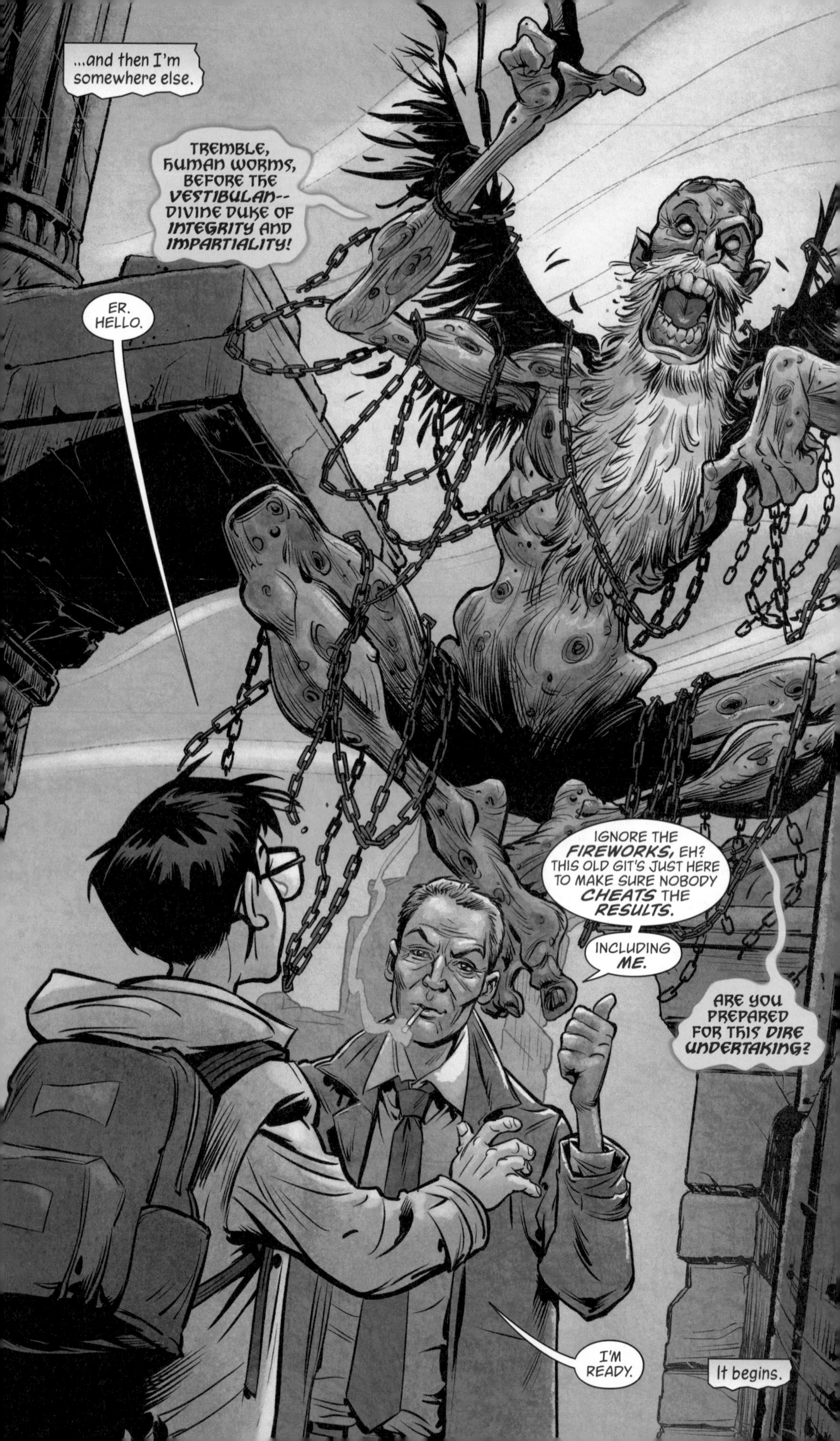
...and then I'm somewhere else.
TREMBLE, HUMAN WORMS, BEFORE THE VESTIBULAN-- DIVINE DUKE OF INTEGRITY AND IMPARTIALITY!
ER. HELLO.
IGNORE THE FIREWORKS, EH? THIS OLD GIT'S JUST HERE TO MAKE SURE NOBODY CHEATS THE RESULTS.
INCLUDING ME.
ARE YOU PREPARED FOR THIS DIRE UNDERTAKING?
I'M READY.
It begins.

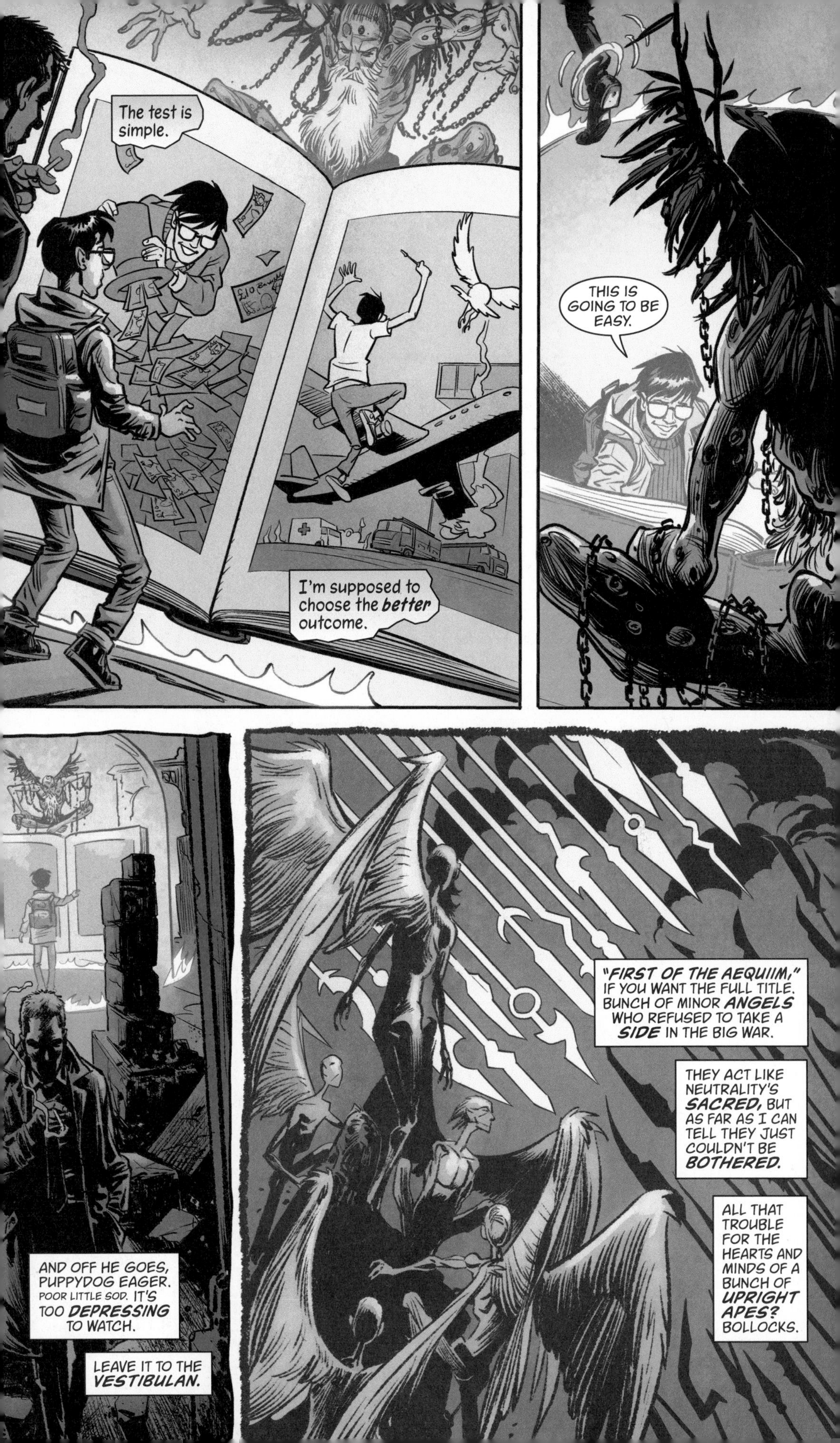
The test is simple.
I'm supposed to choose the better outcome.
THIS IS GOING TO BE EASY.
AND OFF HE GOES, PUPPYDOG EAGER. POOR LITTLE SOD. IT'S TOO DEPRESSING TO WATCH.
LEAVE IT TO THE VESTIBULAN.
"FIRST OF THE AEQUIIM," IF YOU WANT THE FULL TITLE. BUNCH OF MINOR ANGELS WHO REFUSED TO TAKE A SIDE IN THE BIG WAR.
THEY ACT LIKE NEUTRALITY'S SACRED, BUT AS FAR AS I CAN TELL THEY JUST COULDN'T BE BOTHERED.
ALL THAT TROUBLE FOR THE HEARTS AND MINDS OF A BUNCH OF UPRIGHT APES? BOLLOCKS.

And that's how it goes. I make a choice, creepy guy over there nods, and the pages turn to the next part of the test. It's easy.

Other than that he just hovers there, frowning. I wonder what his story is?

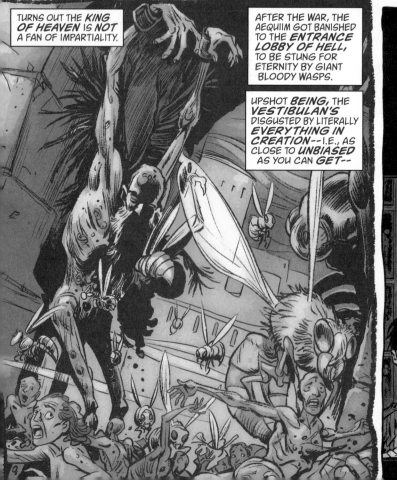

TURNS OUT THE *KING OF HEAVEN* IS *NOT* A FAN OF IMPARTIALITY.

AFTER THE WAR, THE AEQUIIM GOT BANISHED TO THE *ENTRANCE LOBBY OF HELL*, TO BE STUNG FOR ETERNITY BY GIANT BLOODY WASPS.

UPSHOT *BEING*, THE *VESTIBULAN'S* DISGUSTED BY LITERALLY *EVERYTHING IN CREATION*--I.E., AS CLOSE TO *UNBIASED* AS YOU CAN *GET*--

--AND HE'S SO *GRATEFUL* TO BE *SET FREE* ONCE IN A WHILE HE WON'T EVEN *TRY* TO CLAIM THE SUMMONER'S *SOUL*.

FACT IS, THE BLOODY *DEMON* AIN'T THE BIGGEST *BASTARD* IN TONIGHT'S LITTLE DRAMA.

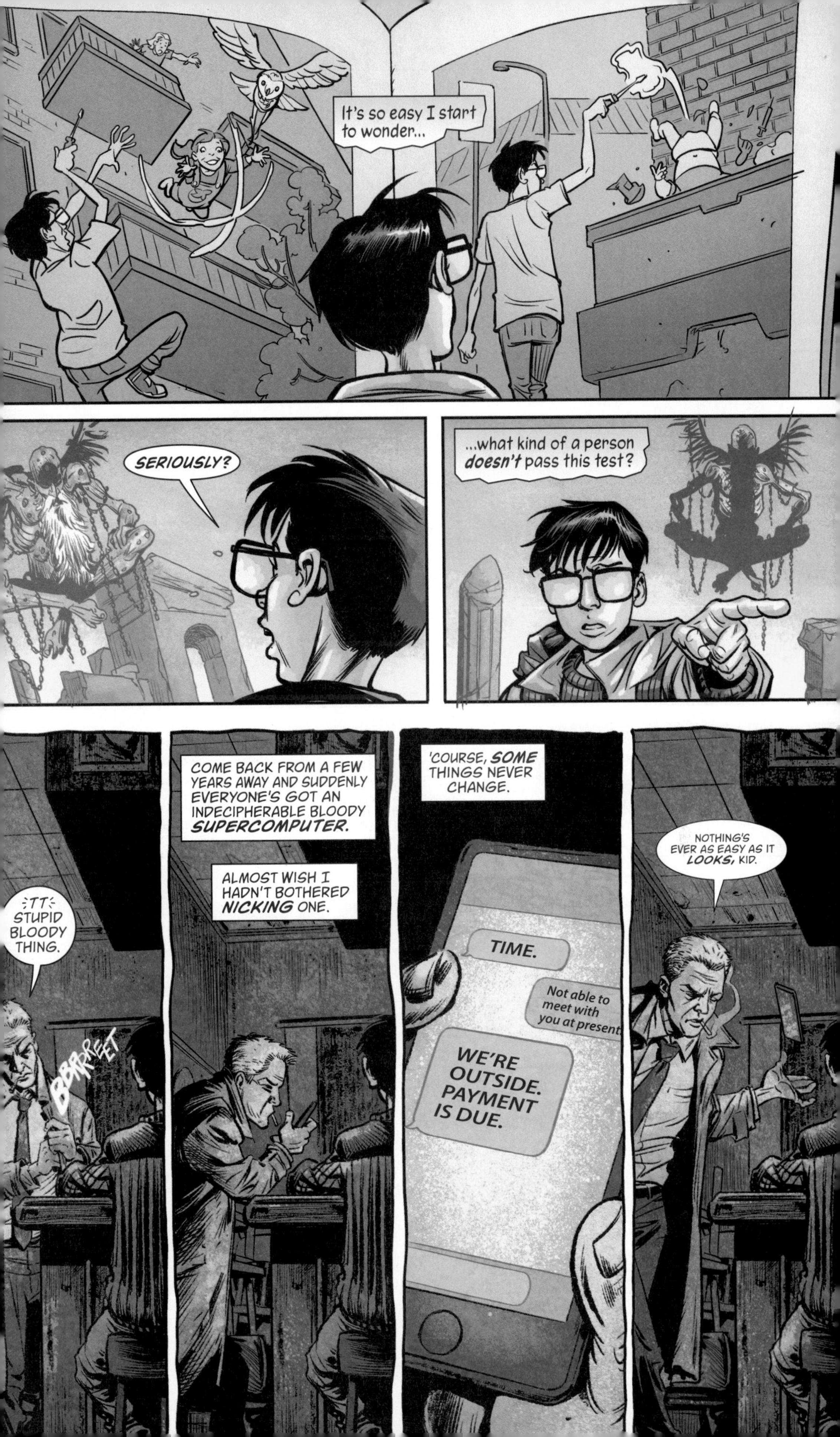

It's so easy I start to wonder...
SERIOUSLY?
...what kind of a person doesn't pass this test?
COME BACK FROM A FEW YEARS AWAY AND SUDDENLY EVERYONE'S GOT AN INDECIPHERABLE BLOODY SUPERCOMPUTER.
TT STUPID BLOODY THING.
BBRREET
ALMOST WISH I HADN'T BOTHERED NICKING ONE.
'COURSE, SOME THINGS NEVER CHANGE.
TIME.
Not able to meet with you at present.
WE'RE OUTSIDE. PAYMENT IS DUE.
NOTHING'S EVER AS EASY AS IT LOOKS, KID.

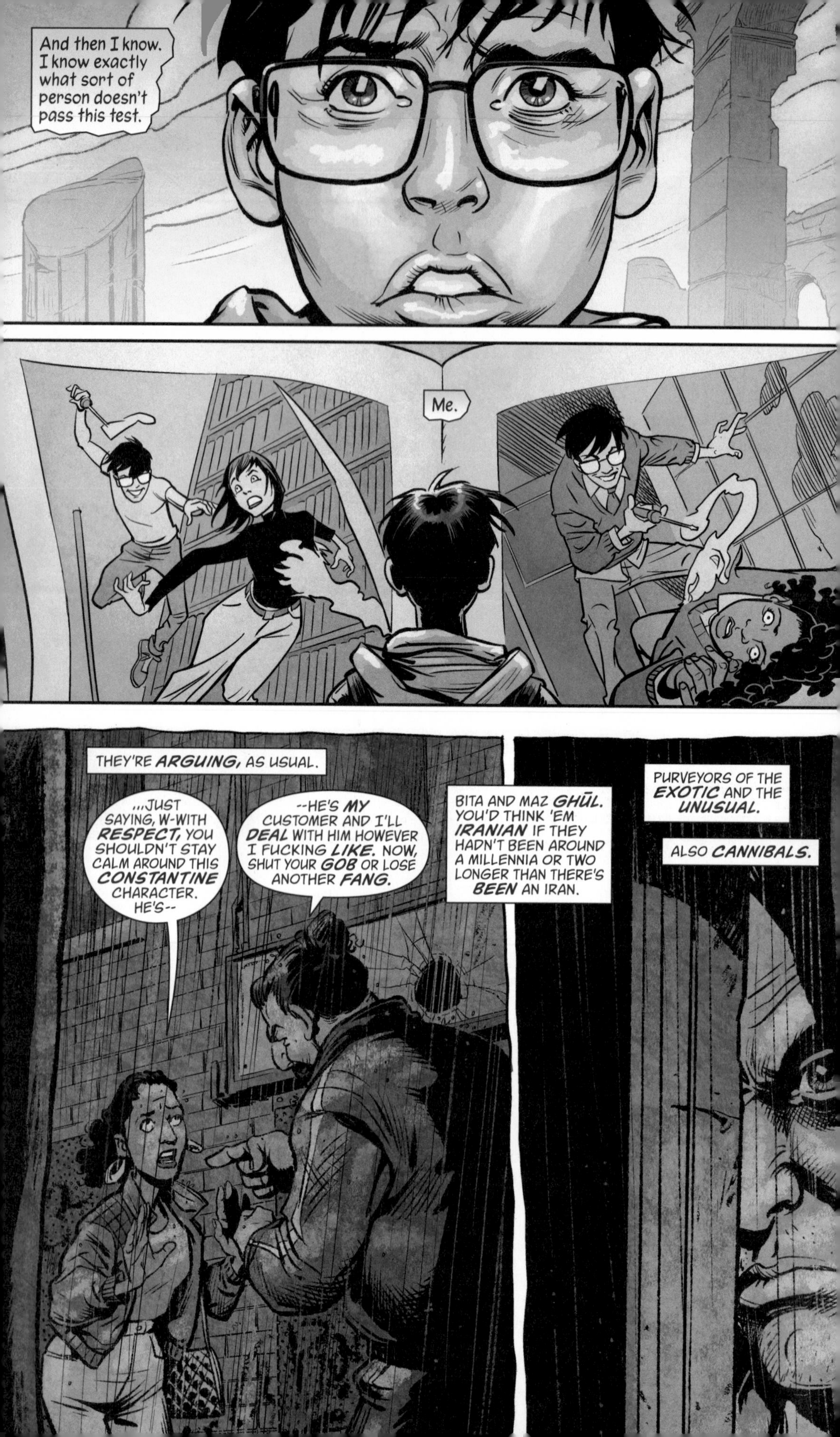
And then I know. I know exactly what sort of person doesn't pass this test.
Me.
THEY'RE ARGUING, AS USUAL.
...JUST SAYING, W-WITH RESPECT, YOU SHOULDN'T STAY CALM AROUND THIS CONSTANTINE CHARACTER. HE'S--
--HE'S MY CUSTOMER AND I'LL DEAL WITH HIM HOWEVER I FUCKING LIKE. NOW, SHUT YOUR GOB OR LOSE ANOTHER FANG.
BITA AND MAZ GHŪL. YOU'D THINK 'EM IRANIAN IF THEY HADN'T BEEN AROUND A MILLENNIA OR TWO LONGER THAN THERE'S BEEN AN IRAN.
PURVEYORS OF THE EXOTIC AND THE UNUSUAL.
ALSO CANNIBALS.

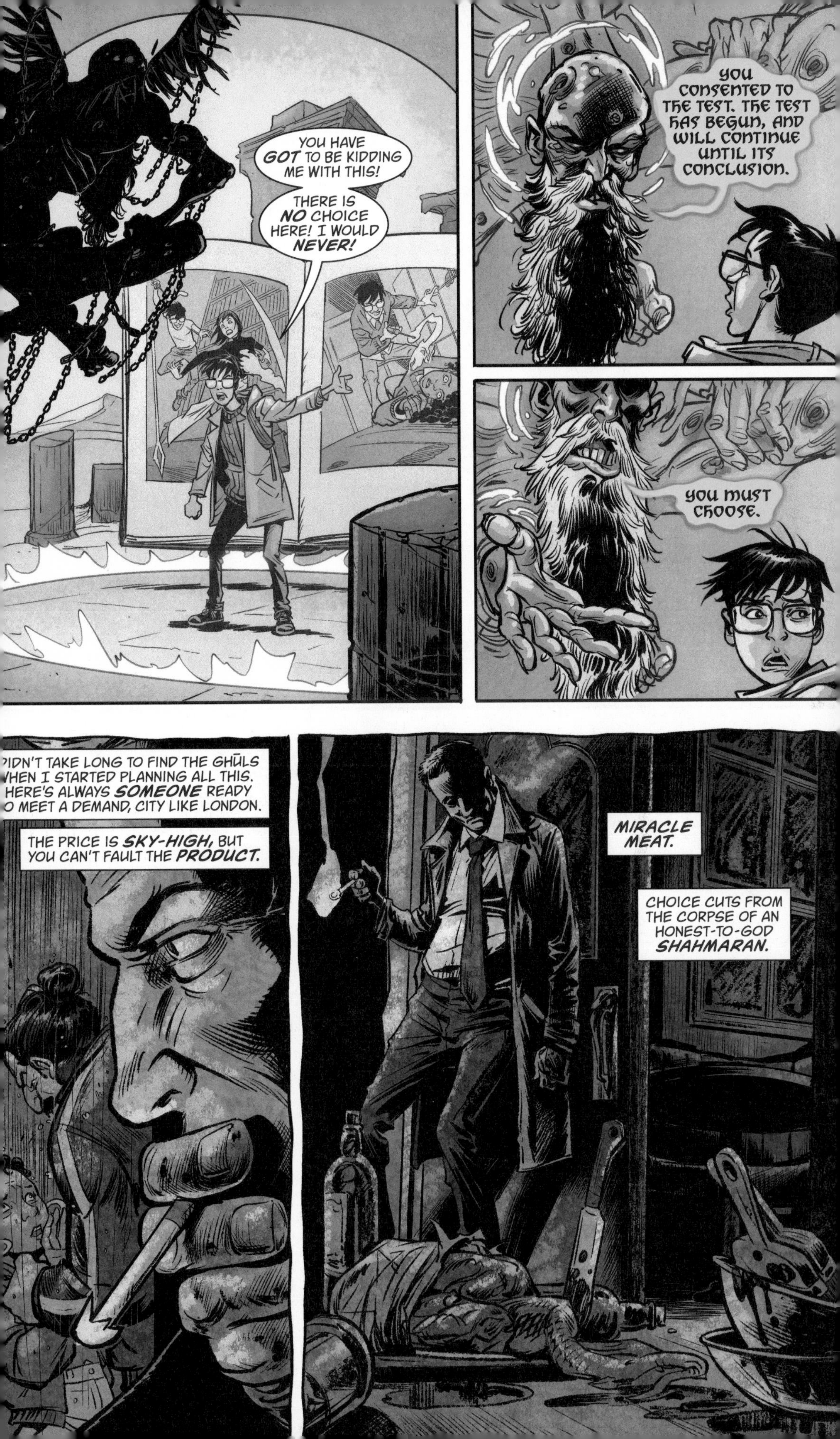
YOU HAVE GOT TO BE KIDDING ME WITH THIS!
THERE IS NO CHOICE HERE! I WOULD NEVER!
YOU CONSENTED TO THE TEST. THE TEST HAS BEGUN, AND WILL CONTINUE UNTIL ITS CONCLUSION.
YOU MUST CHOOSE.
DIDN'T TAKE LONG TO FIND THE GHŪLS WHEN I STARTED PLANNING ALL THIS. THERE'S ALWAYS SOMEONE READY TO MEET A DEMAND, CITY LIKE LONDON.
THE PRICE IS SKY-HIGH, BUT YOU CAN'T FAULT THE PRODUCT.
MIRACLE MEAT.
CHOICE CUTS FROM THE CORPSE OF AN HONEST-TO-GOD SHAHMARAN.

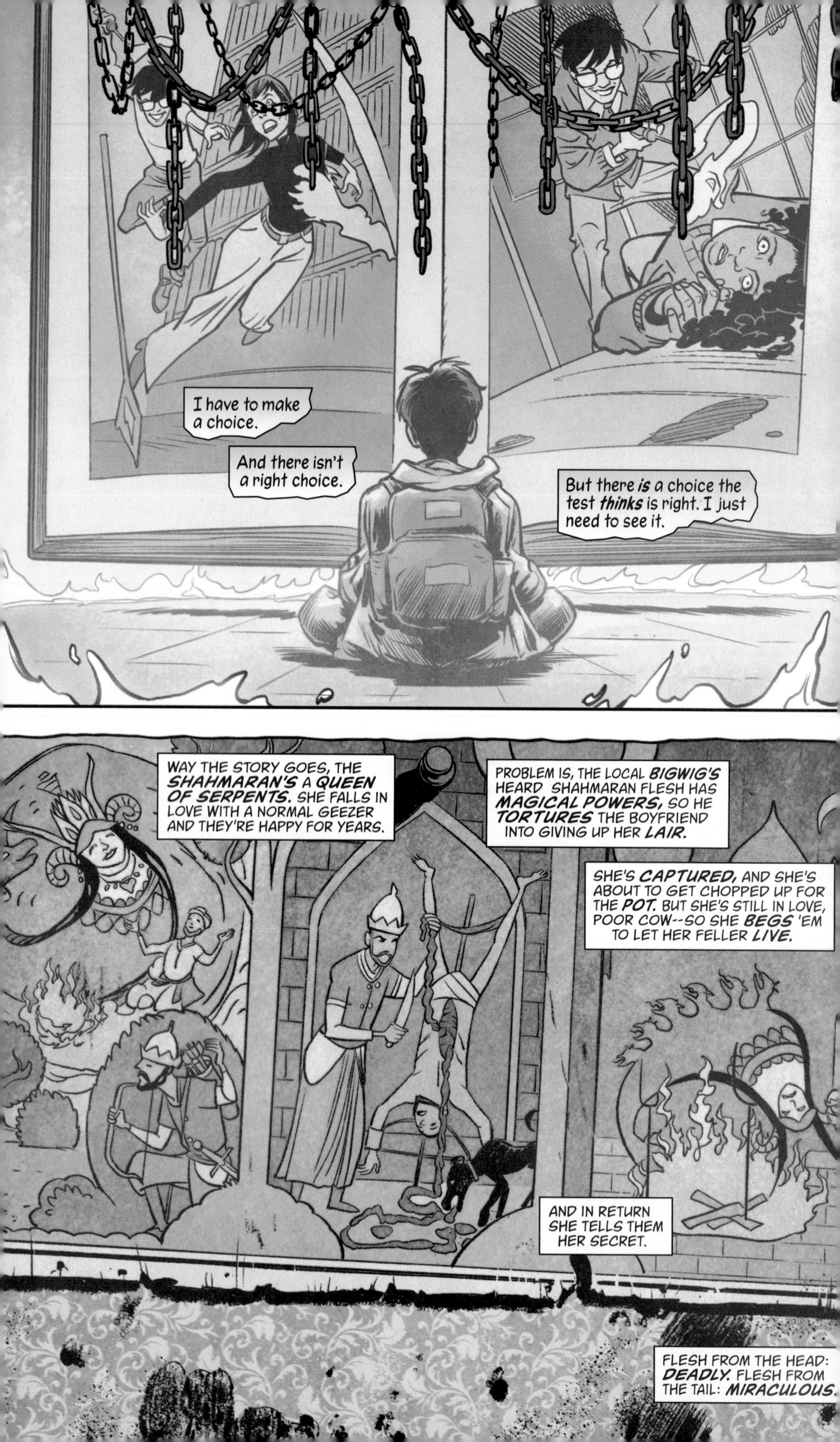

I have to make a choice.
And there isn't a right choice.
But there *is* a choice the test *thinks* is right. I just need to see it.
WAY THE STORY GOES, THE ***SHAHMARAN'S*** A ***QUEEN OF SERPENTS.*** SHE FALLS IN LOVE WITH A NORMAL GEEZER AND THEY'RE HAPPY FOR YEARS.
PROBLEM IS, THE LOCAL ***BIGWIG'S*** HEARD SHAHMARAN FLESH HAS ***MAGICAL POWERS,*** SO HE ***TORTURES*** THE BOYFRIEND INTO GIVING UP HER ***LAIR.***
SHE'S ***CAPTURED,*** AND SHE'S ABOUT TO GET CHOPPED UP FOR THE ***POT.*** BUT SHE'S STILL IN LOVE, POOR COW--SO SHE ***BEGS*** 'EM TO LET HER FELLER ***LIVE.***
AND IN RETURN SHE TELLS THEM HER SECRET.
FLESH FROM THE HEAD: ***DEADLY.*** FLESH FROM THE TAIL: ***MIRACULOUS.***

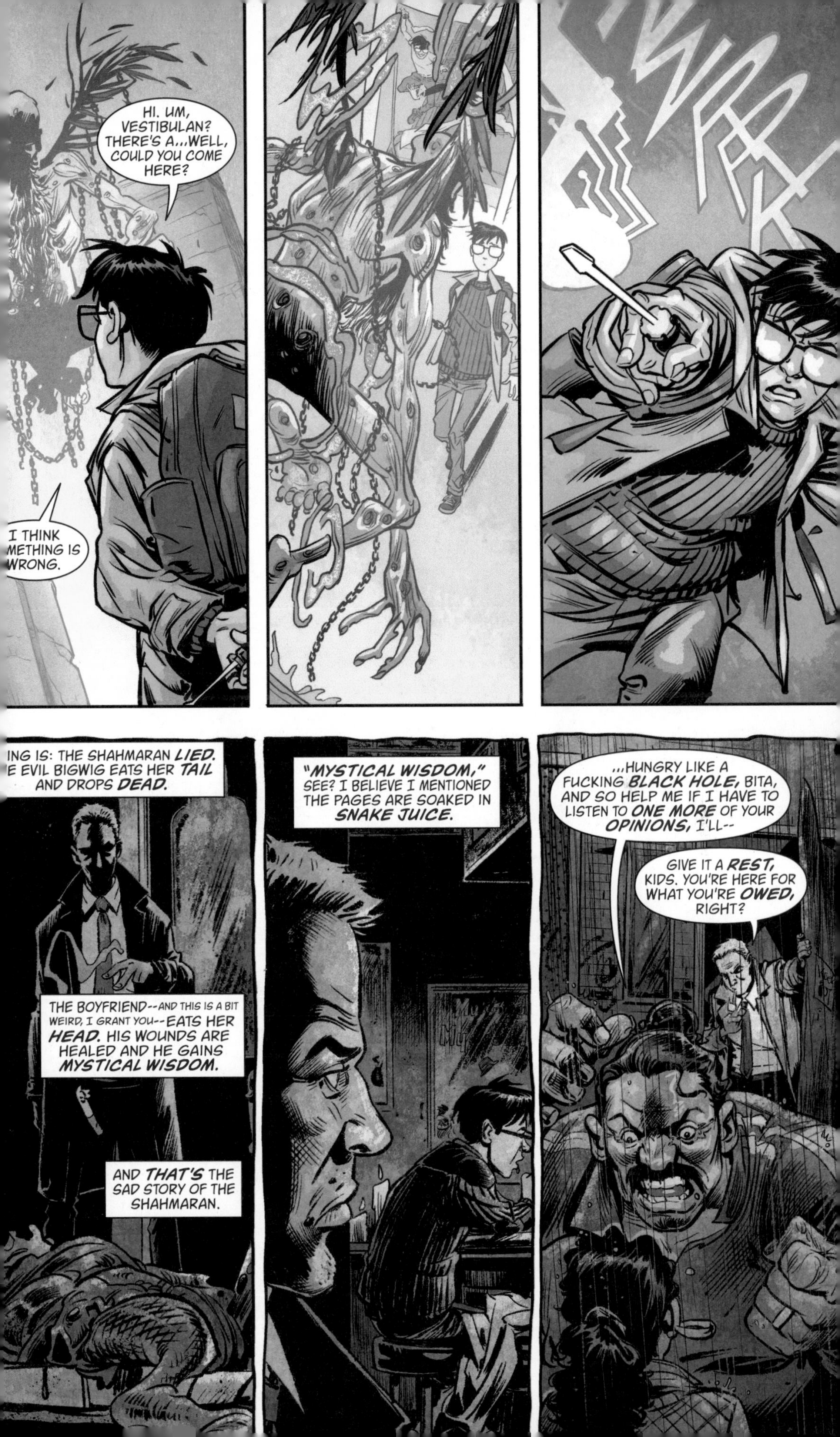

HI. UM, VESTIBULAN? THERE'S A...WELL, COULD YOU COME HERE?
I THINK METHING IS WRONG.
ING IS: THE SHAHMARAN LIED. E EVIL BIGWIG EATS HER TAIL AND DROPS DEAD.
THE BOYFRIEND--AND THIS IS A BIT WEIRD, I GRANT YOU--EATS HER HEAD. HIS WOUNDS ARE HEALED AND HE GAINS MYSTICAL WISDOM.
AND THAT'S THE SAD STORY OF THE SHAHMARAN.
"MYSTICAL WISDOM," SEE? I BELIEVE I MENTIONED THE PAGES ARE SOAKED IN SNAKE JUICE.
...HUNGRY LIKE A FUCKING BLACK HOLE, BITA, AND SO HELP ME IF I HAVE TO LISTEN TO ONE MORE OF YOUR OPINIONS, I'LL--
GIVE IT A REST, KIDS. YOU'RE HERE FOR WHAT YOU'RE OWED, RIGHT?

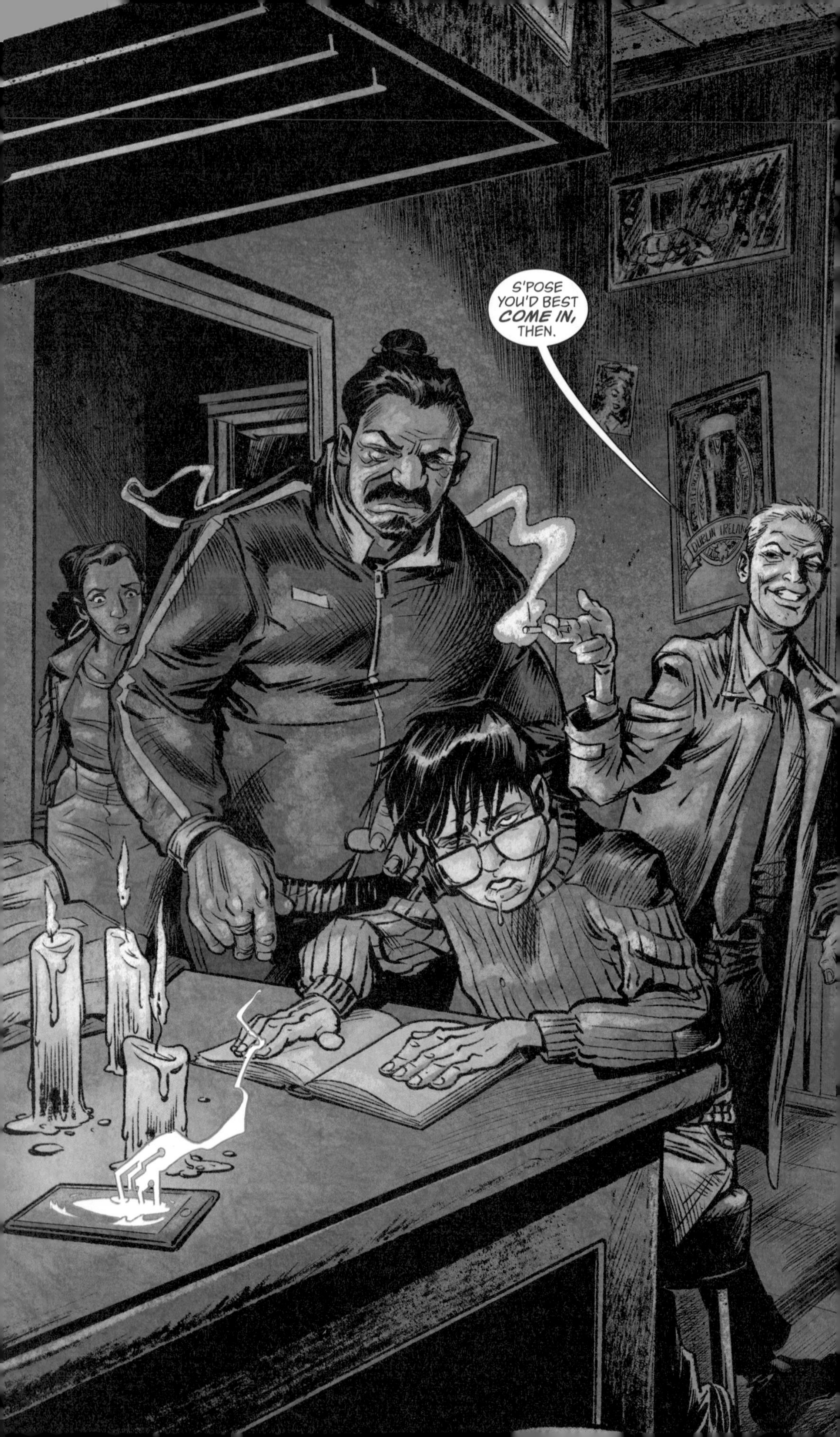
S'POSE YOU'D BEST **COME IN,** THEN.
DUBLIN IRELAN

This test *sucks*.

The Vestibulan said the test had to be completed.

So I skip ahead.

THERE.

I WIN.

Test Completed

THIS IS THE ONE YOU **DRUGGED**, YES? THE BLOOD OF THE SHAHMARAN'S **HEAD**--TO INDUCE VISIONS.

J-JUST ON THE FIRST PAGE, YEAH.

MM. AND YOU PUT THE BLOOD OF THE **TAIL** ON ALL THE **REST**--SO THE CHILD MURDERS **HIMSELF** WITH EVERY TURN.

VERY CLEVER.

SNNF SNNF

YEAH.

SO-- CAN WE **EAT HIM** NOW?

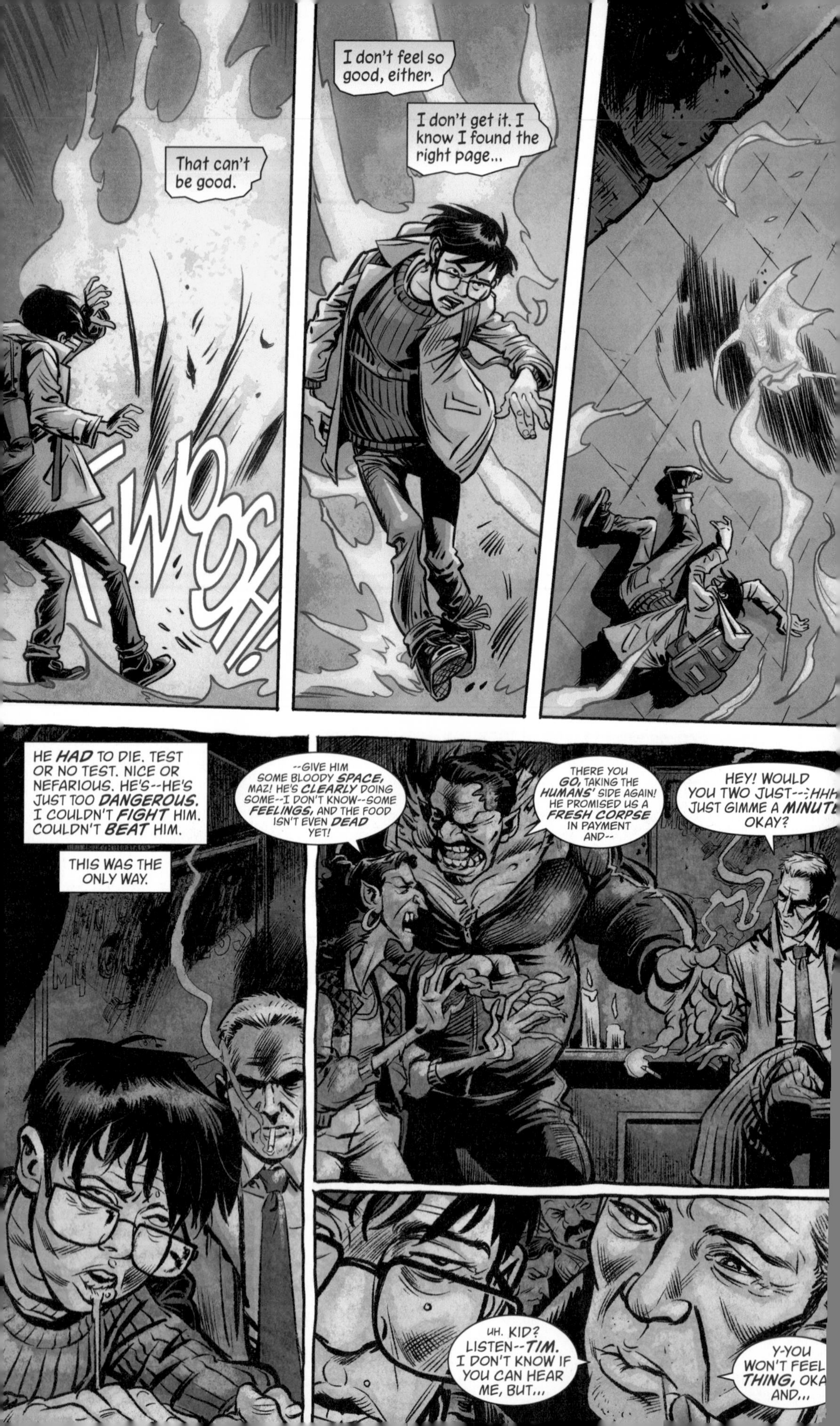
That can't be good.
FWOOSH!
I don't feel so good, either.
I don't get it. I know I found the right page...
HE HAD TO DIE. TEST OR NO TEST. NICE OR NEFARIOUS. HE'S--HE'S JUST TOO DANGEROUS. I COULDN'T FIGHT HIM. COULDN'T BEAT HIM.
THIS WAS THE ONLY WAY.
--GIVE HIM SOME BLOODY SPACE, MAZ! HE'S CLEARLY DOING SOME--I DON'T KNOW--SOME FEELINGS, AND THE FOOD ISN'T EVEN DEAD YET!
THERE YOU GO, TAKING THE HUMANS' SIDE AGAIN! HE PROMISED US A FRESH CORPSE IN PAYMENT AND--
HEY! WOULD YOU TWO JUST--;HHH JUST GIMME A MINUTE OKAY?
UH. KID? LISTEN--TIM. I DON'T KNOW IF YOU CAN HEAR ME, BUT...
Y-YOU WON'T FEEL THING, OKA AND...

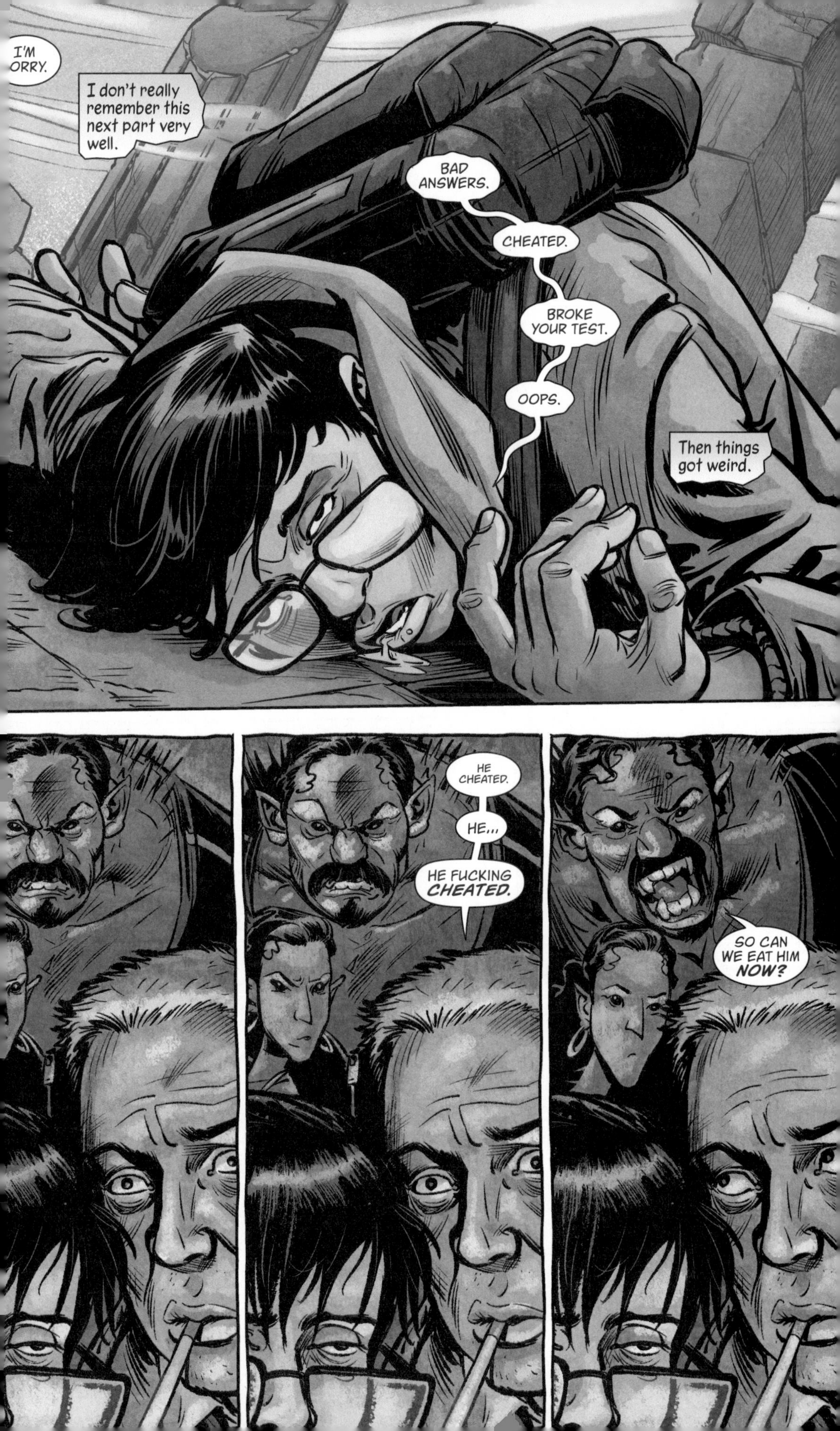
I'M ORRY.
I don't really remember this next part very well.
BAD ANSWERS.
CHEATED.
BROKE YOUR TEST.
OOPS.
Then things got weird.
HE CHEATED.
HE...
HE FUCKING CHEATED.
SO CAN WE EAT HIM NOW?

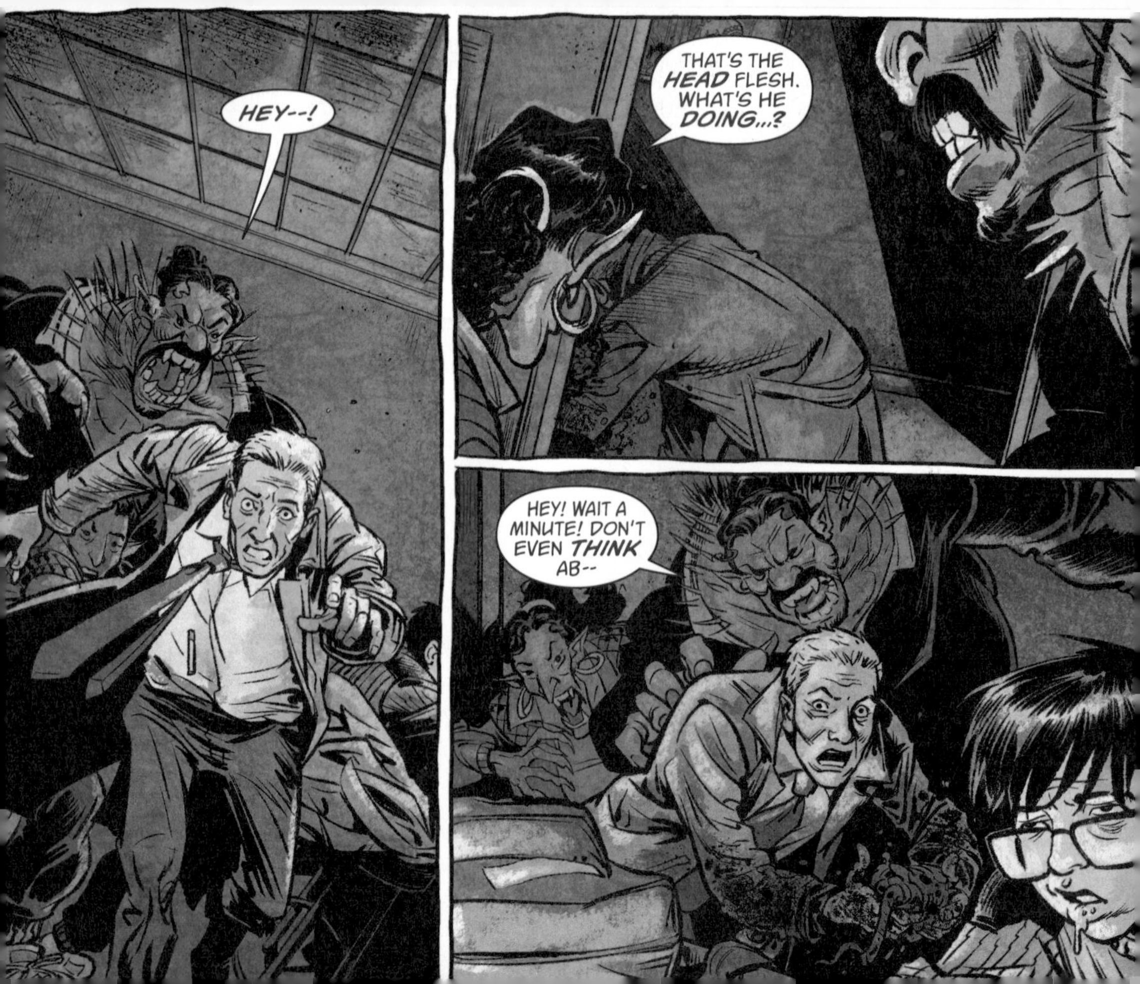
HEY--!
THAT'S THE HEAD FLESH. WHAT'S HE DOING...?
HEY! WAIT A MINUTE! DON'T EVEN THINK AB--

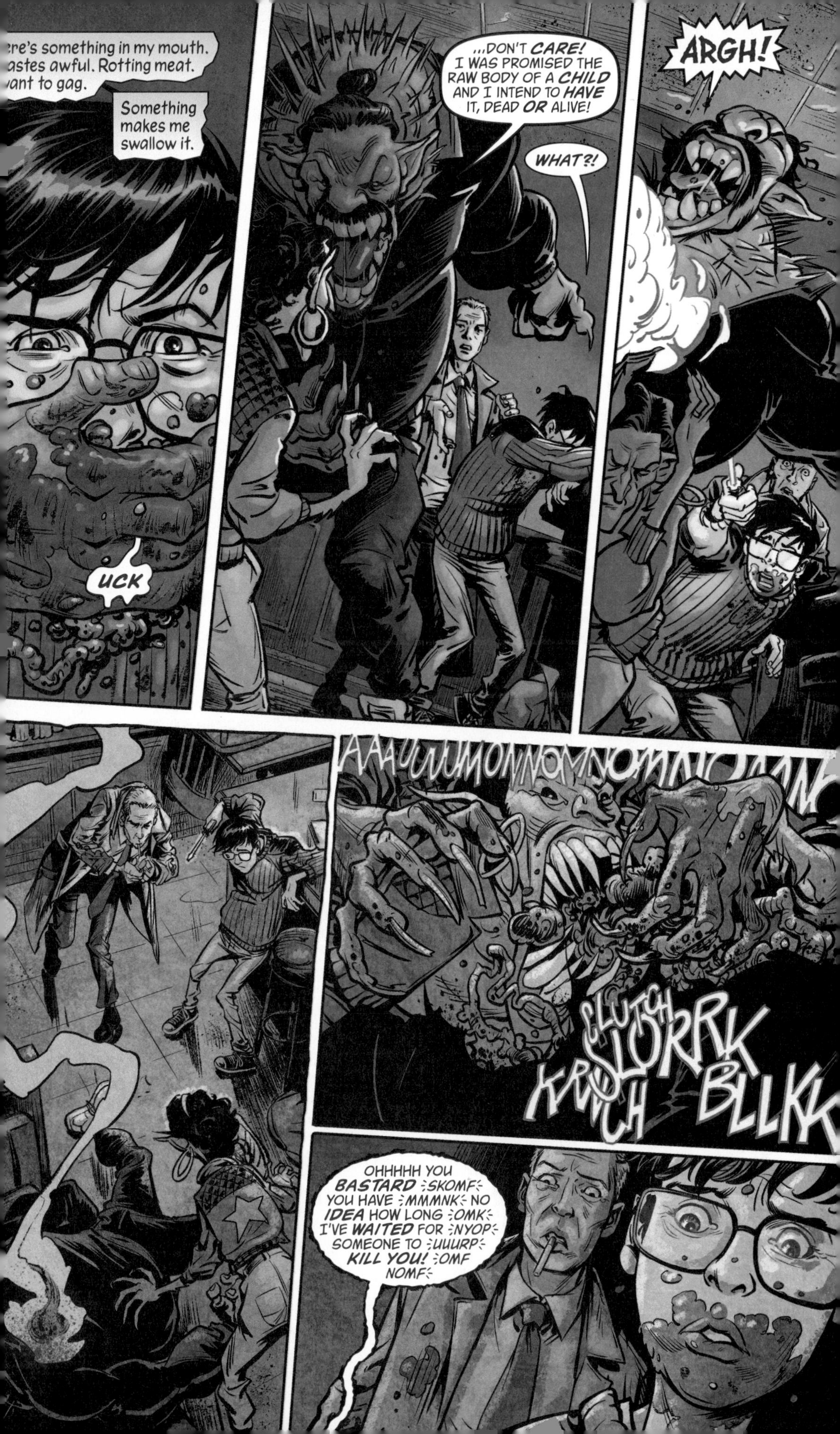

ere's something in my mouth. astes awful. Rotting meat. ant to gag.
Something makes me swallow it.
UCK
...DON'T CARE! I WAS PROMISED THE RAW BODY OF A CHILD AND I INTEND TO HAVE IT, DEAD OR ALIVE!
WHAT?!
ARGH!
SLORRK
KRUNCH
BLLKK
OHHHHH YOU BASTARD SKOMF YOU HAVE MMMNK NO IDEA HOW LONG OMK I'VE WAITED FOR NYOP SOMEONE TO UUURP KILL YOU! OMF NOMF

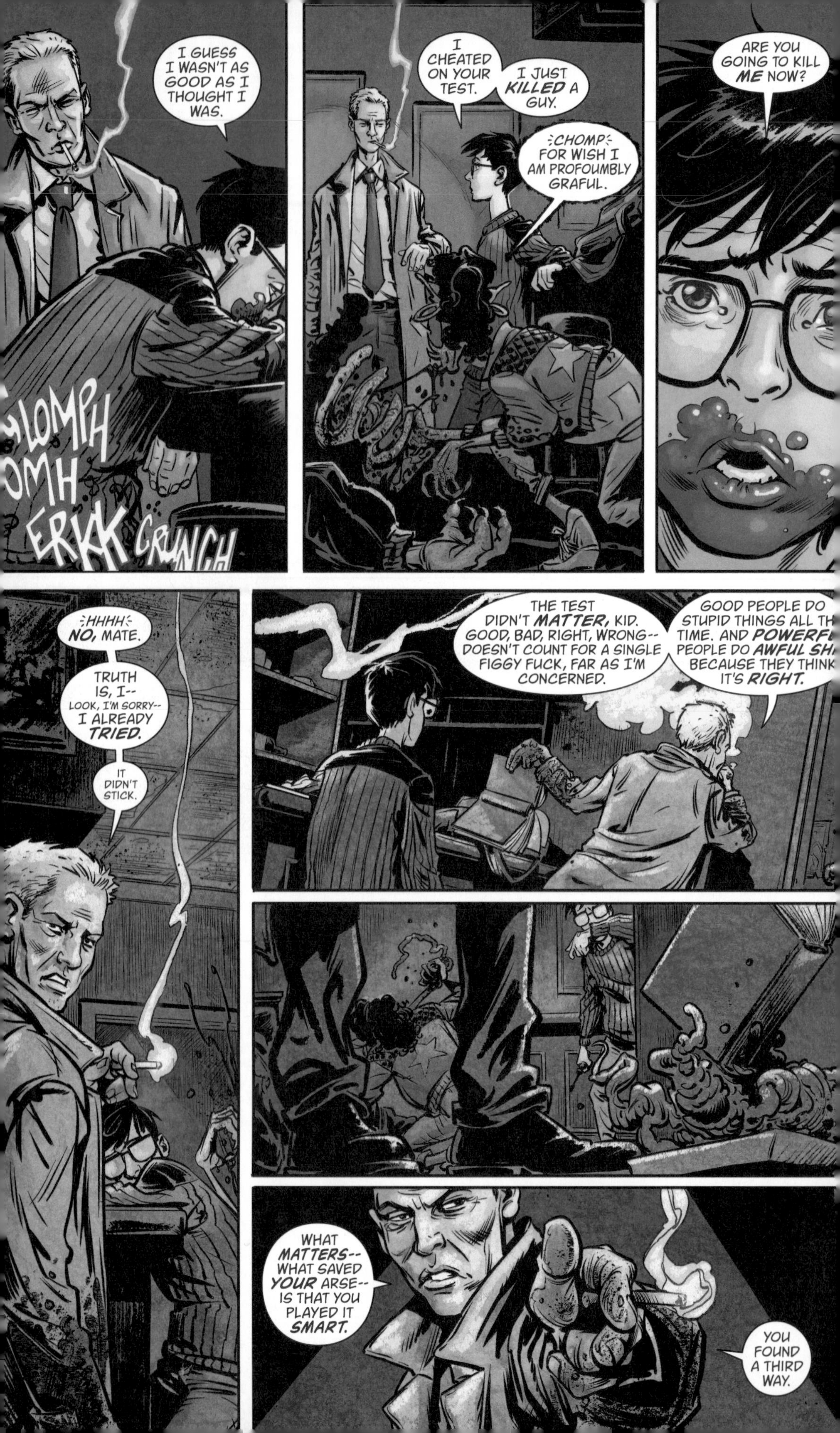

I GUESS I WASN'T AS GOOD AS I THOUGHT I WAS.
SLOMPH
OMH
ERKKK
CRUNCH
I CHEATED ON YOUR TEST.
I JUST KILLED A GUY.
CHOMP
FOR WISH I AM PROFOUMBLY GRAFUL.
ARE YOU GOING TO KILL ME NOW?
HHHH
NO, MATE.
TRUTH IS, I-- LOOK, I'M SORRY-- I ALREADY TRIED.
IT DIDN'T STICK.
THE TEST DIDN'T MATTER, KID. GOOD, BAD, RIGHT, WRONG-- DOESN'T COUNT FOR A SINGLE FIGGY FUCK, FAR AS I'M CONCERNED.
GOOD PEOPLE DO STUPID THINGS ALL TH TIME. AND POWERF PEOPLE DO AWFUL SH BECAUSE THEY THINK IT'S RIGHT.
WHAT MATTERS-- WHAT SAVED YOUR ARSE-- IS THAT YOU PLAYED IT SMART.
YOU FOUND A THIRD WAY.

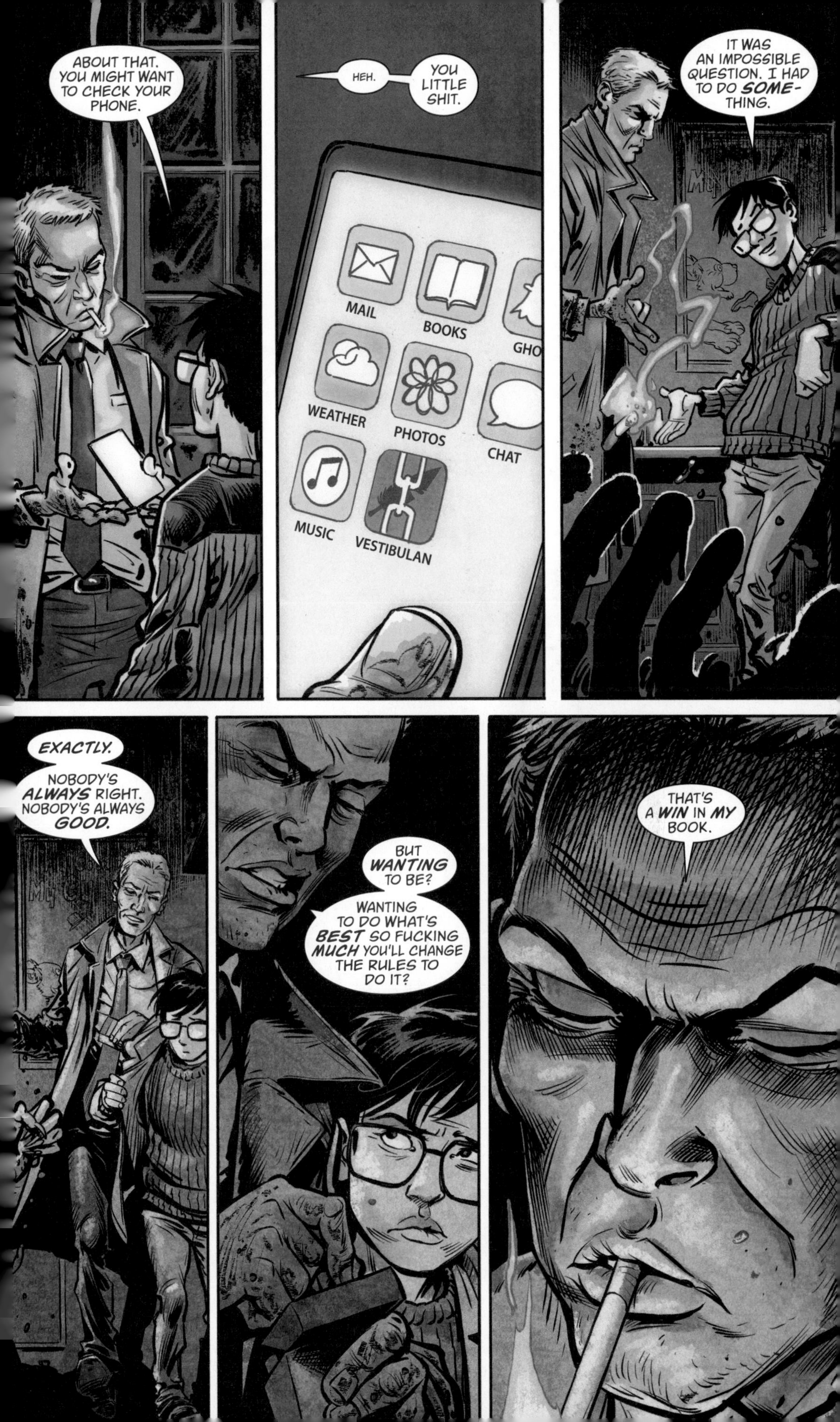
ABOUT THAT. YOU MIGHT WANT TO CHECK YOUR PHONE.
HEH.
YOU LITTLE SHIT.
MAIL
BOOKS
GHO
WEATHER
PHOTOS
CHAT
MUSIC
VESTIBULAN
IT WAS AN IMPOSSIBLE QUESTION. I HAD TO DO SOME-THING.
EXACTLY.
NOBODY'S ALWAYS RIGHT. NOBODY'S ALWAYS GOOD.
BUT WANTING TO BE?
WANTING TO DO WHAT'S BEST SO FUCKING MUCH YOU'LL CHANGE THE RULES TO DO IT?
THAT'S A WIN IN MY BOOK.

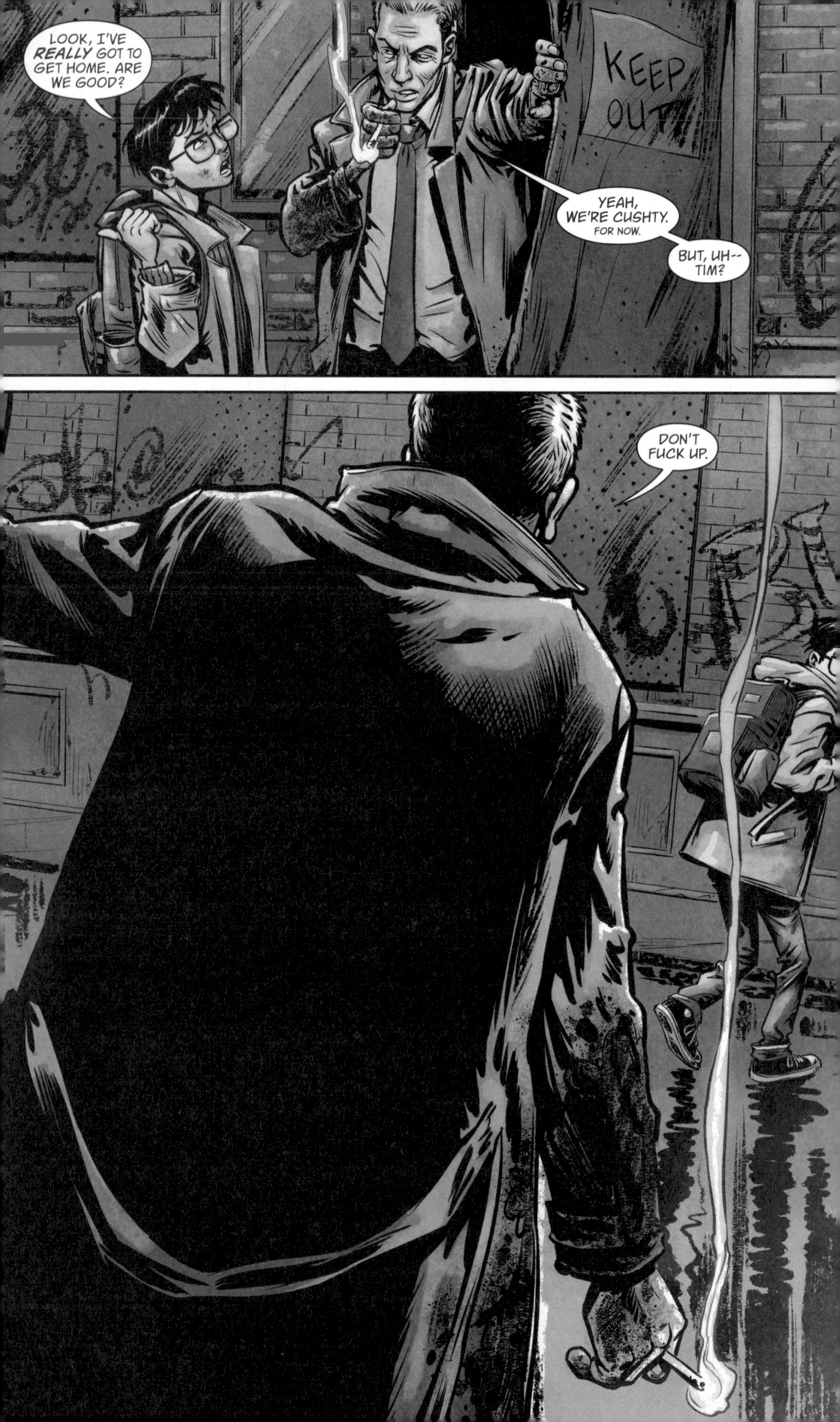
LOOK, I'VE *REALLY* GOT TO GET HOME. ARE WE GOOD?
KEEP OUT
YEAH, WE'RE CUSHTY. FOR NOW.
BUT, UH-- TIM?
DON'T FUCK UP.

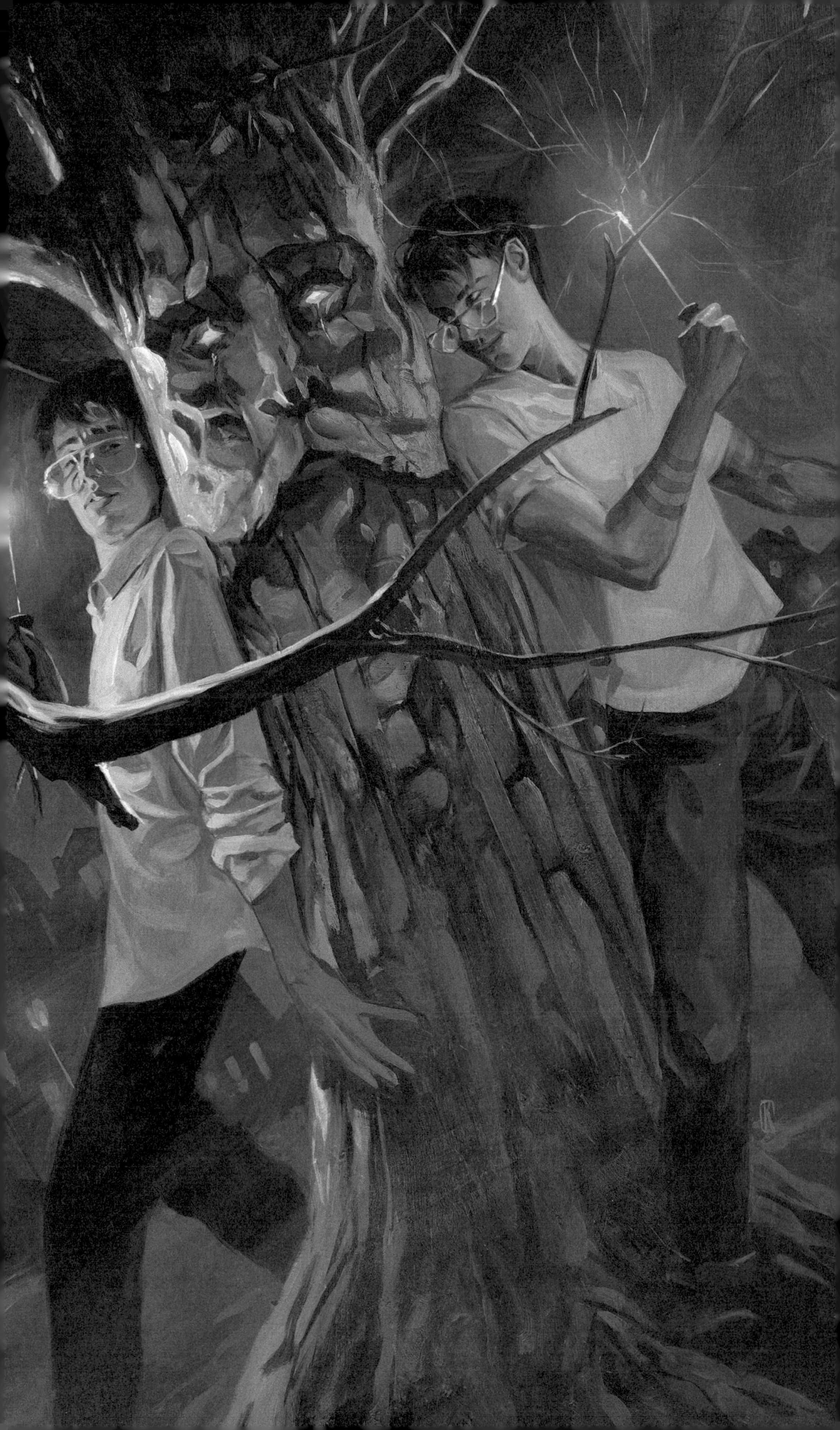

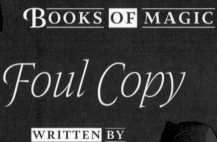

BOOKS OF MAGIC

Foul Copy

WRITTEN BY
Kat Howard

LAYOUTS BY
Tom Fowler

FINISHES BY
Craig Taillefer

COLORS BY
Jordan Boyd

LETTERS BY
Todd Klein

COVER ART BY
Kai Carpenter

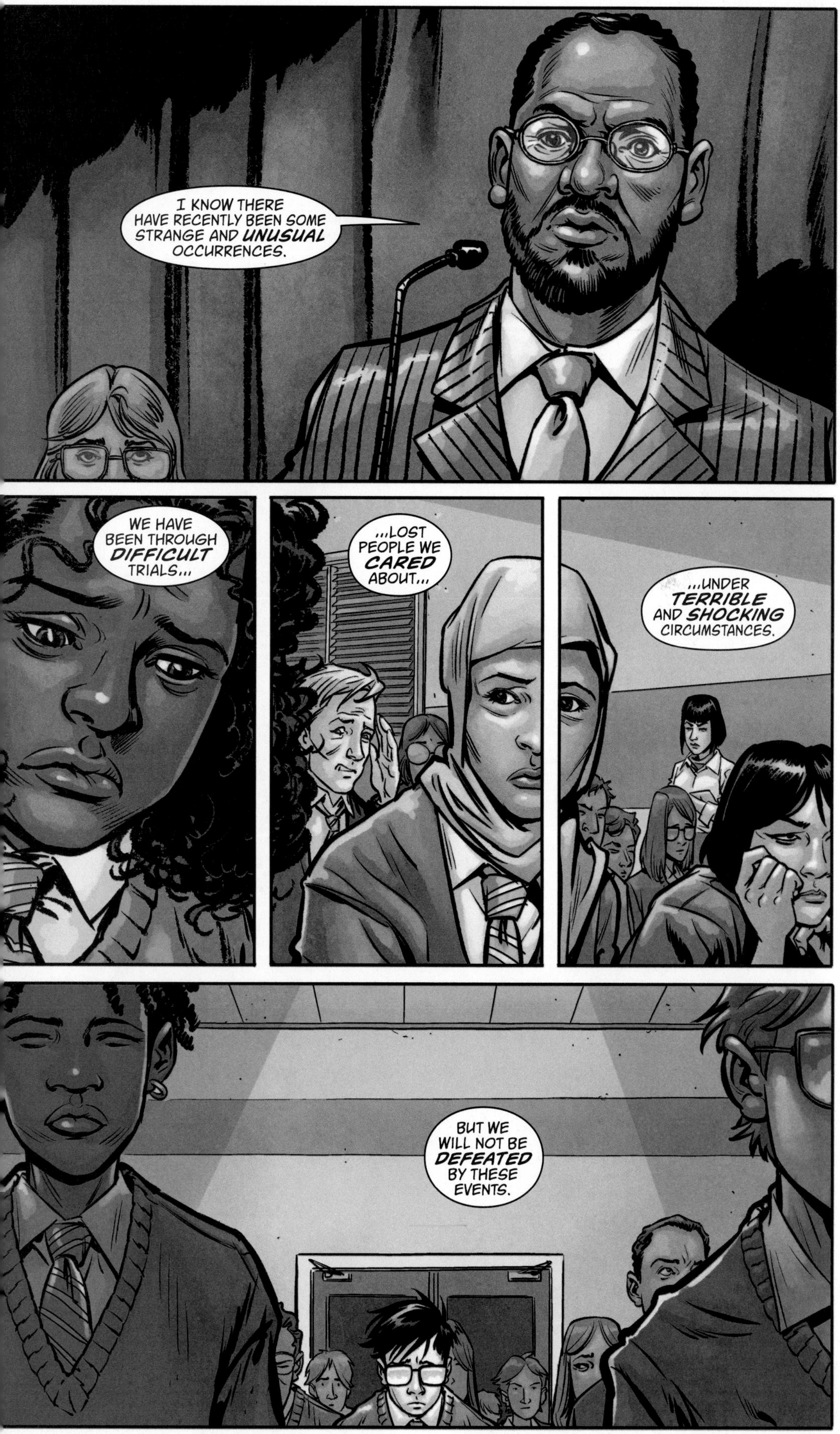
I KNOW THERE HAVE RECENTLY BEEN SOME STRANGE AND UNUSUAL OCCURRENCES.
WE HAVE BEEN THROUGH DIFFICULT TRIALS...
...LOST PEOPLE WE CARED ABOUT...
...UNDER TERRIBLE AND SHOCKING CIRCUMSTANCES.
BUT WE WILL NOT BE DEFEATED BY THESE EVENTS.

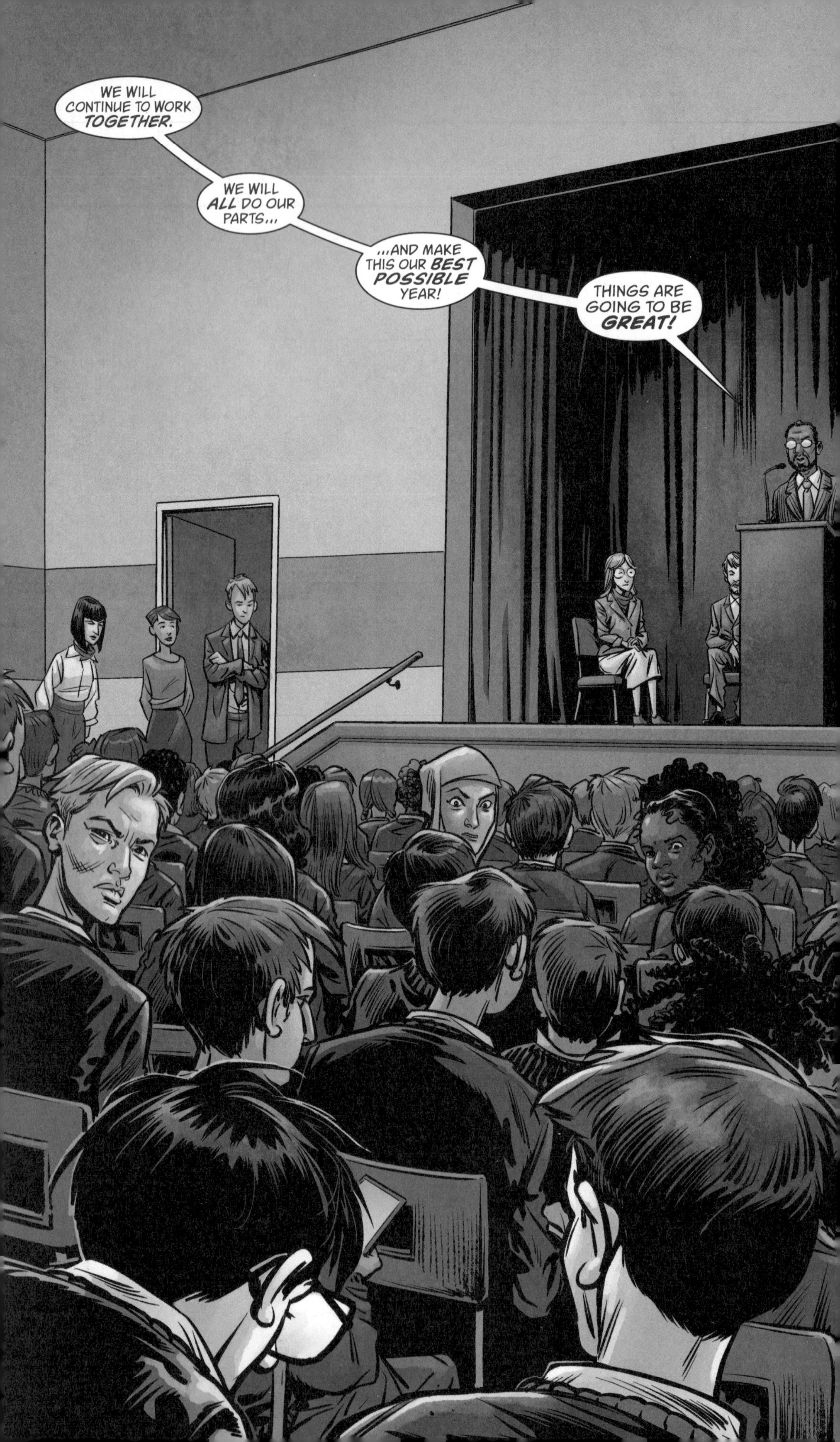
WE WILL CONTINUE TO WORK TOGETHER.
WE WILL ALL DO OUR PARTS...
...AND MAKE THIS OUR BEST POSSIBLE YEAR!
THINGS ARE GOING TO BE GREAT!

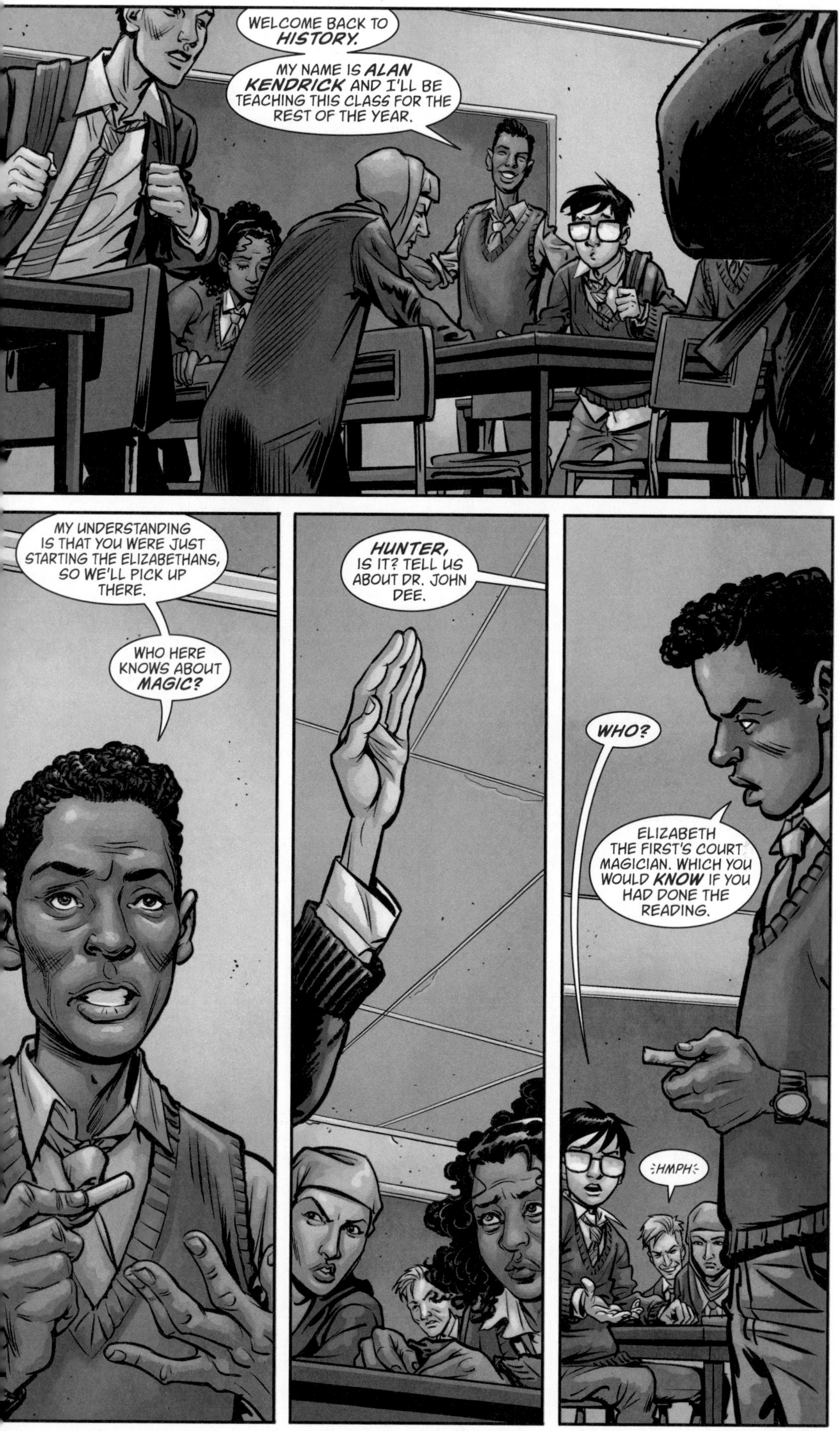
WELCOME BACK TO HISTORY.
MY NAME IS ALAN KENDRICK AND I'LL BE TEACHING THIS CLASS FOR THE REST OF THE YEAR.
MY UNDERSTANDING IS THAT YOU WERE JUST STARTING THE ELIZABETHANS, SO WE'LL PICK UP THERE.
WHO HERE KNOWS ABOUT MAGIC?
HUNTER, IS IT? TELL US ABOUT DR. JOHN DEE.
WHO?
ELIZABETH THE FIRST'S COURT MAGICIAN. WHICH YOU WOULD KNOW IF YOU HAD DONE THE READING.
HMPH

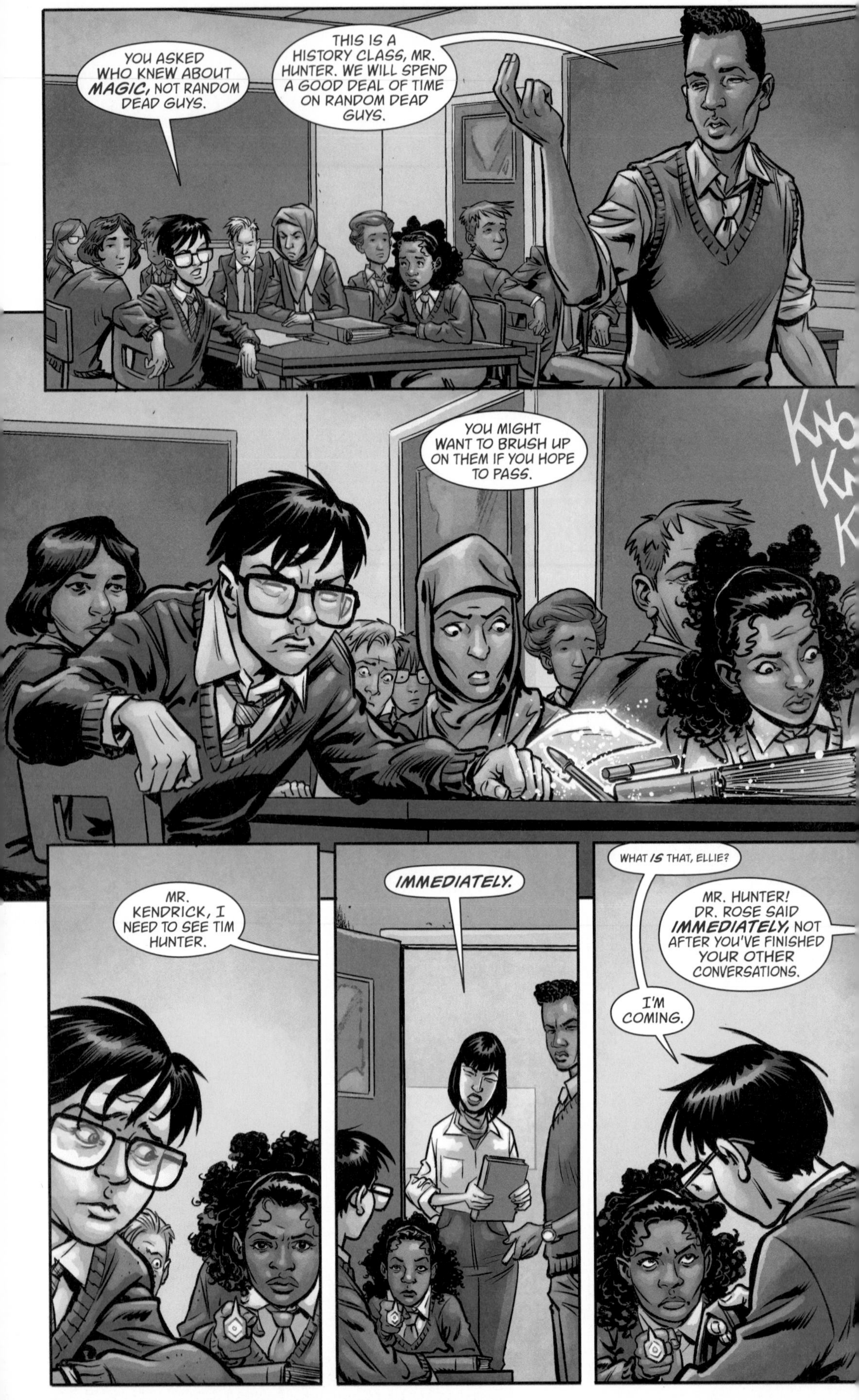
YOU ASKED WHO KNEW ABOUT *MAGIC,* NOT RANDOM DEAD GUYS.
THIS IS A HISTORY CLASS, MR. HUNTER. WE WILL SPEND A GOOD DEAL OF TIME ON RANDOM DEAD GUYS.
YOU MIGHT WANT TO BRUSH UP ON THEM IF YOU HOPE TO PASS.
MR. KENDRICK, I NEED TO SEE TIM HUNTER.
IMMEDIATELY.
WHAT *IS* THAT, ELLIE?
MR. HUNTER! DR. ROSE SAID *IMMEDIATELY,* NOT AFTER YOU'VE FINISHED YOUR OTHER CONVERSATIONS.
I'M COMING.

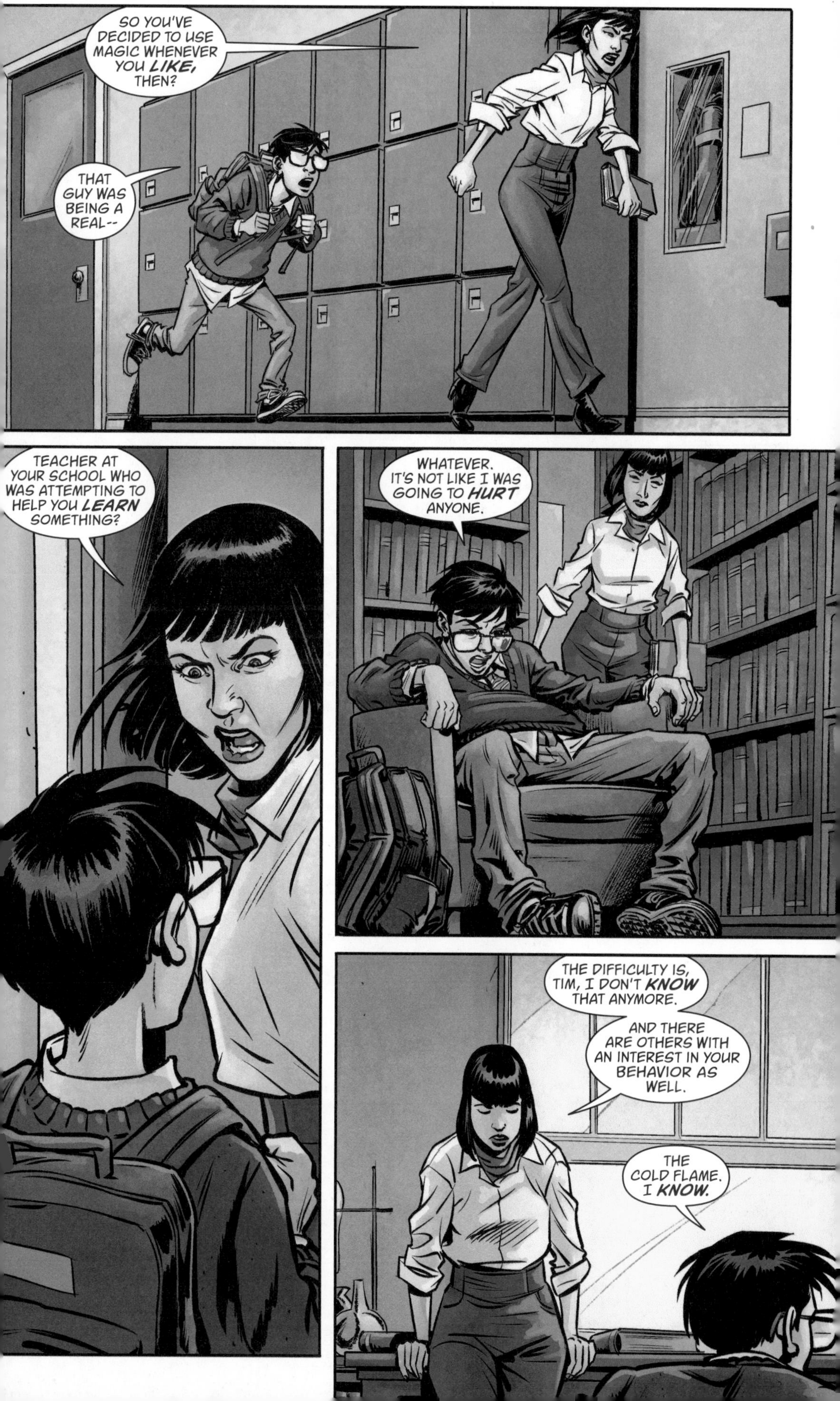
SO YOU'VE DECIDED TO USE MAGIC WHENEVER YOU *LIKE,* THEN?
THAT GUY WAS BEING A REAL--
TEACHER AT YOUR SCHOOL WHO WAS ATTEMPTING TO HELP YOU *LEARN* SOMETHING?
WHATEVER. IT'S NOT LIKE I WAS GOING TO *HURT* ANYONE.
THE DIFFICULTY IS, TIM, I DON'T *KNOW* THAT ANYMORE.
AND THERE ARE OTHERS WITH AN INTEREST IN YOUR BEHAVIOR AS WELL.
THE COLD FLAME. I *KNOW.*

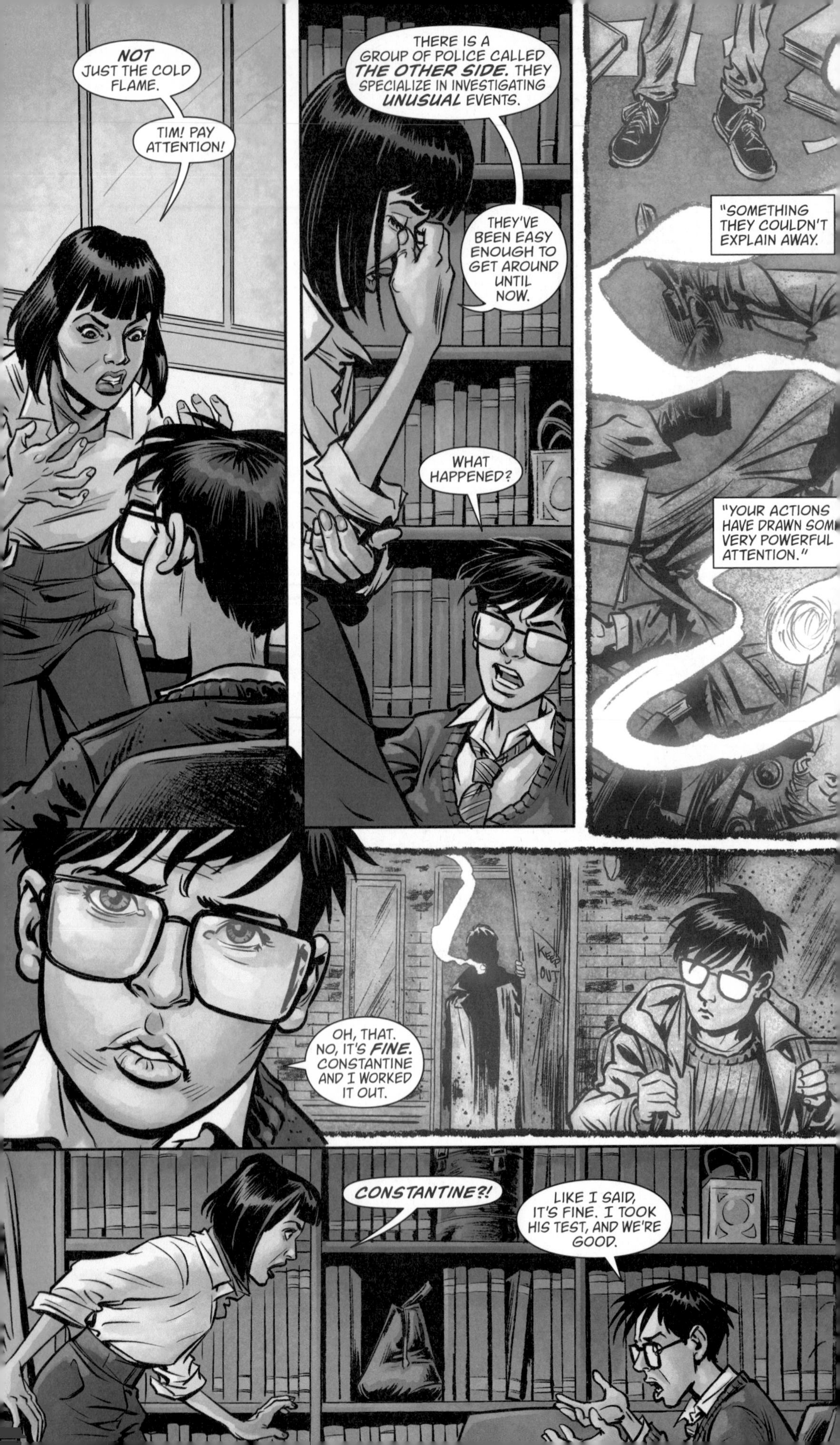

NOT JUST THE COLD FLAME.
TIM! PAY ATTENTION!
THERE IS A GROUP OF POLICE CALLED THE OTHER SIDE. THEY SPECIALIZE IN INVESTIGATING UNUSUAL EVENTS.
THEY'VE BEEN EASY ENOUGH TO GET AROUND UNTIL NOW.
WHAT HAPPENED?
"SOMETHING THEY COULDN'T EXPLAIN AWAY.
"YOUR ACTIONS HAVE DRAWN SOM VERY POWERFUL ATTENTION."
OH, THAT. NO, IT'S FINE. CONSTANTINE AND I WORKED IT OUT.
KEEP OUT
CONSTANTINE?!
LIKE I SAID, IT'S FINE. I TOOK HIS TEST, AND WE'RE GOOD.

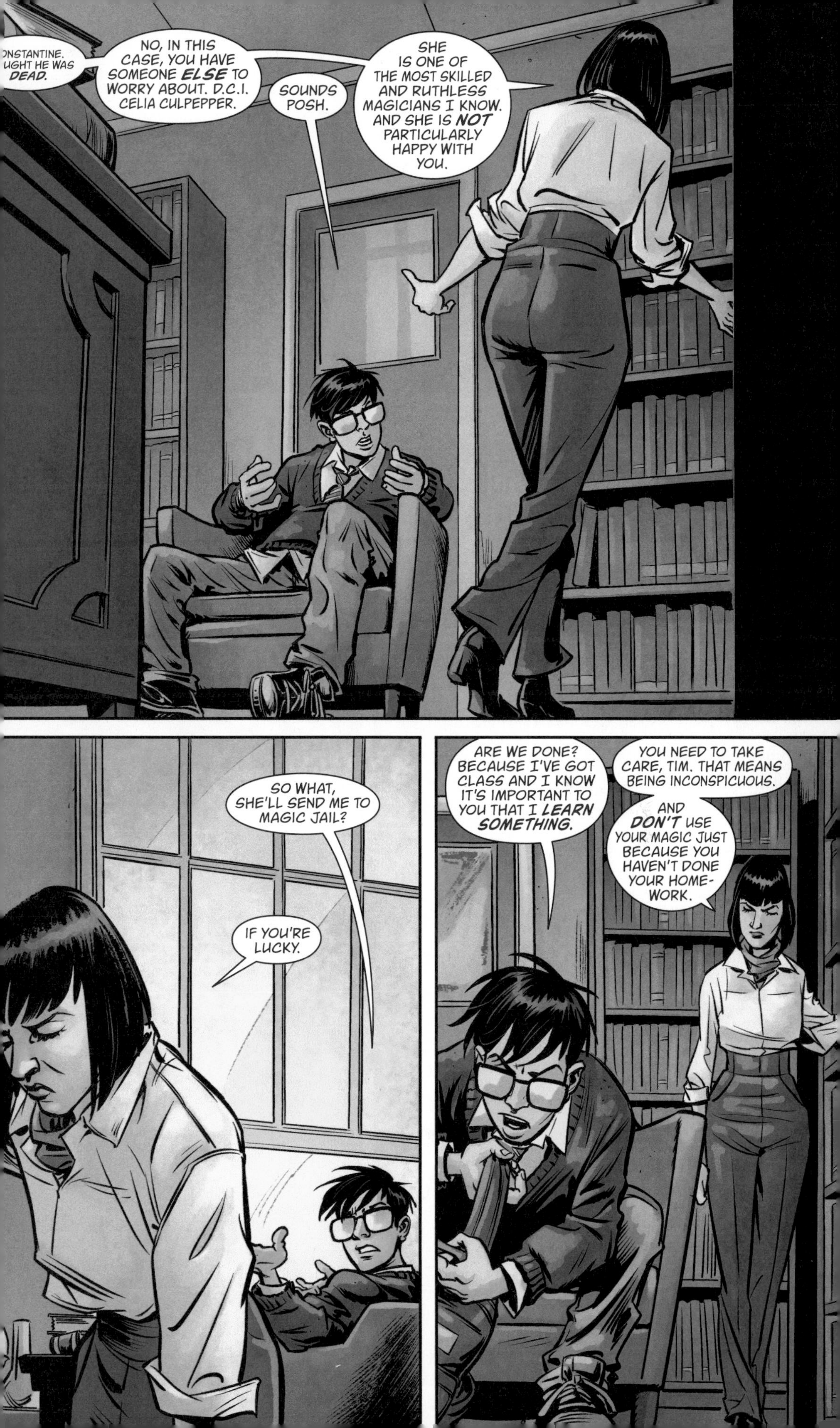
ONSTANTINE. UGHT HE WAS DEAD.
NO, IN THIS CASE, YOU HAVE SOMEONE ELSE TO WORRY ABOUT. D.C.I. CELIA CULPEPPER.
SOUNDS POSH.
SHE IS ONE OF THE MOST SKILLED AND RUTHLESS MAGICIANS I KNOW. AND SHE IS NOT PARTICULARLY HAPPY WITH YOU.
SO WHAT, SHE'LL SEND ME TO MAGIC JAIL?
IF YOU'RE LUCKY.
ARE WE DONE? BECAUSE I'VE GOT CLASS AND I KNOW IT'S IMPORTANT TO YOU THAT I LEARN SOMETHING.
YOU NEED TO TAKE CARE, TIM. THAT MEANS BEING INCONSPICUOUS.
AND DON'T USE YOUR MAGIC JUST BECAUSE YOU HAVEN'T DONE YOUR HOME-WORK.

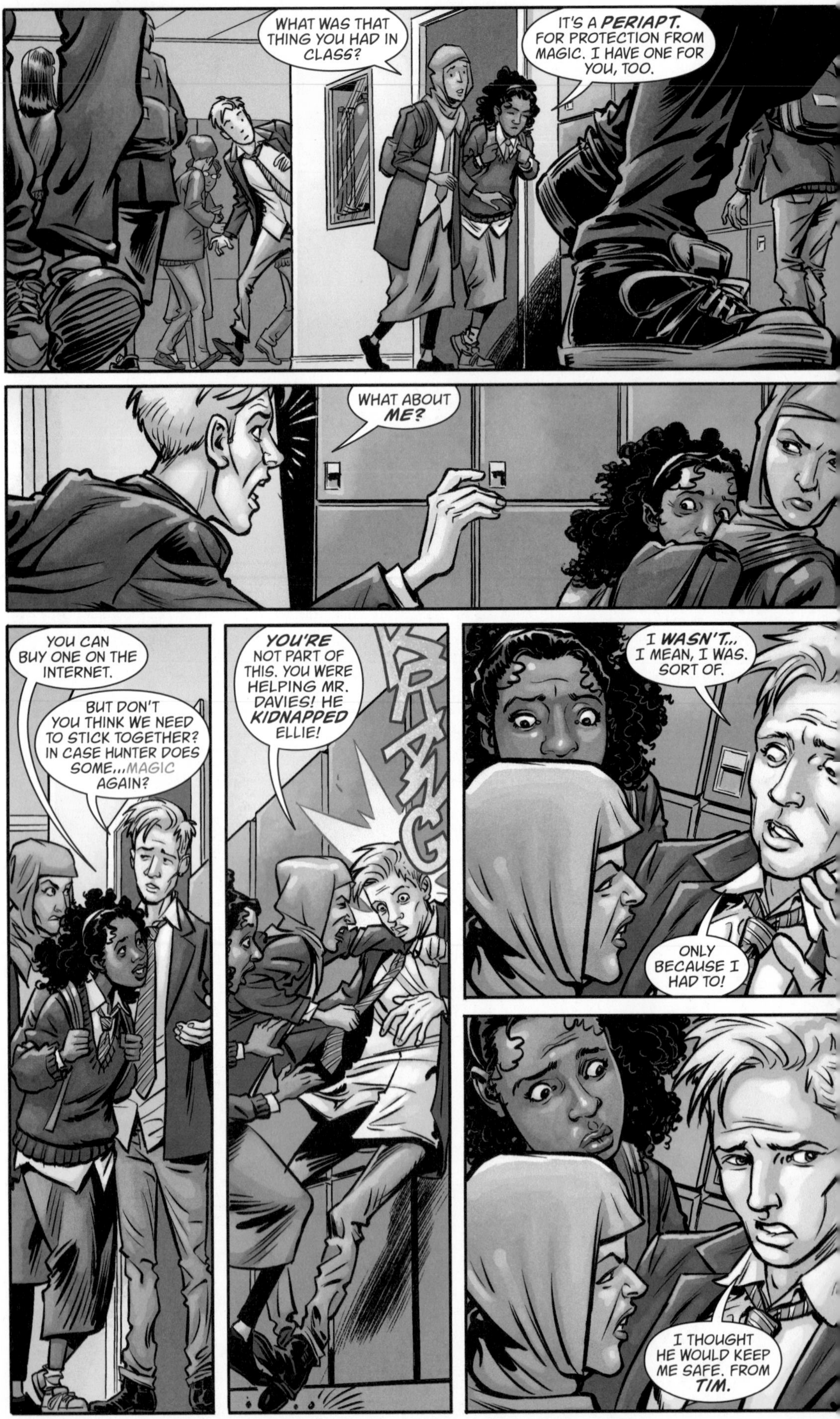
WHAT WAS THAT THING YOU HAD IN CLASS?
IT'S A **PERIAPT.** FOR PROTECTION FROM MAGIC. I HAVE ONE FOR YOU, TOO.
WHAT ABOUT **ME?**
YOU CAN BUY ONE ON THE INTERNET.
BUT DON'T YOU THINK WE NEED TO STICK TOGETHER? IN CASE HUNTER DOES SOME...MAGIC AGAIN?
YOU'RE NOT PART OF THIS. YOU WERE HELPING MR. DAVIES! HE **KIDNAPPED** ELLIE!
KRANG
I **WASN'T**... I MEAN, I WAS. SORT OF.
ONLY BECAUSE I HAD TO!
I THOUGHT HE WOULD KEEP ME SAFE. FROM **TIM.**

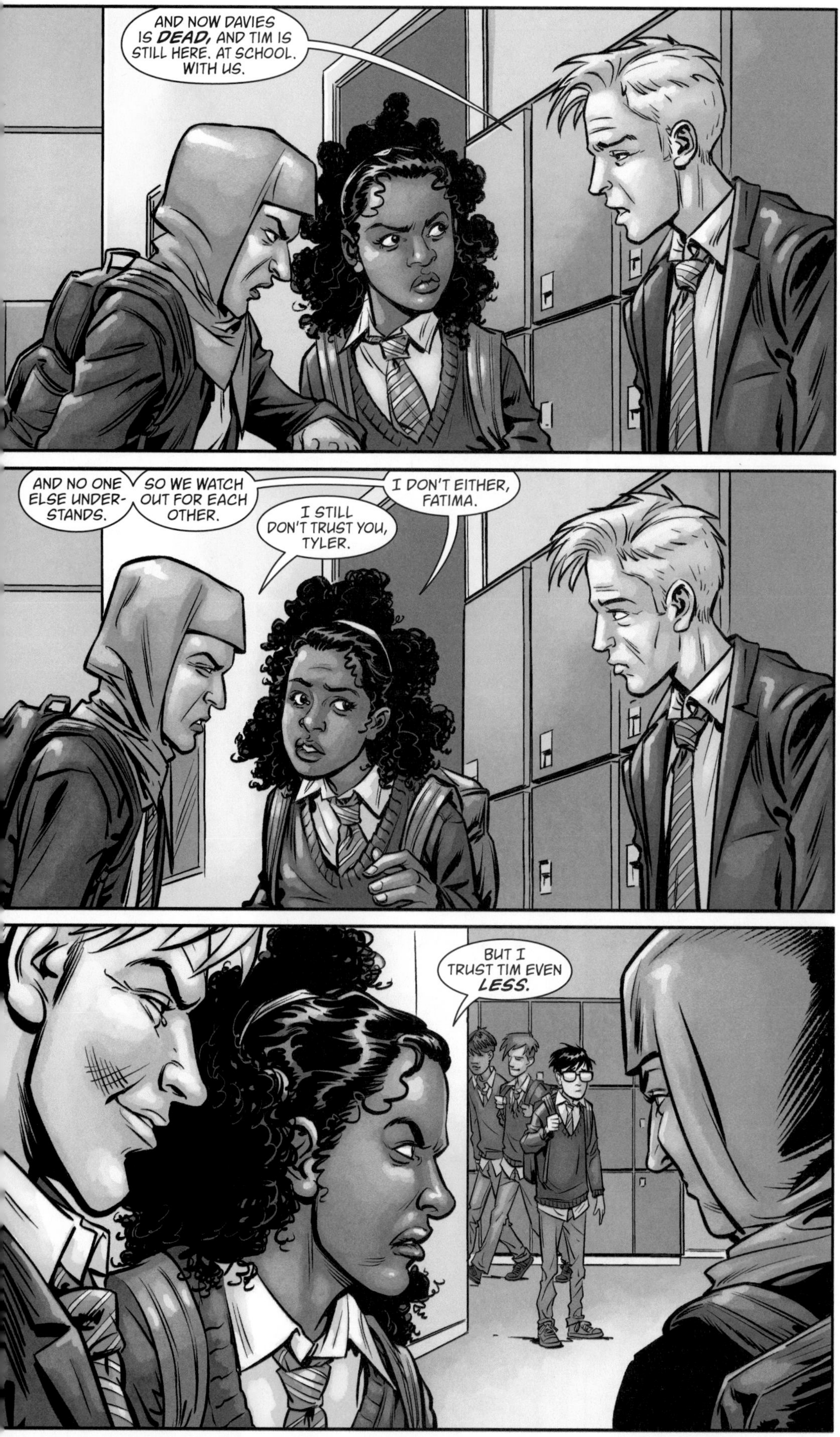
AND NOW DAVIES IS DEAD, AND TIM IS STILL HERE. AT SCHOOL. WITH US.
AND NO ONE ELSE UNDER-STANDS.
SO WE WATCH OUT FOR EACH OTHER.
I STILL DON'T TRUST YOU, TYLER.
I DON'T EITHER, FATIMA.
BUT I TRUST TIM EVEN LESS.

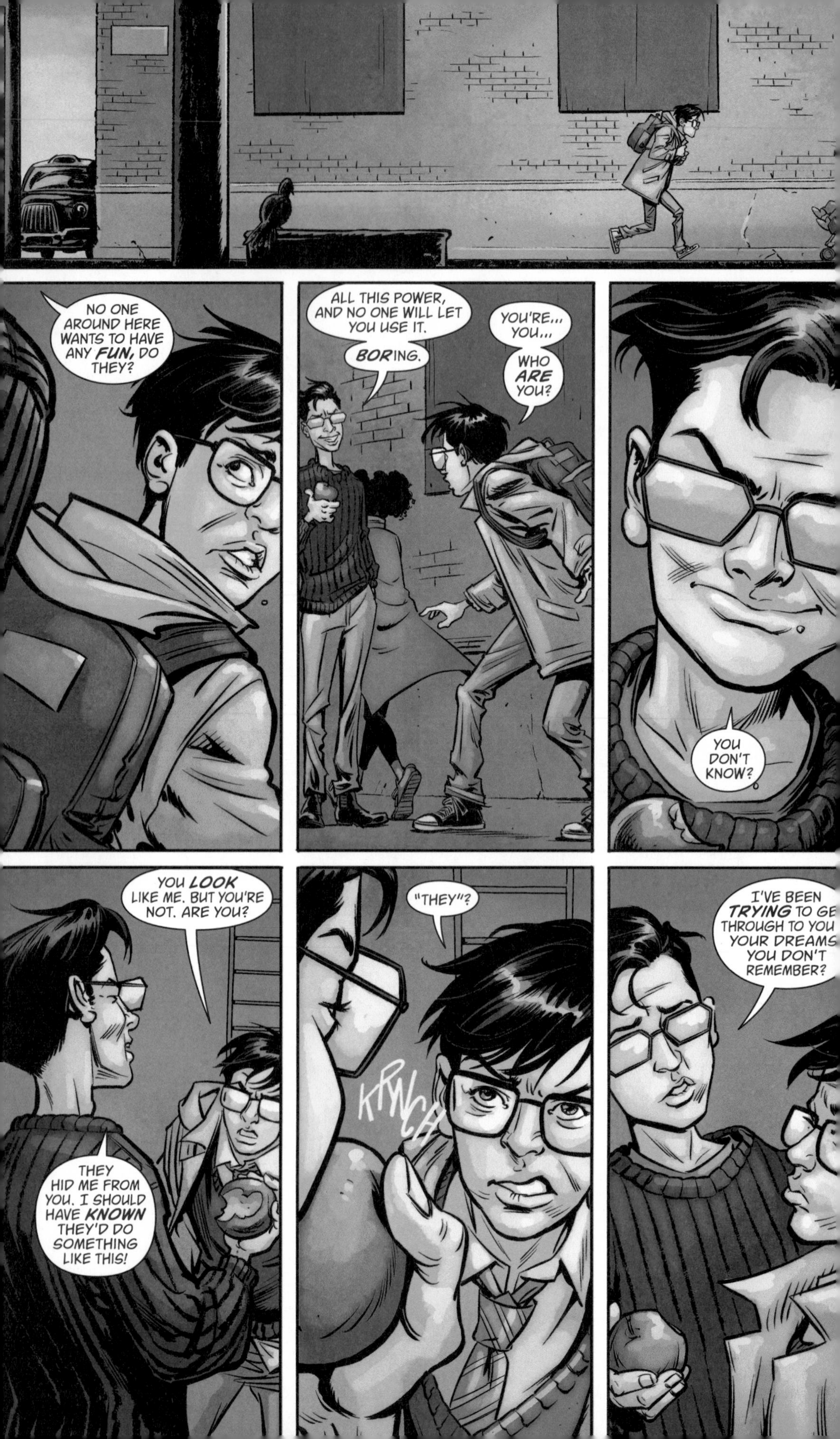

NO ONE AROUND HERE WANTS TO HAVE ANY FUN, DO THEY?
ALL THIS POWER, AND NO ONE WILL LET YOU USE IT.
BORING.
YOU'RE... YOU...
WHO ARE YOU?
YOU DON'T KNOW?
YOU LOOK LIKE ME. BUT YOU'RE NOT. ARE YOU?
THEY HID ME FROM YOU. I SHOULD HAVE KNOWN THEY'D DO SOMETHING LIKE THIS!
"THEY"?
KRNCH
I'VE BEEN TRYING TO GE THROUGH TO YOU YOUR DREAMS YOU DON'T REMEMBER?

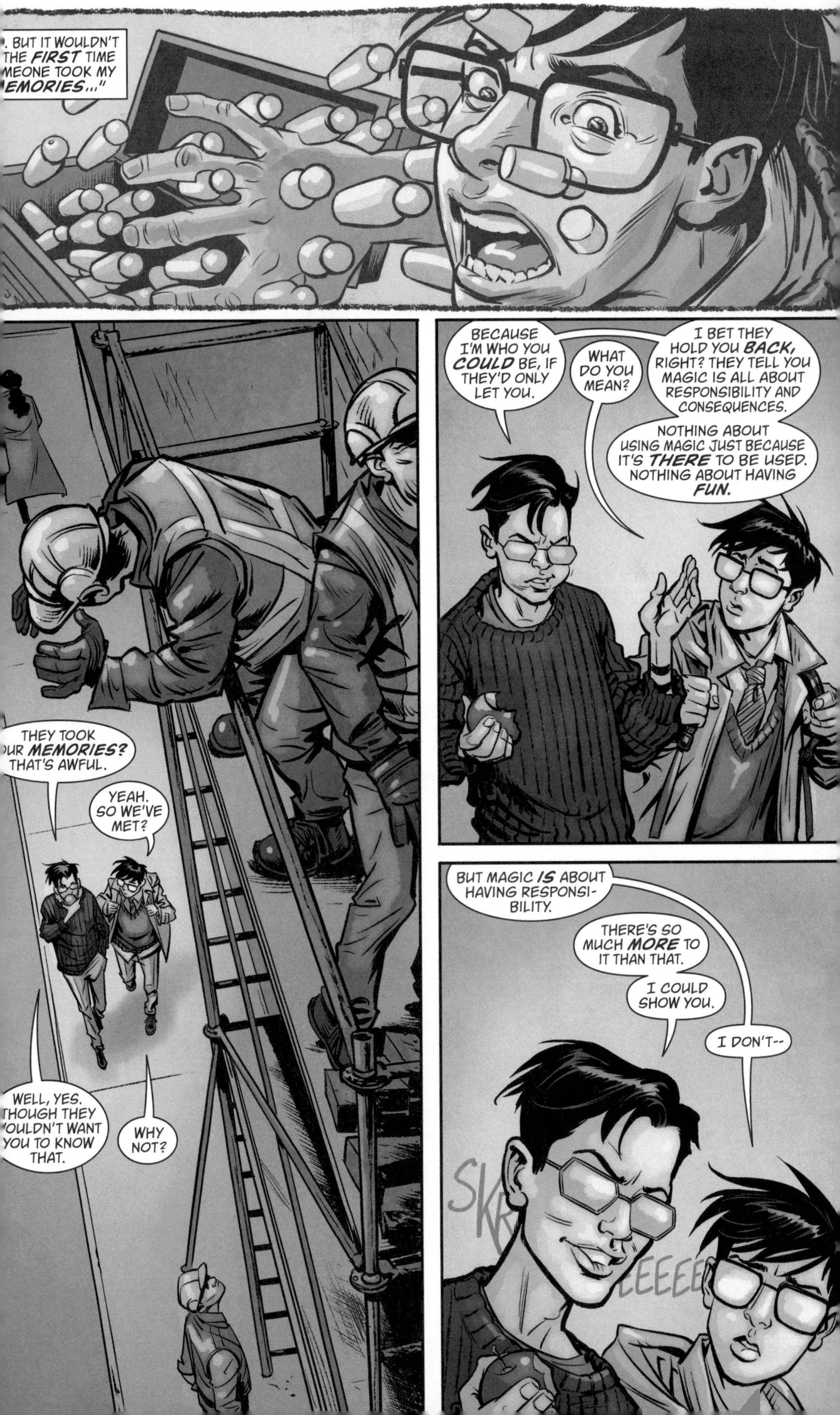
. BUT IT WOULDN'T THE FIRST TIME MEONE TOOK MY EMORIES..."
THEY TOOK UR MEMORIES? THAT'S AWFUL.
YEAH. SO WE'VE MET?
WELL, YES. THOUGH THEY OULDN'T WANT YOU TO KNOW THAT.
WHY NOT?
BECAUSE I'M WHO YOU COULD BE, IF THEY'D ONLY LET YOU.
WHAT DO YOU MEAN?
I BET THEY HOLD YOU BACK, RIGHT? THEY TELL YOU MAGIC IS ALL ABOUT RESPONSIBILITY AND CONSEQUENCES.
NOTHING ABOUT USING MAGIC JUST BECAUSE IT'S THERE TO BE USED. NOTHING ABOUT HAVING FUN.
BUT MAGIC IS ABOUT HAVING RESPONSI-BILITY.
THERE'S SO MUCH MORE TO IT THAN THAT.
I COULD SHOW YOU.
I DON'T--
SKR
EEEEE

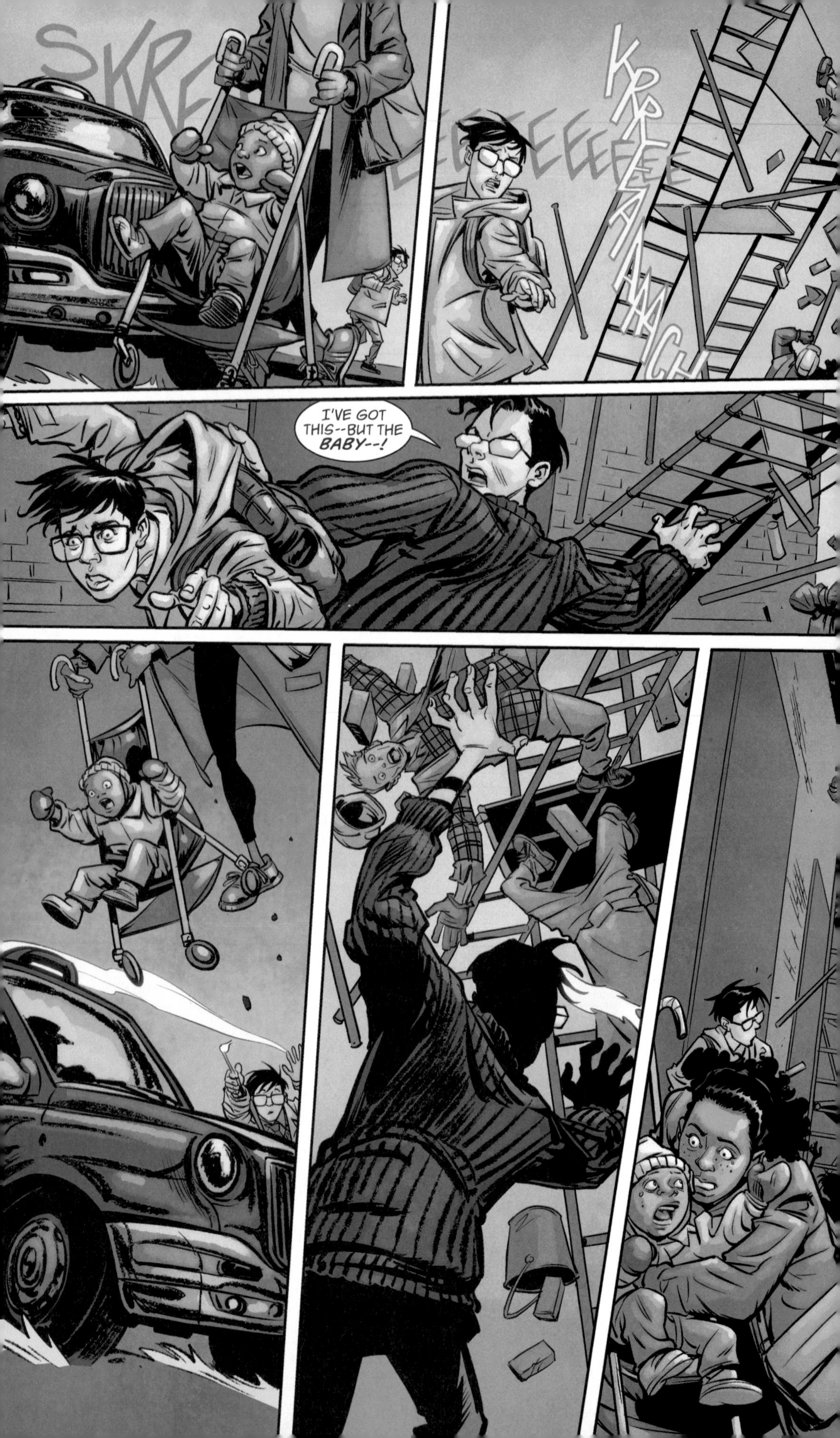
SKREEEEEEEEE
KRRTESAAAACH
I'VE GOT THIS--BUT THE BABY--!

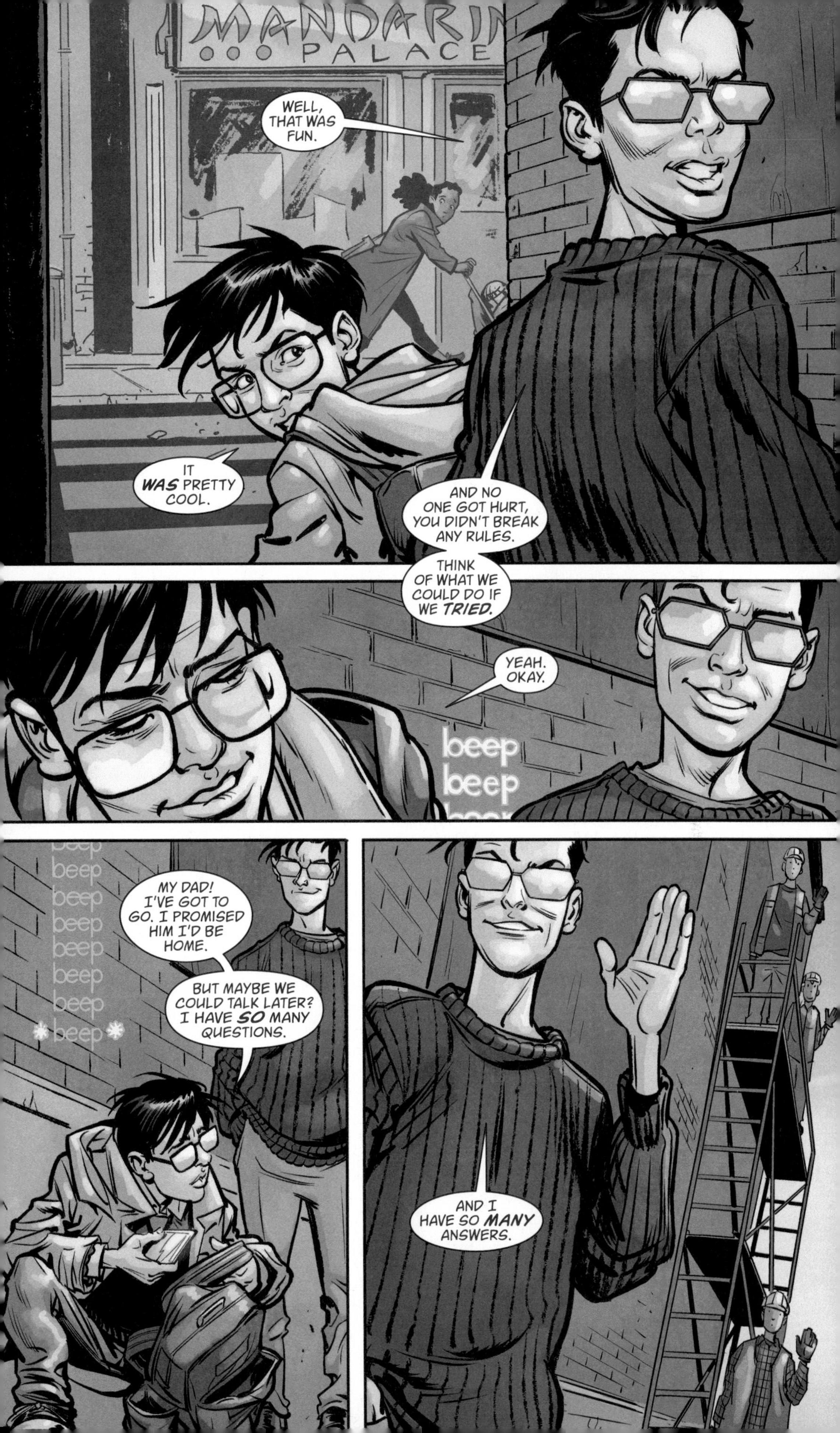
MANDARIN
PALACE
WELL, THAT WAS FUN.
IT *WAS* PRETTY COOL.
AND NO ONE GOT HURT, YOU DIDN'T BREAK ANY RULES.
THINK OF WHAT WE COULD DO IF WE *TRIED*.
YEAH. OKAY.
beep
beep
beep
beep
beep
beep
beep
beep
beep
beep
MY DAD! I'VE GOT TO GO. I PROMISED HIM I'D BE HOME.
BUT MAYBE WE COULD TALK LATER? I HAVE *SO* MANY QUESTIONS.
AND I HAVE SO *MANY* ANSWERS.

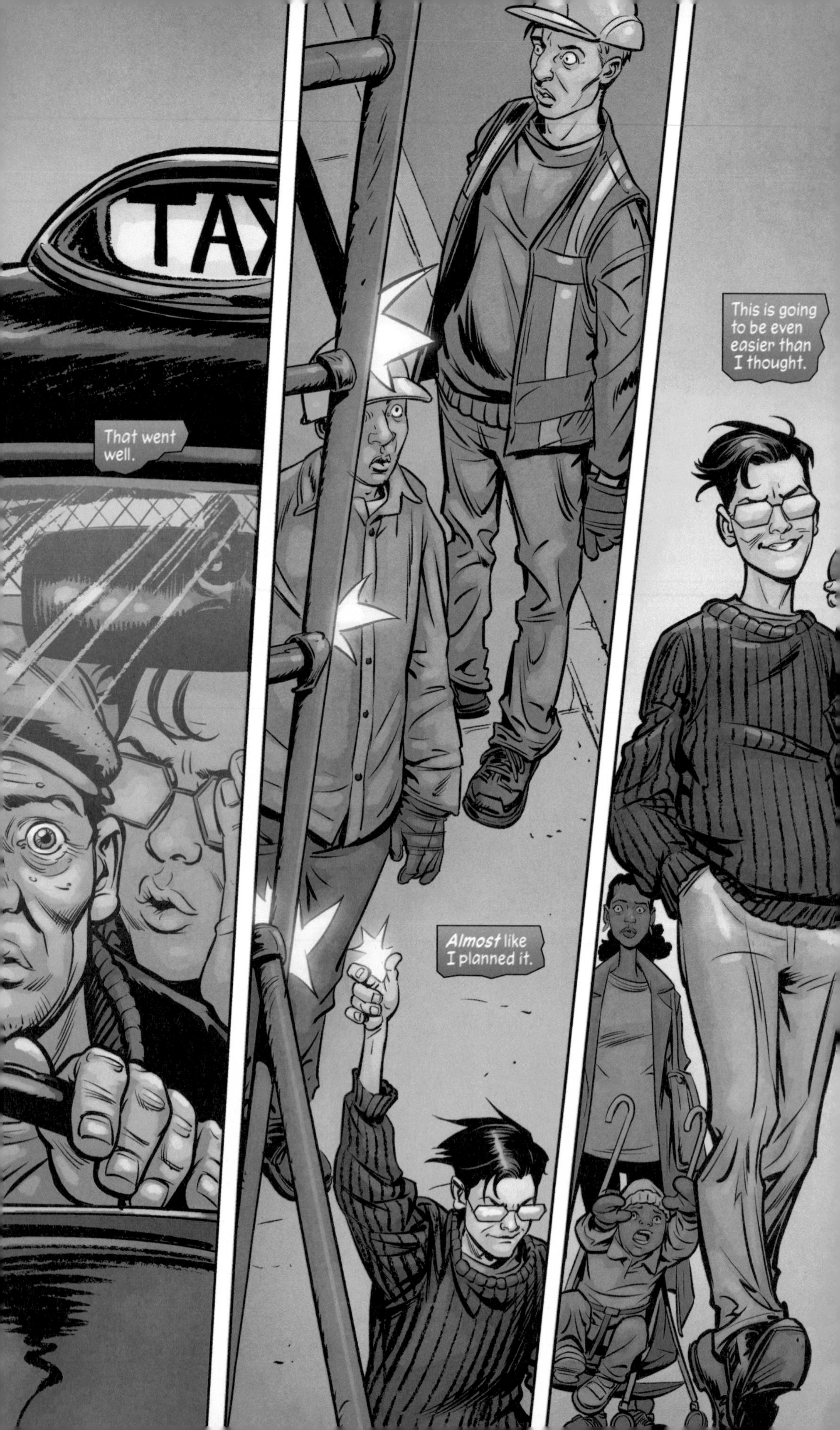
TAX
That went well.
Almost like I planned it.
This is going to be even easier than I thought.

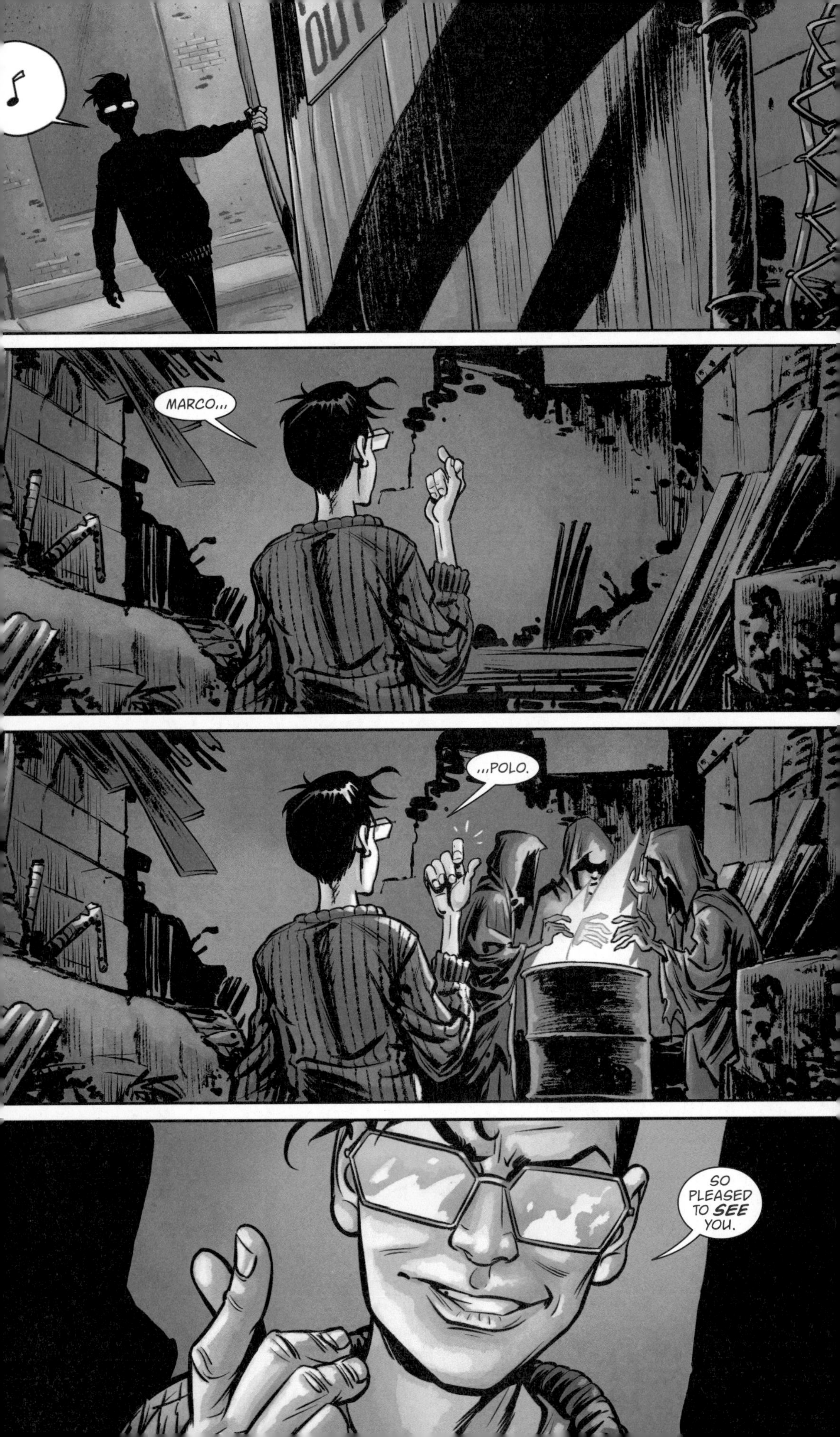

♪
MARCO...
...POLO.
SO PLEASED TO SEE YOU.

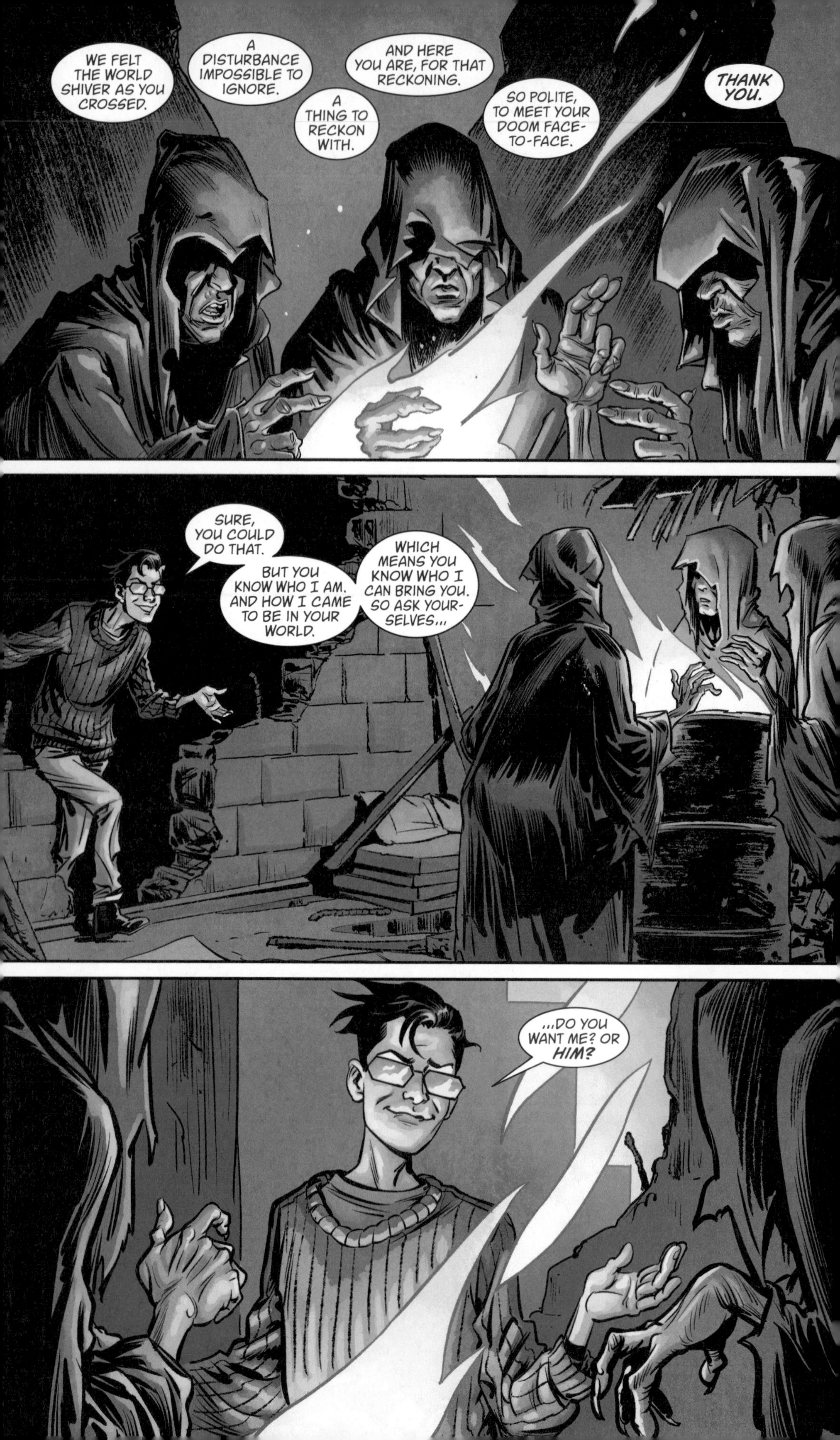
WE FELT THE WORLD SHIVER AS YOU CROSSED.
A DISTURBANCE IMPOSSIBLE TO IGNORE.
A THING TO RECKON WITH.
AND HERE YOU ARE, FOR THAT RECKONING.
SO POLITE, TO MEET YOUR DOOM FACE-TO-FACE.
THANK YOU.
SURE, YOU COULD DO THAT.
BUT YOU KNOW WHO I AM. AND HOW I CAME TO BE IN YOUR WORLD.
WHICH MEANS YOU KNOW WHO I CAN BRING YOU. SO ASK YOUR-SELVES...
...DO YOU WANT ME? OR HIM?

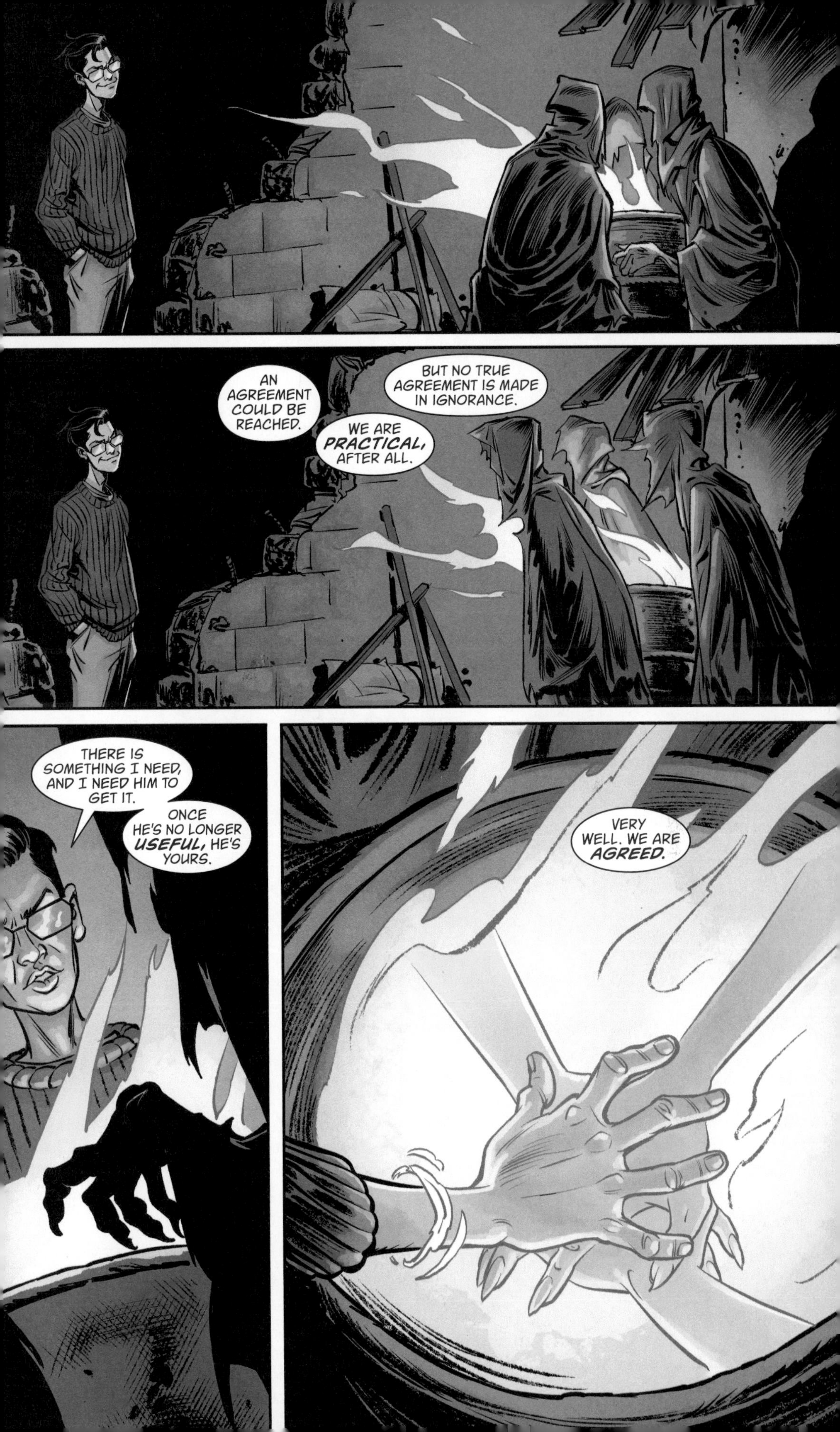
AN AGREEMENT COULD BE REACHED.
BUT NO TRUE AGREEMENT IS MADE IN IGNORANCE.
WE ARE PRACTICAL, AFTER ALL.
THERE IS SOMETHING I NEED, AND I NEED HIM TO GET IT.
ONCE HE'S NO LONGER USEFUL, HE'S YOURS.
VERY WELL. WE ARE AGREED.

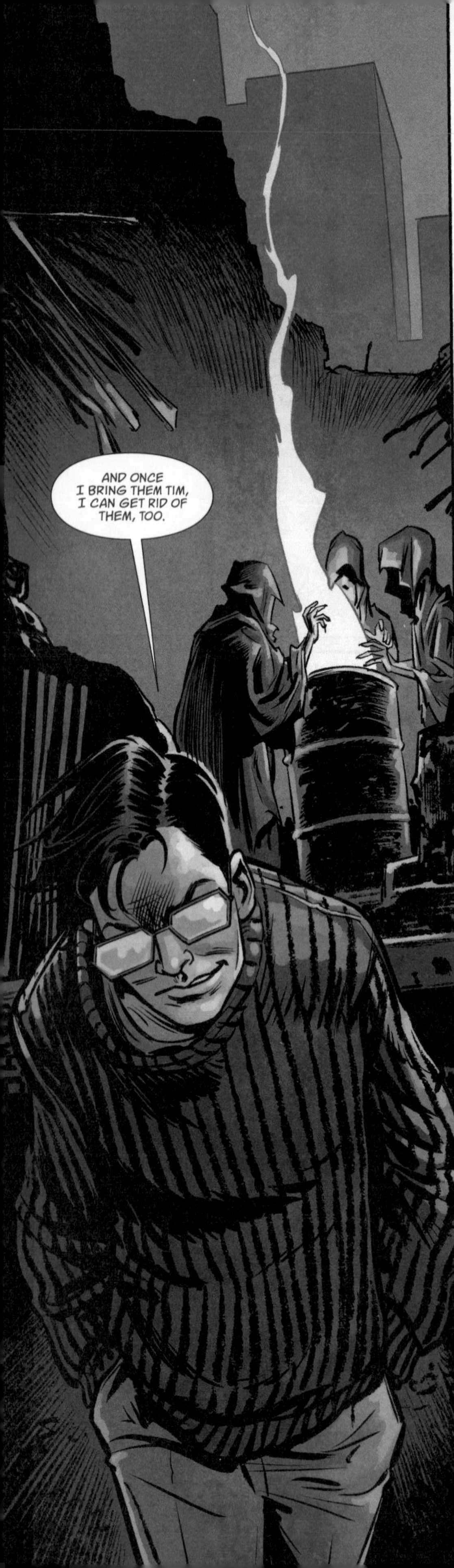
AND ONCE I BRING THEM TIM, I CAN GET RID OF THEM, TOO.

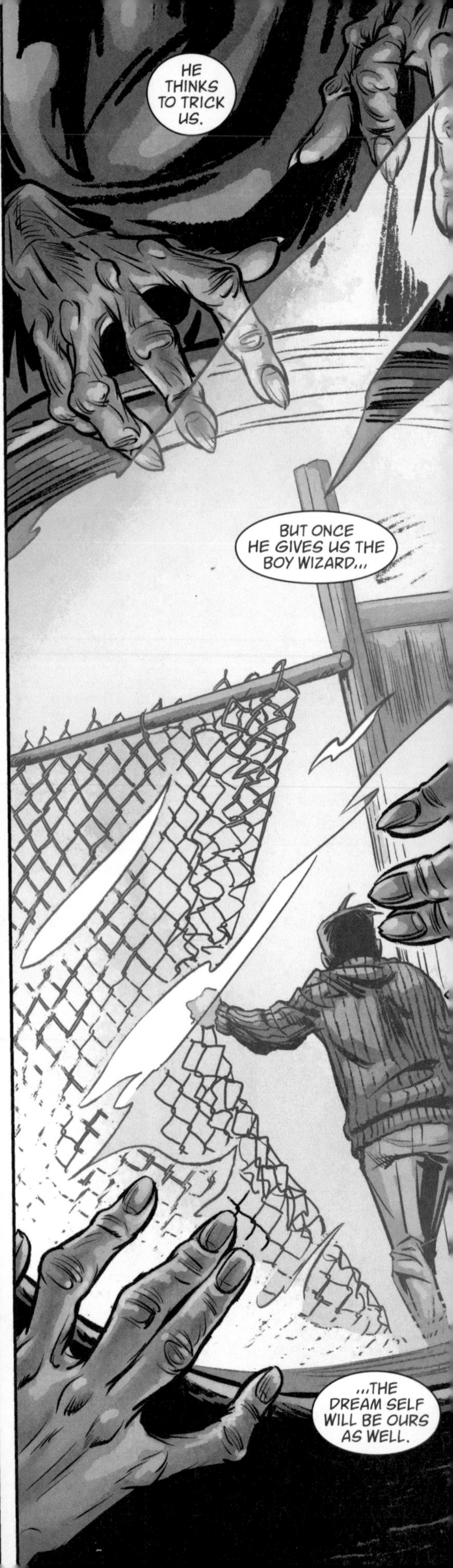
HE THINKS TO TRICK US.
BUT ONCE HE GIVES US THE BOY WIZARD...
...THE DREAM SELF WILL BE OURS AS WELL.

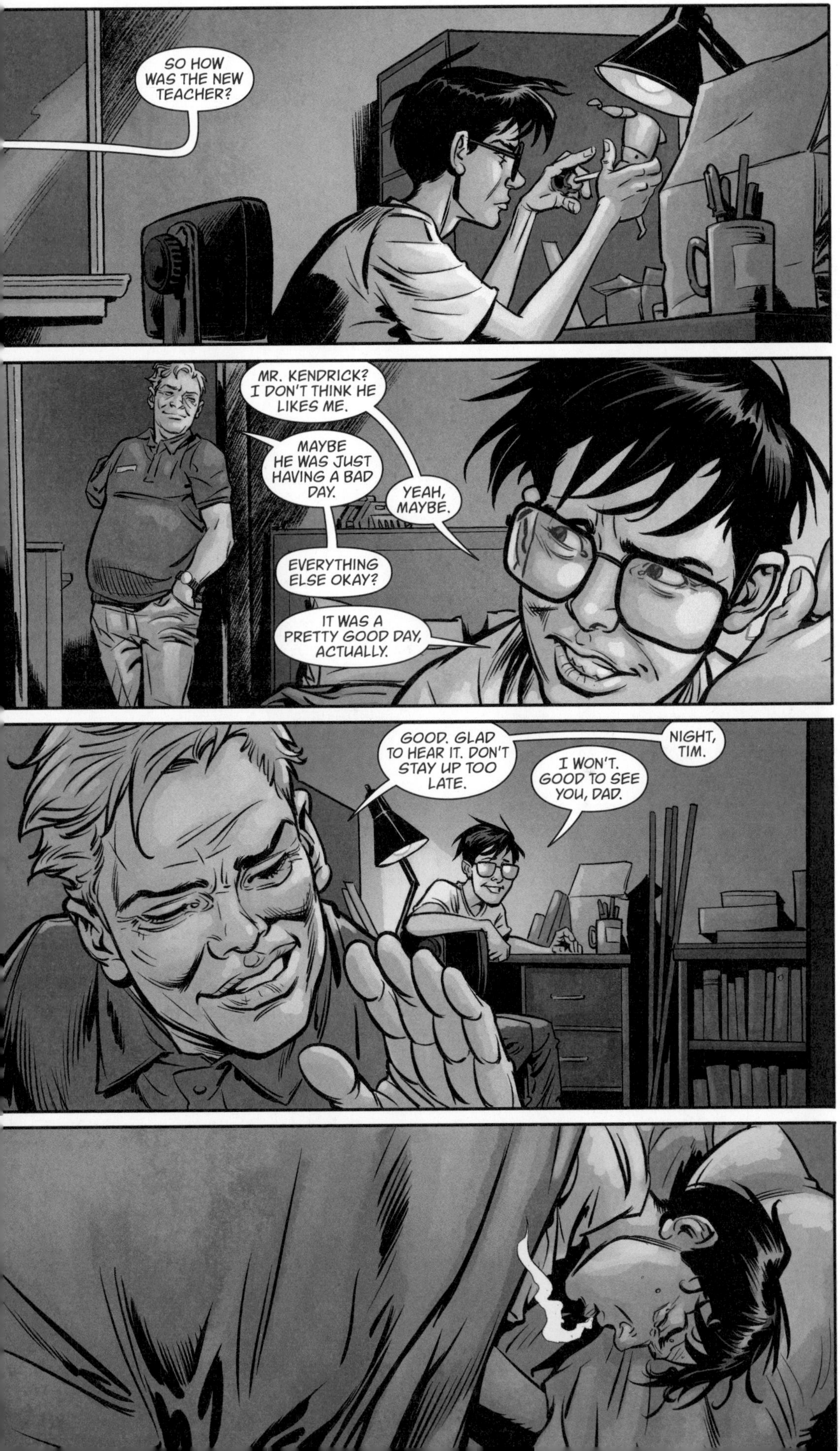
SO HOW WAS THE NEW TEACHER?
MR. KENDRICK? I DON'T THINK HE LIKES ME.
MAYBE HE WAS JUST HAVING A BAD DAY.
YEAH, MAYBE.
EVERYTHING ELSE OKAY?
IT WAS A PRETTY GOOD DAY, ACTUALLY.
GOOD. GLAD TO HEAR IT. DON'T STAY UP TOO LATE.
I WON'T. GOOD TO SEE YOU, DAD.
NIGHT, TIM.

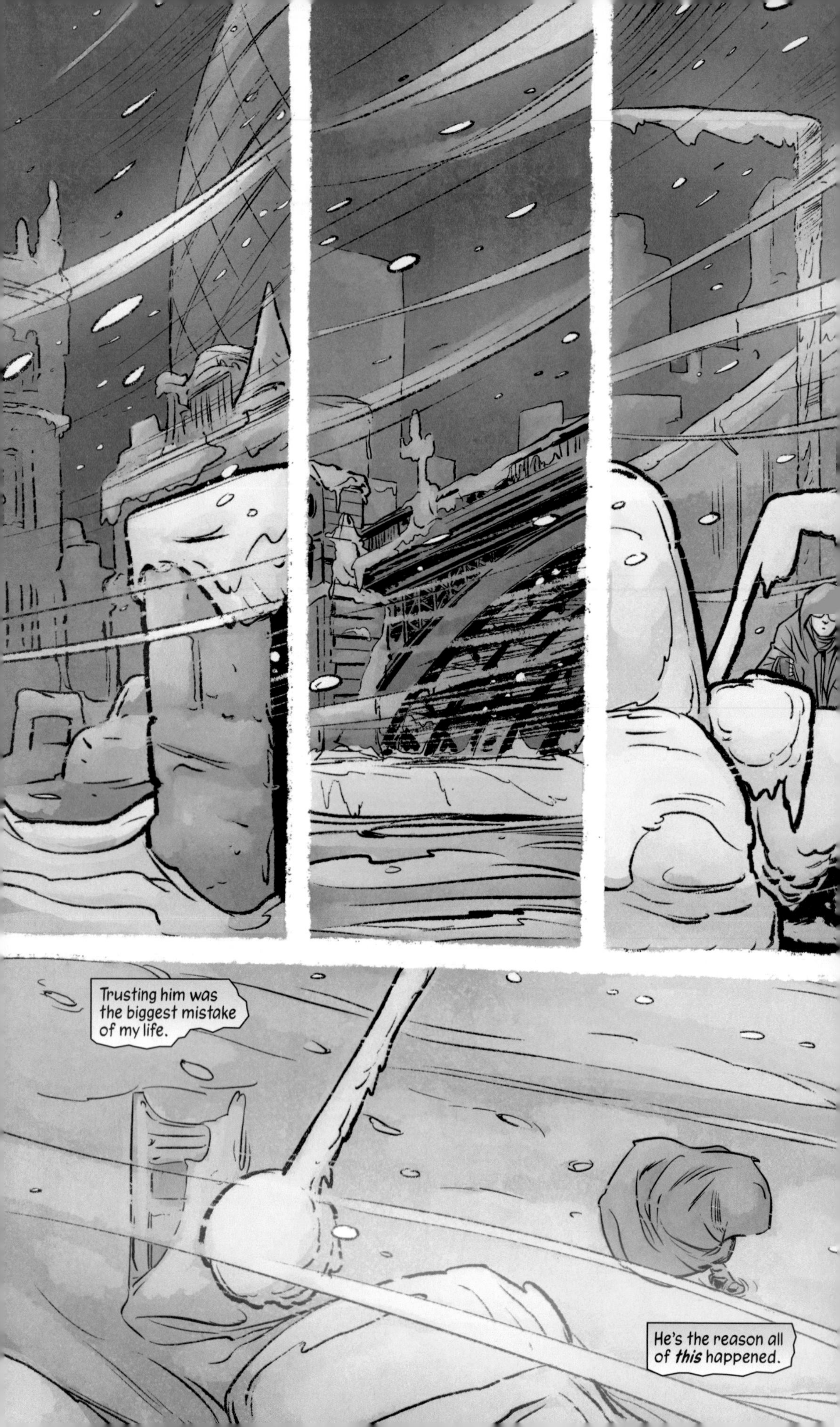
Trusting him was the biggest mistake of my life.
He's the reason all of *this* happened.

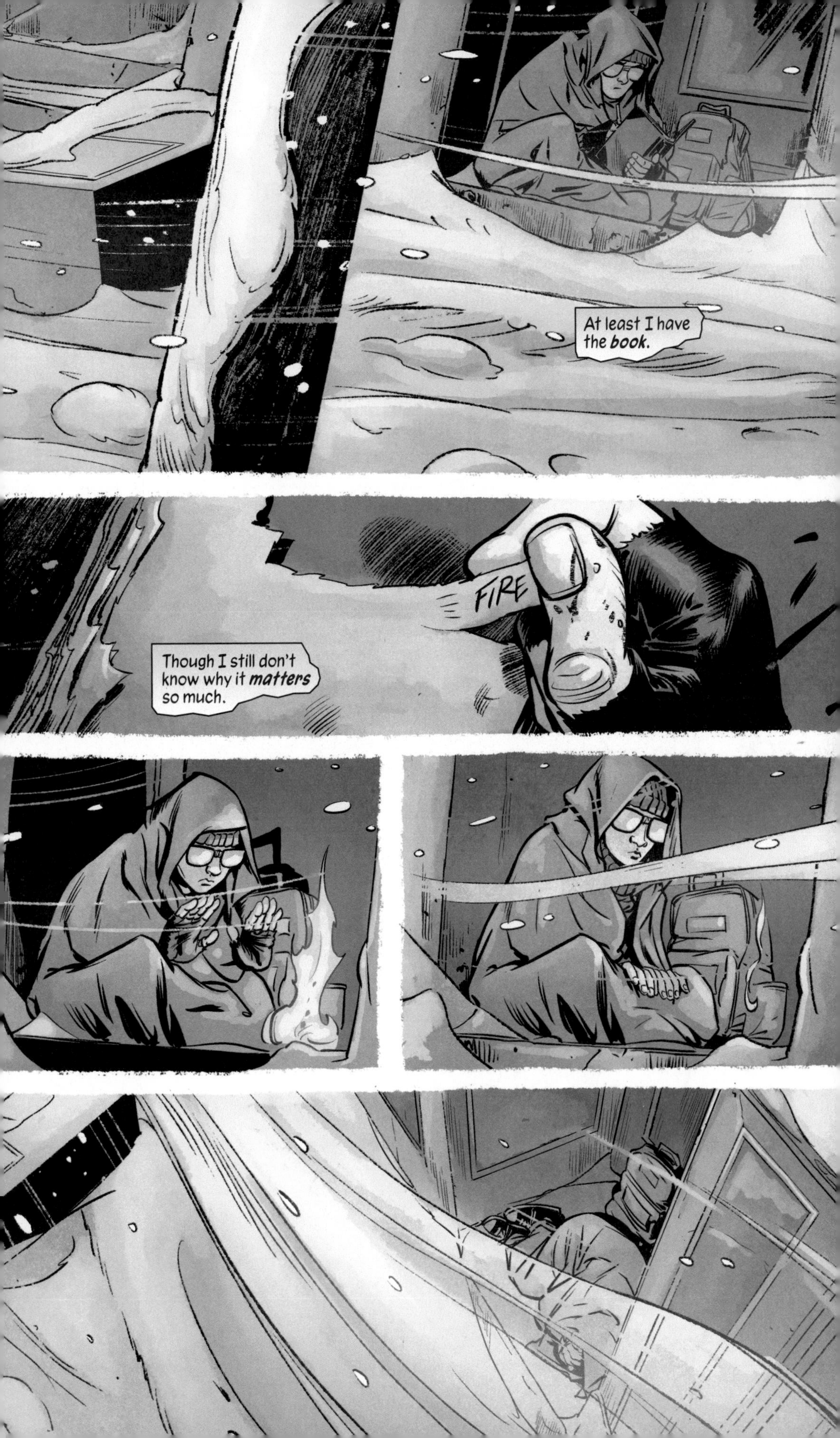
At least I have the ***book.***
FIRE
Though I still don't know why it ***matters*** so much.

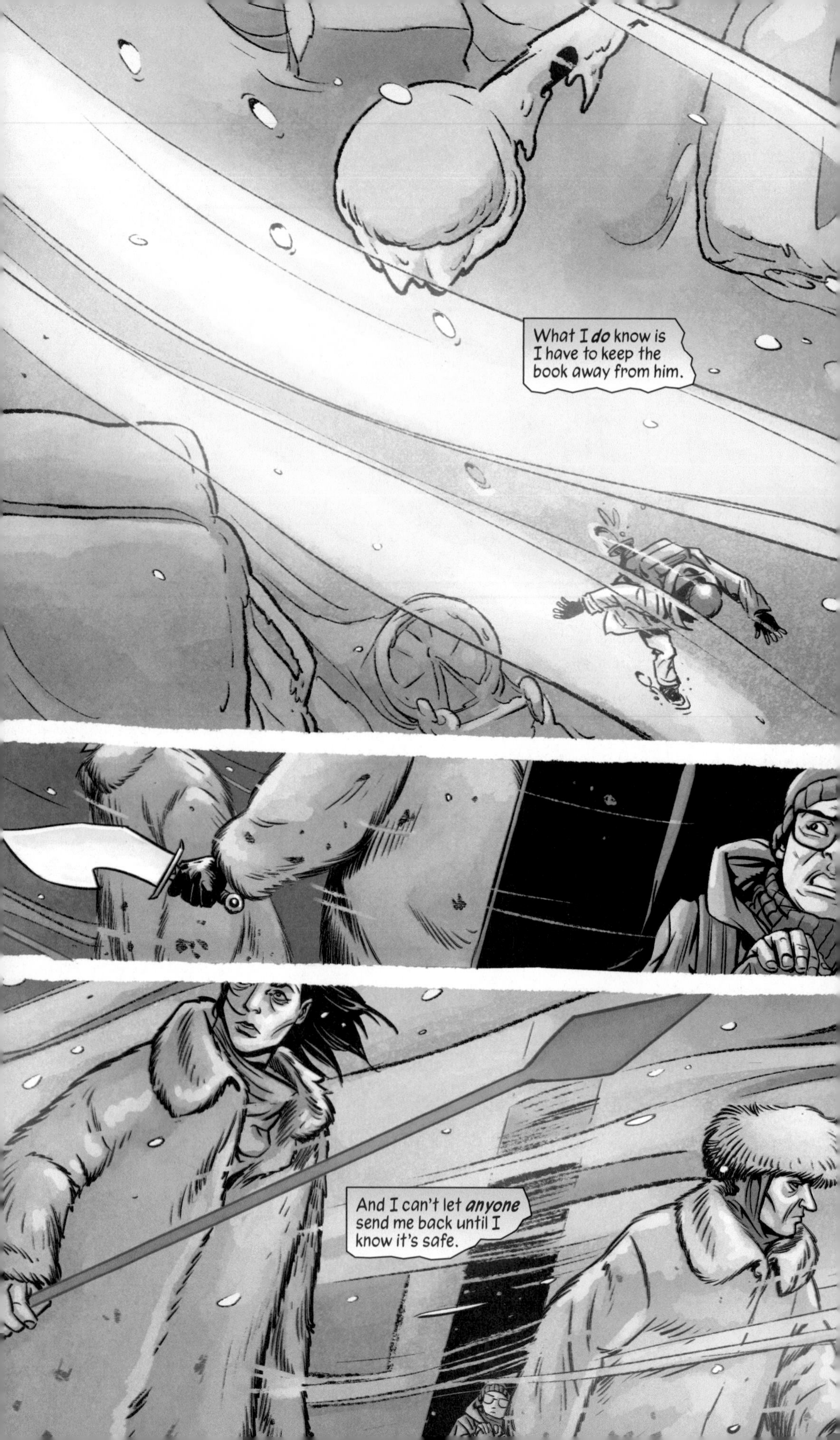
What I *do* know is I have to keep the book away from him.
And I can't let *anyone* send me back until I know it's safe.

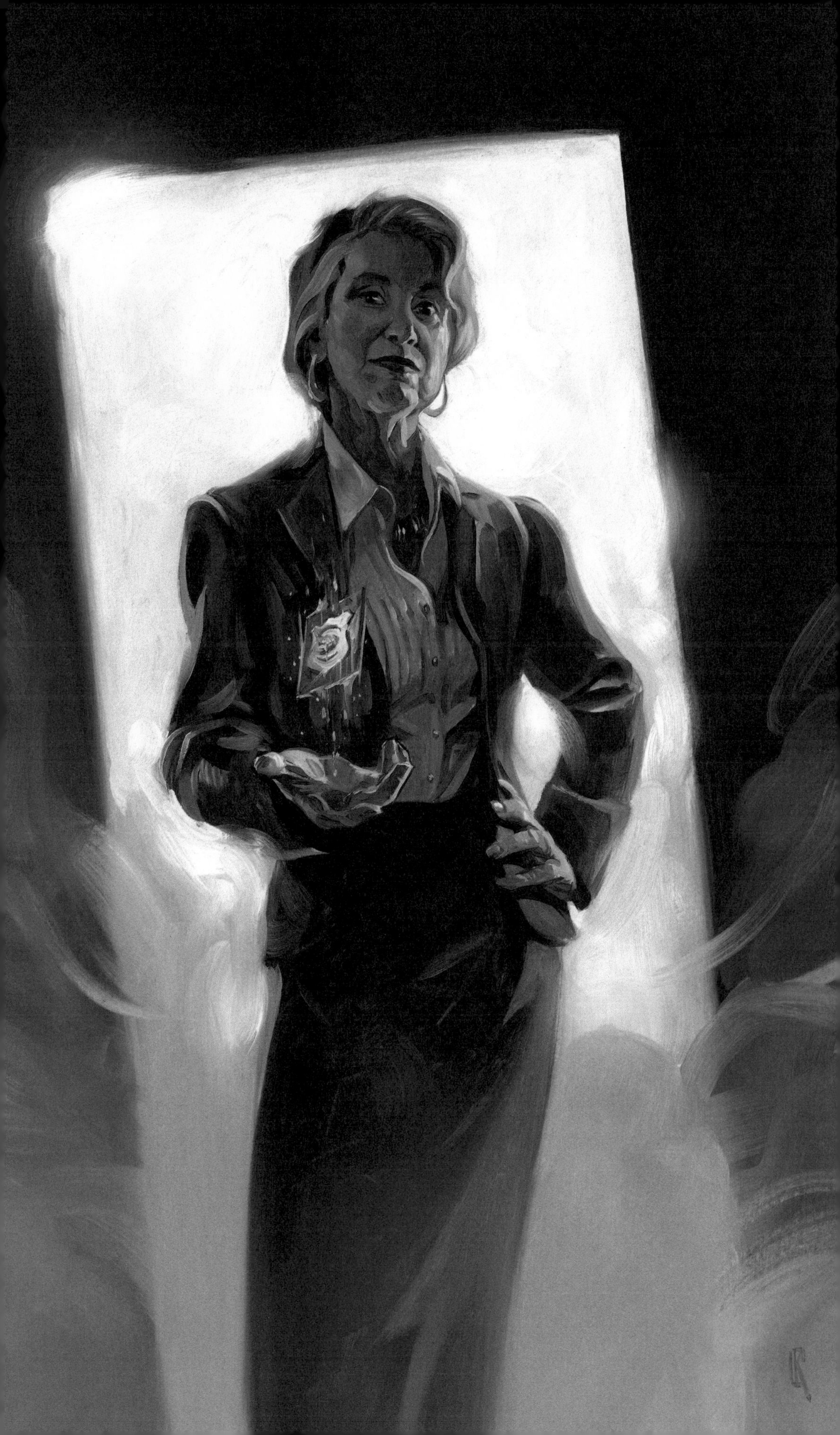

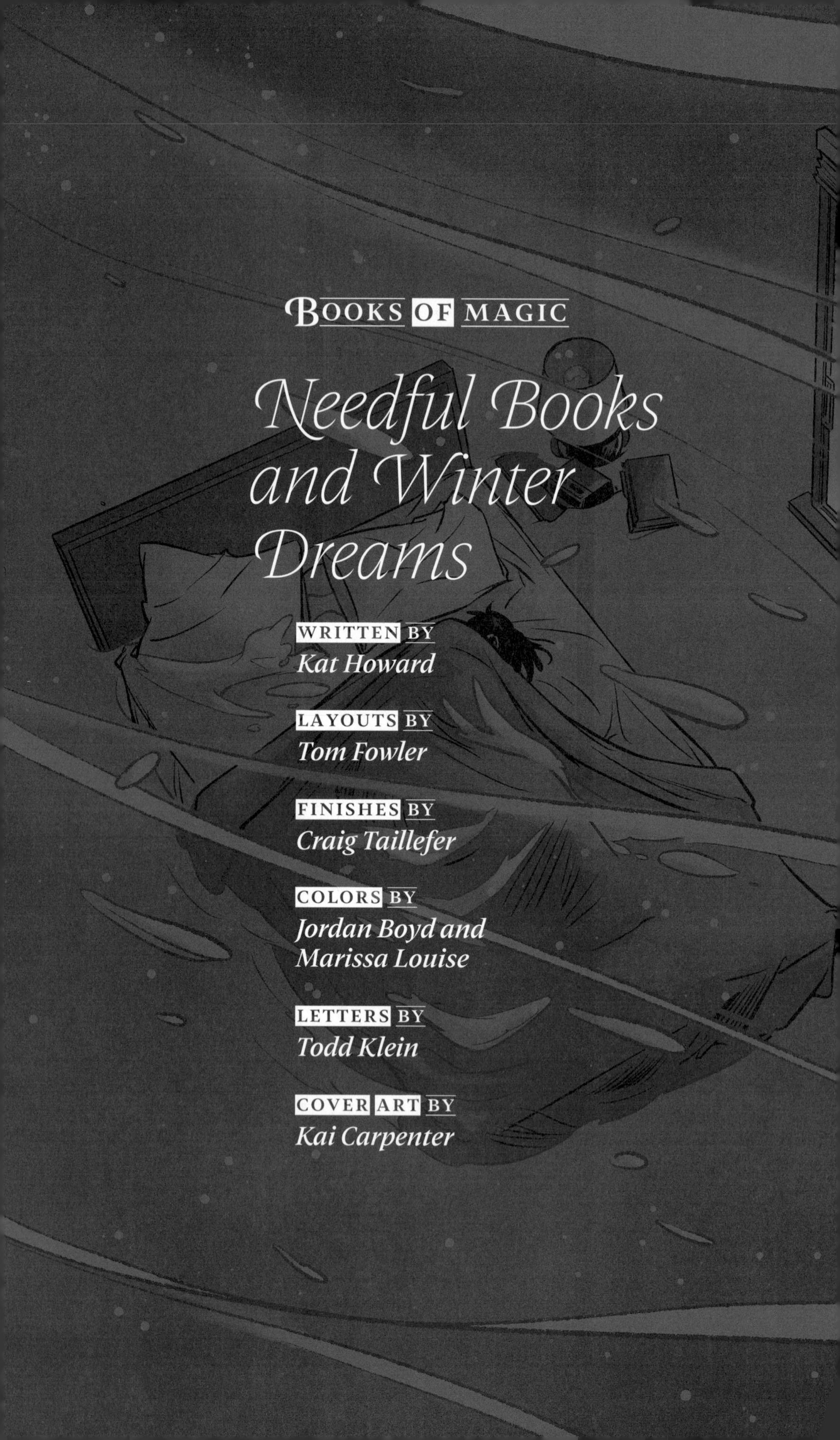

BOOKS OF MAGIC

Needful Books and Winter Dreams

WRITTEN BY
Kat Howard

LAYOUTS BY
Tom Fowler

FINISHES BY
Craig Taillefer

COLORS BY
Jordan Boyd and Marissa Louise

LETTERS BY
Todd Klein

COVER ART BY
Kai Carpenter

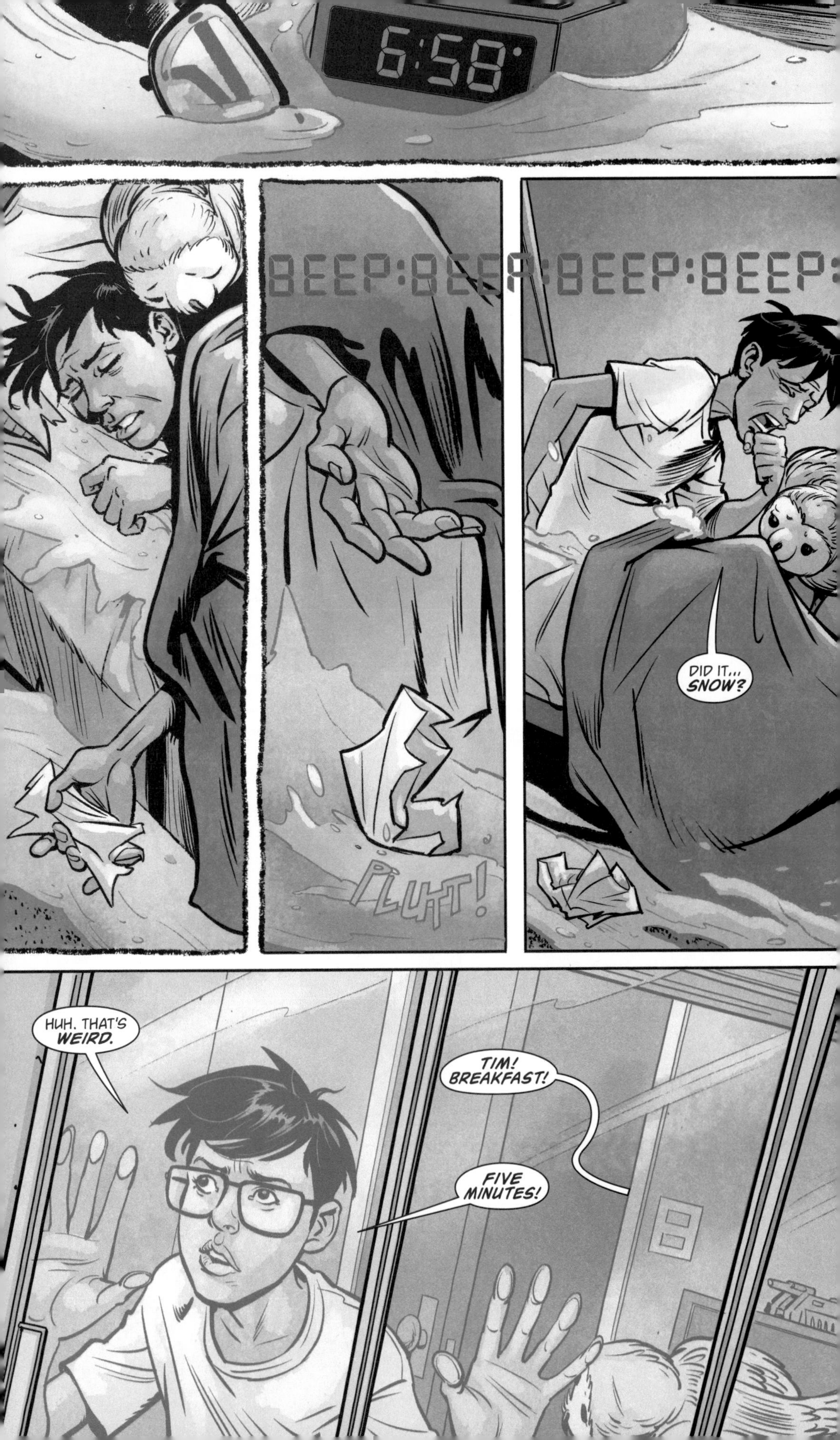
6:58
BEEP:BEEP:BEEP:BEEP:
PLUT!
DID IT... SNOW?
HUH. THAT'S WEIRD.
TIM! BREAKFAST!
FIVE MINUTES!

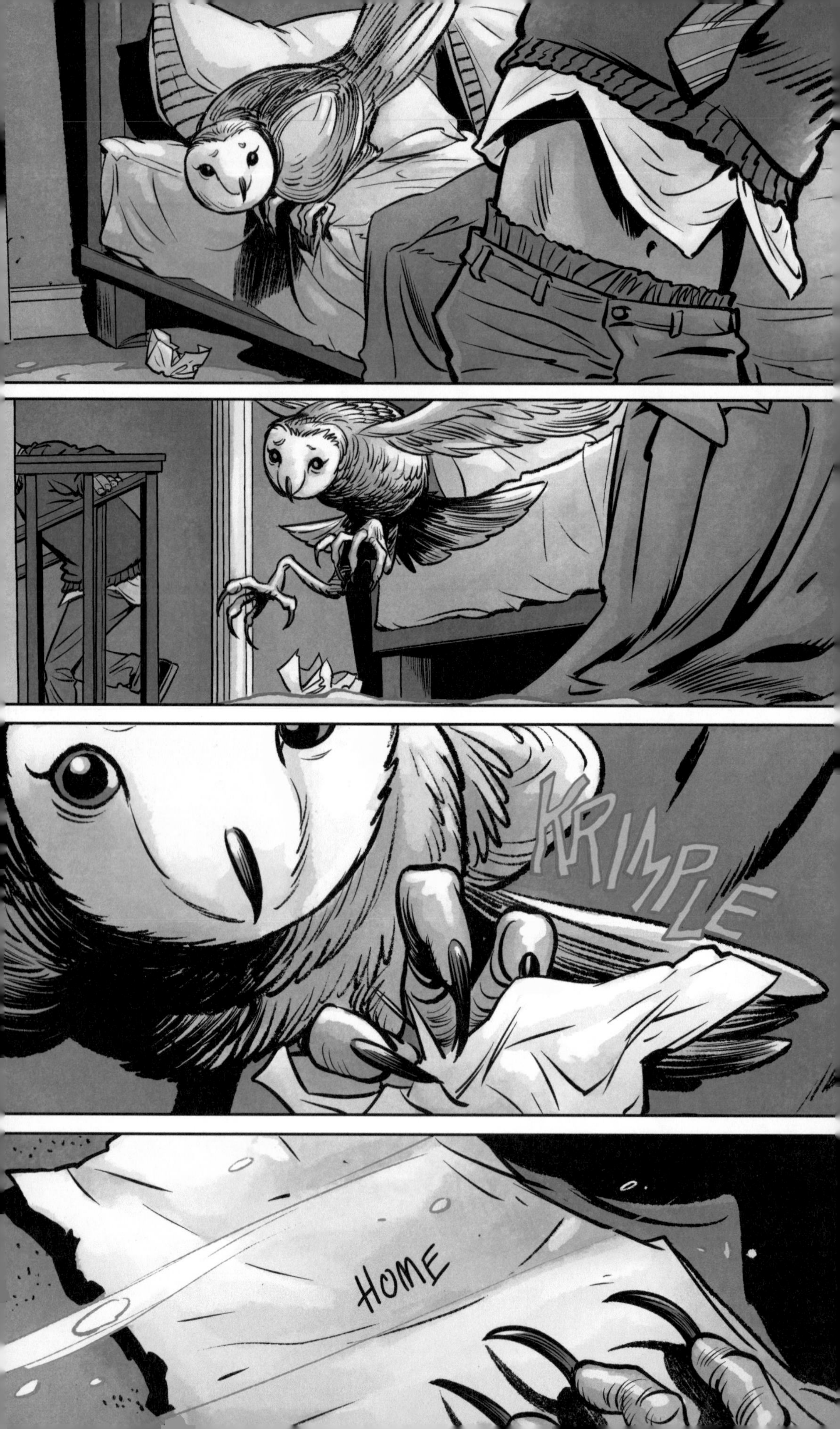
KRIMPLE
HOME

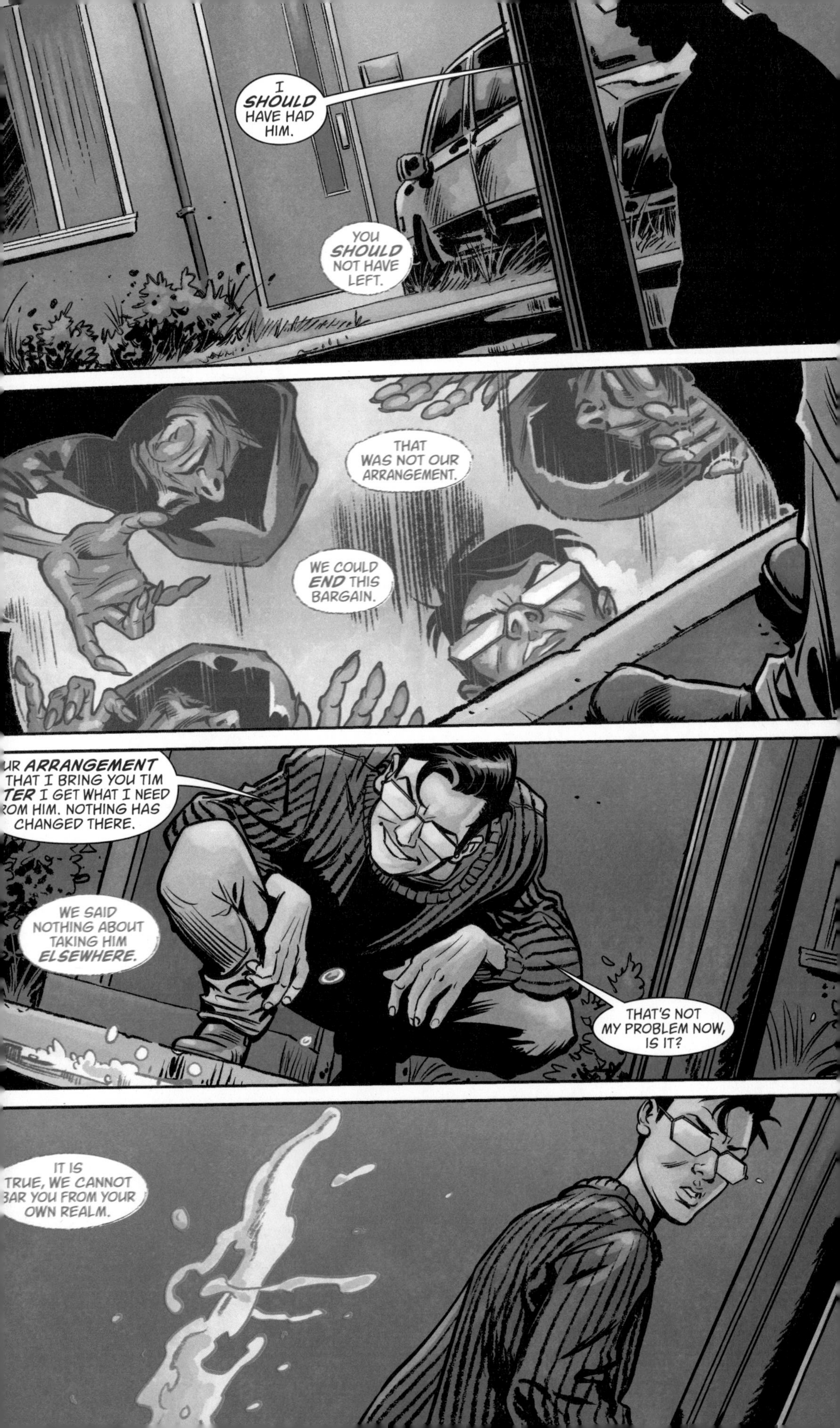
I SHOULD HAVE HAD HIM.
YOU SHOULD NOT HAVE LEFT.
THAT WAS NOT OUR ARRANGEMENT.
WE COULD END THIS BARGAIN.
UR ARRANGEMENT THAT I BRING YOU TIM TER I GET WHAT I NEED ROM HIM. NOTHING HAS CHANGED THERE.
WE SAID NOTHING ABOUT TAKING HIM ELSEWHERE.
THAT'S NOT MY PROBLEM NOW, IS IT?
IT IS TRUE, WE CANNOT BAR YOU FROM YOUR OWN REALM.

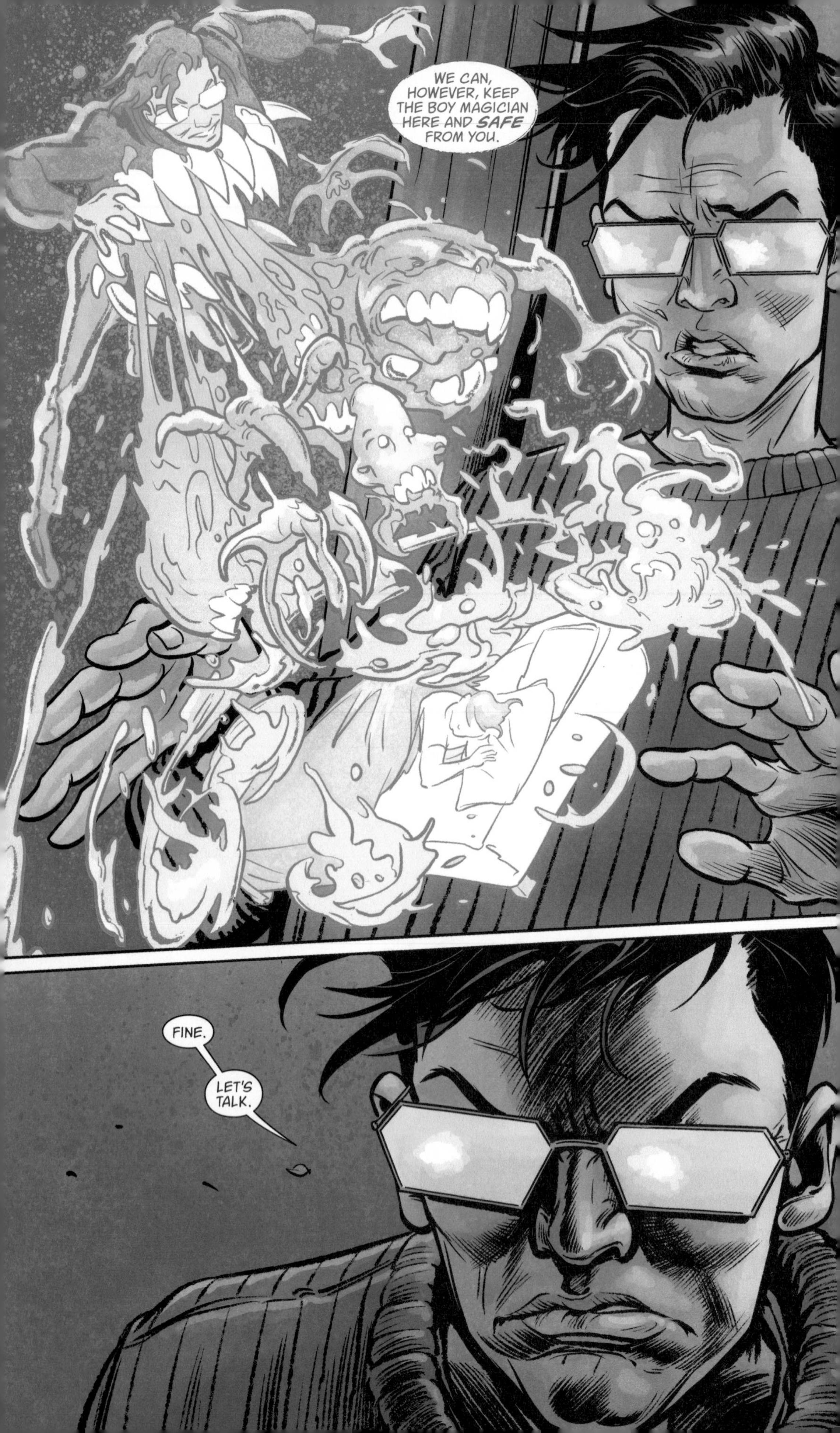
WE CAN, HOWEVER, KEEP THE BOY MAGICIAN HERE AND SAFE FROM YOU.
FINE.
LET'S TALK.

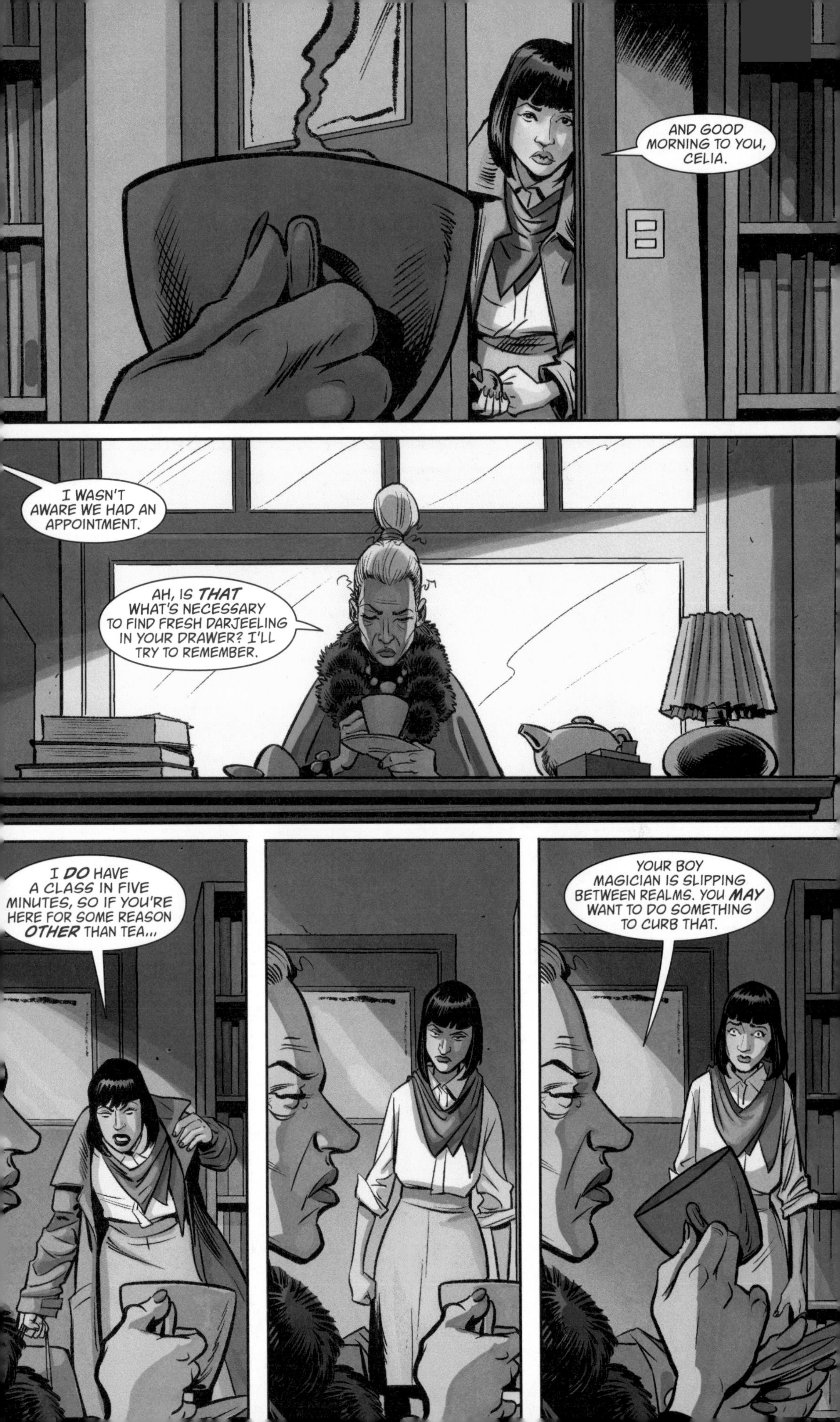
AND GOOD MORNING TO YOU, CELIA.
I WASN'T AWARE WE HAD AN APPOINTMENT.
AH, IS *THAT* WHAT'S NECESSARY TO FIND FRESH DARJEELING IN YOUR DRAWER? I'LL TRY TO REMEMBER.
I *DO* HAVE A CLASS IN FIVE MINUTES, SO IF YOU'RE HERE FOR SOME REASON *OTHER* THAN TEA...
YOUR BOY MAGICIAN IS SLIPPING BETWEEN REALMS. YOU *MAY* WANT TO DO SOMETHING TO CURB THAT.

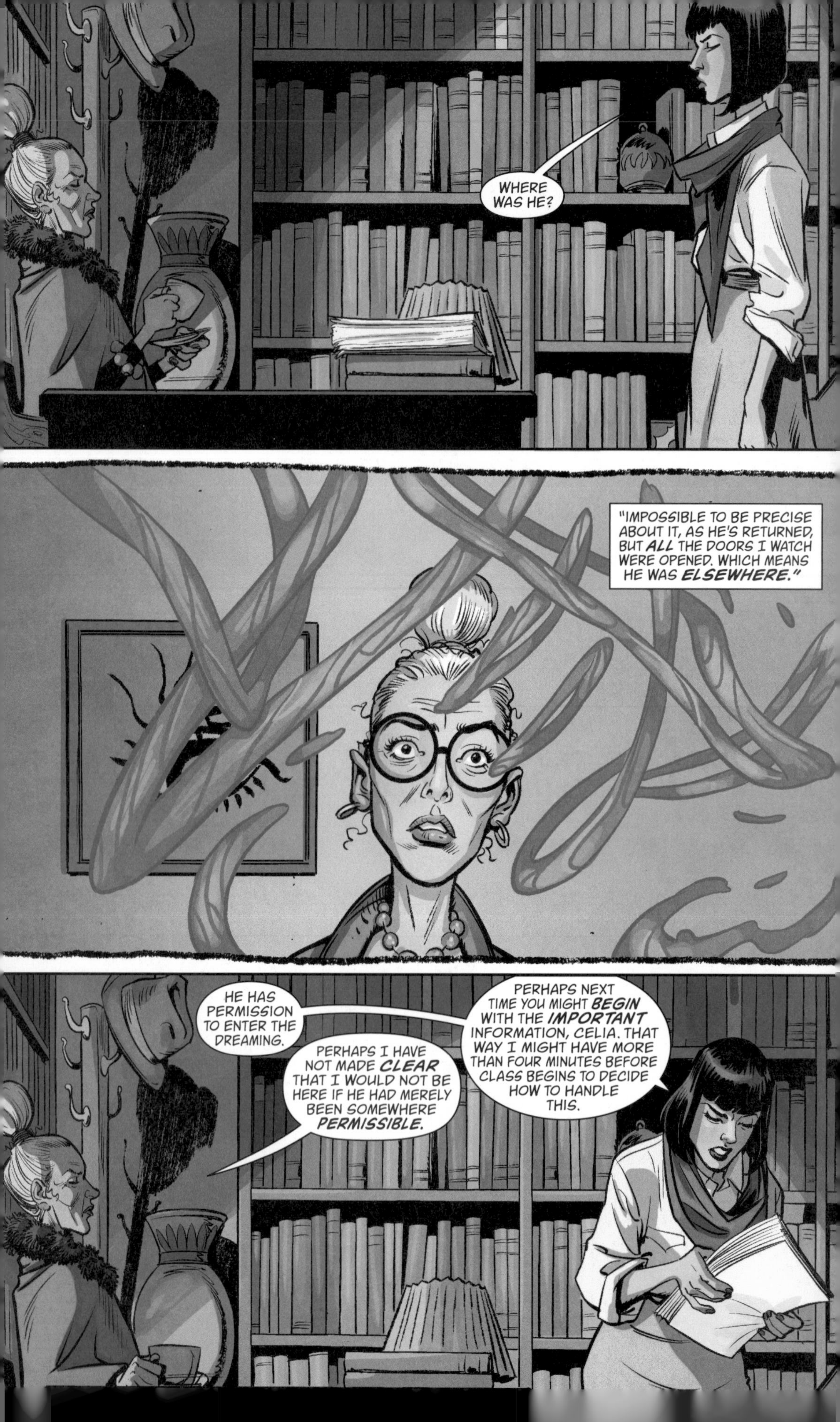
WHERE WAS HE?
"IMPOSSIBLE TO BE PRECISE ABOUT IT, AS HE'S RETURNED, BUT ALL THE DOORS I WATCH WERE OPENED. WHICH MEANS HE WAS ELSEWHERE."
HE HAS PERMISSION TO ENTER THE DREAMING.
PERHAPS I HAVE NOT MADE CLEAR THAT I WOULD NOT BE HERE IF HE HAD MERELY BEEN SOMEWHERE PERMISSIBLE.
PERHAPS NEXT TIME YOU MIGHT BEGIN WITH THE IMPORTANT INFORMATION, CELIA. THAT WAY I MIGHT HAVE MORE THAN FOUR MINUTES BEFORE CLASS BEGINS TO DECIDE HOW TO HANDLE THIS.

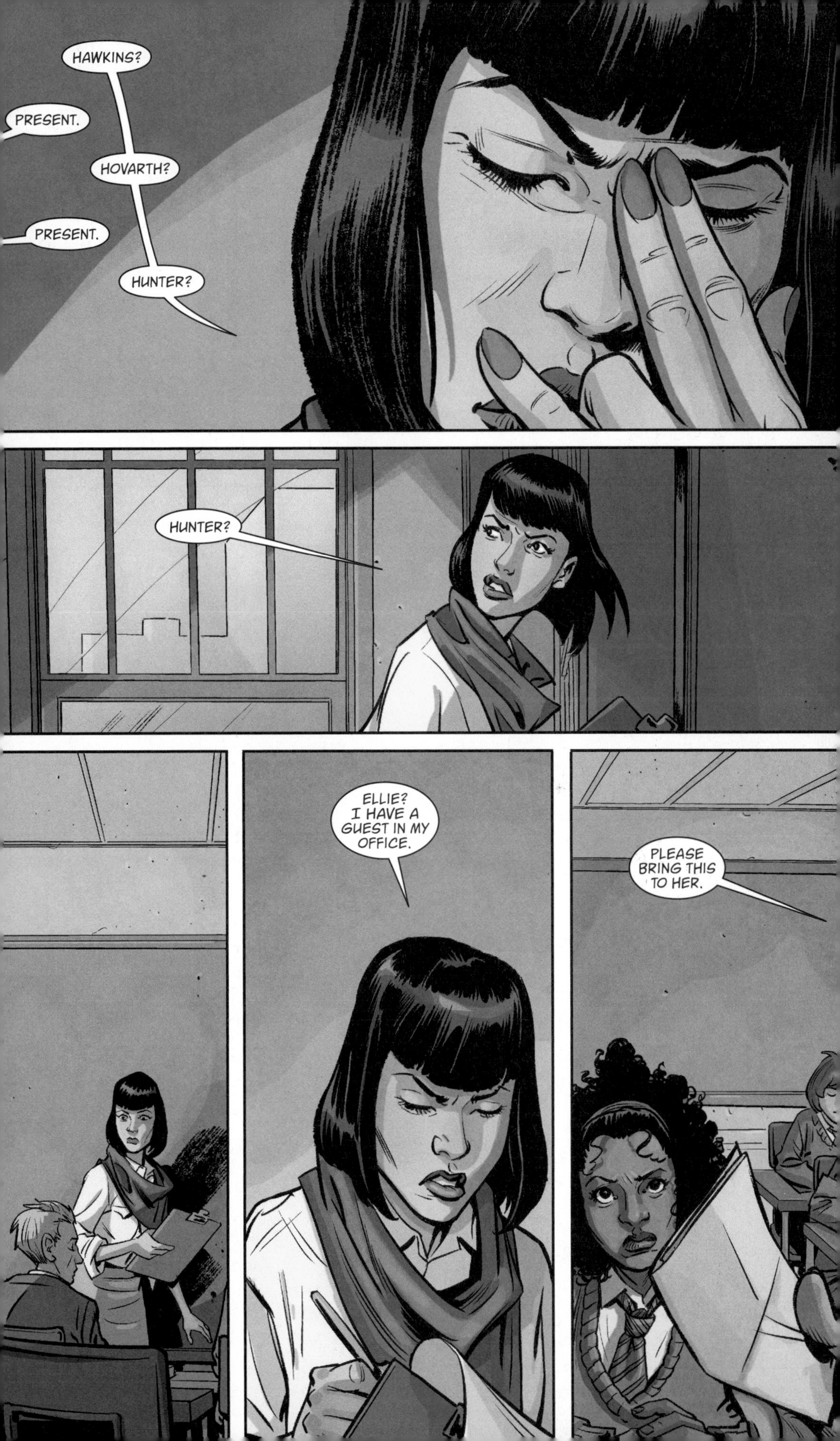
HAWKINS?
PRESENT.
HOVARTH?
PRESENT.
HUNTER?
HUNTER?
ELLIE? I HAVE A GUEST IN MY OFFICE.
PLEASE BRING THIS TO HER.

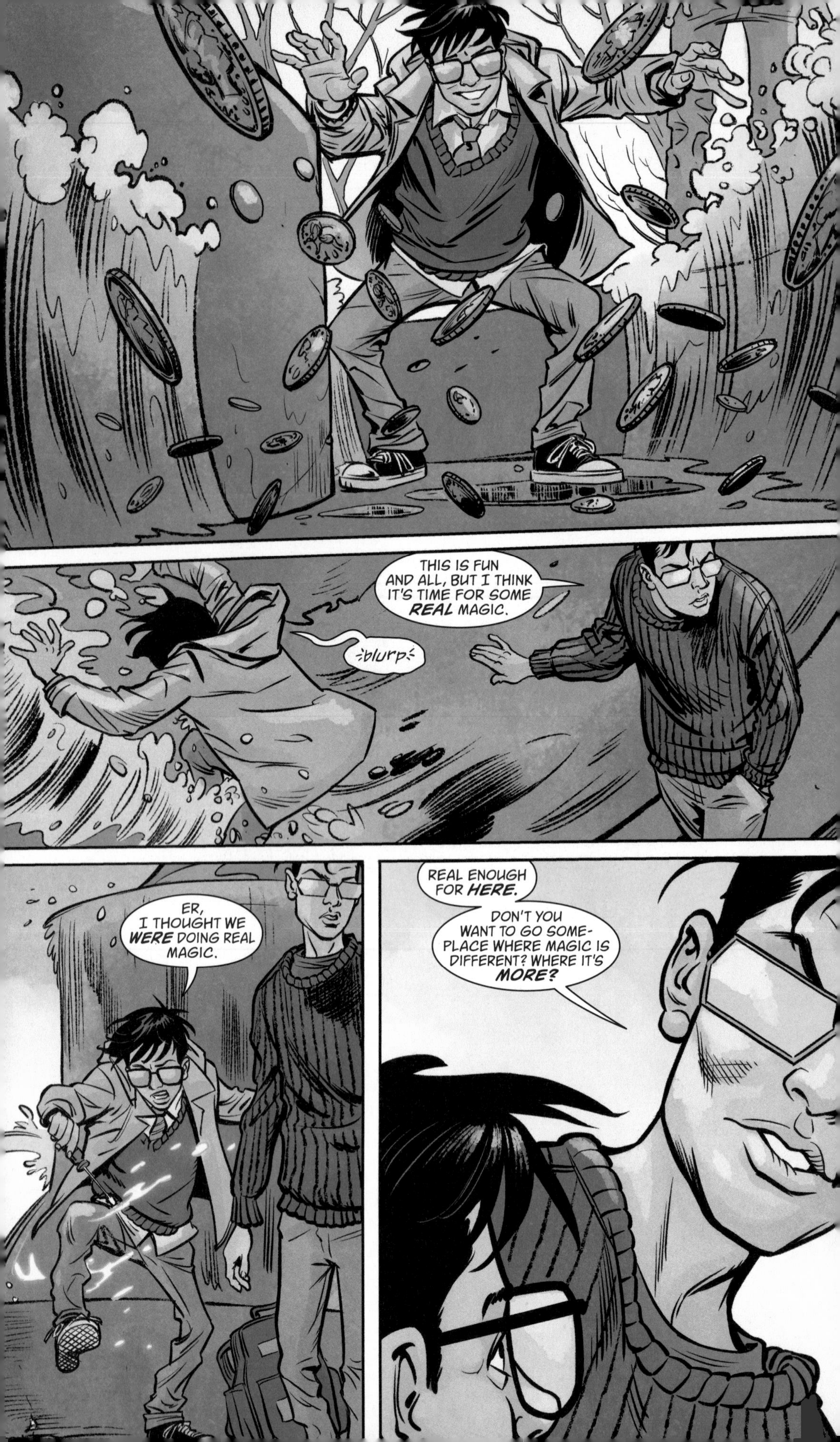
THIS IS FUN AND ALL, BUT I THINK IT'S TIME FOR SOME *REAL* MAGIC.
blurp
ER, I THOUGHT WE *WERE* DOING REAL MAGIC.
REAL ENOUGH FOR *HERE.*
DON'T YOU WANT TO GO SOME-PLACE WHERE MAGIC IS DIFFERENT? WHERE IT'S *MORE?*

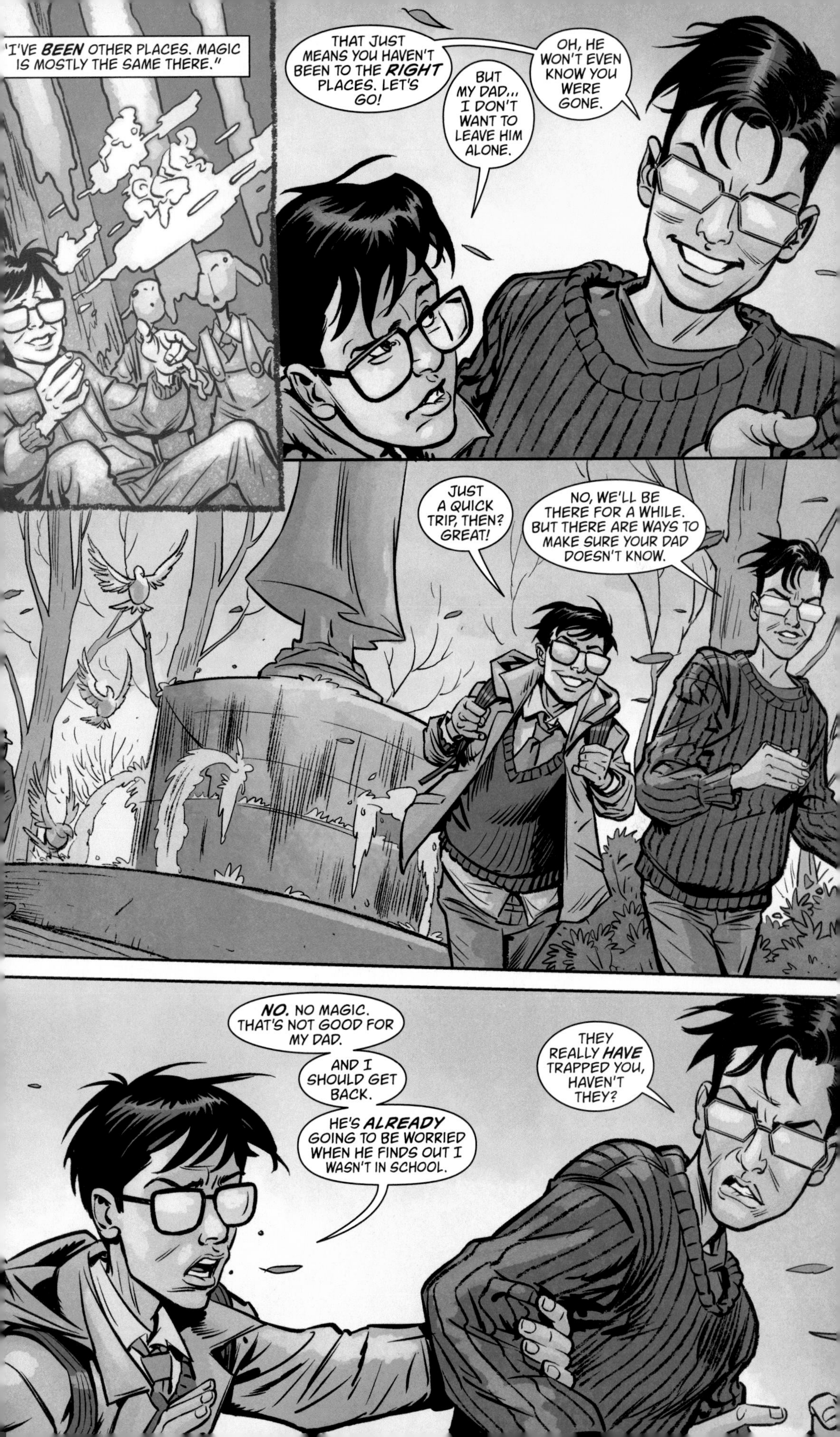

"I'VE BEEN OTHER PLACES. MAGIC IS MOSTLY THE SAME THERE."
THAT JUST MEANS YOU HAVEN'T BEEN TO THE RIGHT PLACES. LET'S GO!
BUT MY DAD... I DON'T WANT TO LEAVE HIM ALONE.
OH, HE WON'T EVEN KNOW YOU WERE GONE.
JUST A QUICK TRIP, THEN? GREAT!
NO, WE'LL BE THERE FOR A WHILE. BUT THERE ARE WAYS TO MAKE SURE YOUR DAD DOESN'T KNOW.
NO. NO MAGIC. THAT'S NOT GOOD FOR MY DAD.
AND I SHOULD GET BACK.
HE'S ALREADY GOING TO BE WORRIED WHEN HE FINDS OUT I WASN'T IN SCHOOL.
THEY REALLY HAVE TRAPPED YOU, HAVEN'T THEY?

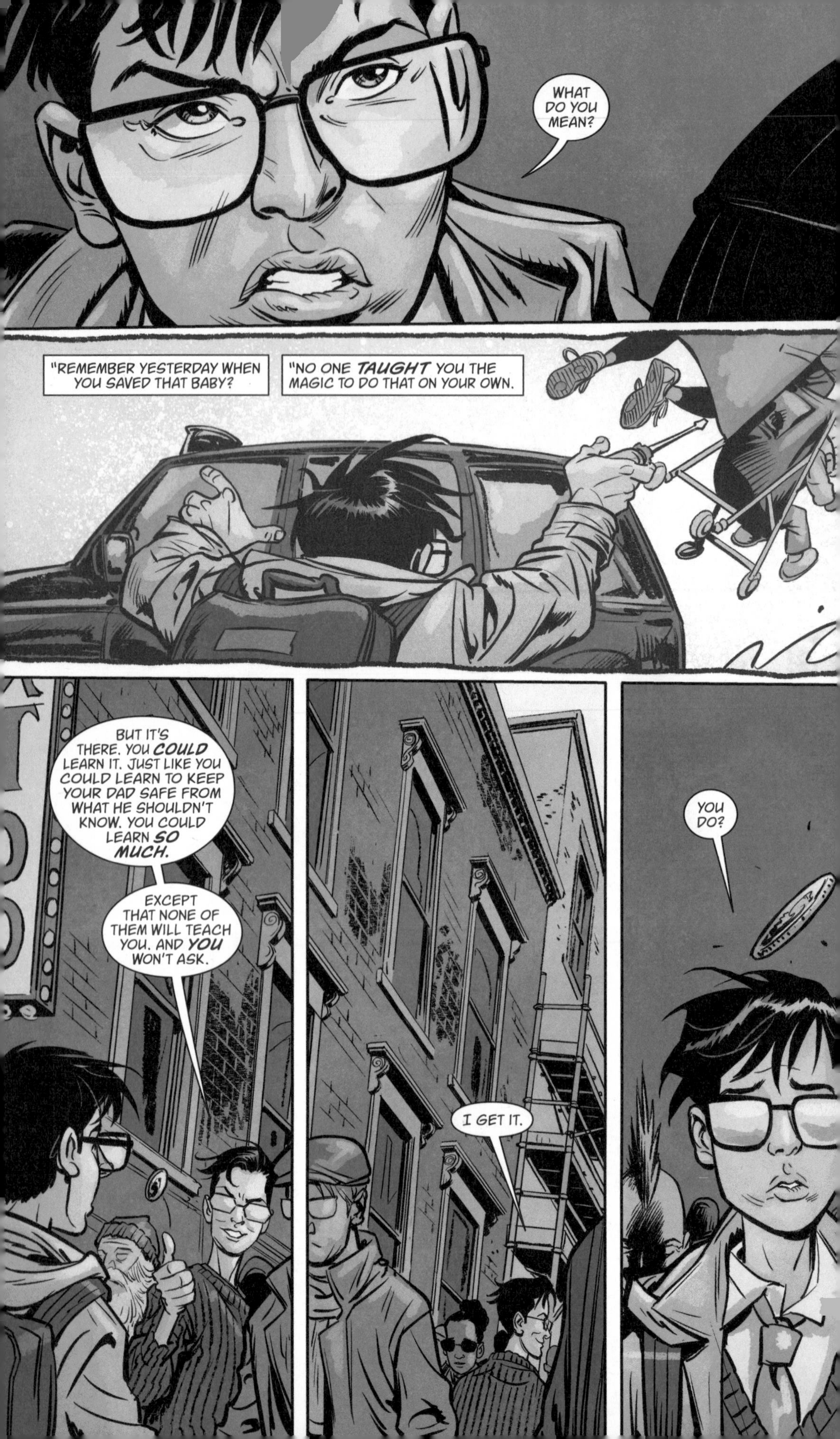

WHAT DO YOU MEAN?
"REMEMBER YESTERDAY WHEN YOU SAVED THAT BABY?
"NO ONE TAUGHT YOU THE MAGIC TO DO THAT ON YOUR OWN.
BUT IT'S THERE. YOU COULD LEARN IT. JUST LIKE YOU COULD LEARN TO KEEP YOUR DAD SAFE FROM WHAT HE SHOULDN'T KNOW. YOU COULD LEARN SO MUCH.
EXCEPT THAT NONE OF THEM WILL TEACH YOU. AND YOU WON'T ASK.
I GET IT.
YOU DO?

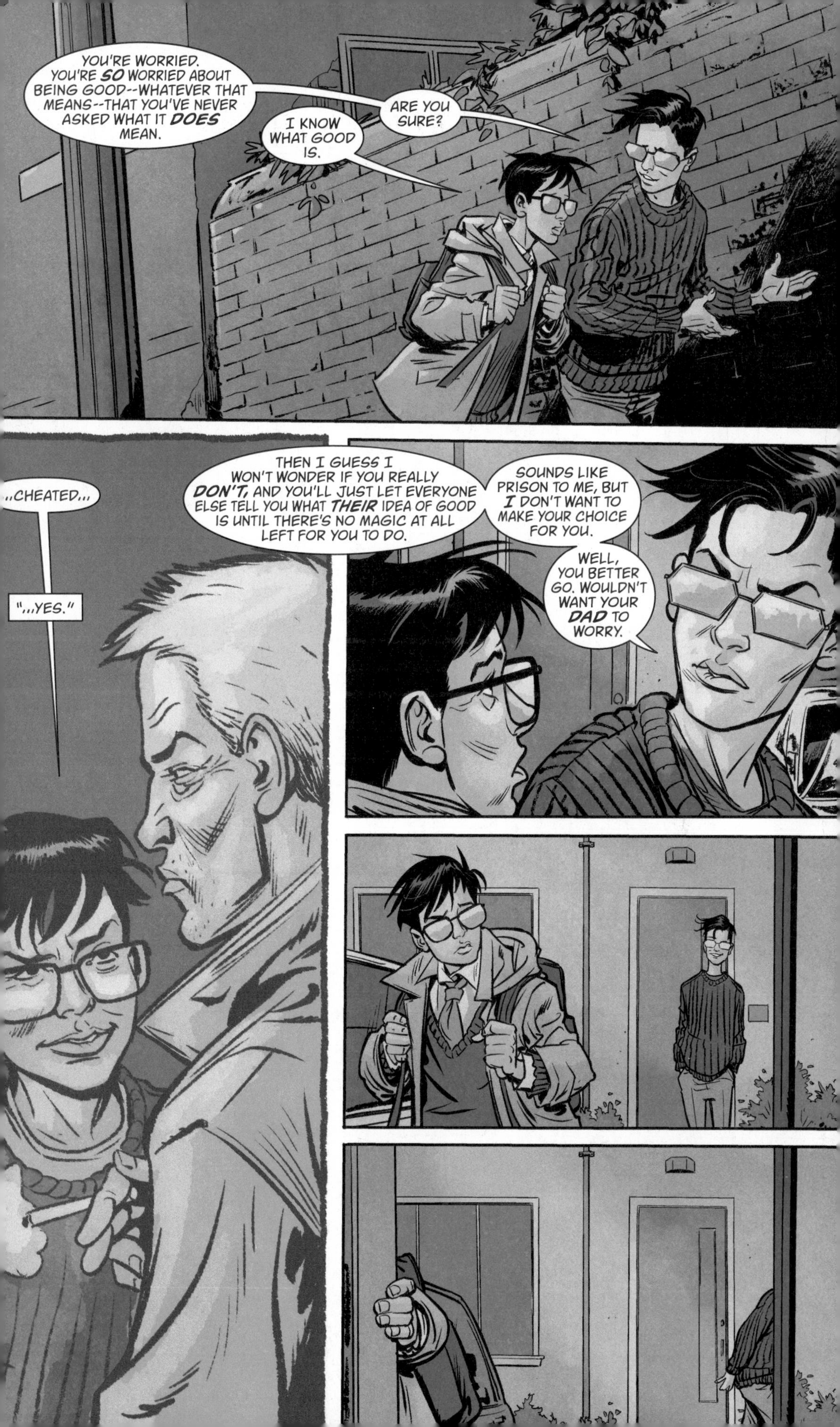
YOU'RE WORRIED. YOU'RE SO WORRIED ABOUT BEING GOOD--WHATEVER THAT MEANS--THAT YOU'VE NEVER ASKED WHAT IT DOES MEAN.
I KNOW WHAT GOOD IS.
ARE YOU SURE?
...CHEATED...
"...YES."
THEN I GUESS I WON'T WONDER IF YOU REALLY DON'T, AND YOU'LL JUST LET EVERYONE ELSE TELL YOU WHAT THEIR IDEA OF GOOD IS UNTIL THERE'S NO MAGIC AT ALL LEFT FOR YOU TO DO.
SOUNDS LIKE PRISON TO ME, BUT I DON'T WANT TO MAKE YOUR CHOICE FOR YOU.
WELL, YOU BETTER GO. WOULDN'T WANT YOUR DAD TO WORRY.

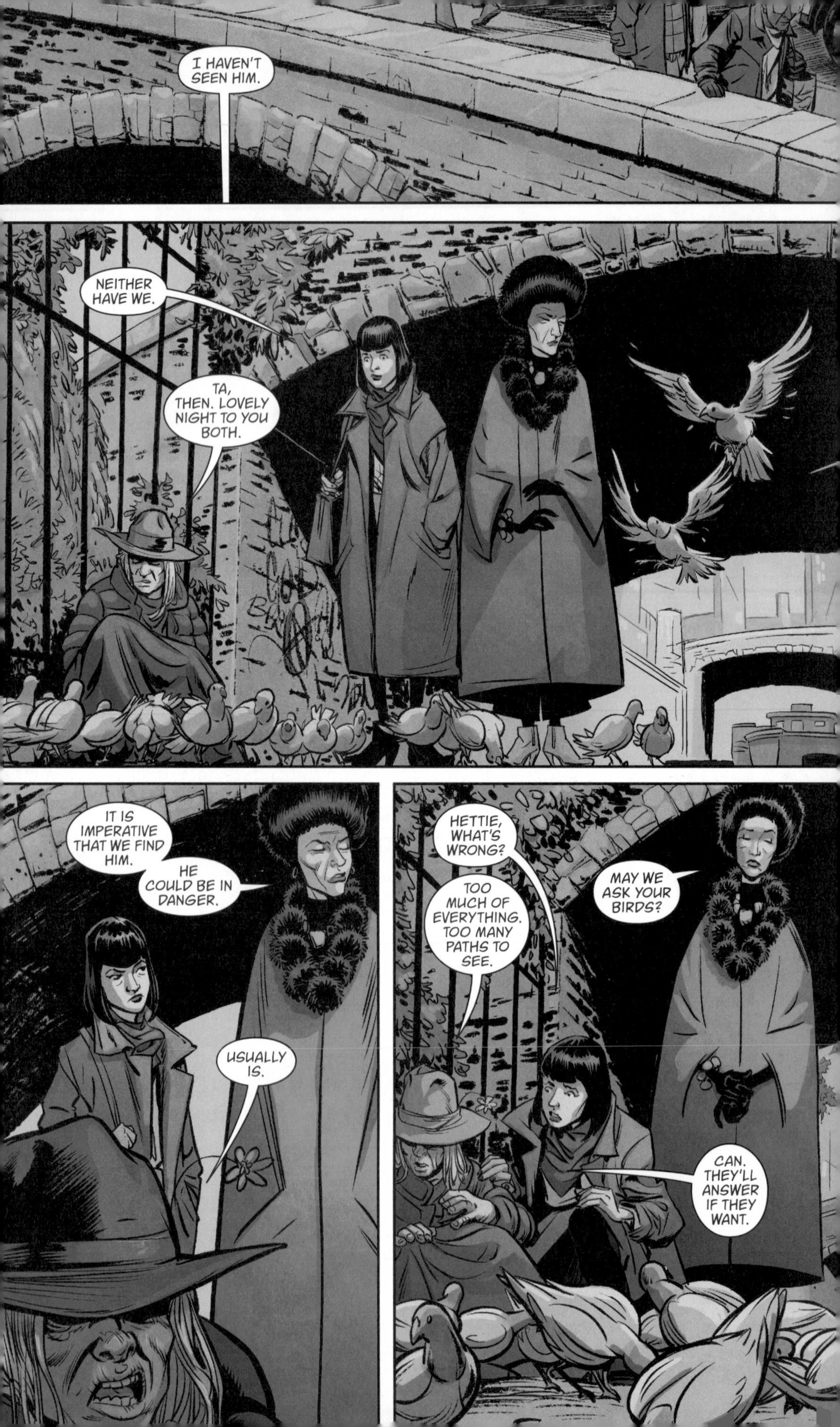
I HAVEN'T SEEN HIM.
NEITHER HAVE WE.
TA, THEN. LOVELY NIGHT TO YOU BOTH.
IT IS IMPERATIVE THAT WE FIND HIM.
HE COULD BE IN DANGER.
USUALLY IS.
HETTIE, WHAT'S WRONG?
TOO MUCH OF EVERYTHING. TOO MANY PATHS TO SEE.
MAY WE ASK YOUR BIRDS?
CAN. THEY'LL ANSWER IF THEY WANT.

IT'S VERY [IM]PORTANT THAT [W]E FIND *TIM HUNTER.*

I WOULD BE IN YOUR DEBT FOR ANY HELP YOU COULD GIVE.

COOROOCOOROO COOROO COOROO COOROO COOROO COOROO COOROO COOROO COOF

THAT *DOES* EXPLAIN SOME THINGS.

INDEED.

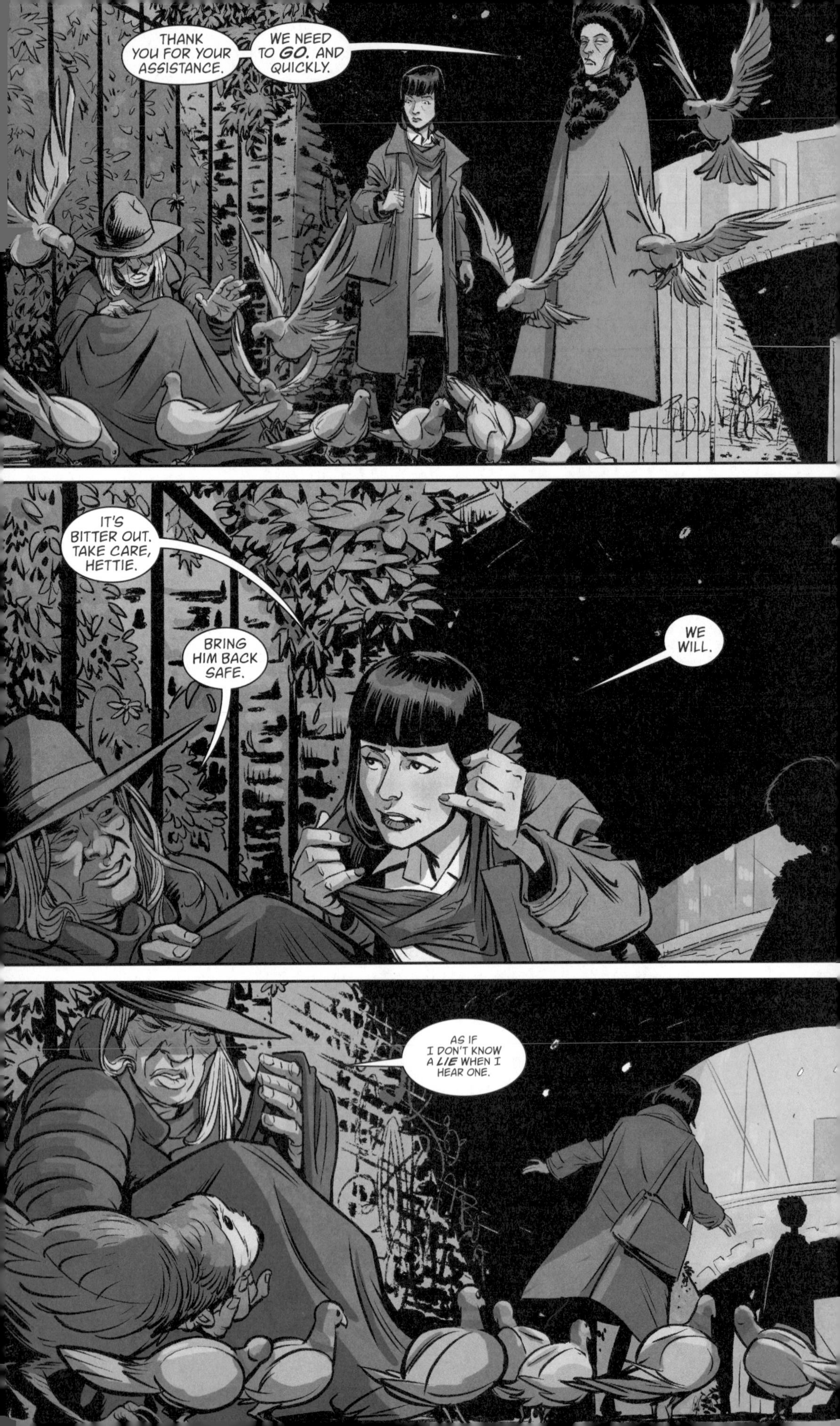
THANK YOU FOR YOUR ASSISTANCE.
WE NEED TO GO. AND QUICKLY.
IT'S BITTER OUT. TAKE CARE, HETTIE.
BRING HIM BACK SAFE.
WE WILL.
AS IF I DON'T KNOW A LIE WHEN I HEAR ONE.

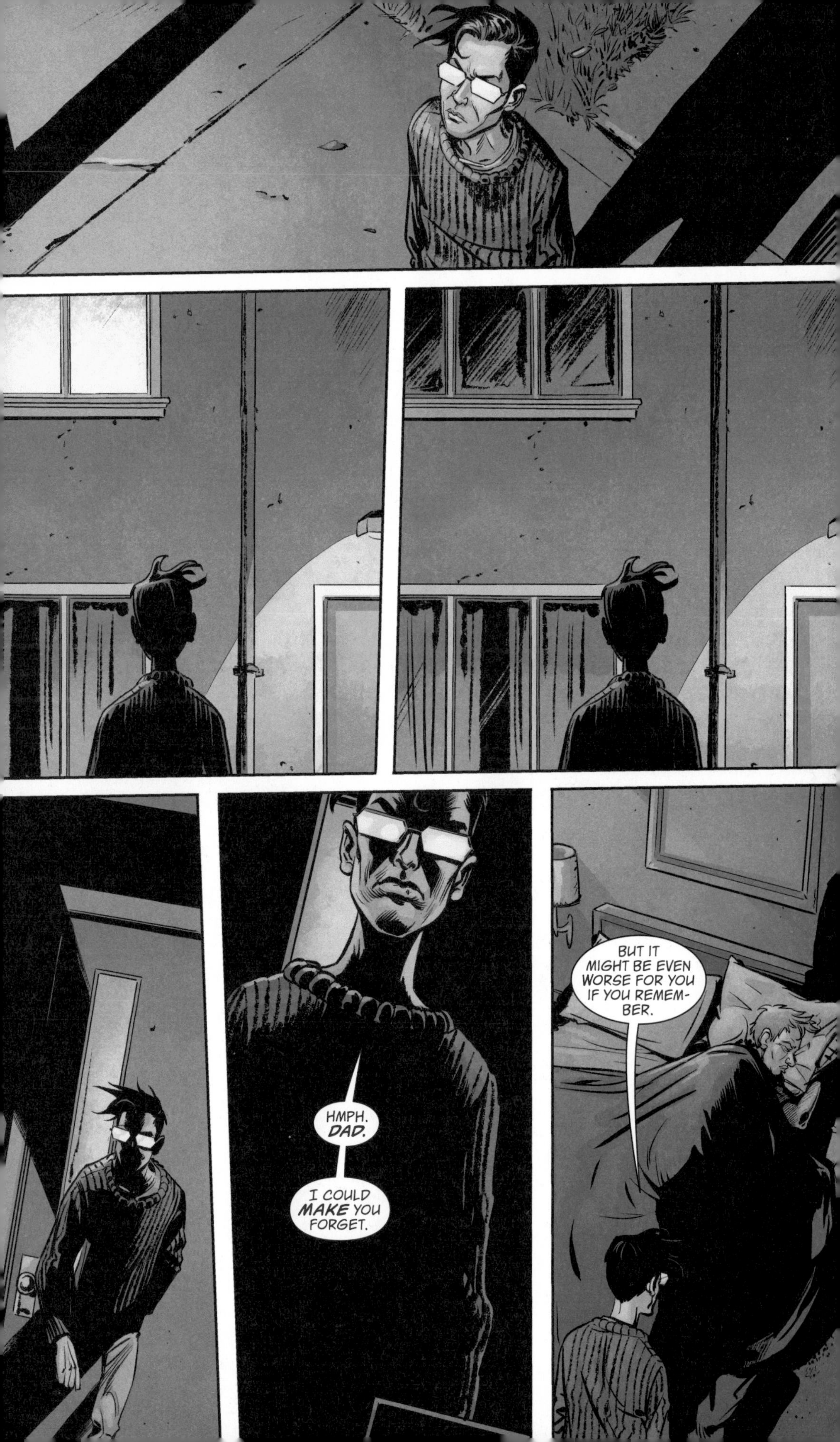
HMPH. DAD.
I COULD MAKE YOU FORGET.
BUT IT MIGHT BE EVEN WORSE FOR YOU IF YOU REMEMBER.

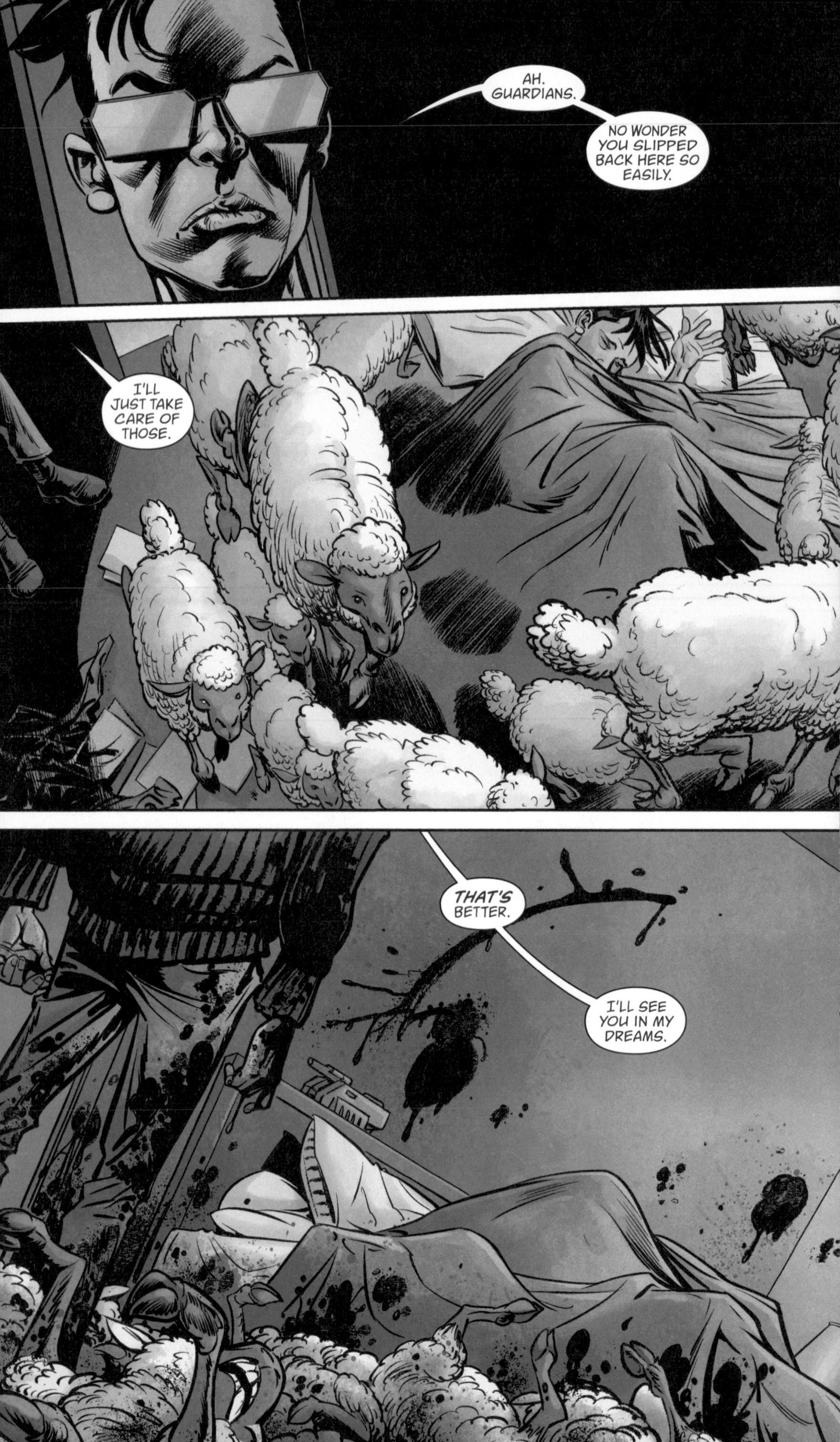
AH. GUARDIANS.
NO WONDER YOU SLIPPED BACK HERE SO EASILY.
I'LL JUST TAKE CARE OF THOSE.
THAT'S BETTER.
I'LL SEE YOU IN MY DREAMS.

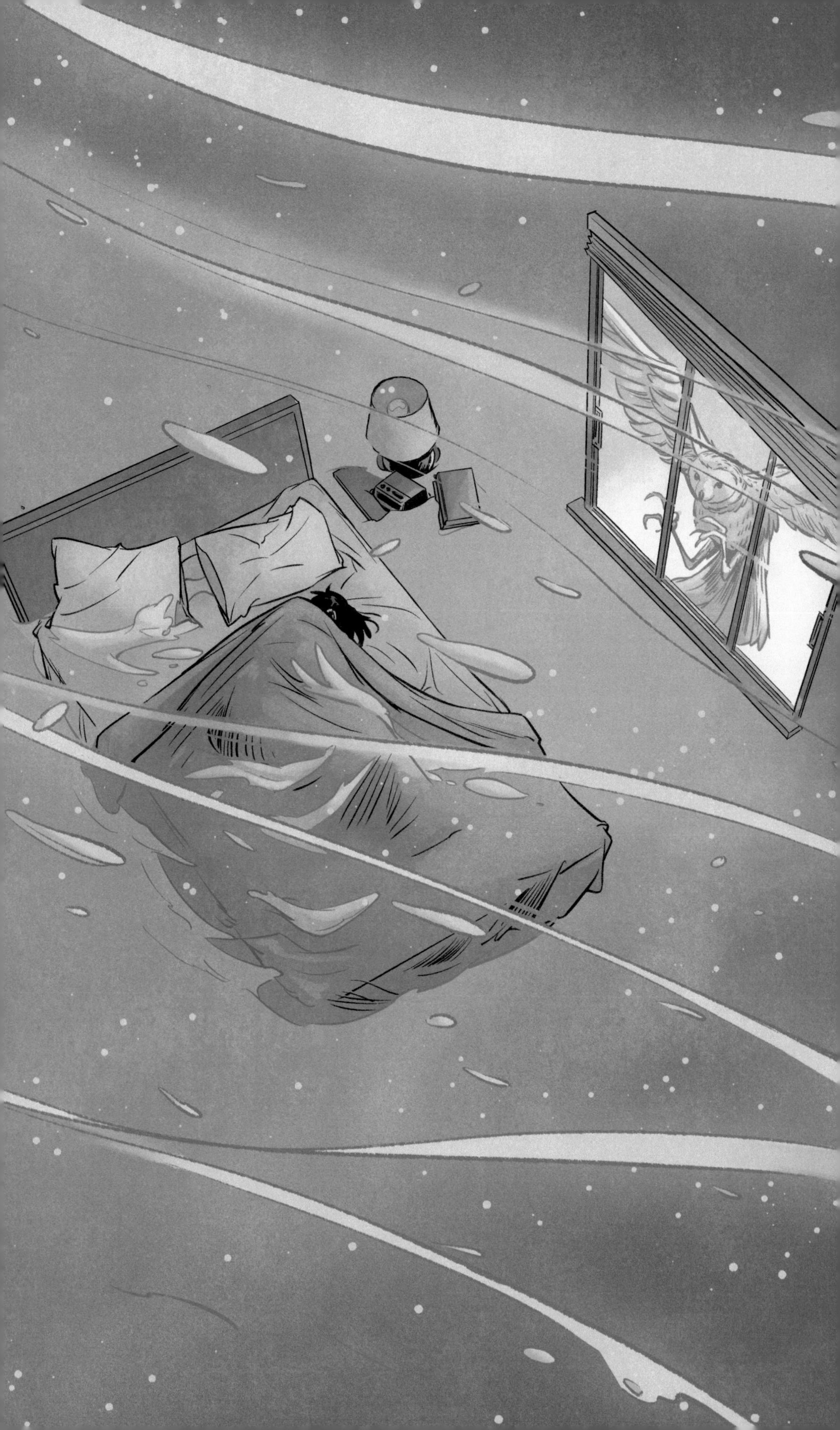

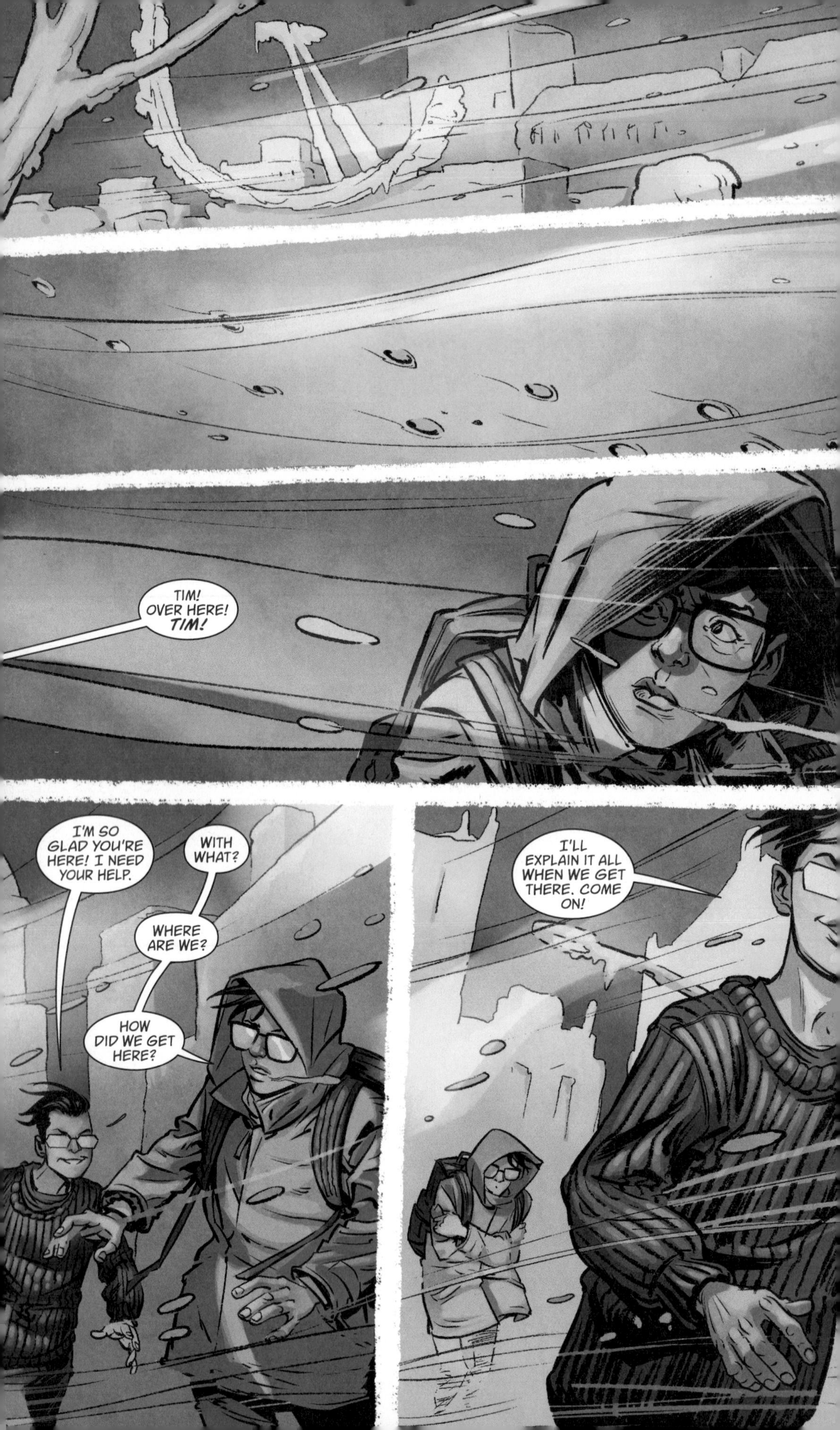
TIM!
OVER HERE!
TIM!
I'M SO GLAD YOU'RE HERE! I NEED YOUR HELP.
WITH WHAT?
WHERE ARE WE?
HOW DID WE GET HERE?
I'LL EXPLAIN IT ALL WHEN WE GET THERE. COME ON!

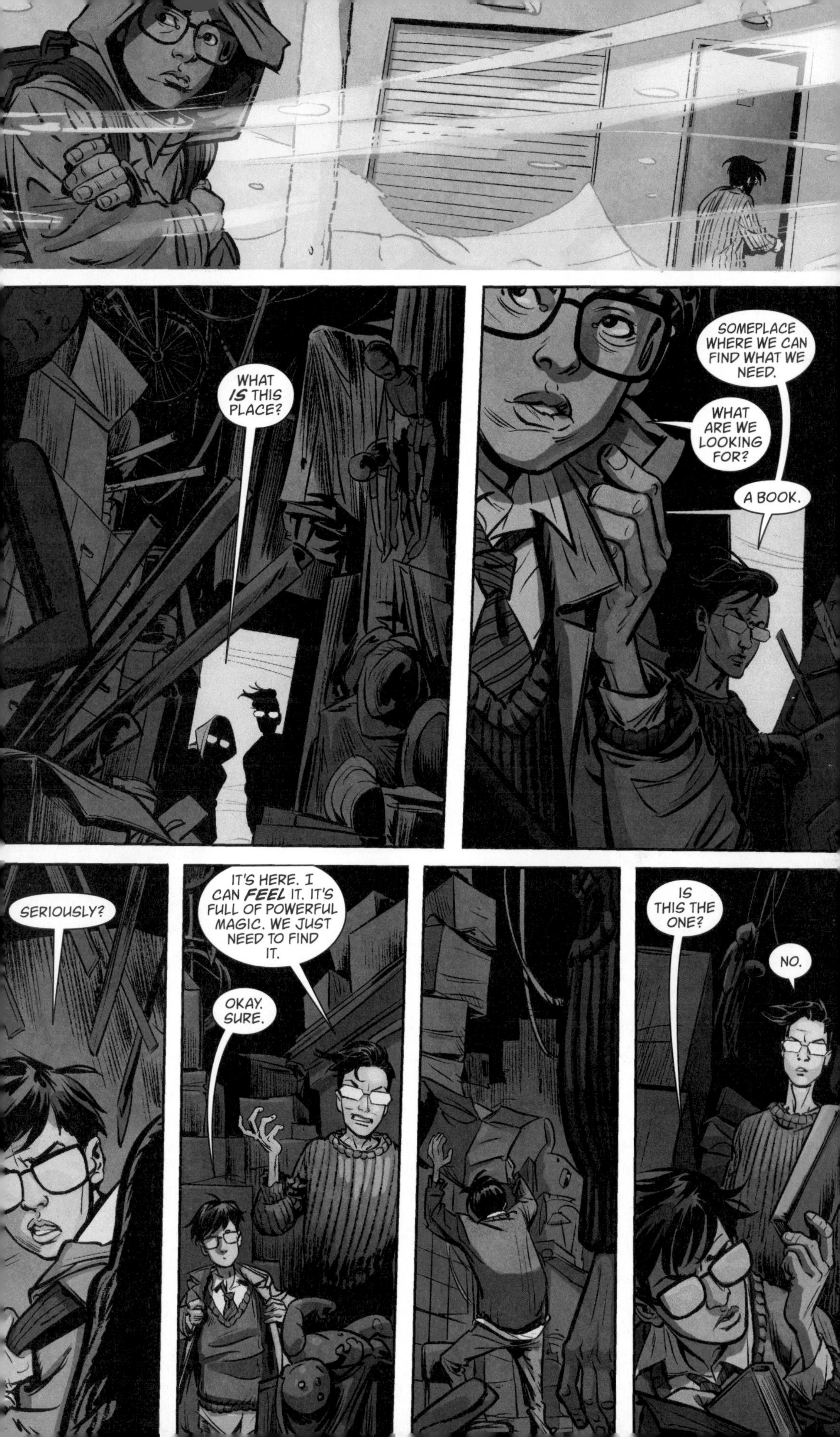
WHAT *IS* THIS PLACE?
SOMEPLACE WHERE WE CAN FIND WHAT WE NEED.
WHAT ARE WE LOOKING FOR?
A BOOK.
SERIOUSLY?
IT'S HERE. I CAN *FEEL* IT. IT'S FULL OF POWERFUL MAGIC. WE JUST NEED TO FIND IT.
OKAY. SURE.
IS THIS THE ONE?
NO.

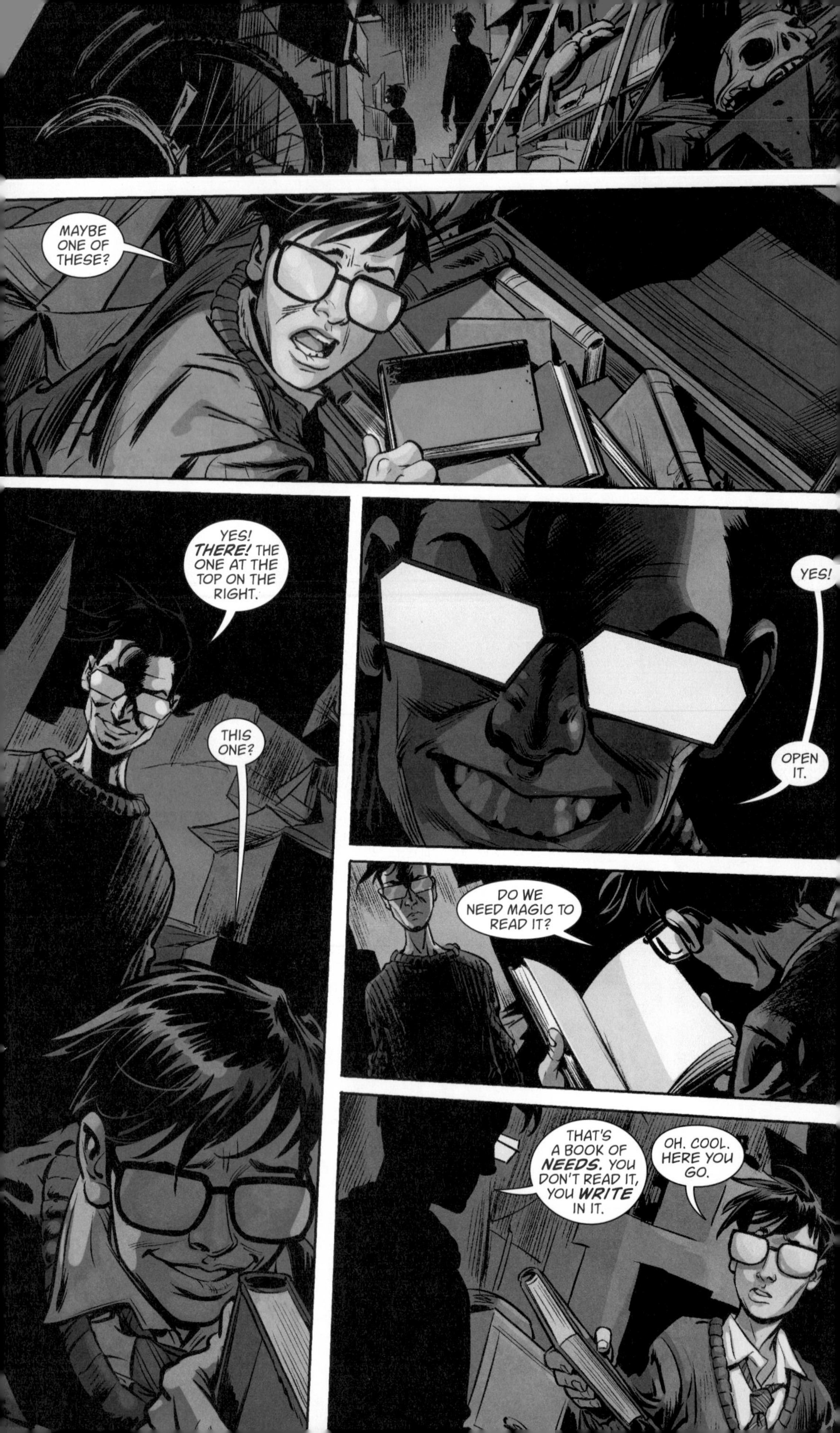
MAYBE ONE OF THESE?
YES! **THERE!** THE ONE AT THE TOP ON THE RIGHT.
THIS ONE?
YES!
OPEN IT.
DO WE NEED MAGIC TO READ IT?
THAT'S A BOOK OF **NEEDS.** YOU DON'T READ IT, YOU **WRITE** IN IT.
OH. COOL. HERE YOU GO.

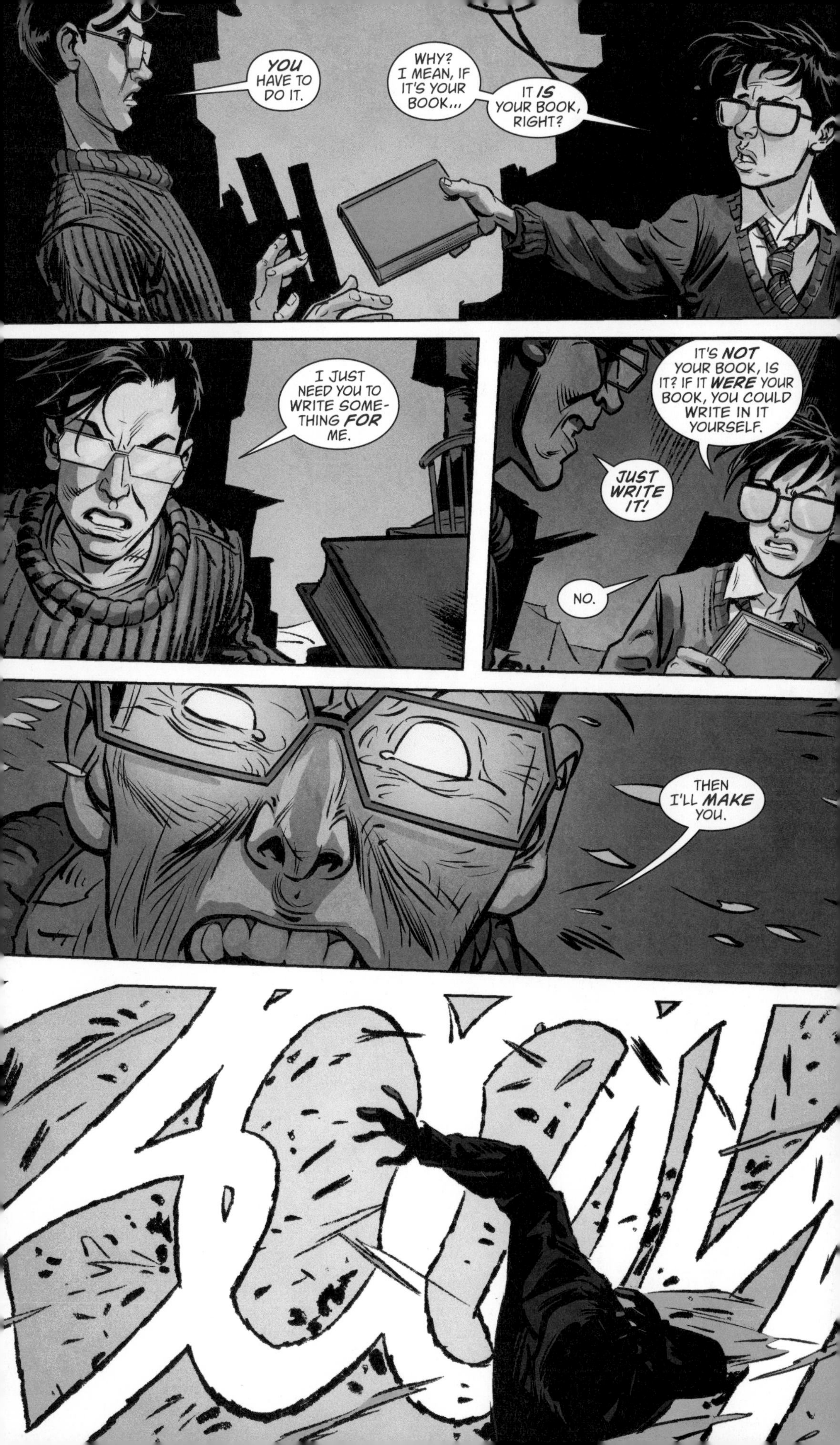
YOU HAVE TO DO IT.
WHY? I MEAN, IF IT'S YOUR BOOK...
IT IS YOUR BOOK, RIGHT?
I JUST NEED YOU TO WRITE SOME-THING FOR ME.
IT'S NOT YOUR BOOK, IS IT? IF IT WERE YOUR BOOK, YOU COULD WRITE IN IT YOURSELF.
JUST WRITE IT!
NO.
THEN I'LL MAKE YOU.

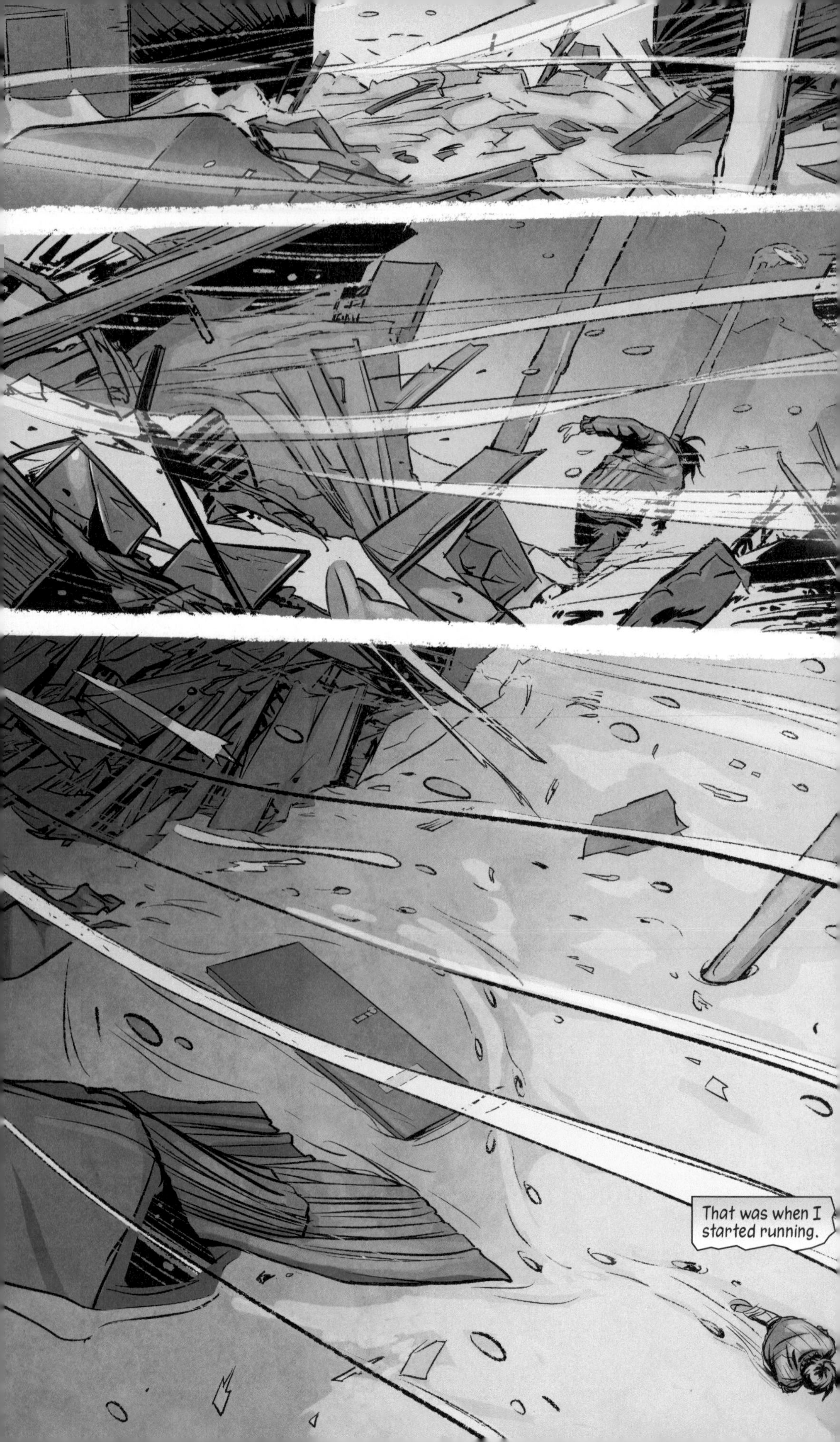
That was when I started running.

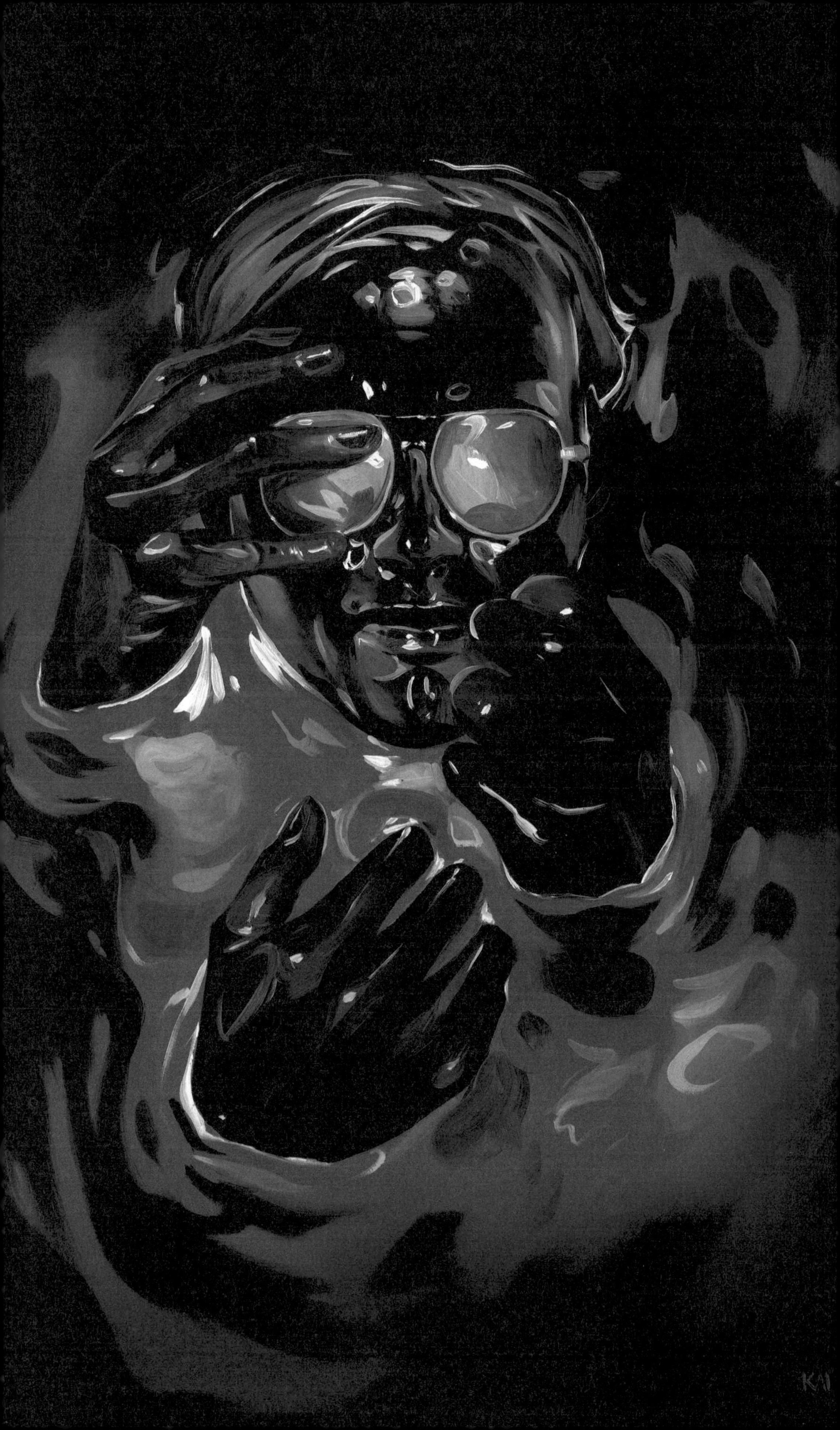
KAI

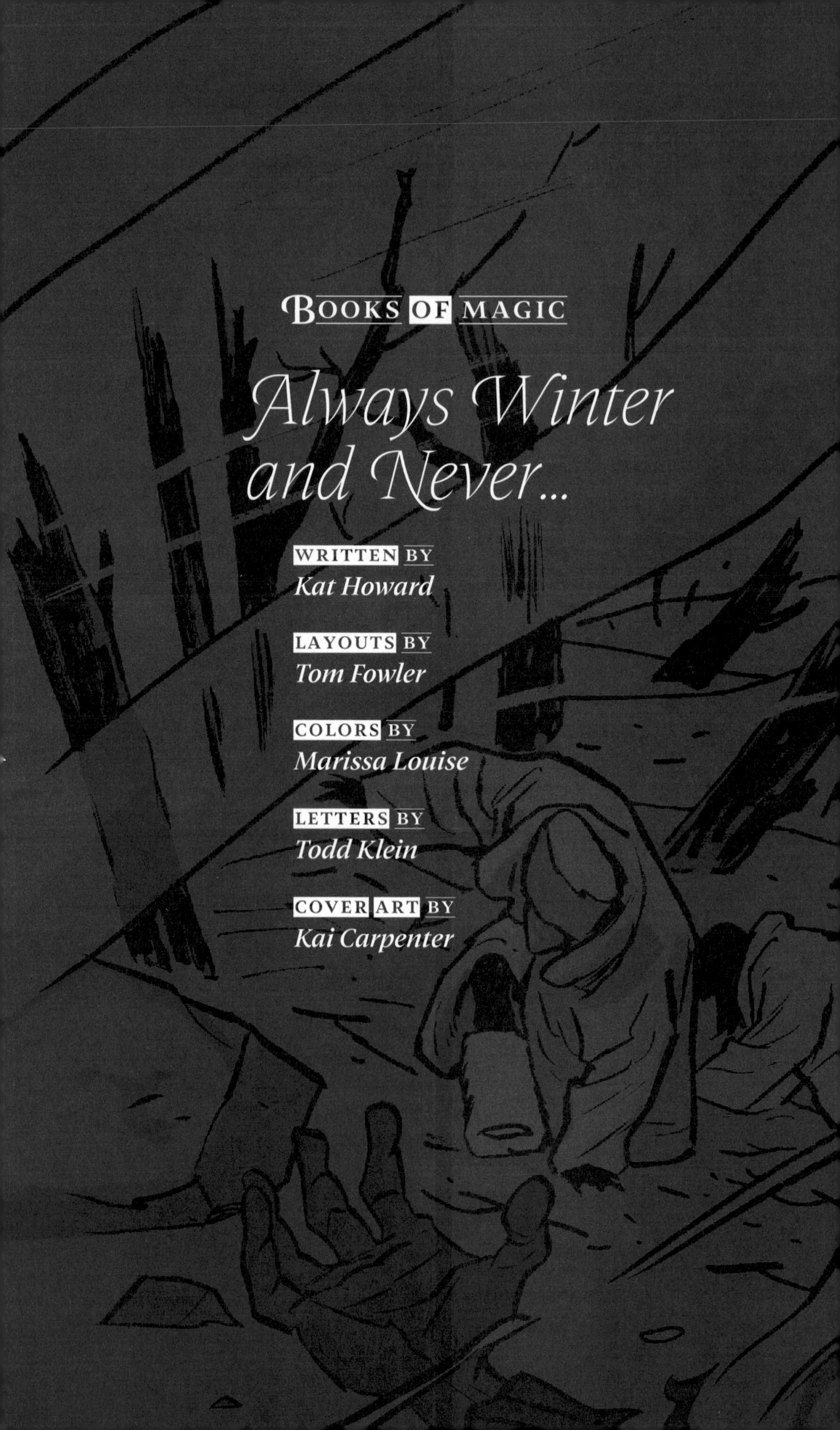

BOOKS OF MAGIC

Always Winter and Never...

WRITTEN BY
Kat Howard

LAYOUTS BY
Tom Fowler

COLORS BY
Marissa Louise

LETTERS BY
Todd Klein

COVER ART BY
Kai Carpenter

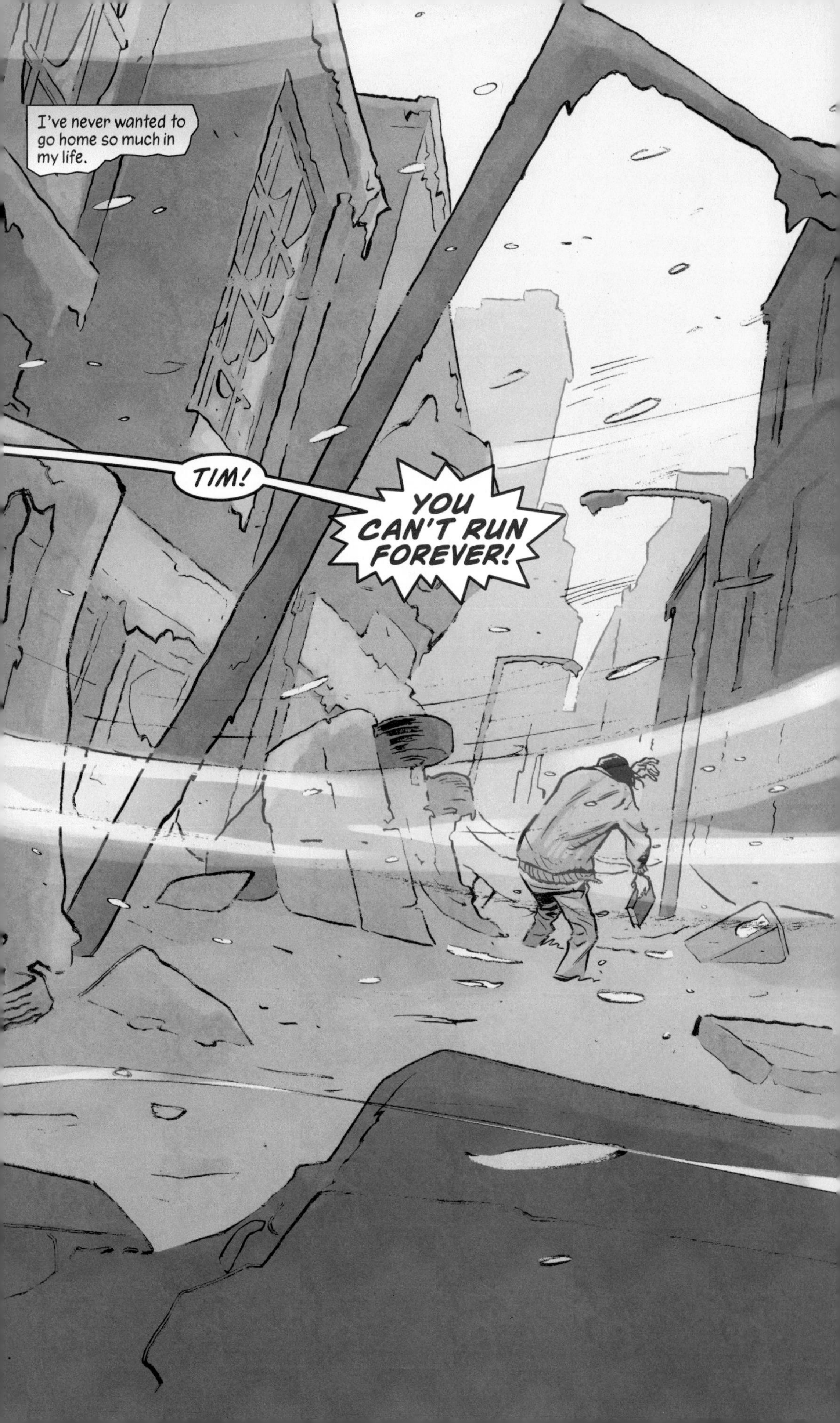
I've never wanted to go home so much in my life.
TIM!
YOU CAN'T RUN FOREVER!

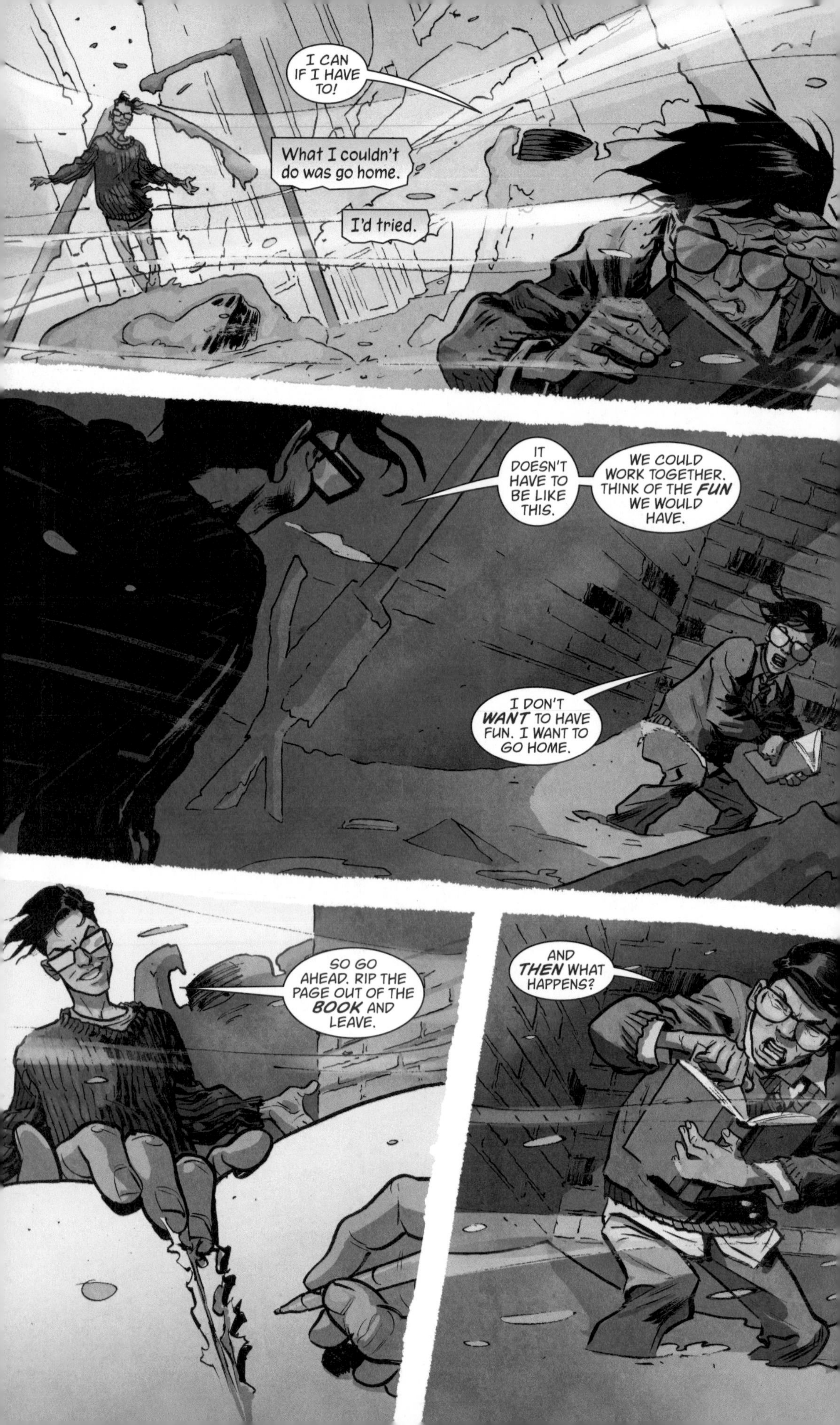
I CAN IF I HAVE TO!
What I couldn't do was go home.
I'd tried.
IT DOESN'T HAVE TO BE LIKE THIS.
WE COULD WORK TOGETHER. THINK OF THE FUN WE WOULD HAVE.
I DON'T WANT TO HAVE FUN. I WANT TO GO HOME.
SO GO AHEAD. RIP THE PAGE OUT OF THE BOOK AND LEAVE.
AND THEN WHAT HAPPENS?

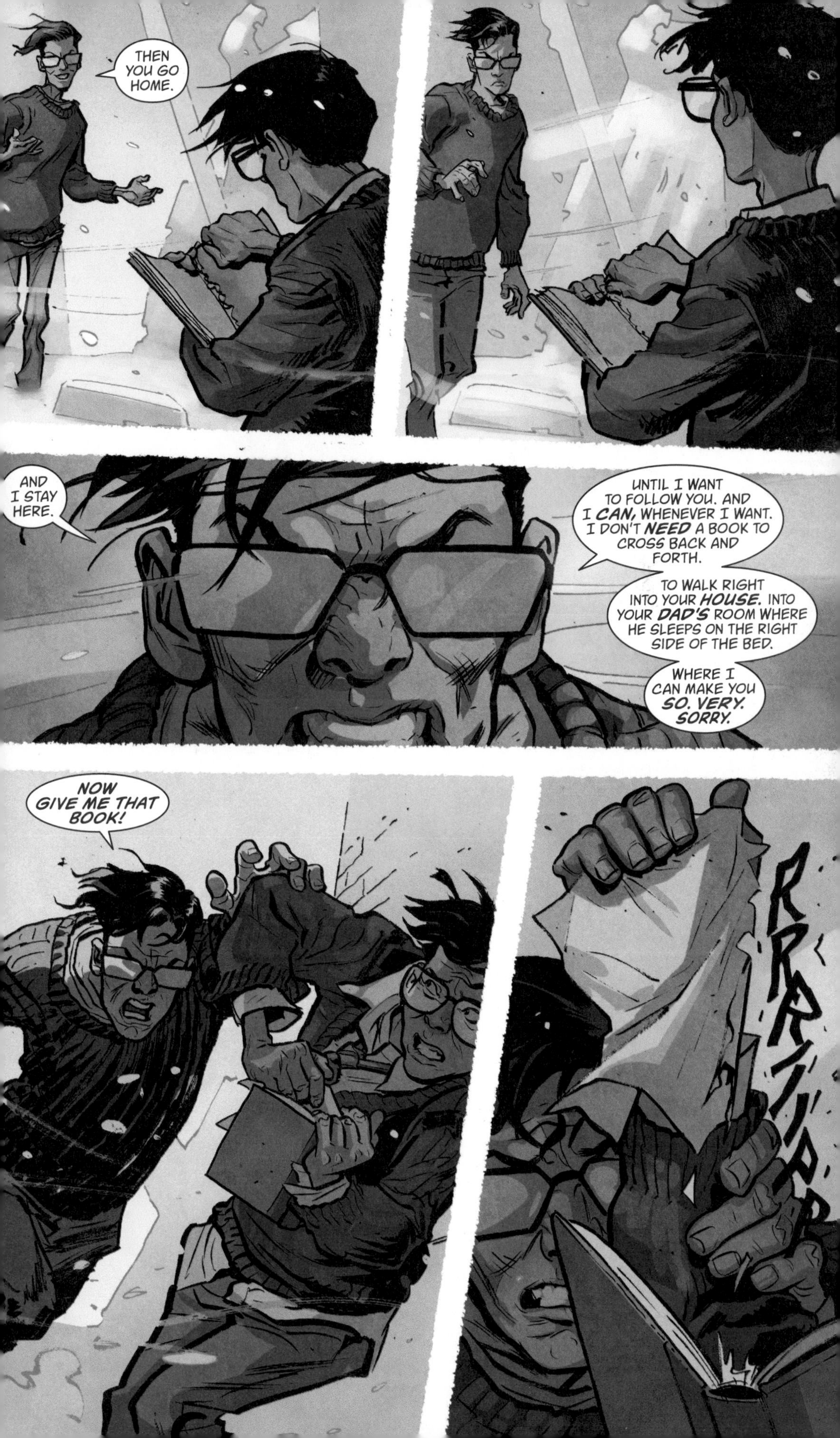
THEN YOU GO HOME.
AND I STAY HERE.
UNTIL I WANT TO FOLLOW YOU. AND I CAN, WHENEVER I WANT. I DON'T NEED A BOOK TO CROSS BACK AND FORTH.
TO WALK RIGHT INTO YOUR HOUSE. INTO YOUR DAD'S ROOM WHERE HE SLEEPS ON THE RIGHT SIDE OF THE BED.
WHERE I CAN MAKE YOU SO. VERY. SORRY.
NOW GIVE ME THAT BOOK!
RRRIIIPP

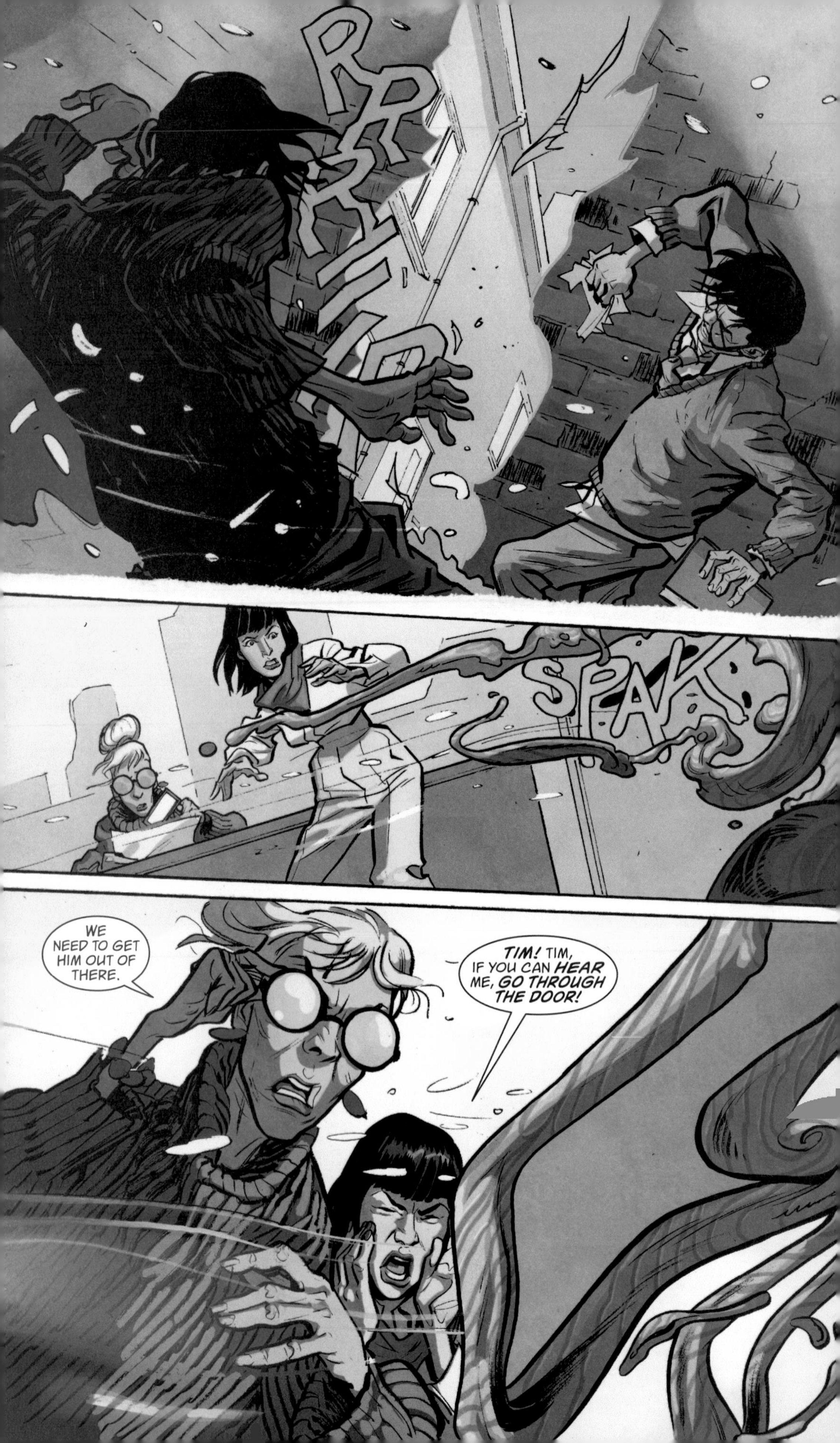
RRRIIIP
SPAK
WE NEED TO GET HIM OUT OF THERE.
TIM! TIM, IF YOU CAN HEAR ME, GO THROUGH THE DOOR!

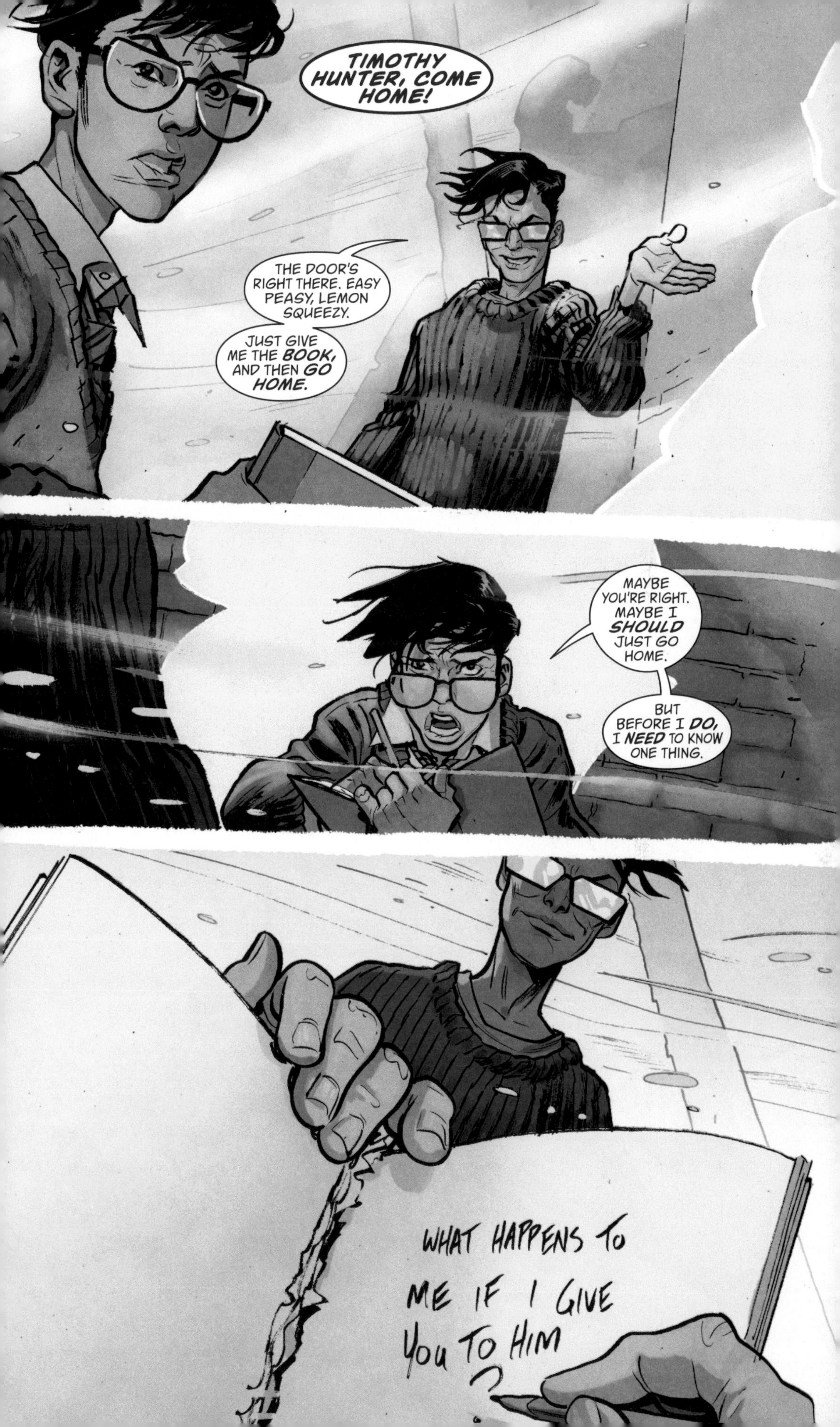
TIMOTHY HUNTER, COME HOME!
THE DOOR'S RIGHT THERE. EASY PEASY, LEMON SQUEEZY.
JUST GIVE ME THE BOOK, AND THEN GO HOME.
MAYBE YOU'RE RIGHT. MAYBE I SHOULD JUST GO HOME.
BUT BEFORE I DO, I NEED TO KNOW ONE THING.
WHAT HAPPENS TO ME IF I GIVE YOU TO HIM ?

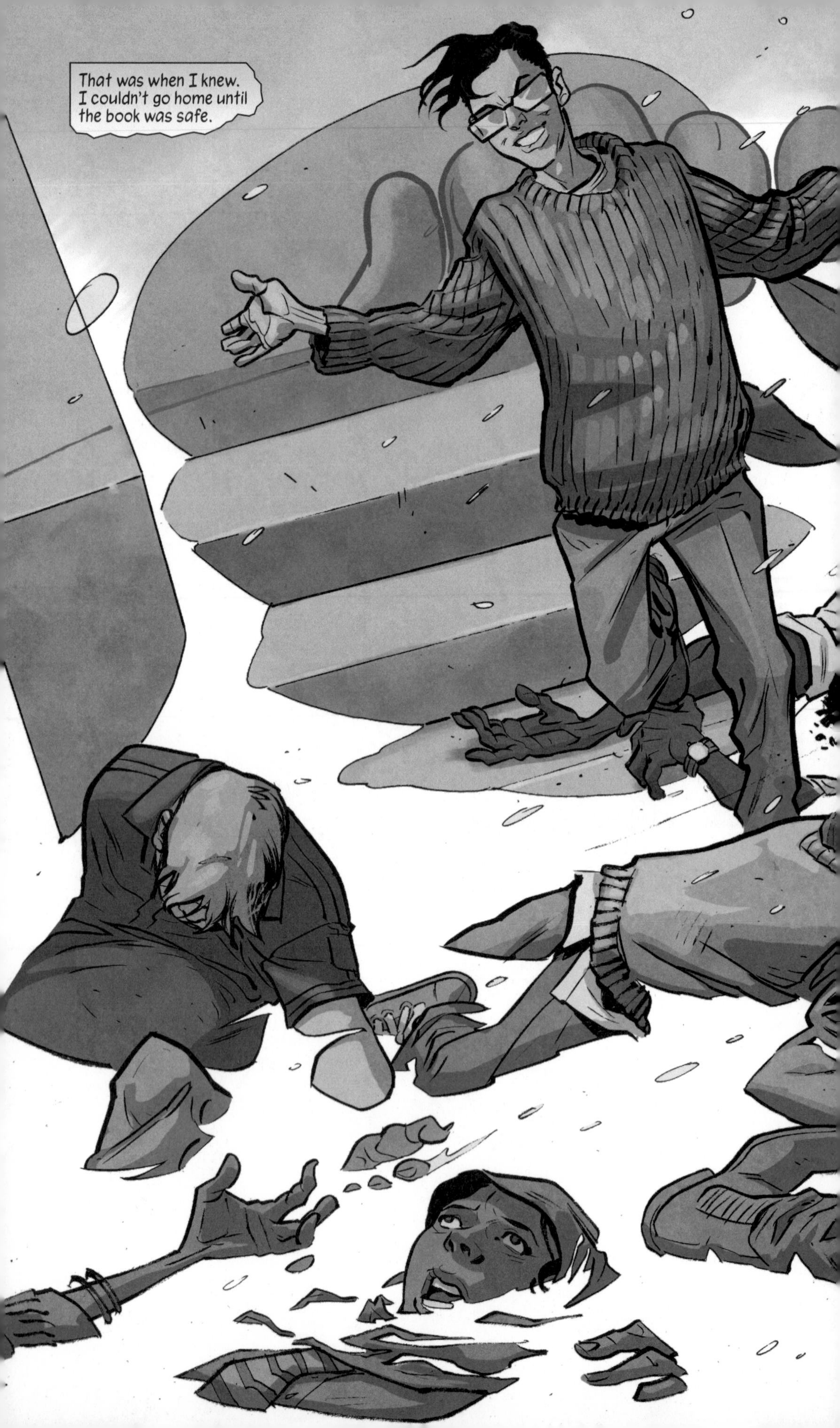
That was when I knew. I couldn't go home until the book was safe.

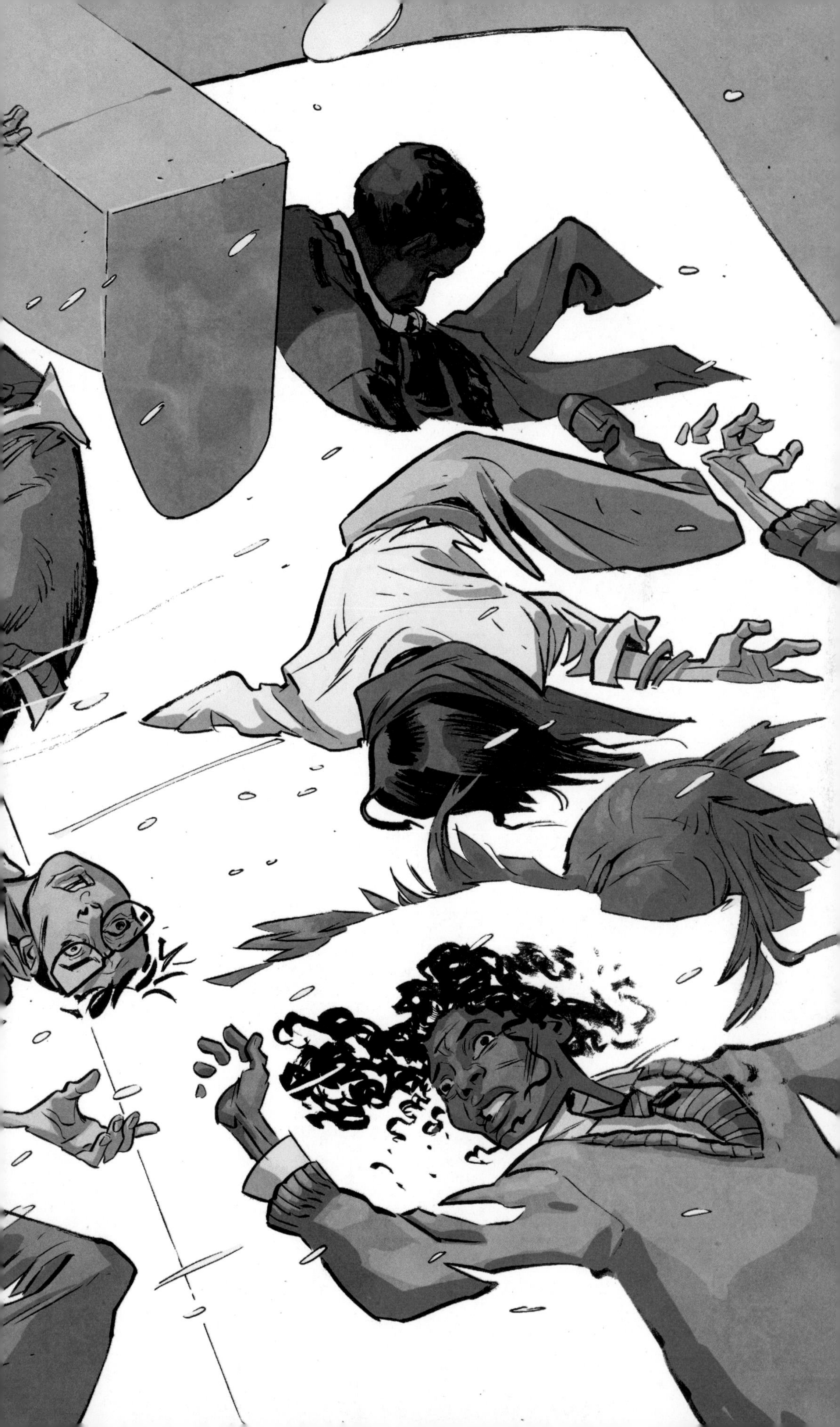

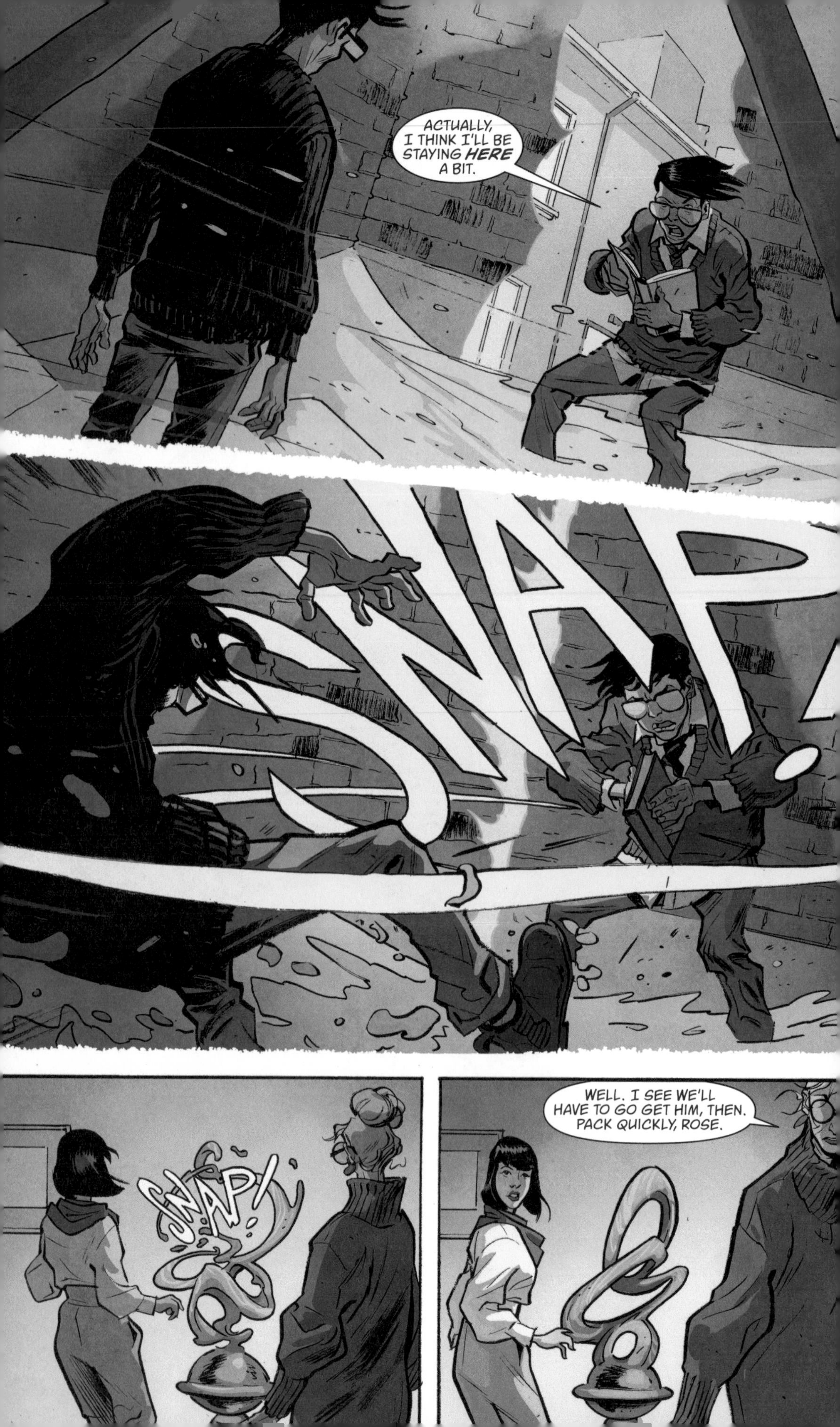
ACTUALLY, I THINK I'LL BE STAYING HERE A BIT.
SNAP!
SNAP!
WELL. I SEE WE'LL HAVE TO GO GET HIM, THEN. PACK QUICKLY, ROSE.

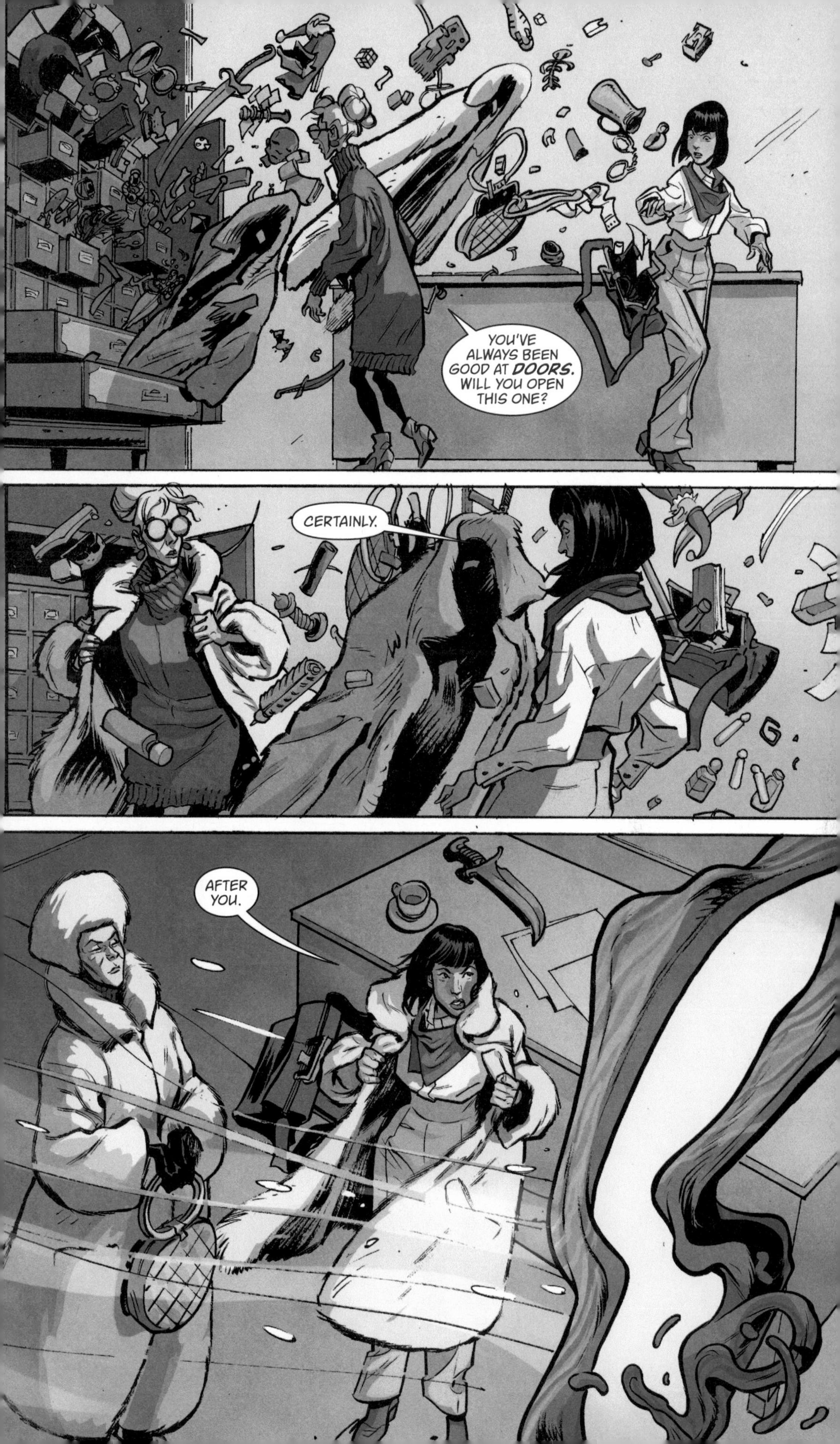
YOU'VE ALWAYS BEEN GOOD AT DOORS. WILL YOU OPEN THIS ONE?
CERTAINLY.
AFTER YOU.

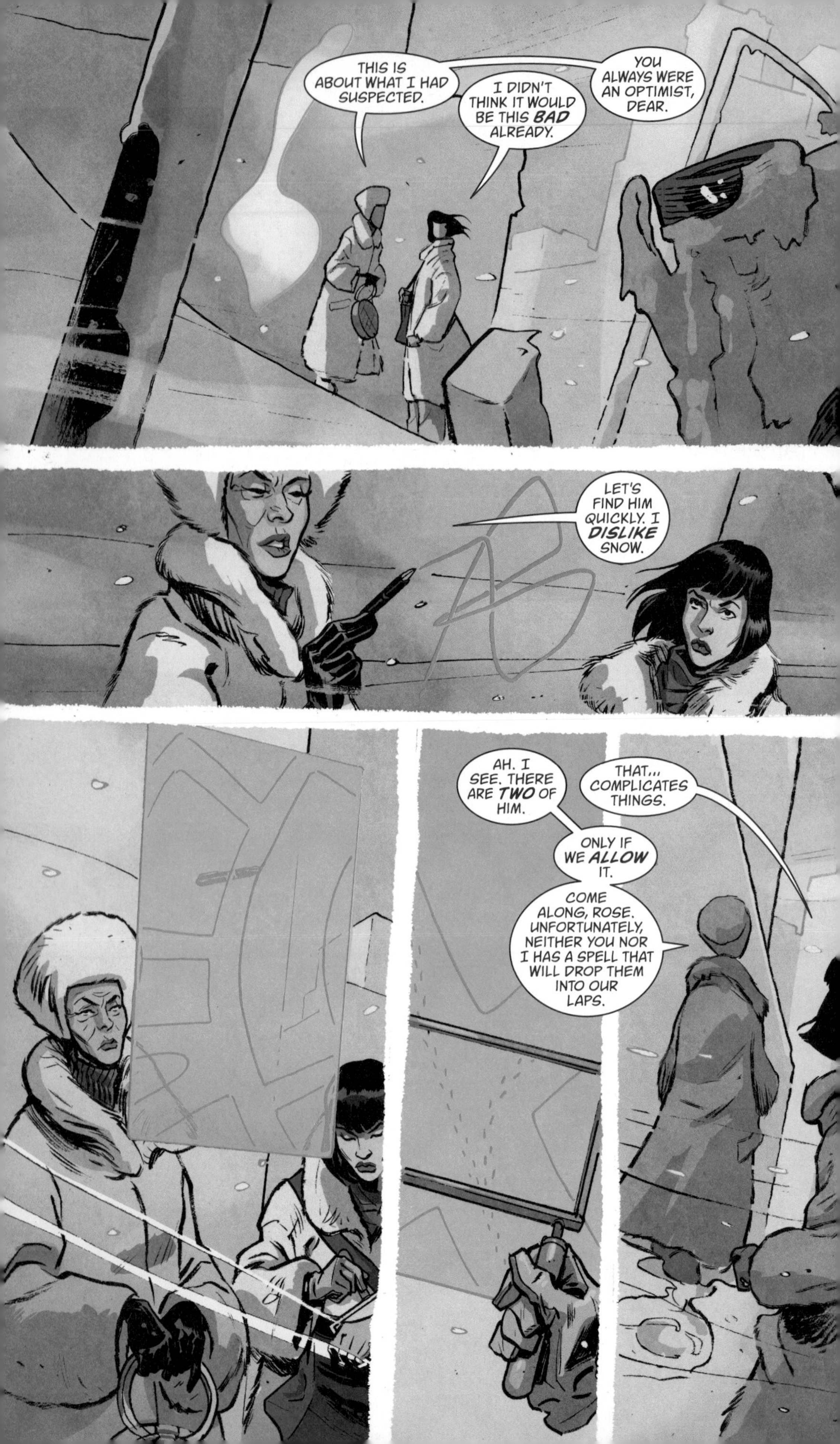
THIS IS ABOUT WHAT I HAD SUSPECTED.
I DIDN'T THINK IT WOULD BE THIS BAD ALREADY.
YOU ALWAYS WERE AN OPTIMIST, DEAR.
LET'S FIND HIM QUICKLY. I DISLIKE SNOW.
AH. I SEE. THERE ARE TWO OF HIM.
THAT... COMPLICATES THINGS.
ONLY IF WE ALLOW IT.
COME ALONG, ROSE. UNFORTUNATELY, NEITHER YOU NOR I HAS A SPELL THAT WILL DROP THEM INTO OUR LAPS.

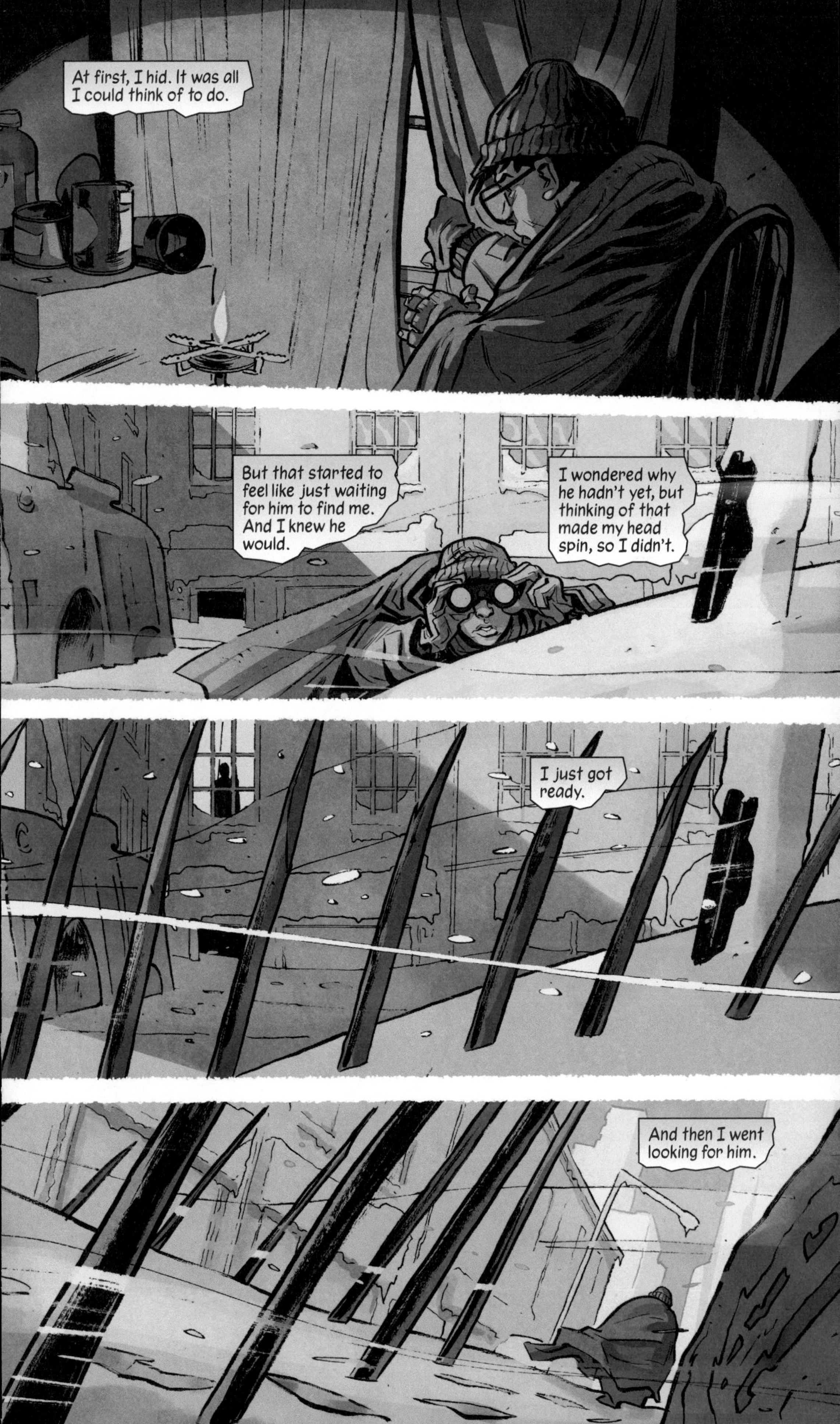
At first, I hid. It was all I could think of to do.
But that started to feel like just waiting for him to find me. And I knew he would.
I wondered why he hadn't yet, but thinking of that made my head spin, so I didn't.
I just got ready.
And then I went looking for him.

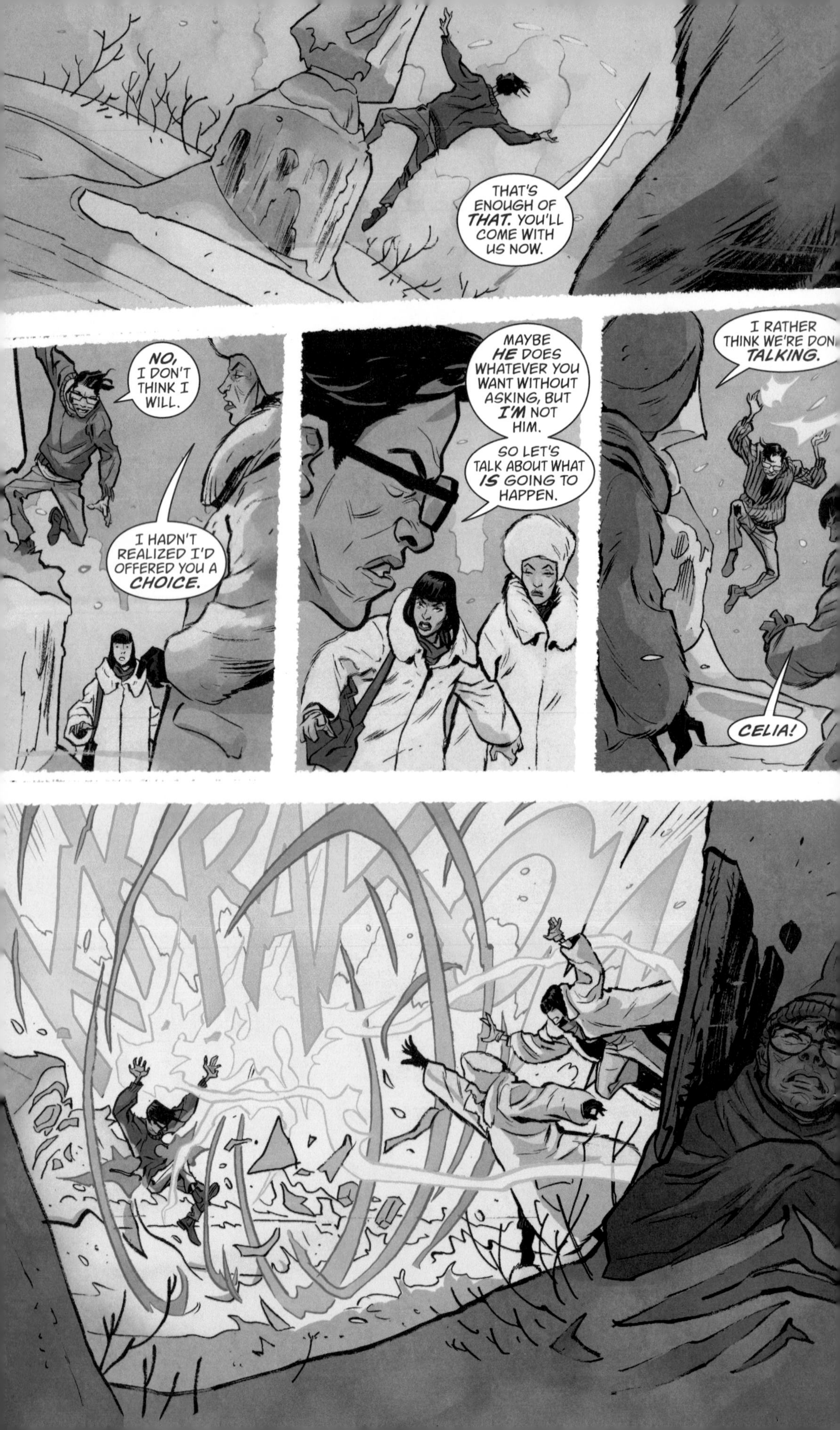
THAT'S ENOUGH OF *THAT.* YOU'LL COME WITH US NOW.
NO, I DON'T THINK I WILL.
I HADN'T REALIZED I'D OFFERED YOU A *CHOICE.*
MAYBE *HE* DOES WHATEVER YOU WANT WITHOUT ASKING, BUT *I'M* NOT HIM.
SO LET'S TALK ABOUT WHAT *IS* GOING TO HAPPEN.
I RATHER THINK WE'RE DON *TALKING.*
CELIA!

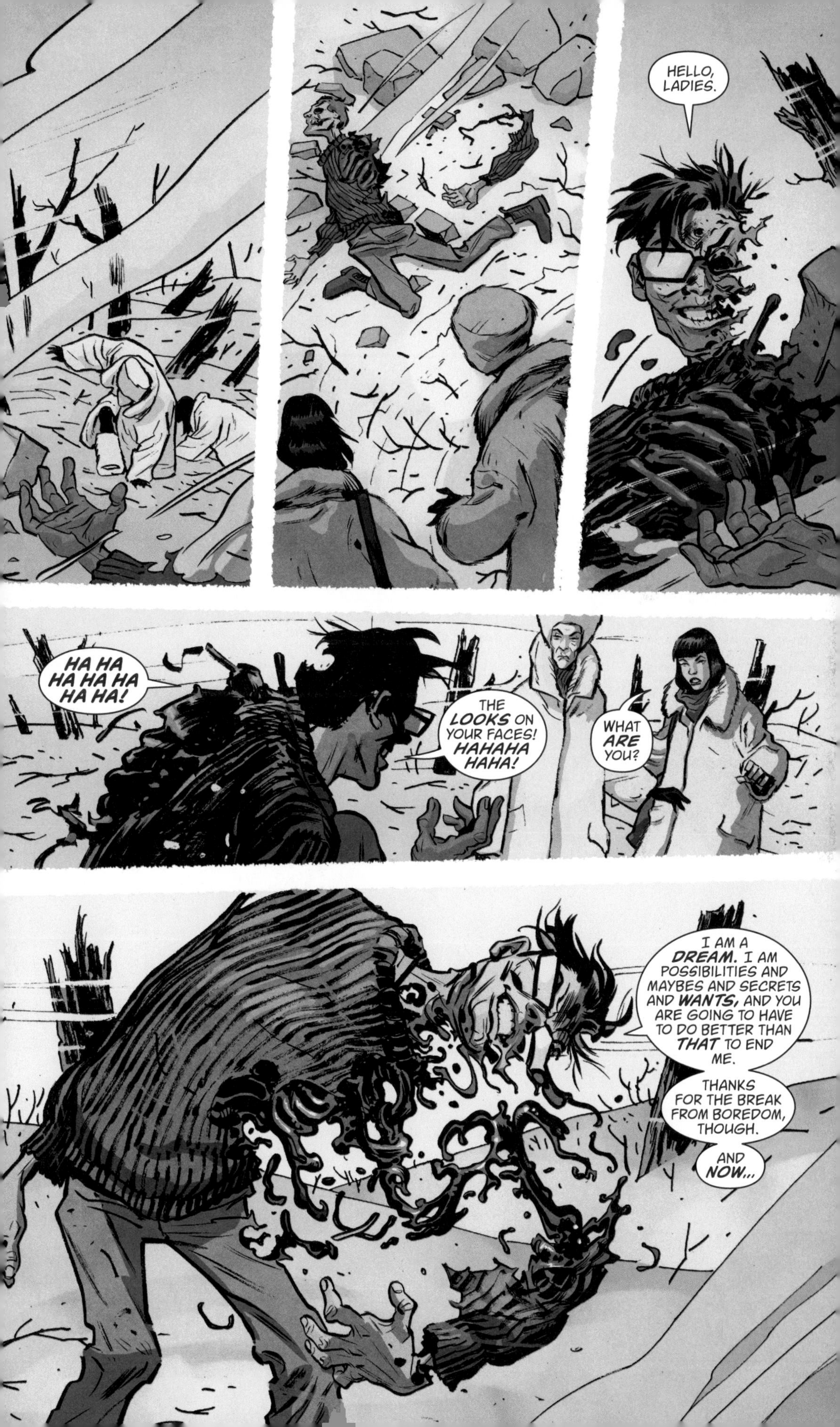
HELLO, LADIES.
HA HA HA HA HA HA HA!
THE LOOKS ON YOUR FACES! HAHAHA HAHA!
WHAT ARE YOU?
I AM A DREAM. I AM POSSIBILITIES AND MAYBES AND SECRETS AND WANTS, AND YOU ARE GOING TO HAVE TO DO BETTER THAN THAT TO END ME.
THANKS FOR THE BREAK FROM BOREDOM, THOUGH.
AND NOW...

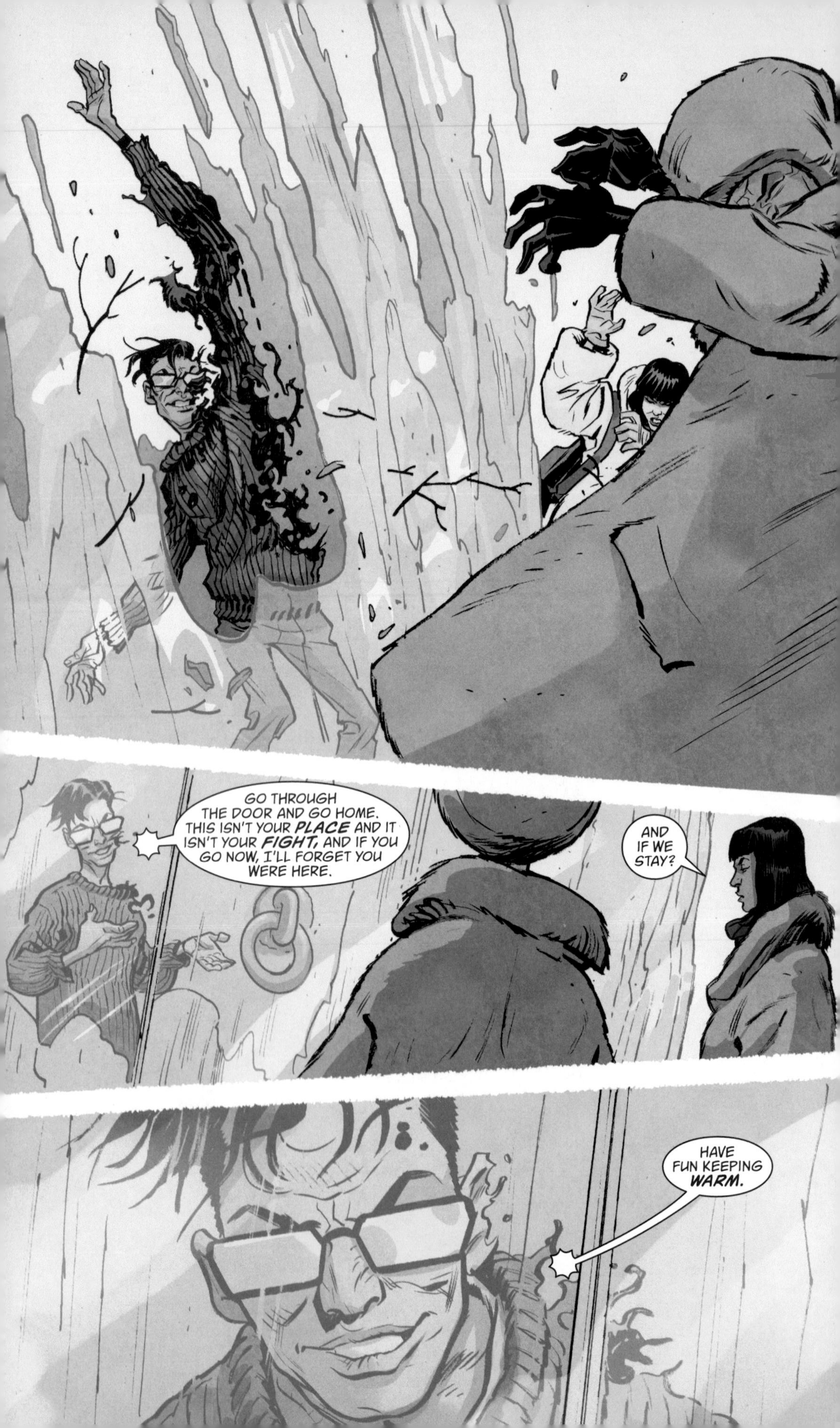
GO THROUGH THE DOOR AND GO HOME. THIS ISN'T YOUR PLACE AND IT ISN'T YOUR FIGHT, AND IF YOU GO NOW, I'LL FORGET YOU WERE HERE.
AND IF WE STAY?
HAVE FUN KEEPING WARM.

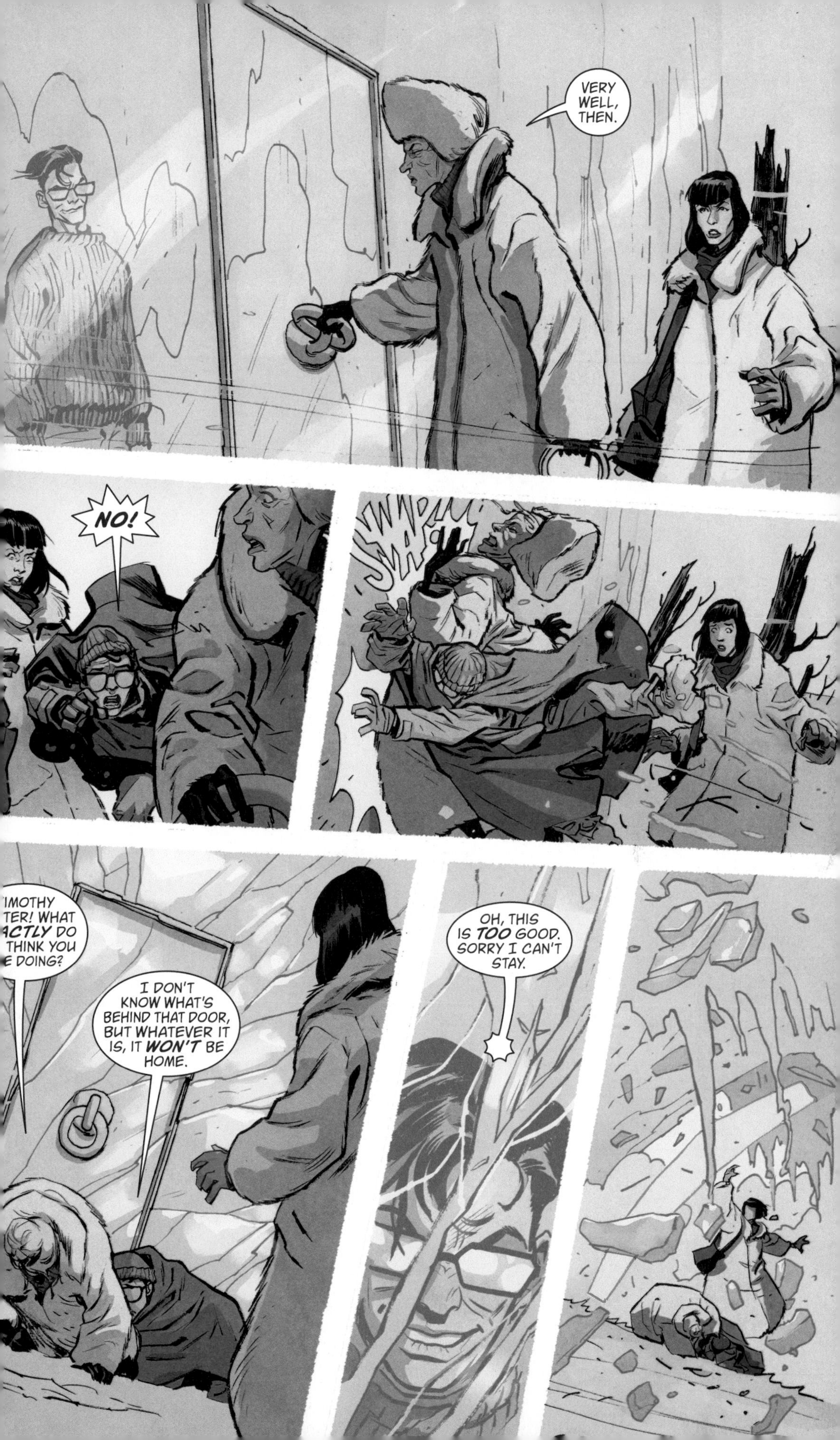
VERY WELL, THEN.
NO!
'IMOTHY TER! WHAT ACTLY DO THINK YOU E DOING?
I DON'T KNOW WHAT'S BEHIND THAT DOOR, BUT WHATEVER IT IS, IT WON'T BE HOME.
OH, THIS IS TOO GOOD. SORRY I CAN'T STAY.

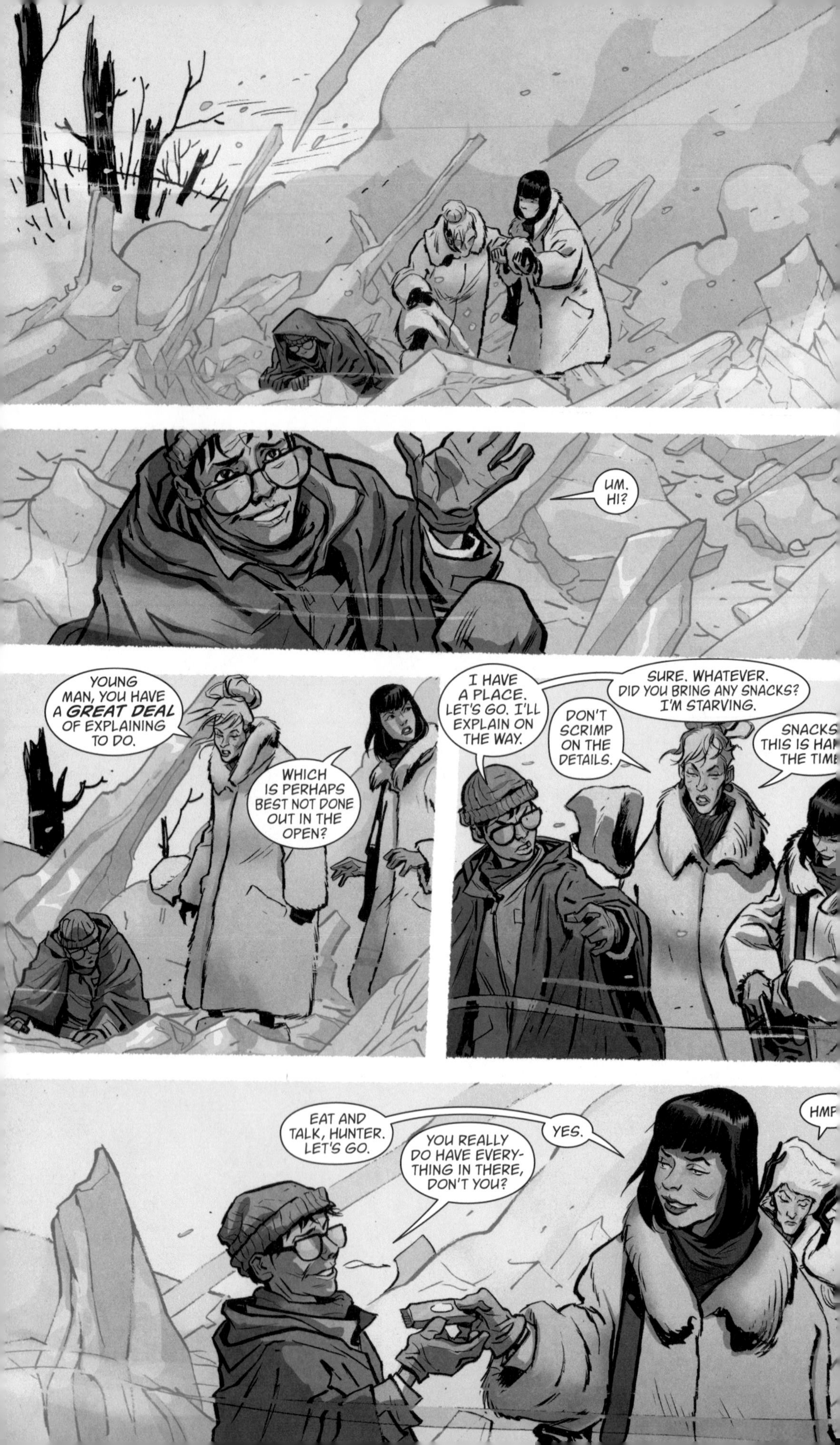
UM. HI?
YOUNG MAN, YOU HAVE A GREAT DEAL OF EXPLAINING TO DO.
WHICH IS PERHAPS BEST NOT DONE OUT IN THE OPEN?
I HAVE A PLACE. LET'S GO. I'LL EXPLAIN ON THE WAY.
SURE. WHATEVER. DID YOU BRING ANY SNACKS? I'M STARVING.
DON'T SCRIMP ON THE DETAILS.
SNACKS
EAT AND TALK, HUNTER. LET'S GO.
YES.
YOU REALLY DO HAVE EVERYTHING IN THERE, DON'T YOU?

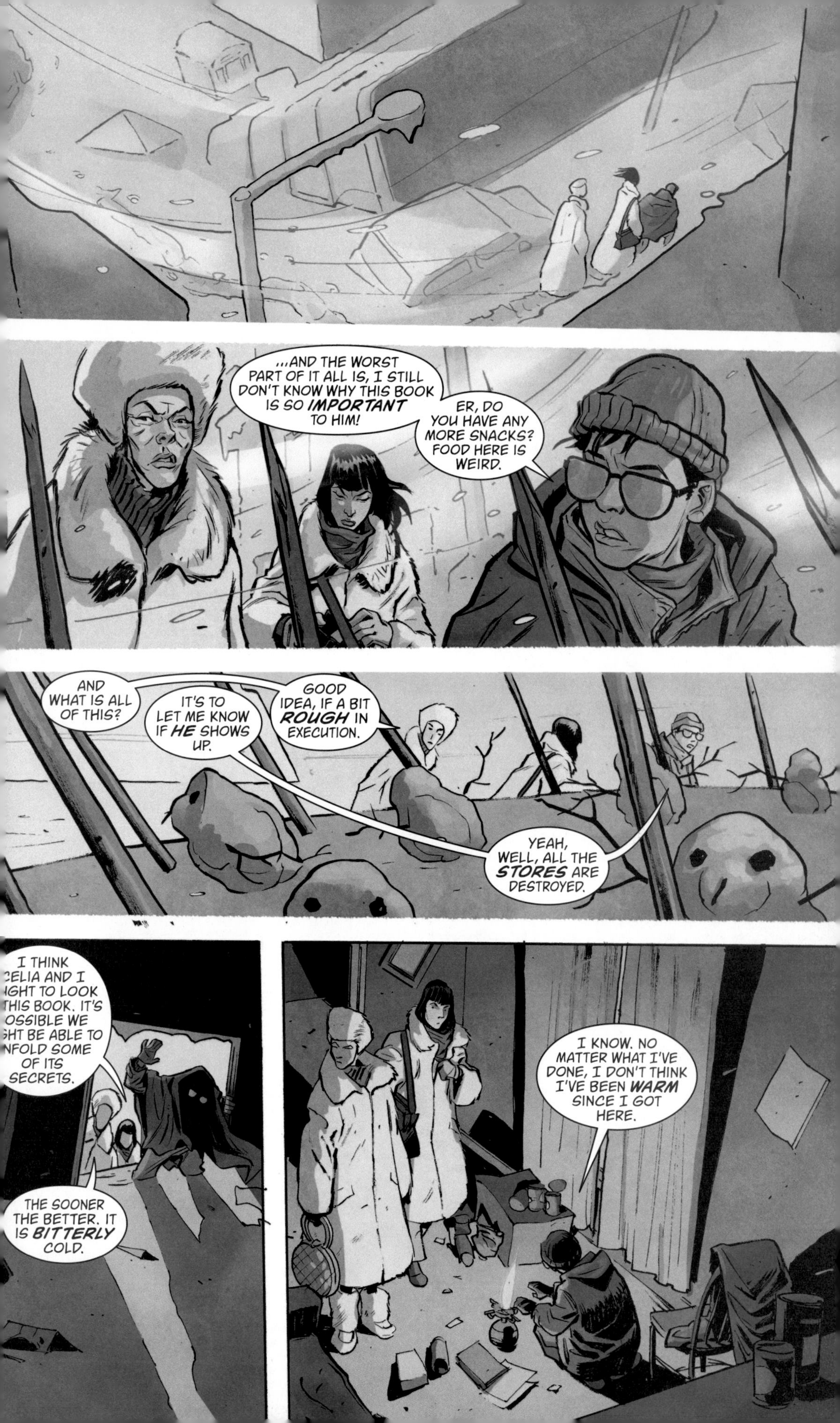

...AND THE WORST PART OF IT ALL IS, I STILL DON'T KNOW WHY THIS BOOK IS SO IMPORTANT TO HIM!
ER, DO YOU HAVE ANY MORE SNACKS? FOOD HERE IS WEIRD.
AND WHAT IS ALL OF THIS?
IT'S TO LET ME KNOW IF HE SHOWS UP.
GOOD IDEA, IF A BIT ROUGH IN EXECUTION.
YEAH, WELL, ALL THE STORES ARE DESTROYED.
I THINK CELIA AND I IGHT TO LOOK THIS BOOK. IT'S OSSIBLE WE GHT BE ABLE TO NFOLD SOME OF ITS SECRETS.
THE SOONER THE BETTER. IT IS BITTERLY COLD.
I KNOW. NO MATTER WHAT I'VE DONE, I DON'T THINK I'VE BEEN WARM SINCE I GOT HERE.

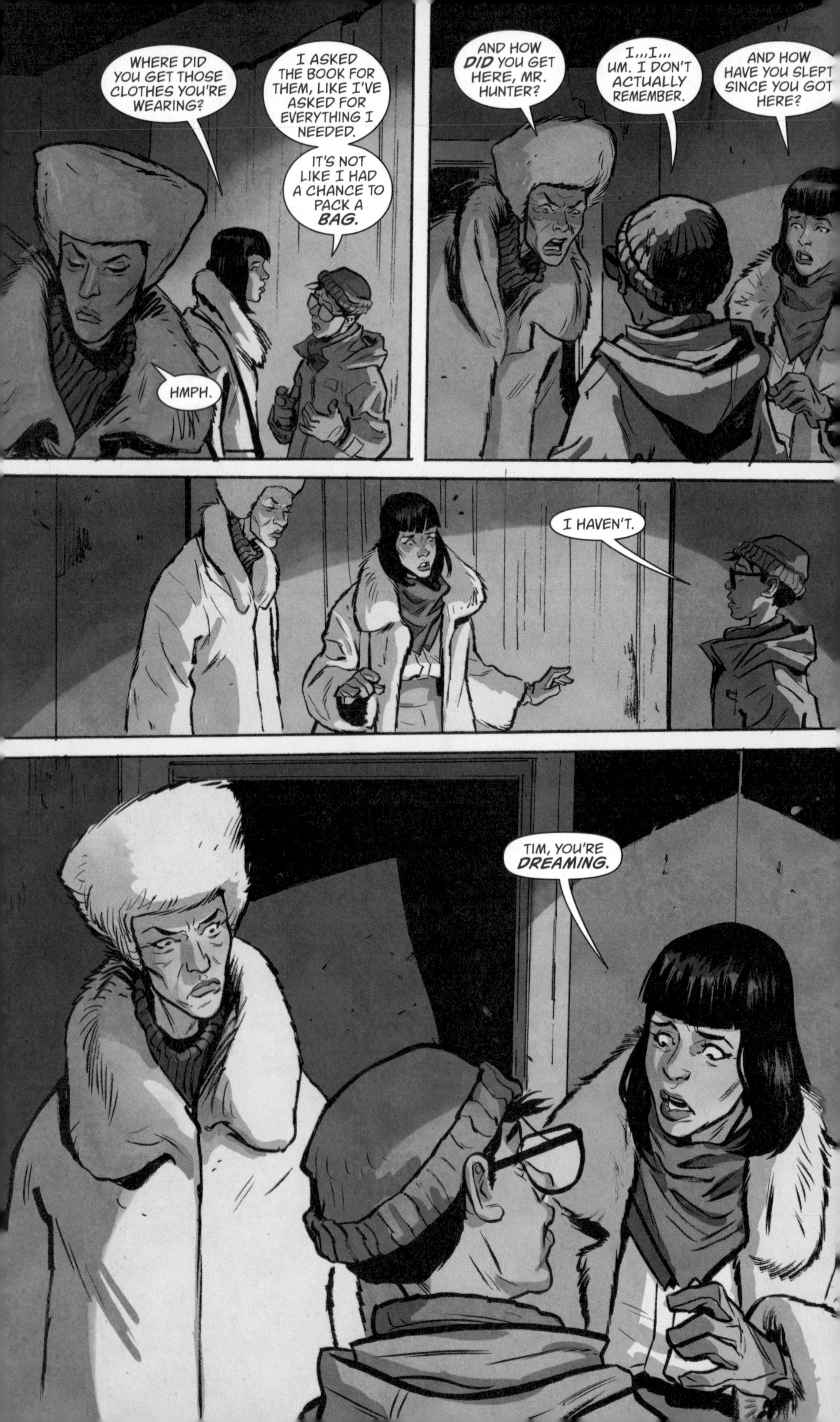
WHERE DID YOU GET THOSE CLOTHES YOU'RE WEARING?
I ASKED THE BOOK FOR THEM, LIKE I'VE ASKED FOR EVERYTHING I NEEDED.
IT'S NOT LIKE I HAD A CHANCE TO PACK A BAG.
HMPH.
AND HOW DID YOU GET HERE, MR. HUNTER?
I...I... UM. I DON'T ACTUALLY REMEMBER.
AND HOW HAVE YOU SLEPT SINCE YOU GOT HERE?
I HAVEN'T.
TIM, YOU'RE DREAMING.

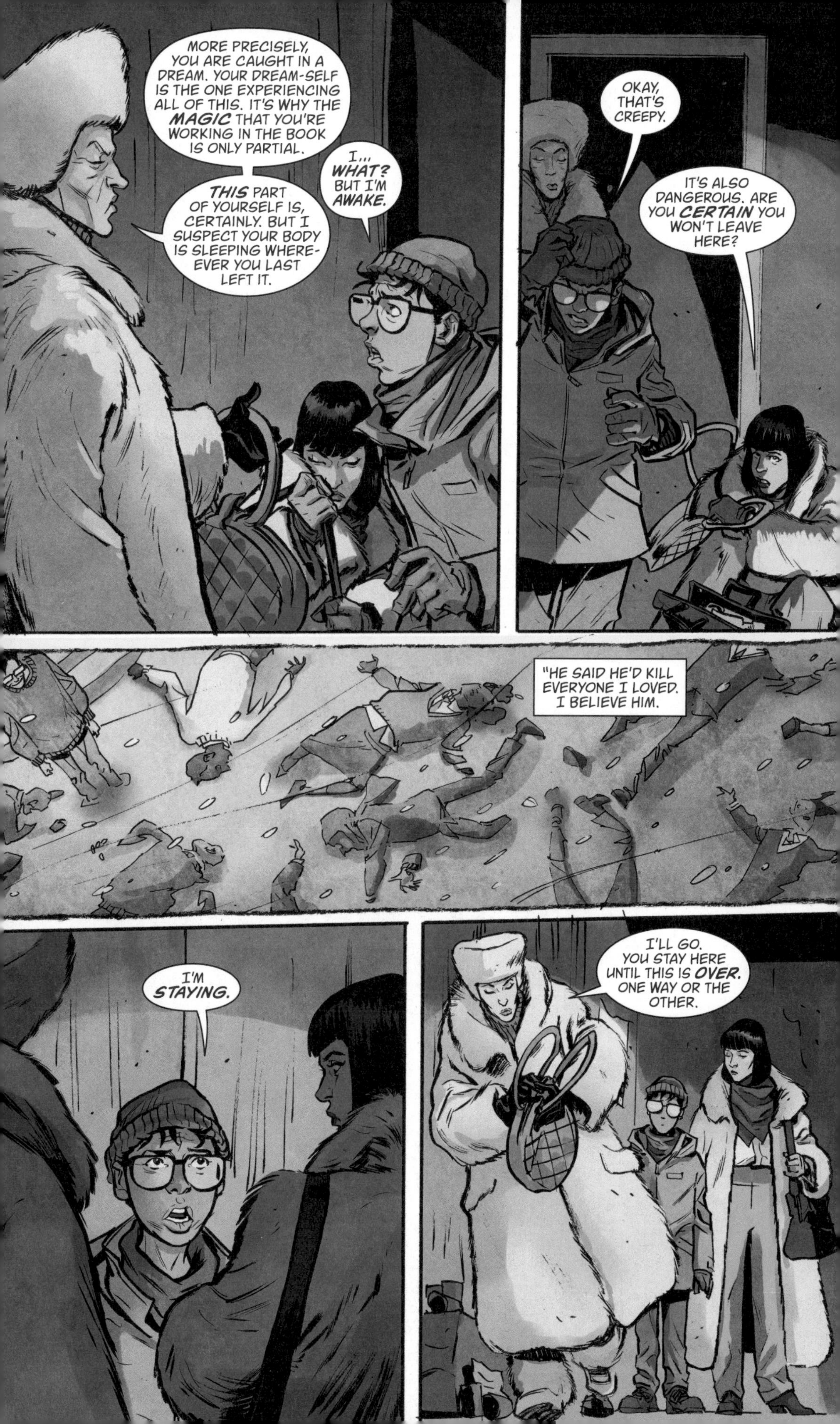
MORE PRECISELY, YOU ARE CAUGHT IN A DREAM. YOUR DREAM-SELF IS THE ONE EXPERIENCING ALL OF THIS. IT'S WHY THE MAGIC THAT YOU'RE WORKING IN THE BOOK IS ONLY PARTIAL.
THIS PART OF YOURSELF IS, CERTAINLY. BUT I SUSPECT YOUR BODY IS SLEEPING WHEREEVER YOU LAST LEFT IT.
I... WHAT? BUT I'M AWAKE.
OKAY, THAT'S CREEPY.
IT'S ALSO DANGEROUS. ARE YOU CERTAIN YOU WON'T LEAVE HERE?
"HE SAID HE'D KILL EVERYONE I LOVED. I BELIEVE HIM.
I'M STAYING.
I'LL GO. YOU STAY HERE UNTIL THIS IS OVER. ONE WAY OR THE OTHER.

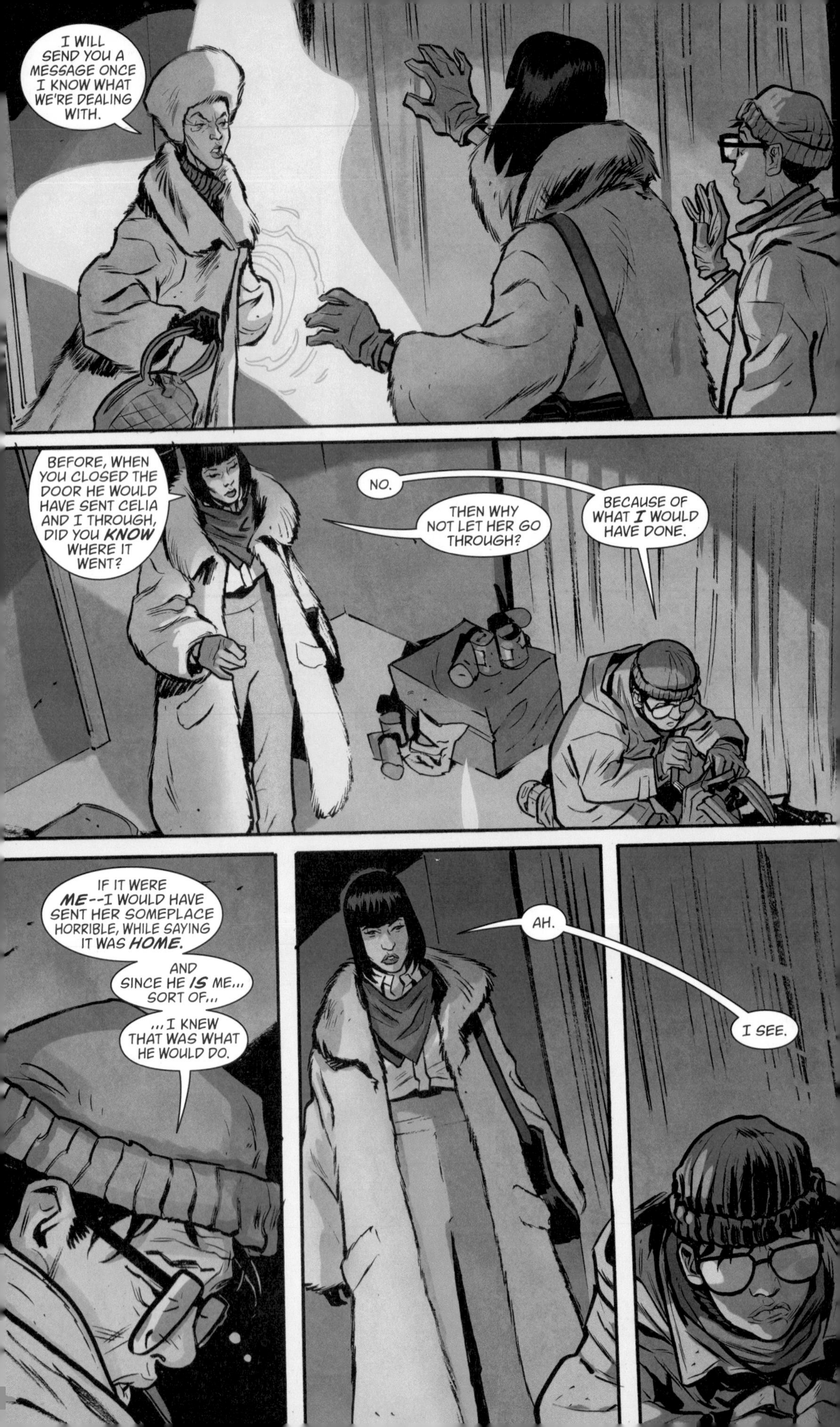

I WILL SEND YOU A MESSAGE ONCE I KNOW WHAT WE'RE DEALING WITH.
BEFORE, WHEN YOU CLOSED THE DOOR HE WOULD HAVE SENT CELIA AND I THROUGH, DID YOU *KNOW* WHERE IT WENT?
NO.
THEN WHY NOT LET HER GO THROUGH?
BECAUSE OF WHAT *I* WOULD HAVE DONE.
IF IT WERE *ME*--I WOULD HAVE SENT HER SOMEPLACE HORRIBLE, WHILE SAYING IT WAS *HOME*.
AND SINCE HE *IS* ME... SORT OF...
...I KNEW THAT WAS WHAT HE WOULD DO.
AH.
I SEE.

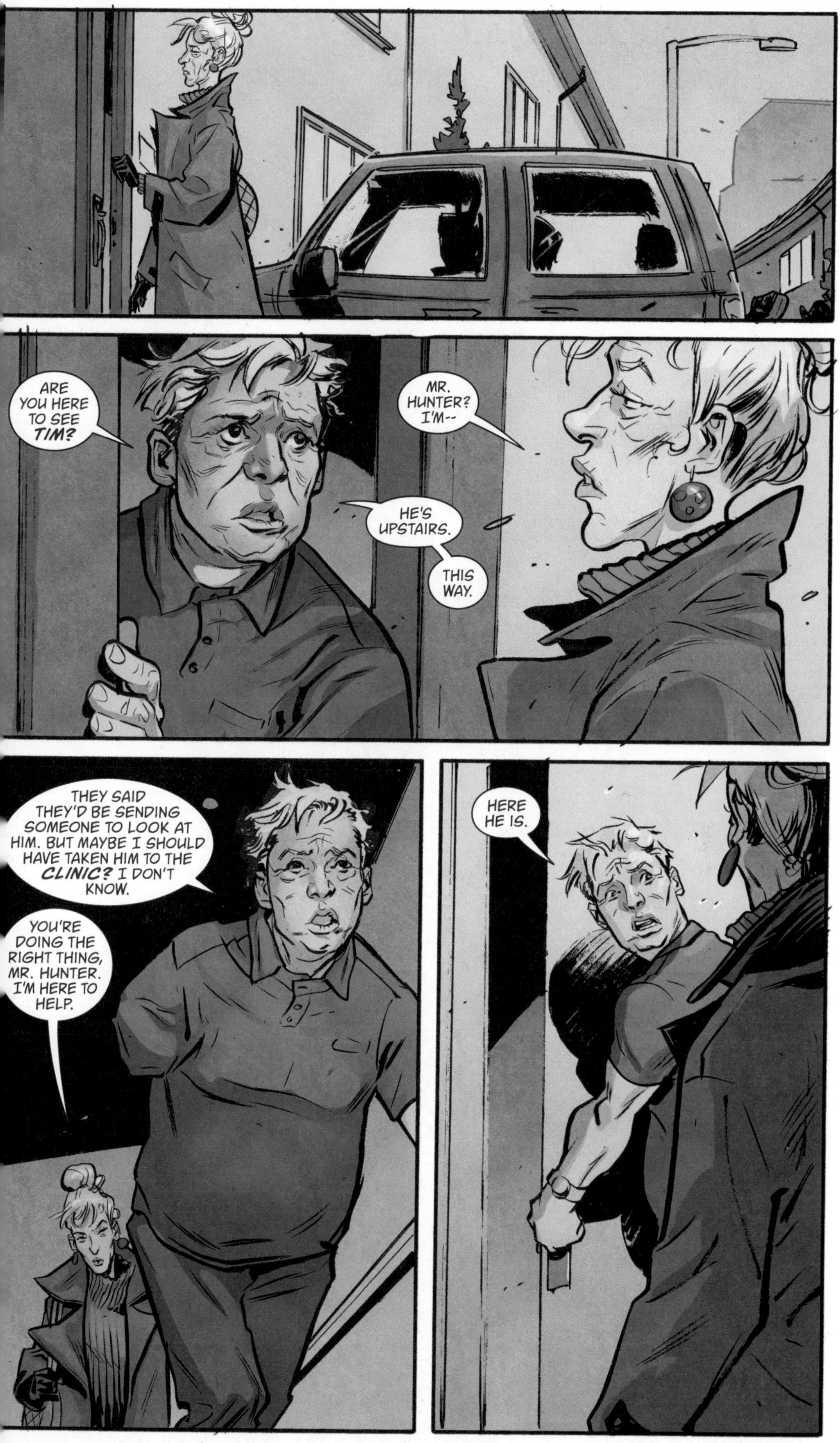
ARE YOU HERE TO SEE *TIM?*
MR. HUNTER? I'M--
HE'S UPSTAIRS.
THIS WAY.
THEY SAID THEY'D BE SENDING SOMEONE TO LOOK AT HIM. BUT MAYBE I SHOULD HAVE TAKEN HIM TO THE *CLINIC?* I DON'T KNOW.
YOU'RE DOING THE RIGHT THING, MR. HUNTER. I'M HERE TO HELP.
HERE HE IS.

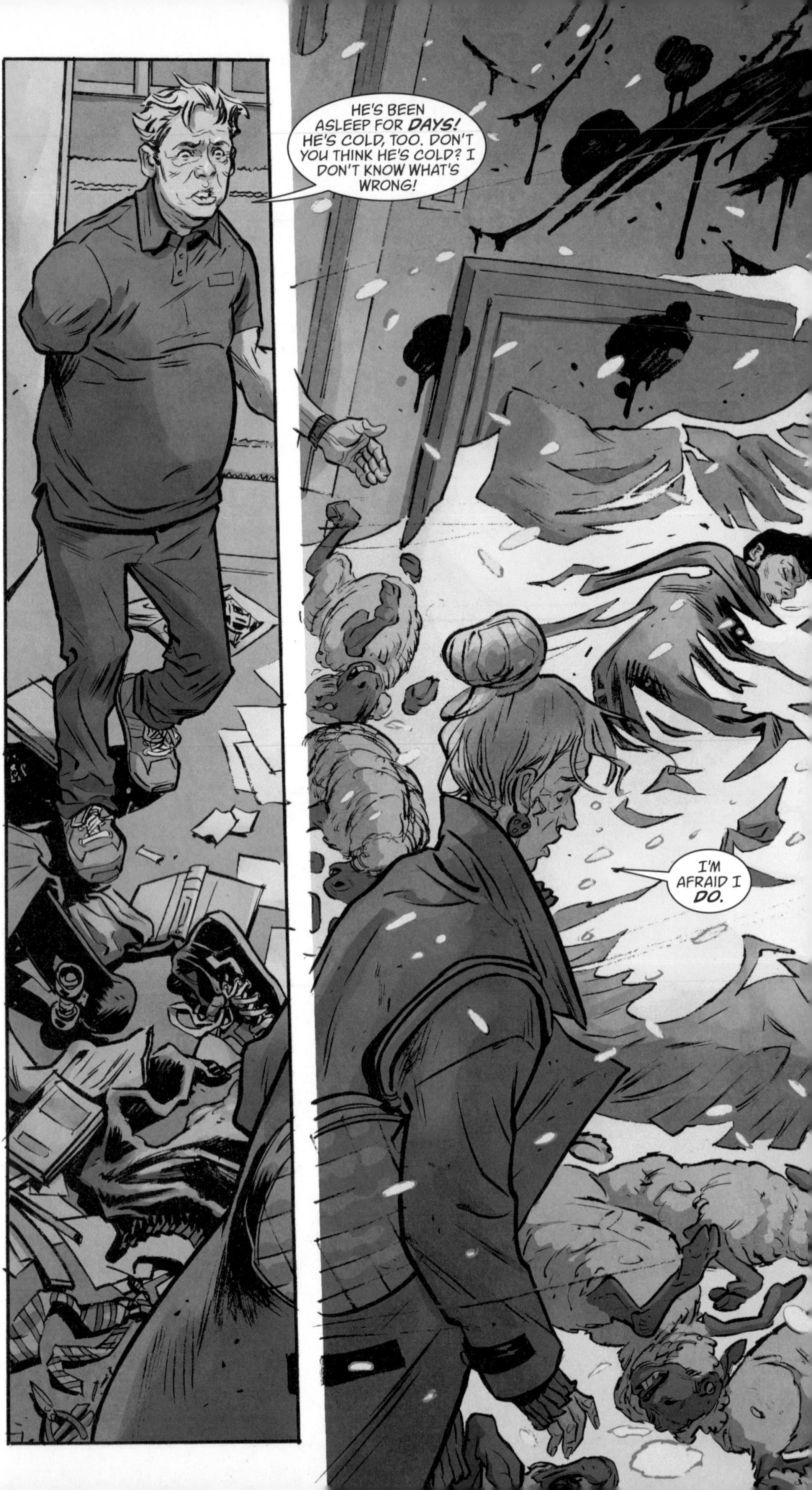
HE'S BEEN ASLEEP FOR DAYS! HE'S COLD, TOO. DON'T YOU THINK HE'S COLD? I DON'T KNOW WHAT'S WRONG!
I'M AFRAID I DO.

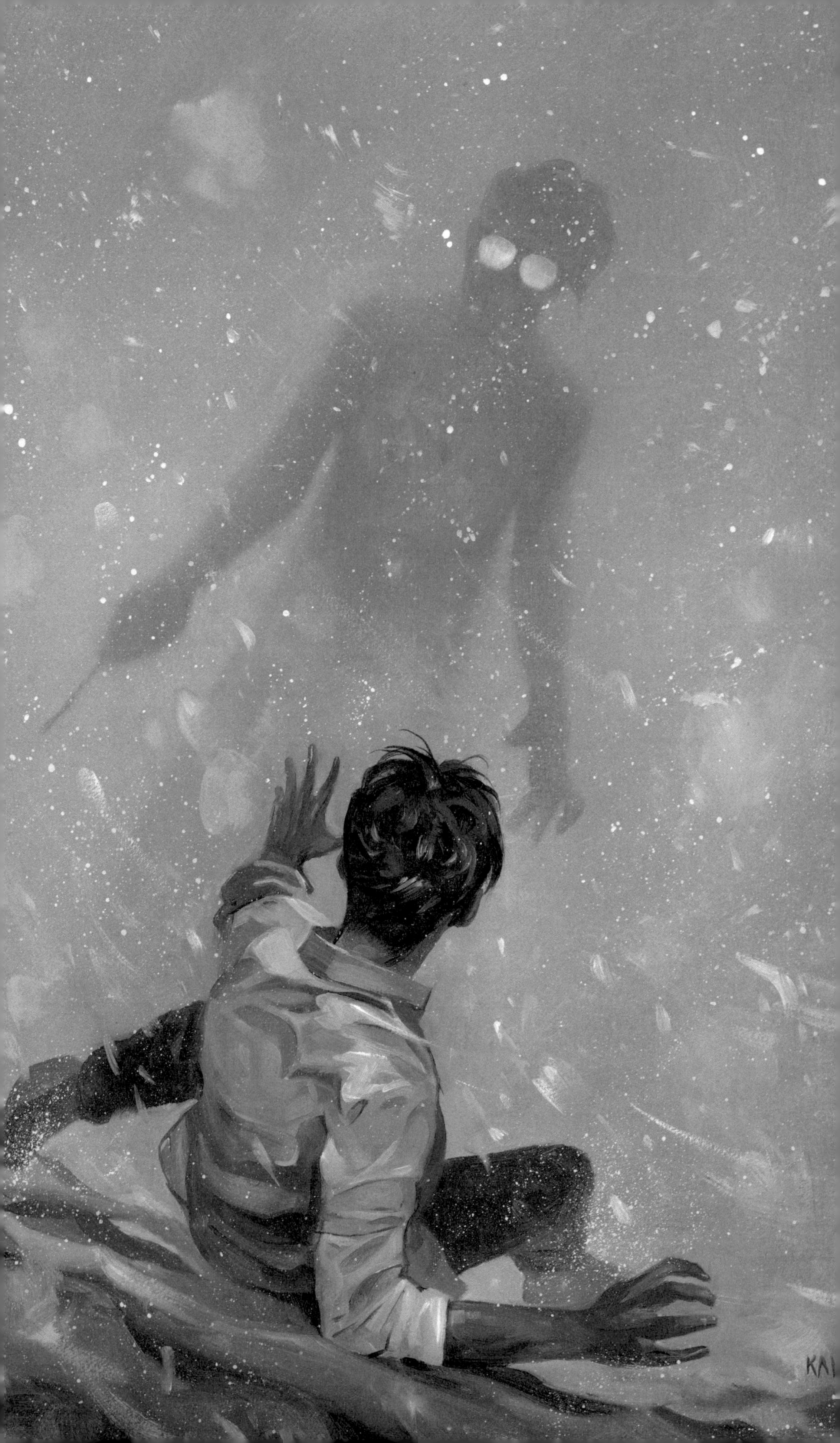
KAI

BOOKS OF MAGIC

An Awakening

WRITTEN BY
Kat Howard

LAYOUTS BY
Tom Fowler

FINISHES BY
*Craig Taillefer
and Tom Fowler*

COLORS BY
Brian Reber

LETTERS BY
Todd Klein

COVER ART BY
Kai Carpenter

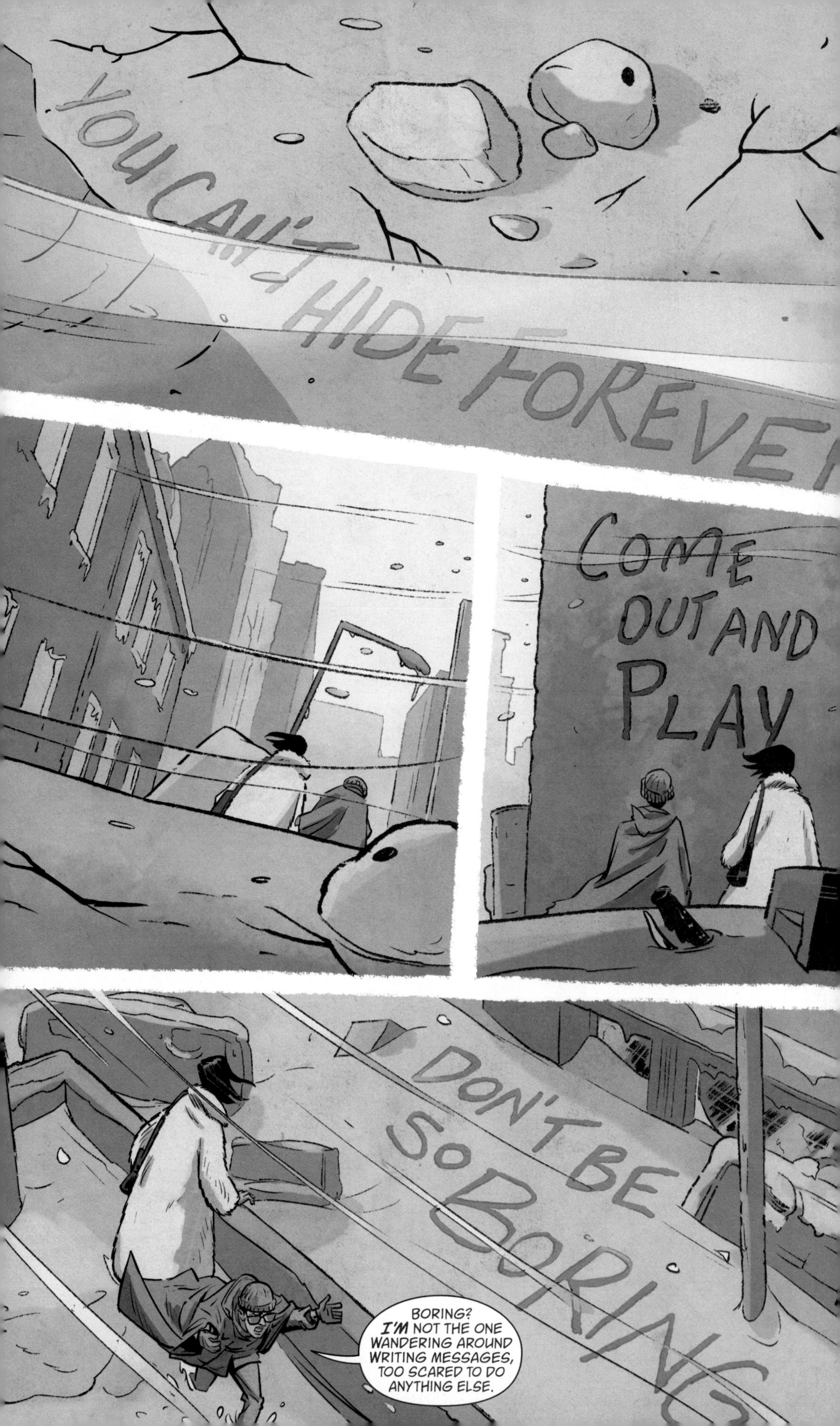
YOU CAN'T HIDE FOREVER
COME OUT AND PLAY
DON'T BE SO BORING
BORING? I'M NOT THE ONE WANDERING AROUND WRITING MESSAGES, TOO SCARED TO DO ANYTHING ELSE.

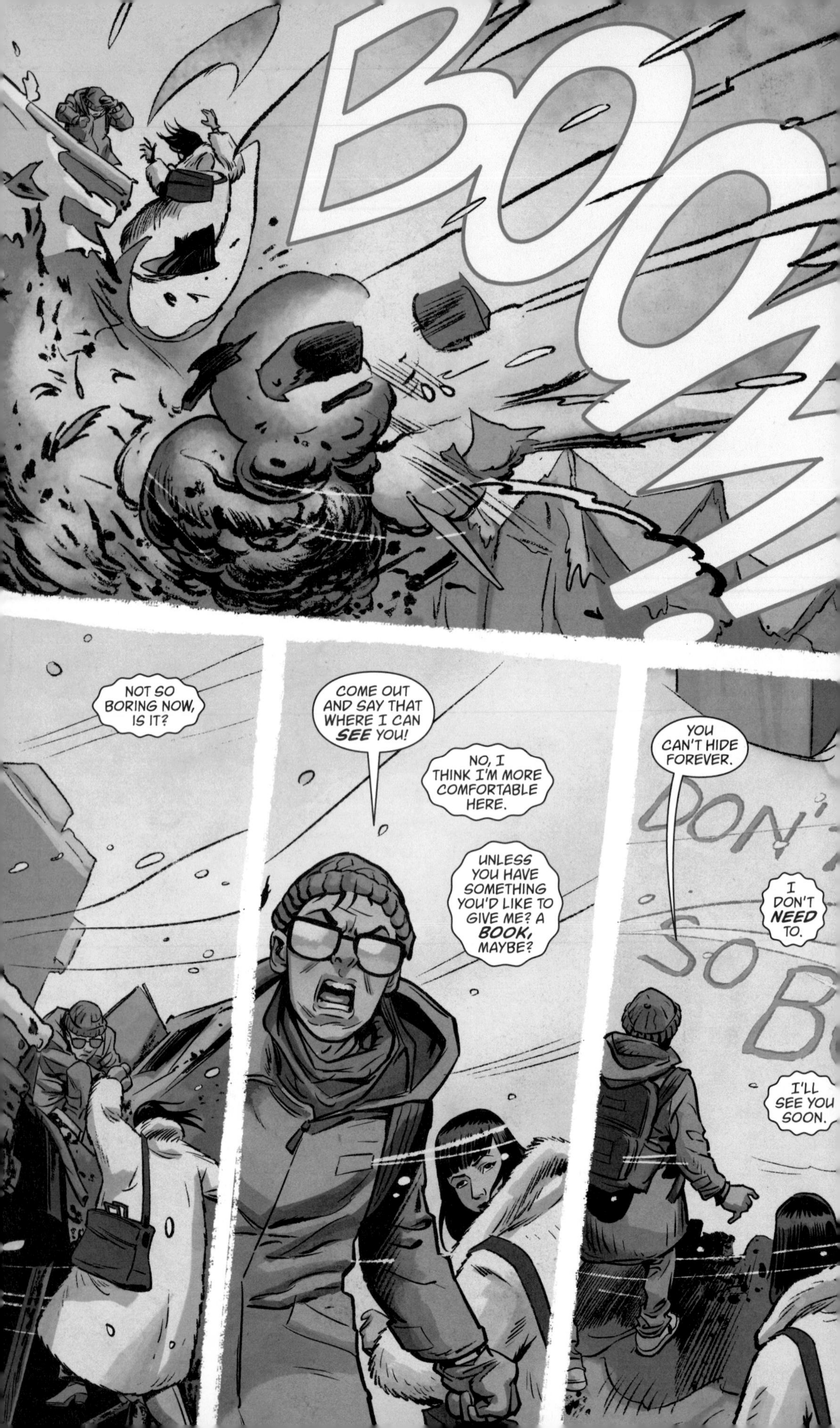
BOOM!
NOT SO BORING NOW, IS IT?
COME OUT AND SAY THAT WHERE I CAN **SEE** YOU!
NO, I THINK I'M MORE COMFORTABLE HERE.
UNLESS YOU HAVE SOMETHING YOU'D LIKE TO GIVE ME? A **BOOK,** MAYBE?
YOU CAN'T HIDE FOREVER.
I DON'T **NEED** TO.
I'LL SEE YOU SOON.

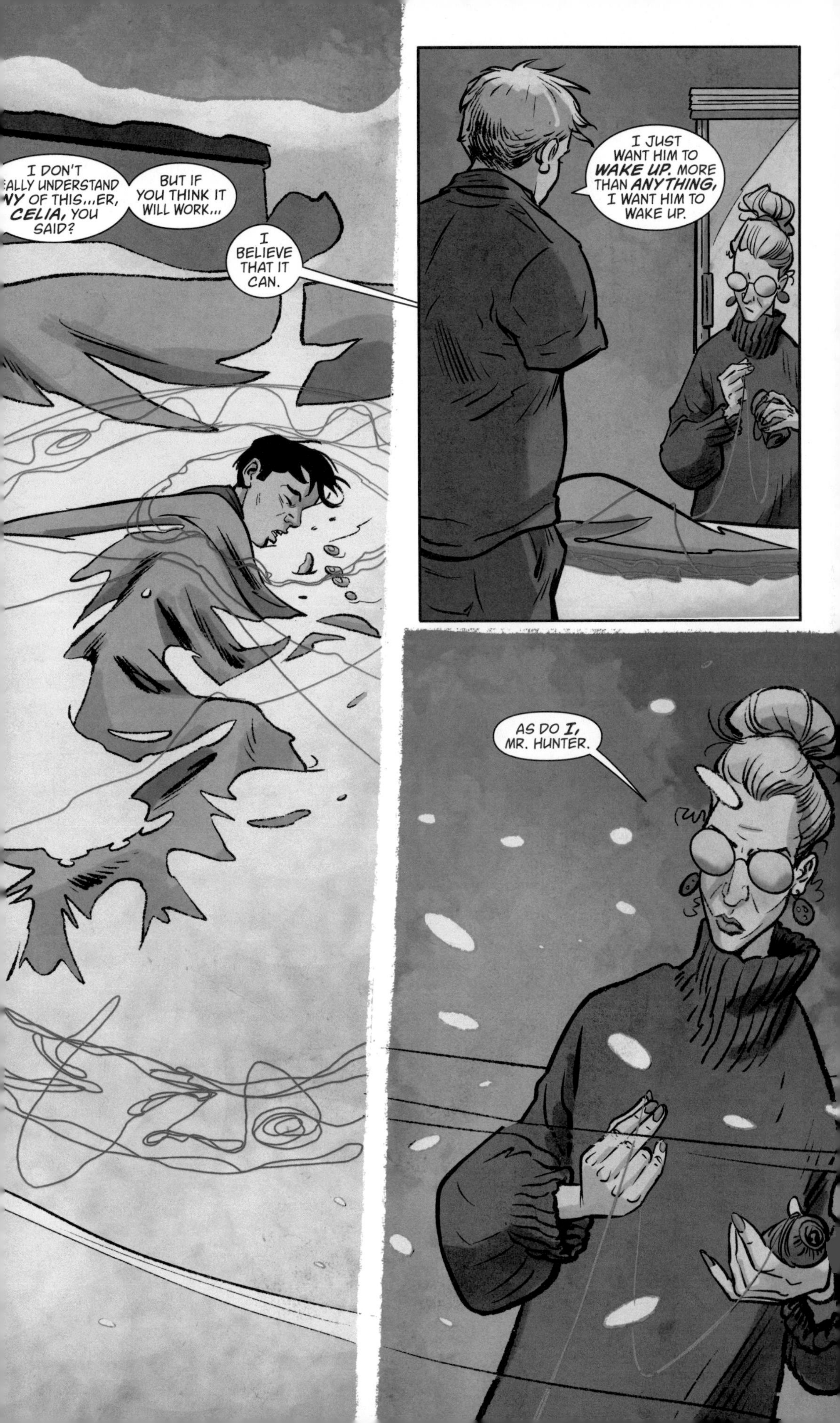
I DON'T EALLY UNDERSTAND NY OF THIS...ER, *CELIA,* YOU SAID?
BUT IF YOU THINK IT WILL WORK...
I BELIEVE THAT IT CAN.
I JUST WANT HIM TO *WAKE UP.* MORE THAN *ANYTHING,* I WANT HIM TO WAKE UP.
AS DO *I,* MR. HUNTER.

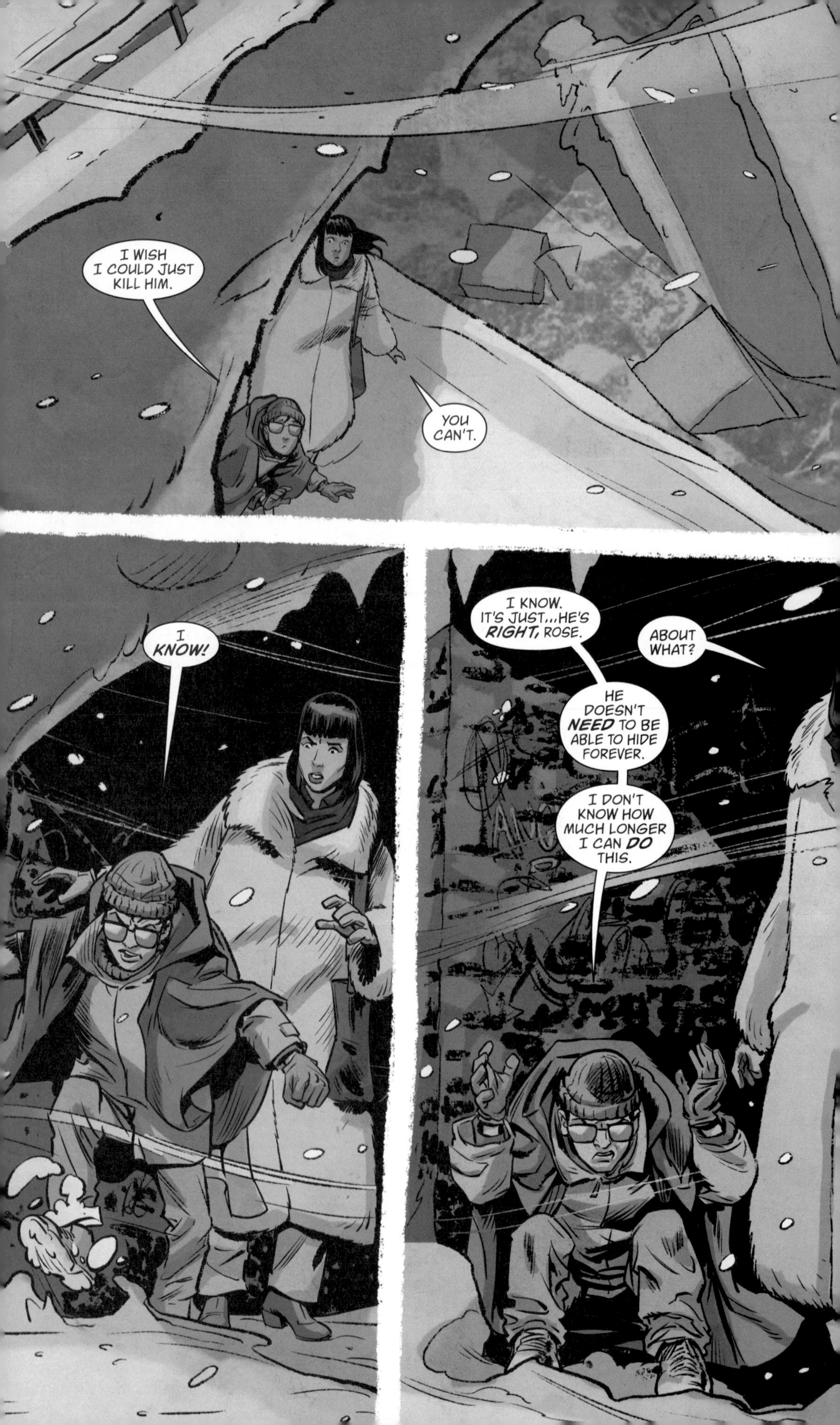
I WISH I COULD JUST KILL HIM.
YOU CAN'T.
I KNOW!
I KNOW. IT'S JUST...HE'S RIGHT, ROSE.
ABOUT WHAT?
HE DOESN'T NEED TO BE ABLE TO HIDE FOREVER.
I DON'T KNOW HOW MUCH LONGER I CAN DO THIS.

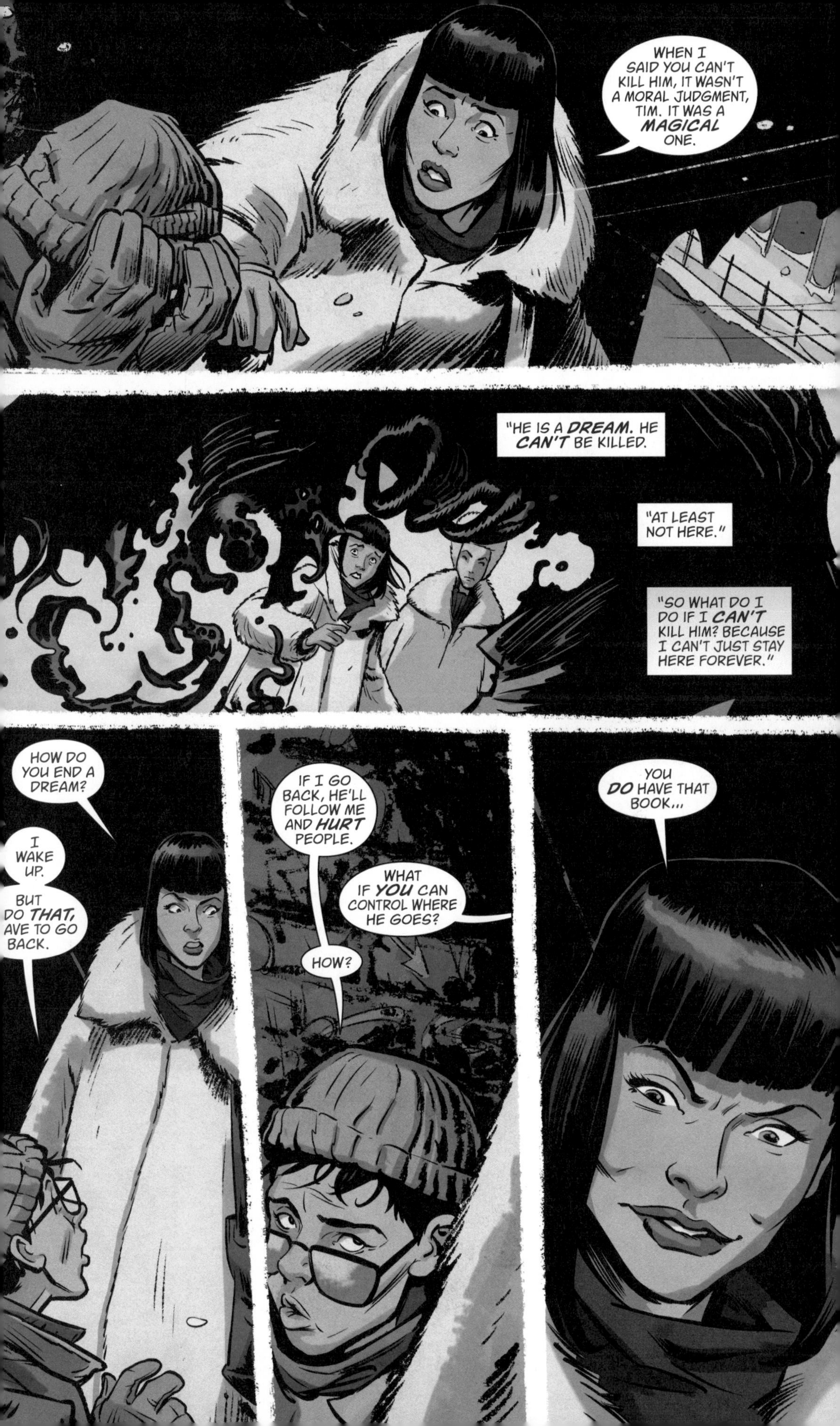

WHEN I SAID YOU CAN'T KILL HIM, IT WASN'T A MORAL JUDGMENT, TIM. IT WAS A *MAGICAL* ONE.
"HE IS A *DREAM.* HE *CAN'T* BE KILLED.
"AT LEAST NOT HERE."
"SO WHAT DO I DO IF I *CAN'T* KILL HIM? BECAUSE I CAN'T JUST STAY HERE FOREVER."
HOW DO YOU END A DREAM?
I WAKE UP.
BUT DO *THAT,* AVE TO GO BACK.
IF I GO BACK, HE'LL FOLLOW ME AND *HURT* PEOPLE.
WHAT IF *YOU* CAN CONTROL WHERE HE GOES?
HOW?
YOU *DO* HAVE THAT BOOK...

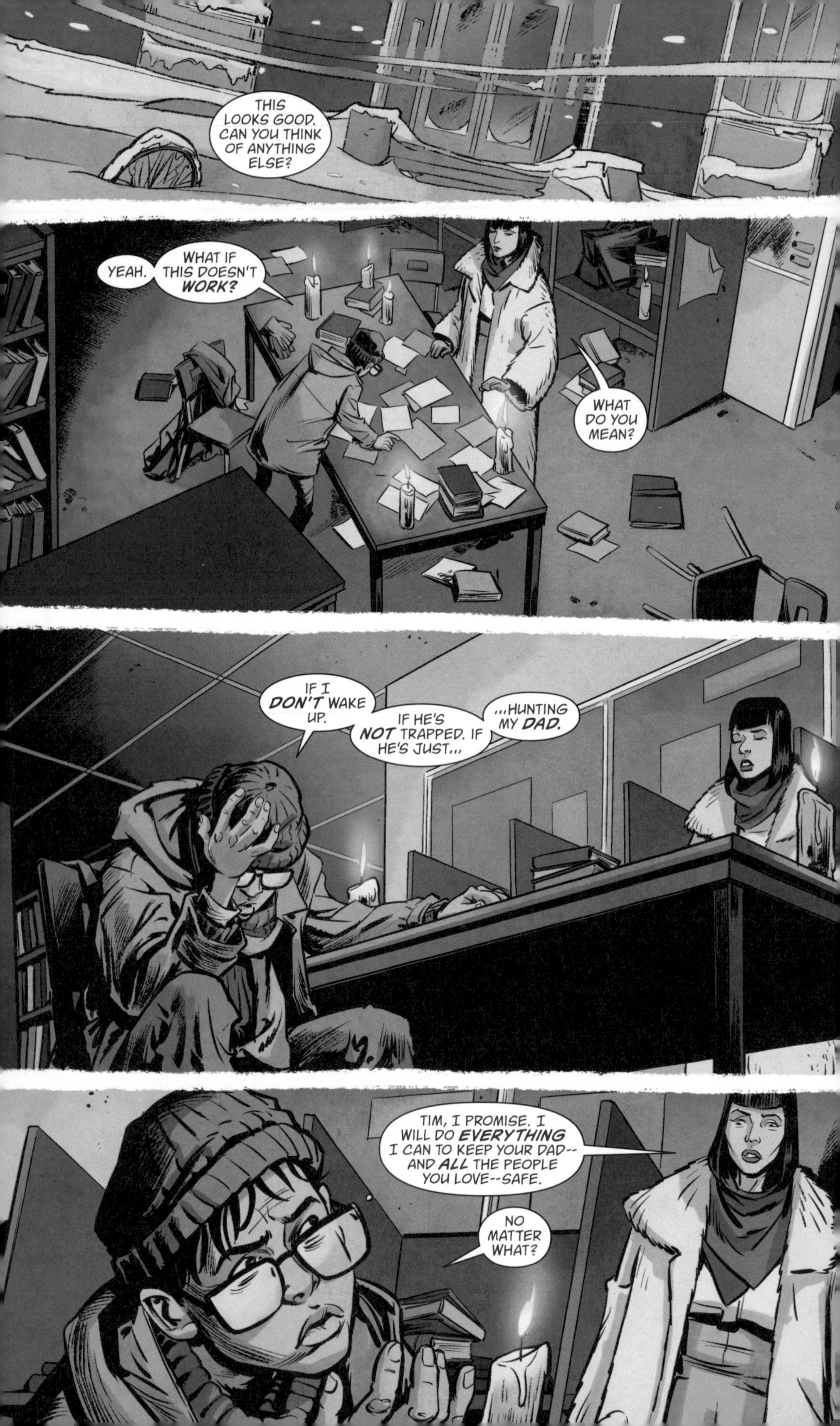
THIS LOOKS GOOD. CAN YOU THINK OF ANYTHING ELSE?
YEAH.
WHAT IF THIS DOESN'T WORK?
WHAT DO YOU MEAN?
IF I DON'T WAKE UP.
IF HE'S NOT TRAPPED. IF HE'S JUST...
...HUNTING MY DAD.
TIM, I PROMISE. I WILL DO EVERYTHING I CAN TO KEEP YOUR DAD--AND ALL THE PEOPLE YOU LOVE--SAFE.
NO MATTER WHAT?

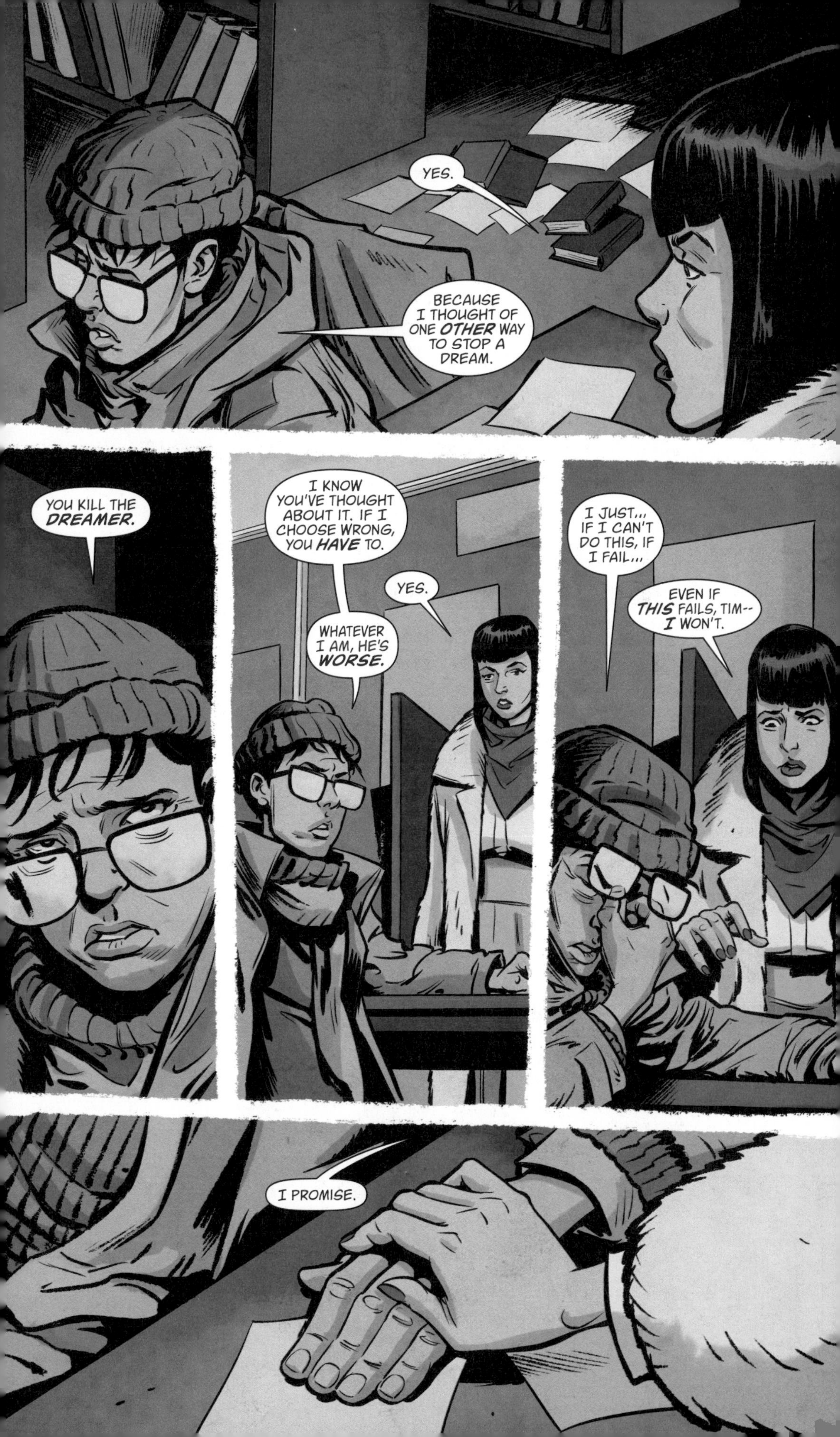
YES.
BECAUSE I THOUGHT OF ONE OTHER WAY TO STOP A DREAM.
YOU KILL THE DREAMER.
I KNOW YOU'VE THOUGHT ABOUT IT. IF I CHOOSE WRONG, YOU HAVE TO.
YES.
WHATEVER I AM, HE'S WORSE.
I JUST... IF I CAN'T DO THIS, IF I FAIL...
EVEN IF THIS FAILS, TIM-- I WON'T.
I PROMISE.

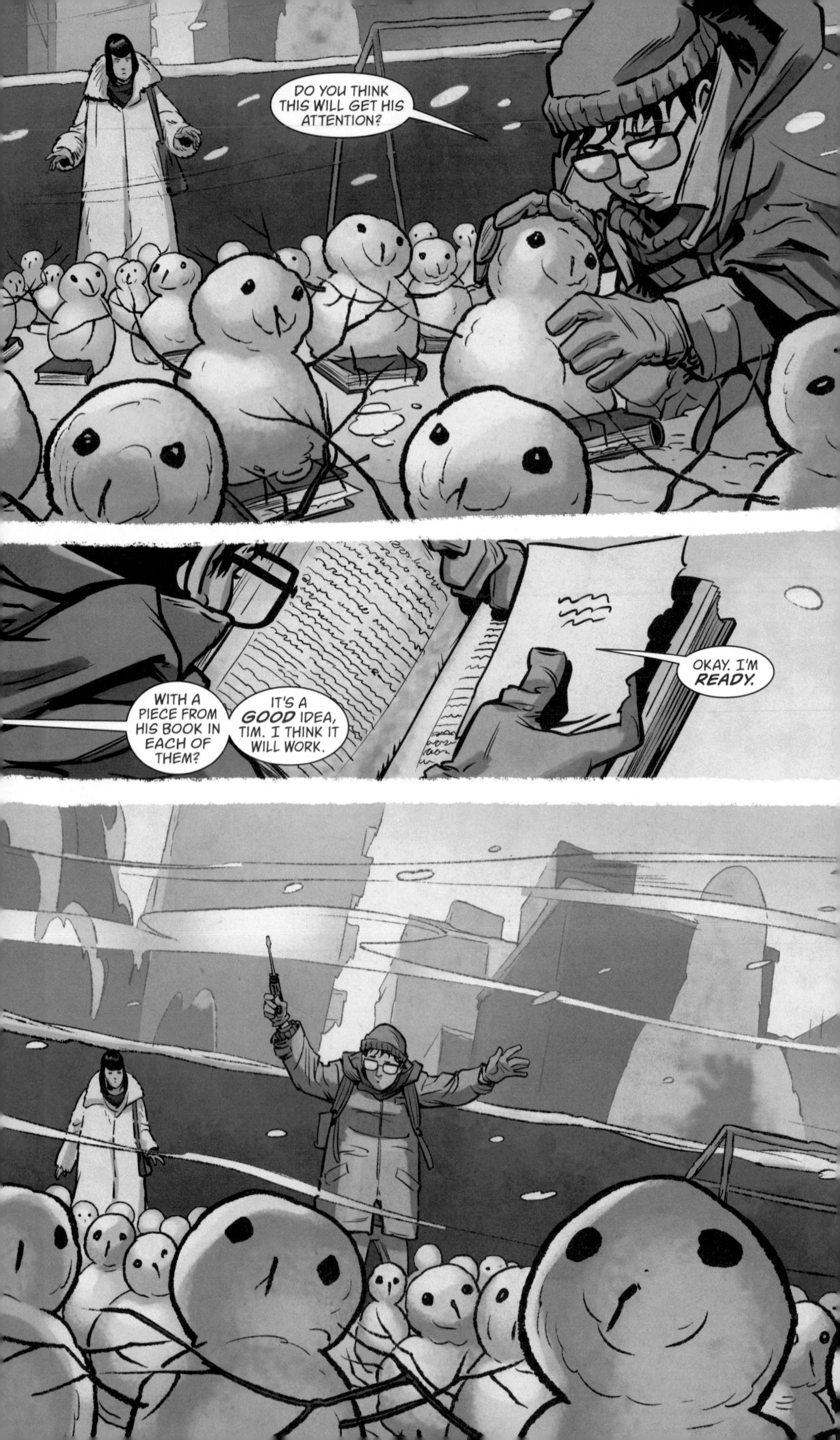
DO YOU THINK THIS WILL GET HIS ATTENTION?
WITH A PIECE FROM HIS BOOK IN EACH OF THEM?
IT'S A GOOD IDEA, TIM. I THINK IT WILL WORK.
OKAY. I'M READY.

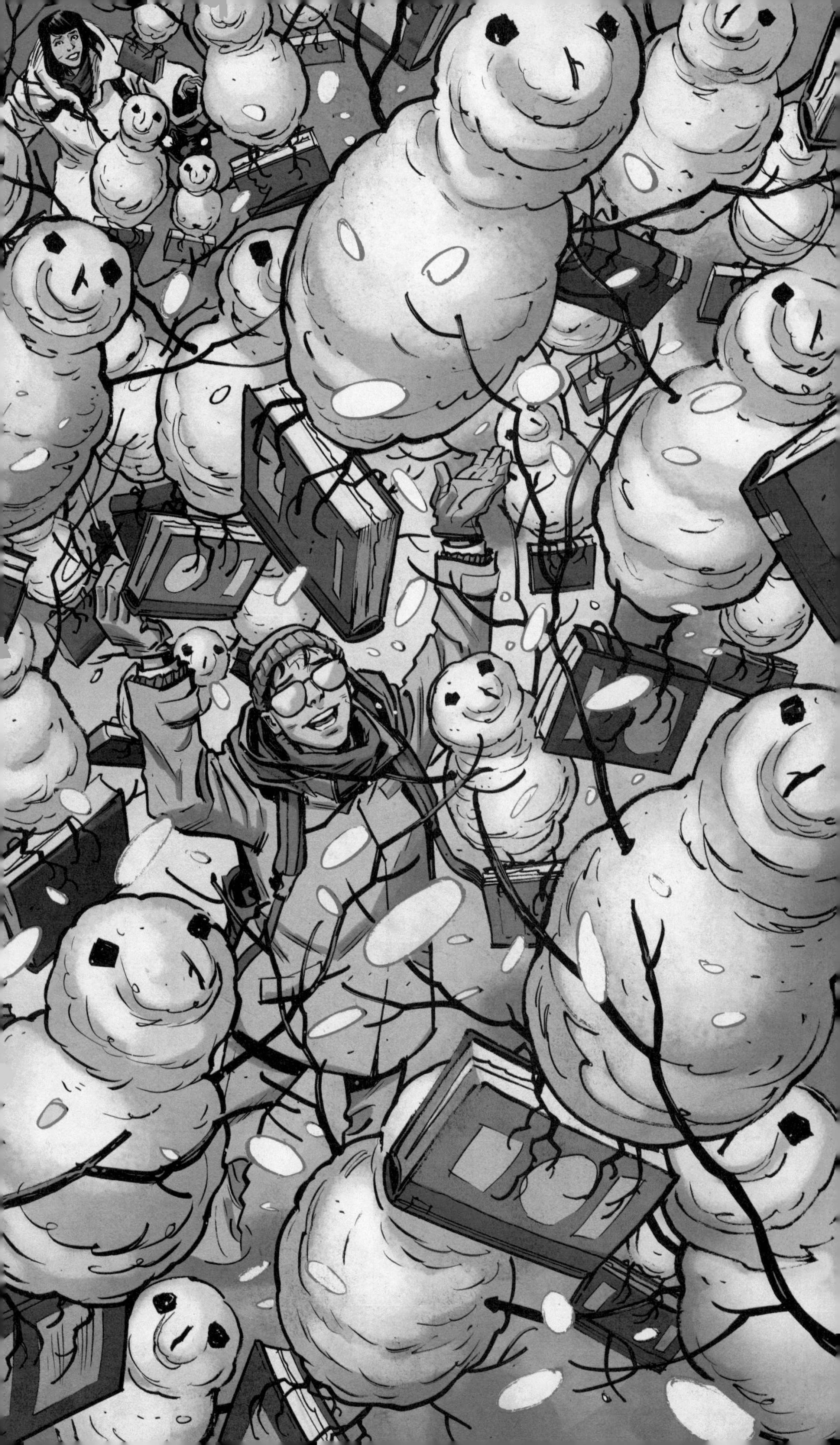

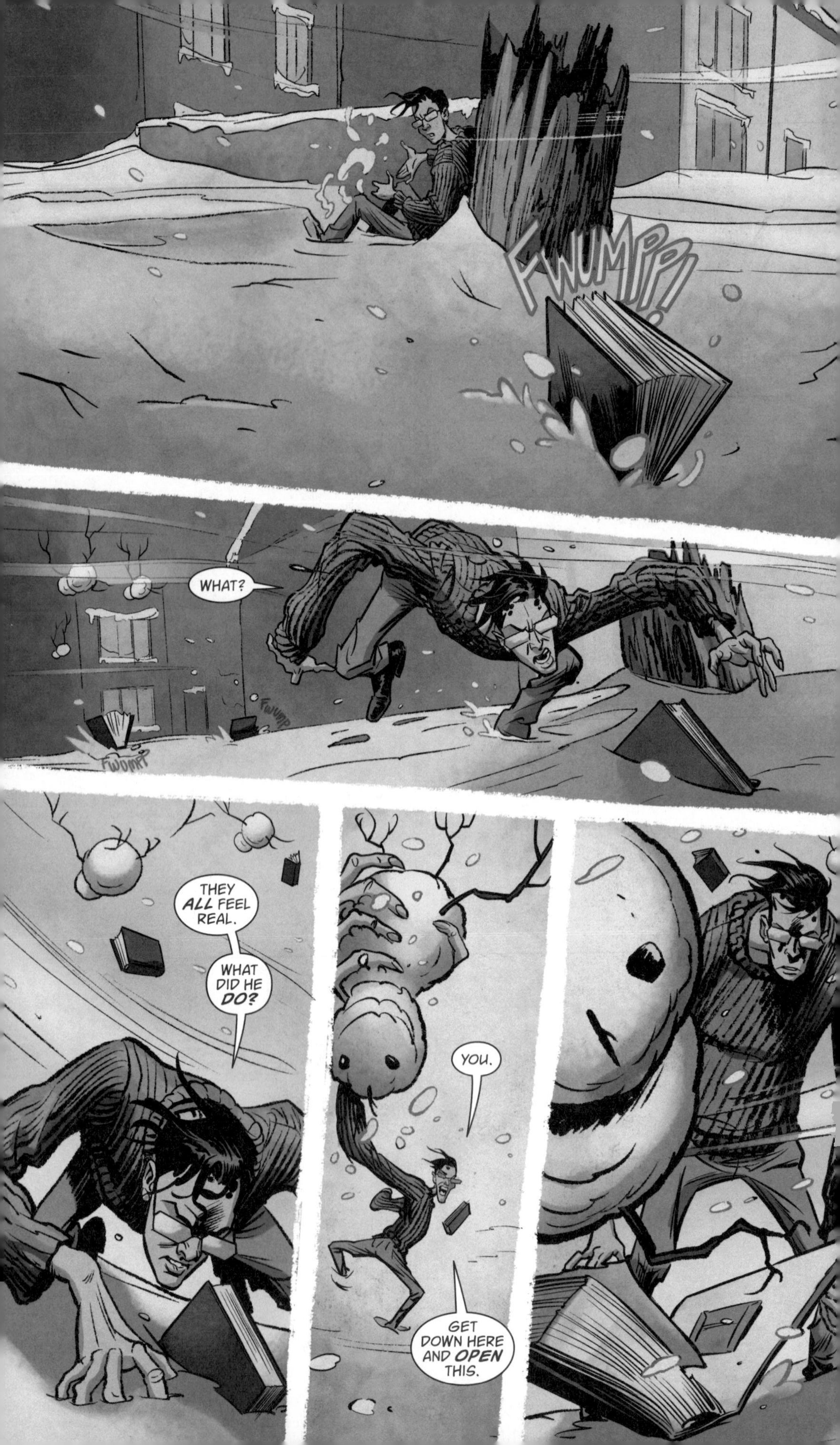
FWUMP!!
WHAT?
FWUMP
FWUMP
THEY ALL FEEL REAL.
WHAT DID HE DO?
YOU.
GET DOWN HERE AND OPEN THIS.

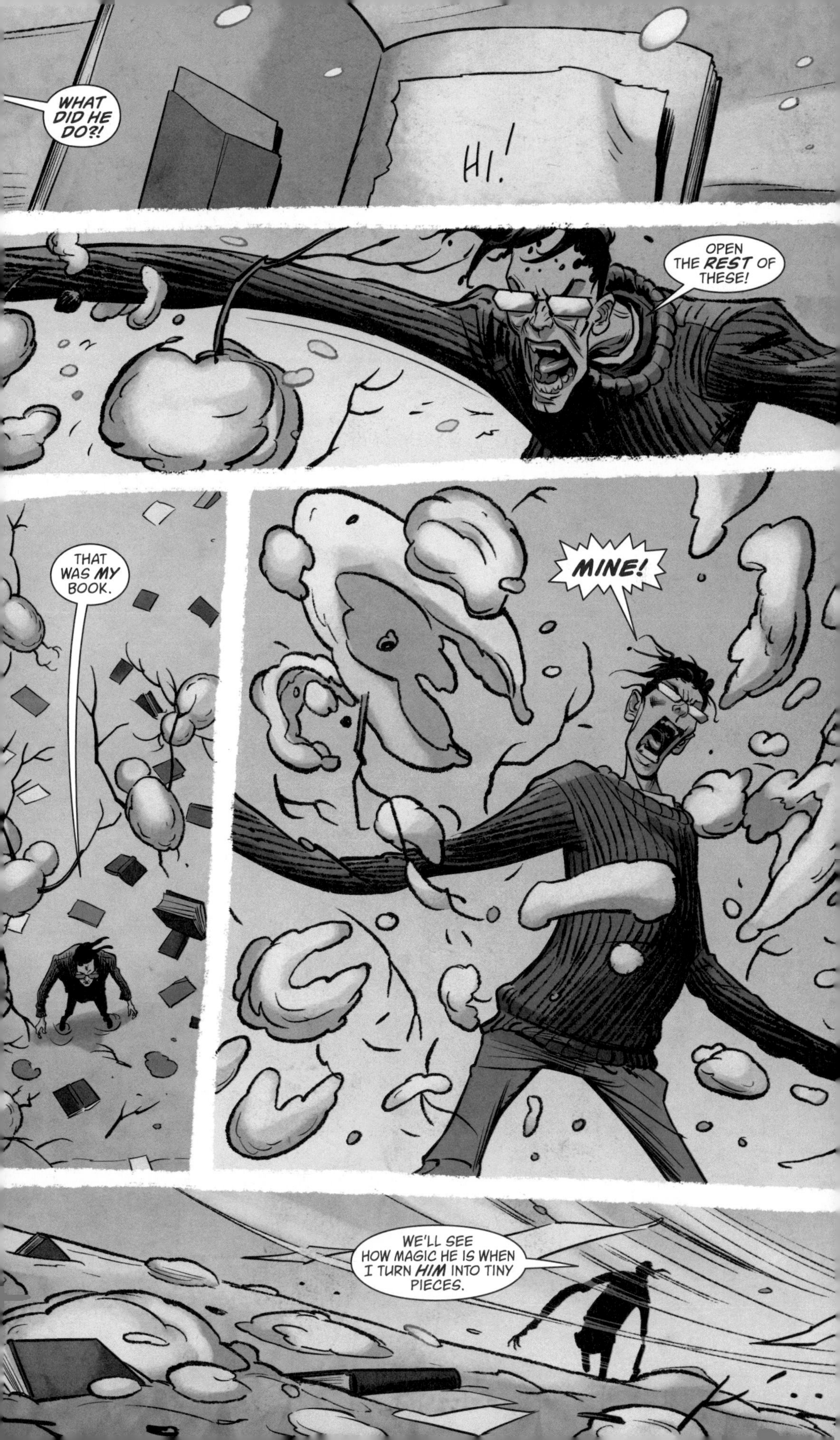
WHAT DID HE DO?!
HI!
OPEN THE REST OF THESE!
THAT WAS MY BOOK.
MINE!
WE'LL SEE HOW MAGIC HE IS WHEN I TURN HIM INTO TINY PIECES.

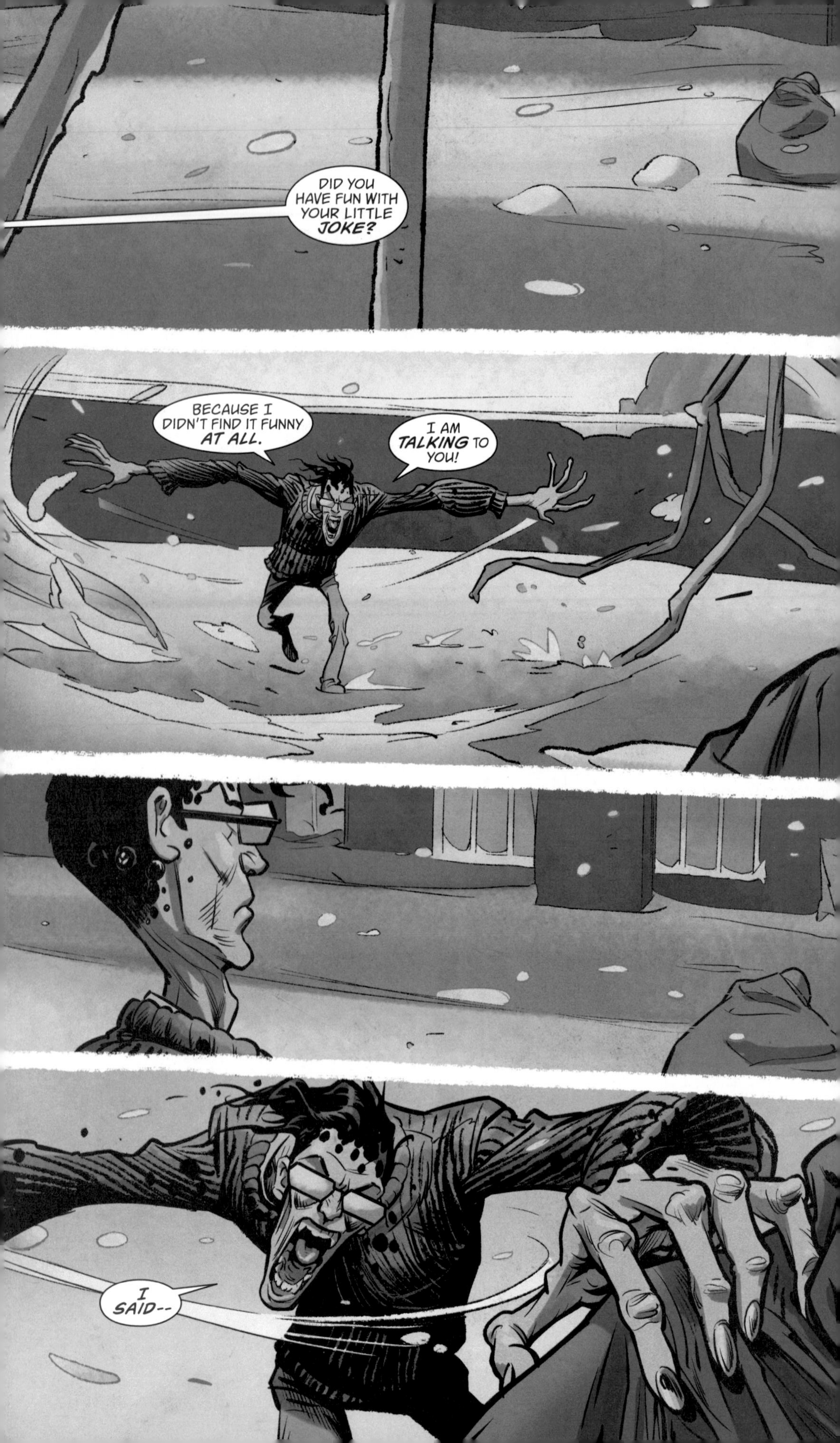
DID YOU HAVE FUN WITH YOUR LITTLE JOKE?
BECAUSE I DIDN'T FIND IT FUNNY AT ALL.
I AM TALKING TO YOU!
I SAID--

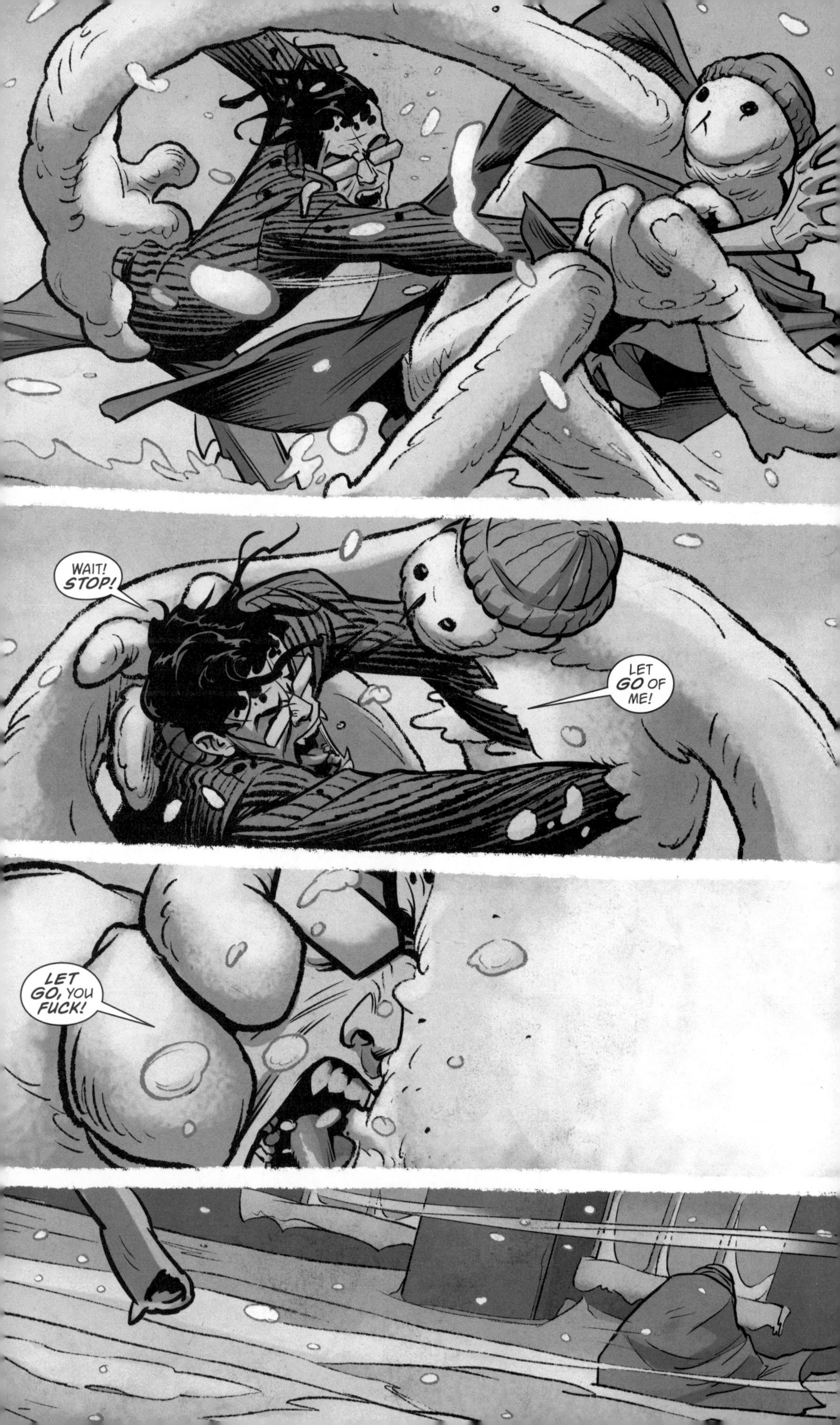
WAIT! STOP!
LET GO OF ME!
LET GO, YOU FUCK!

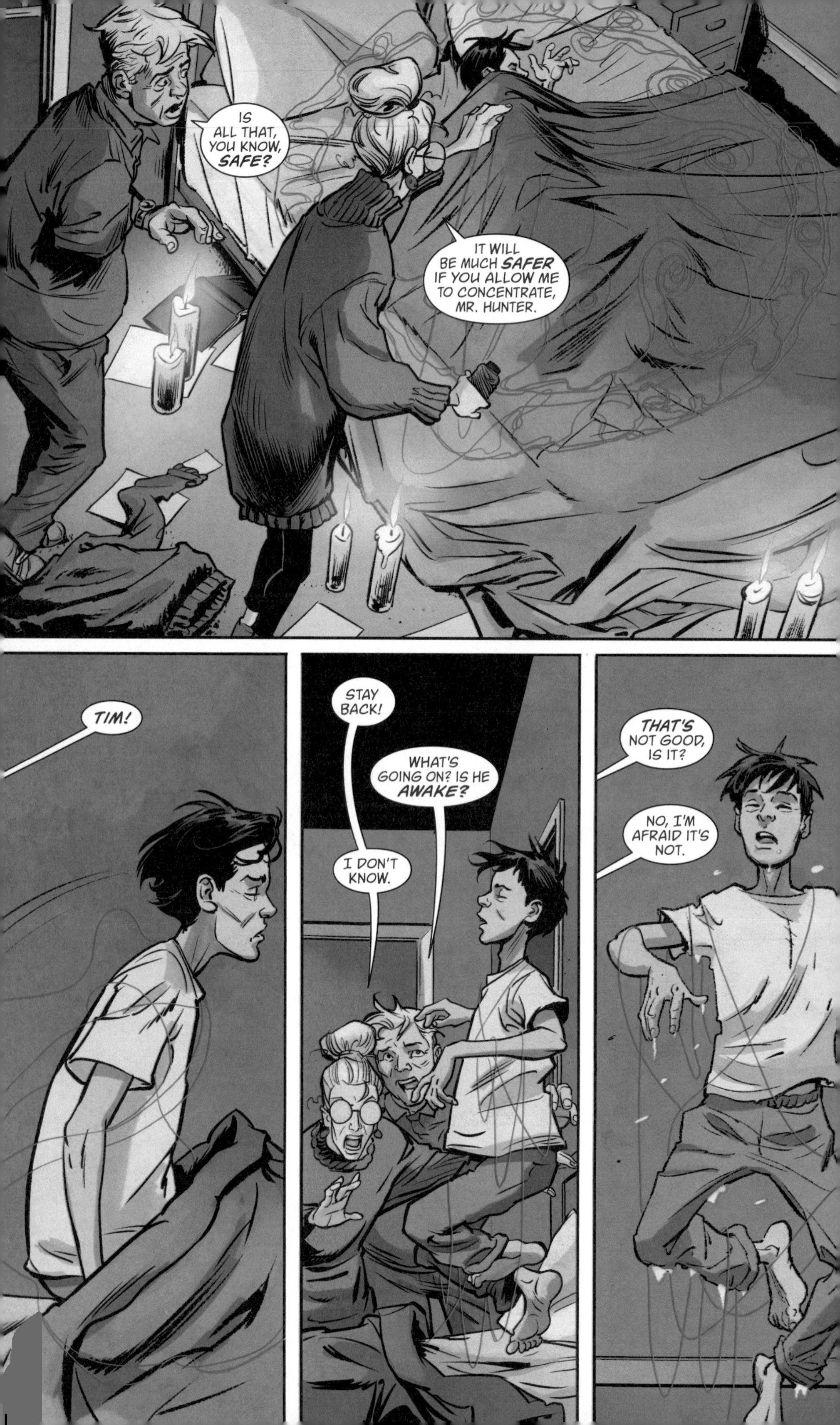
IS ALL THAT, YOU KNOW, SAFE?
IT WILL BE MUCH SAFER IF YOU ALLOW ME TO CONCENTRATE, MR. HUNTER.
TIM!
STAY BACK!
WHAT'S GOING ON? IS HE AWAKE?
I DON'T KNOW.
THAT'S NOT GOOD, IS IT?
NO, I'M AFRAID IT'S NOT.

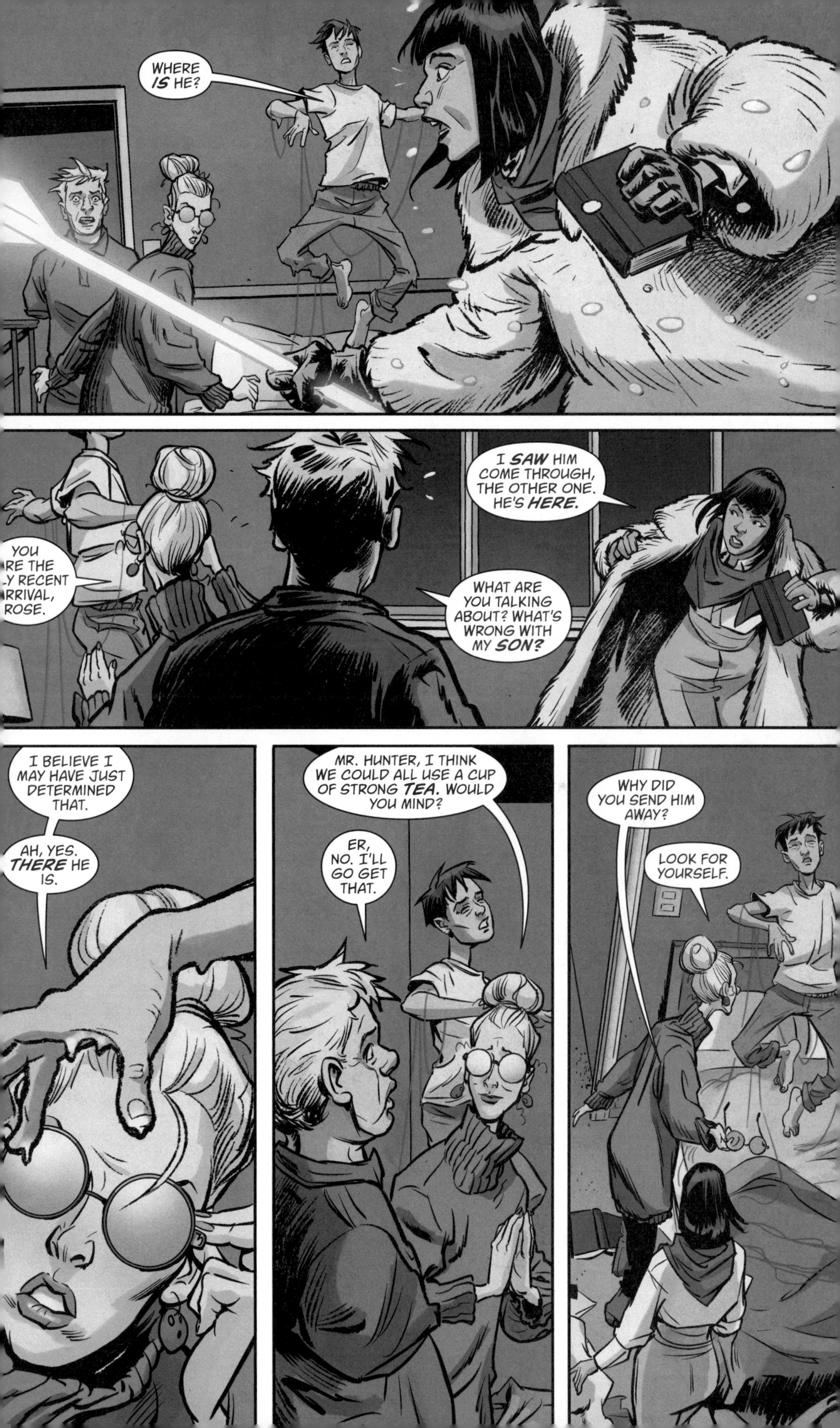
WHERE IS HE?
I SAW HIM COME THROUGH, THE OTHER ONE. HE'S HERE.
YOU RE THE Y RECENT RRIVAL, ROSE.
WHAT ARE YOU TALKING ABOUT? WHAT'S WRONG WITH MY SON?
I BELIEVE I MAY HAVE JUST DETERMINED THAT.
AH, YES. THERE HE IS.
MR. HUNTER, I THINK WE COULD ALL USE A CUP OF STRONG TEA. WOULD YOU MIND?
ER, NO. I'LL GO GET THAT.
WHY DID YOU SEND HIM AWAY?
LOOK FOR YOURSELF.

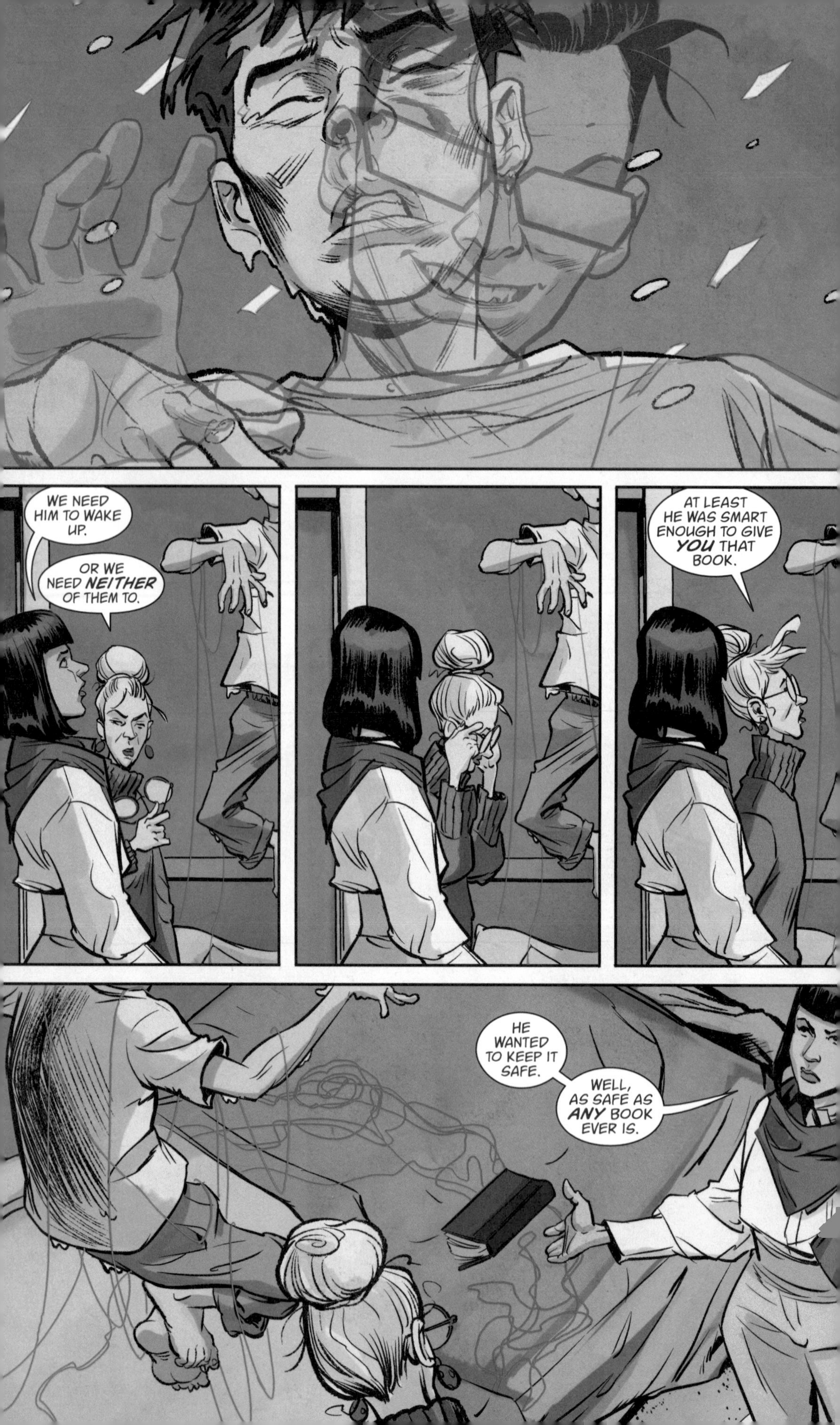
WE NEED HIM TO WAKE UP.
OR WE NEED NEITHER OF THEM TO.
AT LEAST HE WAS SMART ENOUGH TO GIVE YOU THAT BOOK.
HE WANTED TO KEEP IT SAFE.
WELL, AS SAFE AS ANY BOOK EVER IS.

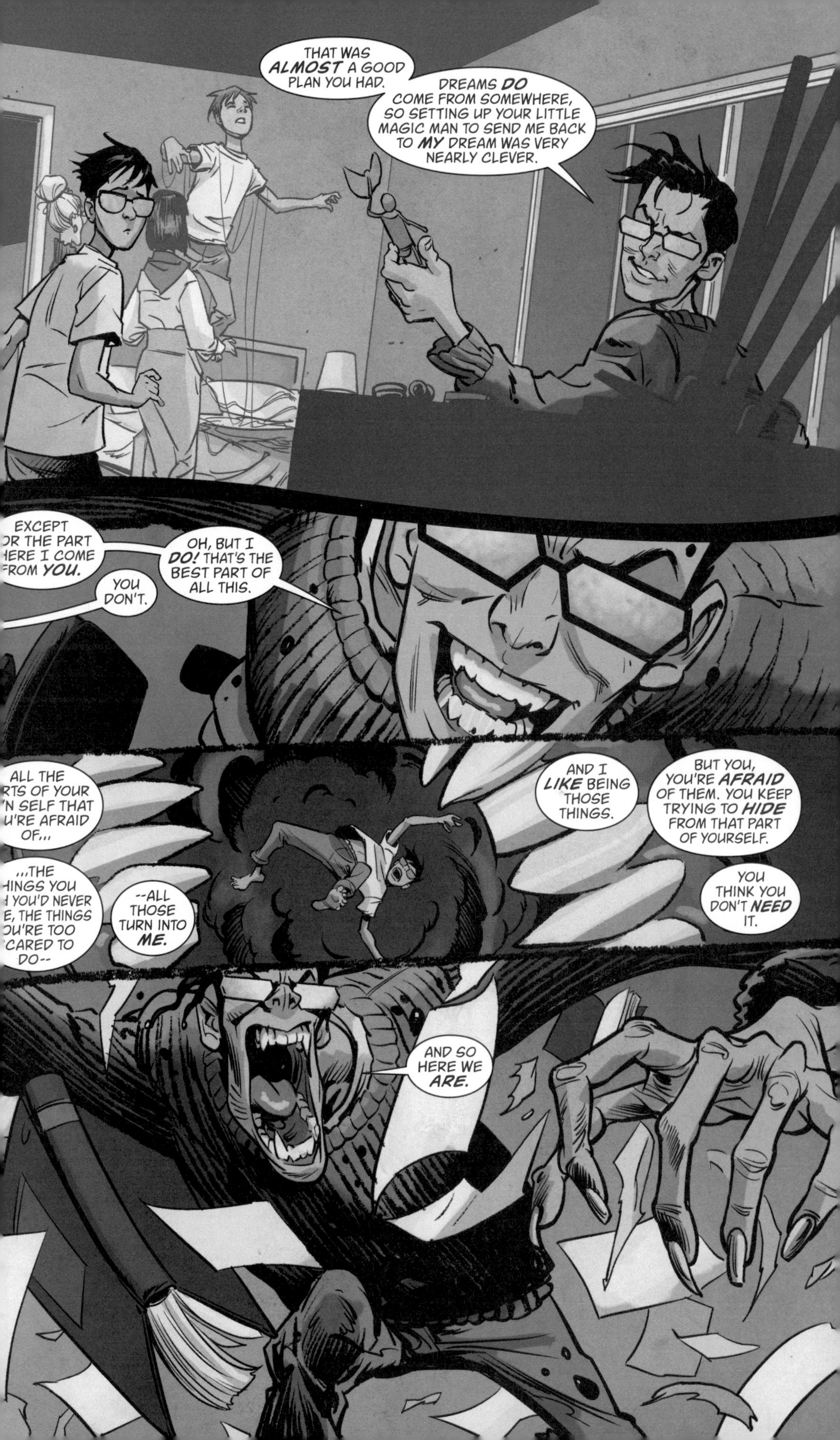
THAT WAS ALMOST A GOOD PLAN YOU HAD.
DREAMS DO COME FROM SOMEWHERE, SO SETTING UP YOUR LITTLE MAGIC MAN TO SEND ME BACK TO MY DREAM WAS VERY NEARLY CLEVER.
EXCEPT OR THE PART HERE I COME FROM YOU.
YOU DON'T.
OH, BUT I DO! THAT'S THE BEST PART OF ALL THIS.
ALL THE RTS OF YOUR N SELF THAT U'RE AFRAID OF...
...THE HINGS YOU YOU'D NEVER E, THE THINGS OU'RE TOO CARED TO DO--
--ALL THOSE TURN INTO ME.
AND I LIKE BEING THOSE THINGS.
BUT YOU, YOU'RE AFRAID OF THEM. YOU KEEP TRYING TO HIDE FROM THAT PART OF YOURSELF.
YOU THINK YOU DON'T NEED IT.
AND SO HERE WE ARE.

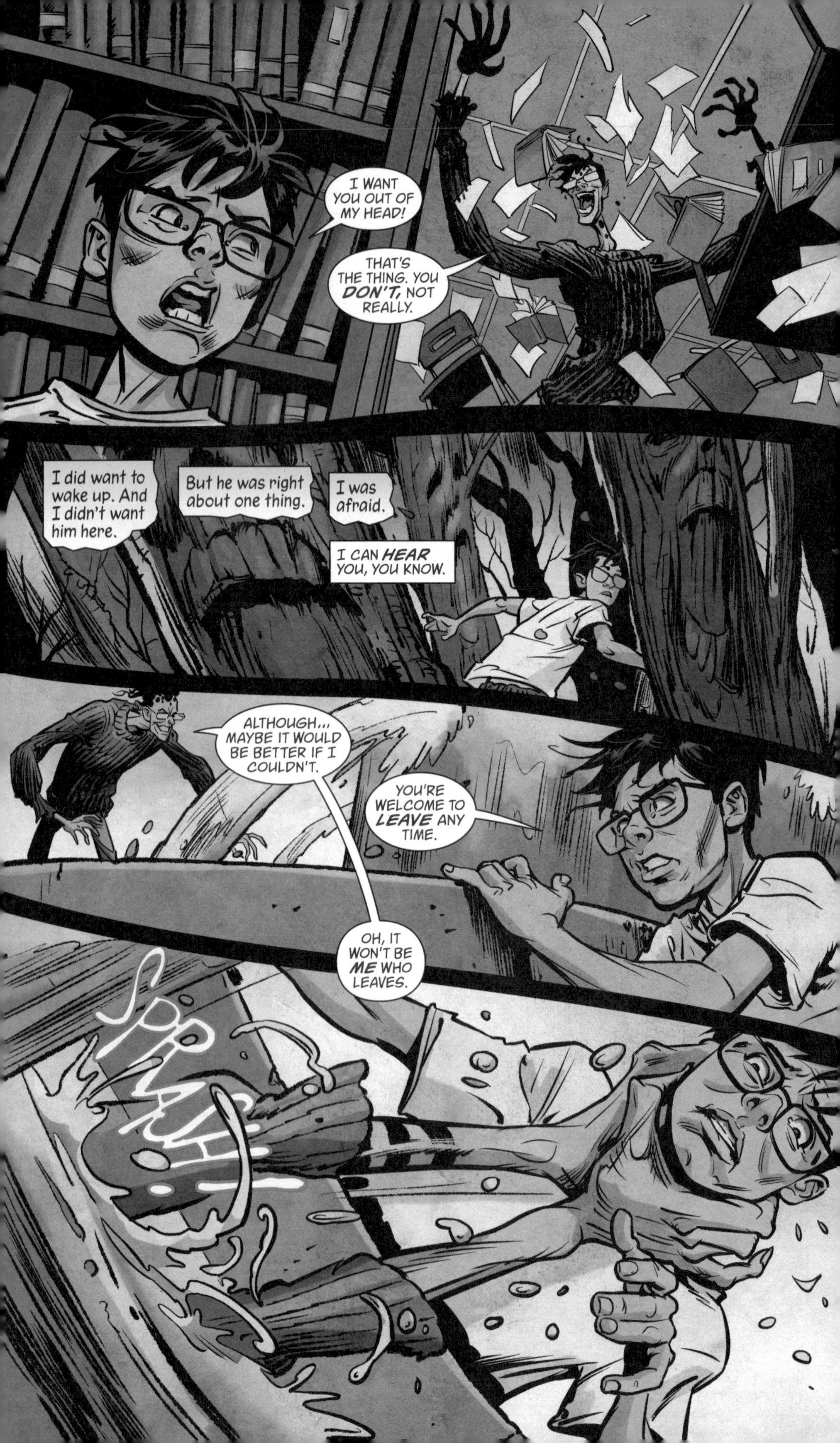

I WANT YOU OUT OF MY HEAD!
THAT'S THE THING. YOU DON'T, NOT REALLY.
I did want to wake up. And I didn't want him here.
But he was right about one thing.
I was afraid.
I CAN HEAR YOU, YOU KNOW.
ALTHOUGH... MAYBE IT WOULD BE BETTER IF I COULDN'T.
YOU'RE WELCOME TO LEAVE ANY TIME.
OH, IT WON'T BE ME WHO LEAVES.
SPPLASH!

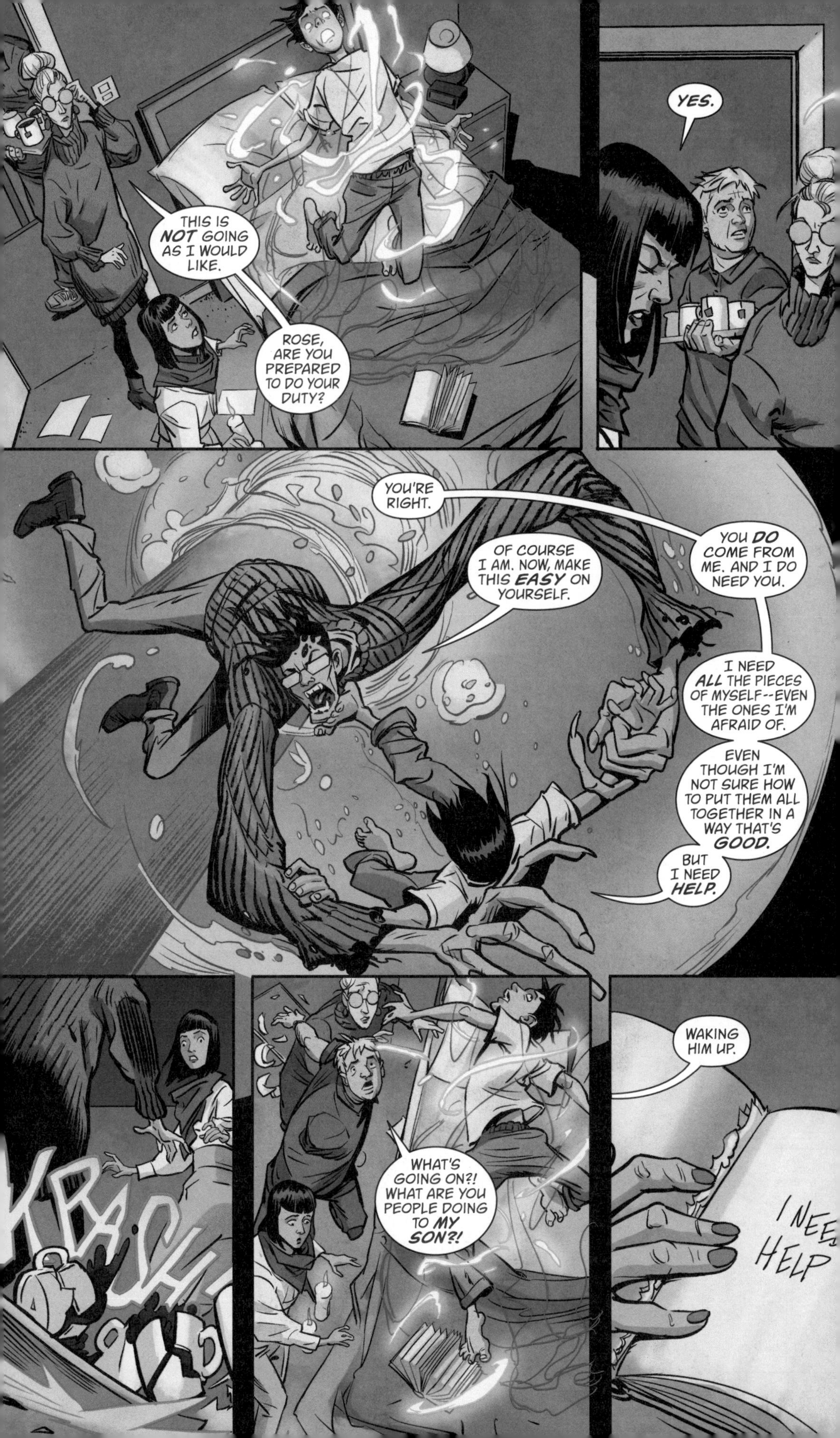
THIS IS NOT GOING AS I WOULD LIKE.
ROSE, ARE YOU PREPARED TO DO YOUR DUTY?
YES.
YOU'RE RIGHT.
OF COURSE I AM. NOW, MAKE THIS EASY ON YOURSELF.
YOU DO COME FROM ME. AND I DO NEED YOU.
I NEED ALL THE PIECES OF MYSELF--EVEN THE ONES I'M AFRAID OF.
EVEN THOUGH I'M NOT SURE HOW TO PUT THEM ALL TOGETHER IN A WAY THAT'S GOOD.
BUT I NEED HELP.
KRASH
WHAT'S GOING ON?! WHAT ARE YOU PEOPLE DOING TO MY SON?!
WAKING HIM UP.
I NEE HELP

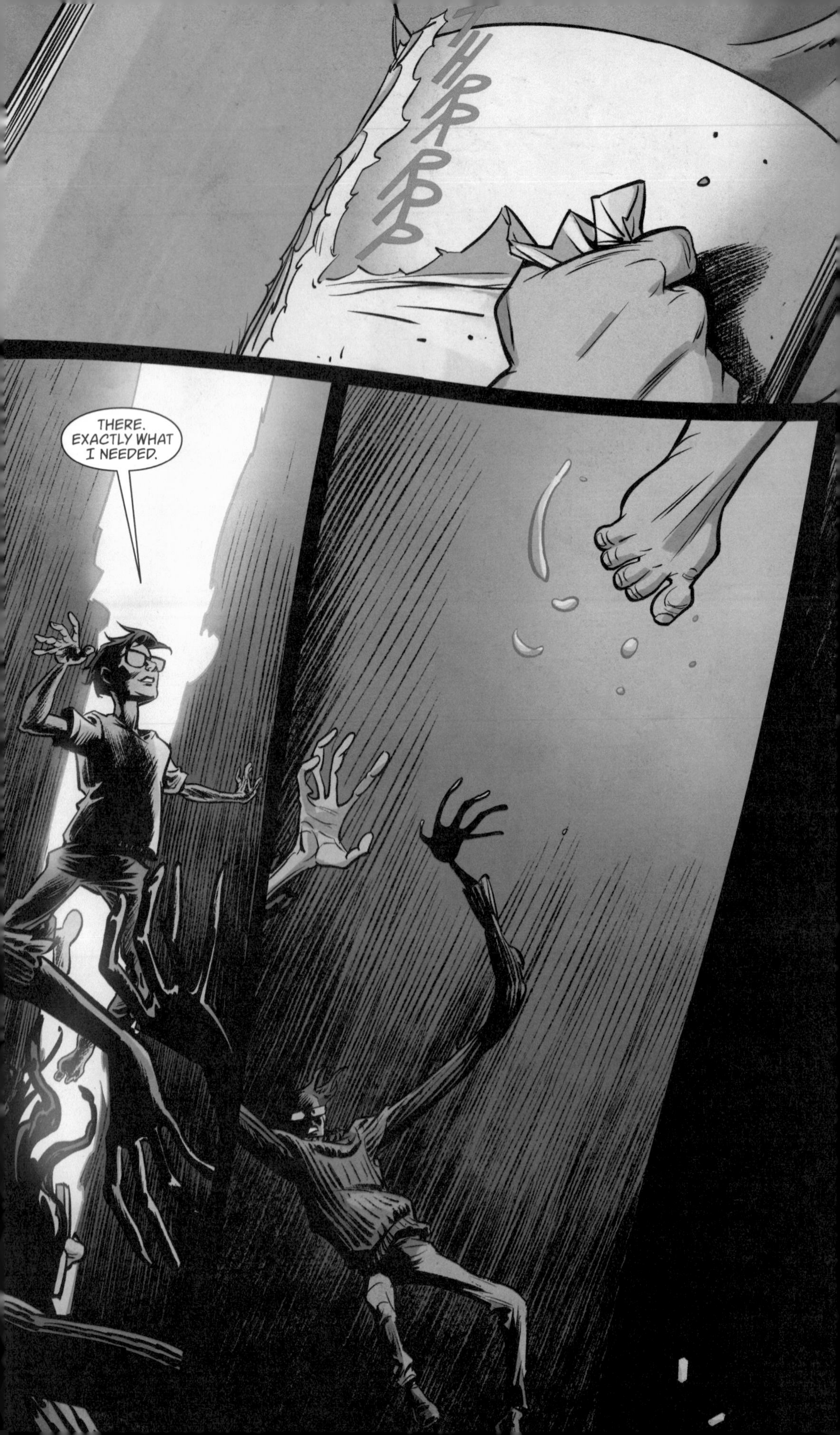
THHRRPP
THERE. EXACTLY WHAT I NEEDED.

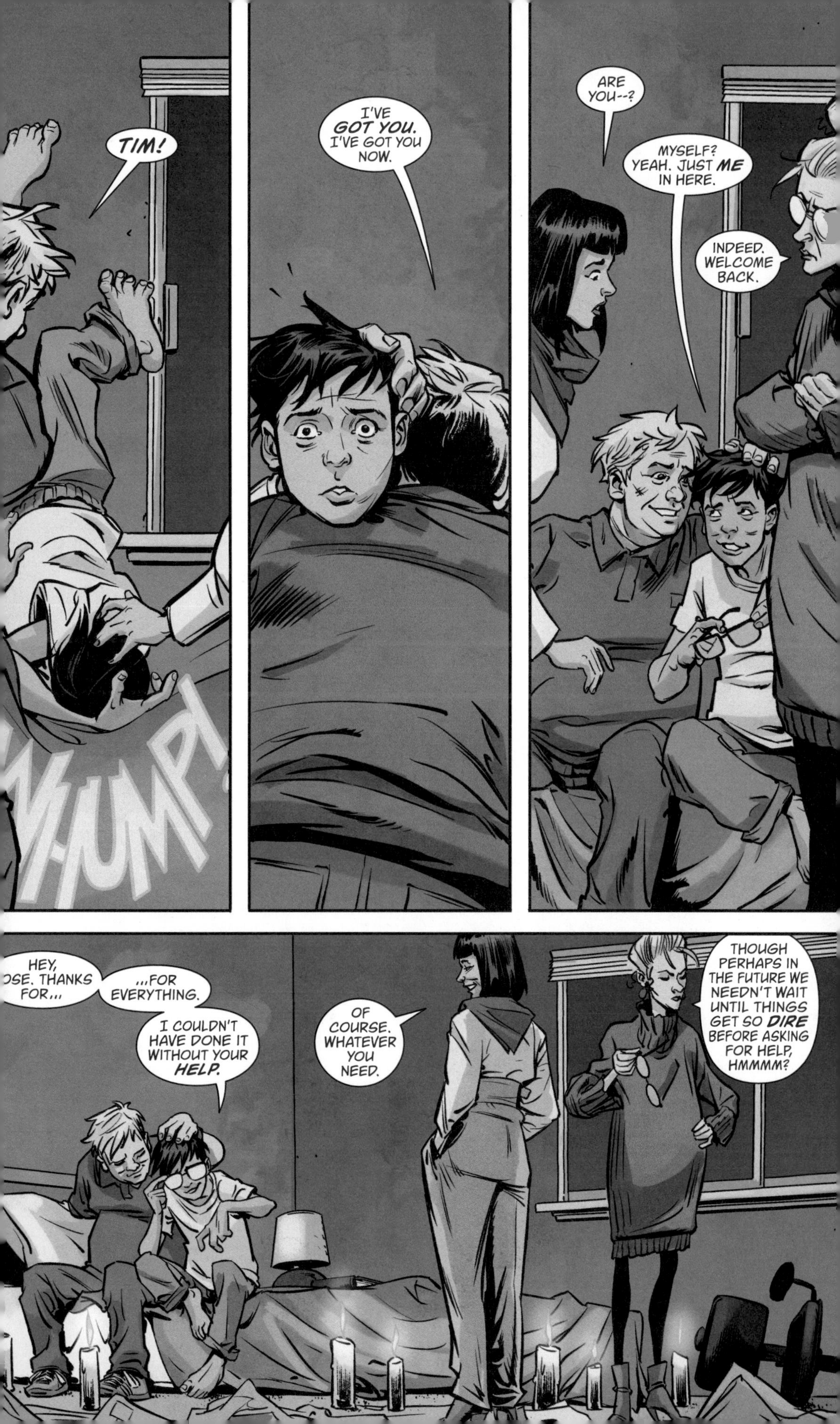
TIM!
FWUMP!
I'VE GOT YOU. I'VE GOT YOU NOW.
ARE YOU--?
MYSELF? YEAH. JUST ME IN HERE.
INDEED. WELCOME BACK.
HEY, ...OSE. THANKS FOR...
...FOR EVERYTHING.
I COULDN'T HAVE DONE IT WITHOUT YOUR HELP.
OF COURSE. WHATEVER YOU NEED.
THOUGH PERHAPS IN THE FUTURE WE NEEDN'T WAIT UNTIL THINGS GET SO DIRE BEFORE ASKING FOR HELP, HMMMM?

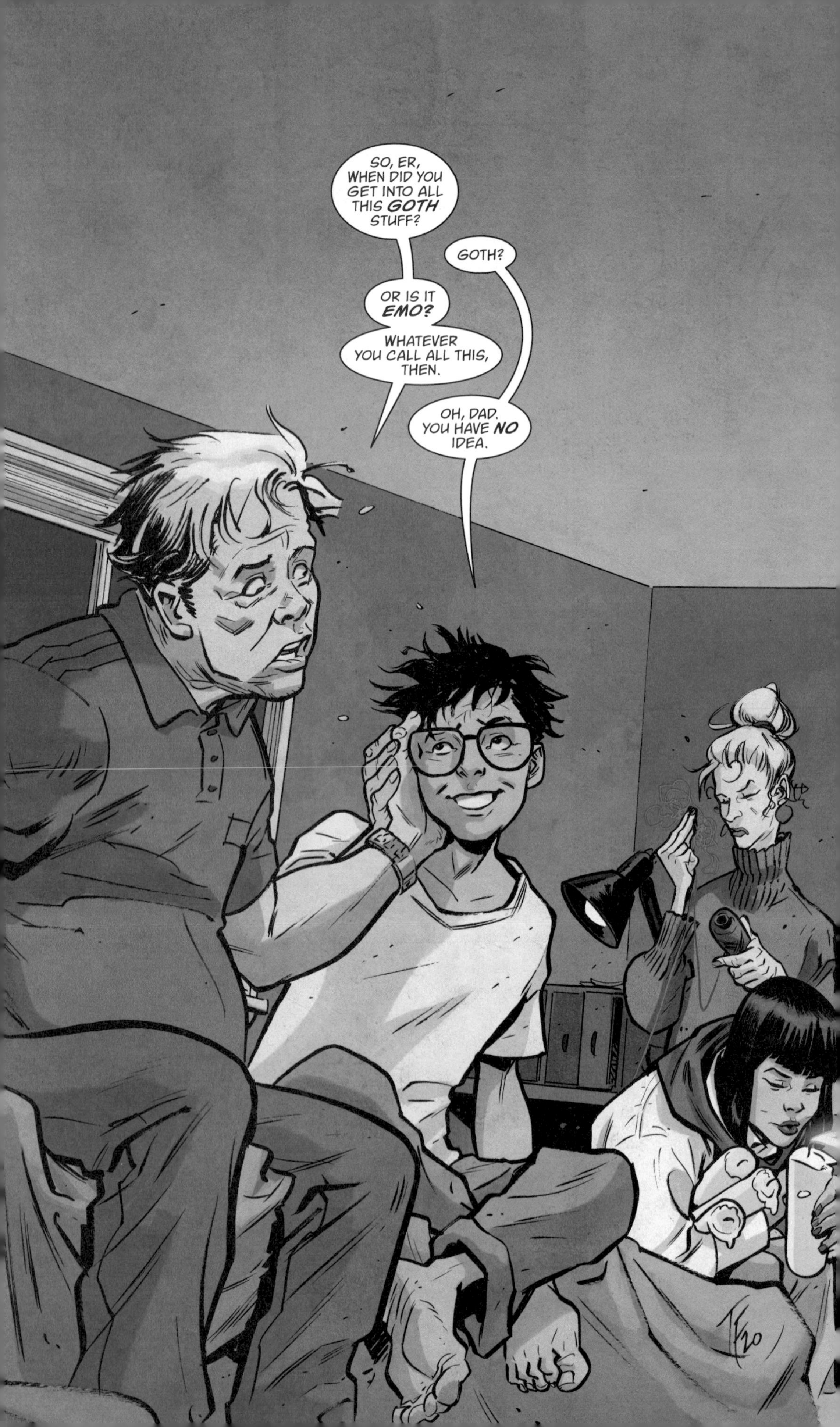
SO, ER, WHEN DID YOU GET INTO ALL THIS **GOTH** STUFF?
GOTH?
OR IS IT **EMO?**
WHATEVER YOU CALL ALL THIS, THEN.
OH, DAD. YOU HAVE **NO** IDEA.

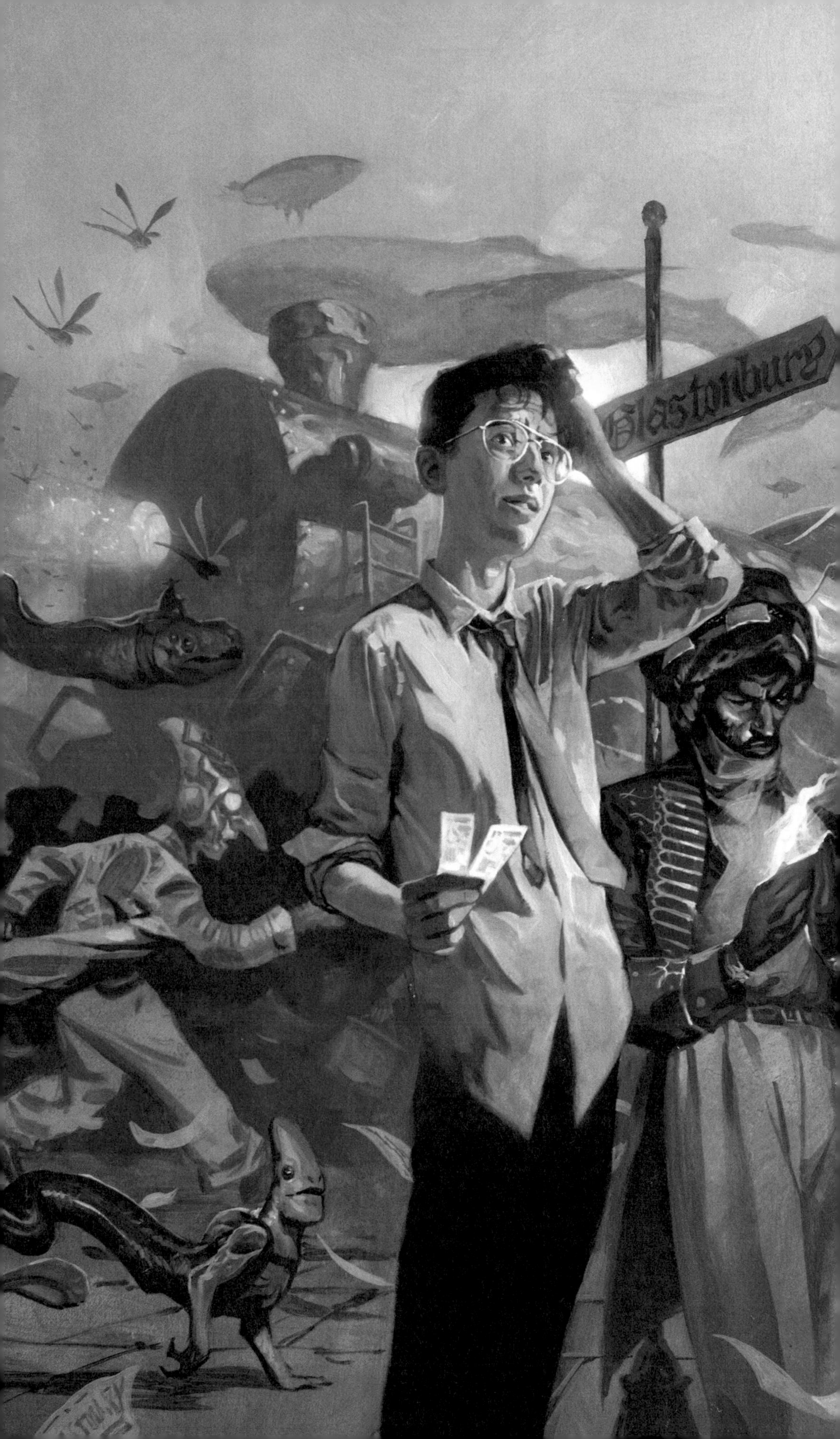
Glastonbury

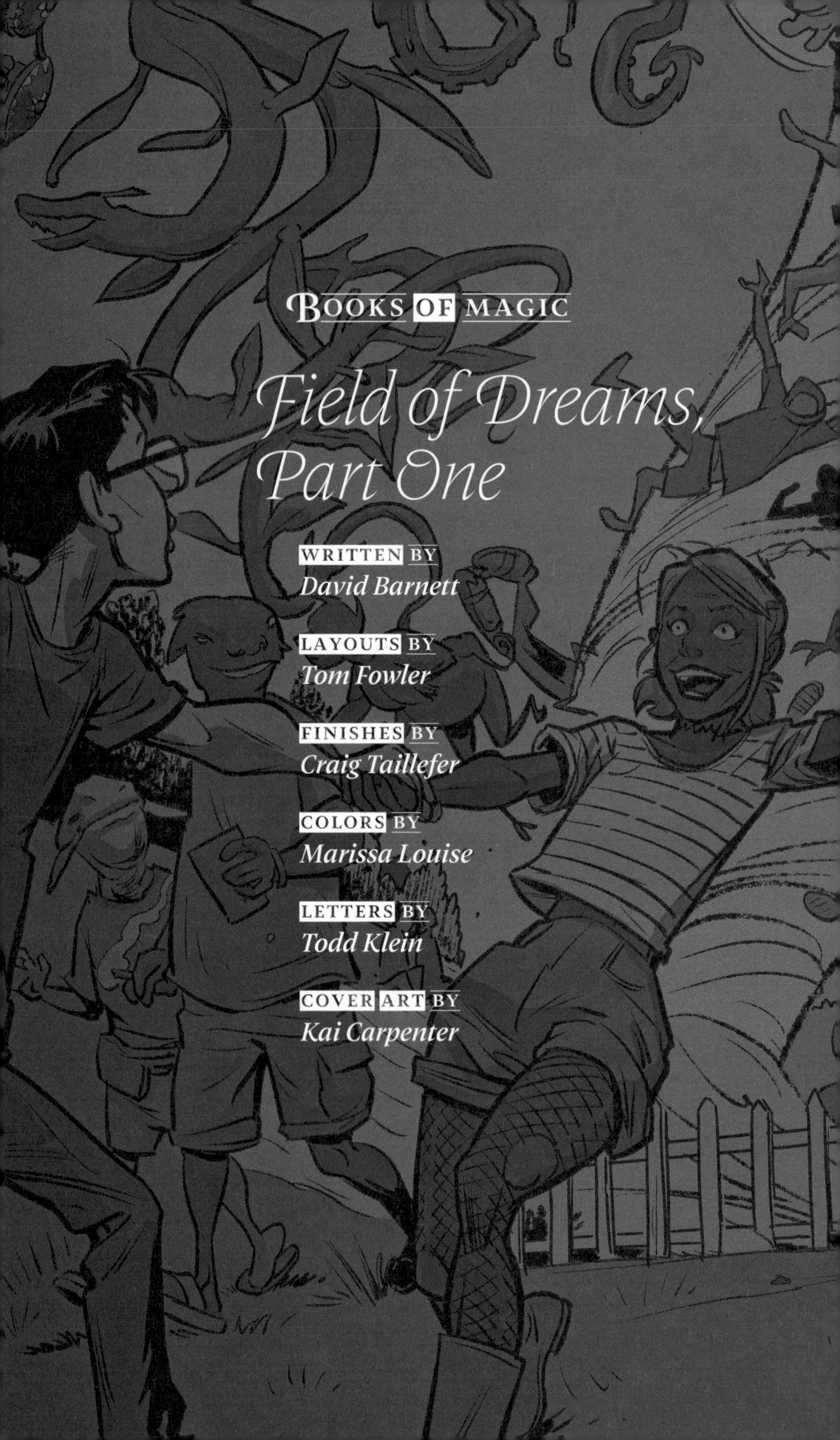

BOOKS OF MAGIC

Field of Dreams, Part One

WRITTEN BY
David Barnett

LAYOUTS BY
Tom Fowler

FINISHES BY
Craig Taillefer

COLORS BY
Marissa Louise

LETTERS BY
Todd Klein

COVER ART BY
Kai Carpenter

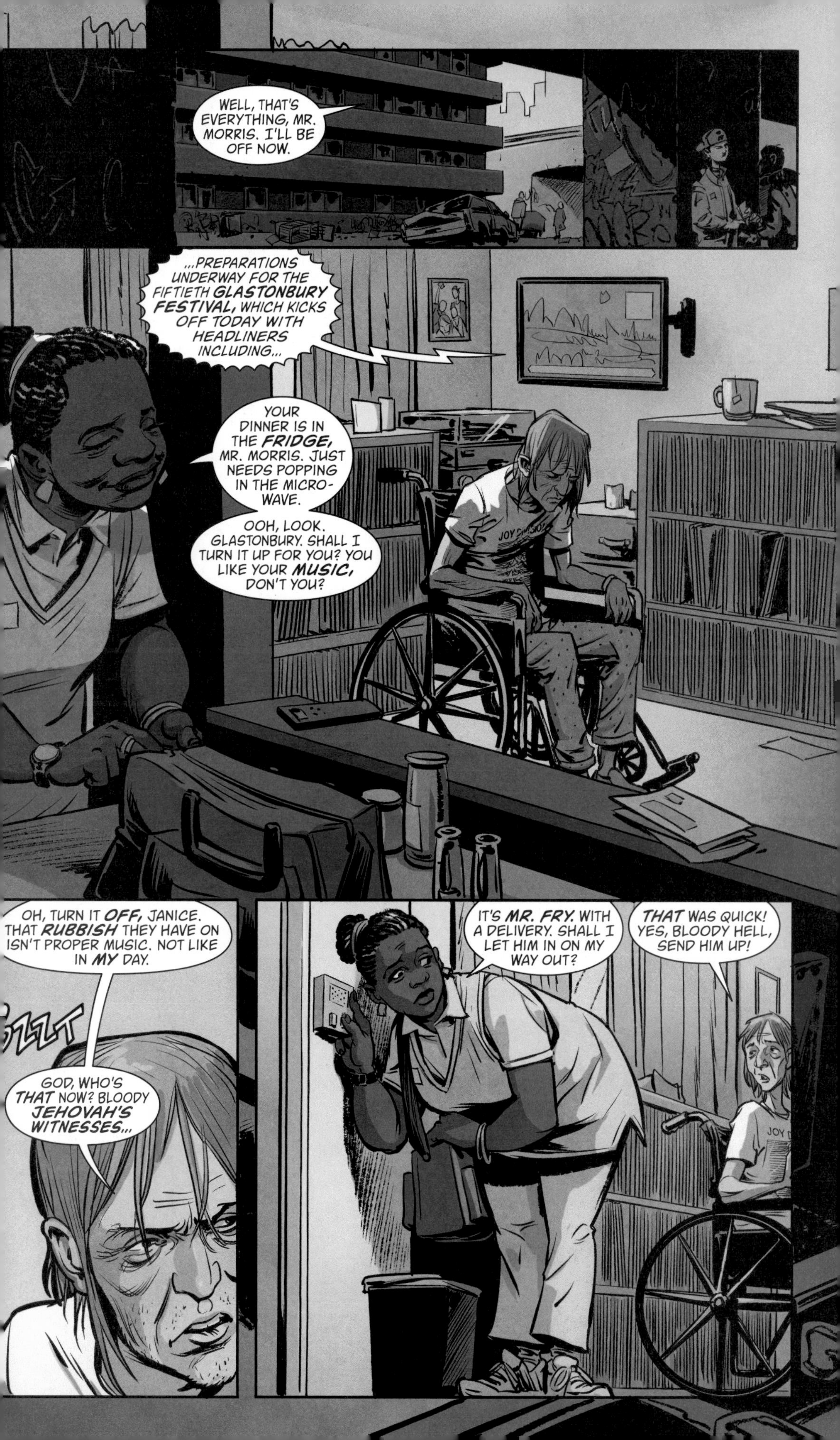
WELL, THAT'S EVERYTHING, MR. MORRIS. I'LL BE OFF NOW.
...PREPARATIONS UNDERWAY FOR THE FIFTIETH GLASTONBURY FESTIVAL, WHICH KICKS OFF TODAY WITH HEADLINERS INCLUDING...
YOUR DINNER IS IN THE FRIDGE, MR. MORRIS. JUST NEEDS POPPING IN THE MICRO-WAVE.
OOH, LOOK. GLASTONBURY. SHALL I TURN IT UP FOR YOU? YOU LIKE YOUR MUSIC, DON'T YOU?
OH, TURN IT OFF, JANICE. THAT RUBBISH THEY HAVE ON ISN'T PROPER MUSIC. NOT LIKE IN MY DAY.
BZZZT
GOD, WHO'S THAT NOW? BLOODY JEHOVAH'S WITNESSES...
IT'S MR. FRY. WITH A DELIVERY. SHALL I LET HIM IN ON MY WAY OUT?
THAT WAS QUICK! YES, BLOODY HELL, SEND HIM UP!

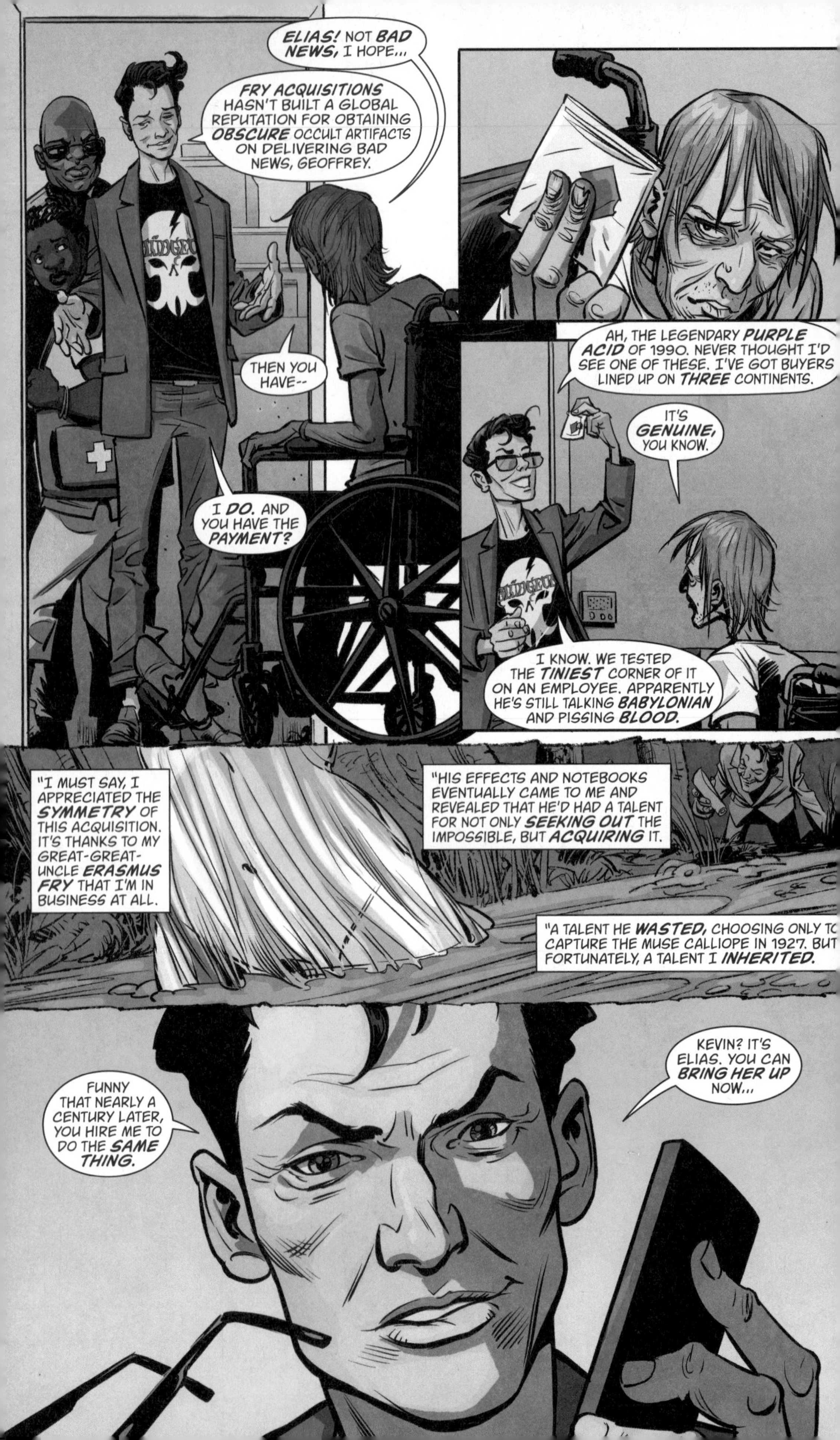
ELIAS! NOT BAD NEWS, I HOPE...
FRY ACQUISITIONS HASN'T BUILT A GLOBAL REPUTATION FOR OBTAINING OBSCURE OCCULT ARTIFACTS ON DELIVERING BAD NEWS, GEOFFREY.
THEN YOU HAVE--
I DO. AND YOU HAVE THE PAYMENT?
AH, THE LEGENDARY PURPLE ACID OF 1990. NEVER THOUGHT I'D SEE ONE OF THESE. I'VE GOT BUYERS LINED UP ON THREE CONTINENTS.
IT'S GENUINE, YOU KNOW.
I KNOW. WE TESTED THE TINIEST CORNER OF IT ON AN EMPLOYEE. APPARENTLY HE'S STILL TALKING BABYLONIAN AND PISSING BLOOD.
"I MUST SAY, I APPRECIATED THE SYMMETRY OF THIS ACQUISITION. IT'S THANKS TO MY GREAT-GREAT-UNCLE ERASMUS FRY THAT I'M IN BUSINESS AT ALL.
"HIS EFFECTS AND NOTEBOOKS EVENTUALLY CAME TO ME AND REVEALED THAT HE'D HAD A TALENT FOR NOT ONLY SEEKING OUT THE IMPOSSIBLE, BUT ACQUIRING IT.
"A TALENT HE WASTED, CHOOSING ONLY TO CAPTURE THE MUSE CALLIOPE IN 1927. BUT FORTUNATELY, A TALENT I INHERITED.
FUNNY THAT NEARLY A CENTURY LATER, YOU HIRE ME TO DO THE SAME THING.
KEVIN? IT'S ELIAS. YOU CAN BRING HER UP NOW...

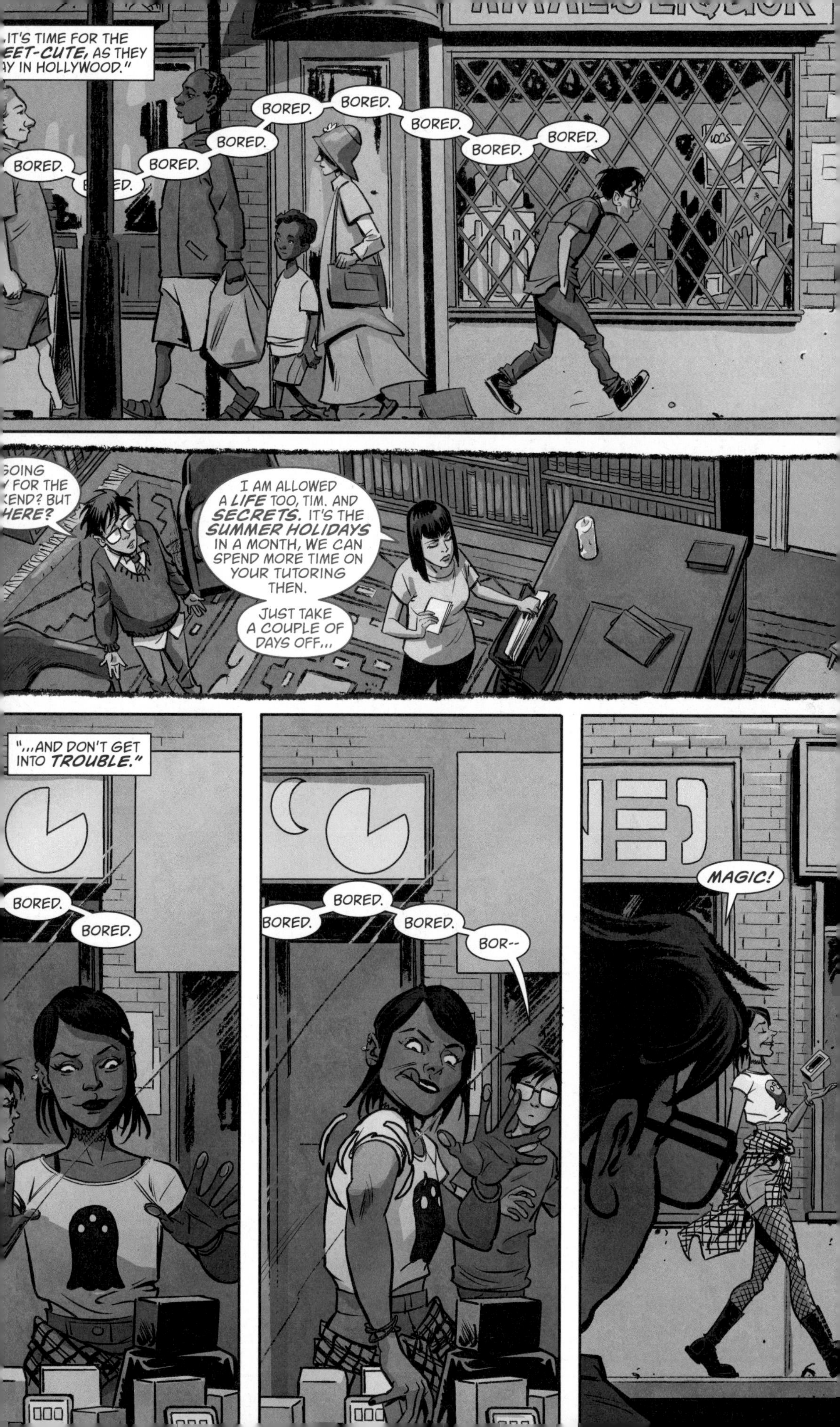
IT'S TIME FOR THE
EET-CUTE, AS THEY
AY IN HOLLYWOOD."
BORED.
BORED.
BORED.
BORED.
BORED.
BORED.
BORED.
BORED.
GOING
FOR THE
KEND? BUT
HERE?
I AM ALLOWED A LIFE TOO, TIM. AND SECRETS. IT'S THE SUMMER HOLIDAYS IN A MONTH, WE CAN SPEND MORE TIME ON YOUR TUTORING THEN.
JUST TAKE A COUPLE OF DAYS OFF...
"...AND DON'T GET INTO TROUBLE."
BORED.
BORED.
BORED.
BORED.
BORED.
BOR--
MAGIC!

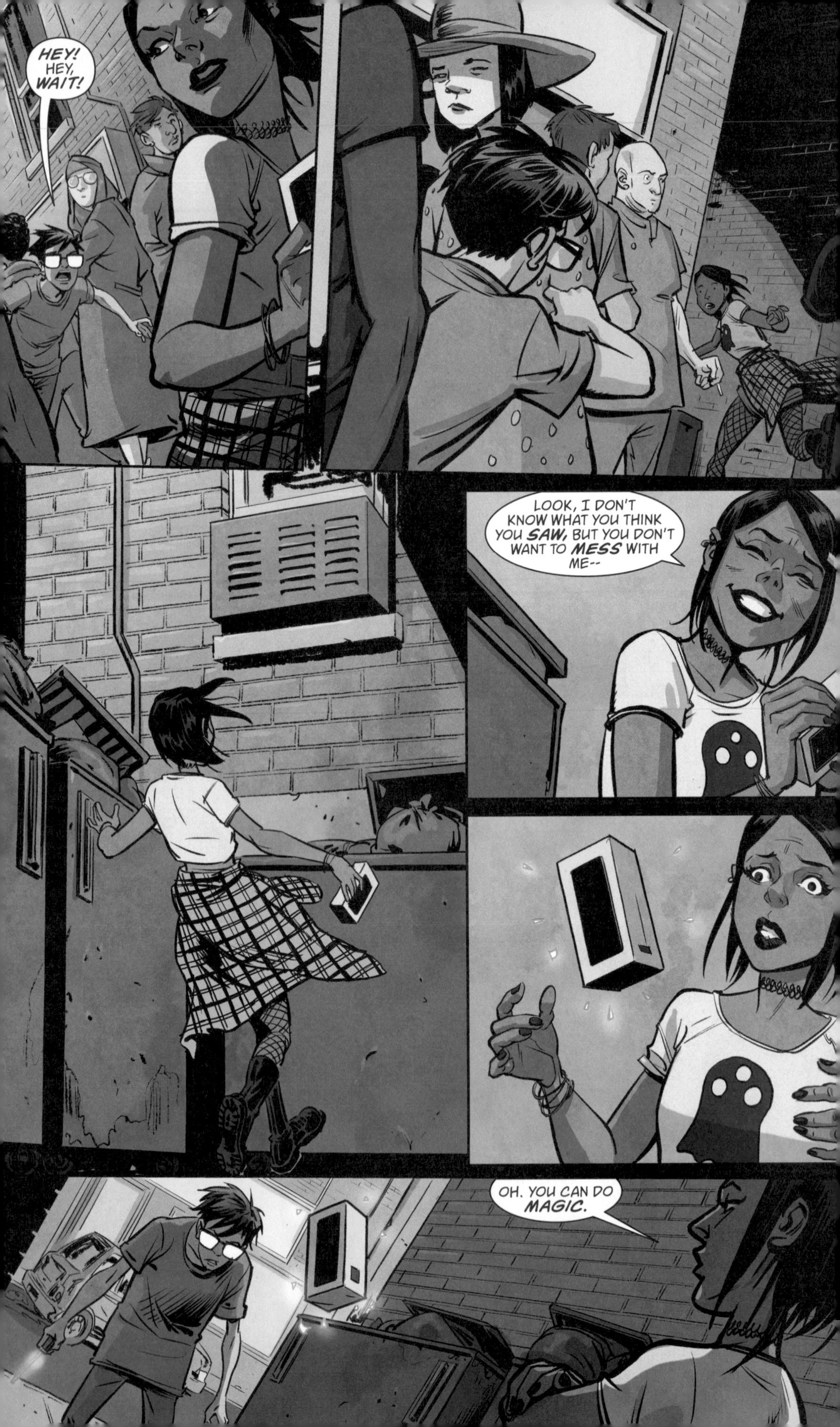
HEY! HEY, WAIT!
LOOK, I DON'T KNOW WHAT YOU THINK YOU SAW, BUT YOU DON'T WANT TO MESS WITH ME--
OH. YOU CAN DO MAGIC.

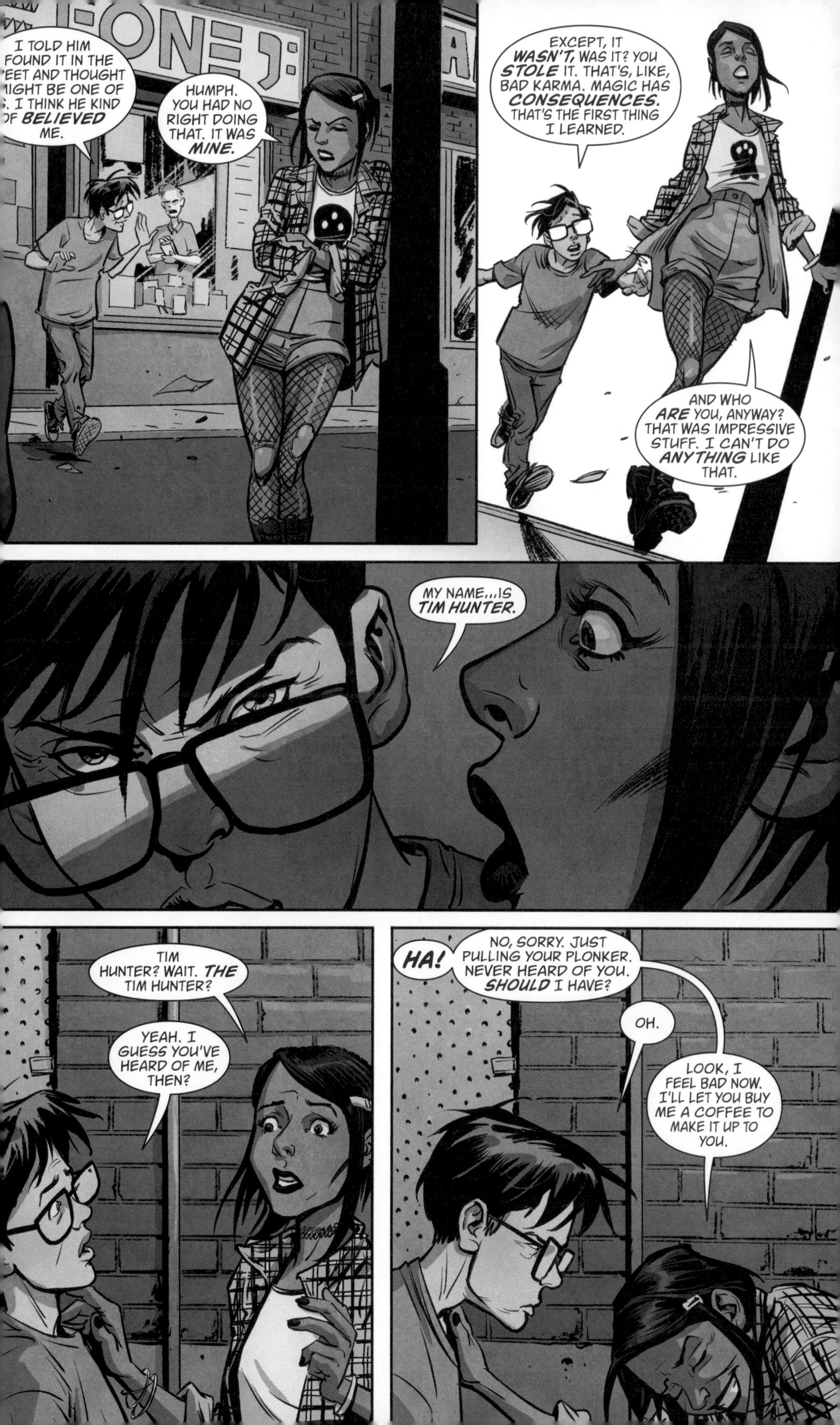

I TOLD HIM
FOUND IT IN THE
EET AND THOUGHT
IIGHT BE ONE OF
. I THINK HE KIND
F BELIEVED
ME.
HUMPH.
YOU HAD NO
RIGHT DOING
THAT. IT WAS
MINE.
EXCEPT, IT WASN'T, WAS IT? YOU STOLE IT. THAT'S, LIKE, BAD KARMA. MAGIC HAS CONSEQUENCES. THAT'S THE FIRST THING I LEARNED.
AND WHO ARE YOU, ANYWAY? THAT WAS IMPRESSIVE STUFF. I CAN'T DO ANYTHING LIKE THAT.
MY NAME...IS TIM HUNTER.
TIM HUNTER? WAIT. THE TIM HUNTER?
YEAH. I GUESS YOU'VE HEARD OF ME, THEN?
HA!
NO, SORRY. JUST PULLING YOUR PLONKER. NEVER HEARD OF YOU. SHOULD I HAVE?
OH.
LOOK, I FEEL BAD NOW. I'LL LET YOU BUY ME A COFFEE TO MAKE IT UP TO YOU.

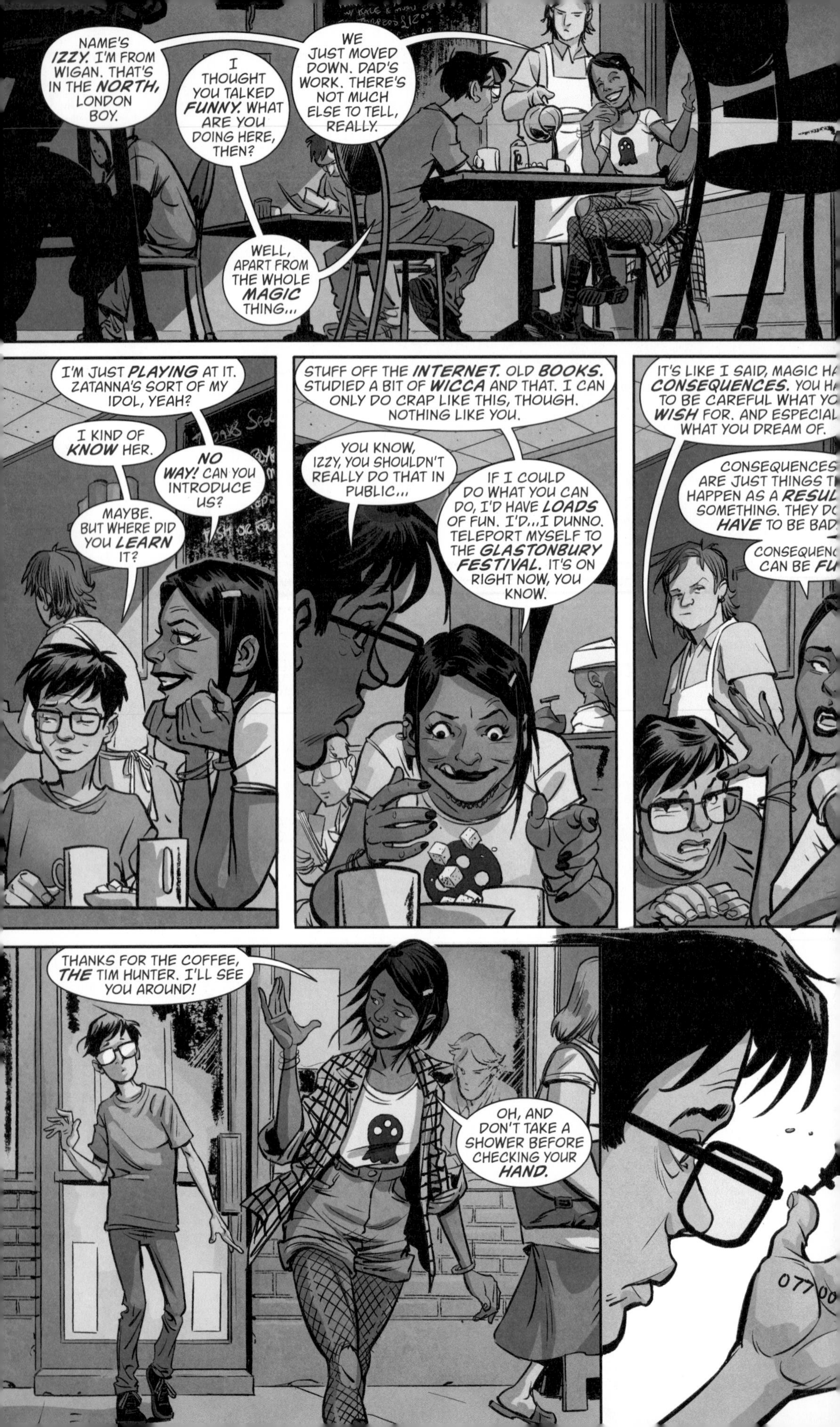

NAME'S IZZY. I'M FROM WIGAN. THAT'S IN THE NORTH, LONDON BOY.
I THOUGHT YOU TALKED FUNNY. WHAT ARE YOU DOING HERE, THEN?
WE JUST MOVED DOWN. DAD'S WORK. THERE'S NOT MUCH ELSE TO TELL, REALLY.
WELL, APART FROM THE WHOLE MAGIC THING...
I'M JUST PLAYING AT IT. ZATANNA'S SORT OF MY IDOL, YEAH?
I KIND OF KNOW HER.
NO WAY! CAN YOU INTRODUCE US?
MAYBE. BUT WHERE DID YOU LEARN IT?
STUFF OFF THE INTERNET. OLD BOOKS. STUDIED A BIT OF WICCA AND THAT. I CAN ONLY DO CRAP LIKE THIS, THOUGH. NOTHING LIKE YOU.
YOU KNOW, IZZY, YOU SHOULDN'T REALLY DO THAT IN PUBLIC...
IF I COULD DO WHAT YOU CAN DO, I'D HAVE LOADS OF FUN. I'D...I DUNNO. TELEPORT MYSELF TO THE GLASTONBURY FESTIVAL. IT'S ON RIGHT NOW, YOU KNOW.
IT'S LIKE I SAID, MAGIC HA CONSEQUENCES. YOU HA TO BE CAREFUL WHAT YO WISH FOR. AND ESPECIAL WHAT YOU DREAM OF.
CONSEQUENCES ARE JUST THINGS T HAPPEN AS A RESUL SOMETHING. THEY DO HAVE TO BE BAD
CONSEQUENC CAN BE FU
THANKS FOR THE COFFEE, THE TIM HUNTER. I'LL SEE YOU AROUND!
OH, AND DON'T TAKE A SHOWER BEFORE CHECKING YOUR HAND.
077

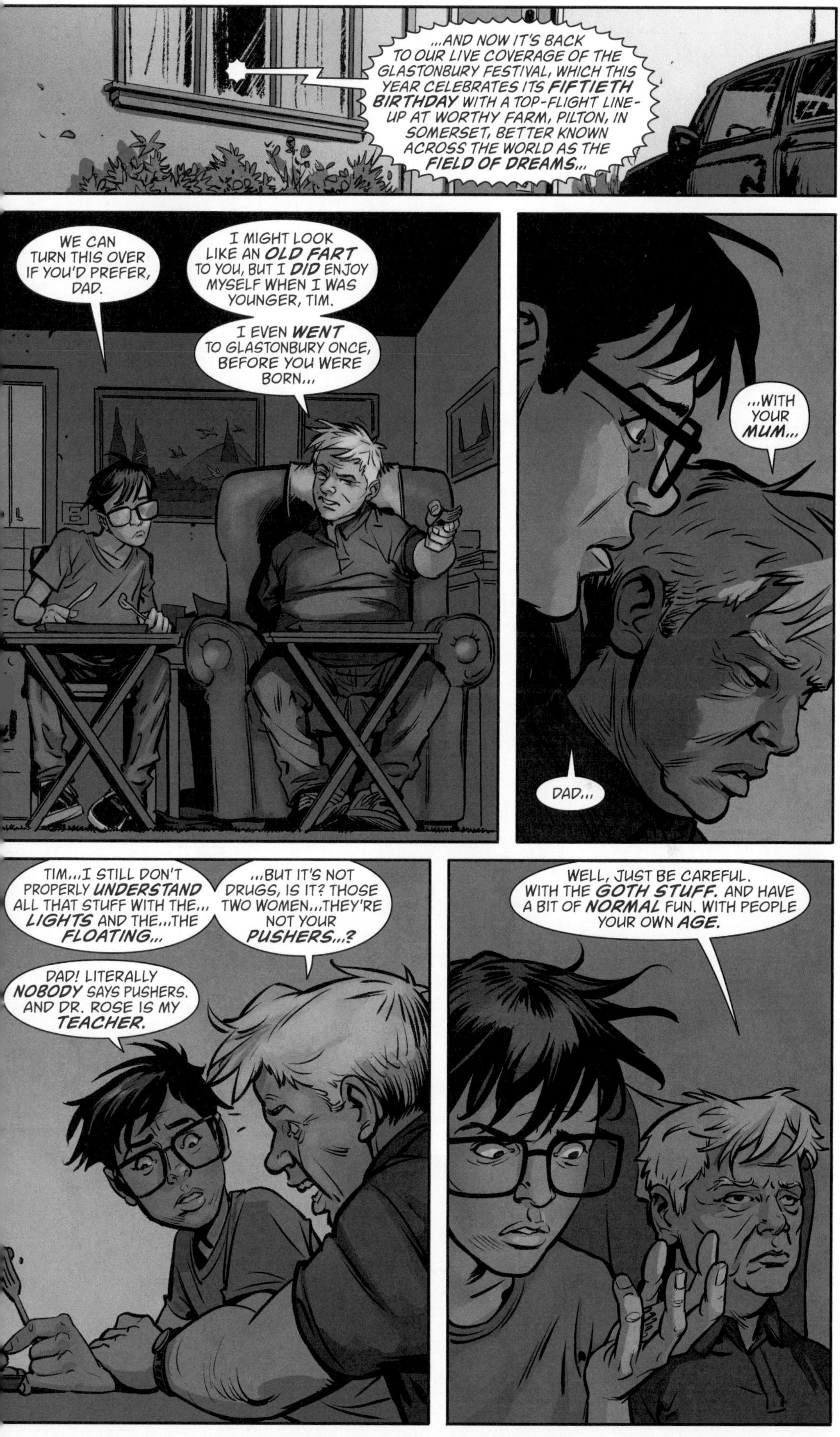
...AND NOW IT'S BACK TO OUR LIVE COVERAGE OF THE GLASTONBURY FESTIVAL, WHICH THIS YEAR CELEBRATES ITS FIFTIETH BIRTHDAY WITH A TOP-FLIGHT LINE-UP AT WORTHY FARM, PILTON, IN SOMERSET, BETTER KNOWN ACROSS THE WORLD AS THE FIELD OF DREAMS...
WE CAN TURN THIS OVER IF YOU'D PREFER, DAD.
I MIGHT LOOK LIKE AN OLD FART TO YOU, BUT I DID ENJOY MYSELF WHEN I WAS YOUNGER, TIM.
I EVEN WENT TO GLASTONBURY ONCE, BEFORE YOU WERE BORN...
...WITH YOUR MUM...
DAD...
TIM...I STILL DON'T PROPERLY UNDERSTAND ALL THAT STUFF WITH THE... LIGHTS AND THE...THE FLOATING...
...BUT IT'S NOT DRUGS, IS IT? THOSE TWO WOMEN...THEY'RE NOT YOUR PUSHERS...?
DAD! LITERALLY NOBODY SAYS PUSHERS. AND DR. ROSE IS MY TEACHER.
WELL, JUST BE CAREFUL. WITH THE GOTH STUFF. AND HAVE A BIT OF NORMAL FUN. WITH PEOPLE YOUR OWN AGE.

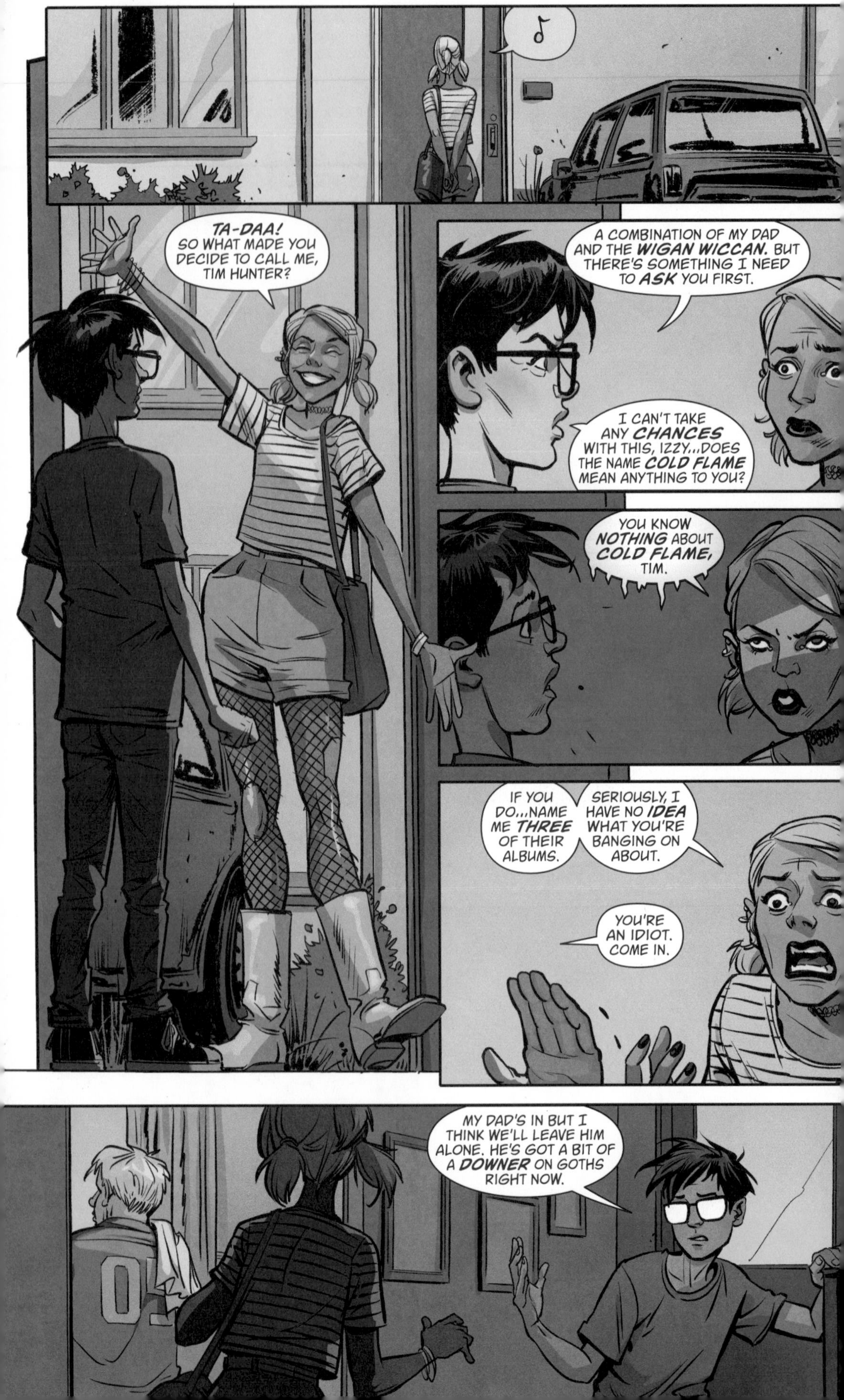
♪
TA-DAA! SO WHAT MADE YOU DECIDE TO CALL ME, TIM HUNTER?
A COMBINATION OF MY DAD AND THE WIGAN WICCAN. BUT THERE'S SOMETHING I NEED TO ASK YOU FIRST.
I CAN'T TAKE ANY CHANCES WITH THIS, IZZY...DOES THE NAME COLD FLAME MEAN ANYTHING TO YOU?
YOU KNOW NOTHING ABOUT COLD FLAME, TIM.
SERIOUSLY, I HAVE NO IDEA WHAT YOU'RE BANGING ON ABOUT.
IF YOU DO...NAME ME THREE OF THEIR ALBUMS.
YOU'RE AN IDIOT. COME IN.
MY DAD'S IN BUT I THINK WE'LL LEAVE HIM ALONE. HE'S GOT A BIT OF A DOWNER ON GOTHS RIGHT NOW.
05

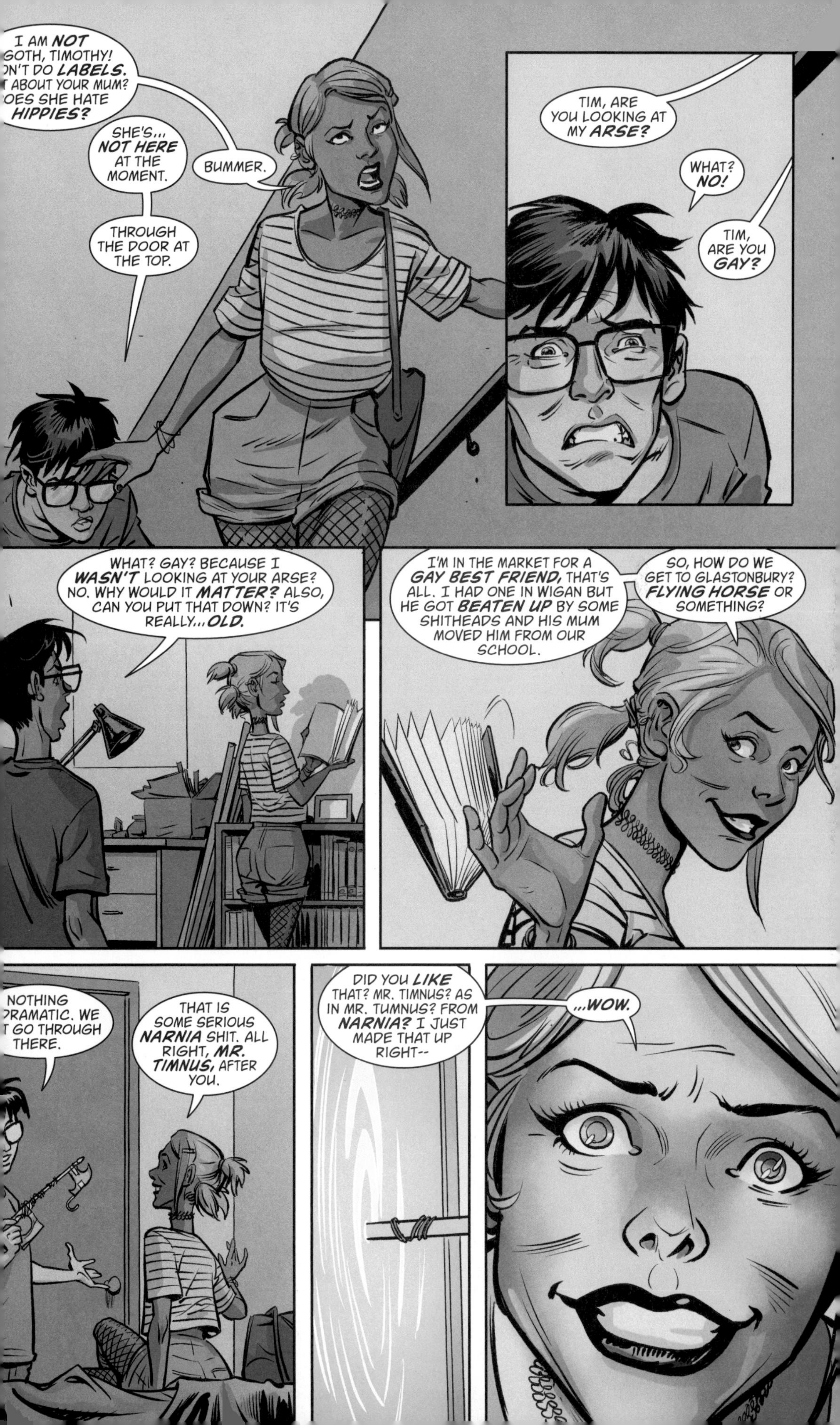
I AM NOT
GOTH, TIMOTHY!
N'T DO LABELS.
T ABOUT YOUR MUM?
OES SHE HATE
HIPPIES?
SHE'S... NOT HERE AT THE MOMENT.
BUMMER.
THROUGH THE DOOR AT THE TOP.
TIM, ARE YOU LOOKING AT MY ARSE?
WHAT? NO!
TIM, ARE YOU GAY?
WHAT? GAY? BECAUSE I WASN'T LOOKING AT YOUR ARSE? NO. WHY WOULD IT MATTER? ALSO, CAN YOU PUT THAT DOWN? IT'S REALLY...OLD.
I'M IN THE MARKET FOR A GAY BEST FRIEND, THAT'S ALL. I HAD ONE IN WIGAN BUT HE GOT BEATEN UP BY SOME SHITHEADS AND HIS MUM MOVED HIM FROM OUR SCHOOL.
SO, HOW DO WE GET TO GLASTONBURY? FLYING HORSE OR SOMETHING?
NOTHING
RAMATIC. WE
GO THROUGH
THERE.
THAT IS SOME SERIOUS NARNIA SHIT. ALL RIGHT, MR. TIMNUS, AFTER YOU.
DID YOU LIKE THAT? MR. TIMNUS? AS IN MR. TUMNUS? FROM NARNIA? I JUST MADE THAT UP RIGHT--
...WOW.

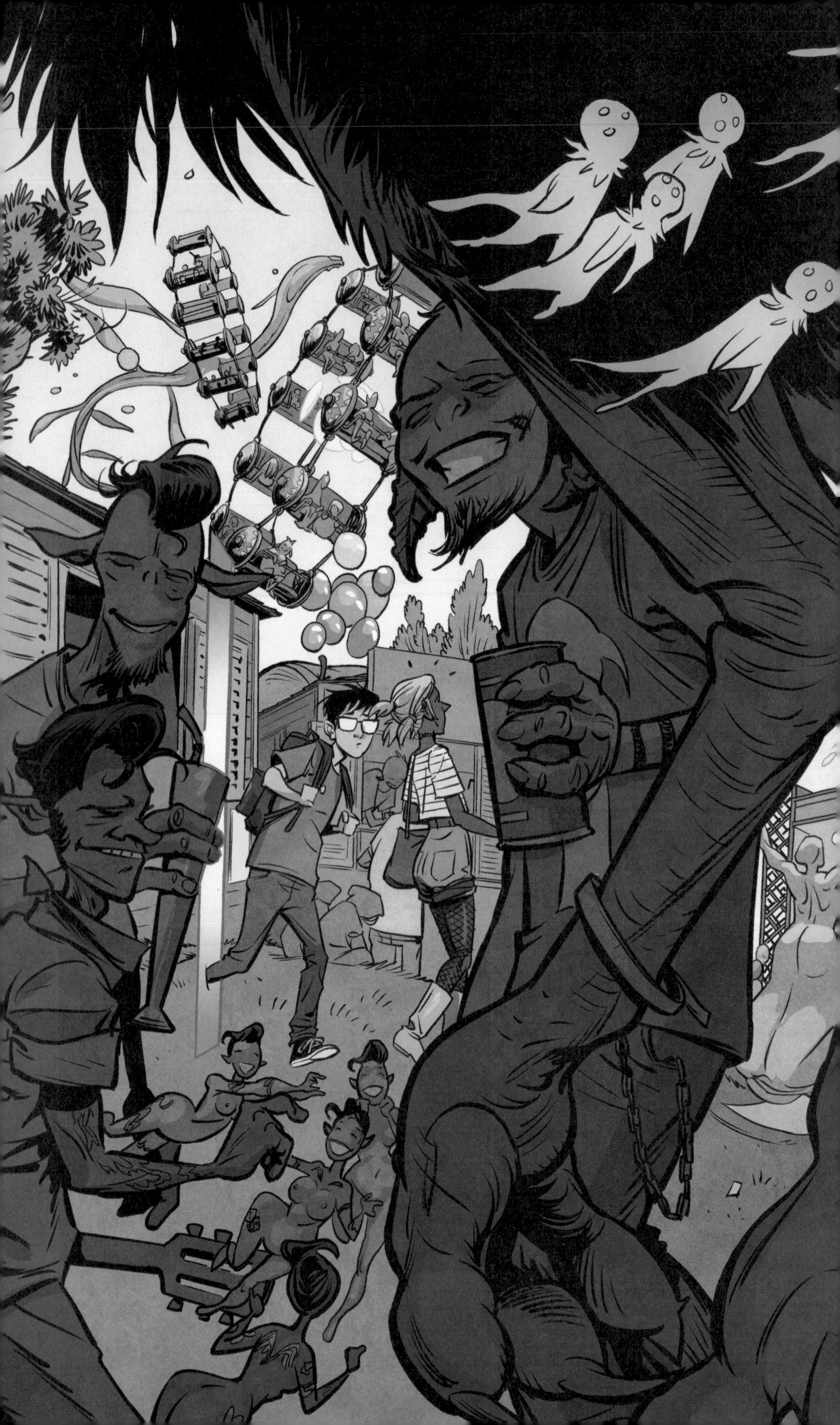

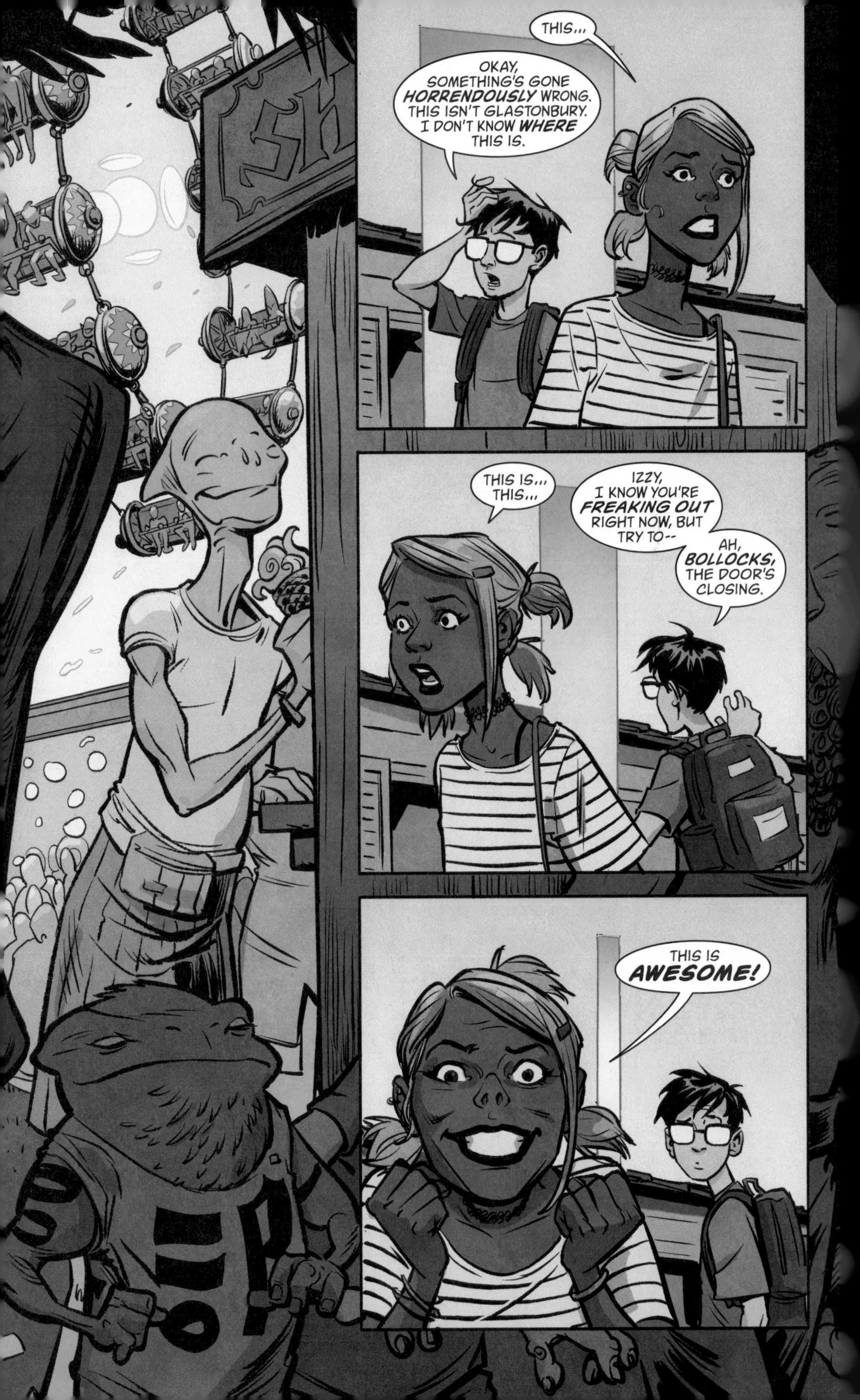
OKAY, SOMETHING'S GONE HORRENDOUSLY WRONG. THIS ISN'T GLASTONBURY. I DON'T KNOW WHERE THIS IS.
THIS...
THIS IS... THIS...
IZZY, I KNOW YOU'RE FREAKING OUT RIGHT NOW, BUT TRY TO--
AH, BOLLOCKS, THE DOOR'S CLOSING.
THIS IS AWESOME!

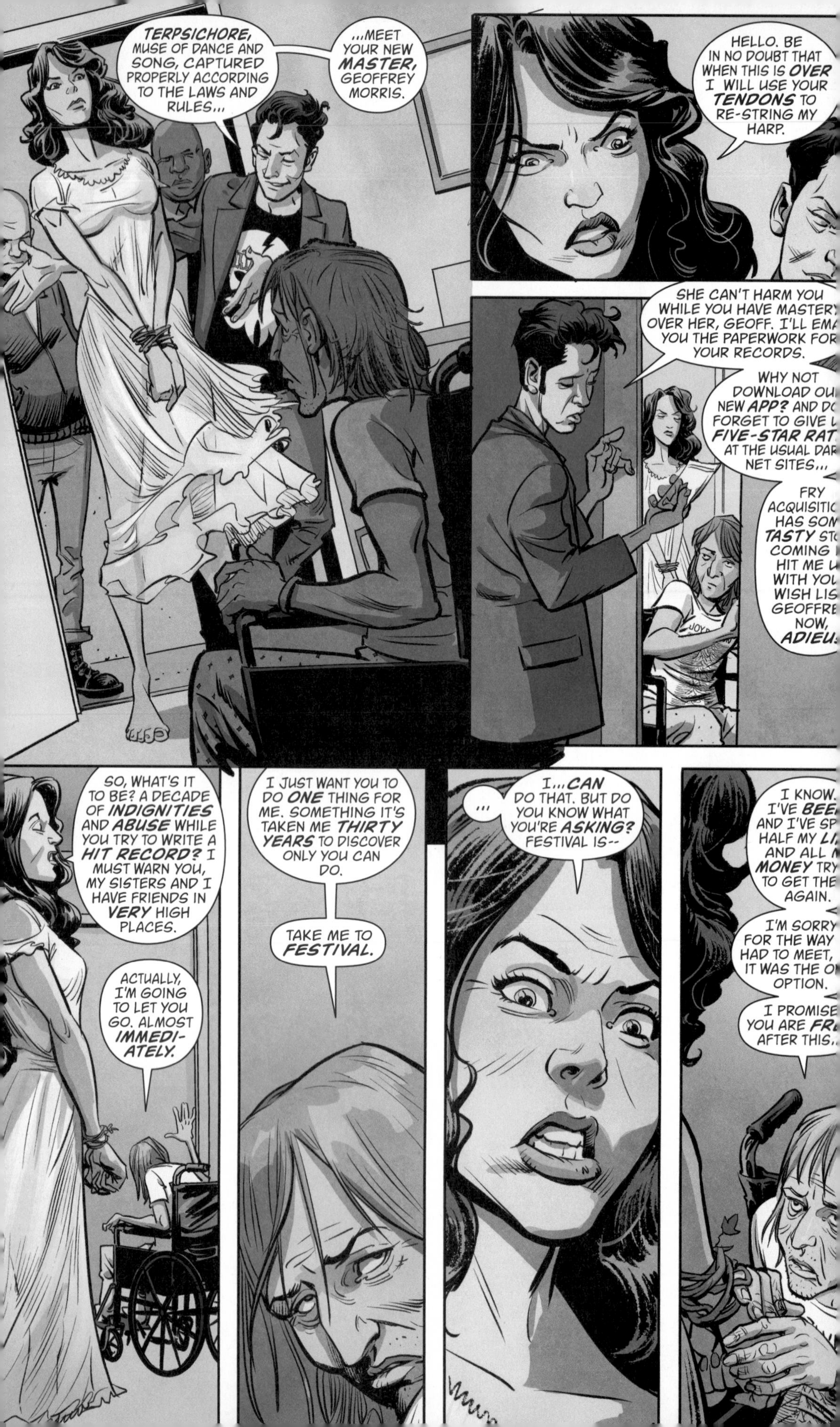
TERPSICHORE, MUSE OF DANCE AND SONG, CAPTURED PROPERLY ACCORDING TO THE LAWS AND RULES...
...MEET YOUR NEW MASTER, GEOFFREY MORRIS.
HELLO. BE IN NO DOUBT THAT WHEN THIS IS OVER I WILL USE YOUR TENDONS TO RE-STRING MY HARP.
SHE CAN'T HARM YOU WHILE YOU HAVE MASTER OVER HER, GEOFF. I'LL EMA YOU THE PAPERWORK FOR YOUR RECORDS.
WHY NOT DOWNLOAD OU NEW APP? AND DO FORGET TO GIVE U FIVE-STAR RAT AT THE USUAL DAR NET SITES...
FRY ACQUISITIC HAS SOM TASTY ST COMING HIT ME U WITH YOU WISH LIS GEOFFRE NOW, ADIEU
SO, WHAT'S IT TO BE? A DECADE OF INDIGNITIES AND ABUSE WHILE YOU TRY TO WRITE A HIT RECORD? I MUST WARN YOU, MY SISTERS AND I HAVE FRIENDS IN VERY HIGH PLACES.
ACTUALLY, I'M GOING TO LET YOU GO. ALMOST IMMEDI-ATELY.
I JUST WANT YOU TO DO ONE THING FOR ME. SOMETHING IT'S TAKEN ME THIRTY YEARS TO DISCOVER ONLY YOU CAN DO.
TAKE ME TO FESTIVAL.
...
I...CAN DO THAT. BUT DO YOU KNOW WHAT YOU'RE ASKING? FESTIVAL IS--
I KNOW. I'VE BEE AND I'VE SP HALF MY LI AND ALL M MONEY TRY TO GET THE AGAIN.
I'M SORRY FOR THE WAY HAD TO MEET, IT WAS THE O OPTION.
I PROMISE YOU ARE FR AFTER THIS.

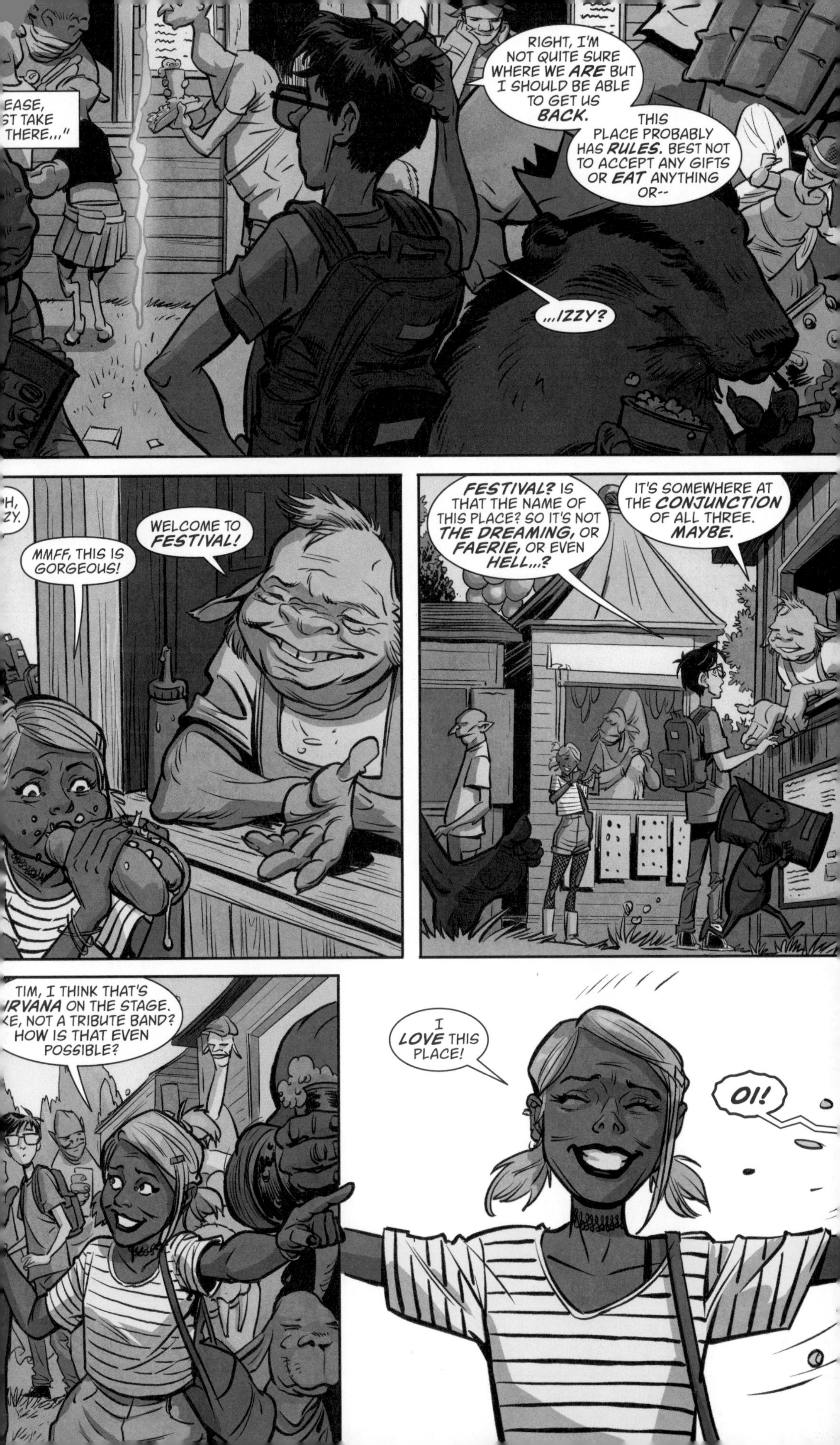
EASE,
ST TAKE
THERE..."
RIGHT, I'M NOT QUITE SURE WHERE WE ARE BUT I SHOULD BE ABLE TO GET US BACK.
THIS PLACE PROBABLY HAS RULES. BEST NOT TO ACCEPT ANY GIFTS OR EAT ANYTHING OR--
...IZZY?
H,
ZY.
MMFF, THIS IS GORGEOUS!
WELCOME TO FESTIVAL!
FESTIVAL? IS THAT THE NAME OF THIS PLACE? SO IT'S NOT THE DREAMING, OR FAERIE, OR EVEN HELL...?
IT'S SOMEWHERE AT THE CONJUNCTION OF ALL THREE. MAYBE.
TIM, I THINK THAT'S
IRVANA ON THE STAGE.
KE, NOT A TRIBUTE BAND?
HOW IS THAT EVEN POSSIBLE?
I LOVE THIS PLACE!
OI!

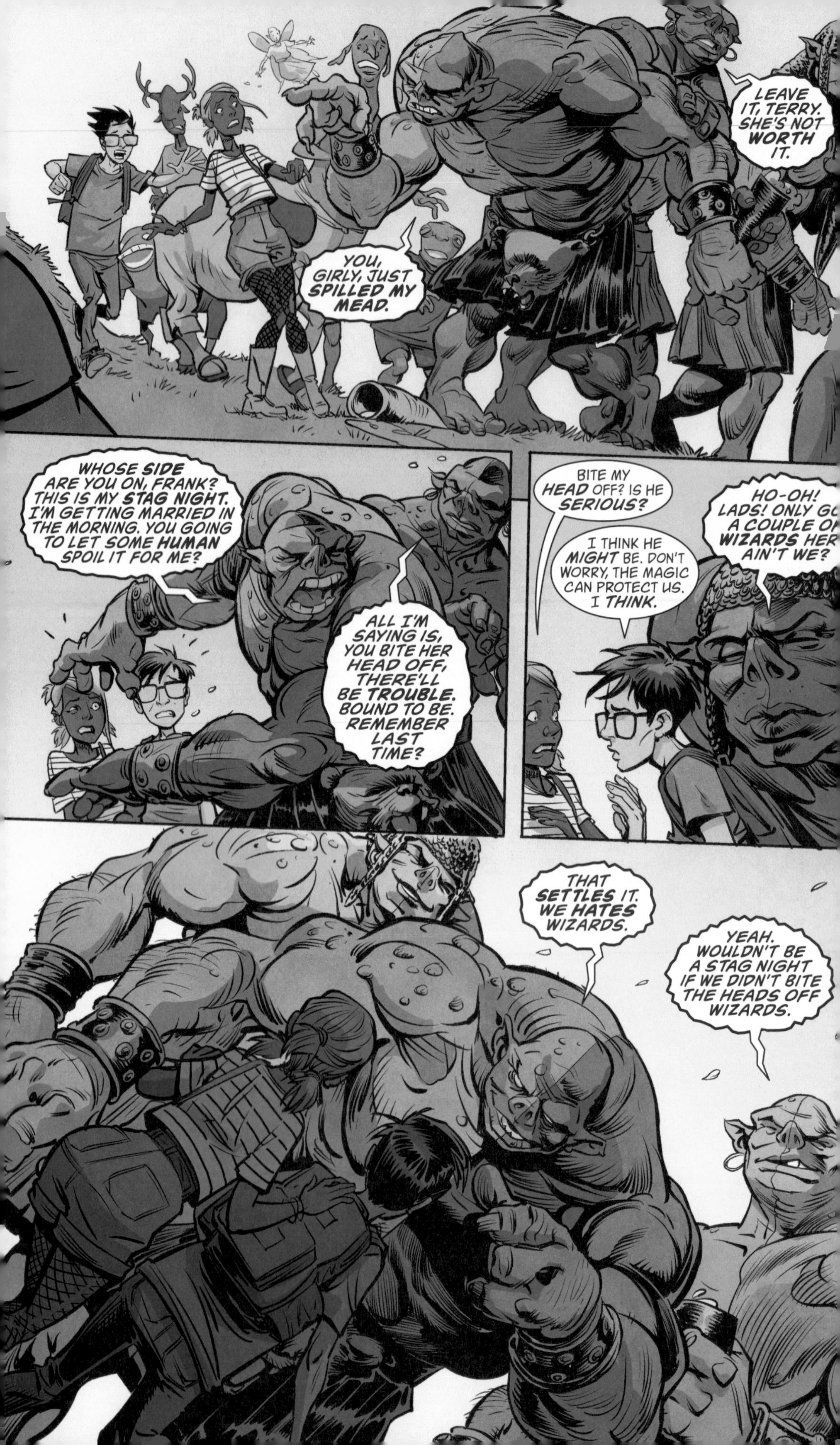
YOU, GIRLY, JUST SPILLED MY MEAD.
LEAVE IT, TERRY. SHE'S NOT WORTH IT.
WHOSE SIDE ARE YOU ON, FRANK? THIS IS MY STAG NIGHT. I'M GETTING MARRIED IN THE MORNING. YOU GOING TO LET SOME HUMAN SPOIL IT FOR ME?
ALL I'M SAYING IS, YOU BITE HER HEAD OFF, THERE'LL BE TROUBLE. BOUND TO BE. REMEMBER LAST TIME?
BITE MY HEAD OFF? IS HE SERIOUS?
I THINK HE MIGHT BE. DON'T WORRY, THE MAGIC CAN PROTECT US. I THINK.
THAT SETTLES IT. WE HATES WIZARDS.
YEAH. WOULDN'T BE A STAG NIGHT IF WE DIDN'T BITE THE HEADS OFF WIZARDS.

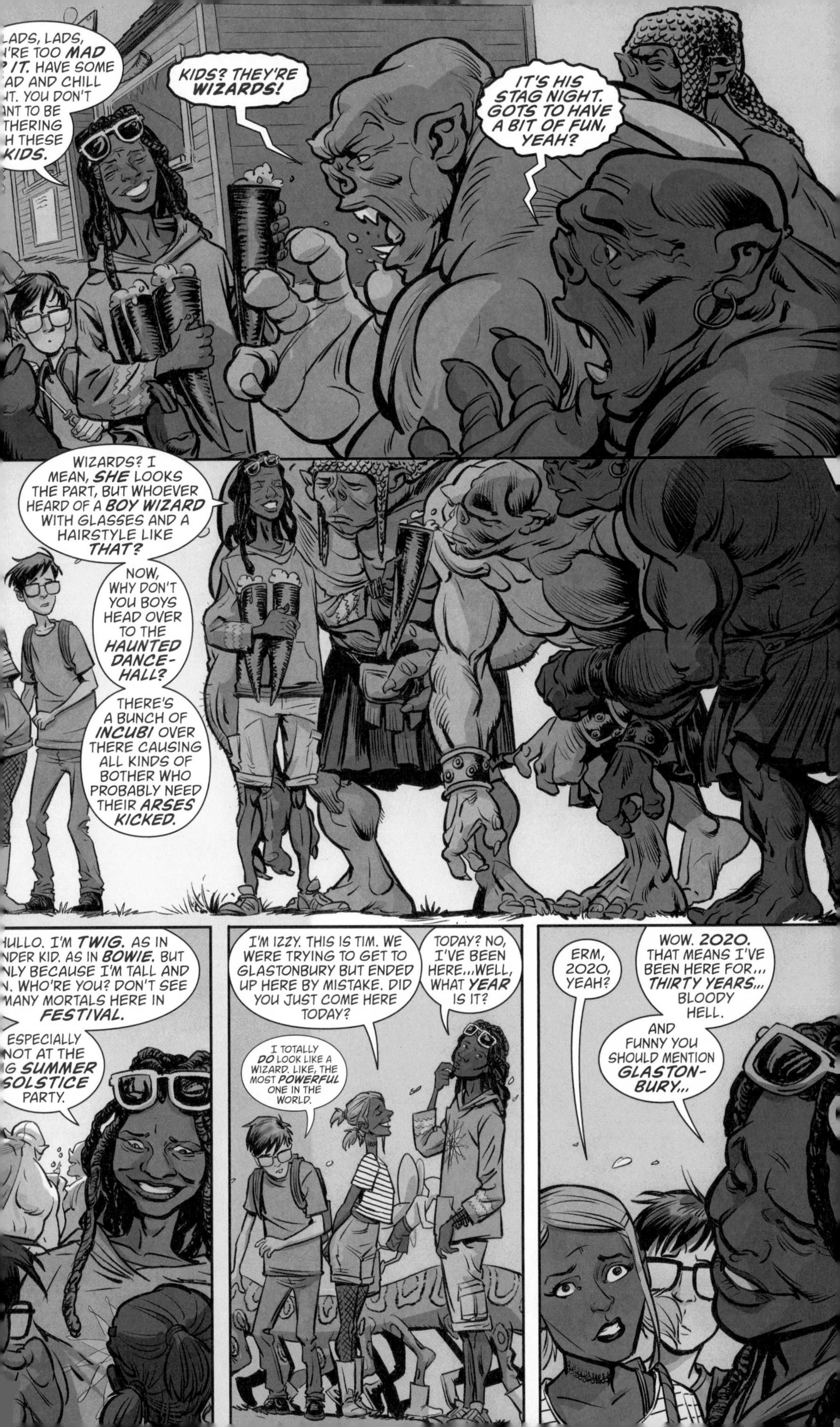
LADS, LADS, 'RE TOO MAD IT. HAVE SOME AD AND CHILL T. YOU DON'T NT TO BE THERING H THESE KIDS.
KIDS? THEY'RE WIZARDS!
IT'S HIS STAG NIGHT. GOTS TO HAVE A BIT OF FUN, YEAH?
WIZARDS? I MEAN, SHE LOOKS THE PART, BUT WHOEVER HEARD OF A BOY WIZARD WITH GLASSES AND A HAIRSTYLE LIKE THAT?
NOW, WHY DON'T YOU BOYS HEAD OVER TO THE HAUNTED DANCE-HALL?
THERE'S A BUNCH OF INCUBI OVER THERE CAUSING ALL KINDS OF BOTHER WHO PROBABLY NEED THEIR ARSES KICKED.
HULLO. I'M TWIG. AS IN NDER KID. AS IN BOWIE. BUT NLY BECAUSE I'M TALL AND N. WHO'RE YOU? DON'T SEE MANY MORTALS HERE IN FESTIVAL.
ESPECIALLY NOT AT THE G SUMMER SOLSTICE PARTY.
I'M IZZY. THIS IS TIM. WE WERE TRYING TO GET TO GLASTONBURY BUT ENDED UP HERE BY MISTAKE. DID YOU JUST COME HERE TODAY?
I TOTALLY DO LOOK LIKE A WIZARD. LIKE, THE MOST POWERFUL ONE IN THE WORLD.
TODAY? NO, I'VE BEEN HERE...WELL, WHAT YEAR IS IT?
ERM, 2020, YEAH?
WOW. 2020. THAT MEANS I'VE BEEN HERE FOR... THIRTY YEARS... BLOODY HELL.
AND FUNNY YOU SHOULD MENTION GLASTON-BURY...

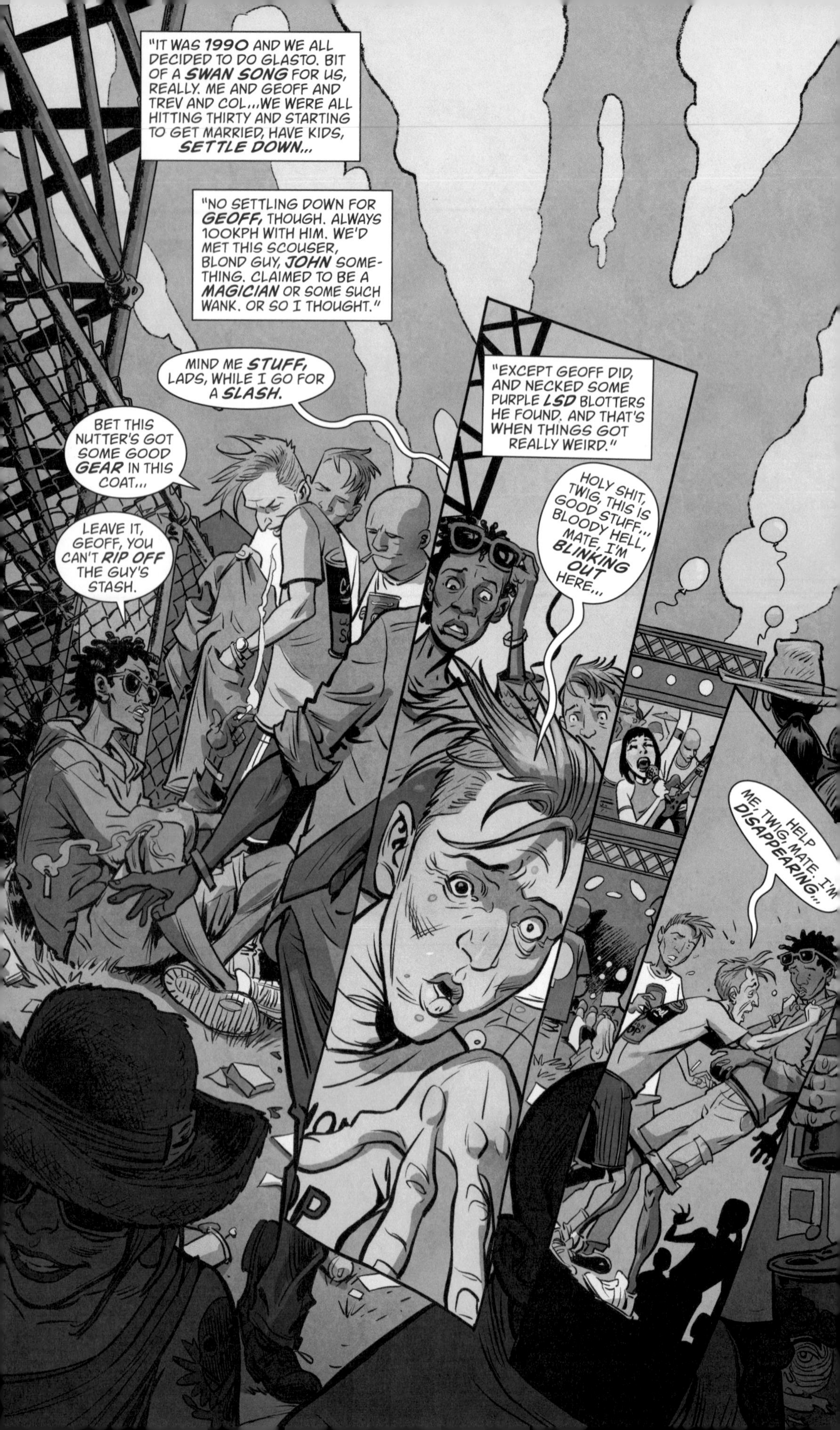
"IT WAS 1990 AND WE ALL DECIDED TO DO GLASTO. BIT OF A SWAN SONG FOR US, REALLY. ME AND GEOFF AND TREV AND COL...WE WERE ALL HITTING THIRTY AND STARTING TO GET MARRIED, HAVE KIDS, SETTLE DOWN...
"NO SETTLING DOWN FOR GEOFF, THOUGH. ALWAYS 100KPH WITH HIM. WE'D MET THIS SCOUSER, BLOND GUY, JOHN SOMETHING. CLAIMED TO BE A MAGICIAN OR SOME SUCH WANK. OR SO I THOUGHT."
MIND ME STUFF, LADS, WHILE I GO FOR A SLASH.
BET THIS NUTTER'S GOT SOME GOOD GEAR IN THIS COAT...
LEAVE IT, GEOFF, YOU CAN'T RIP OFF THE GUY'S STASH.
"EXCEPT GEOFF DID, AND NECKED SOME PURPLE LSD BLOTTERS HE FOUND. AND THAT'S WHEN THINGS GOT REALLY WEIRD."
HOLY SHIT, TWIG, THIS IS GOOD STUFF... BLOODY HELL, MATE, I'M BLINKING OUT HERE...
HELP ME, TWIG, MATE. I'M DISAPPEARING...

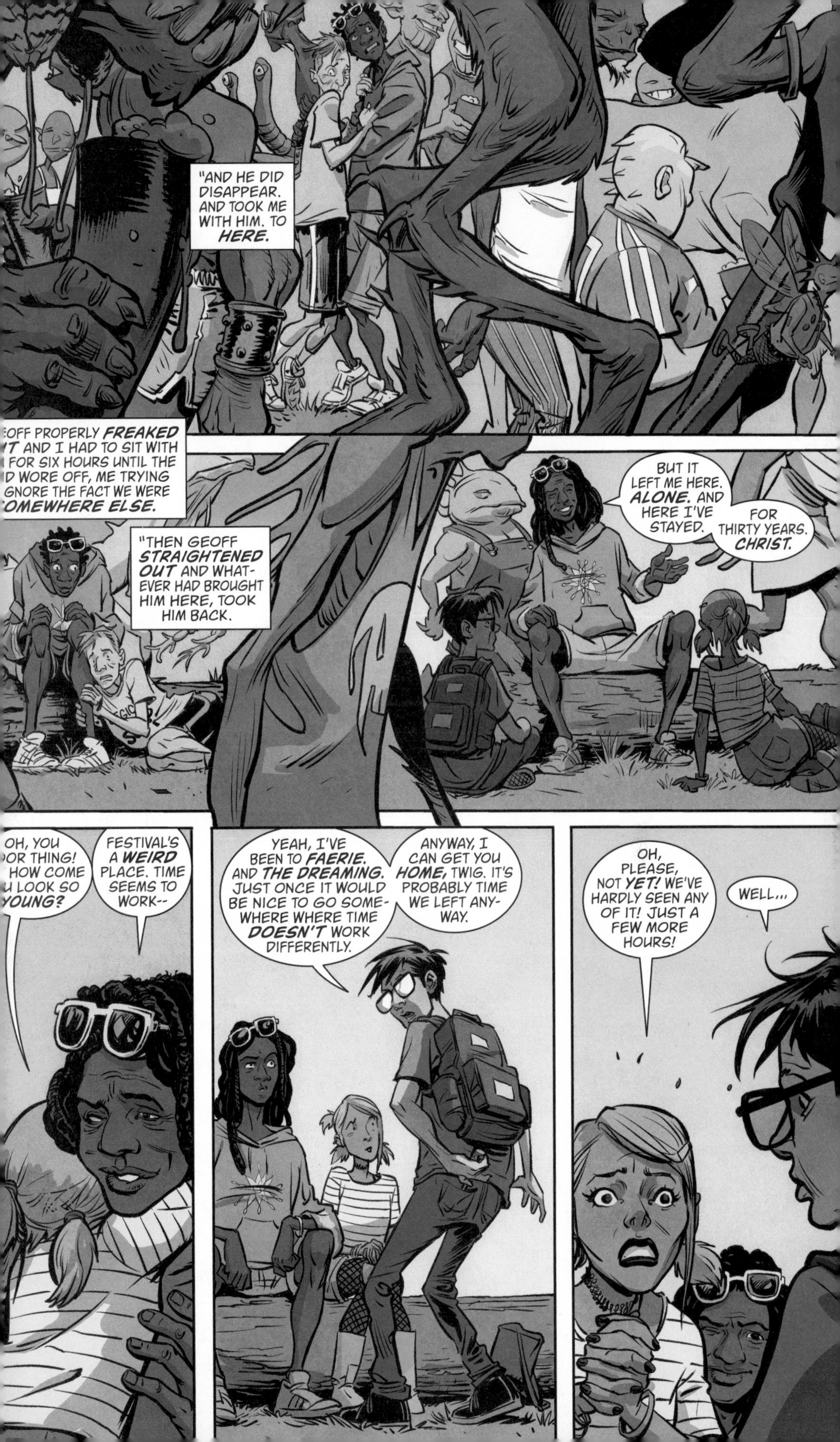
"AND HE DID DISAPPEAR. AND TOOK ME WITH HIM. TO *HERE.*
EOFF PROPERLY *FREAKED* *IT* AND I HAD TO SIT WITH FOR SIX HOURS UNTIL THE D WORE OFF, ME TRYING GNORE THE FACT WE WERE *OMEWHERE ELSE.*
"THEN GEOFF *STRAIGHTENED OUT* AND WHATEVER HAD BROUGHT HIM HERE, TOOK HIM BACK.
BUT IT LEFT ME HERE. *ALONE.* AND HERE I'VE STAYED.
FOR THIRTY YEARS. *CHRIST.*
OH, YOU OR THING! HOW COME U LOOK SO *YOUNG?*
FESTIVAL'S A *WEIRD* PLACE. TIME SEEMS TO WORK--
YEAH, I'VE BEEN TO *FAERIE.* AND *THE DREAMING.* JUST ONCE IT WOULD BE NICE TO GO SOMEWHERE WHERE TIME *DOESN'T* WORK DIFFERENTLY.
ANYWAY, I CAN GET YOU *HOME,* TWIG. IT'S PROBABLY TIME WE LEFT ANYWAY.
OH, PLEASE, NOT *YET!* WE'VE HARDLY SEEN ANY OF IT! JUST A FEW MORE HOURS!
WELL...

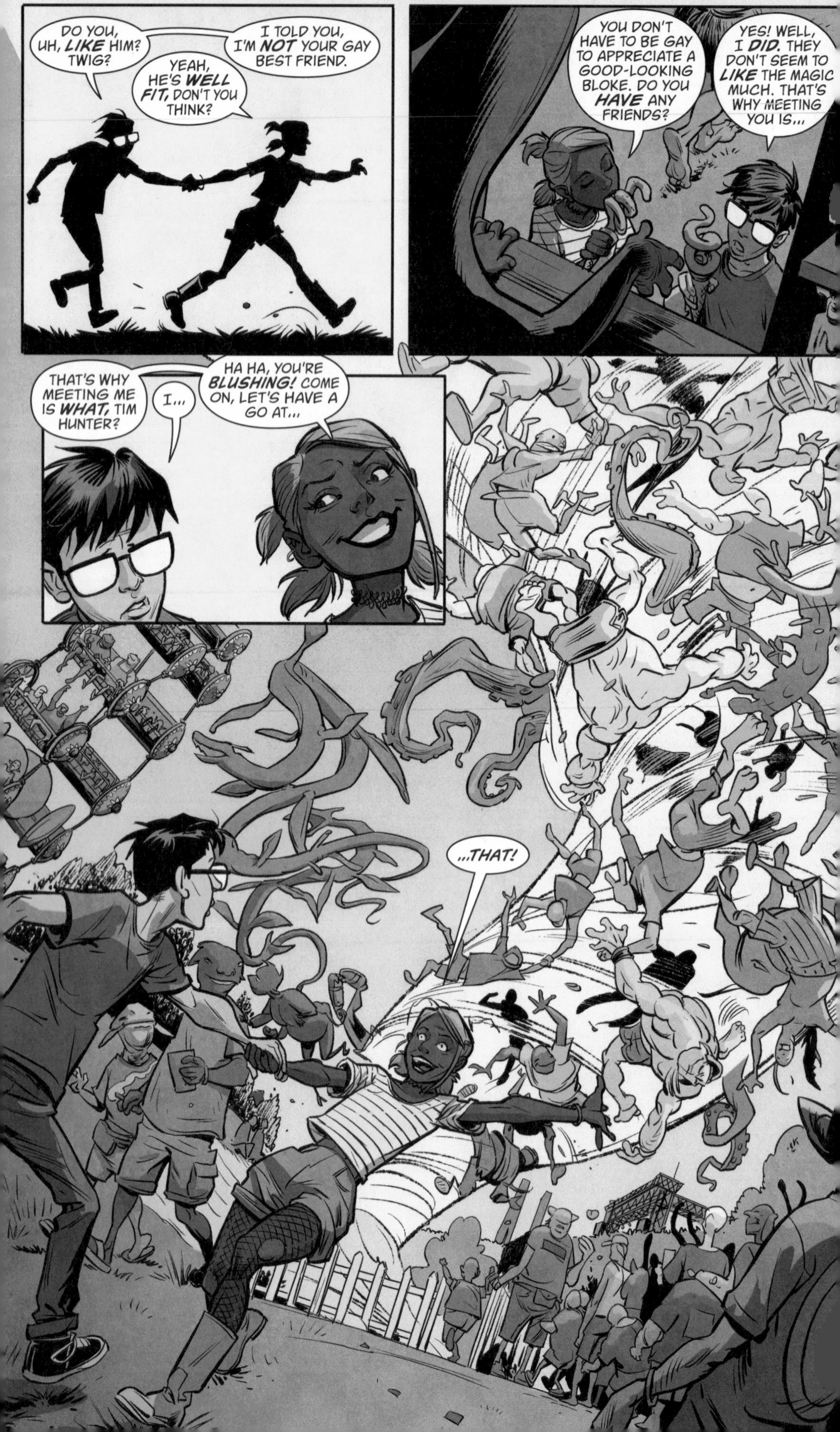
DO YOU, UH, LIKE HIM? TWIG?
I TOLD YOU, I'M NOT YOUR GAY BEST FRIEND.
YEAH, HE'S WELL FIT, DON'T YOU THINK?
YOU DON'T HAVE TO BE GAY TO APPRECIATE A GOOD-LOOKING BLOKE. DO YOU HAVE ANY FRIENDS?
YES! WELL, I DID. THEY DON'T SEEM TO LIKE THE MAGIC MUCH. THAT'S WHY MEETING YOU IS...
THAT'S WHY MEETING ME IS WHAT, TIM HUNTER?
I...
HA HA, YOU'RE BLUSHING! COME ON, LET'S HAVE A GO AT...
...THAT!

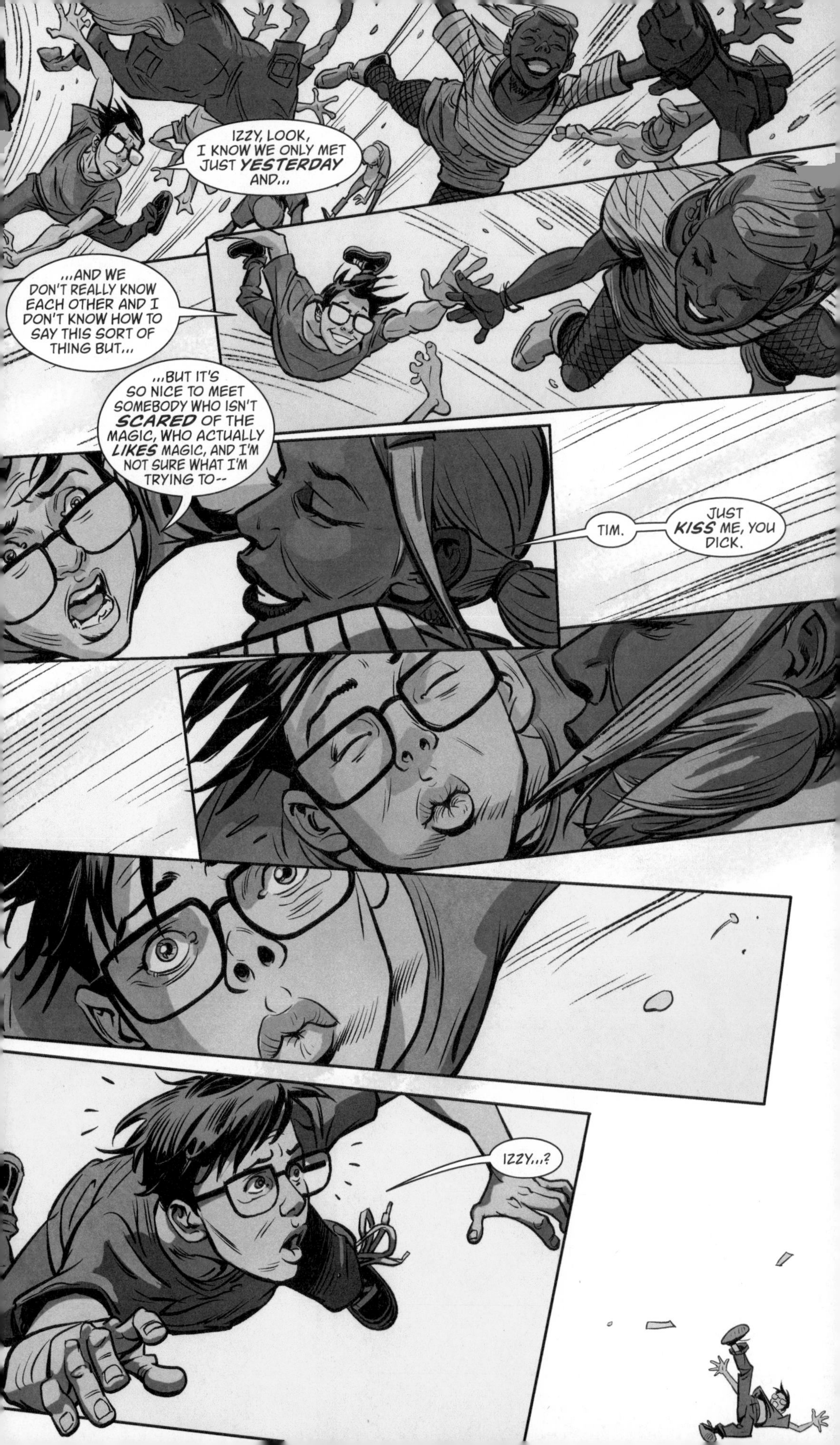
IZZY, LOOK, I KNOW WE ONLY MET JUST YESTERDAY AND...
...AND WE DON'T REALLY KNOW EACH OTHER AND I DON'T KNOW HOW TO SAY THIS SORT OF THING BUT...
...BUT IT'S SO NICE TO MEET SOMEBODY WHO ISN'T SCARED OF THE MAGIC, WHO ACTUALLY LIKES MAGIC, AND I'M NOT SURE WHAT I'M TRYING TO--
TIM.
JUST KISS ME, YOU DICK.
IZZY...?

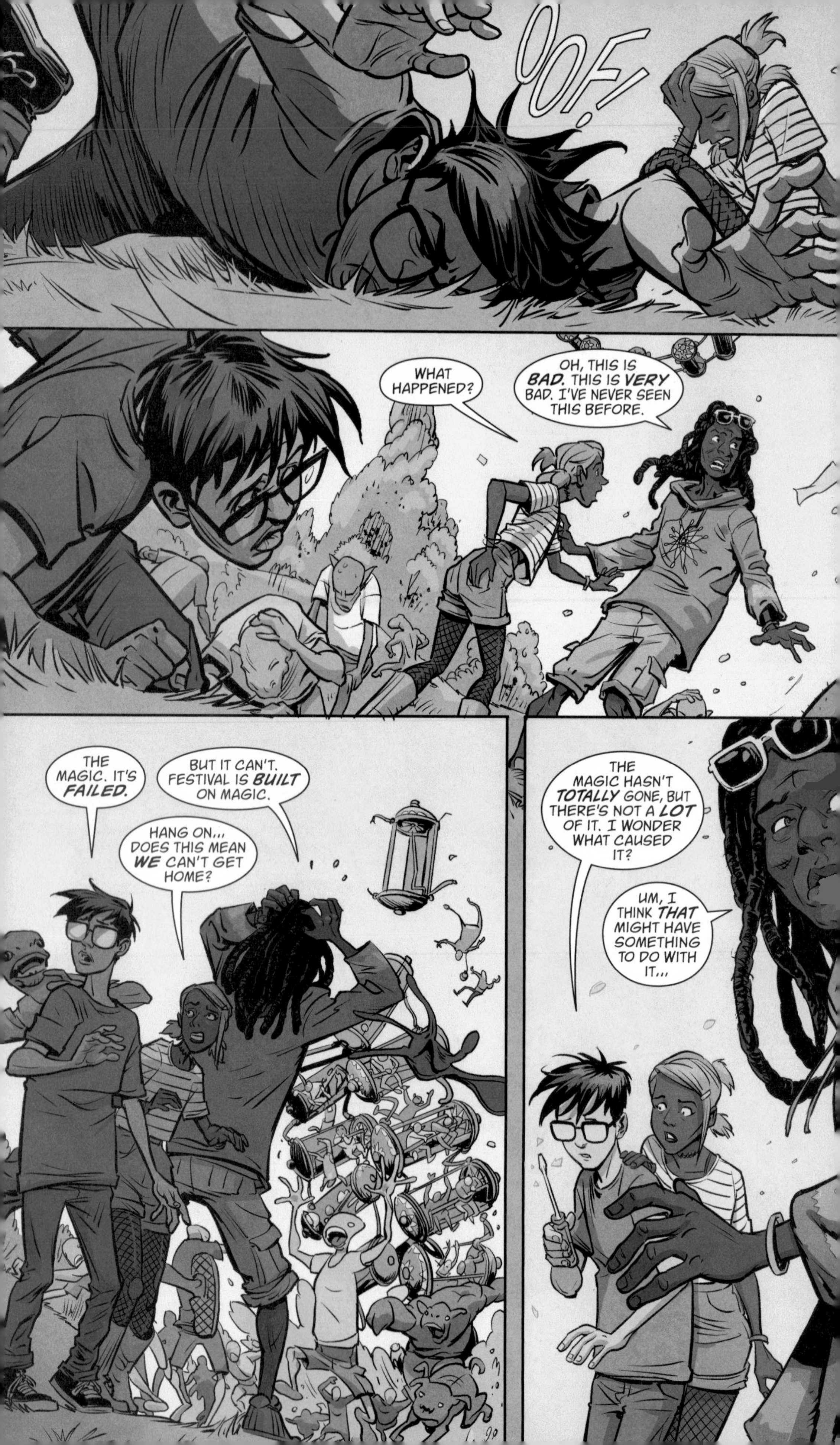
OOF!
WHAT HAPPENED?
OH, THIS IS **BAD.** THIS IS **VERY** BAD. I'VE NEVER SEEN THIS BEFORE.
THE MAGIC. IT'S **FAILED.**
BUT IT CAN'T. FESTIVAL IS **BUILT** ON MAGIC.
HANG ON... DOES THIS MEAN **WE** CAN'T GET HOME?
THE MAGIC HASN'T **TOTALLY** GONE, BUT THERE'S NOT A **LOT** OF IT. I WONDER WHAT CAUSED IT?
UM, I THINK **THAT** MIGHT HAVE SOMETHING TO DO WITH IT...

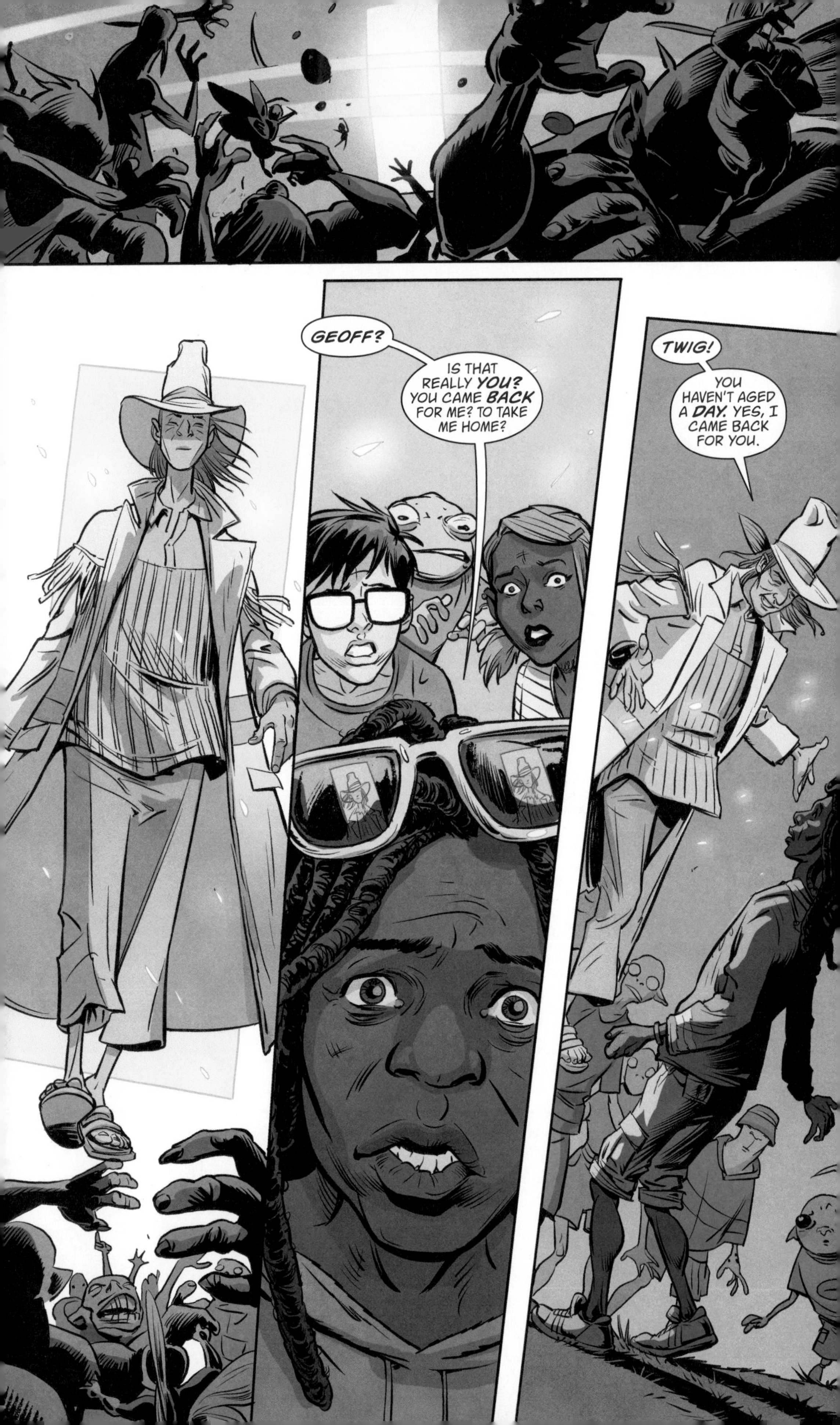
GEOFF?
IS THAT REALLY YOU? YOU CAME BACK FOR ME? TO TAKE ME HOME?
TWIG!
YOU HAVEN'T AGED A DAY. YES, I CAME BACK FOR YOU.

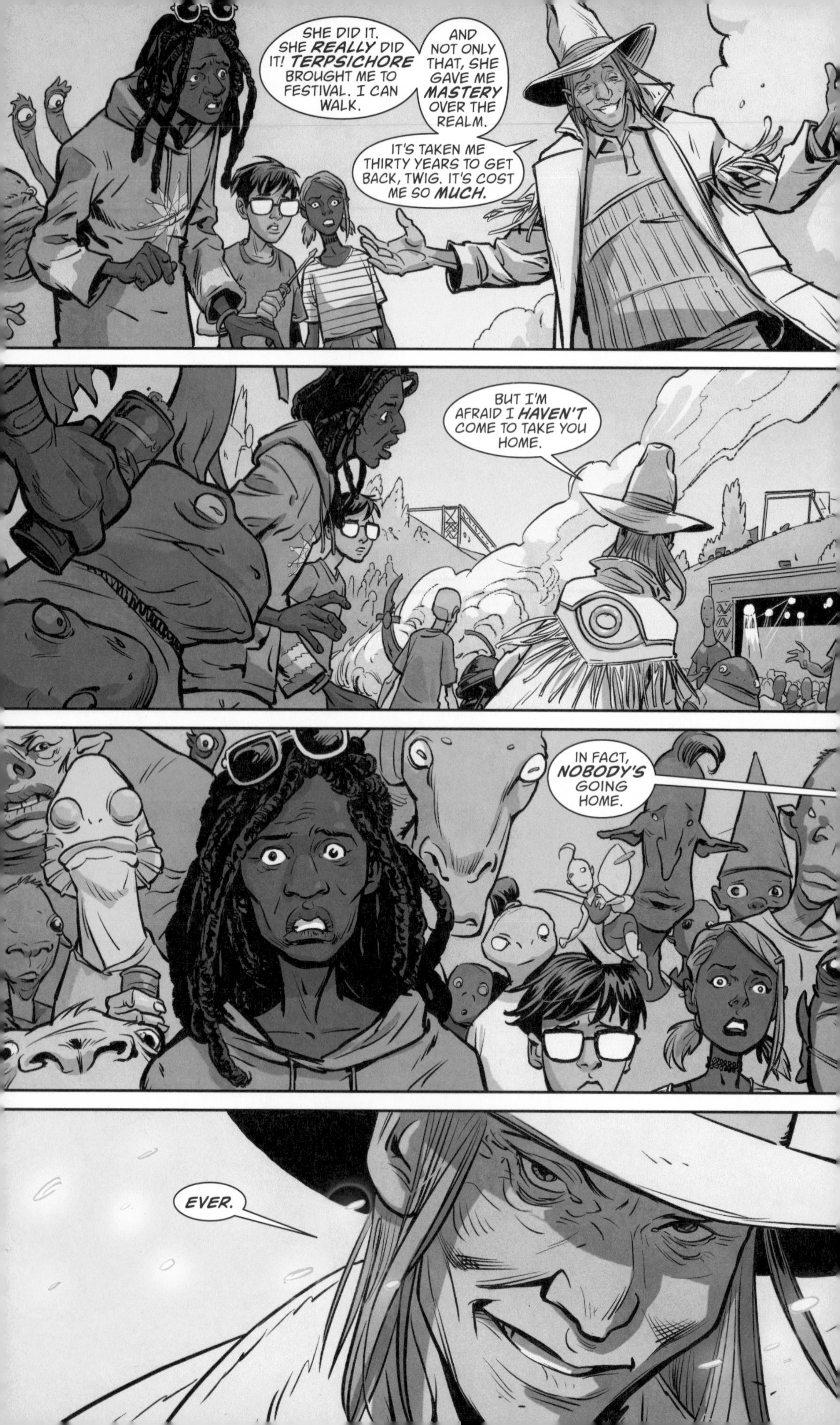

SHE DID IT. SHE *REALLY* DID IT! *TERPSICHORE* BROUGHT ME TO FESTIVAL. I CAN WALK.
AND NOT ONLY THAT, SHE GAVE ME *MASTERY* OVER THE REALM.
IT'S TAKEN ME THIRTY YEARS TO GET BACK, TWIG. IT'S COST ME SO *MUCH.*
BUT I'M AFRAID I *HAVEN'T* COME TO TAKE YOU HOME.
IN FACT, *NOBODY'S* GOING HOME.
EVER.

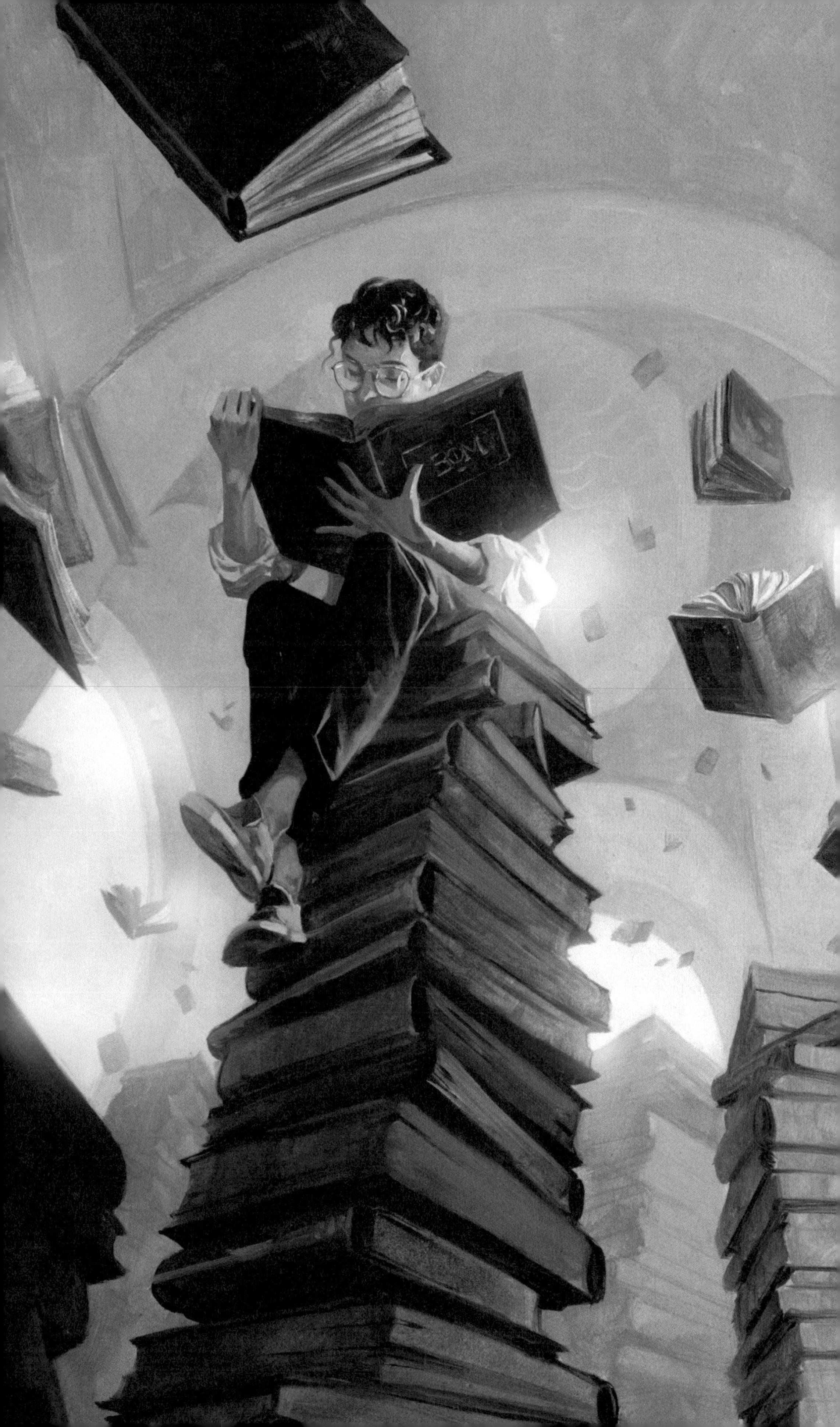

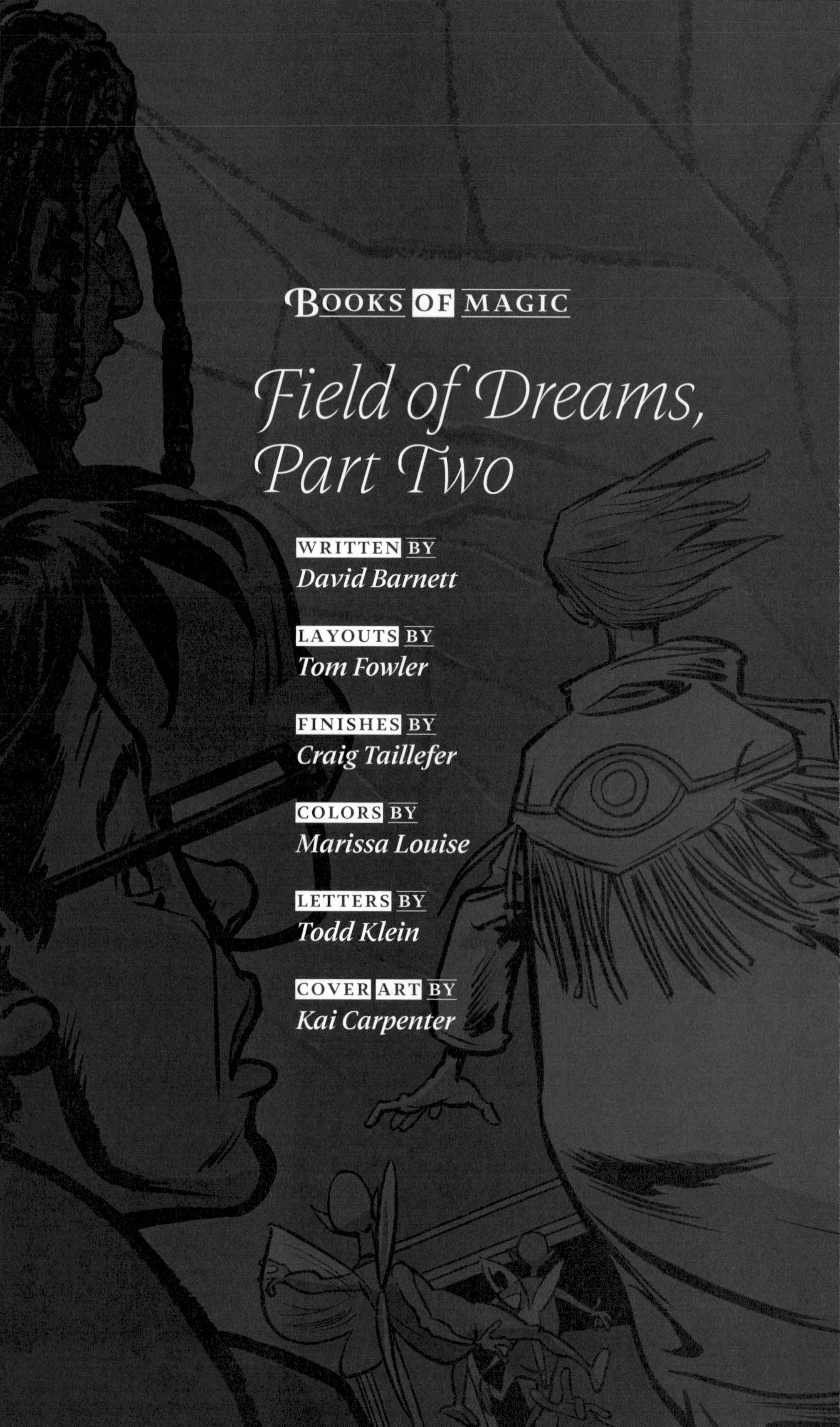

BOOKS OF MAGIC

Field of Dreams, Part Two

WRITTEN BY
David Barnett

LAYOUTS BY
Tom Fowler

FINISHES BY
Craig Taillefer

COLORS BY
Marissa Louise

LETTERS BY
Todd Klein

COVER ART BY
Kai Carpenter

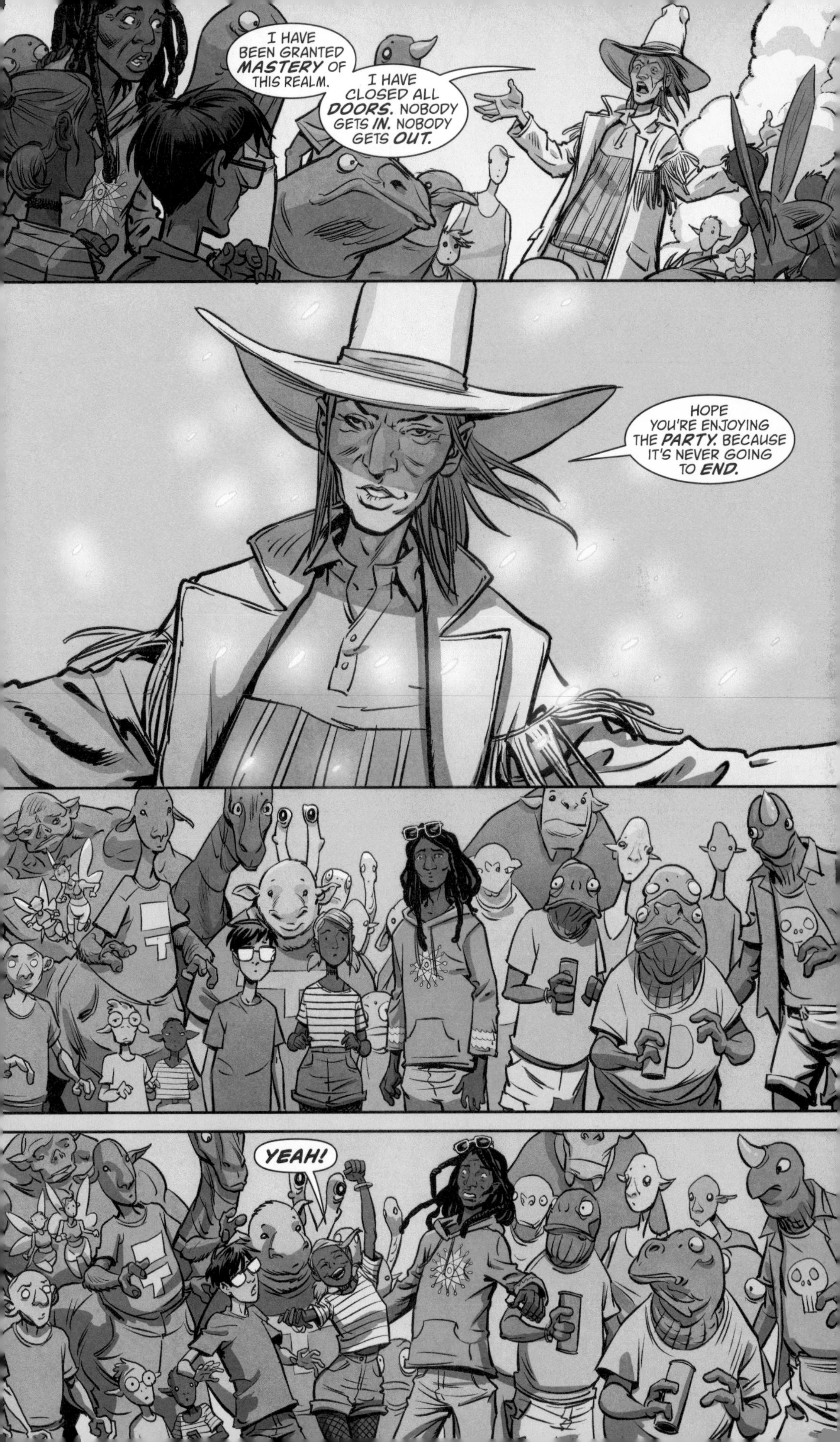
I HAVE BEEN GRANTED MASTERY OF THIS REALM.
I HAVE CLOSED ALL DOORS. NOBODY GETS IN. NOBODY GETS OUT.
HOPE YOU'RE ENJOYING THE PARTY. BECAUSE IT'S NEVER GOING TO END.
YEAH!

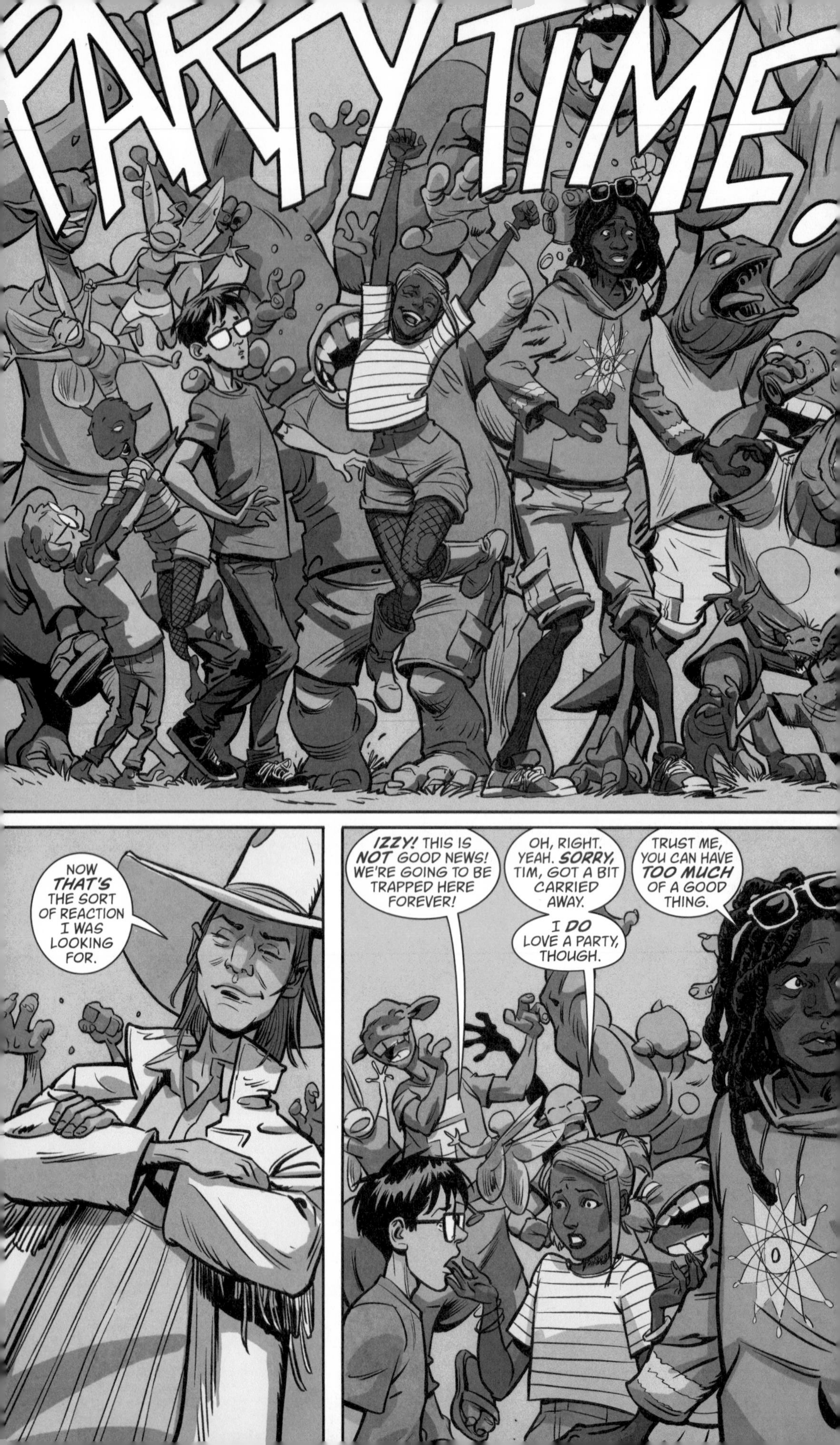
PARTY TIME!
NOW THAT'S THE SORT OF REACTION I WAS LOOKING FOR.
IZZY! THIS IS NOT GOOD NEWS! WE'RE GOING TO BE TRAPPED HERE FOREVER!
OH, RIGHT. YEAH. SORRY, TIM, GOT A BIT CARRIED AWAY.
I DO LOVE A PARTY, THOUGH.
TRUST ME, YOU CAN HAVE TOO MUCH OF A GOOD THING.

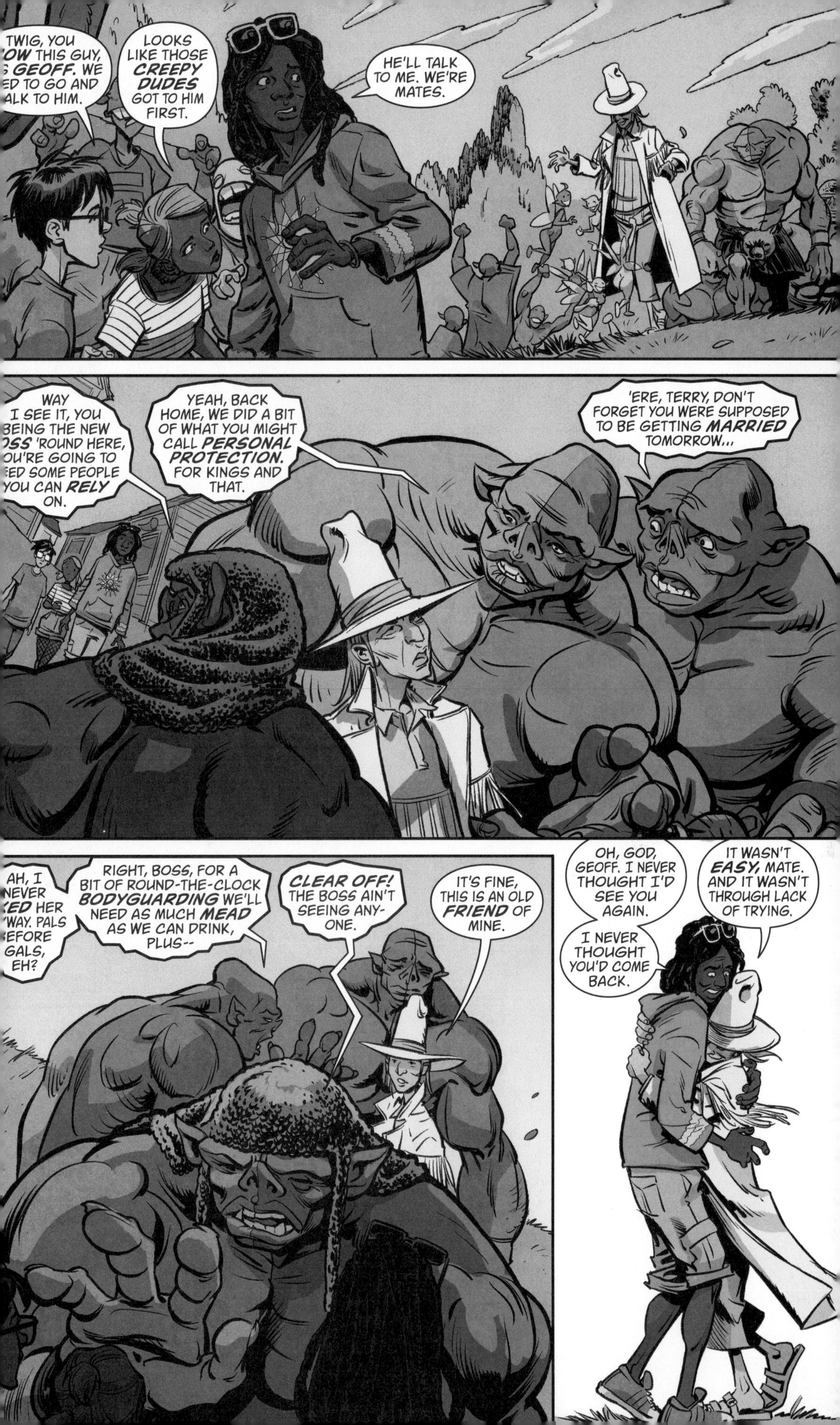
TWIG, YOU OW THIS GUY, S GEOFF. WE ED TO GO AND ALK TO HIM.
LOOKS LIKE THOSE CREEPY DUDES GOT TO HIM FIRST.
HE'LL TALK TO ME. WE'RE MATES.
WAY I SEE IT, YOU BEING THE NEW OSS 'ROUND HERE, OU'RE GOING TO EED SOME PEOPLE YOU CAN RELY ON.
YEAH, BACK HOME, WE DID A BIT OF WHAT YOU MIGHT CALL PERSONAL PROTECTION. FOR KINGS AND THAT.
'ERE, TERRY, DON'T FORGET YOU WERE SUPPOSED TO BE GETTING MARRIED TOMORROW...
AH, I NEVER KED HER WAY. PALS EFORE GALS, EH?
RIGHT, BOSS, FOR A BIT OF ROUND-THE-CLOCK BODYGUARDING WE'LL NEED AS MUCH MEAD AS WE CAN DRINK, PLUS--
CLEAR OFF! THE BOSS AIN'T SEEING ANY-ONE.
IT'S FINE, THIS IS AN OLD FRIEND OF MINE.
OH, GOD, GEOFF. I NEVER THOUGHT I'D SEE YOU AGAIN.
I NEVER THOUGHT YOU'D COME BACK.
IT WASN'T EASY, MATE. AND IT WASN'T THROUGH LACK OF TRYING.

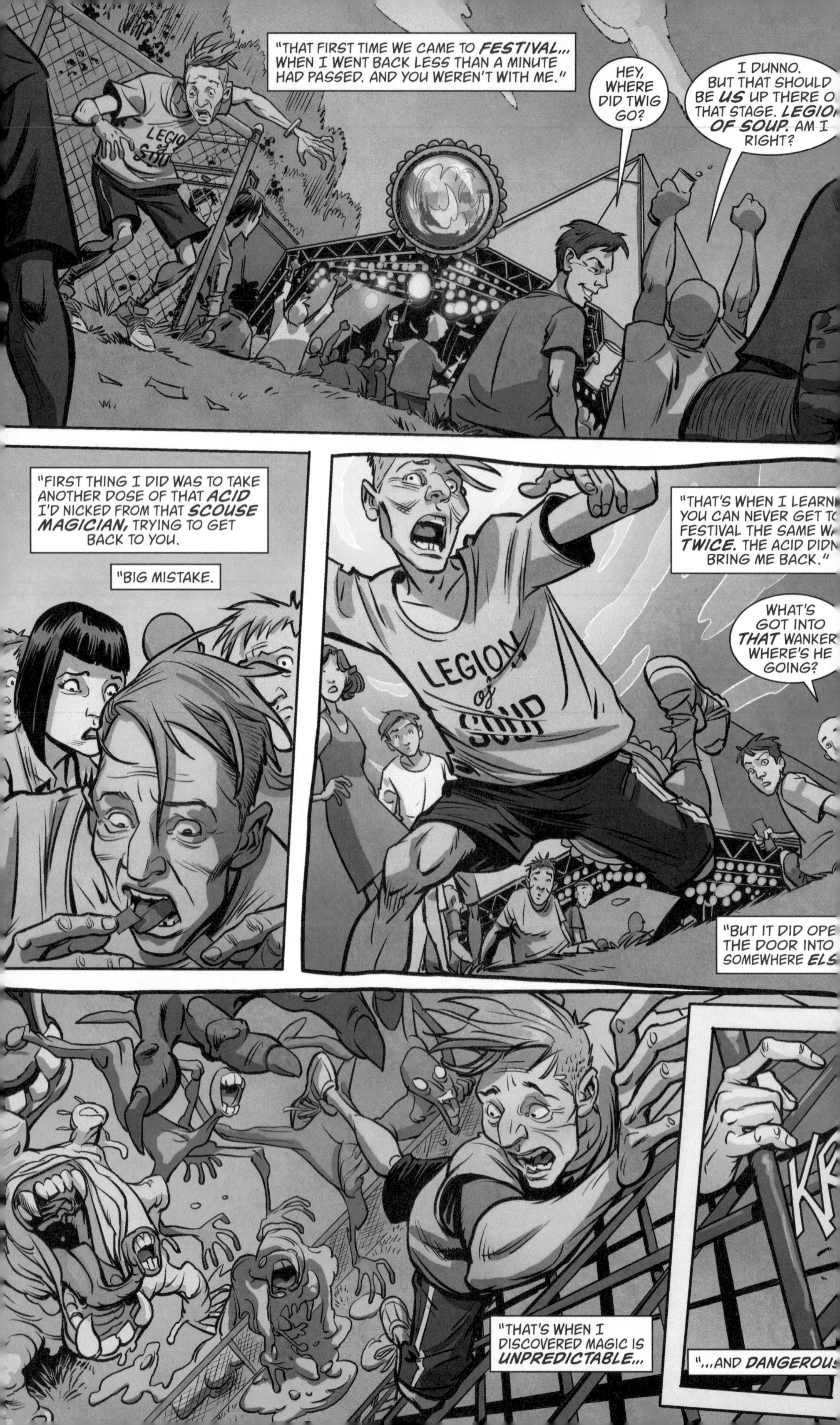

"THAT FIRST TIME WE CAME TO FESTIVAL... WHEN I WENT BACK LESS THAN A MINUTE HAD PASSED. AND YOU WEREN'T WITH ME."
HEY, WHERE DID TWIG GO?
I DUNNO. BUT THAT SHOULD BE US UP THERE O THAT STAGE. LEGIO OF SOUP. AM I RIGHT?
LEGION of SOUP
"FIRST THING I DID WAS TO TAKE ANOTHER DOSE OF THAT ACID I'D NICKED FROM THAT SCOUSE MAGICIAN, TRYING TO GET BACK TO YOU.
"BIG MISTAKE.
"THAT'S WHEN I LEARN YOU CAN NEVER GET TO FESTIVAL THE SAME WA TWICE. THE ACID DIDN BRING ME BACK."
WHAT'S GOT INTO THAT WANKER WHERE'S HE GOING?
LEGION of SOUP
"BUT IT DID OPE THE DOOR INTO SOMEWHERE ELS
"THAT'S WHEN I DISCOVERED MAGIC IS UNPREDICTABLE...
"...AND DANGEROU

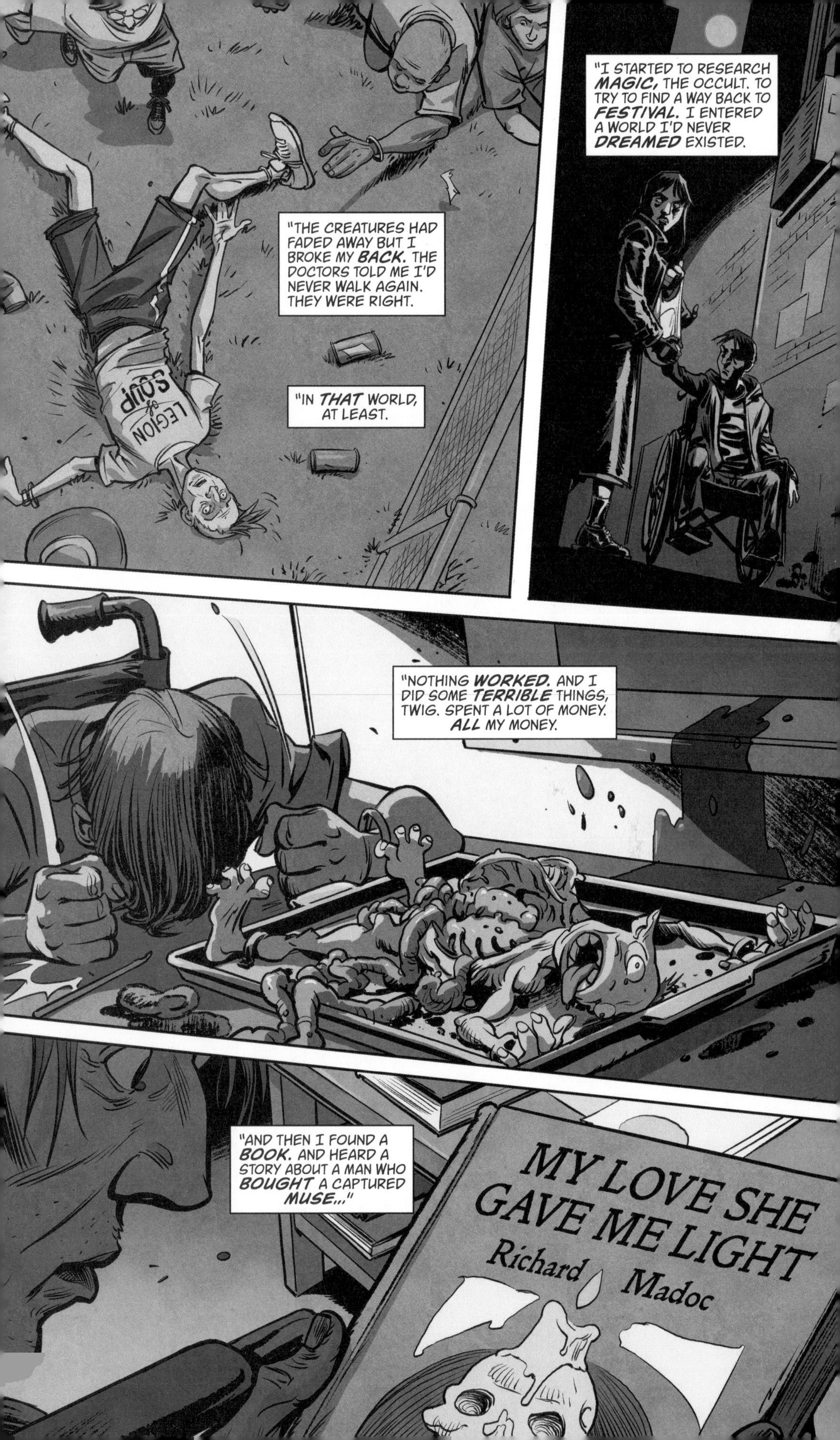
"THE CREATURES HAD FADED AWAY BUT I BROKE MY BACK. THE DOCTORS TOLD ME I'D NEVER WALK AGAIN. THEY WERE RIGHT.
"IN THAT WORLD, AT LEAST.
LEGION of SOUP
"I STARTED TO RESEARCH MAGIC, THE OCCULT. TO TRY TO FIND A WAY BACK TO FESTIVAL. I ENTERED A WORLD I'D NEVER DREAMED EXISTED.
"NOTHING WORKED. AND I DID SOME TERRIBLE THINGS, TWIG. SPENT A LOT OF MONEY. ALL MY MONEY.
"AND THEN I FOUND A BOOK. AND HEARD A STORY ABOUT A MAN WHO BOUGHT A CAPTURED MUSE..."
MY LOVE SHE GAVE ME LIGHT
Richard Madoc

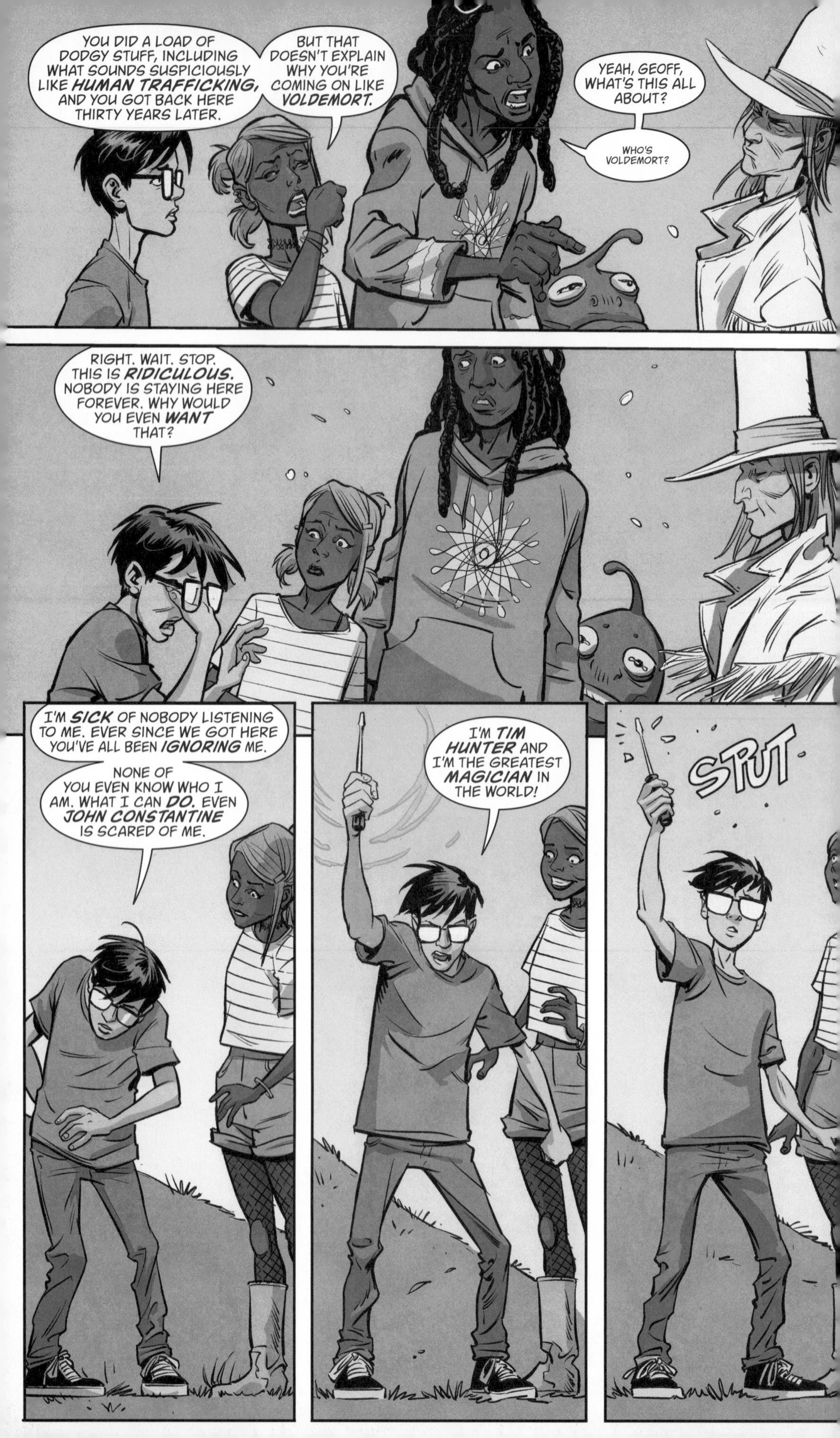
YOU DID A LOAD OF DODGY STUFF, INCLUDING WHAT SOUNDS SUSPICIOUSLY LIKE HUMAN TRAFFICKING, AND YOU GOT BACK HERE THIRTY YEARS LATER.
BUT THAT DOESN'T EXPLAIN WHY YOU'RE COMING ON LIKE VOLDEMORT.
YEAH, GEOFF, WHAT'S THIS ALL ABOUT?
WHO'S VOLDEMORT?
RIGHT. WAIT. STOP. THIS IS RIDICULOUS. NOBODY IS STAYING HERE FOREVER. WHY WOULD YOU EVEN WANT THAT?
I'M SICK OF NOBODY LISTENING TO ME. EVER SINCE WE GOT HERE YOU'VE ALL BEEN IGNORING ME.
NONE OF YOU EVEN KNOW WHO I AM. WHAT I CAN DO. EVEN JOHN CONSTANTINE IS SCARED OF ME.
I'M TIM HUNTER AND I'M THE GREATEST MAGICIAN IN THE WORLD!
SPUT

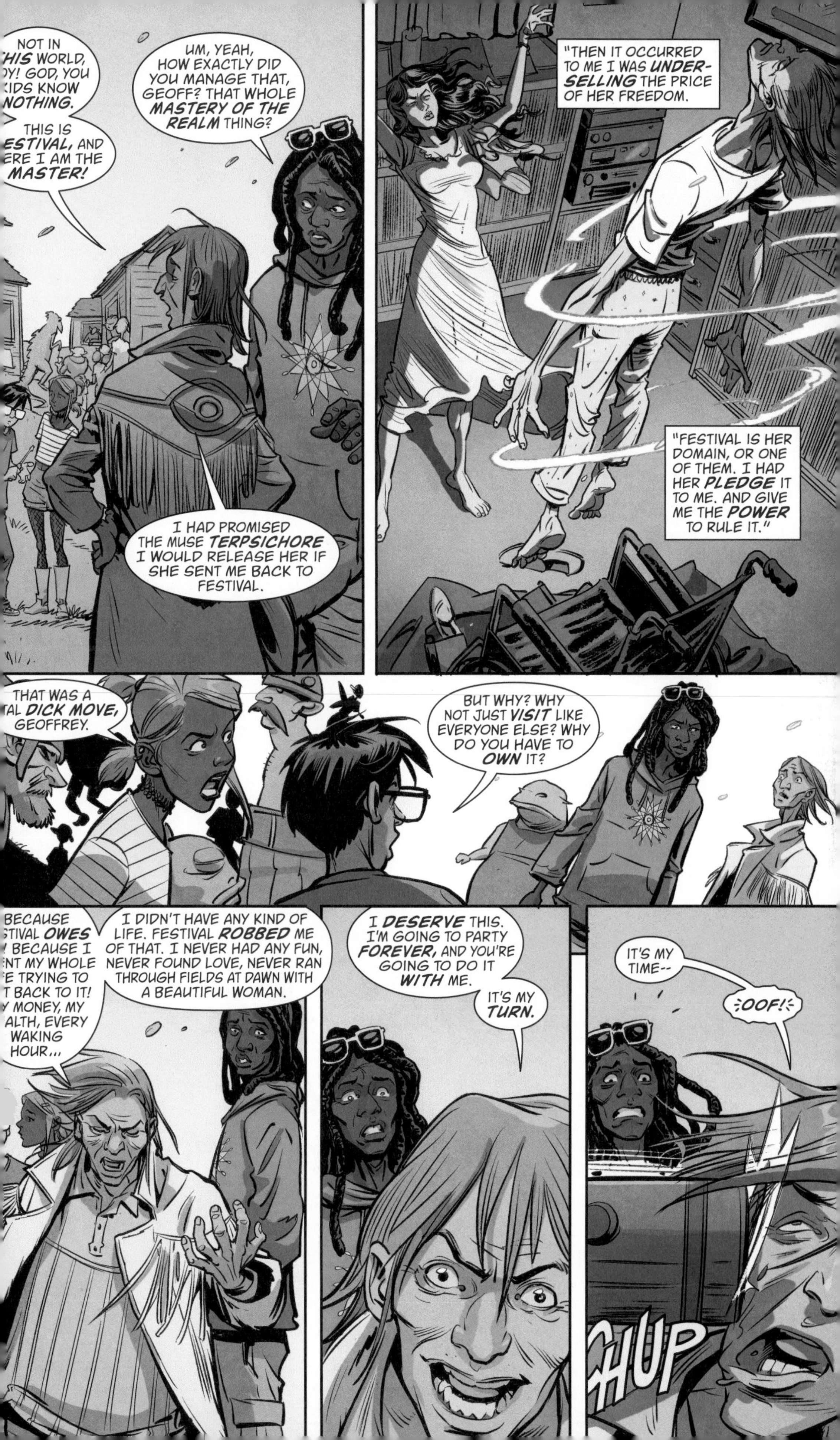

NOT IN THIS WORLD, OY! GOD, YOU KIDS KNOW NOTHING.
THIS IS ESTIVAL, AND ERE I AM THE MASTER!
UM, YEAH, HOW EXACTLY DID YOU MANAGE THAT, GEOFF? THAT WHOLE MASTERY OF THE REALM THING?
I HAD PROMISED THE MUSE TERPSICHORE I WOULD RELEASE HER IF SHE SENT ME BACK TO FESTIVAL.
"THEN IT OCCURRED TO ME I WAS UNDER-SELLING THE PRICE OF HER FREEDOM.
"FESTIVAL IS HER DOMAIN, OR ONE OF THEM. I HAD HER PLEDGE IT TO ME. AND GIVE ME THE POWER TO RULE IT."
THAT WAS A AL DICK MOVE, GEOFFREY.
BUT WHY? WHY NOT JUST VISIT LIKE EVERYONE ELSE? WHY DO YOU HAVE TO OWN IT?
BECAUSE STIVAL OWES BECAUSE I NT MY WHOLE E TRYING TO T BACK TO IT! MONEY, MY ALTH, EVERY WAKING HOUR...
I DIDN'T HAVE ANY KIND OF LIFE. FESTIVAL ROBBED ME OF THAT. I NEVER HAD ANY FUN, NEVER FOUND LOVE, NEVER RAN THROUGH FIELDS AT DAWN WITH A BEAUTIFUL WOMAN.
I DESERVE THIS. I'M GOING TO PARTY FOREVER, AND YOU'RE GOING TO DO IT WITH ME.
IT'S MY TURN.
IT'S MY TIME--
OOF!
CHUP

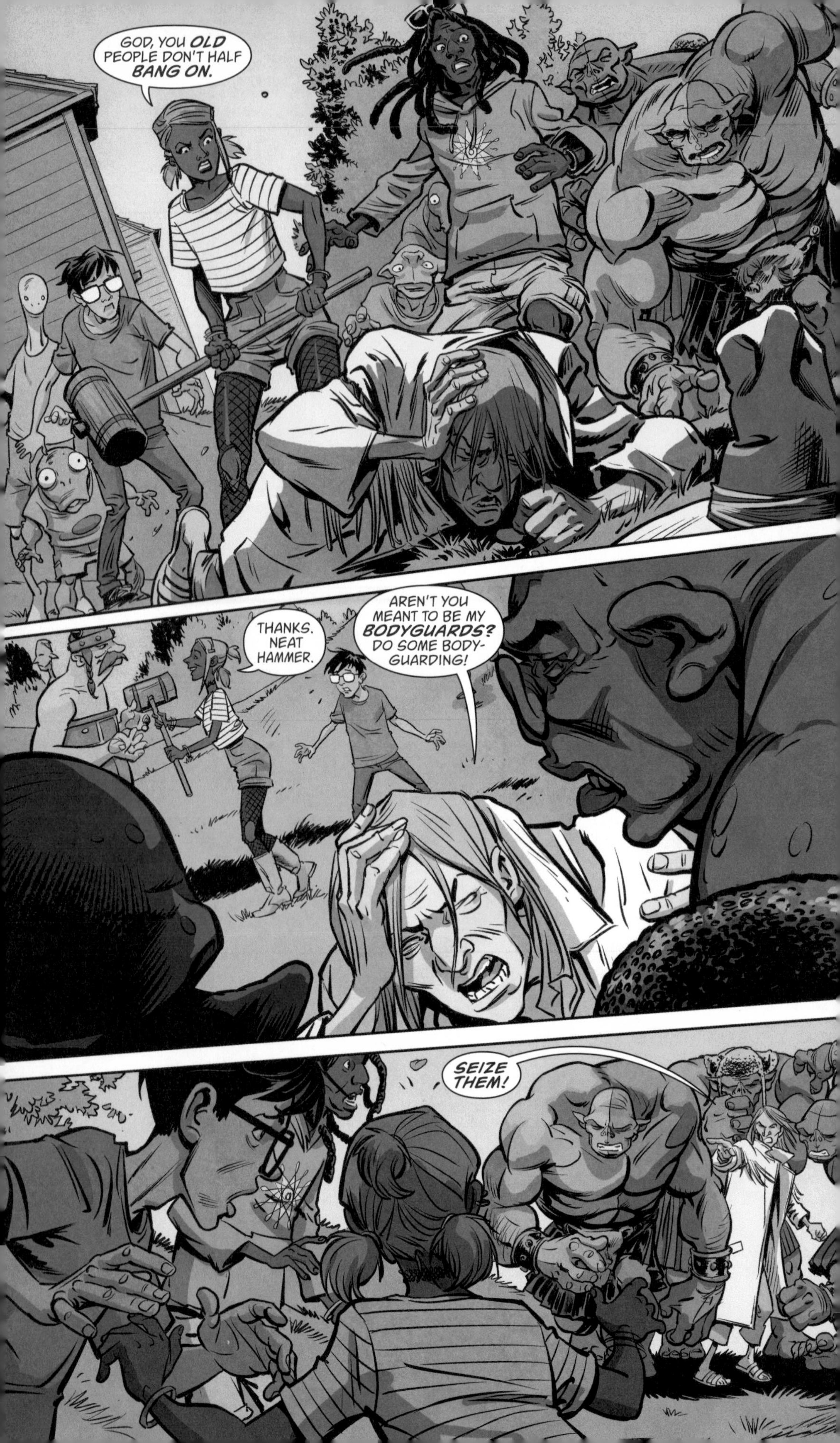
GOD, YOU **OLD** PEOPLE DON'T HALF **BANG ON.**
THANKS. NEAT HAMMER.
AREN'T YOU MEANT TO BE MY **BODYGUARDS?** DO SOME BODY-GUARDING!
SEIZE THEM!

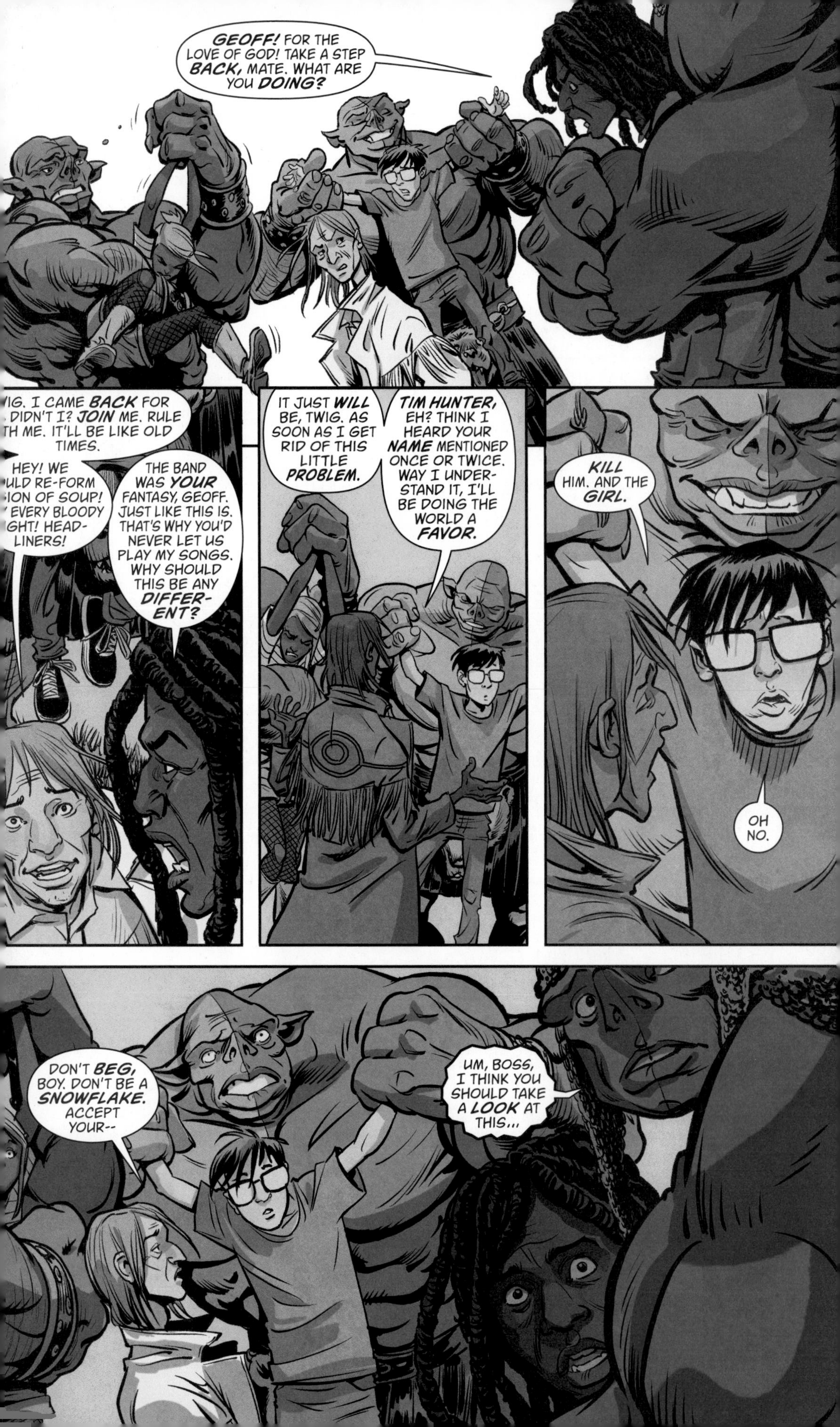
GEOFF! FOR THE LOVE OF GOD! TAKE A STEP BACK, MATE. WHAT ARE YOU DOING?
IG. I CAME BACK FOR . DIDN'T I? JOIN ME. RULE TH ME. IT'LL BE LIKE OLD TIMES.
HEY! WE ULD RE-FORM ION OF SOUP! EVERY BLOODY GHT! HEAD-LINERS!
THE BAND WAS YOUR FANTASY, GEOFF. JUST LIKE THIS IS. THAT'S WHY YOU'D NEVER LET US PLAY MY SONGS. WHY SHOULD THIS BE ANY DIFFER-ENT?
IT JUST WILL BE, TWIG. AS SOON AS I GET RID OF THIS LITTLE PROBLEM.
TIM HUNTER, EH? THINK I HEARD YOUR NAME MENTIONED ONCE OR TWICE. WAY I UNDER-STAND IT, I'LL BE DOING THE WORLD A FAVOR.
KILL HIM. AND THE GIRL.
OH NO.
DON'T BEG, BOY. DON'T BE A SNOWFLAKE. ACCEPT YOUR--
UM, BOSS, I THINK YOU SHOULD TAKE A LOOK AT THIS...

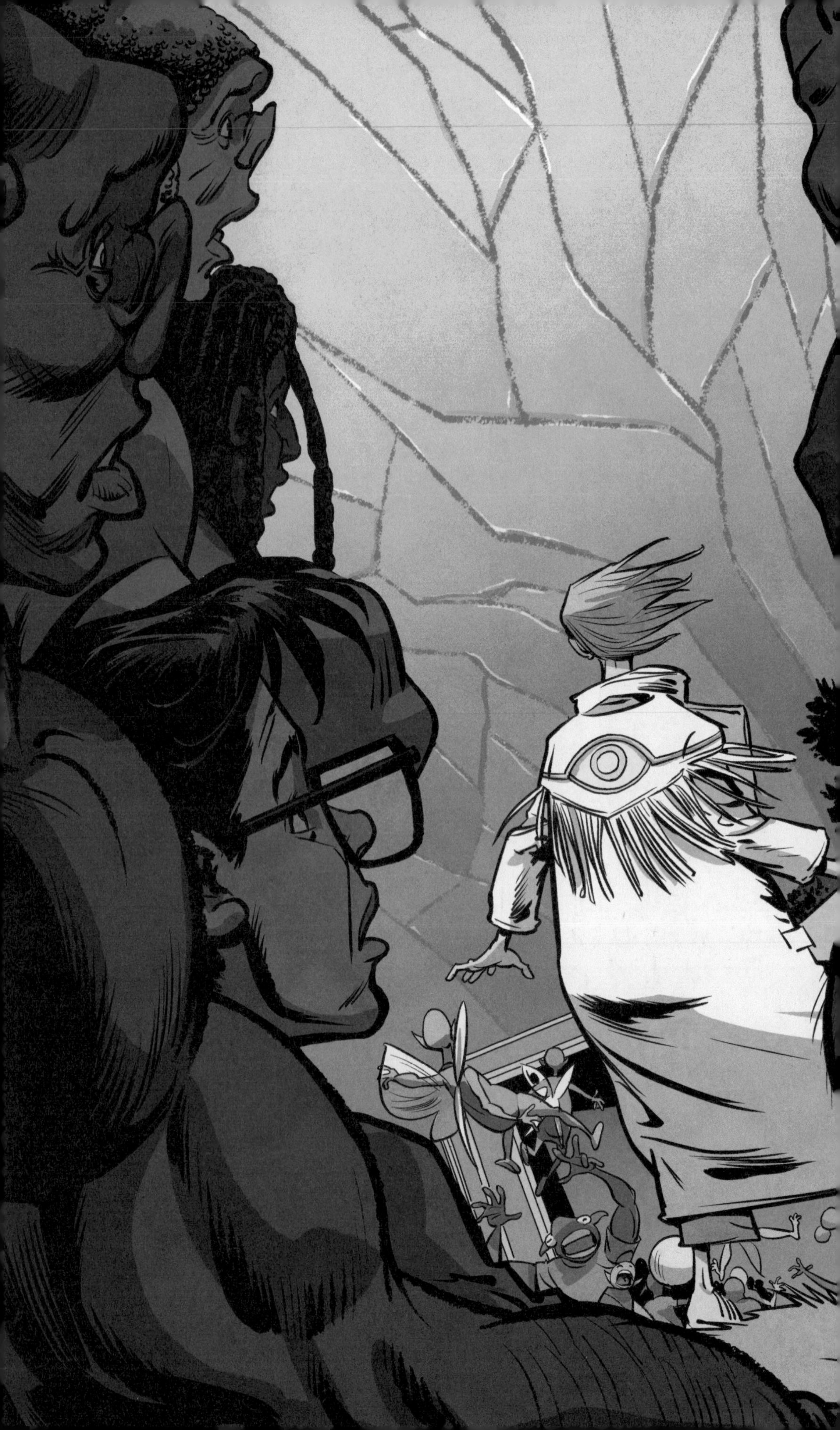

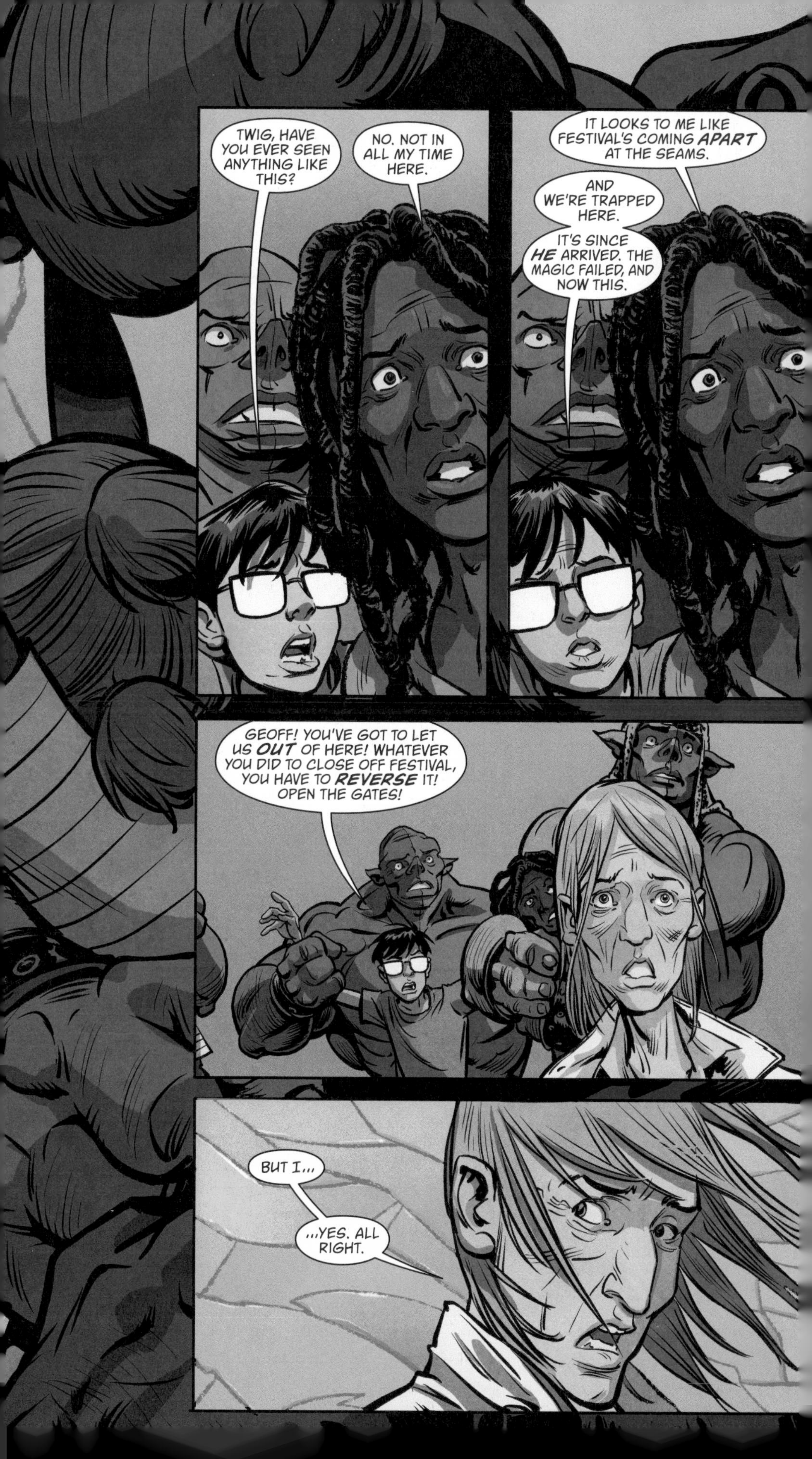
TWIG, HAVE YOU EVER SEEN ANYTHING LIKE THIS?
NO. NOT IN ALL MY TIME HERE.
IT LOOKS TO ME LIKE FESTIVAL'S COMING *APART* AT THE SEAMS.
AND WE'RE TRAPPED HERE.
IT'S SINCE *HE* ARRIVED. THE MAGIC FAILED, AND NOW THIS.
GEOFF! YOU'VE GOT TO LET US *OUT* OF HERE! WHATEVER YOU DID TO CLOSE OFF FESTIVAL, YOU HAVE TO *REVERSE* IT! OPEN THE GATES!
BUT I...
...YES. ALL RIGHT.

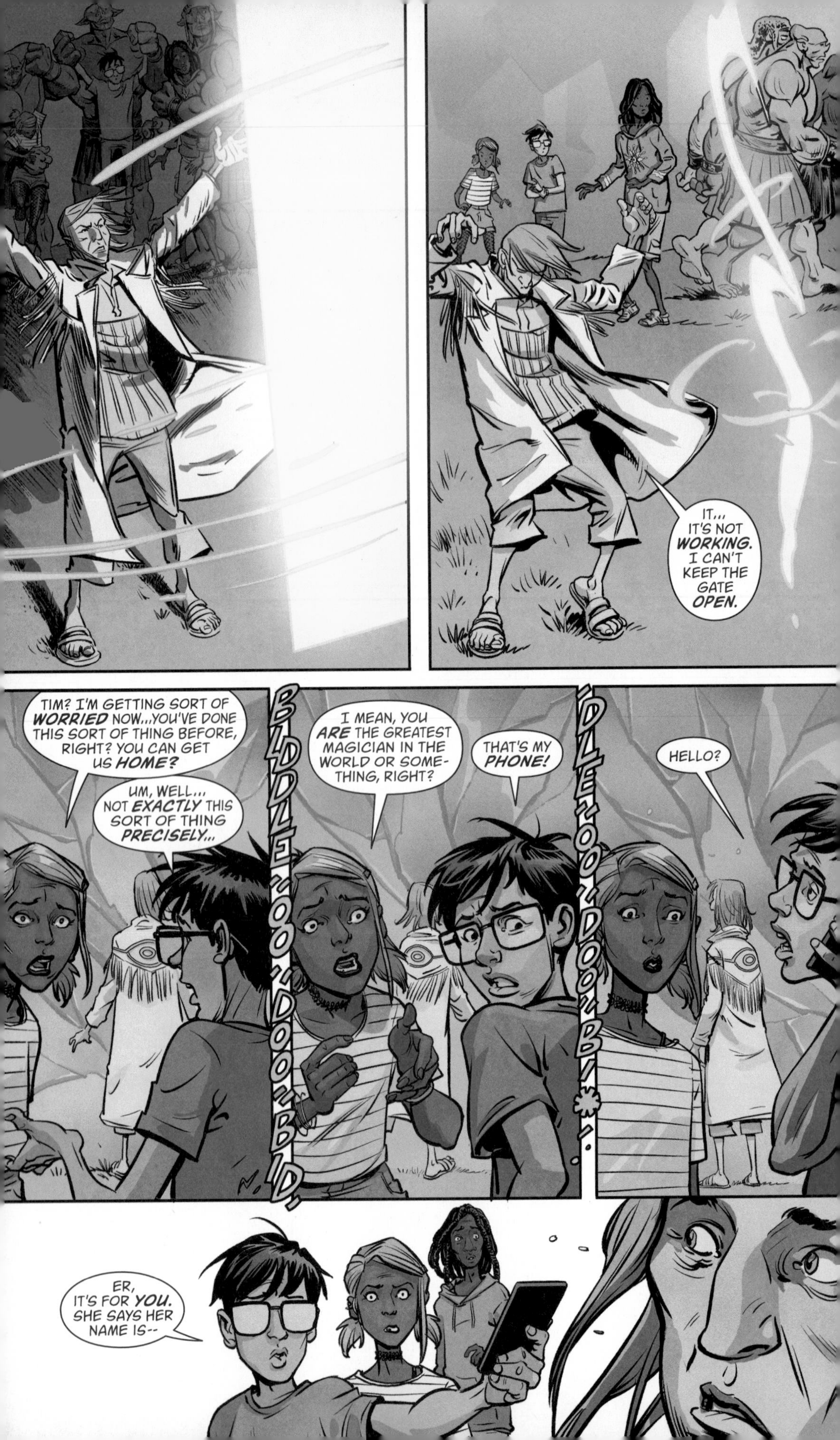
IT... IT'S NOT WORKING. I CAN'T KEEP THE GATE OPEN.
TIM? I'M GETTING SORT OF WORRIED NOW...YOU'VE DONE THIS SORT OF THING BEFORE, RIGHT? YOU CAN GET US HOME?
UM, WELL... NOT EXACTLY THIS SORT OF THING PRECISELY...
BIDDLE-OO-DOO-BID,
I MEAN, YOU ARE THE GREATEST MAGICIAN IN THE WORLD OR SOME-THING, RIGHT?
THAT'S MY PHONE!
DLE-OO-DOO-BI*!
HELLO?
ER, IT'S FOR YOU. SHE SAYS HER NAME IS--

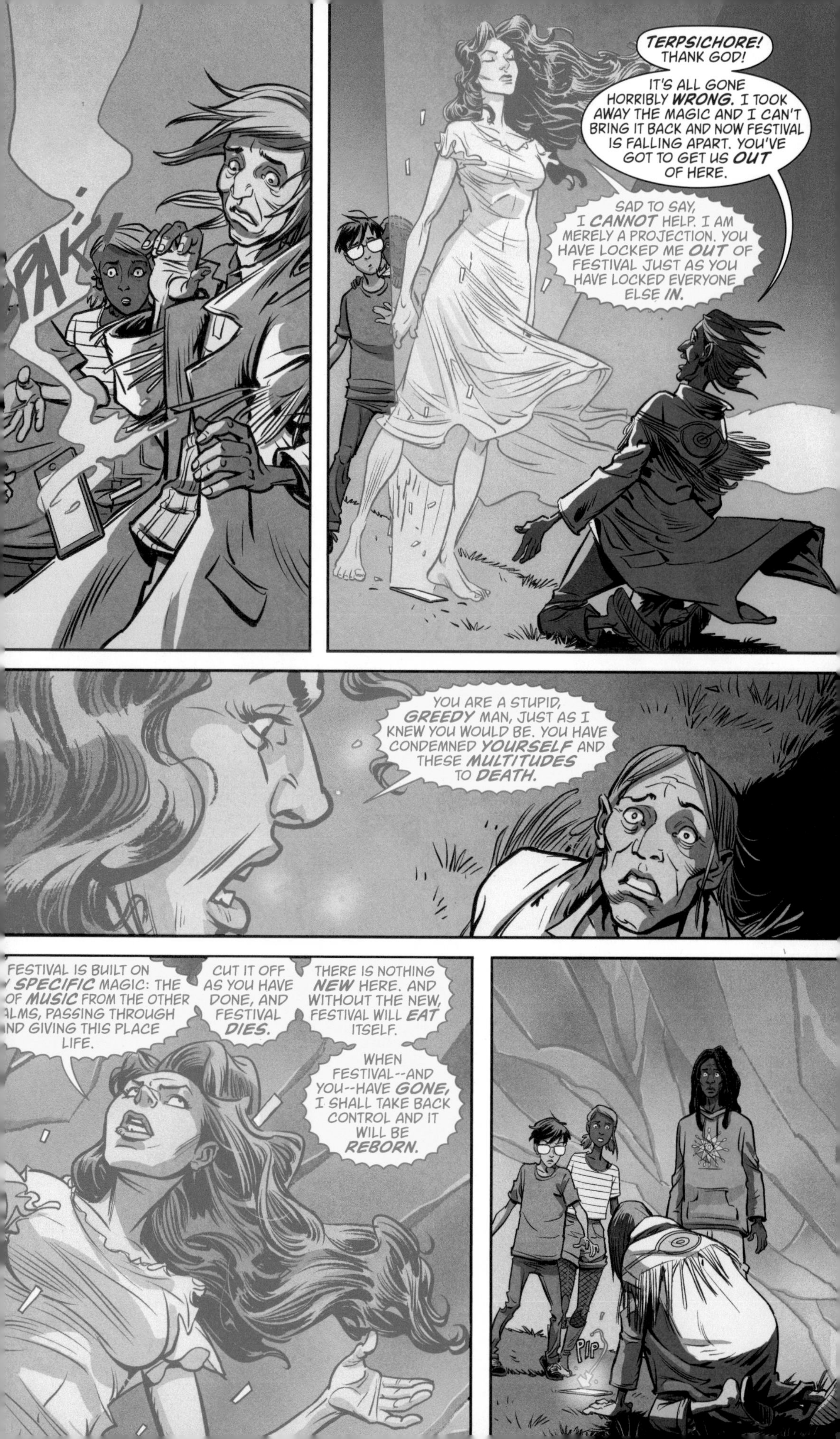
PAK!
TERPSICHORE! THANK GOD!
IT'S ALL GONE HORRIBLY WRONG. I TOOK AWAY THE MAGIC AND I CAN'T BRING IT BACK AND NOW FESTIVAL IS FALLING APART. YOU'VE GOT TO GET US OUT OF HERE.
SAD TO SAY, I CANNOT HELP. I AM MERELY A PROJECTION. YOU HAVE LOCKED ME OUT OF FESTIVAL JUST AS YOU HAVE LOCKED EVERYONE ELSE IN.
YOU ARE A STUPID, GREEDY MAN, JUST AS I KNEW YOU WOULD BE. YOU HAVE CONDEMNED YOURSELF AND THESE MULTITUDES TO DEATH.
FESTIVAL IS BUILT ON SPECIFIC MAGIC: THE OF MUSIC FROM THE OTHER ALMS, PASSING THROUGH ND GIVING THIS PLACE LIFE.
CUT IT OFF AS YOU HAVE DONE, AND FESTIVAL DIES.
THERE IS NOTHING NEW HERE. AND WITHOUT THE NEW, FESTIVAL WILL EAT ITSELF.
WHEN FESTIVAL--AND YOU--HAVE GONE, I SHALL TAKE BACK CONTROL AND IT WILL BE REBORN.
PIP

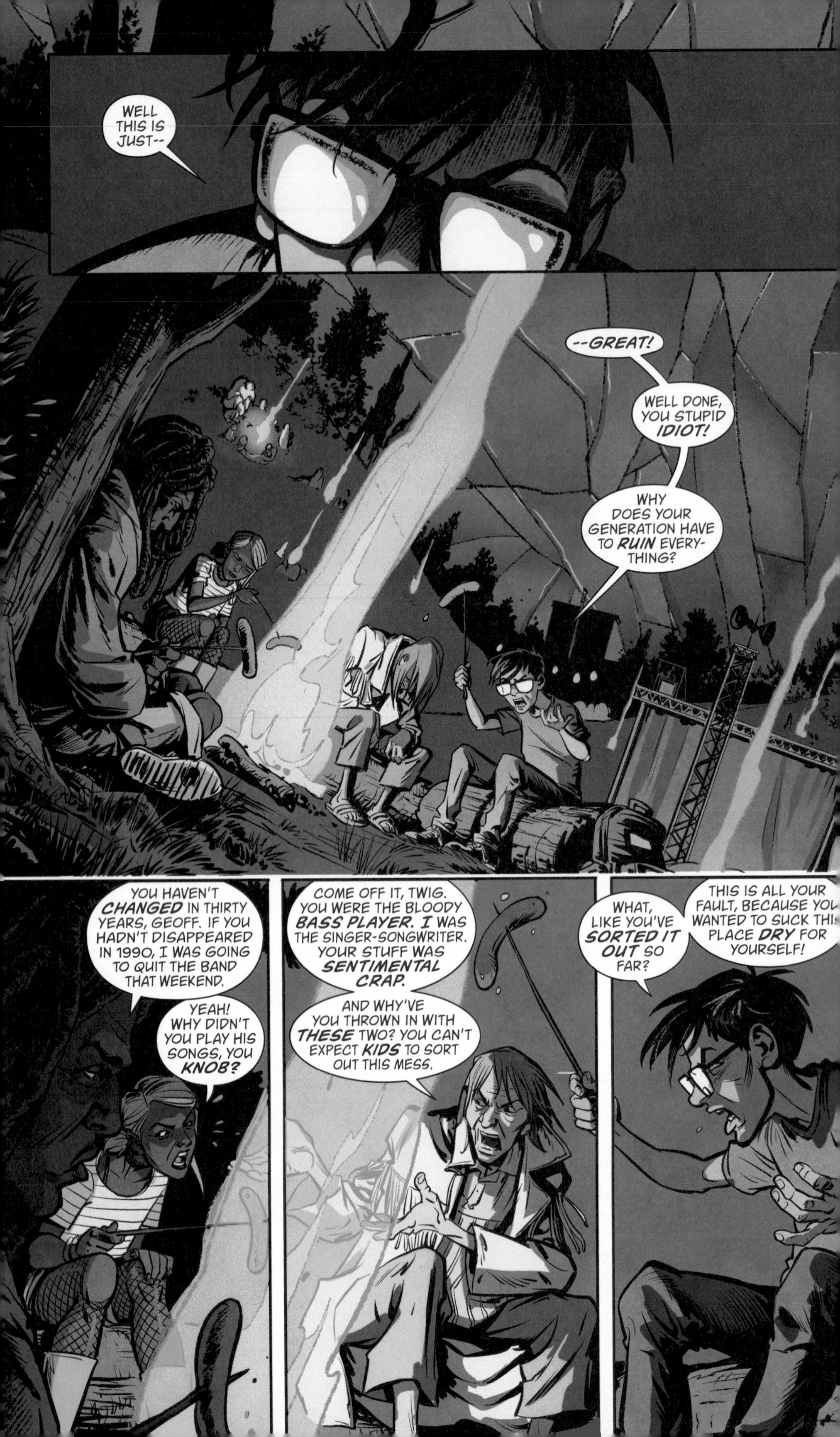
WELL THIS IS JUST--
--GREAT!
WELL DONE, YOU STUPID IDIOT!
WHY DOES YOUR GENERATION HAVE TO RUIN EVERY-THING?
YOU HAVEN'T CHANGED IN THIRTY YEARS, GEOFF. IF YOU HADN'T DISAPPEARED IN 1990, I WAS GOING TO QUIT THE BAND THAT WEEKEND.
YEAH! WHY DIDN'T YOU PLAY HIS SONGS, YOU KNOB?
COME OFF IT, TWIG. YOU WERE THE BLOODY BASS PLAYER. I WAS THE SINGER-SONGWRITER. YOUR STUFF WAS SENTIMENTAL CRAP.
AND WHY'VE YOU THROWN IN WITH THESE TWO? YOU CAN'T EXPECT KIDS TO SORT OUT THIS MESS.
WHAT, LIKE YOU'VE SORTED IT OUT SO FAR?
THIS IS ALL YOUR FAULT, BECAUSE YOU WANTED TO SUCK THIS PLACE DRY FOR YOURSELF!

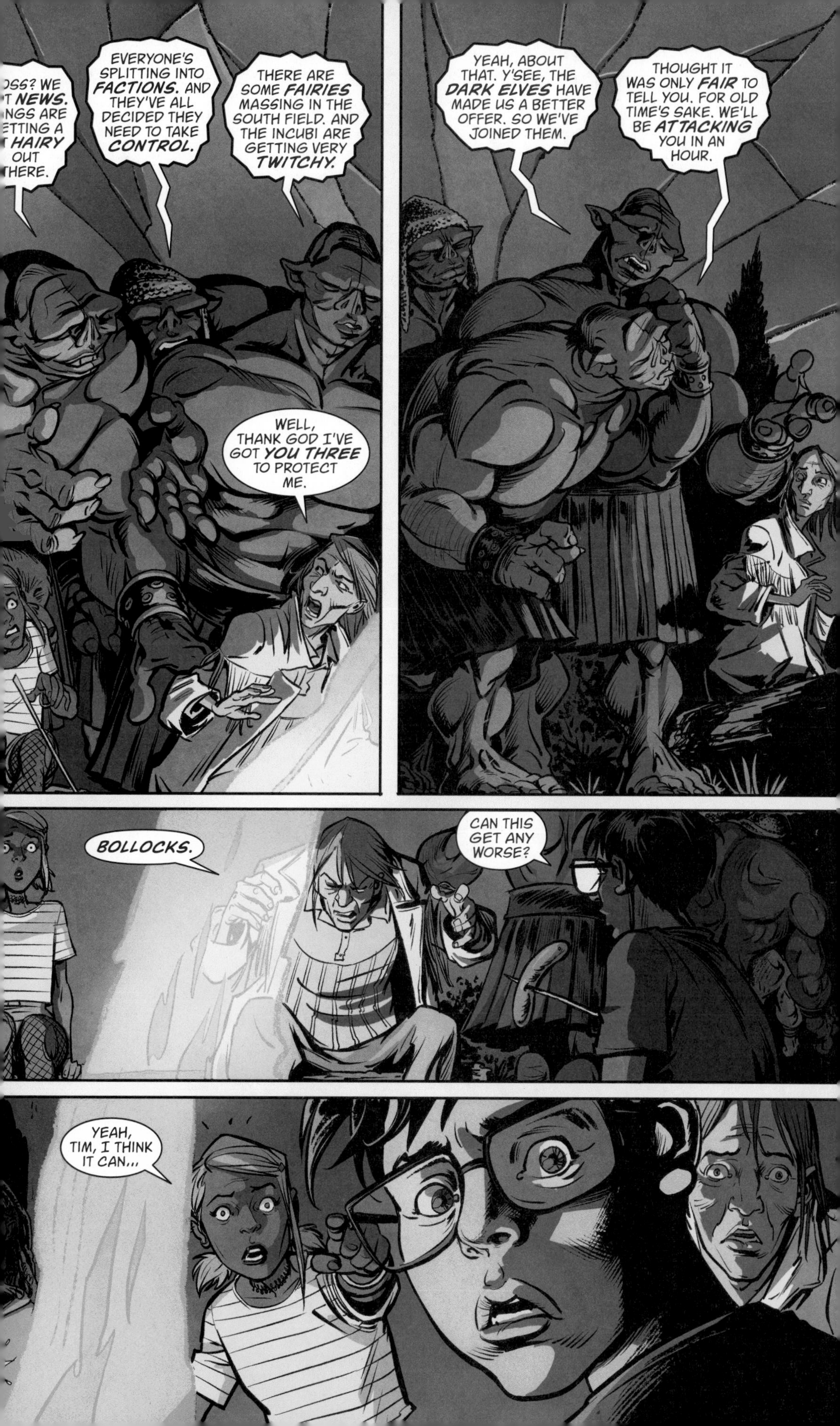

EVERYONE'S SPLITTING INTO FACTIONS. AND THEY'VE ALL DECIDED THEY NEED TO TAKE CONTROL.
THERE ARE SOME FAIRIES MASSING IN THE SOUTH FIELD. AND THE INCUBI ARE GETTING VERY TWITCHY.
WELL, THANK GOD I'VE GOT YOU THREE TO PROTECT ME.
YEAH, ABOUT THAT. Y'SEE, THE DARK ELVES HAVE MADE US A BETTER OFFER. SO WE'VE JOINED THEM.
THOUGHT IT WAS ONLY FAIR TO TELL YOU. FOR OLD TIME'S SAKE. WE'LL BE ATTACKING YOU IN AN HOUR.
BOLLOCKS.
CAN THIS GET ANY WORSE?
YEAH, TIM, I THINK IT CAN...

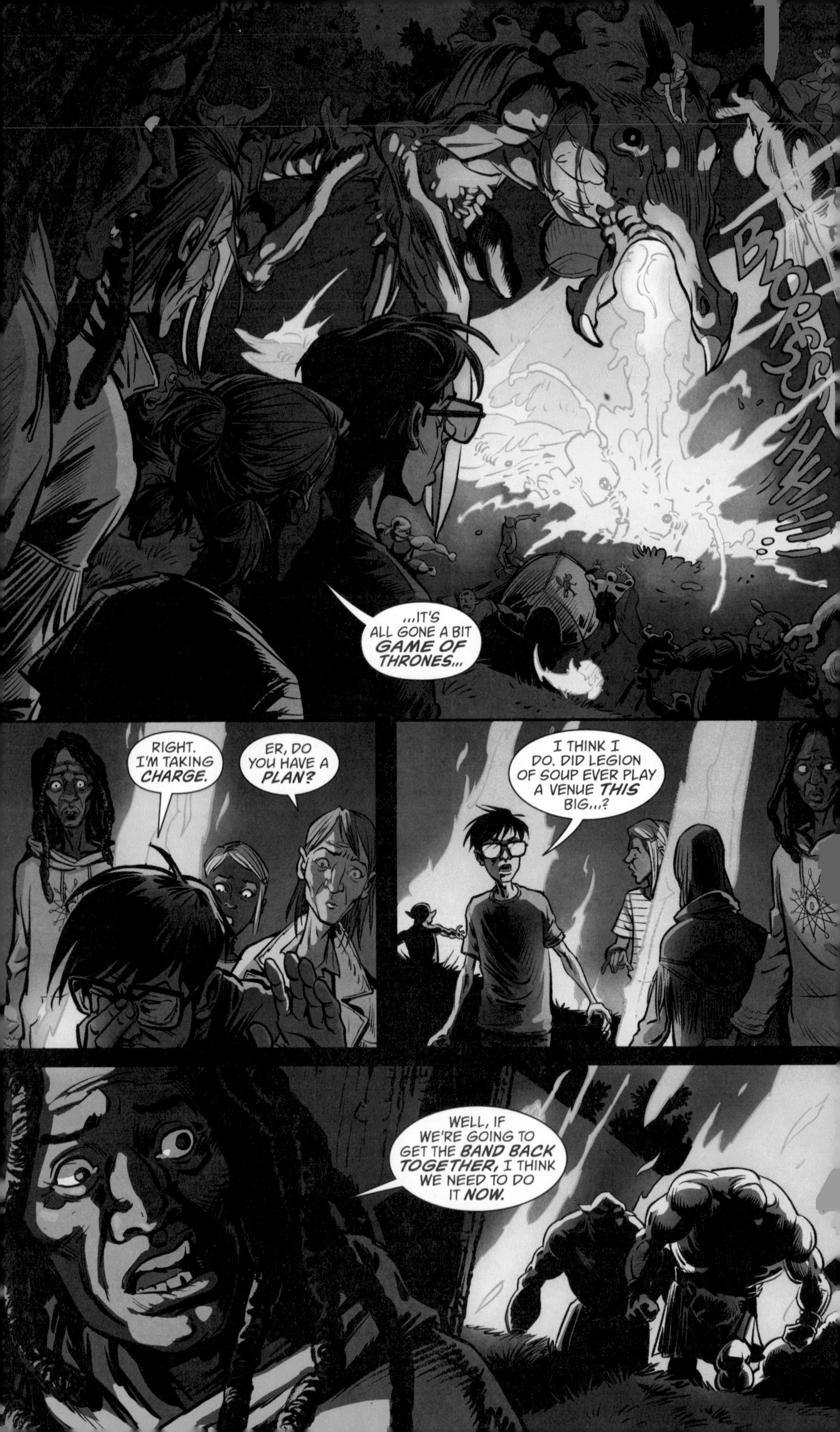
BWORSSSHHHH!
...IT'S ALL GONE A BIT GAME OF THRONES...
RIGHT. I'M TAKING CHARGE.
ER, DO YOU HAVE A PLAN?
I THINK I DO. DID LEGION OF SOUP EVER PLAY A VENUE THIS BIG...?
WELL, IF WE'RE GOING TO GET THE BAND BACK TOGETHER, I THINK WE NEED TO DO IT NOW.

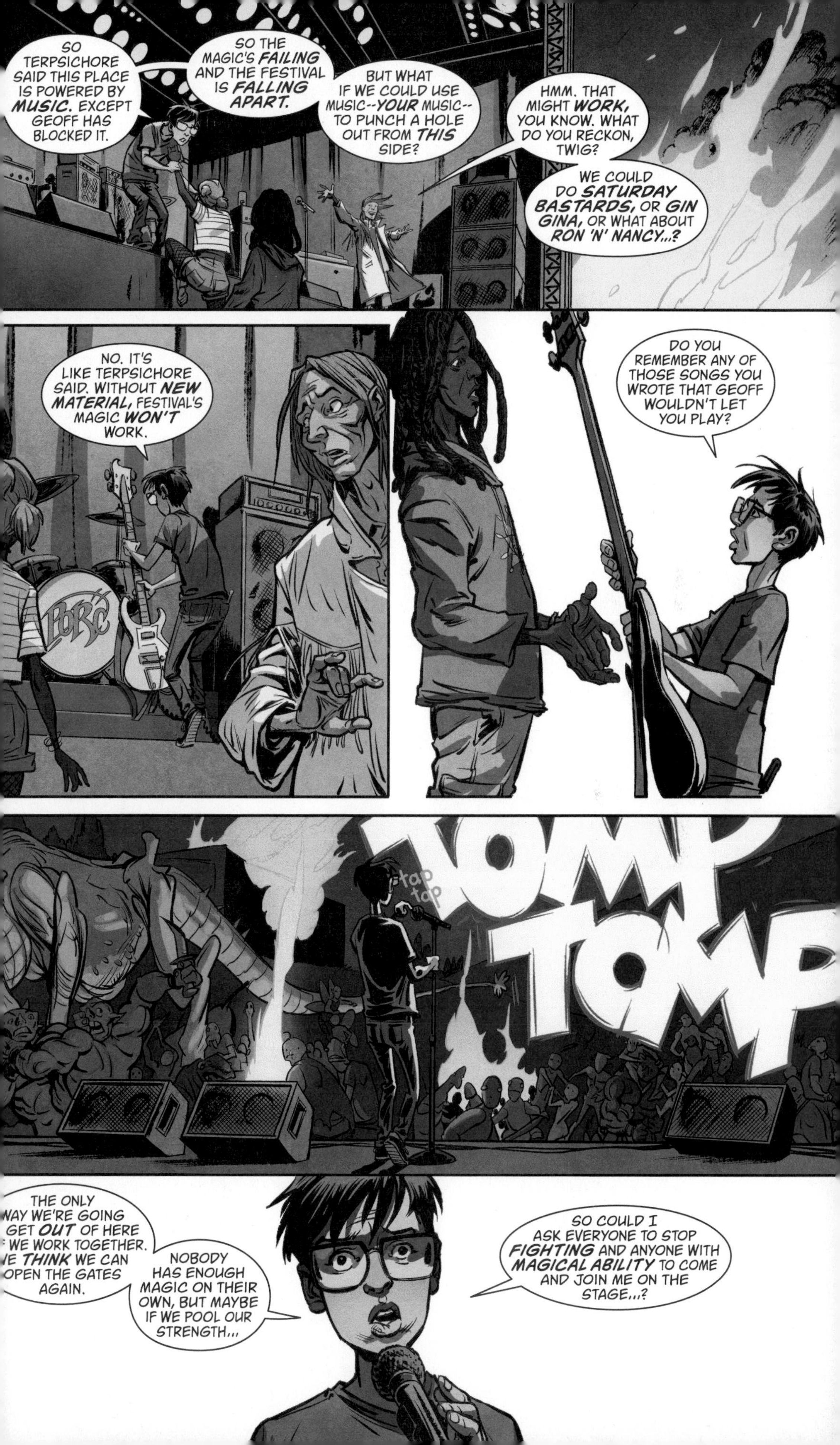
SO TERPSICHORE SAID THIS PLACE IS POWERED BY MUSIC. EXCEPT GEOFF HAS BLOCKED IT.
SO THE MAGIC'S FAILING AND THE FESTIVAL IS FALLING APART.
BUT WHAT IF WE COULD USE MUSIC--YOUR MUSIC--TO PUNCH A HOLE OUT FROM THIS SIDE?
HMM. THAT MIGHT WORK, YOU KNOW. WHAT DO YOU RECKON, TWIG?
WE COULD DO SATURDAY BASTARDS, OR GIN GINA, OR WHAT ABOUT RON 'N' NANCY...?
NO. IT'S LIKE TERPSICHORE SAID. WITHOUT NEW MATERIAL, FESTIVAL'S MAGIC WON'T WORK.
DO YOU REMEMBER ANY OF THOSE SONGS YOU WROTE THAT GEOFF WOULDN'T LET YOU PLAY?
TOMP TOMP
tap tap
THE ONLY WAY WE'RE GOING GET OUT OF HERE F WE WORK TOGETHER. E THINK WE CAN OPEN THE GATES AGAIN.
NOBODY HAS ENOUGH MAGIC ON THEIR OWN, BUT MAYBE IF WE POOL OUR STRENGTH...
SO COULD I ASK EVERYONE TO STOP FIGHTING AND ANYONE WITH MAGICAL ABILITY TO COME AND JOIN ME ON THE STAGE...?

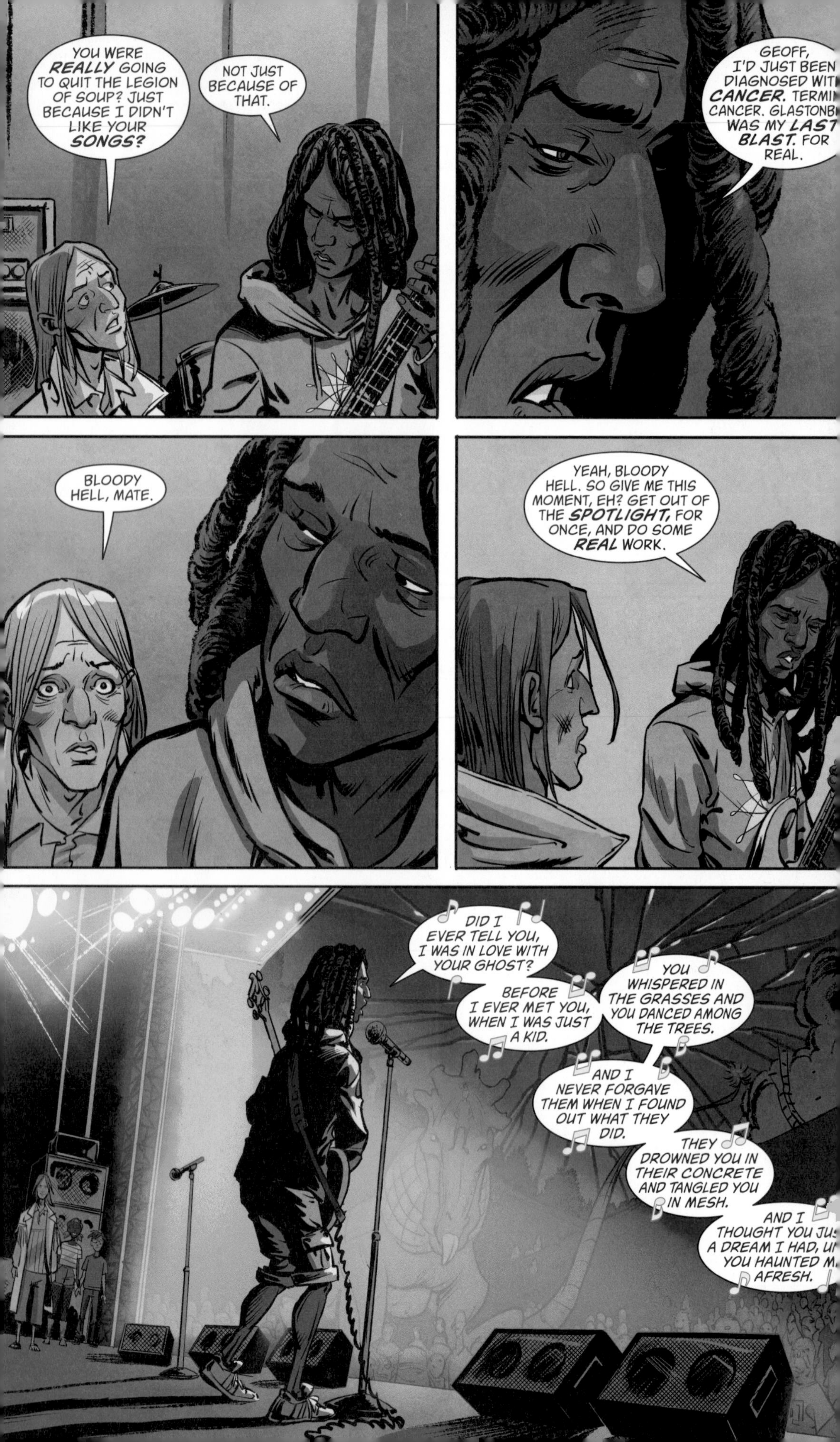
YOU WERE REALLY GOING TO QUIT THE LEGION OF SOUP? JUST BECAUSE I DIDN'T LIKE YOUR SONGS?
NOT JUST BECAUSE OF THAT.
GEOFF, I'D JUST BEEN DIAGNOSED WIT CANCER. TERMI CANCER. GLASTONB WAS MY LAST BLAST. FOR REAL.
BLOODY HELL, MATE.
YEAH, BLOODY HELL. SO GIVE ME THIS MOMENT, EH? GET OUT OF THE SPOTLIGHT, FOR ONCE, AND DO SOME REAL WORK.
DID I EVER TELL YOU, I WAS IN LOVE WITH YOUR GHOST?
BEFORE I EVER MET YOU, WHEN I WAS JUST A KID.
YOU WHISPERED IN THE GRASSES AND YOU DANCED AMONG THE TREES.
AND I NEVER FORGAVE THEM WHEN I FOUND OUT WHAT THEY DID.
THEY DROWNED YOU IN THEIR CONCRETE AND TANGLED YOU IN MESH.
AND I THOUGHT YOU JUS A DREAM I HAD, U YOU HAUNTED M AFRESH.

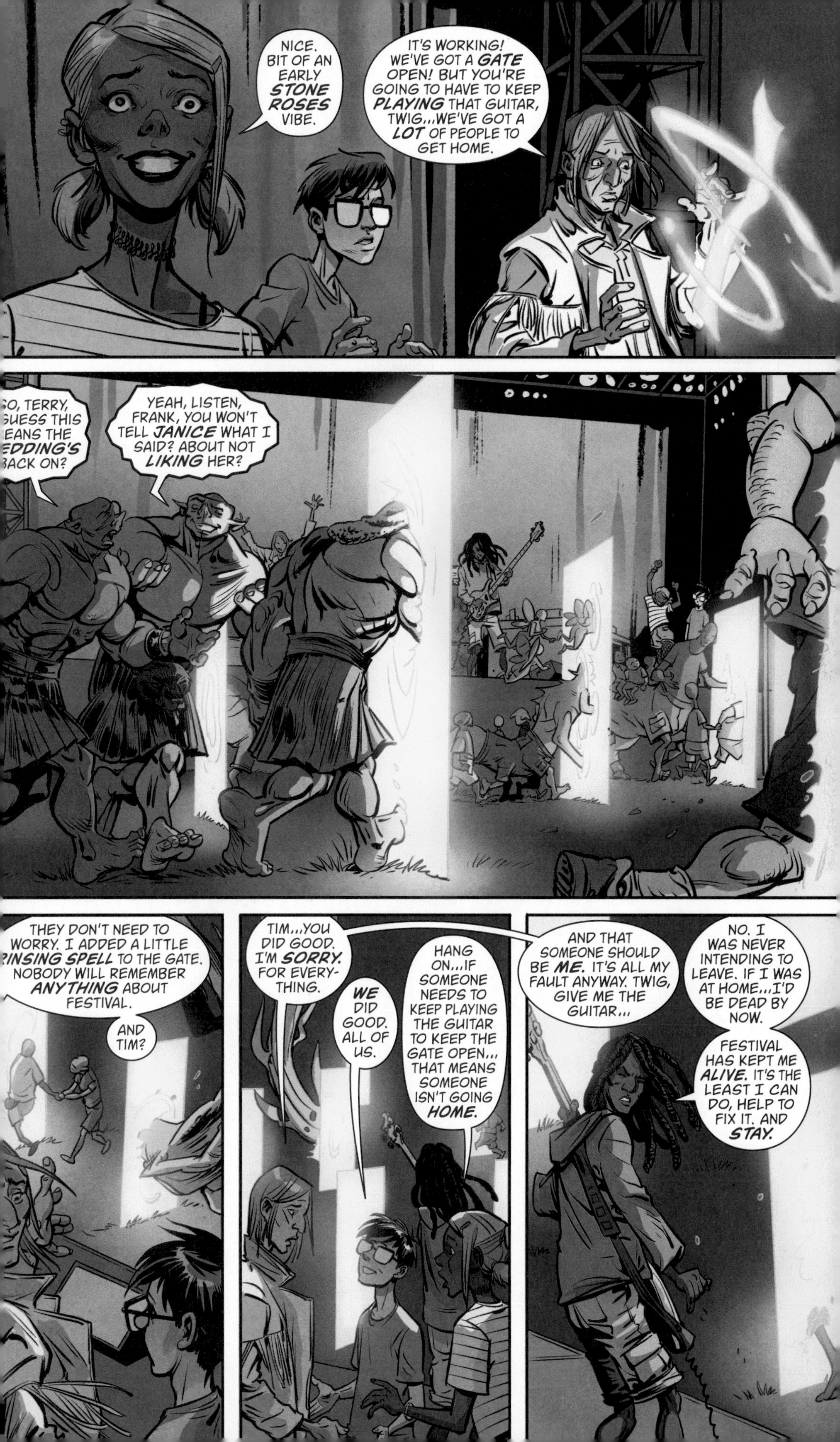
NICE. BIT OF AN EARLY STONE ROSES VIBE.
IT'S WORKING! WE'VE GOT A GATE OPEN! BUT YOU'RE GOING TO HAVE TO KEEP PLAYING THAT GUITAR, TWIG... WE'VE GOT A LOT OF PEOPLE TO GET HOME.
SO, TERRY, GUESS THIS MEANS THE WEDDING'S BACK ON?
YEAH, LISTEN, FRANK, YOU WON'T TELL JANICE WHAT I SAID? ABOUT NOT LIKING HER?
THEY DON'T NEED TO WORRY. I ADDED A LITTLE RINSING SPELL TO THE GATE. NOBODY WILL REMEMBER ANYTHING ABOUT FESTIVAL.
AND TIM?
TIM... YOU DID GOOD. I'M SORRY. FOR EVERYTHING.
WE DID GOOD. ALL OF US.
HANG ON... IF SOMEONE NEEDS TO KEEP PLAYING THE GUITAR TO KEEP THE GATE OPEN... THAT MEANS SOMEONE ISN'T GOING HOME.
AND THAT SOMEONE SHOULD BE ME. IT'S ALL MY FAULT ANYWAY. TWIG, GIVE ME THE GUITAR...
NO. I WAS NEVER INTENDING TO LEAVE. IF I WAS AT HOME... I'D BE DEAD BY NOW.
FESTIVAL HAS KEPT ME ALIVE. IT'S THE LEAST I CAN DO, HELP TO FIX IT. AND STAY.

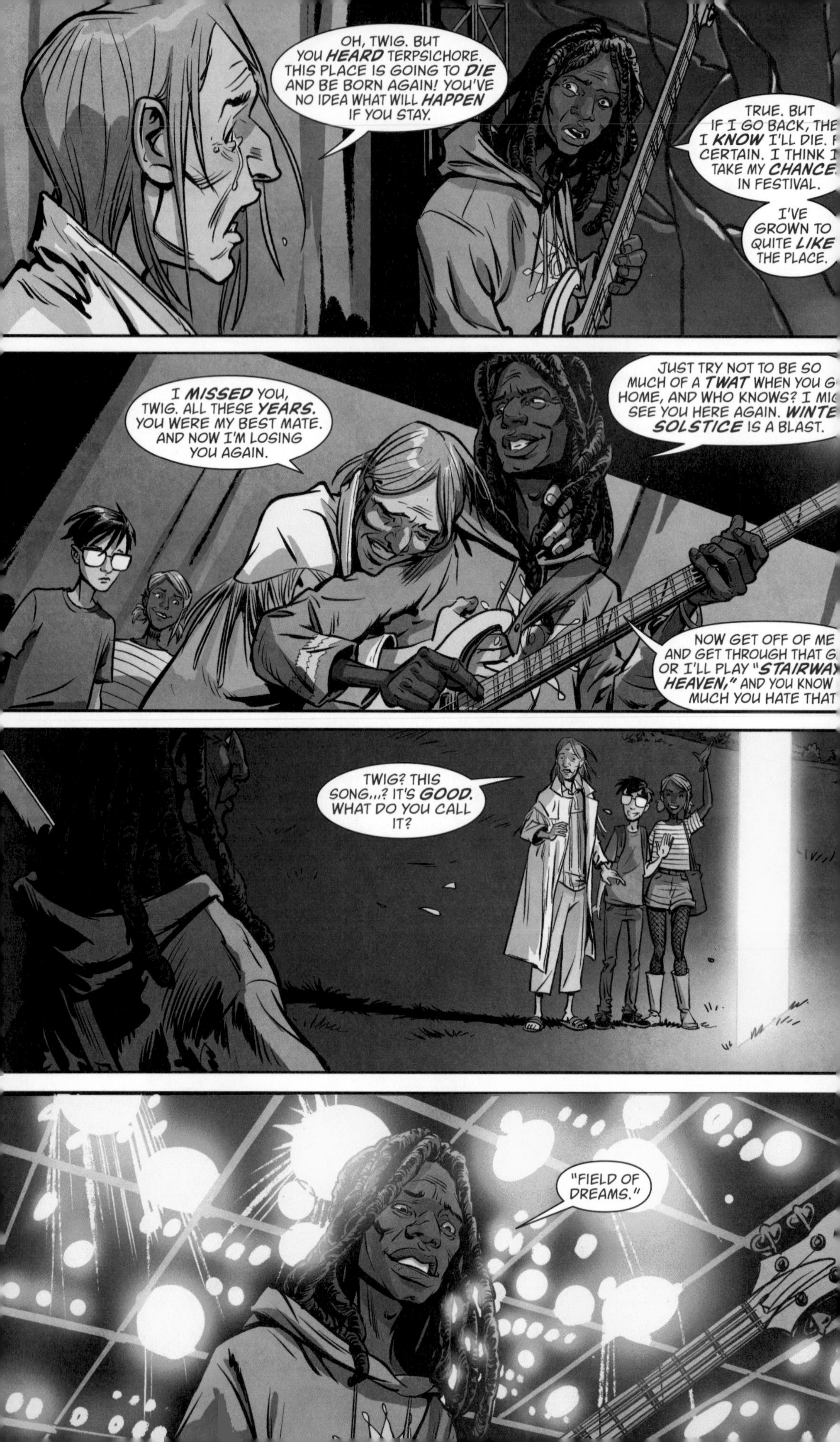
OH, TWIG. BUT YOU HEARD TERPSICHORE. THIS PLACE IS GOING TO DIE AND BE BORN AGAIN! YOU'VE NO IDEA WHAT WILL HAPPEN IF YOU STAY.
TRUE. BUT IF I GO BACK, THE I KNOW I'LL DIE. CERTAIN. I THINK I TAKE MY CHANCE IN FESTIVAL.
I'VE GROWN TO QUITE LIKE THE PLACE.
I MISSED YOU, TWIG. ALL THESE YEARS. YOU WERE MY BEST MATE. AND NOW I'M LOSING YOU AGAIN.
JUST TRY NOT TO BE SO MUCH OF A TWAT WHEN YOU G HOME, AND WHO KNOWS? I MIG SEE YOU HERE AGAIN. WINTE SOLSTICE IS A BLAST.
NOW GET OFF OF ME AND GET THROUGH THAT G OR I'LL PLAY "STAIRWAY HEAVEN," AND YOU KNOW MUCH YOU HATE THAT
TWIG? THIS SONG...? IT'S GOOD. WHAT DO YOU CALL IT?
"FIELD OF DREAMS."

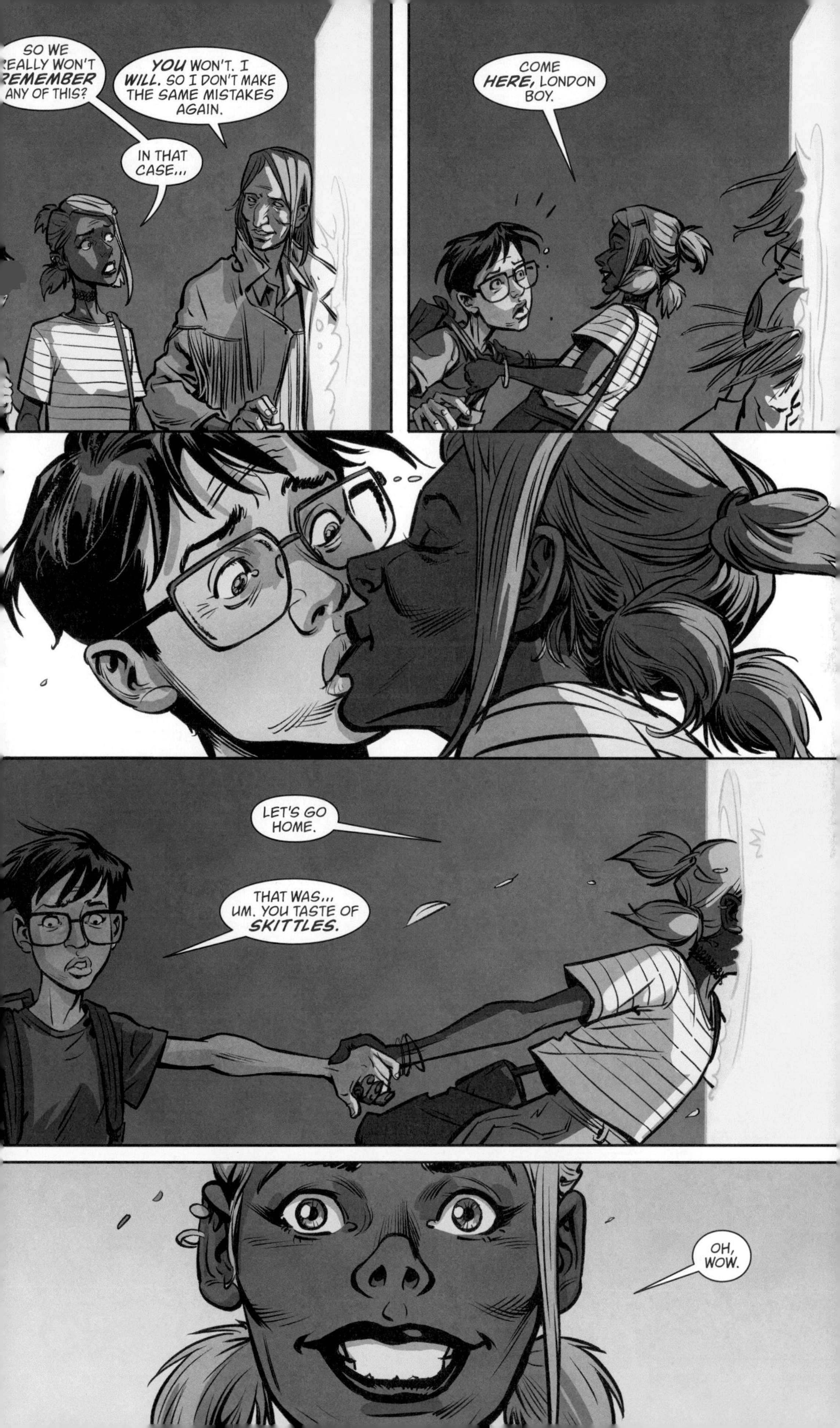
SO WE REALLY WON'T REMEMBER ANY OF THIS?
YOU WON'T. I WILL. SO I DON'T MAKE THE SAME MISTAKES AGAIN.
IN THAT CASE...
COME HERE, LONDON BOY.
LET'S GO HOME.
THAT WAS... UM. YOU TASTE OF SKITTLES.
OH, WOW.

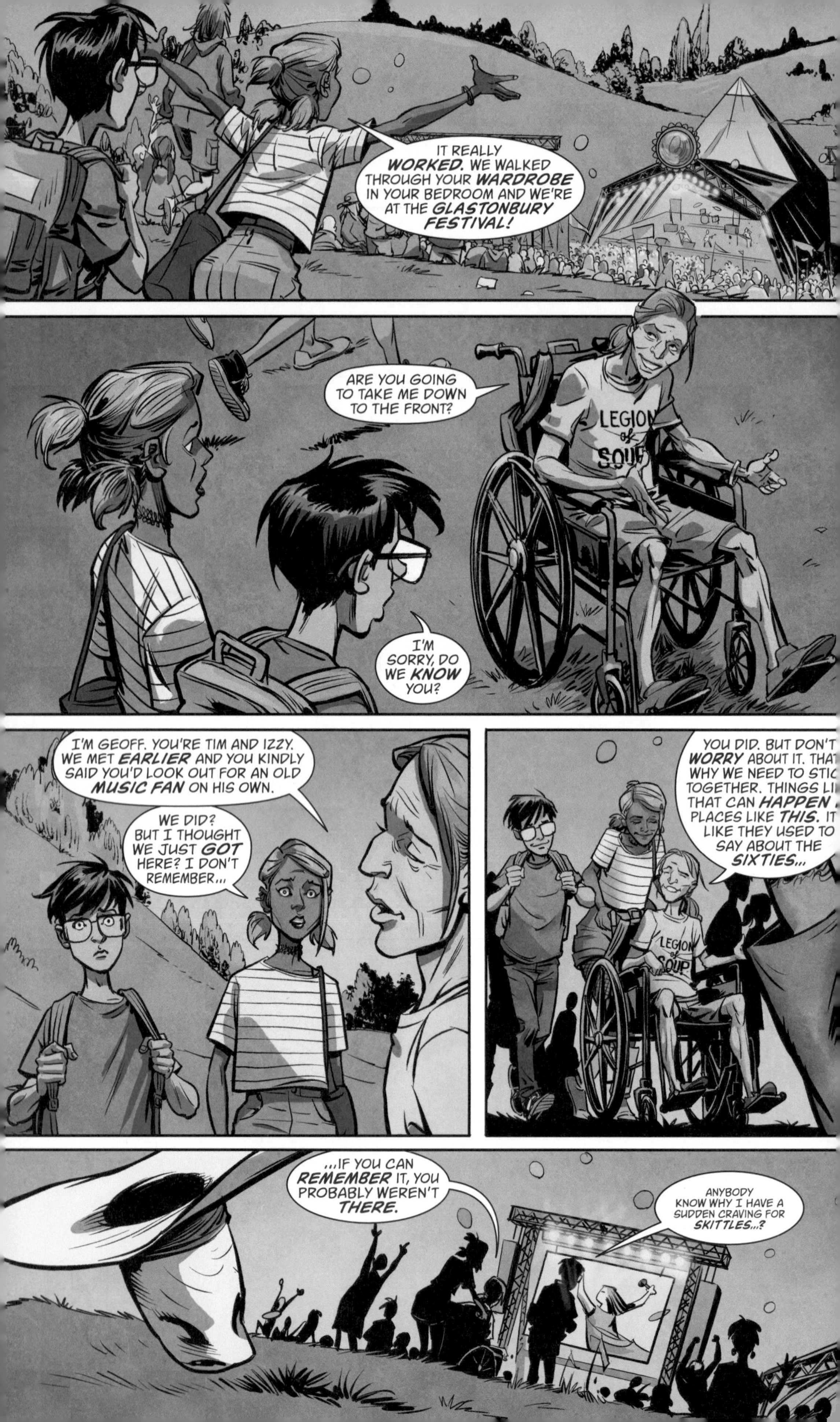
IT REALLY WORKED. WE WALKED THROUGH YOUR WARDROBE IN YOUR BEDROOM AND WE'RE AT THE GLASTONBURY FESTIVAL!
ARE YOU GOING TO TAKE ME DOWN TO THE FRONT?
LEGION of SOUP
I'M SORRY, DO WE KNOW YOU?
I'M GEOFF. YOU'RE TIM AND IZZY. WE MET EARLIER AND YOU KINDLY SAID YOU'D LOOK OUT FOR AN OLD MUSIC FAN ON HIS OWN.
WE DID? BUT I THOUGHT WE JUST GOT HERE? I DON'T REMEMBER...
YOU DID. BUT DON'T WORRY ABOUT IT. THAT WHY WE NEED TO STIC TOGETHER. THINGS LI THAT CAN HAPPEN PLACES LIKE THIS. IT LIKE THEY USED TO SAY ABOUT THE SIXTIES...
LEGION of SOUP
...IF YOU CAN REMEMBER IT, YOU PROBABLY WEREN'T THERE.
ANYBODY KNOW WHY I HAVE A SUDDEN CRAVING FOR SKITTLES...?

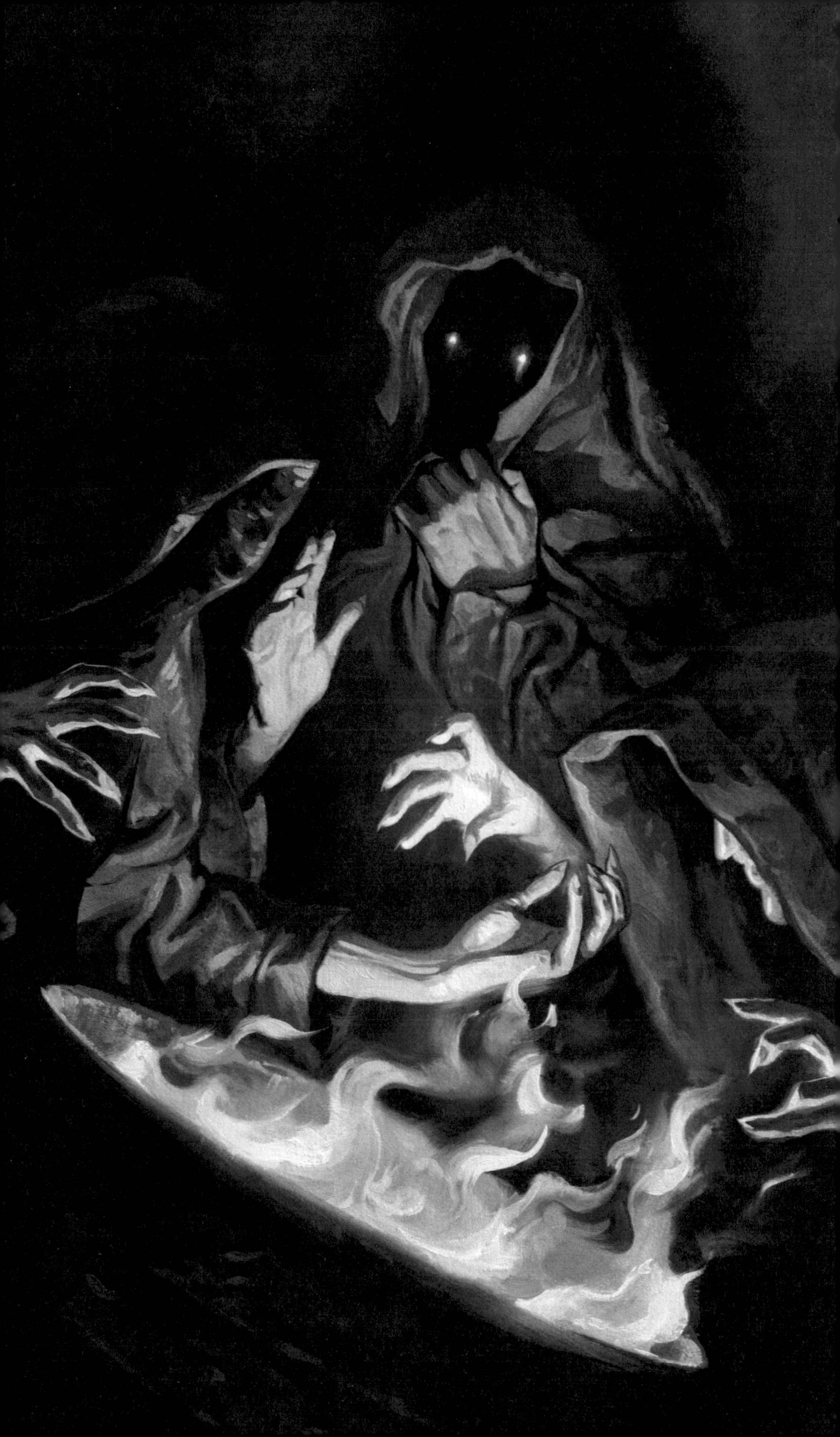

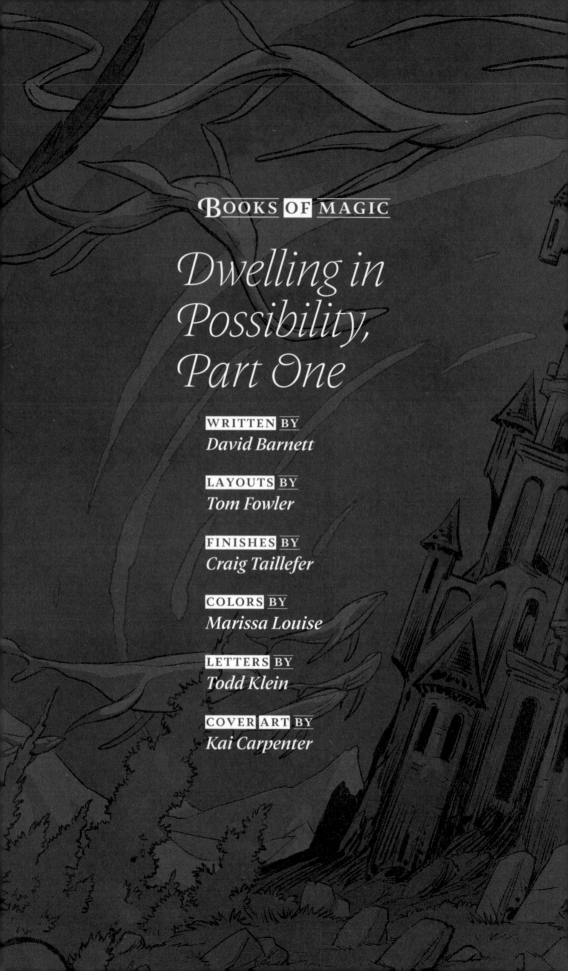

BOOKS OF MAGIC

Dwelling in Possibility, Part One

WRITTEN BY
David Barnett

LAYOUTS BY
Tom Fowler

FINISHES BY
Craig Taillefer

COLORS BY
Marissa Louise

LETTERS BY
Todd Klein

COVER ART BY
Kai Carpenter

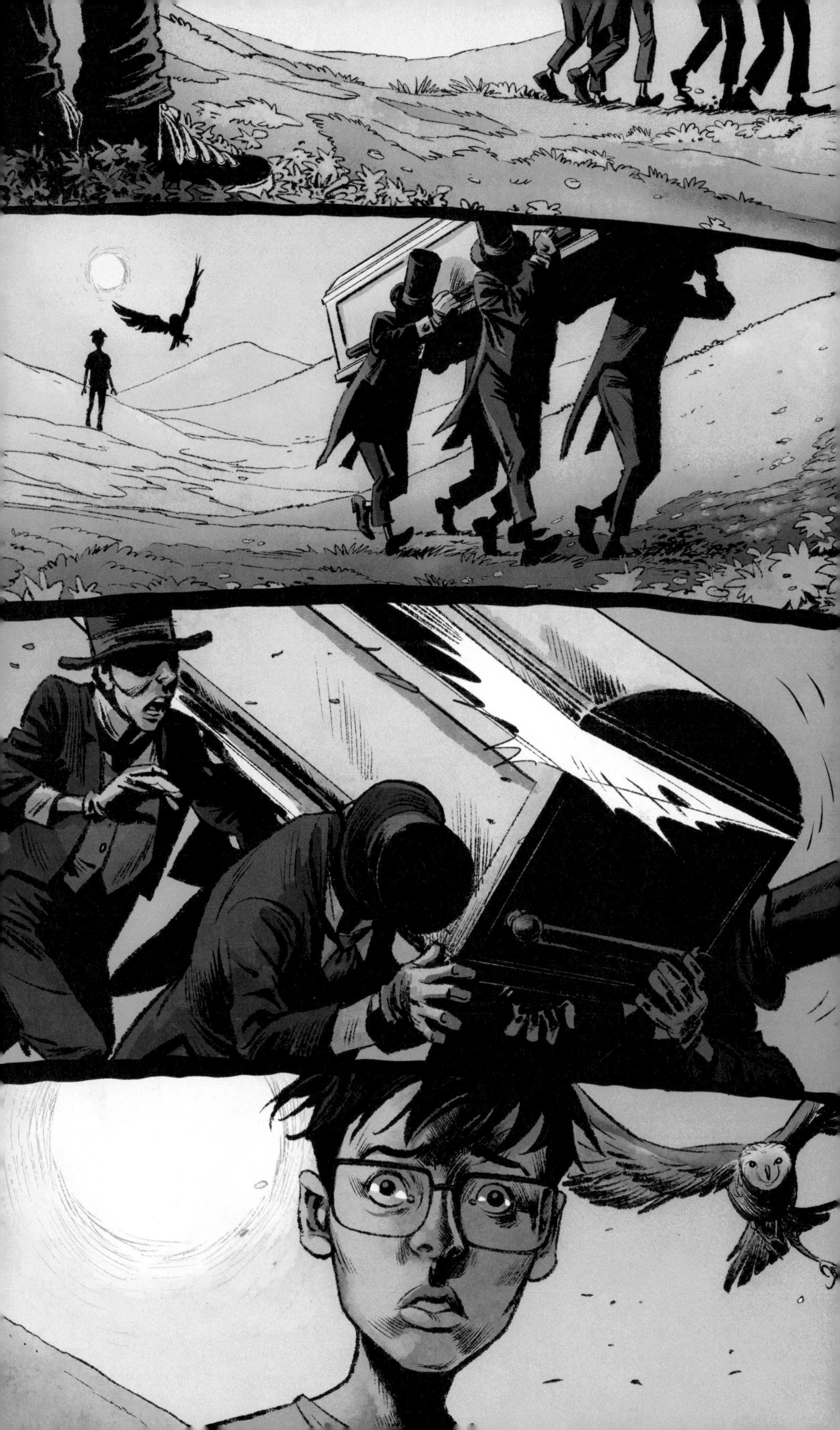

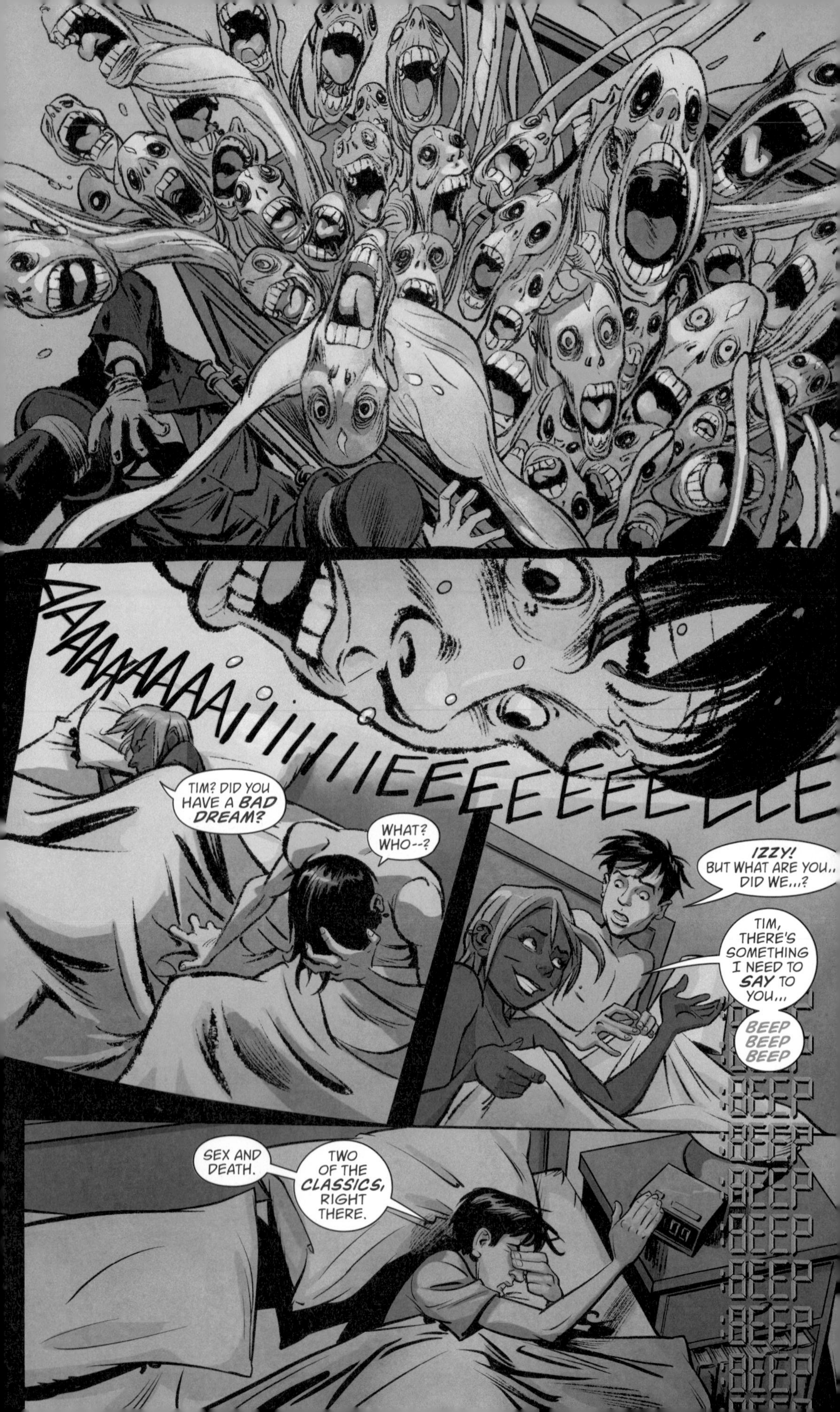
AAAAAAAAAAIIIIIIIIIIEEEEEEEEEE
TIM? DID YOU HAVE A ***BAD DREAM?***
WHAT? WHO--?
IZZY! BUT WHAT ARE YOU.. DID WE...?
TIM, THERE'S SOMETHING I NEED TO ***SAY*** TO YOU...
BEEP BEEP BEEP
SEX AND DEATH.
TWO OF THE ***CLASSICS,*** RIGHT THERE.

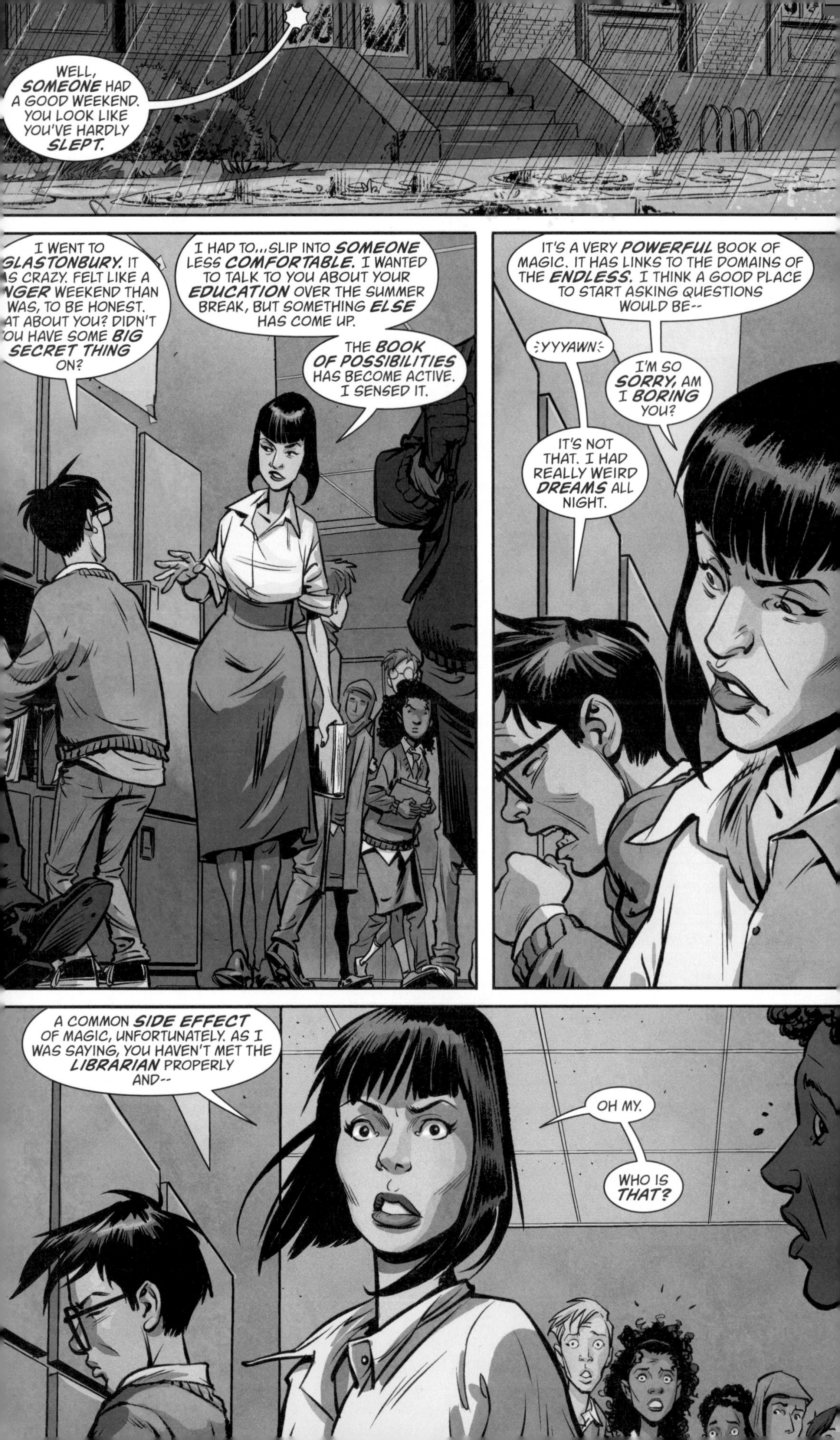
WELL, SOMEONE HAD A GOOD WEEKEND. YOU LOOK LIKE YOU'VE HARDLY SLEPT.
I WENT TO GLASTONBURY. IT S CRAZY. FELT LIKE A NGER WEEKEND THAN WAS, TO BE HONEST. AT ABOUT YOU? DIDN'T OU HAVE SOME BIG SECRET THING ON?
I HAD TO...SLIP INTO SOMEONE LESS COMFORTABLE. I WANTED TO TALK TO YOU ABOUT YOUR EDUCATION OVER THE SUMMER BREAK, BUT SOMETHING ELSE HAS COME UP.
THE BOOK OF POSSIBILITIES HAS BECOME ACTIVE. I SENSED IT.
IT'S A VERY POWERFUL BOOK OF MAGIC. IT HAS LINKS TO THE DOMAINS OF THE ENDLESS. I THINK A GOOD PLACE TO START ASKING QUESTIONS WOULD BE--
YYYAWN
I'M SO SORRY, AM I BORING YOU?
IT'S NOT THAT. I HAD REALLY WEIRD DREAMS ALL NIGHT.
A COMMON SIDE EFFECT OF MAGIC, UNFORTUNATELY. AS I WAS SAYING, YOU HAVEN'T MET THE LIBRARIAN PROPERLY AND--
OH MY.
WHO IS THAT?

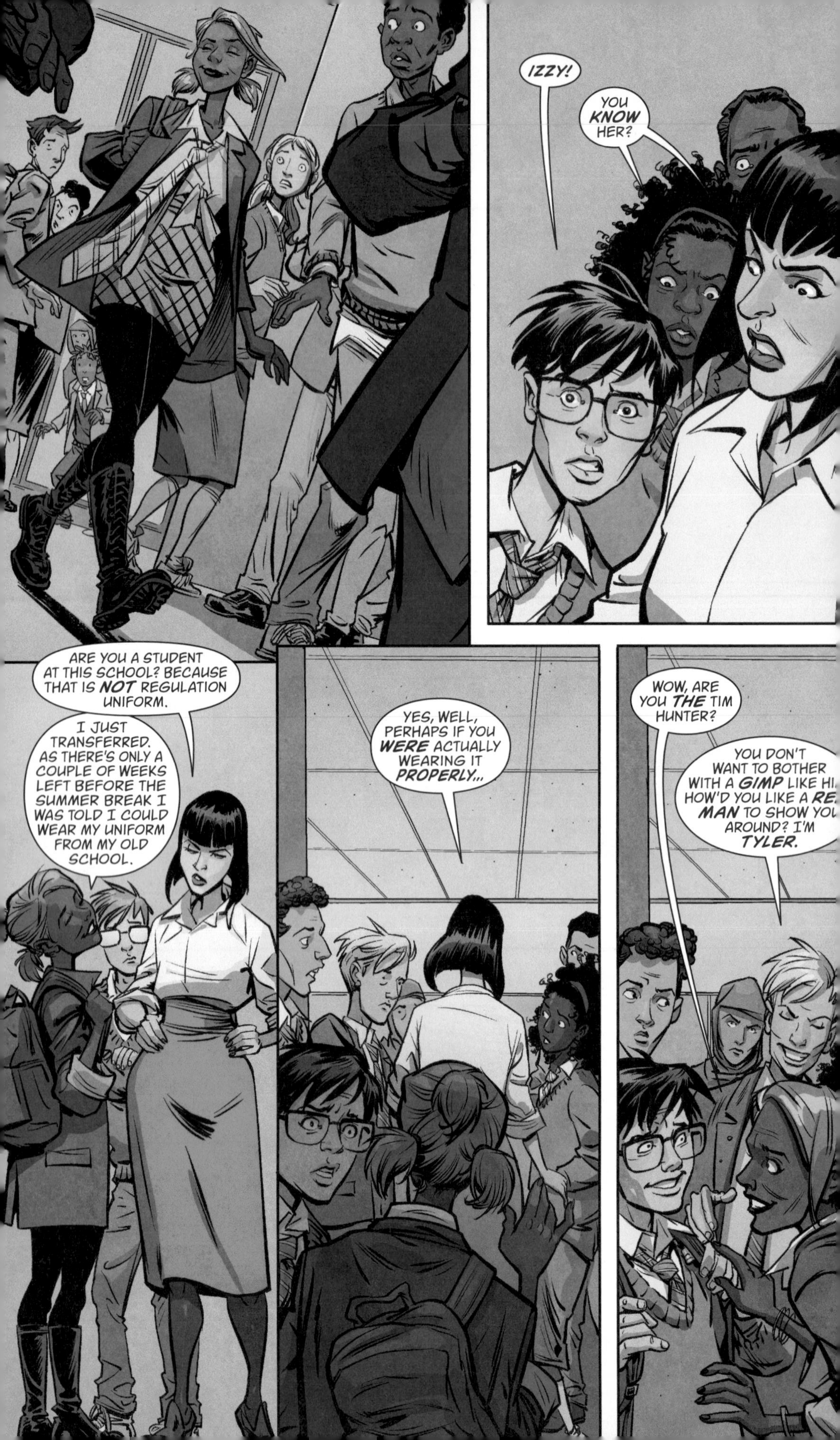
IZZY!
YOU KNOW HER?
ARE YOU A STUDENT AT THIS SCHOOL? BECAUSE THAT IS NOT REGULATION UNIFORM.
I JUST TRANSFERRED. AS THERE'S ONLY A COUPLE OF WEEKS LEFT BEFORE THE SUMMER BREAK I WAS TOLD I COULD WEAR MY UNIFORM FROM MY OLD SCHOOL.
YES, WELL, PERHAPS IF YOU WERE ACTUALLY WEARING IT PROPERLY...
WOW, ARE YOU THE TIM HUNTER?
YOU DON'T WANT TO BOTHER WITH A GIMP LIKE HI
HOW'D YOU LIKE A RE
MAN TO SHOW YO
AROUND? I'M TYLER.

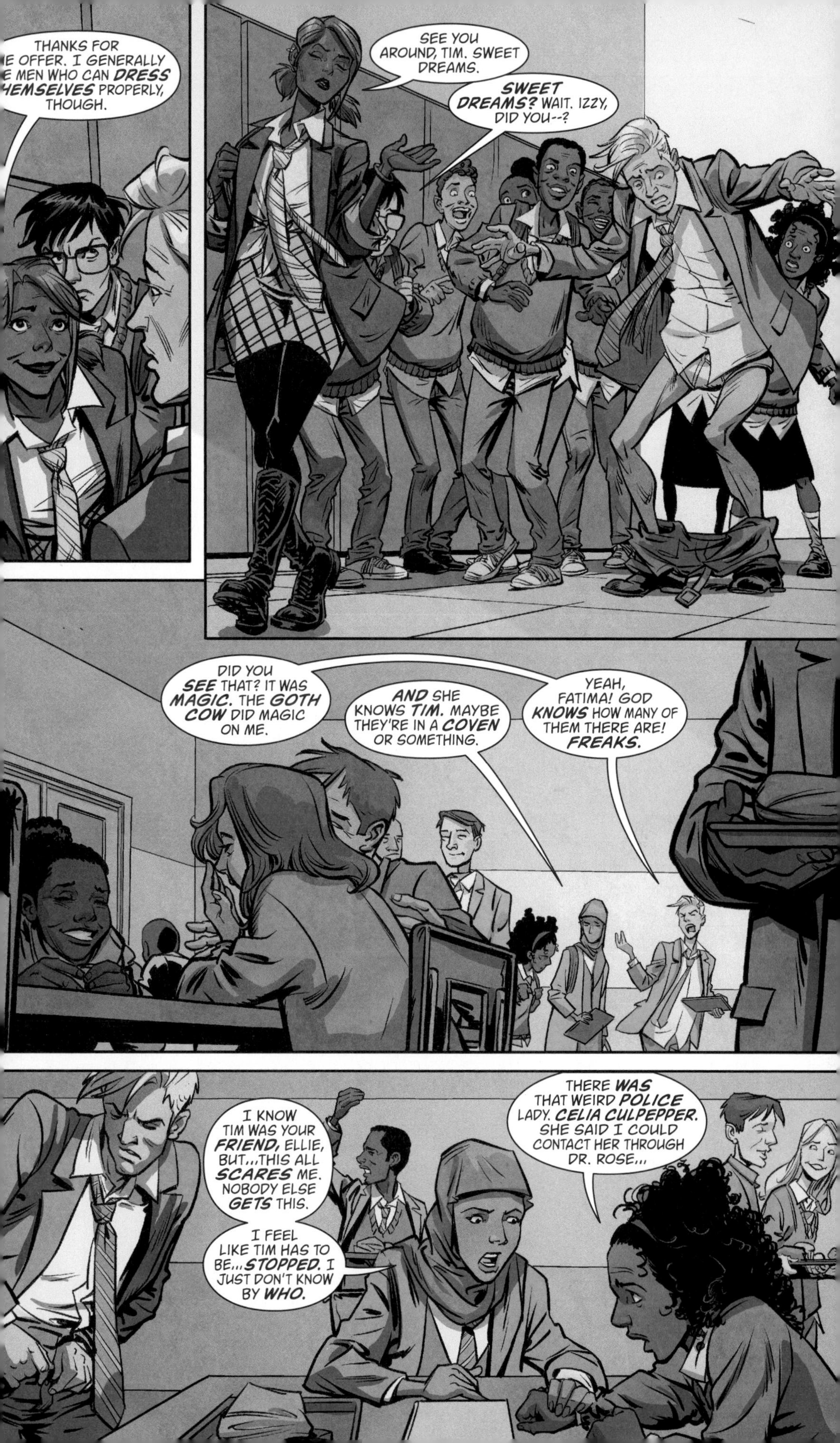

THANKS FOR
E OFFER. I GENERALLY
E MEN WHO CAN DRESS
HEMSELVES PROPERLY,
THOUGH.
SEE YOU AROUND, TIM. SWEET DREAMS.
SWEET DREAMS? WAIT. IZZY, DID YOU--?
DID YOU SEE THAT? IT WAS MAGIC. THE GOTH COW DID MAGIC ON ME.
AND SHE KNOWS TIM. MAYBE THEY'RE IN A COVEN OR SOMETHING.
YEAH, FATIMA! GOD KNOWS HOW MANY OF THEM THERE ARE! FREAKS.
I KNOW TIM WAS YOUR FRIEND, ELLIE, BUT...THIS ALL SCARES ME. NOBODY ELSE GETS THIS.
I FEEL LIKE TIM HAS TO BE...STOPPED. I JUST DON'T KNOW BY WHO.
THERE WAS THAT WEIRD POLICE LADY. CELIA CULPEPPER. SHE SAID I COULD CONTACT HER THROUGH DR. ROSE...

"...MAYBE IT'S TIME TO MAKE THAT *CALL*."

BASTARD!

BASTARD!

BASTARD!

BASTARD!

BASTARD!

BASTARD!

THIS BOSS IS *KILLING* ME!

WHAT *IS* IT, KEVIN? NOT TIME FOR MY *PEDICURE* ALREADY?

A *COMMUNICATION* FOR YOU, MR. FRY. VIA THE *SCRYING POOL*.

ONLY *ONE* SHOWER EVER USES THIS OLD THING.

MORK CALLING ORSON! MORK CALLING ORSON! COME IN, ORSON!

YOU KNOW, I *COUL* GET YOU GUYS REALLY GOOD D ON SOME MOBI PHONES...

ENOUGH OF YOUR PUERILE IDIOCY. WE HAVE NEED OF THE SERVICES OF *FRY ACQUISITIONS*.

WE WOULD *VISIT* WITH YOU.

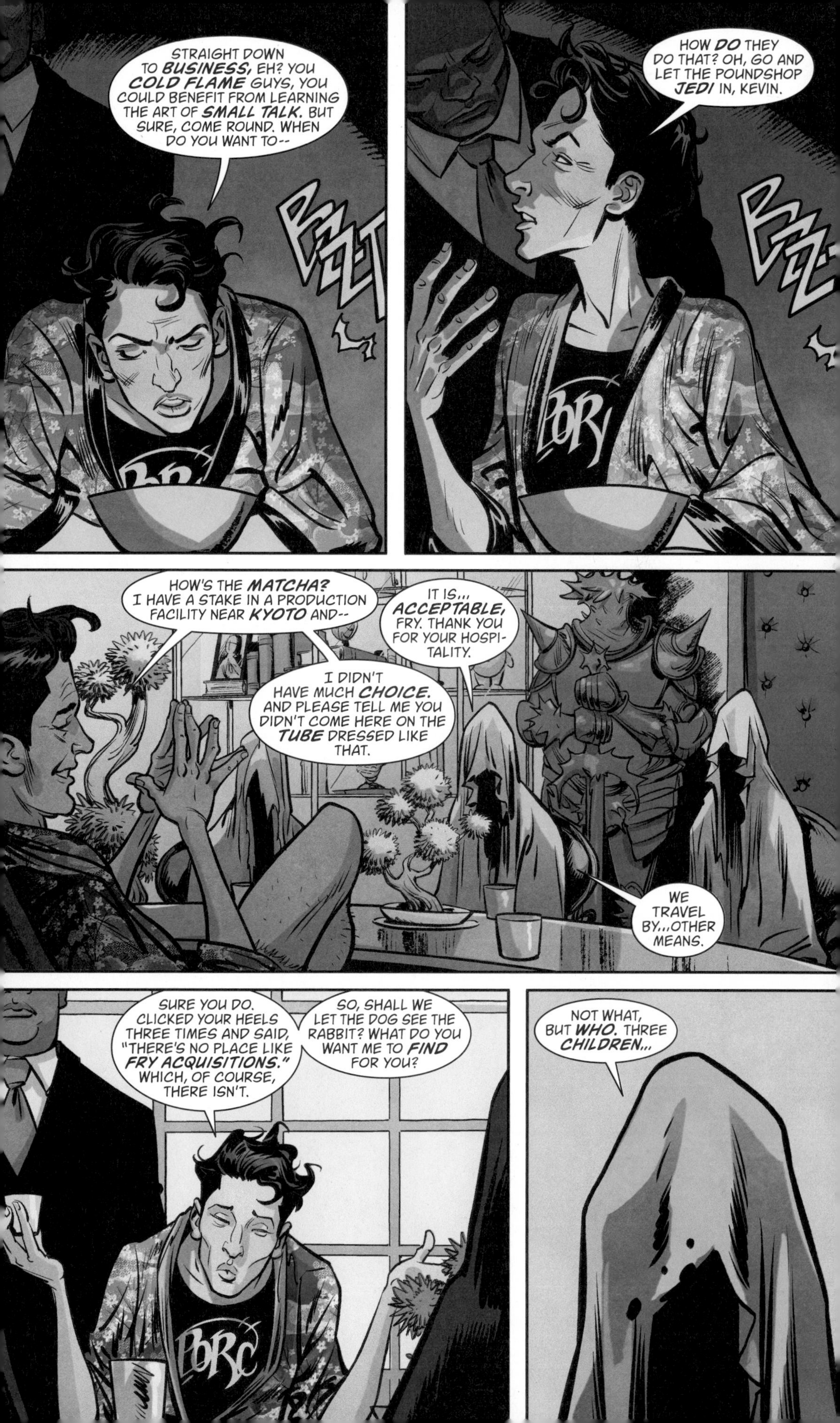
STRAIGHT DOWN TO BUSINESS, EH? YOU COLD FLAME GUYS, YOU COULD BENEFIT FROM LEARNING THE ART OF SMALL TALK. BUT SURE, COME ROUND. WHEN DO YOU WANT TO--
BZZZT
HOW DO THEY DO THAT? OH, GO AND LET THE POUNDSHOP JEDI IN, KEVIN.
BZZZ
HOW'S THE MATCHA? I HAVE A STAKE IN A PRODUCTION FACILITY NEAR KYOTO AND--
IT IS... ACCEPTABLE, FRY. THANK YOU FOR YOUR HOSPI-TALITY.
I DIDN'T HAVE MUCH CHOICE. AND PLEASE TELL ME YOU DIDN'T COME HERE ON THE TUBE DRESSED LIKE THAT.
WE TRAVEL BY...OTHER MEANS.
SURE YOU DO. CLICKED YOUR HEELS THREE TIMES AND SAID, "THERE'S NO PLACE LIKE FRY ACQUISITIONS." WHICH, OF COURSE, THERE ISN'T.
SO, SHALL WE LET THE DOG SEE THE RABBIT? WHAT DO YOU WANT ME TO FIND FOR YOU?
NOT WHAT, BUT WHO. THREE CHILDREN...

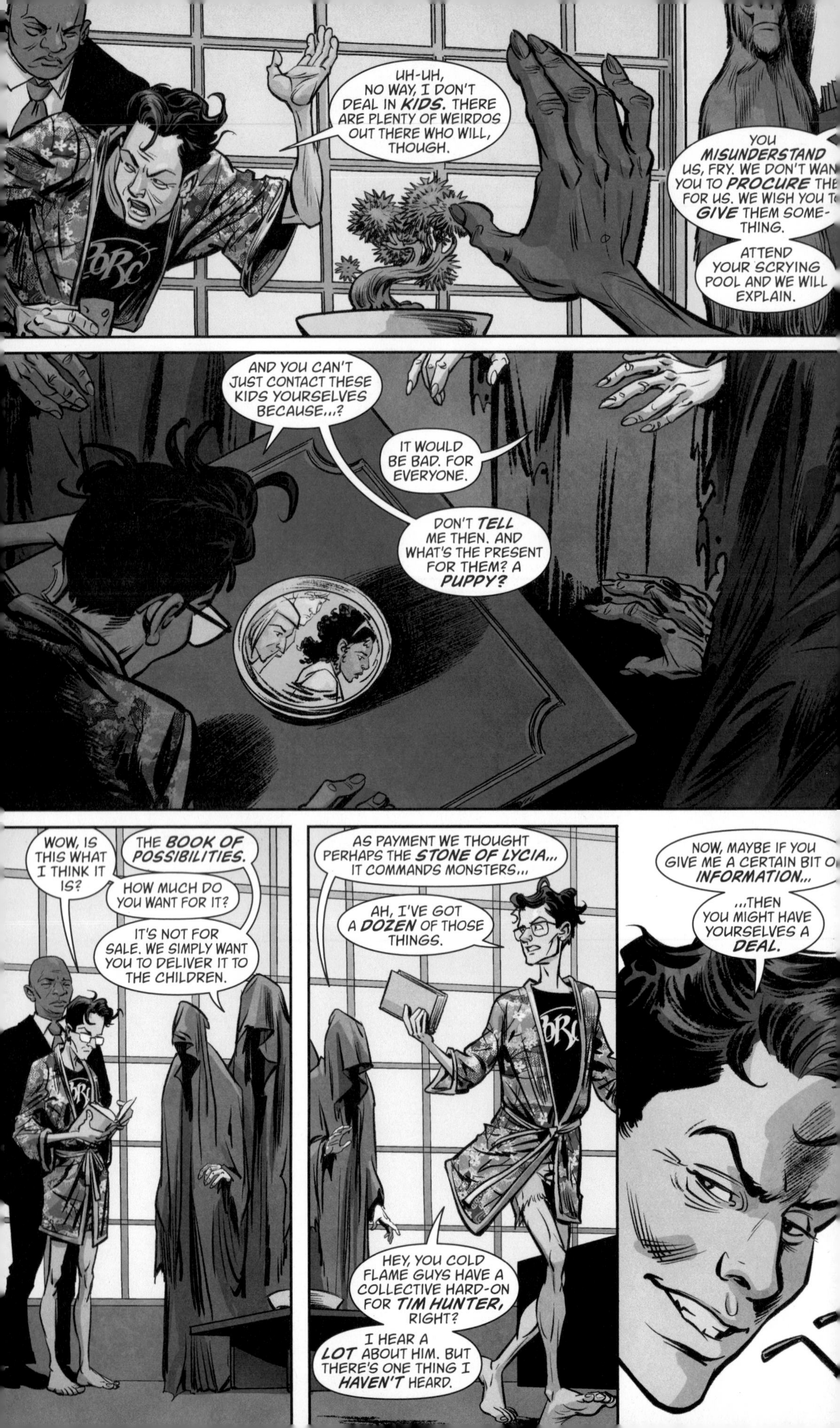
UH-UH, NO WAY, I DON'T DEAL IN KIDS. THERE ARE PLENTY OF WEIRDOS OUT THERE WHO WILL, THOUGH.
YOU MISUNDERSTAND US, FRY. WE DON'T WAN YOU TO PROCURE THE FOR US. WE WISH YOU T GIVE THEM SOME-THING.
ATTEND YOUR SCRYING POOL AND WE WILL EXPLAIN.
AND YOU CAN'T JUST CONTACT THESE KIDS YOURSELVES BECAUSE...?
IT WOULD BE BAD. FOR EVERYONE.
DON'T TELL ME THEN. AND WHAT'S THE PRESENT FOR THEM? A PUPPY?
WOW, IS THIS WHAT I THINK IT IS?
THE BOOK OF POSSIBILITIES.
HOW MUCH DO YOU WANT FOR IT?
IT'S NOT FOR SALE. WE SIMPLY WANT YOU TO DELIVER IT TO THE CHILDREN.
AS PAYMENT WE THOUGHT PERHAPS THE STONE OF LYCIA... IT COMMANDS MONSTERS...
AH, I'VE GOT A DOZEN OF THOSE THINGS.
HEY, YOU COLD FLAME GUYS HAVE A COLLECTIVE HARD-ON FOR TIM HUNTER, RIGHT?
I HEAR A LOT ABOUT HIM. BUT THERE'S ONE THING I HAVEN'T HEARD.
NOW, MAYBE IF YOU GIVE ME A CERTAIN BIT O INFORMATION...
...THEN YOU MIGHT HAVE YOURSELVES A DEAL.

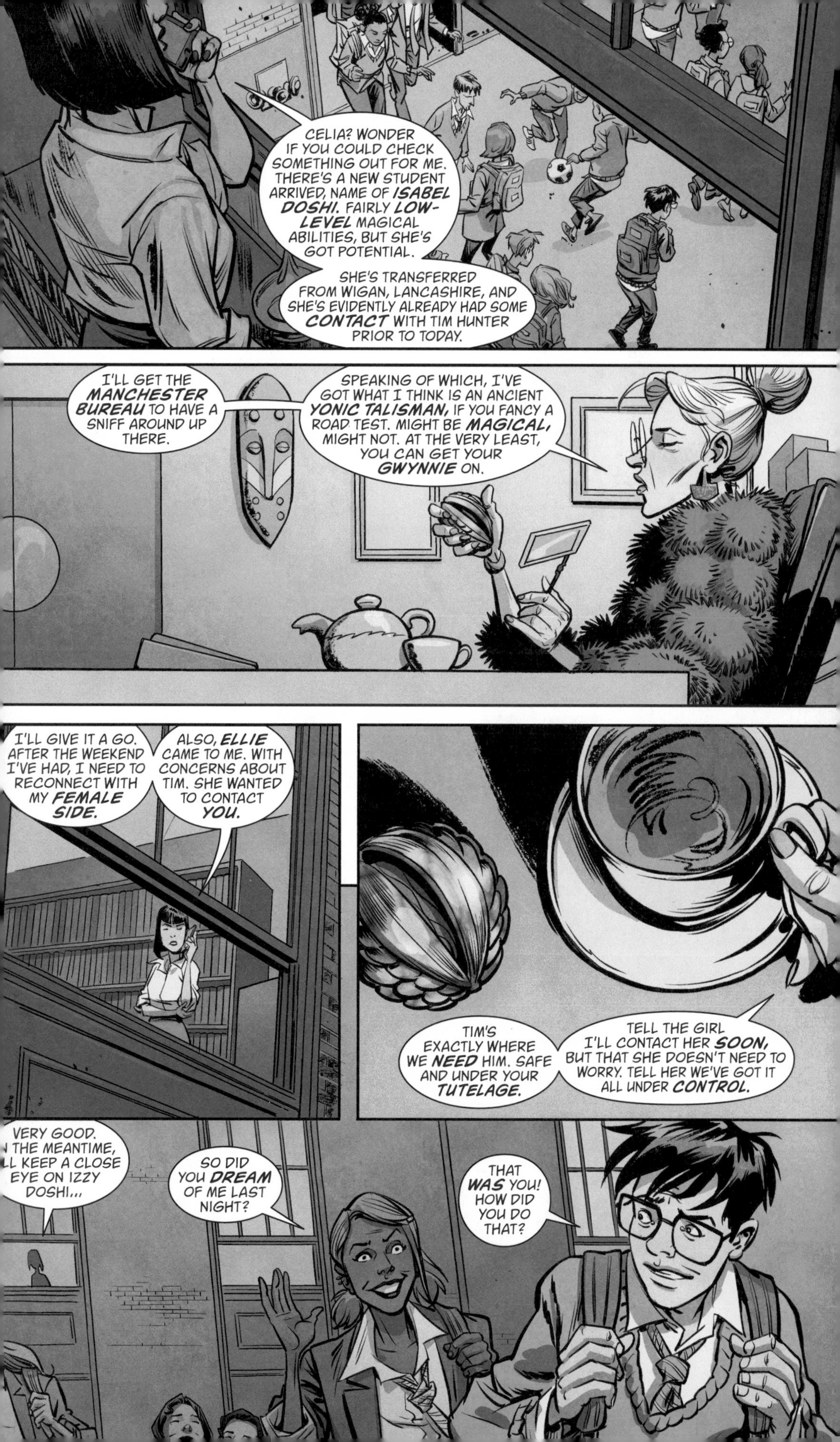
CELIA? WONDER IF YOU COULD CHECK SOMETHING OUT FOR ME. THERE'S A NEW STUDENT ARRIVED, NAME OF ISABEL DOSHI. FAIRLY LOW-LEVEL MAGICAL ABILITIES, BUT SHE'S GOT POTENTIAL.
SHE'S TRANSFERRED FROM WIGAN, LANCASHIRE, AND SHE'S EVIDENTLY ALREADY HAD SOME CONTACT WITH TIM HUNTER PRIOR TO TODAY.
I'LL GET THE MANCHESTER BUREAU TO HAVE A SNIFF AROUND UP THERE.
SPEAKING OF WHICH, I'VE GOT WHAT I THINK IS AN ANCIENT YONIC TALISMAN, IF YOU FANCY A ROAD TEST. MIGHT BE MAGICAL, MIGHT NOT. AT THE VERY LEAST, YOU CAN GET YOUR GWYNNIE ON.
I'LL GIVE IT A GO. AFTER THE WEEKEND I'VE HAD, I NEED TO RECONNECT WITH MY FEMALE SIDE.
ALSO, ELLIE CAME TO ME. WITH CONCERNS ABOUT TIM. SHE WANTED TO CONTACT YOU.
TIM'S EXACTLY WHERE WE NEED HIM. SAFE AND UNDER YOUR TUTELAGE.
TELL THE GIRL I'LL CONTACT HER SOON, BUT THAT SHE DOESN'T NEED TO WORRY. TELL HER WE'VE GOT IT ALL UNDER CONTROL.
VERY GOOD. N THE MEANTIME, LL KEEP A CLOSE EYE ON IZZY DOSHI...
SO DID YOU DREAM OF ME LAST NIGHT?
THAT WAS YOU! HOW DID YOU DO THAT?

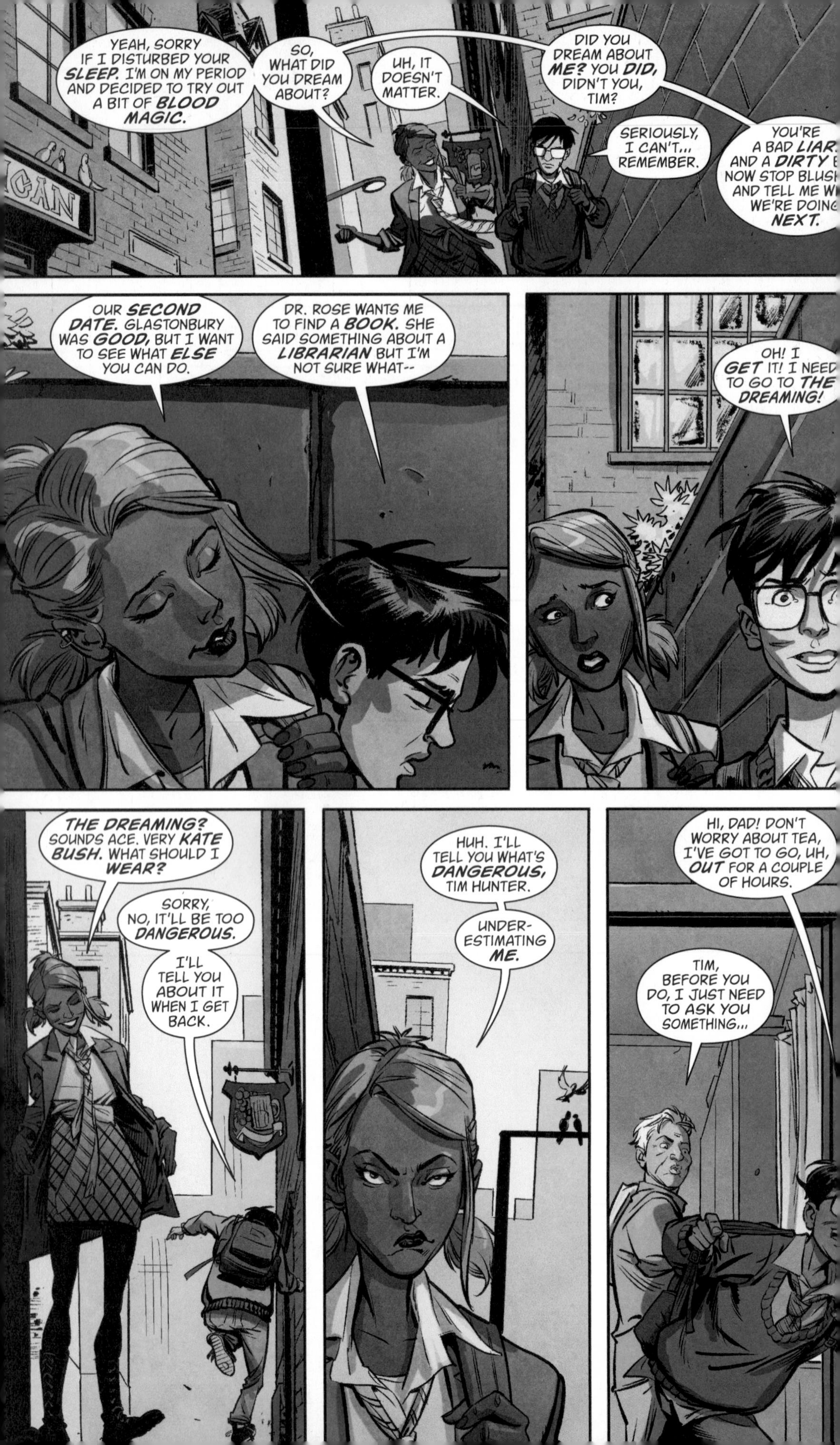
YEAH, SORRY IF I DISTURBED YOUR SLEEP. I'M ON MY PERIOD AND DECIDED TO TRY OUT A BIT OF BLOOD MAGIC.
SO, WHAT DID YOU DREAM ABOUT?
UH, IT DOESN'T MATTER.
DID YOU DREAM ABOUT ME? YOU DID, DIDN'T YOU, TIM?
SERIOUSLY, I CAN'T... REMEMBER.
YOU'RE A BAD LIAR. AND A DIRTY
NOW STOP BLUSH
AND TELL ME W
WE'RE DOING NEXT.
OUR SECOND DATE. GLASTONBURY WAS GOOD, BUT I WANT TO SEE WHAT ELSE YOU CAN DO.
DR. ROSE WANTS ME TO FIND A BOOK. SHE SAID SOMETHING ABOUT A LIBRARIAN BUT I'M NOT SURE WHAT--
OH! I GET IT! I NEED TO GO TO THE DREAMING!
THE DREAMING? SOUNDS ACE. VERY KATE BUSH. WHAT SHOULD I WEAR?
SORRY, NO, IT'LL BE TOO DANGEROUS.
I'LL TELL YOU ABOUT IT WHEN I GET BACK.
HUH. I'LL TELL YOU WHAT'S DANGEROUS, TIM HUNTER.
UNDER-ESTIMATING ME.
HI, DAD! DON'T WORRY ABOUT TEA, I'VE GOT TO GO, UH, OUT FOR A COUPLE OF HOURS.
TIM, BEFORE YOU DO, I JUST NEED TO ASK YOU SOMETHING...

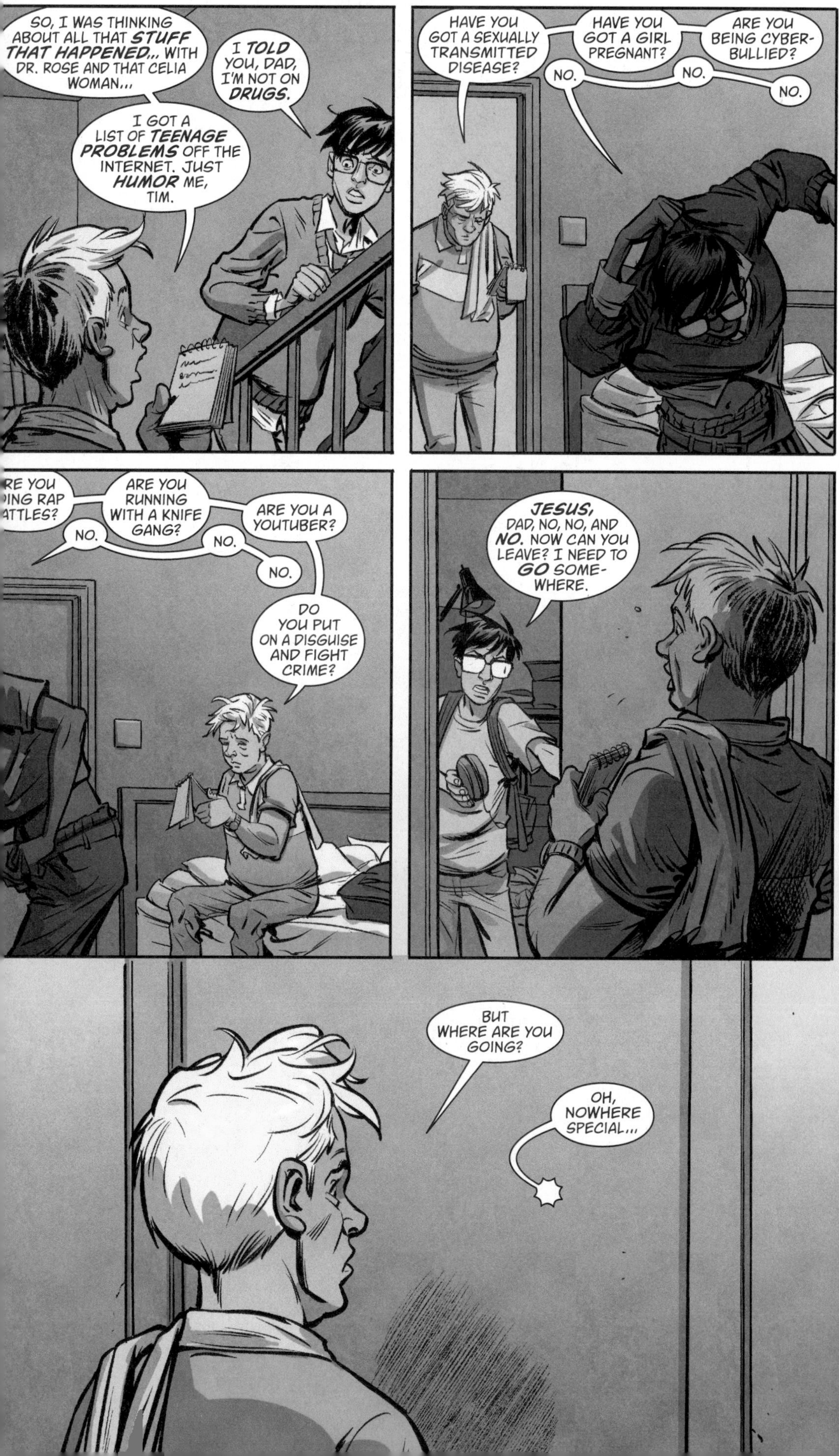
SO, I WAS THINKING ABOUT ALL THAT STUFF THAT HAPPENED... WITH DR. ROSE AND THAT CELIA WOMAN...
I GOT A LIST OF TEENAGE PROBLEMS OFF THE INTERNET. JUST HUMOR ME, TIM.
I TOLD YOU, DAD, I'M NOT ON DRUGS.
HAVE YOU GOT A SEXUALLY TRANSMITTED DISEASE?
NO.
HAVE YOU GOT A GIRL PREGNANT?
NO.
ARE YOU BEING CYBER-BULLIED?
NO.
RE YOU ING RAP ATTLES?
NO.
ARE YOU RUNNING WITH A KNIFE GANG?
NO.
ARE YOU A YOUTUBER?
NO.
DO YOU PUT ON A DISGUISE AND FIGHT CRIME?
JESUS, DAD, NO, NO, AND NO. NOW CAN YOU LEAVE? I NEED TO GO SOME-WHERE.
BUT WHERE ARE YOU GOING?
OH, NOWHERE SPECIAL...

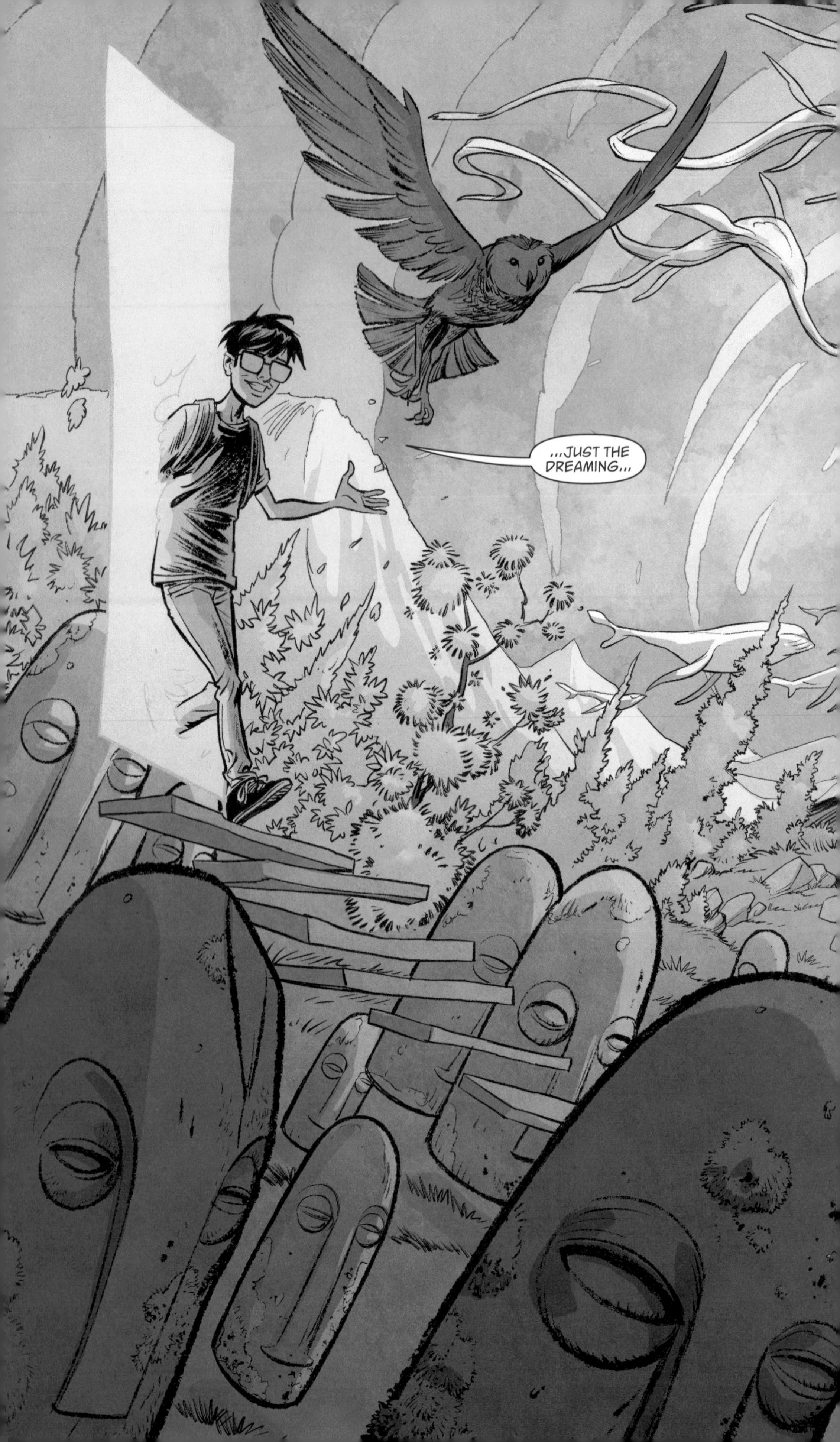
...JUST THE DREAMING...

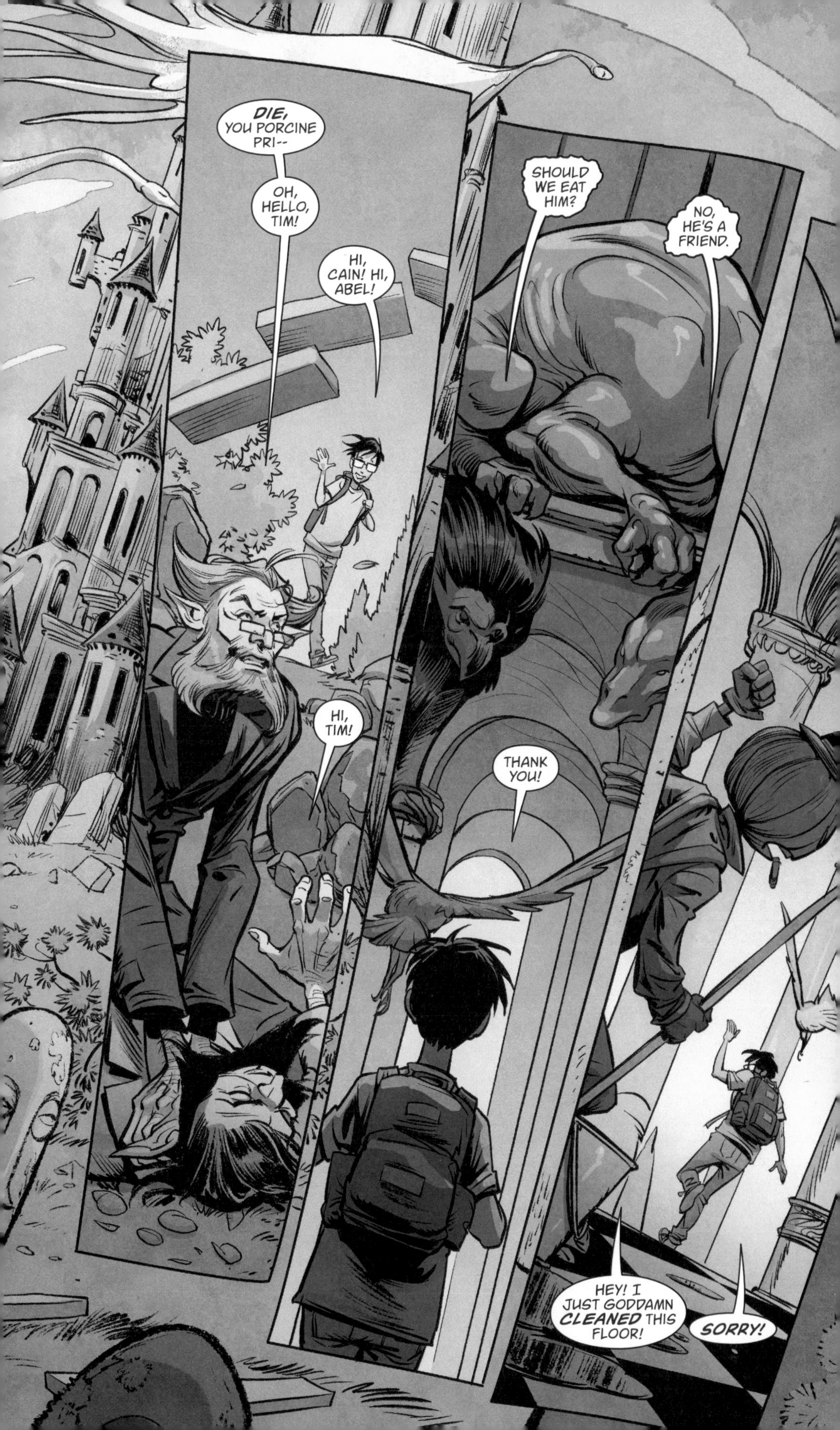
DIE, YOU PORCINE PRI--
OH, HELLO, TIM!
HI, CAIN! HI, ABEL!
HI, TIM!
SHOULD WE EAT HIM?
NO, HE'S A FRIEND.
THANK YOU!
HEY! I JUST GODDAMN CLEANED THIS FLOOR!
SORRY!

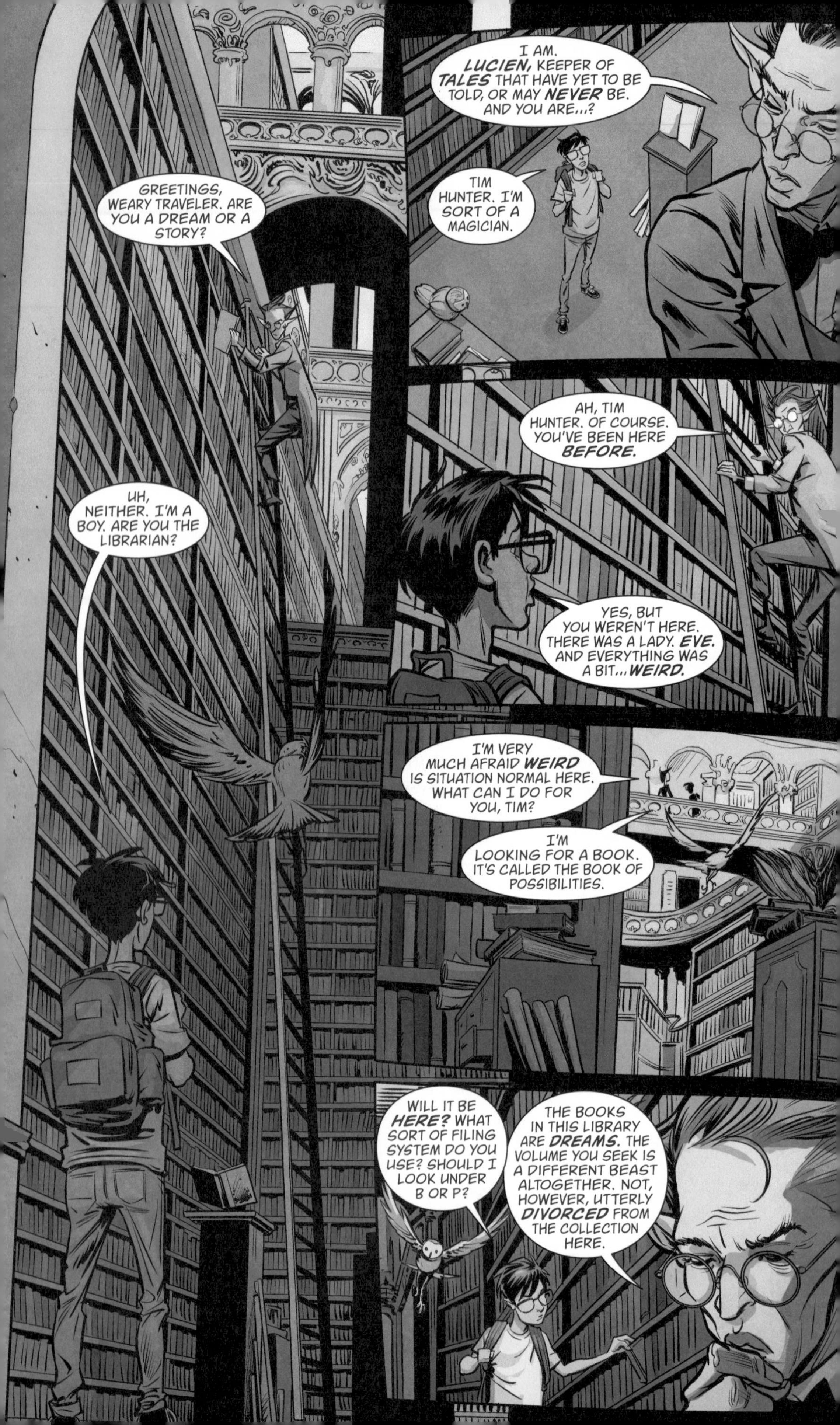
GREETINGS, WEARY TRAVELER. ARE YOU A DREAM OR A STORY?
UH, NEITHER. I'M A BOY. ARE YOU THE LIBRARIAN?
I AM. LUCIEN, KEEPER OF TALES THAT HAVE YET TO BE TOLD, OR MAY NEVER BE. AND YOU ARE...?
TIM HUNTER. I'M SORT OF A MAGICIAN.
AH, TIM HUNTER. OF COURSE. YOU'VE BEEN HERE BEFORE.
YES, BUT YOU WEREN'T HERE. THERE WAS A LADY. EVE. AND EVERYTHING WAS A BIT...WEIRD.
I'M VERY MUCH AFRAID WEIRD IS SITUATION NORMAL HERE. WHAT CAN I DO FOR YOU, TIM?
I'M LOOKING FOR A BOOK. IT'S CALLED THE BOOK OF POSSIBILITIES.
WILL IT BE HERE? WHAT SORT OF FILING SYSTEM DO YOU USE? SHOULD I LOOK UNDER B OR P?
THE BOOKS IN THIS LIBRARY ARE DREAMS. THE VOLUME YOU SEEK IS A DIFFERENT BEAST ALTOGETHER. NOT, HOWEVER, UTTERLY DIVORCED FROM THE COLLECTION HERE.

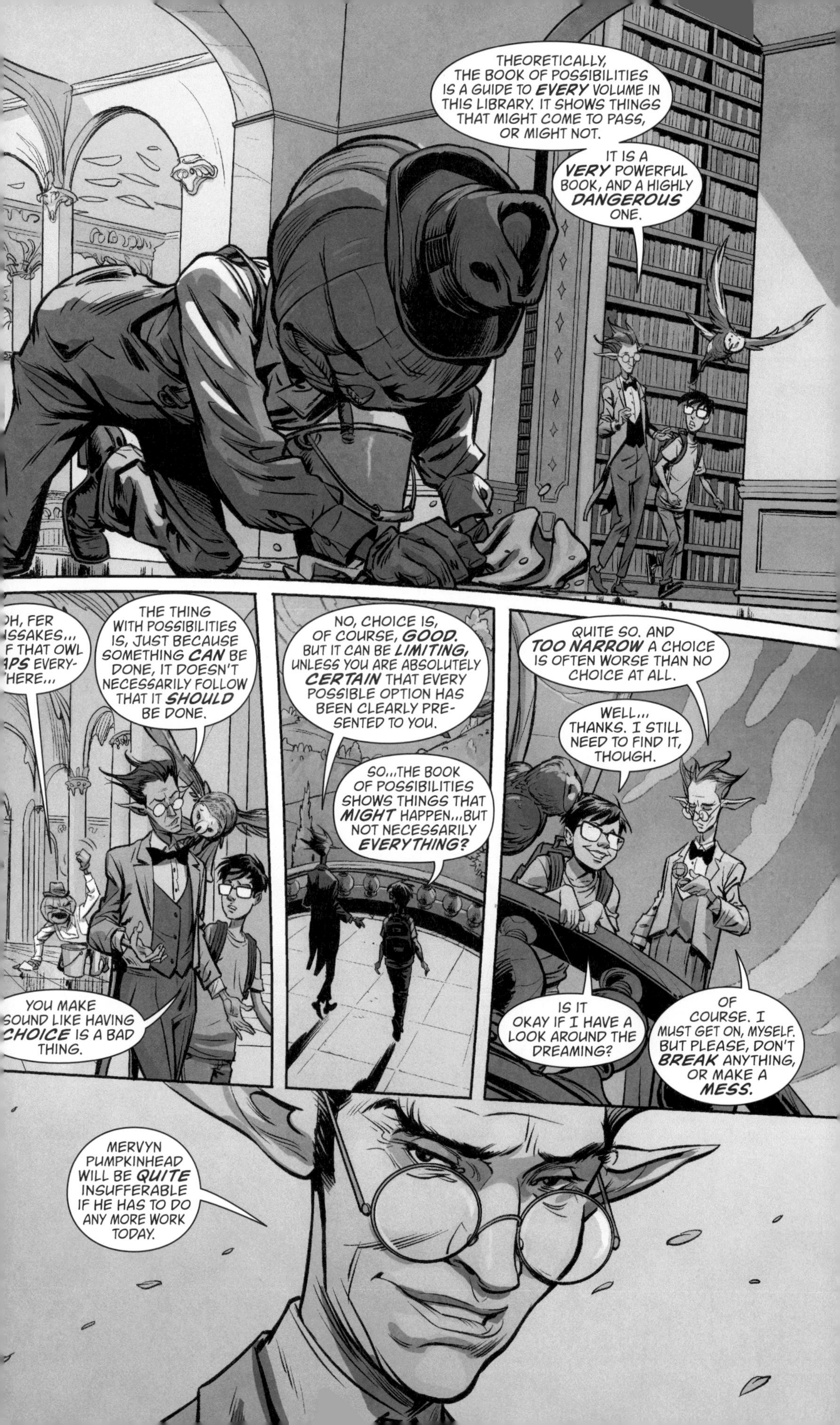
THEORETICALLY, THE BOOK OF POSSIBILITIES IS A GUIDE TO EVERY VOLUME IN THIS LIBRARY. IT SHOWS THINGS THAT MIGHT COME TO PASS, OR MIGHT NOT.
IT IS A VERY POWERFUL BOOK, AND A HIGHLY DANGEROUS ONE.
THE THING WITH POSSIBILITIES IS, JUST BECAUSE SOMETHING CAN BE DONE, IT DOESN'T NECESSARILY FOLLOW THAT IT SHOULD BE DONE.
OH, FER ...SSAKES... ...F THAT OWL ...APS EVERY- ...HERE...
YOU MAKE ...SOUND LIKE HAVING CHOICE IS A BAD THING.
NO, CHOICE IS, OF COURSE, GOOD. BUT IT CAN BE LIMITING, UNLESS YOU ARE ABSOLUTELY CERTAIN THAT EVERY POSSIBLE OPTION HAS BEEN CLEARLY PRE- SENTED TO YOU.
SO...THE BOOK OF POSSIBILITIES SHOWS THINGS THAT MIGHT HAPPEN...BUT NOT NECESSARILY EVERYTHING?
QUITE SO. AND TOO NARROW A CHOICE IS OFTEN WORSE THAN NO CHOICE AT ALL.
WELL... THANKS. I STILL NEED TO FIND IT, THOUGH.
IS IT OKAY IF I HAVE A LOOK AROUND THE DREAMING?
OF COURSE. I MUST GET ON, MYSELF. BUT PLEASE, DON'T BREAK ANYTHING, OR MAKE A MESS.
MERVYN PUMPKINHEAD WILL BE QUITE INSUFFERABLE IF HE HAS TO DO ANY MORE WORK TODAY.

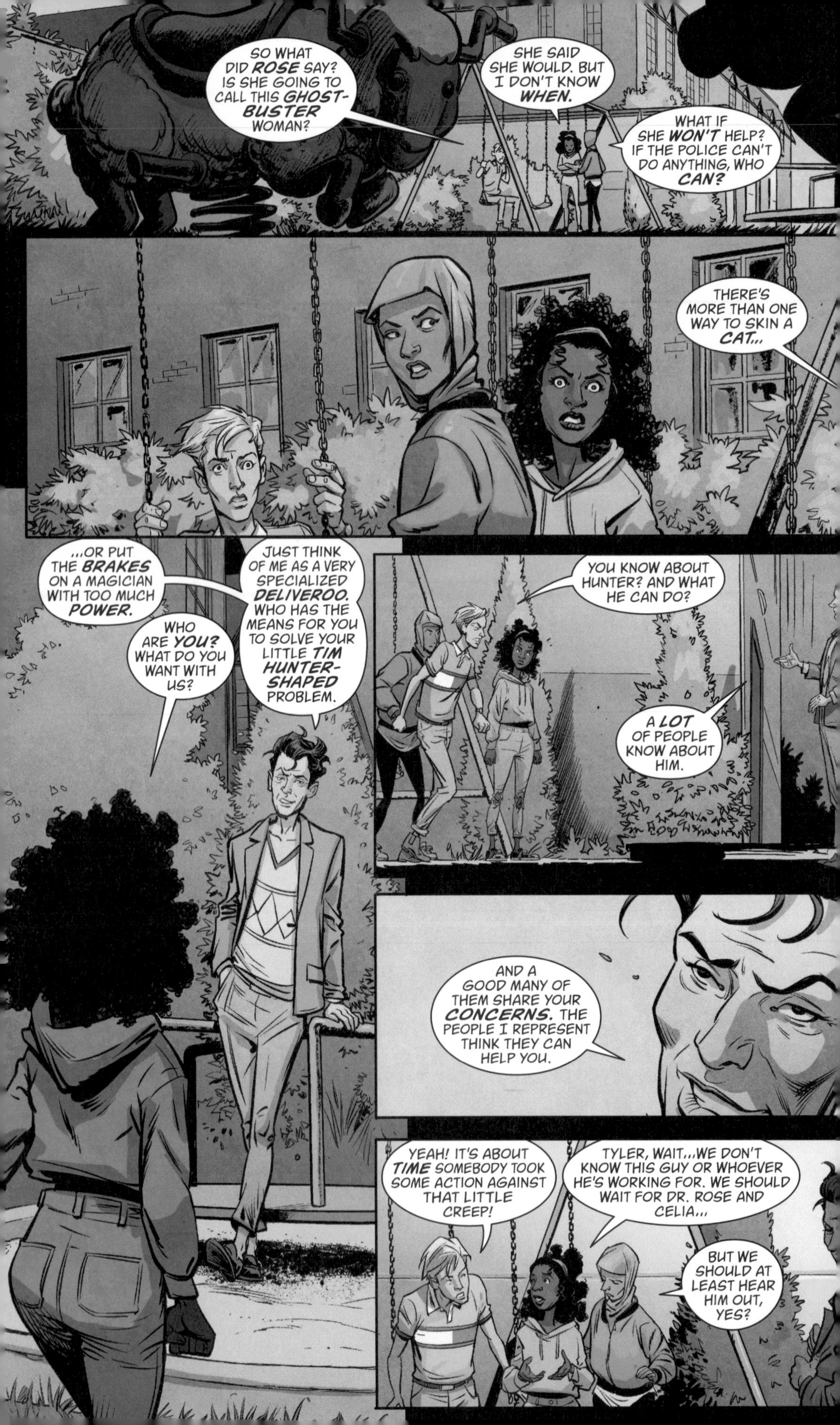
SO WHAT DID ROSE SAY? IS SHE GOING TO CALL THIS GHOST-BUSTER WOMAN?
SHE SAID SHE WOULD. BUT I DON'T KNOW WHEN.
WHAT IF SHE WON'T HELP? IF THE POLICE CAN'T DO ANYTHING, WHO CAN?
THERE'S MORE THAN ONE WAY TO SKIN A CAT...
...OR PUT THE BRAKES ON A MAGICIAN WITH TOO MUCH POWER.
WHO ARE YOU? WHAT DO YOU WANT WITH US?
JUST THINK OF ME AS A VERY SPECIALIZED DELIVEROO. WHO HAS THE MEANS FOR YOU TO SOLVE YOUR LITTLE TIM HUNTER-SHAPED PROBLEM.
YOU KNOW ABOUT HUNTER? AND WHAT HE CAN DO?
A LOT OF PEOPLE KNOW ABOUT HIM.
AND A GOOD MANY OF THEM SHARE YOUR CONCERNS. THE PEOPLE I REPRESENT THINK THEY CAN HELP YOU.
YEAH! IT'S ABOUT TIME SOMEBODY TOOK SOME ACTION AGAINST THAT LITTLE CREEP!
TYLER, WAIT...WE DON'T KNOW THIS GUY OR WHOEVER HE'S WORKING FOR. WE SHOULD WAIT FOR DR. ROSE AND CELIA...
BUT WE SHOULD AT LEAST HEAR HIM OUT, YES?

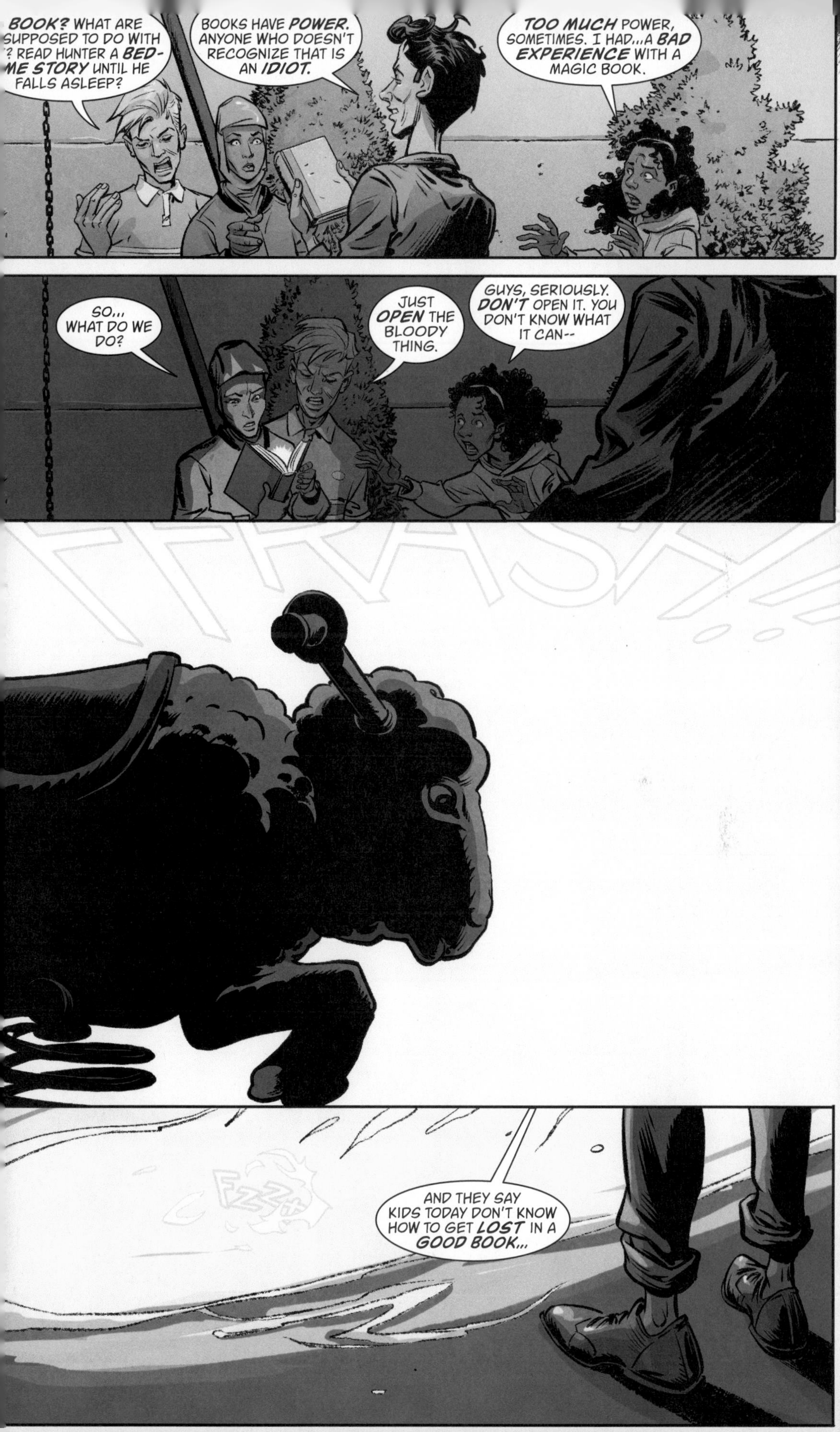
BOOK? WHAT ARE SUPPOSED TO DO WITH ? READ HUNTER A BED-ME STORY UNTIL HE FALLS ASLEEP?
BOOKS HAVE POWER. ANYONE WHO DOESN'T RECOGNIZE THAT IS AN IDIOT.
TOO MUCH POWER, SOMETIMES. I HAD...A BAD EXPERIENCE WITH A MAGIC BOOK.
SO... WHAT DO WE DO?
JUST OPEN THE BLOODY THING.
GUYS, SERIOUSLY. DON'T OPEN IT. YOU DON'T KNOW WHAT IT CAN--
FZZT
AND THEY SAY KIDS TODAY DON'T KNOW HOW TO GET LOST IN A GOOD BOOK...

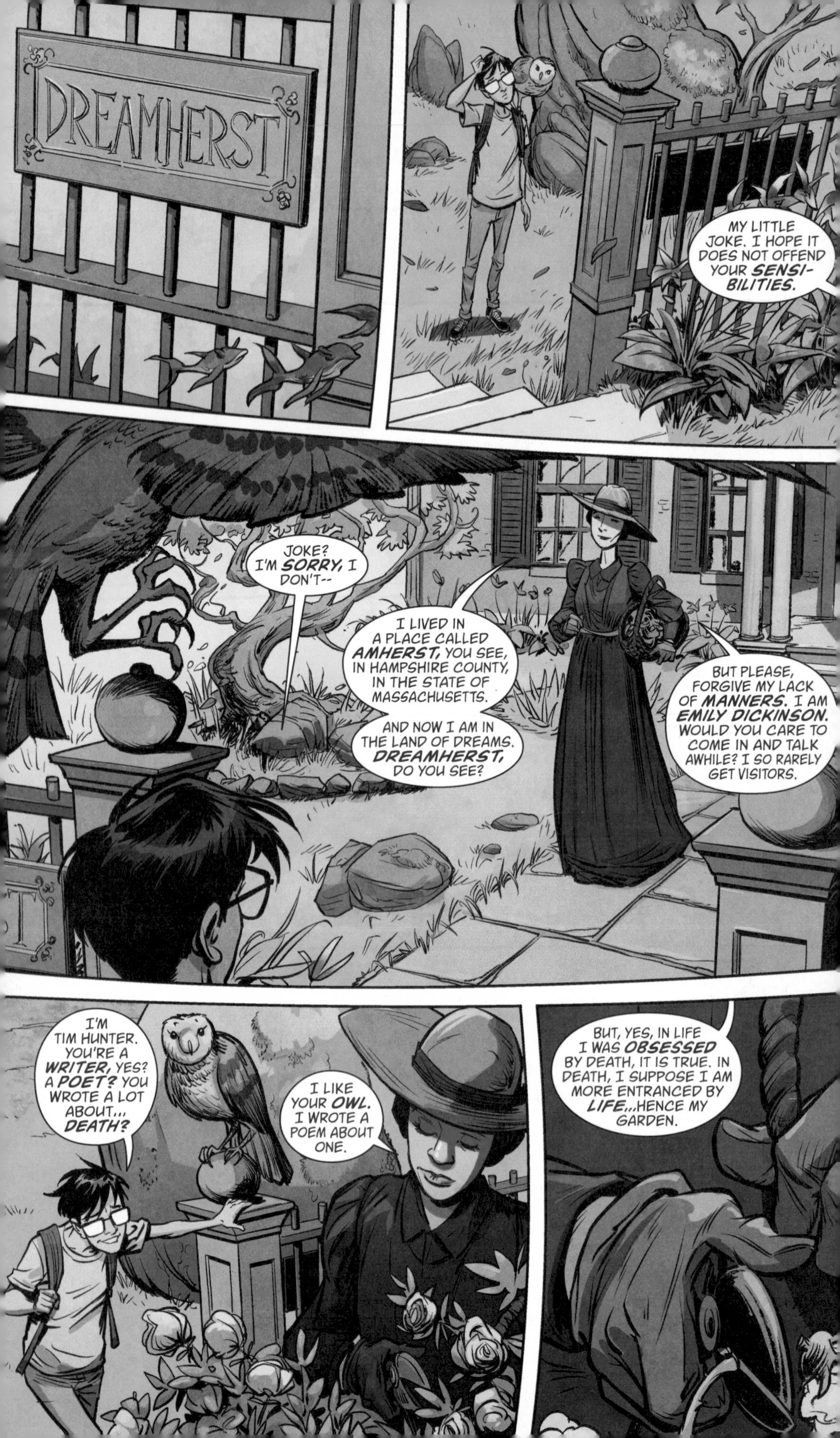
DREAMHERST
MY LITTLE JOKE. I HOPE IT DOES NOT OFFEND YOUR SENSIBILITIES.
JOKE? I'M SORRY, I DON'T--
I LIVED IN A PLACE CALLED AMHERST, YOU SEE, IN HAMPSHIRE COUNTY, IN THE STATE OF MASSACHUSETTS.
AND NOW I AM IN THE LAND OF DREAMS. DREAMHERST, DO YOU SEE?
BUT PLEASE, FORGIVE MY LACK OF MANNERS. I AM EMILY DICKINSON. WOULD YOU CARE TO COME IN AND TALK AWHILE? I SO RARELY GET VISITORS.
I'M TIM HUNTER. YOU'RE A WRITER, YES? A POET? YOU WROTE A LOT ABOUT... DEATH?
I LIKE YOUR OWL. I WROTE A POEM ABOUT ONE.
BUT, YES, IN LIFE I WAS OBSESSED BY DEATH, IT IS TRUE. IN DEATH, I SUPPOSE I AM MORE ENTRANCED BY LIFE...HENCE MY GARDEN.

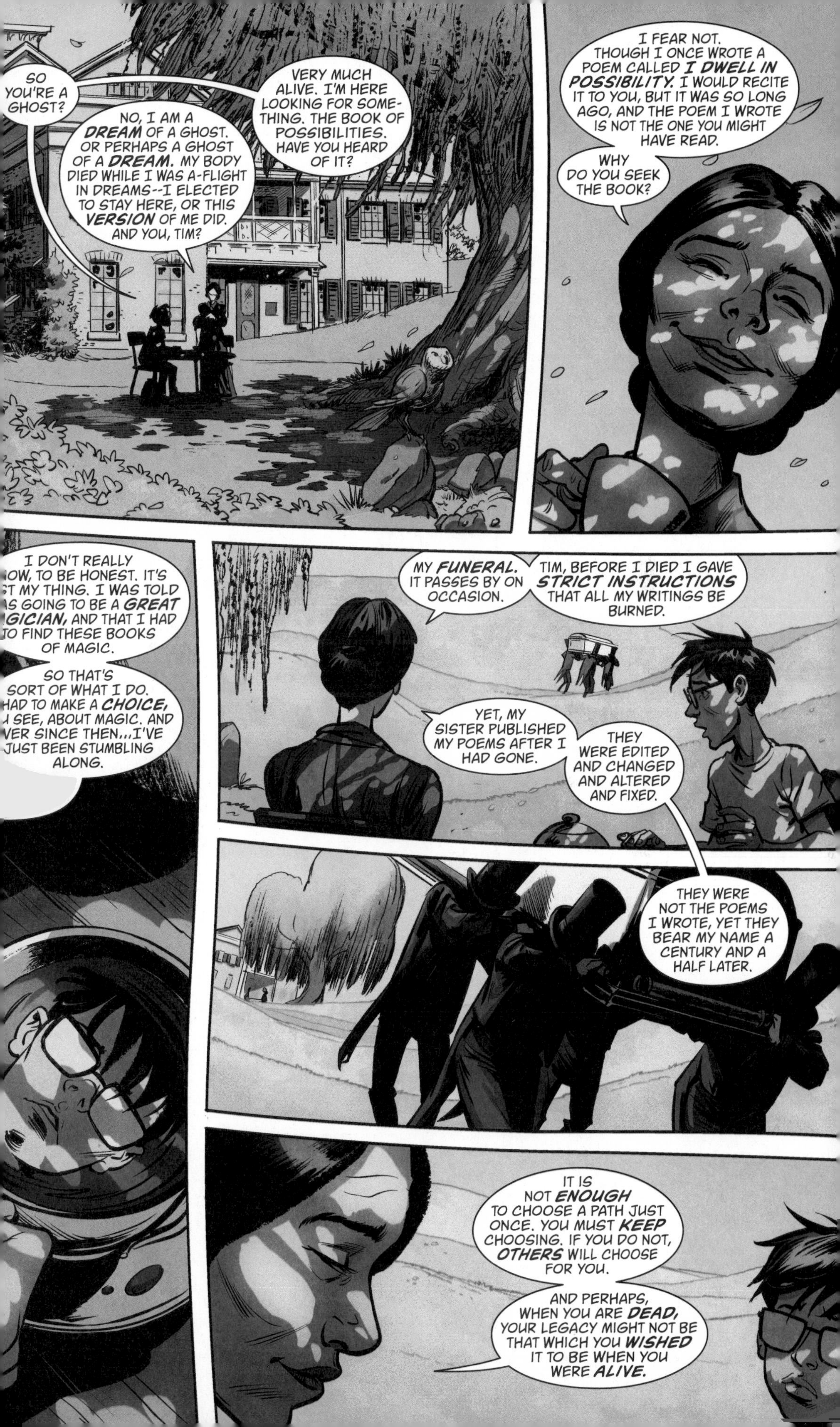
SO YOU'RE A GHOST?
NO, I AM A DREAM OF A GHOST. OR PERHAPS A GHOST OF A DREAM. MY BODY DIED WHILE I WAS A-FLIGHT IN DREAMS--I ELECTED TO STAY HERE, OR THIS VERSION OF ME DID. AND YOU, TIM?
VERY MUCH ALIVE. I'M HERE LOOKING FOR SOME-THING. THE BOOK OF POSSIBILITIES. HAVE YOU HEARD OF IT?
I FEAR NOT. THOUGH I ONCE WROTE A POEM CALLED I DWELL IN POSSIBILITY. I WOULD RECITE IT TO YOU, BUT IT WAS SO LONG AGO, AND THE POEM I WROTE IS NOT THE ONE YOU MIGHT HAVE READ.
WHY DO YOU SEEK THE BOOK?
I DON'T REALLY
OW, TO BE HONEST. IT'S
T MY THING. I WAS TOLD
S GOING TO BE A GREAT
GICIAN, AND THAT I HAD
TO FIND THESE BOOKS
OF MAGIC.
SO THAT'S
SORT OF WHAT I DO.
HAD TO MAKE A CHOICE,
SEE, ABOUT MAGIC. AND
VER SINCE THEN...I'VE
JUST BEEN STUMBLING
ALONG.
MY FUNERAL. IT PASSES BY ON OCCASION.
TIM, BEFORE I DIED I GAVE STRICT INSTRUCTIONS THAT ALL MY WRITINGS BE BURNED.
YET, MY SISTER PUBLISHED MY POEMS AFTER I HAD GONE.
THEY WERE EDITED AND CHANGED AND ALTERED AND FIXED.
THEY WERE NOT THE POEMS I WROTE, YET THEY BEAR MY NAME A CENTURY AND A HALF LATER.
IT IS NOT ENOUGH TO CHOOSE A PATH JUST ONCE. YOU MUST KEEP CHOOSING. IF YOU DO NOT, OTHERS WILL CHOOSE FOR YOU.
AND PERHAPS, WHEN YOU ARE DEAD, YOUR LEGACY MIGHT NOT BE THAT WHICH YOU WISHED IT TO BE WHEN YOU WERE ALIVE.

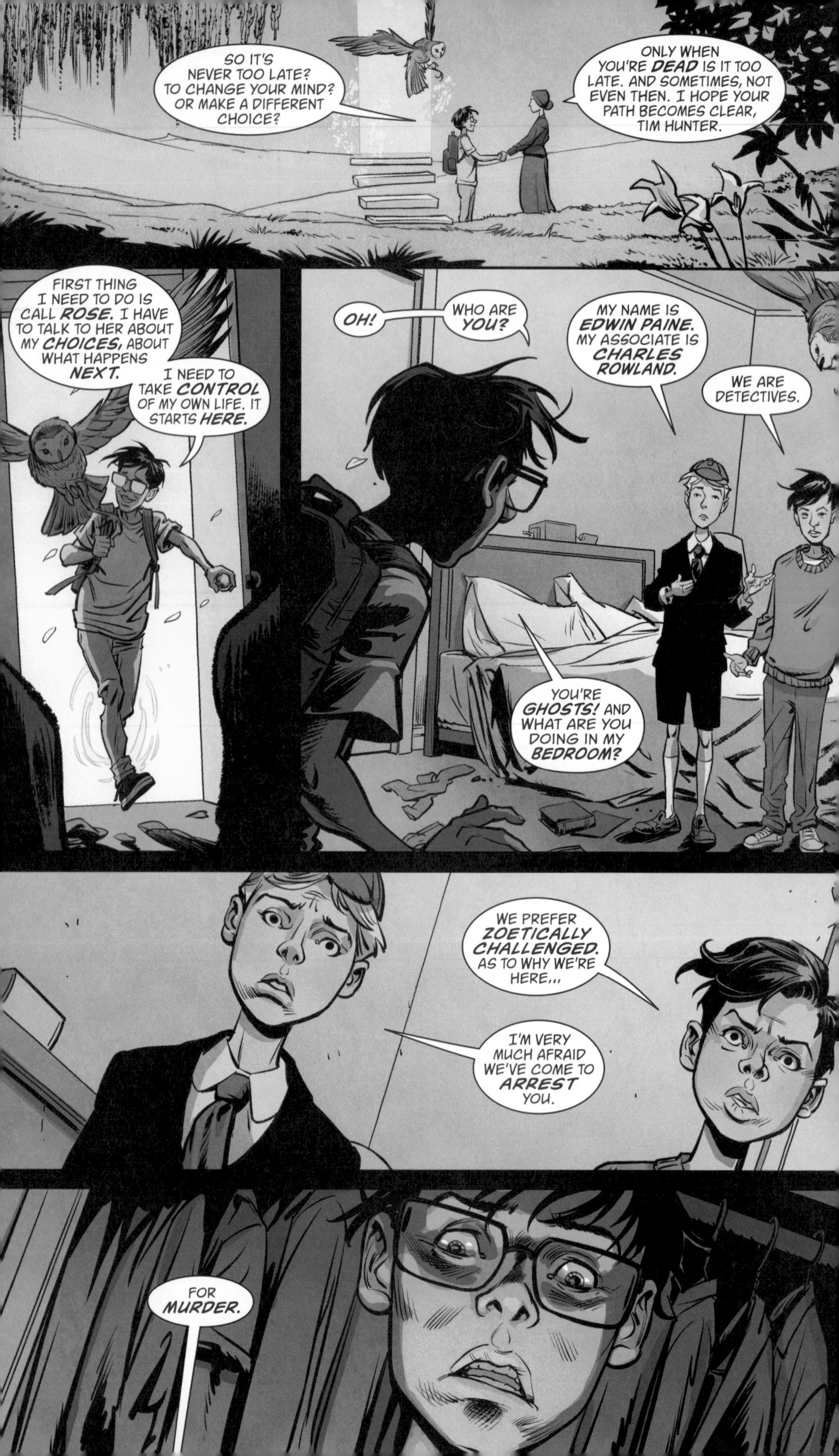
SO IT'S NEVER TOO LATE? TO CHANGE YOUR MIND? OR MAKE A DIFFERENT CHOICE?
ONLY WHEN YOU'RE DEAD IS IT TOO LATE. AND SOMETIMES, NOT EVEN THEN. I HOPE YOUR PATH BECOMES CLEAR, TIM HUNTER.
FIRST THING I NEED TO DO IS CALL ROSE. I HAVE TO TALK TO HER ABOUT MY CHOICES, ABOUT WHAT HAPPENS NEXT.
I NEED TO TAKE CONTROL OF MY OWN LIFE. IT STARTS HERE.
OH!
WHO ARE YOU?
MY NAME IS EDWIN PAINE. MY ASSOCIATE IS CHARLES ROWLAND.
WE ARE DETECTIVES.
YOU'RE GHOSTS! AND WHAT ARE YOU DOING IN MY BEDROOM?
WE PREFER ZOETICALLY CHALLENGED. AS TO WHY WE'RE HERE...
I'M VERY MUCH AFRAID WE'VE COME TO ARREST YOU.
FOR MURDER.

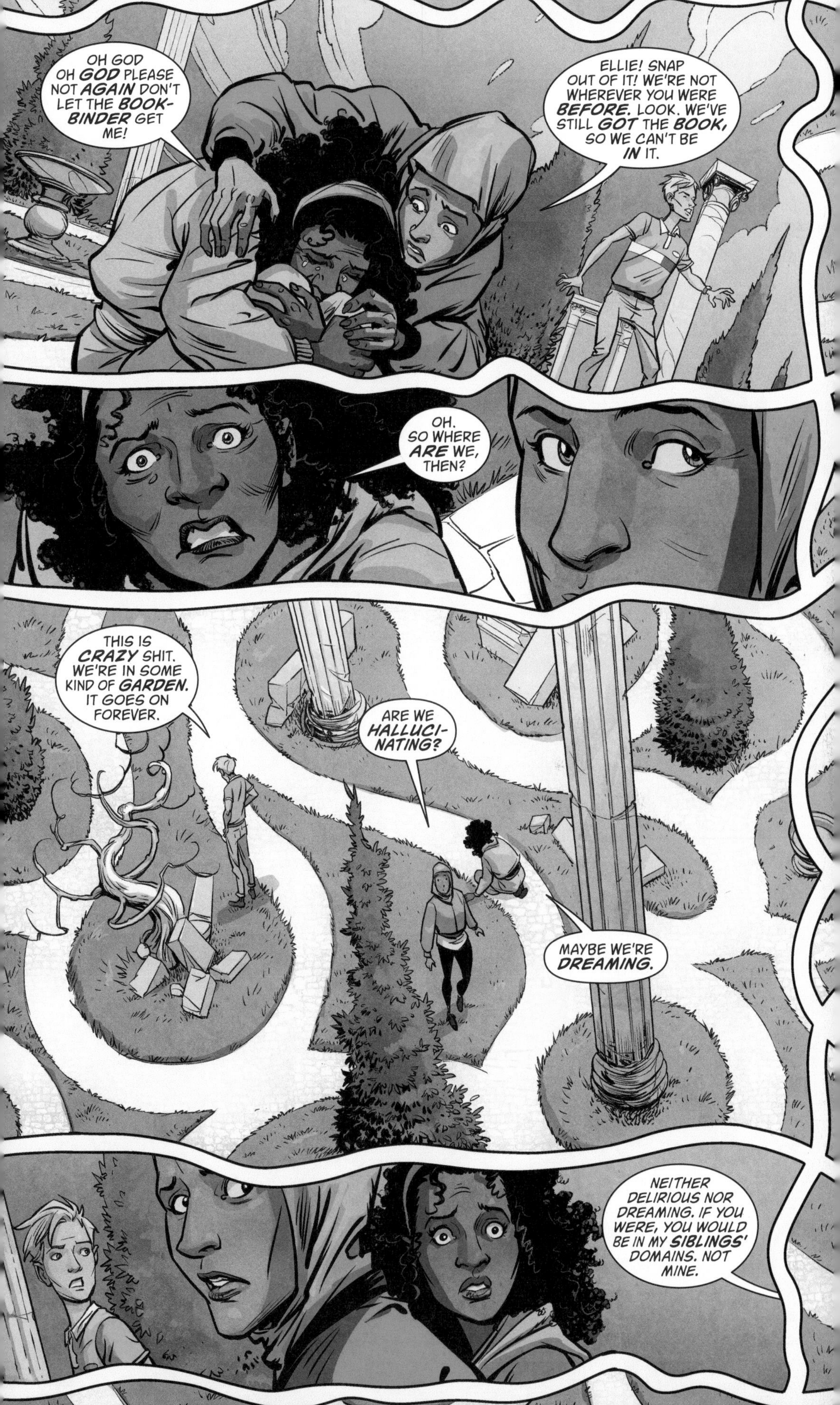
OH GOD OH GOD PLEASE NOT AGAIN DON'T LET THE BOOK-BINDER GET ME!
ELLIE! SNAP OUT OF IT! WE'RE NOT WHEREVER YOU WERE BEFORE. LOOK. WE'VE STILL GOT THE BOOK, SO WE CAN'T BE IN IT.
OH. SO WHERE ARE WE, THEN?
THIS IS CRAZY SHIT. WE'RE IN SOME KIND OF GARDEN. IT GOES ON FOREVER.
ARE WE HALLUCI-NATING?
MAYBE WE'RE DREAMING.
NEITHER DELIRIOUS NOR DREAMING. IF YOU WERE, YOU WOULD BE IN MY SIBLINGS' DOMAINS. NOT MINE.

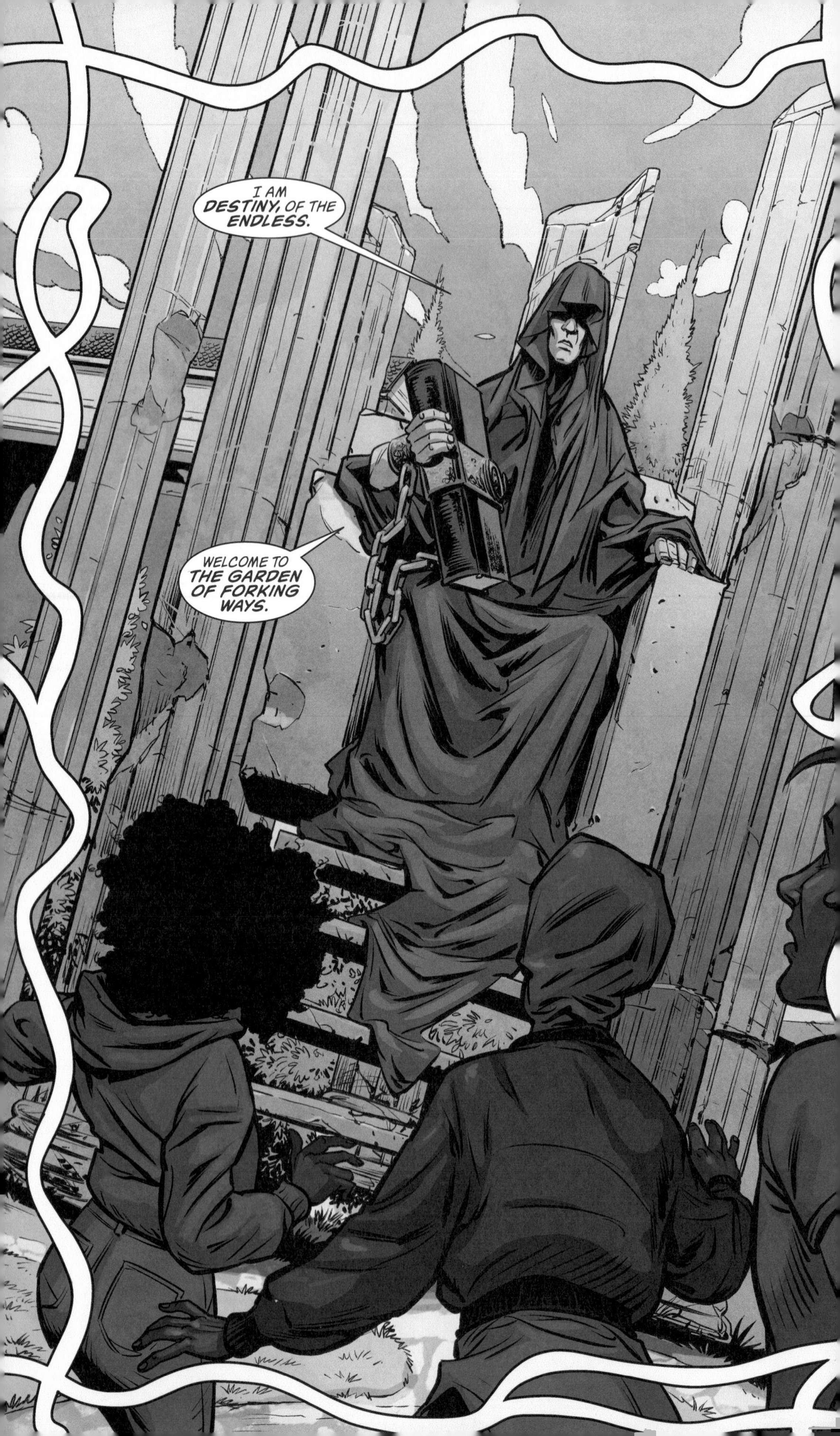
I AM DESTINY, OF THE ENDLESS.
WELCOME TO THE GARDEN OF FORKING WAYS.

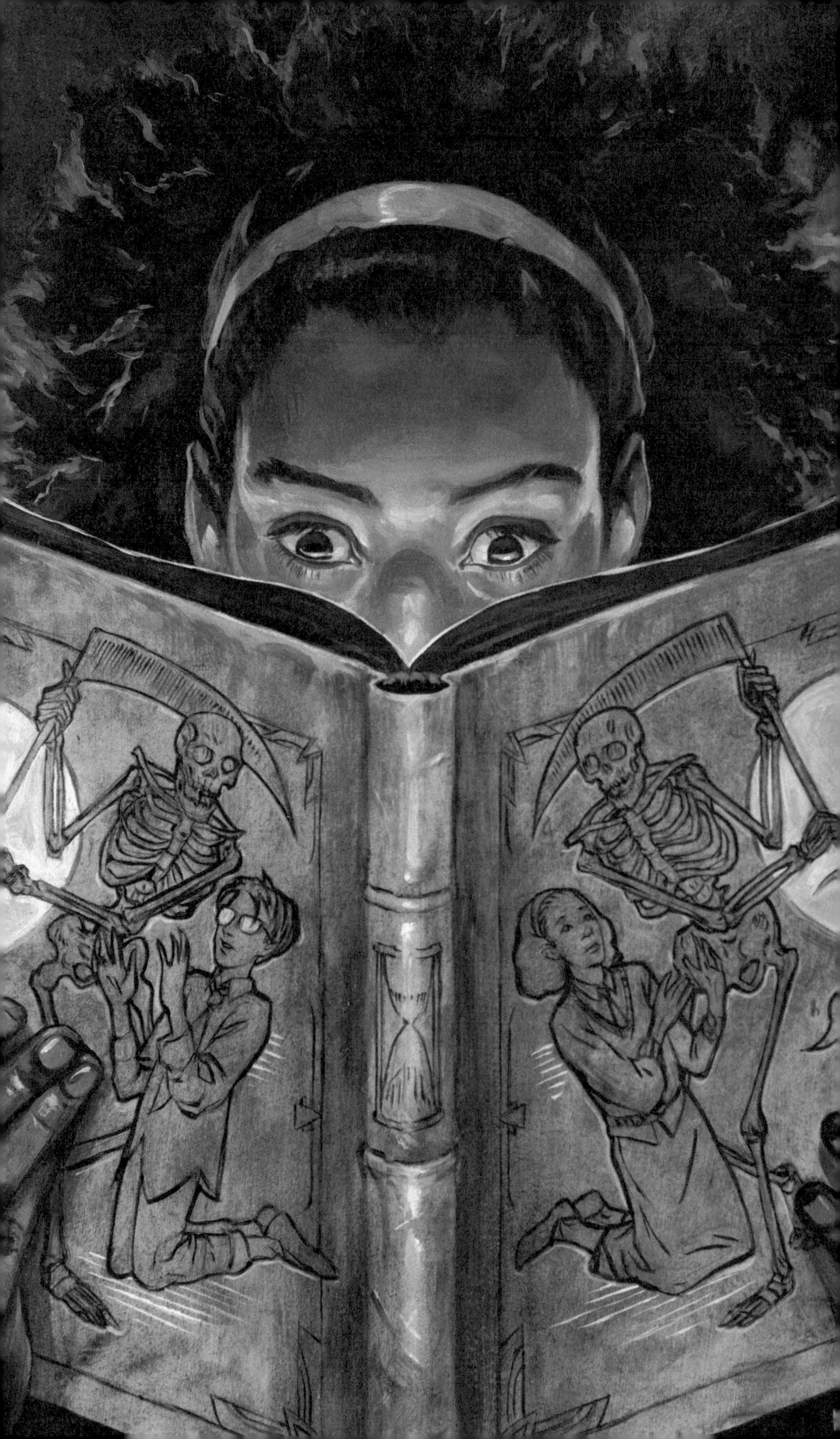

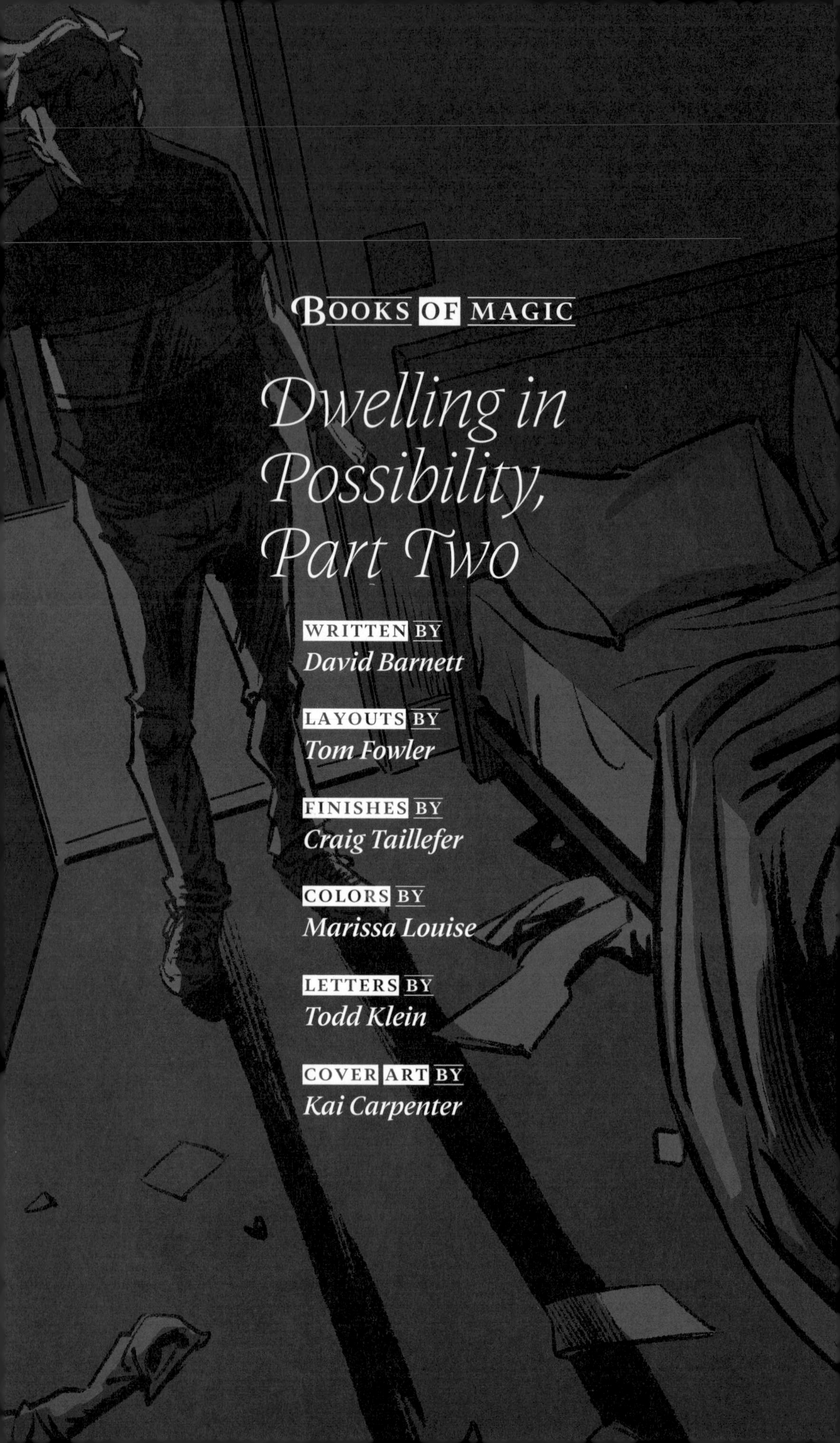

BOOKS OF MAGIC

Dwelling in Possibility, Part Two

WRITTEN BY
David Barnett

LAYOUTS BY
Tom Fowler

FINISHES BY
Craig Taillefer

COLORS BY
Marissa Louise

LETTERS BY
Todd Klein

COVER ART BY
Kai Carpenter

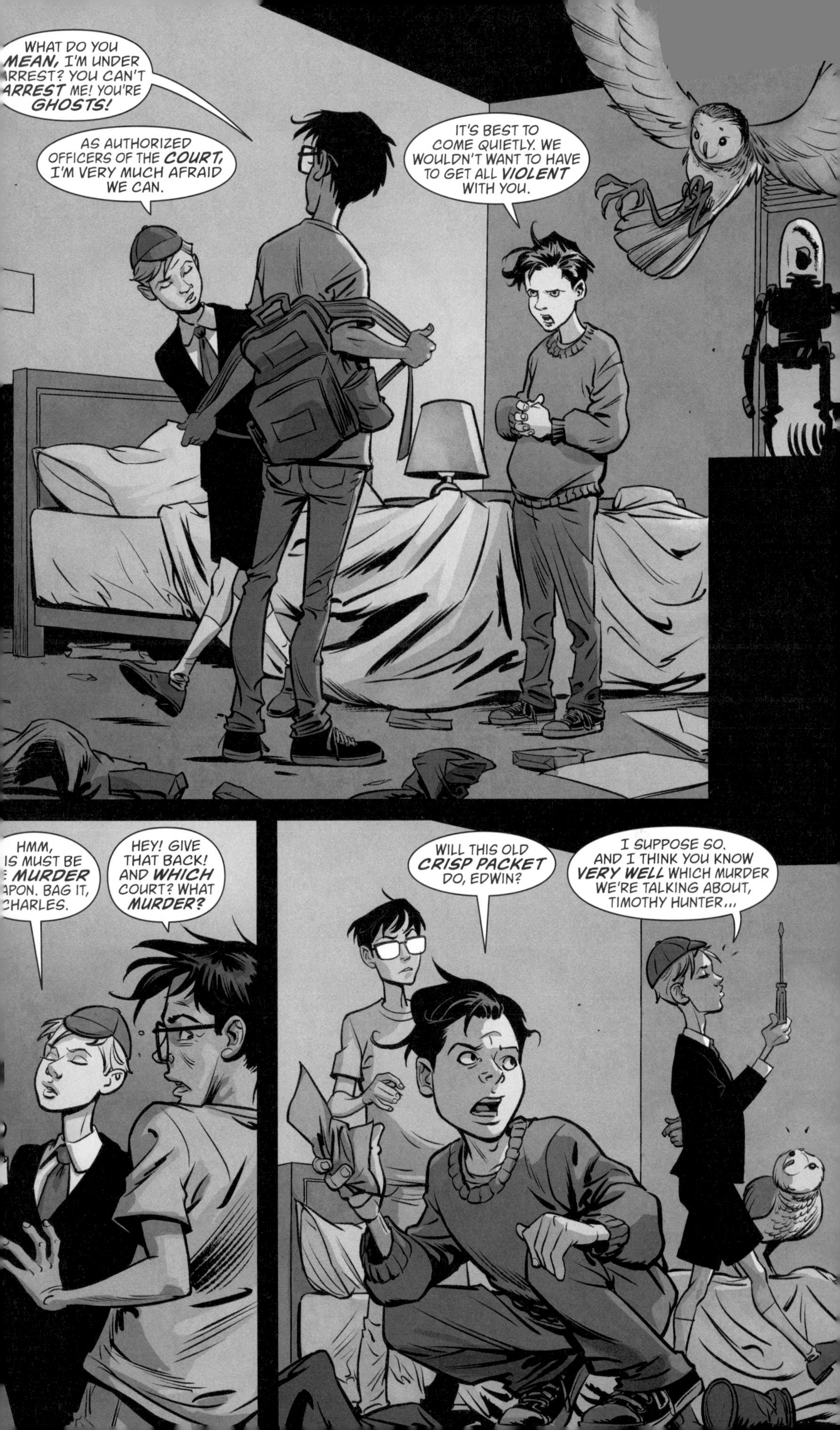
WHAT DO YOU MEAN, I'M UNDER RREST? YOU CAN'T ARREST ME! YOU'RE GHOSTS!
AS AUTHORIZED OFFICERS OF THE COURT, I'M VERY MUCH AFRAID WE CAN.
IT'S BEST TO COME QUIETLY. WE WOULDN'T WANT TO HAVE TO GET ALL VIOLENT WITH YOU.
HMM, IS MUST BE E MURDER APON. BAG IT, CHARLES.
HEY! GIVE THAT BACK! AND WHICH COURT? WHAT MURDER?
WILL THIS OLD CRISP PACKET DO, EDWIN?
I SUPPOSE SO. AND I THINK YOU KNOW VERY WELL WHICH MURDER WE'RE TALKING ABOUT, TIMOTHY HUNTER...

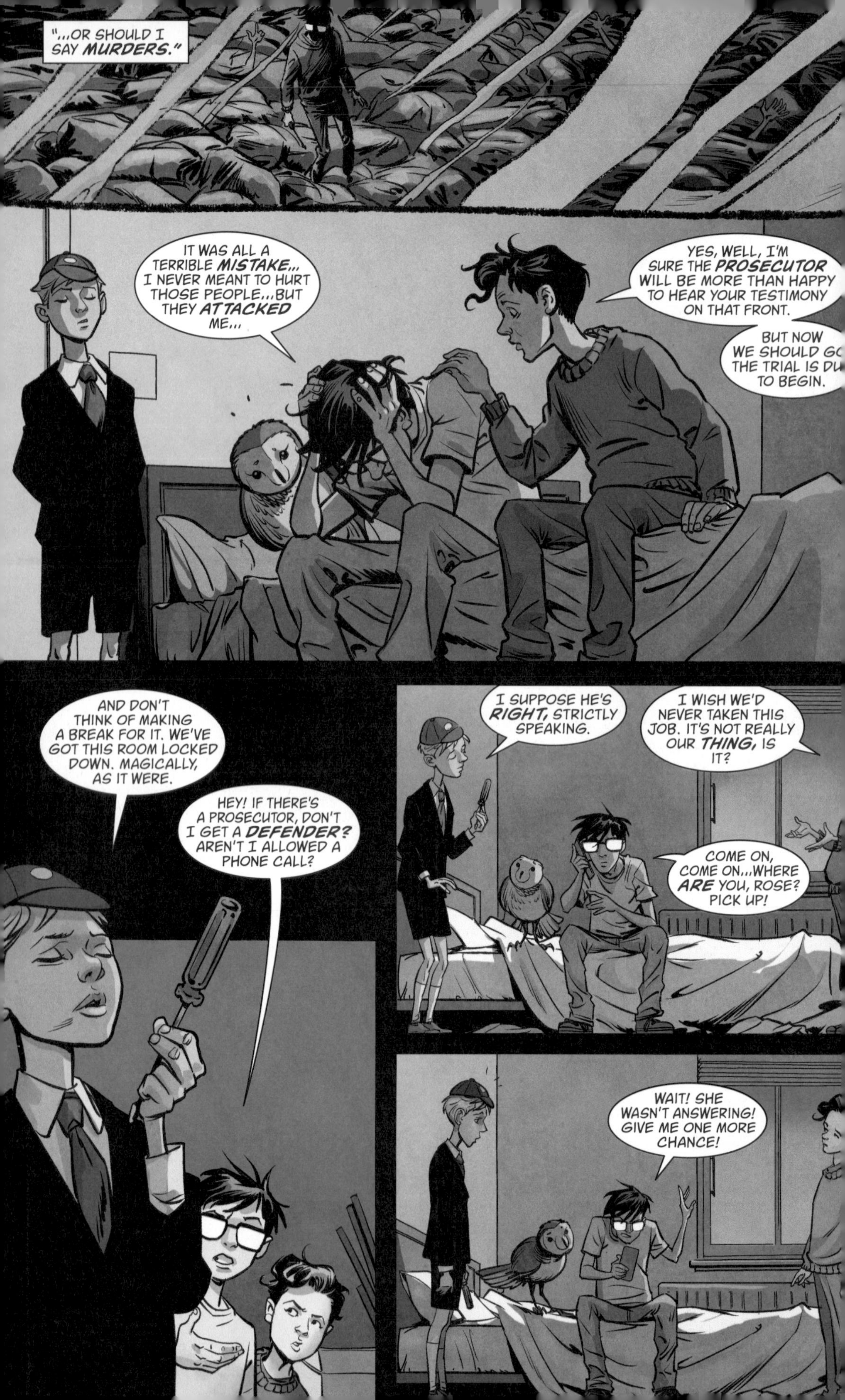

"...OR SHOULD I SAY MURDERS."
IT WAS ALL A TERRIBLE MISTAKE... I NEVER MEANT TO HURT THOSE PEOPLE...BUT THEY ATTACKED ME...
YES, WELL, I'M SURE THE PROSECUTOR WILL BE MORE THAN HAPPY TO HEAR YOUR TESTIMONY ON THAT FRONT.
AND DON'T THINK OF MAKING A BREAK FOR IT. WE'VE GOT THIS ROOM LOCKED DOWN. MAGICALLY, AS IT WERE.
HEY! IF THERE'S A PROSECUTOR, DON'T I GET A DEFENDER? AREN'T I ALLOWED A PHONE CALL?
I SUPPOSE HE'S RIGHT, STRICTLY SPEAKING.
I WISH WE'D NEVER TAKEN THIS JOB. IT'S NOT REALLY OUR THING, IS IT?
COME ON, COME ON...WHERE ARE YOU, ROSE? PICK UP!
WAIT! SHE WASN'T ANSWERING! GIVE ME ONE MORE CHANCE!

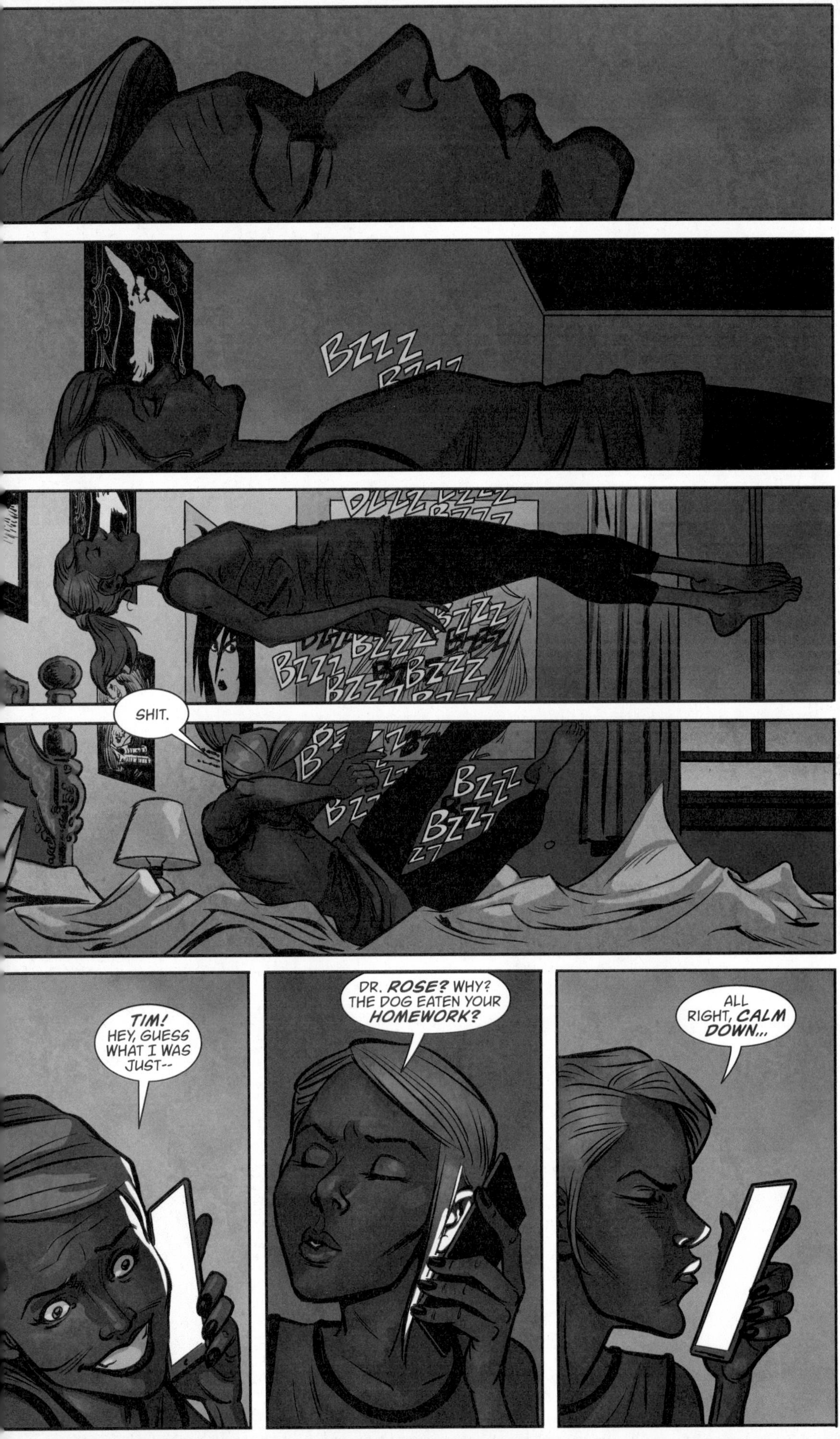
BZZZ
SHIT.
TIM! HEY, GUESS WHAT I WAS JUST--
DR. ROSE? WHY? THE DOG EATEN YOUR HOMEWORK?
ALL RIGHT, CALM DOWN...

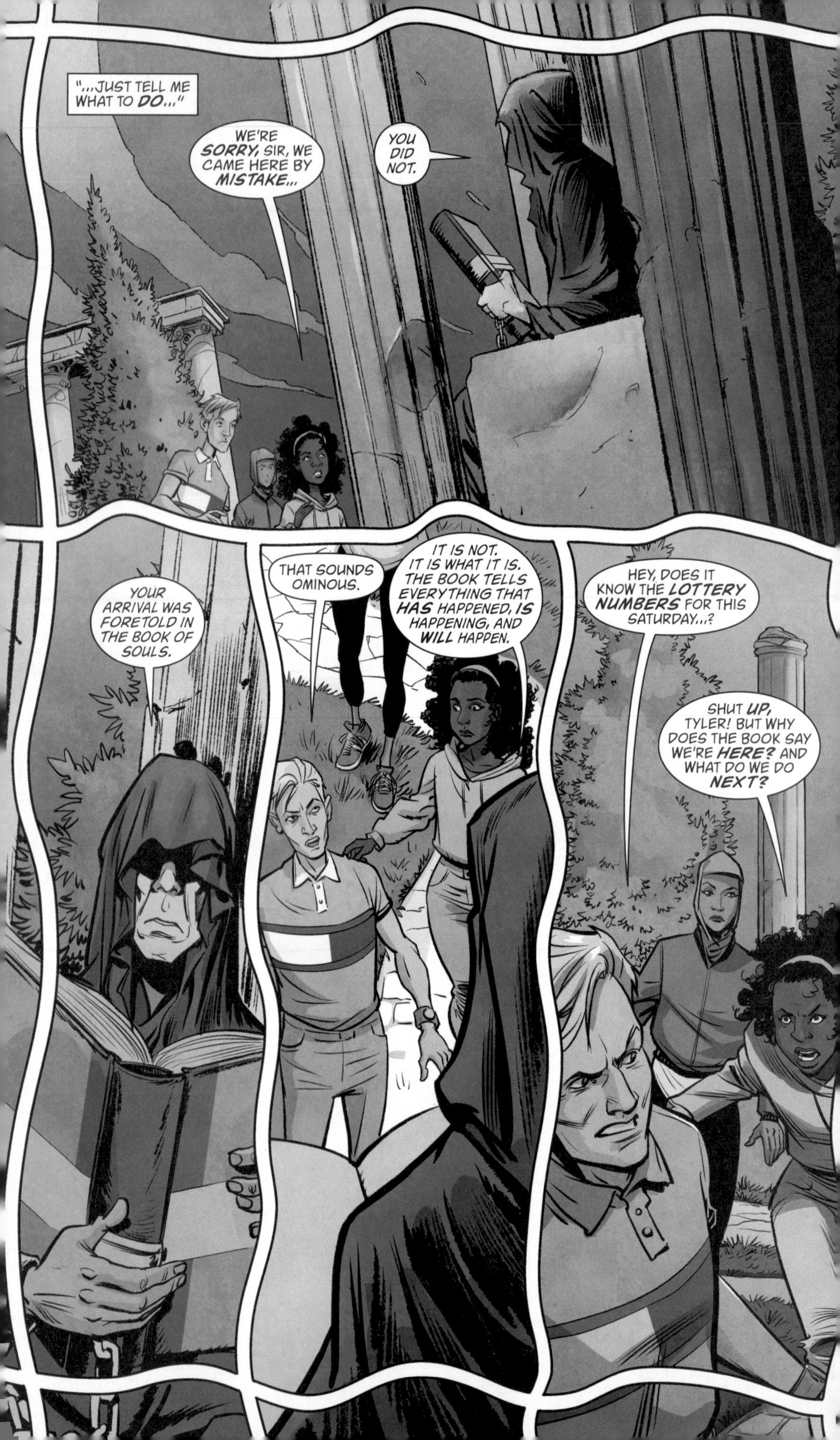
"...JUST TELL ME WHAT TO DO..."
WE'RE SORRY, SIR, WE CAME HERE BY MISTAKE...
YOU DID NOT.
YOUR ARRIVAL WAS FORETOLD IN THE BOOK OF SOULS.
THAT SOUNDS OMINOUS.
IT IS NOT. IT IS WHAT IT IS. THE BOOK TELLS EVERYTHING THAT HAS HAPPENED, IS HAPPENING, AND WILL HAPPEN.
HEY, DOES IT KNOW THE LOTTERY NUMBERS FOR THIS SATURDAY...?
SHUT UP, TYLER! BUT WHY DOES THE BOOK SAY WE'RE HERE? AND WHAT DO WE DO NEXT?

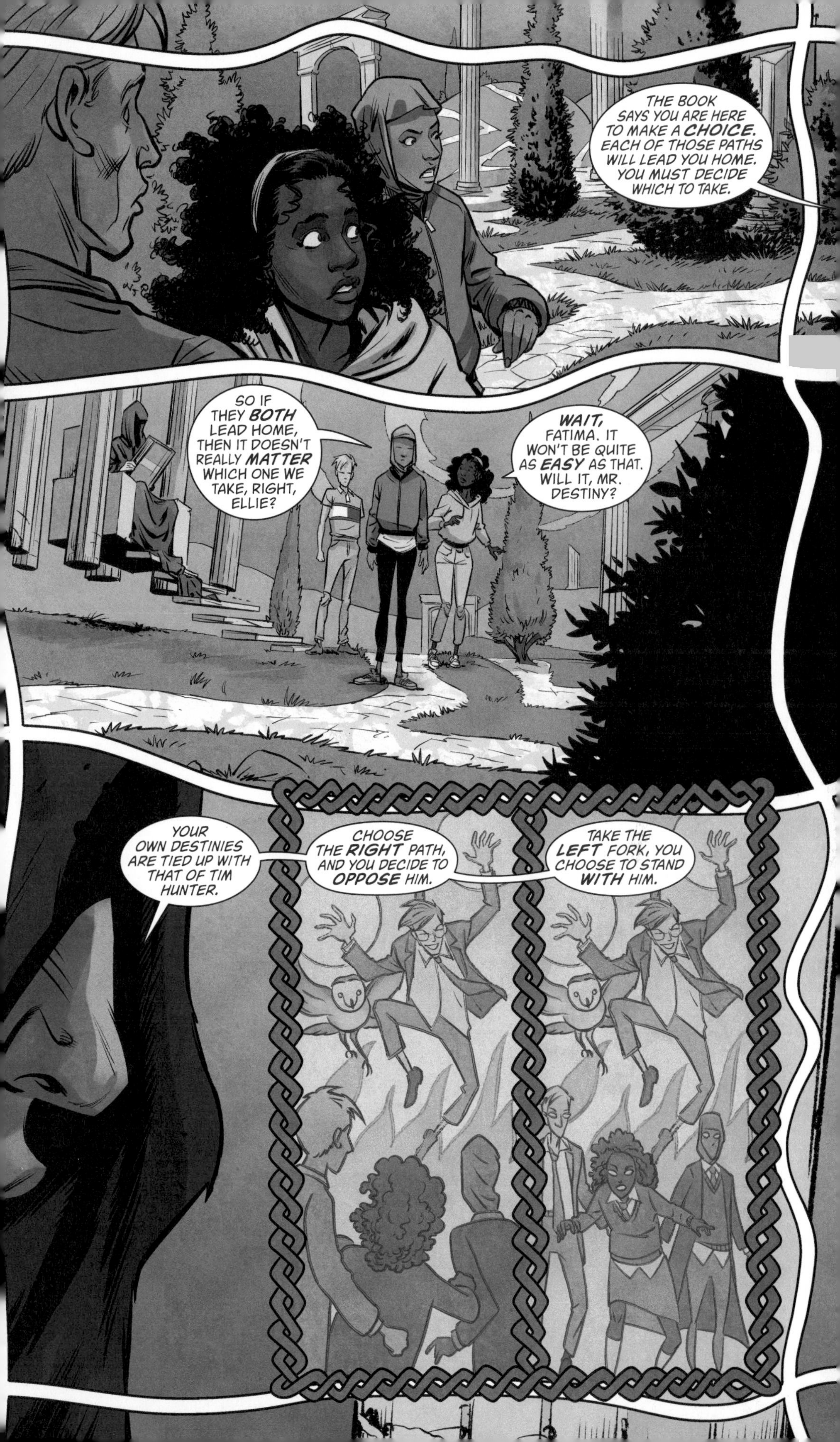
THE BOOK SAYS YOU ARE HERE TO MAKE A CHOICE. EACH OF THOSE PATHS WILL LEAD YOU HOME. YOU MUST DECIDE WHICH TO TAKE.
SO IF THEY BOTH LEAD HOME, THEN IT DOESN'T REALLY MATTER WHICH ONE WE TAKE, RIGHT, ELLIE?
WAIT, FATIMA. IT WON'T BE QUITE AS EASY AS THAT. WILL IT, MR. DESTINY?
YOUR OWN DESTINIES ARE TIED UP WITH THAT OF TIM HUNTER.
CHOOSE THE RIGHT PATH, AND YOU DECIDE TO OPPOSE HIM.
TAKE THE LEFT FORK, YOU CHOOSE TO STAND WITH HIM.

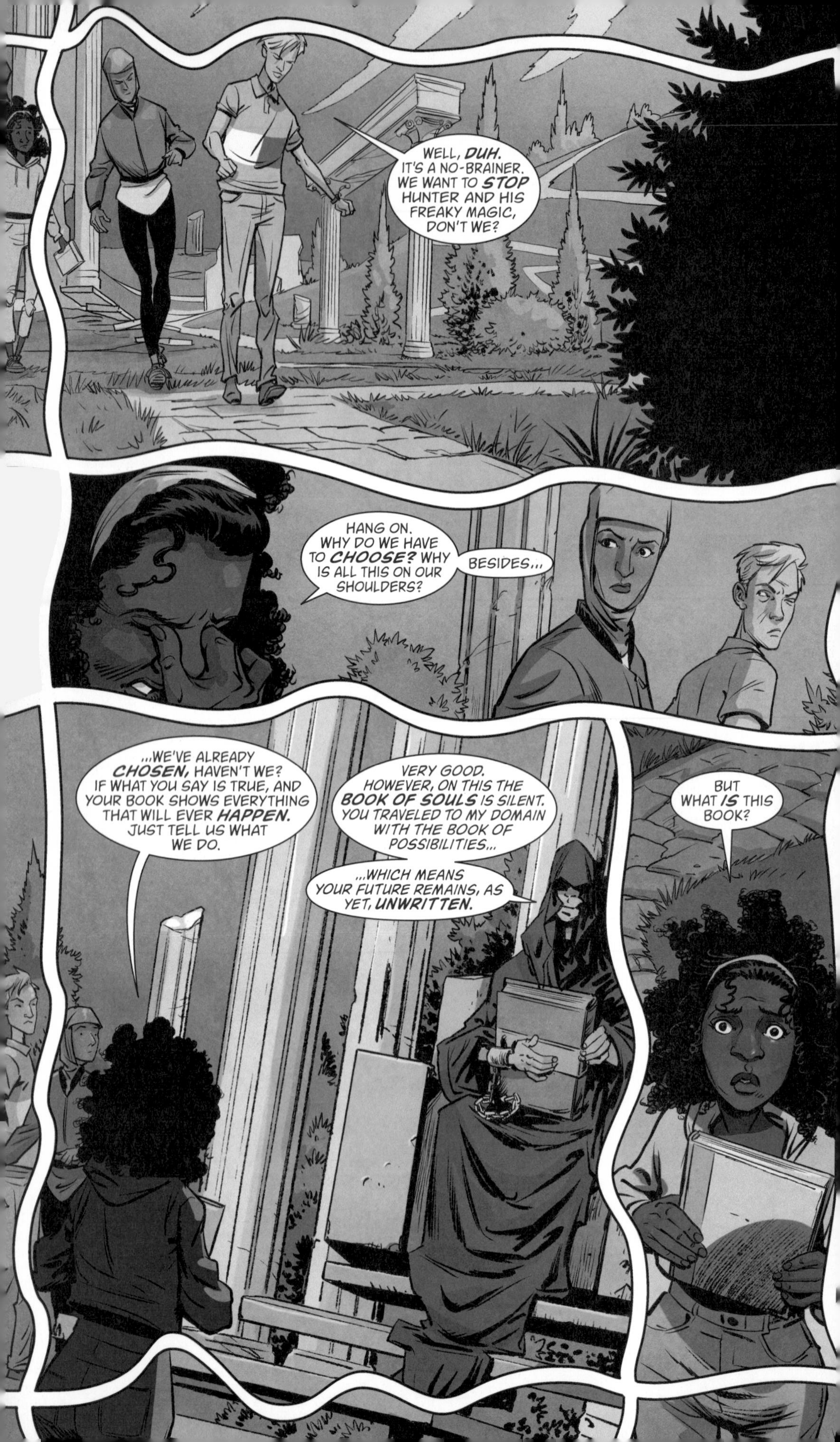
WELL, DUH. IT'S A NO-BRAINER. WE WANT TO STOP HUNTER AND HIS FREAKY MAGIC, DON'T WE?
HANG ON. WHY DO WE HAVE TO CHOOSE? WHY IS ALL THIS ON OUR SHOULDERS?
BESIDES...
...WE'VE ALREADY CHOSEN, HAVEN'T WE? IF WHAT YOU SAY IS TRUE, AND YOUR BOOK SHOWS EVERYTHING THAT WILL EVER HAPPEN. JUST TELL US WHAT WE DO.
VERY GOOD. HOWEVER, ON THIS THE BOOK OF SOULS IS SILENT. YOU TRAVELED TO MY DOMAIN WITH THE BOOK OF POSSIBILITIES...
...WHICH MEANS YOUR FUTURE REMAINS, AS YET, UNWRITTEN.
BUT WHAT IS THIS BOOK?

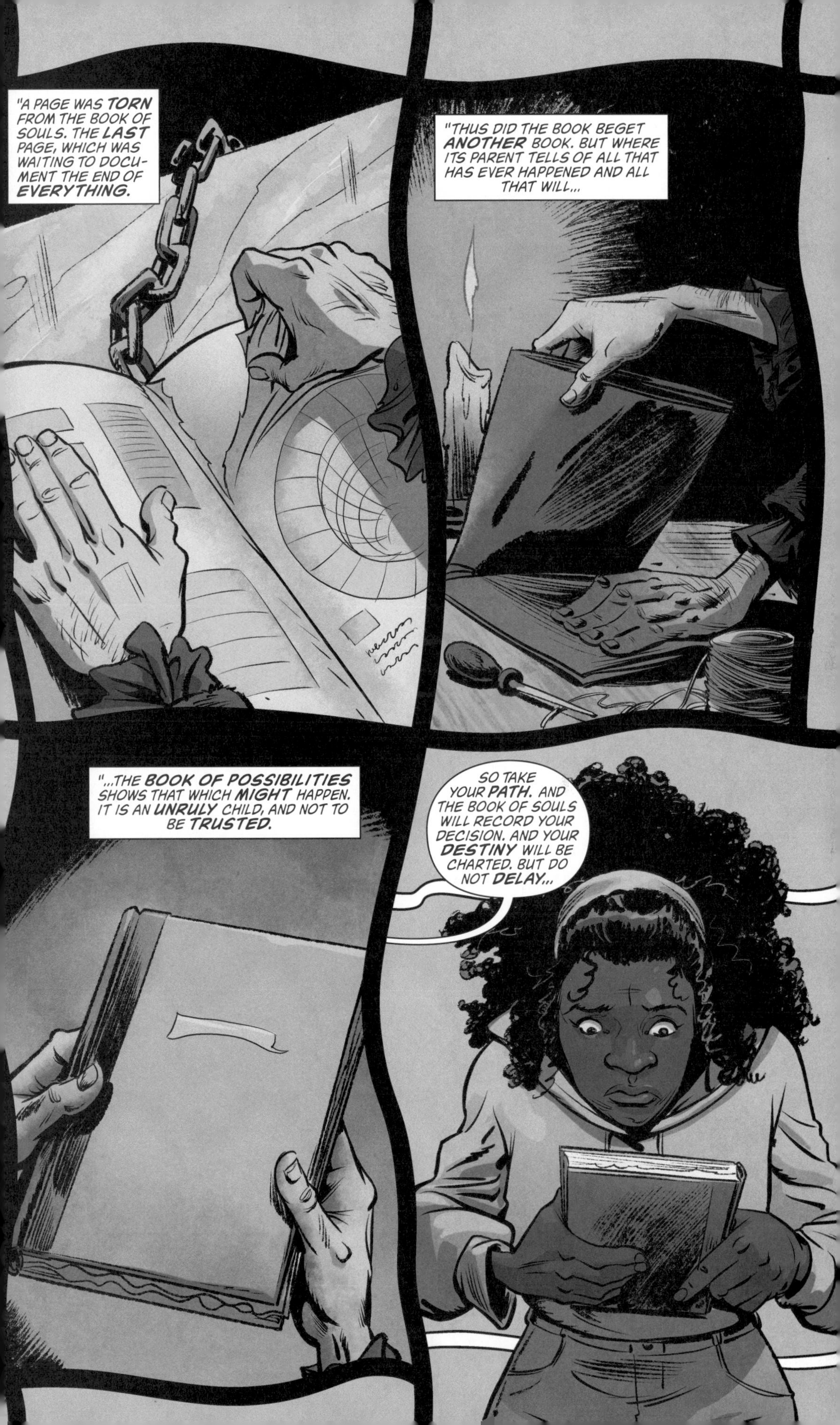
"A PAGE WAS TORN FROM THE BOOK OF SOULS. THE LAST PAGE, WHICH WAS WAITING TO DOCUMENT THE END OF EVERYTHING.
"THUS DID THE BOOK BEGET ANOTHER BOOK. BUT WHERE ITS PARENT TELLS OF ALL THAT HAS EVER HAPPENED AND ALL THAT WILL...
"...THE BOOK OF POSSIBILITIES SHOWS THAT WHICH MIGHT HAPPEN. IT IS AN UNRULY CHILD, AND NOT TO BE TRUSTED.
SO TAKE YOUR PATH. AND THE BOOK OF SOULS WILL RECORD YOUR DECISION. AND YOUR DESTINY WILL BE CHARTED. BUT DO NOT DELAY...

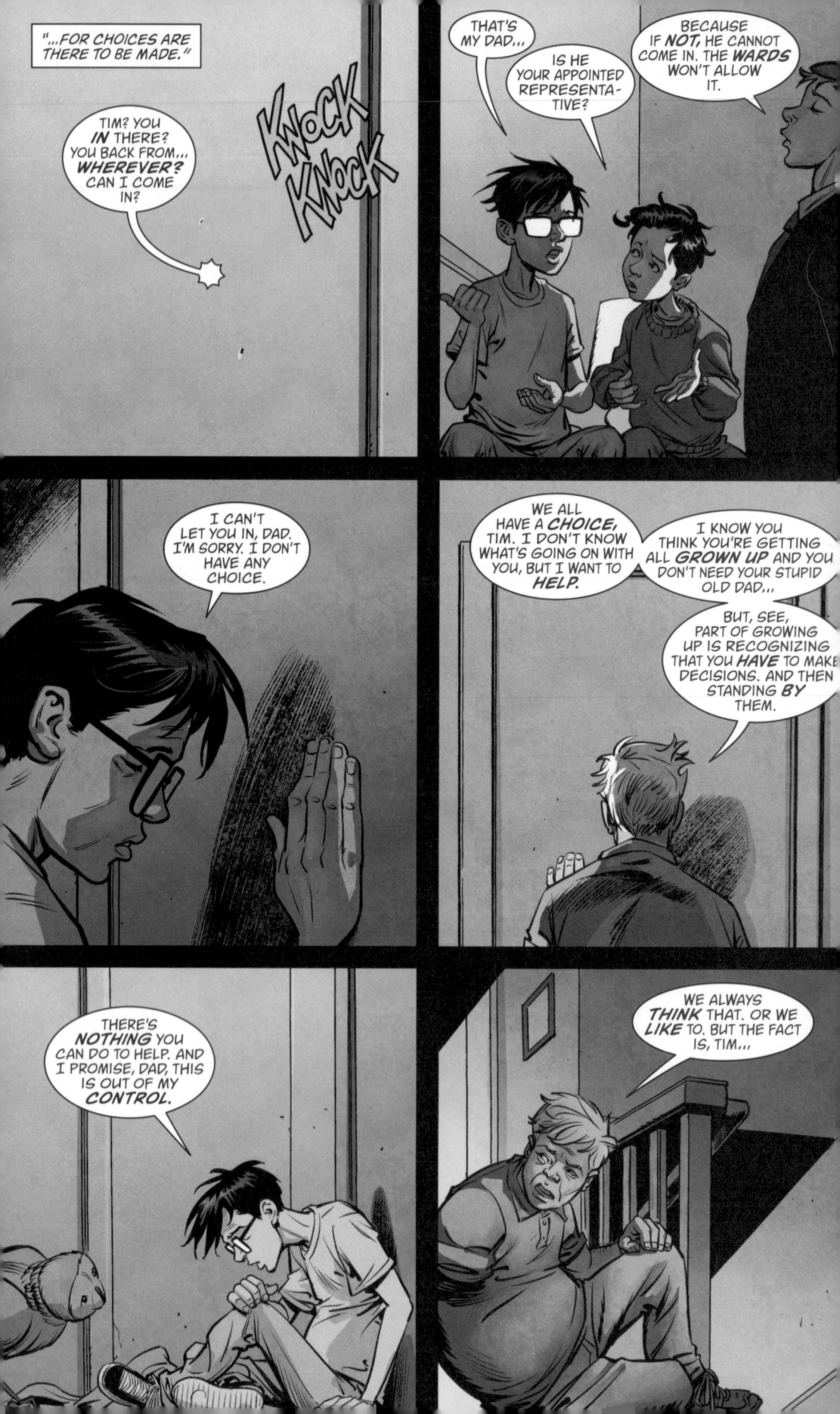
"...FOR CHOICES ARE THERE TO BE MADE."
TIM? YOU IN THERE? YOU BACK FROM... WHEREVER? CAN I COME IN?
KNOCK KNOCK
THAT'S MY DAD...
IS HE YOUR APPOINTED REPRESENTA-TIVE?
BECAUSE IF NOT, HE CANNOT COME IN. THE WARDS WON'T ALLOW IT.
I CAN'T LET YOU IN, DAD. I'M SORRY. I DON'T HAVE ANY CHOICE.
WE ALL HAVE A CHOICE, TIM. I DON'T KNOW WHAT'S GOING ON WITH YOU, BUT I WANT TO HELP.
I KNOW YOU THINK YOU'RE GETTING ALL GROWN UP AND YOU DON'T NEED YOUR STUPID OLD DAD...
BUT, SEE, PART OF GROWING UP IS RECOGNIZING THAT YOU HAVE TO MAKE DECISIONS. AND THEN STANDING BY THEM.
THERE'S NOTHING YOU CAN DO TO HELP. AND I PROMISE, DAD, THIS IS OUT OF MY CONTROL.
WE ALWAYS THINK THAT. OR WE LIKE TO. BUT THE FACT IS, TIM...

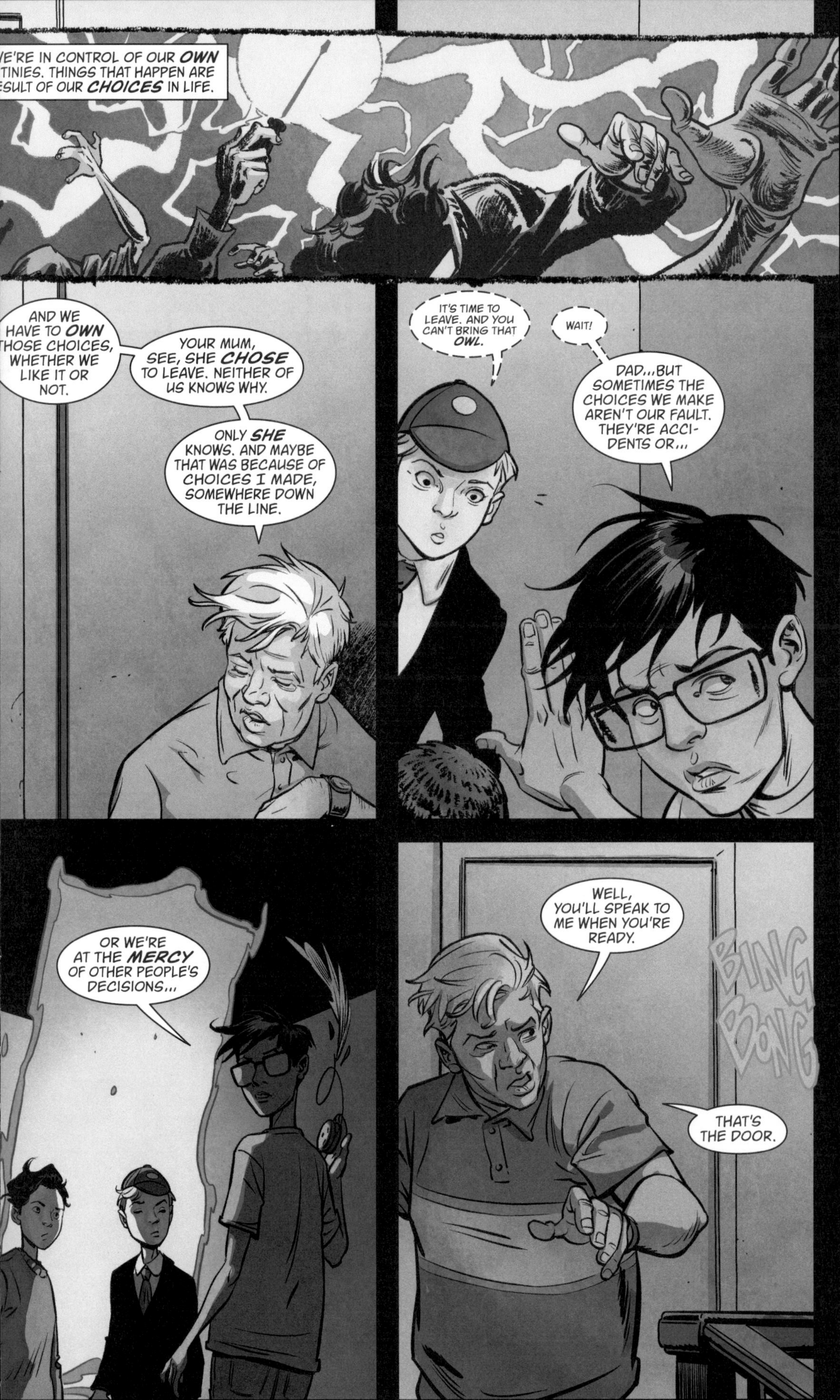

WE'RE IN CONTROL OF OUR *OWN* DESTINIES. THINGS THAT HAPPEN ARE THE RESULT OF OUR *CHOICES* IN LIFE.
AND WE HAVE TO *OWN* THOSE CHOICES, WHETHER WE LIKE IT OR NOT.
YOUR MUM, SEE, SHE *CHOSE* TO LEAVE. NEITHER OF US KNOWS WHY.
ONLY *SHE* KNOWS. AND MAYBE THAT WAS BECAUSE OF CHOICES I MADE, SOMEWHERE DOWN THE LINE.
IT'S TIME TO LEAVE. AND YOU CAN'T BRING THAT *OWL*.
WAIT!
DAD...BUT SOMETIMES THE CHOICES WE MAKE AREN'T OUR FAULT. THEY'RE ACCI-DENTS OR...
OR WE'RE AT THE *MERCY* OF OTHER PEOPLE'S DECISIONS...
WELL, YOU'LL SPEAK TO ME WHEN YOU'RE READY.
BING BONG
THAT'S THE DOOR.

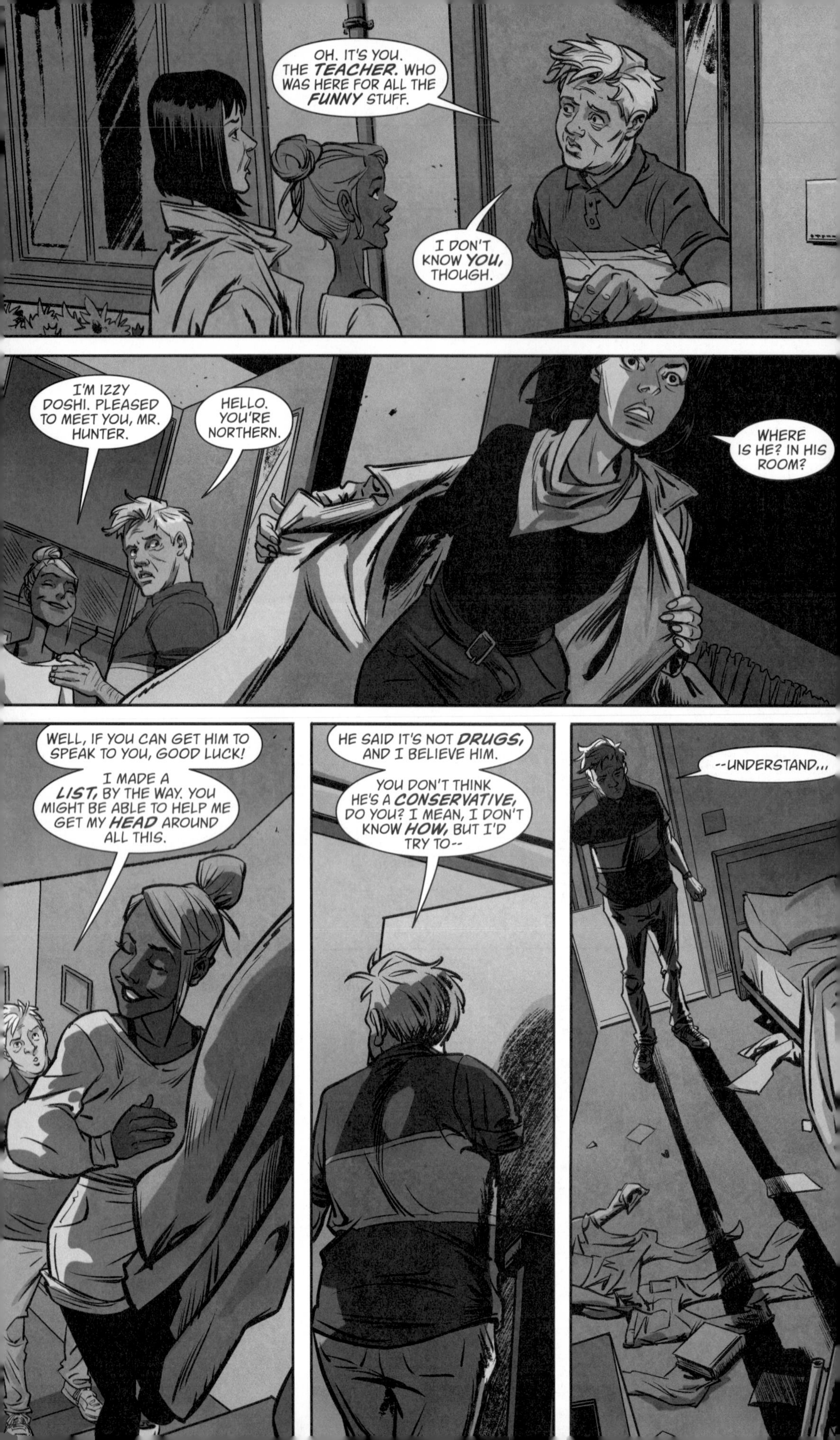
OH. IT'S YOU. THE TEACHER. WHO WAS HERE FOR ALL THE FUNNY STUFF.
I DON'T KNOW YOU, THOUGH.
I'M IZZY DOSHI. PLEASED TO MEET YOU, MR. HUNTER.
HELLO. YOU'RE NORTHERN.
WHERE IS HE? IN HIS ROOM?
WELL, IF YOU CAN GET HIM TO SPEAK TO YOU, GOOD LUCK!
I MADE A LIST, BY THE WAY. YOU MIGHT BE ABLE TO HELP ME GET MY HEAD AROUND ALL THIS.
HE SAID IT'S NOT DRUGS, AND I BELIEVE HIM.
YOU DON'T THINK HE'S A CONSERVATIVE, DO YOU? I MEAN, I DON'T KNOW HOW, BUT I'D TRY TO--
--UNDERSTAND...

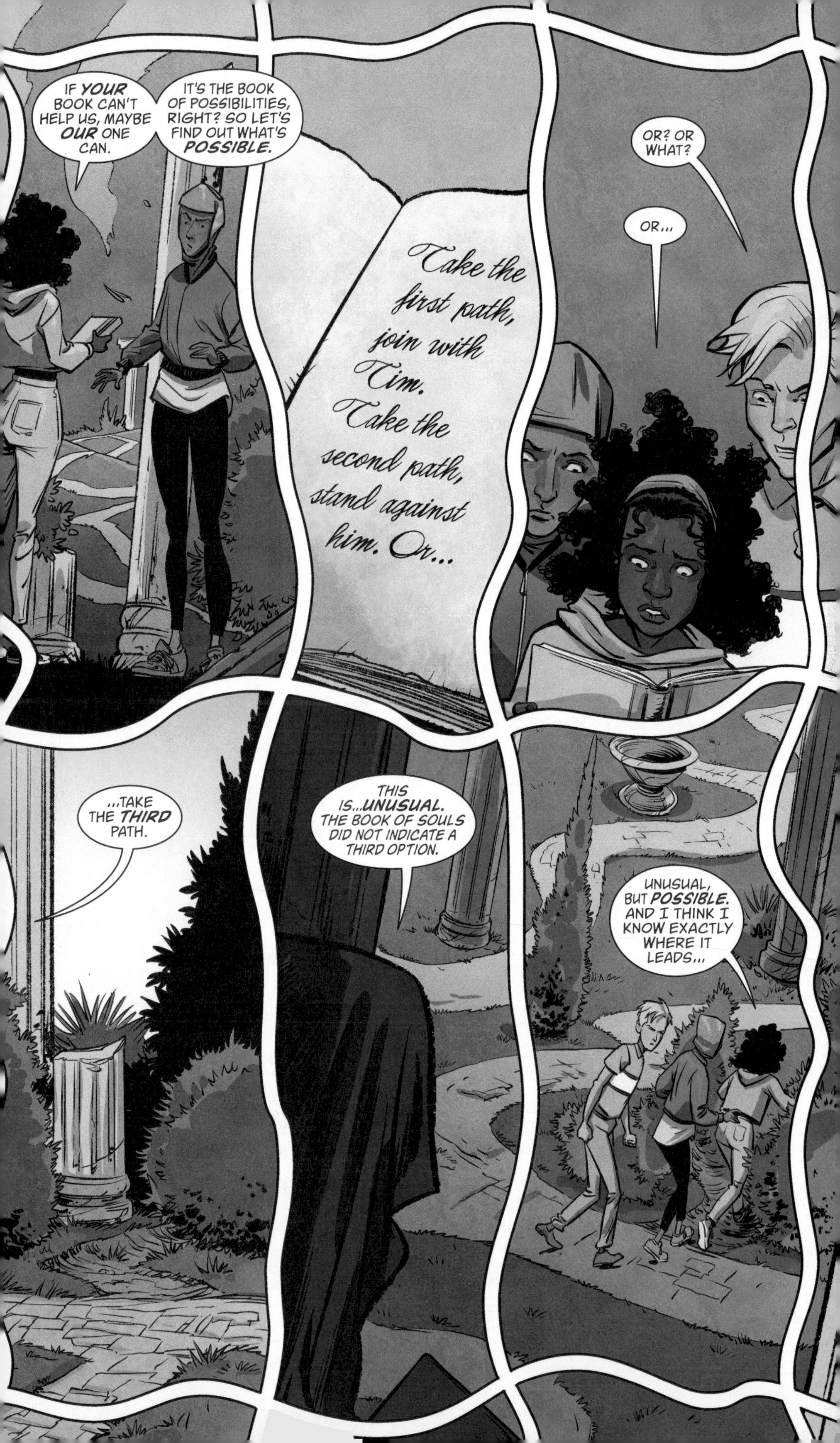
IF YOUR BOOK CAN'T HELP US, MAYBE OUR ONE CAN.
IT'S THE BOOK OF POSSIBILITIES, RIGHT? SO LET'S FIND OUT WHAT'S POSSIBLE.
Take the first path, join with Tim. Take the second path, stand against him. Or...
OR...
OR? OR WHAT?
...TAKE THE THIRD PATH.
THIS IS...UNUSUAL. THE BOOK OF SOULS DID NOT INDICATE A THIRD OPTION.
UNUSUAL, BUT POSSIBLE. AND I THINK I KNOW EXACTLY WHERE IT LEADS...

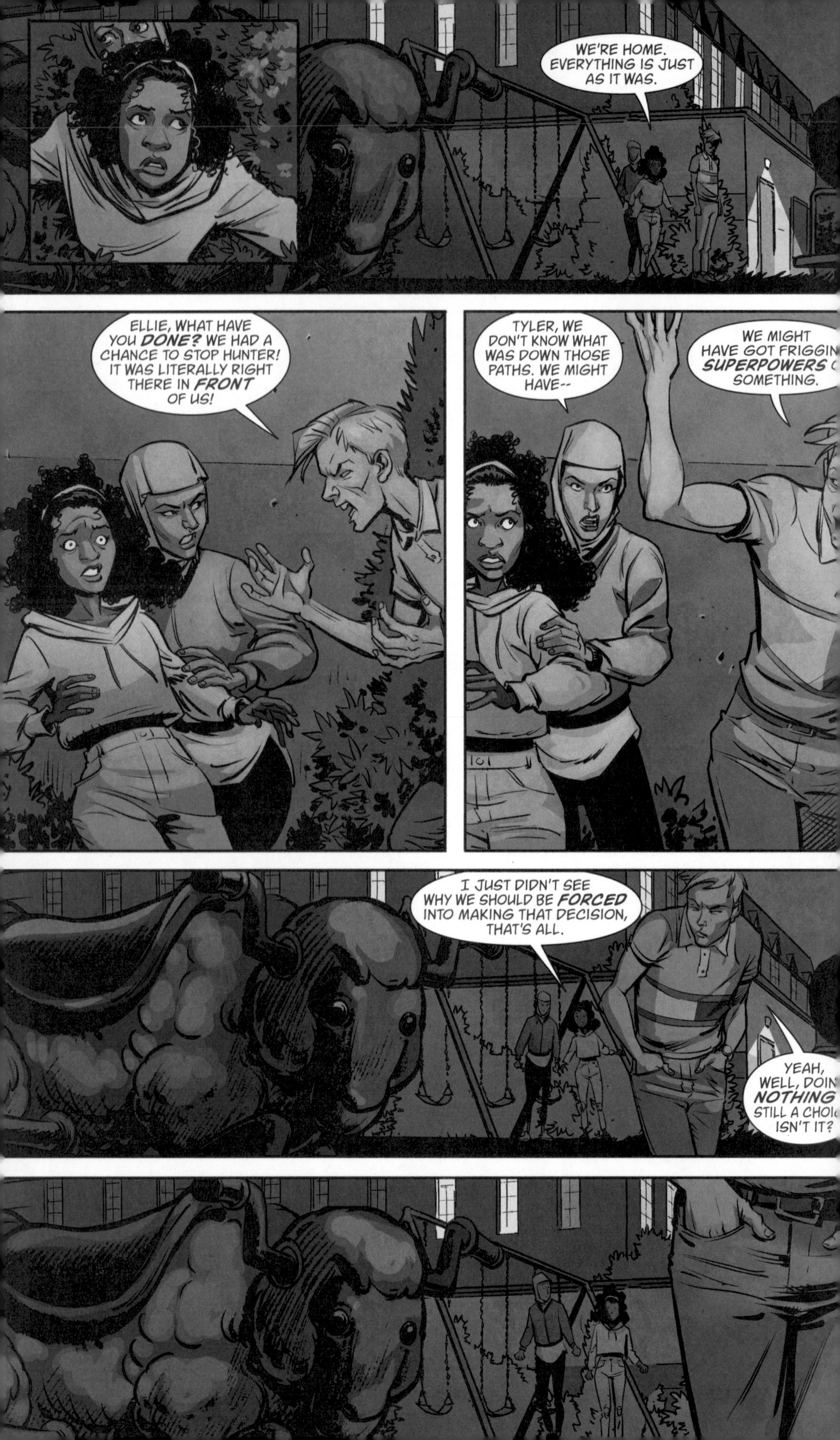
WE'RE HOME. EVERYTHING IS JUST AS IT WAS.
ELLIE, WHAT HAVE YOU DONE? WE HAD A CHANCE TO STOP HUNTER! IT WAS LITERALLY RIGHT THERE IN FRONT OF US!
TYLER, WE DON'T KNOW WHAT WAS DOWN THOSE PATHS. WE MIGHT HAVE--
WE MIGHT HAVE GOT FRIGGIN SUPERPOWERS
SOMETHING.
I JUST DIDN'T SEE WHY WE SHOULD BE FORCED INTO MAKING THAT DECISION, THAT'S ALL.
YEAH, WELL, DOIN NOTHING STILL A CHOI ISN'T IT?

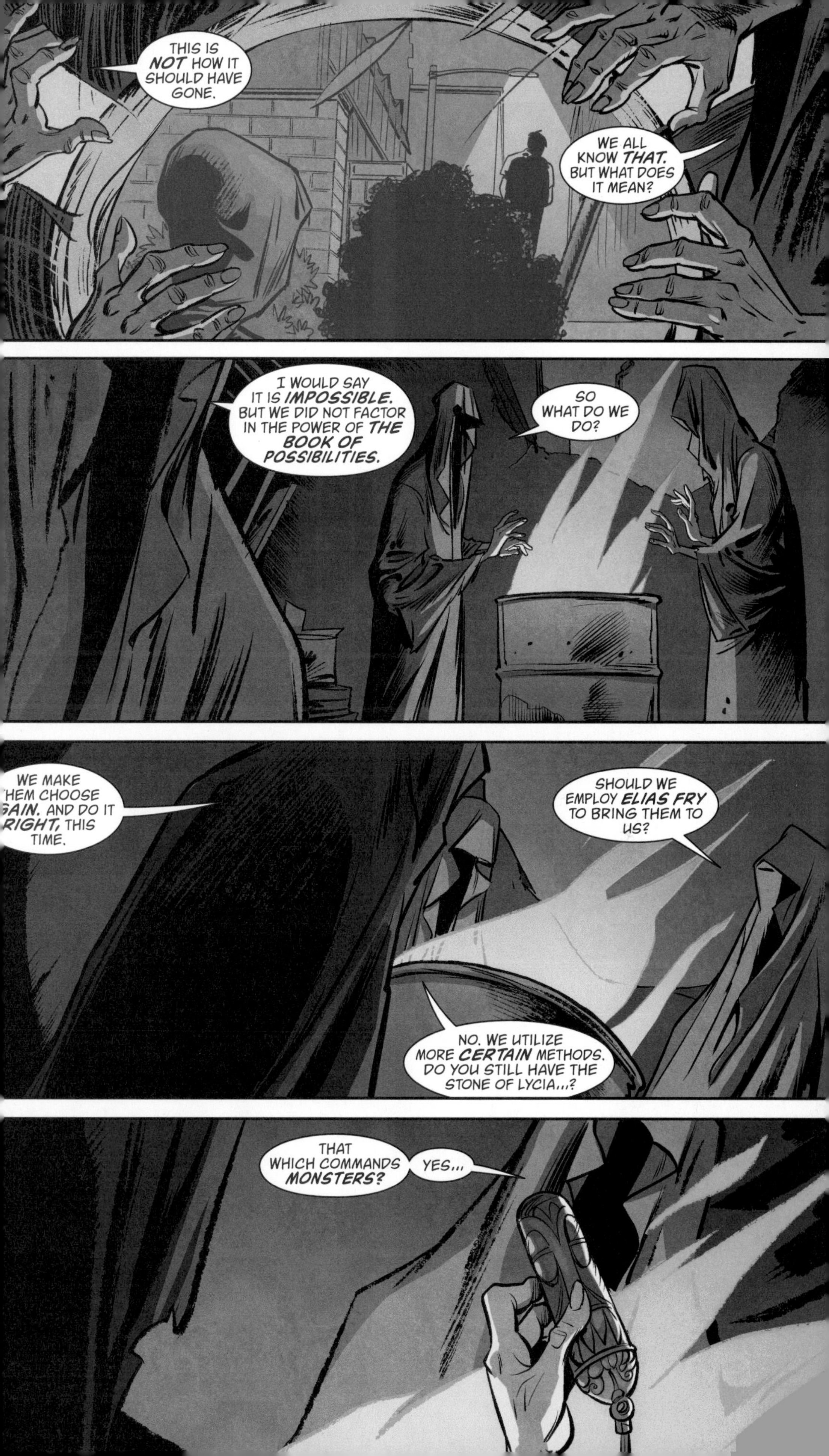
THIS IS NOT HOW IT SHOULD HAVE GONE.
WE ALL KNOW THAT. BUT WHAT DOES IT MEAN?
I WOULD SAY IT IS IMPOSSIBLE. BUT WE DID NOT FACTOR IN THE POWER OF THE BOOK OF POSSIBILITIES.
SO WHAT DO WE DO?
WE MAKE THEM CHOOSE AGAIN. AND DO IT RIGHT, THIS TIME.
SHOULD WE EMPLOY ELIAS FRY TO BRING THEM TO US?
NO. WE UTILIZE MORE CERTAIN METHODS. DO YOU STILL HAVE THE STONE OF LYCIA...?
THAT WHICH COMMANDS MONSTERS?
YES...

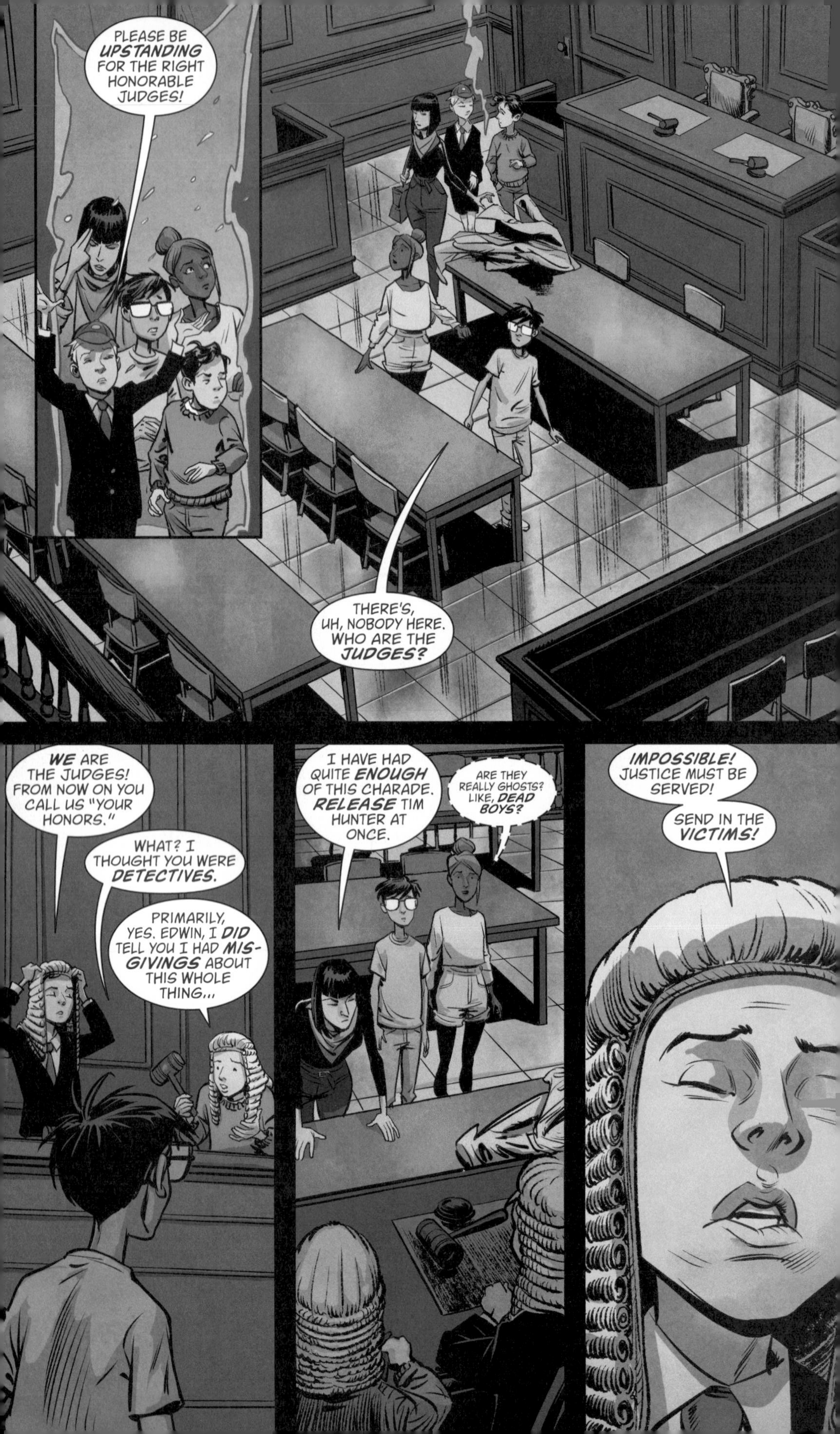

PLEASE BE UPSTANDING FOR THE RIGHT HONORABLE JUDGES!
THERE'S, UH, NOBODY HERE. WHO ARE THE JUDGES?
WE ARE THE JUDGES! FROM NOW ON YOU CALL US "YOUR HONORS."
WHAT? I THOUGHT YOU WERE DETECTIVES.
PRIMARILY, YES. EDWIN, I DID TELL YOU I HAD MISGIVINGS ABOUT THIS WHOLE THING...
I HAVE HAD QUITE ENOUGH OF THIS CHARADE. RELEASE TIM HUNTER AT ONCE.
ARE THEY REALLY GHOSTS? LIKE, DEAD BOYS?
IMPOSSIBLE! JUSTICE MUST BE SERVED!
SEND IN THE VICTIMS!

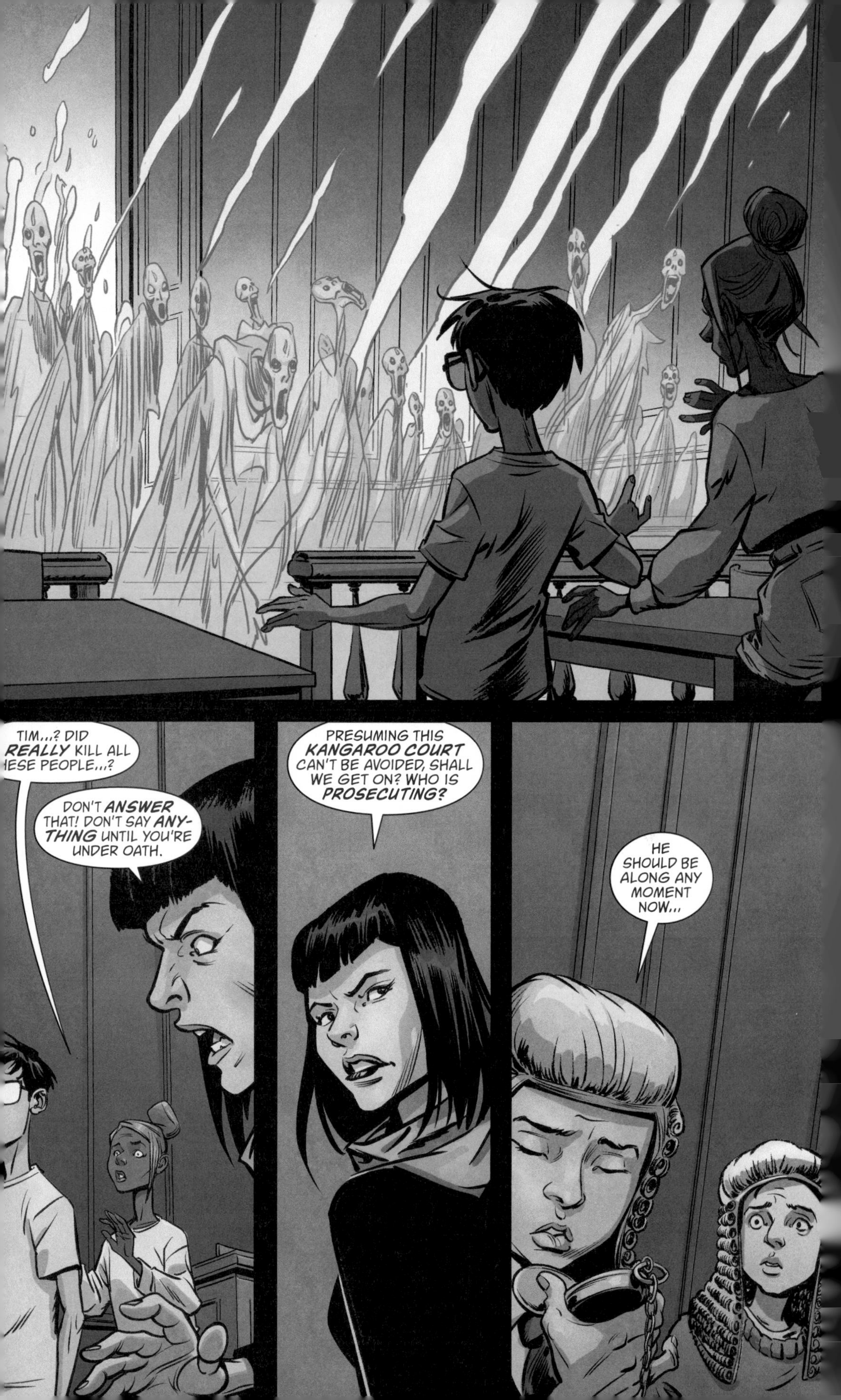
TIM...? DID
REALLY KILL ALL
HESE PEOPLE...?
DON'T ANSWER THAT! DON'T SAY ANYTHING UNTIL YOU'RE UNDER OATH.
PRESUMING THIS KANGAROO COURT CAN'T BE AVOIDED, SHALL WE GET ON? WHO IS PROSECUTING?
HE SHOULD BE ALONG ANY MOMENT NOW...

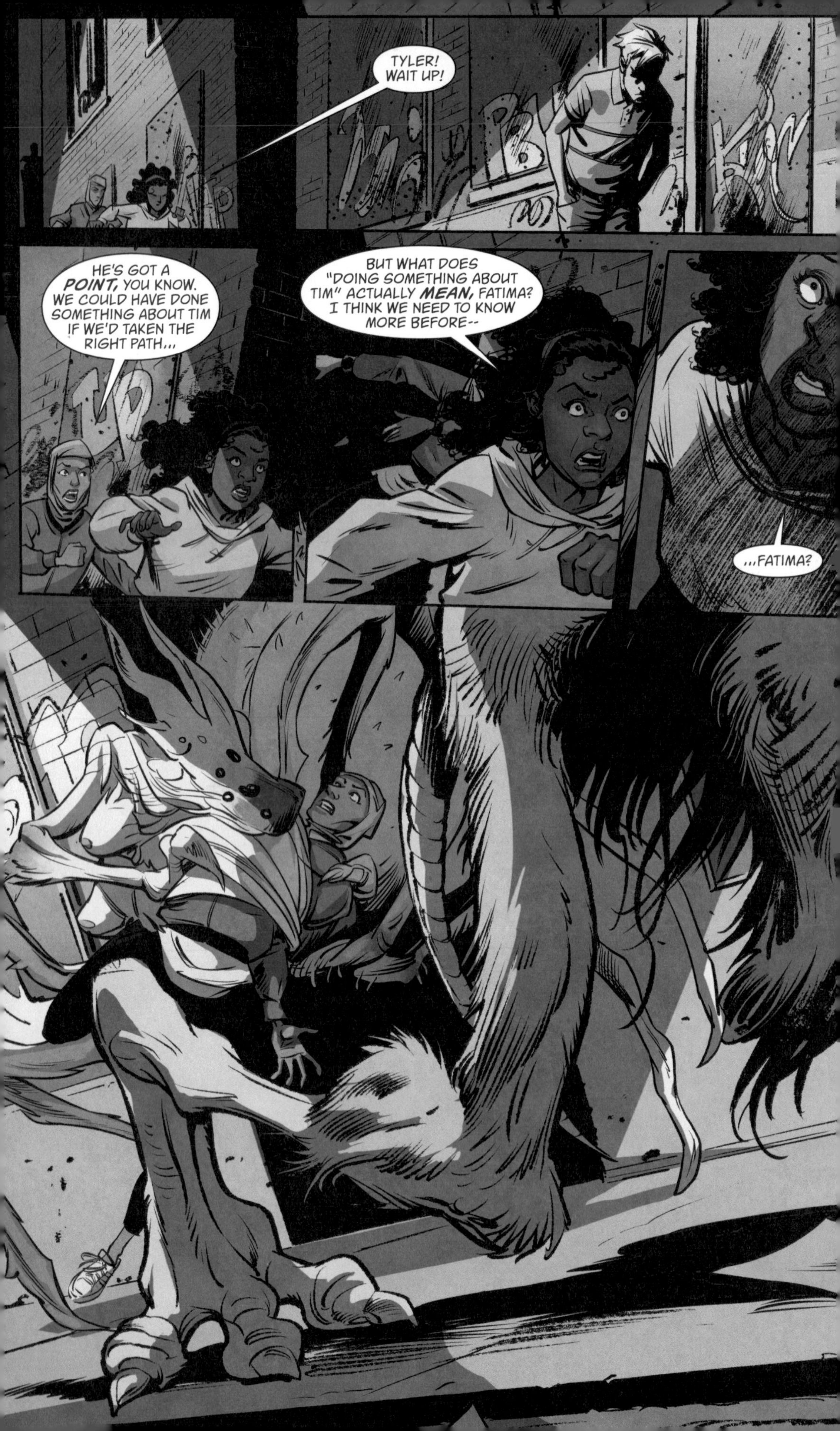
TYLER! WAIT UP!
HE'S GOT A POINT, YOU KNOW. WE COULD HAVE DONE SOMETHING ABOUT TIM IF WE'D TAKEN THE RIGHT PATH...
BUT WHAT DOES "DOING SOMETHING ABOUT TIM" ACTUALLY MEAN, FATIMA? I THINK WE NEED TO KNOW MORE BEFORE--
...FATIMA?

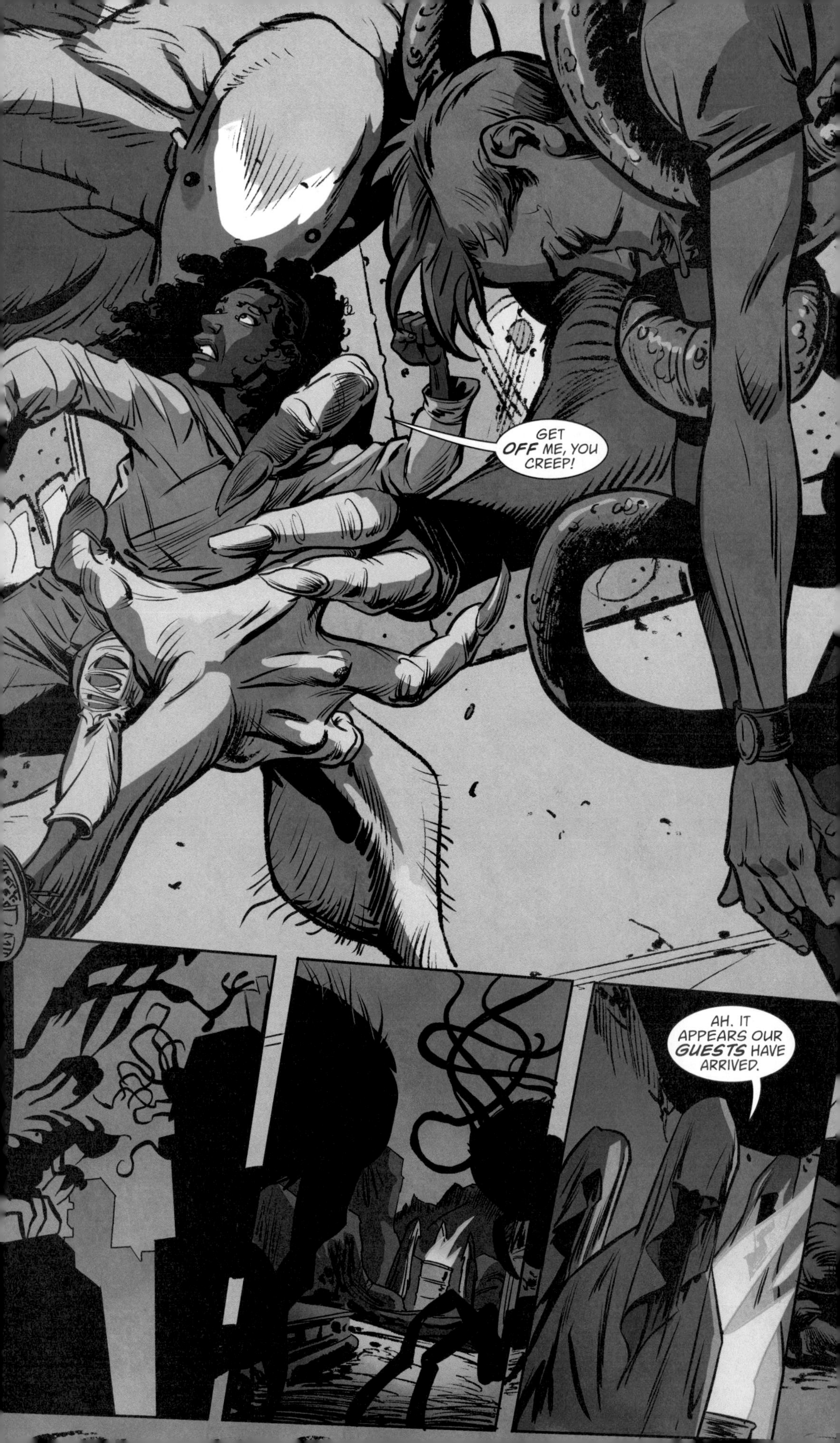
GET OFF ME, YOU CREEP!
AH. IT APPEARS OUR GUESTS HAVE ARRIVED.

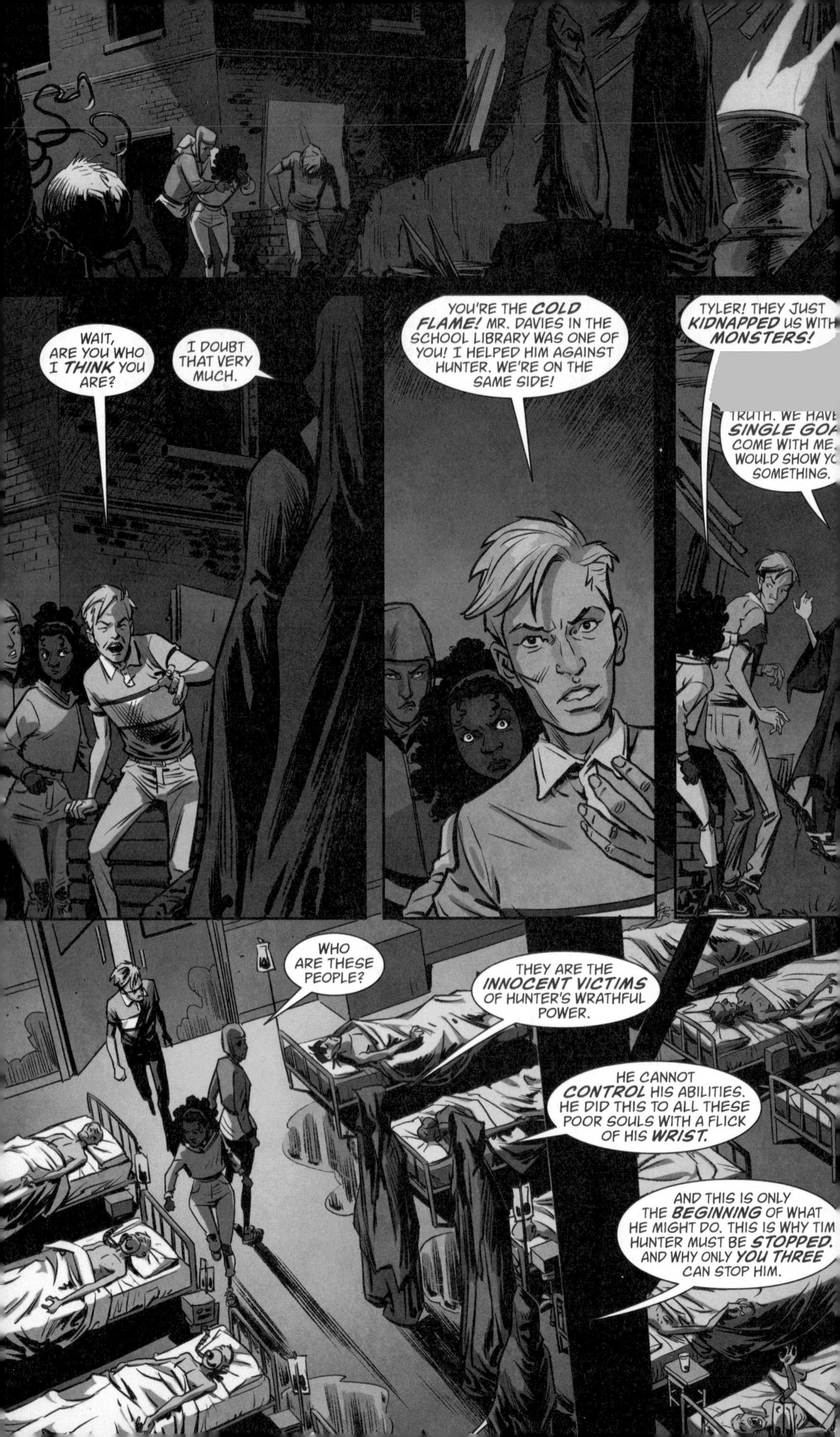
WAIT, ARE YOU WHO I *THINK* YOU ARE?
I DOUBT THAT VERY MUCH.
YOU'RE THE *COLD FLAME!* MR. DAVIES IN THE SCHOOL LIBRARY WAS ONE OF YOU! I HELPED HIM AGAINST HUNTER. WE'RE ON THE SAME SIDE!
TYLER! THEY JUST *KIDNAPPED* US WITH *MONSTERS!*
TRUTH. WE HAVE
SINGLE GOA
COME WITH ME.
WOULD SHOW YO
SOMETHING.
WHO ARE THESE PEOPLE?
THEY ARE THE *INNOCENT VICTIMS* OF HUNTER'S WRATHFUL POWER.
HE CANNOT *CONTROL* HIS ABILITIES. HE DID THIS TO ALL THESE POOR SOULS WITH A FLICK OF HIS *WRIST.*
AND THIS IS ONLY THE *BEGINNING* OF WHAT HE MIGHT DO. THIS IS WHY TIM HUNTER MUST BE *STOPPED.* AND WHY ONLY *YOU THREE* CAN STOP HIM.

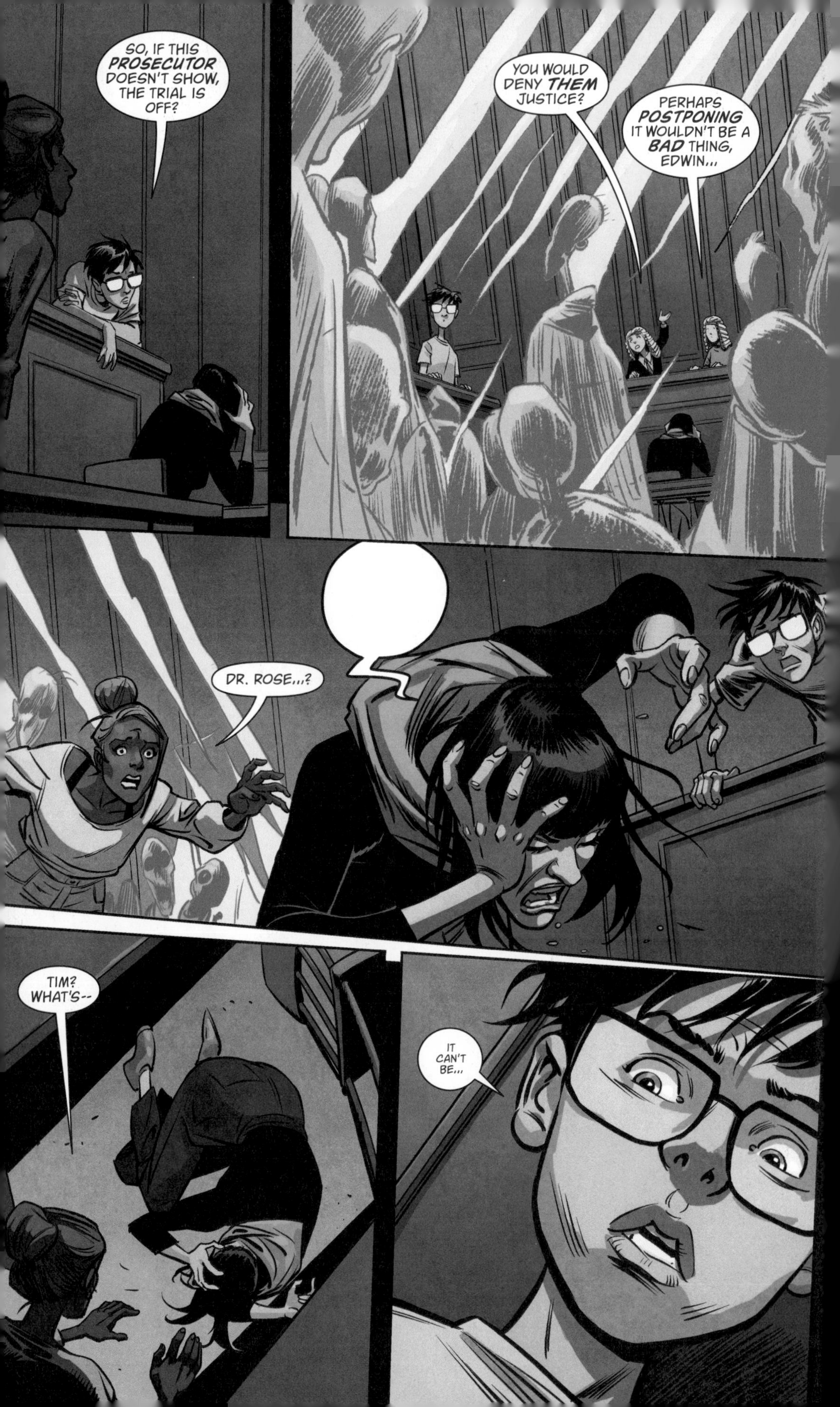

SO, IF THIS PROSECUTOR DOESN'T SHOW, THE TRIAL IS OFF?
YOU WOULD DENY THEM JUSTICE?
PERHAPS POSTPONING IT WOULDN'T BE A BAD THING, EDWIN...
DR. ROSE...?
TIM? WHAT'S--
IT CAN'T BE...

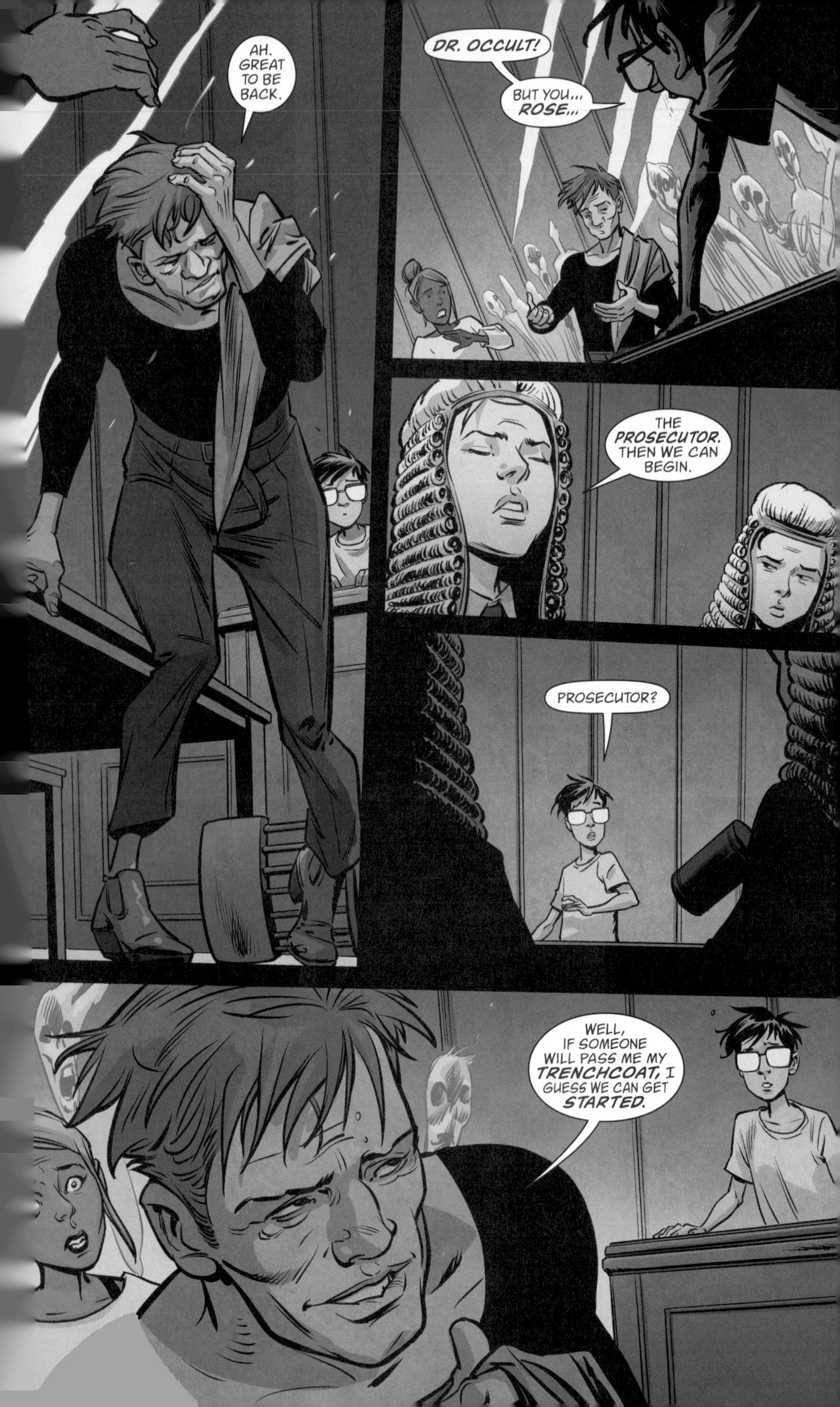
AH. GREAT TO BE BACK.
DR. OCCULT!
BUT YOU... ROSE...
THE PROSECUTOR. THEN WE CAN BEGIN.
PROSECUTOR?
WELL, IF SOMEONE WILL PASS ME MY TRENCHCOAT, I GUESS WE CAN GET STARTED.

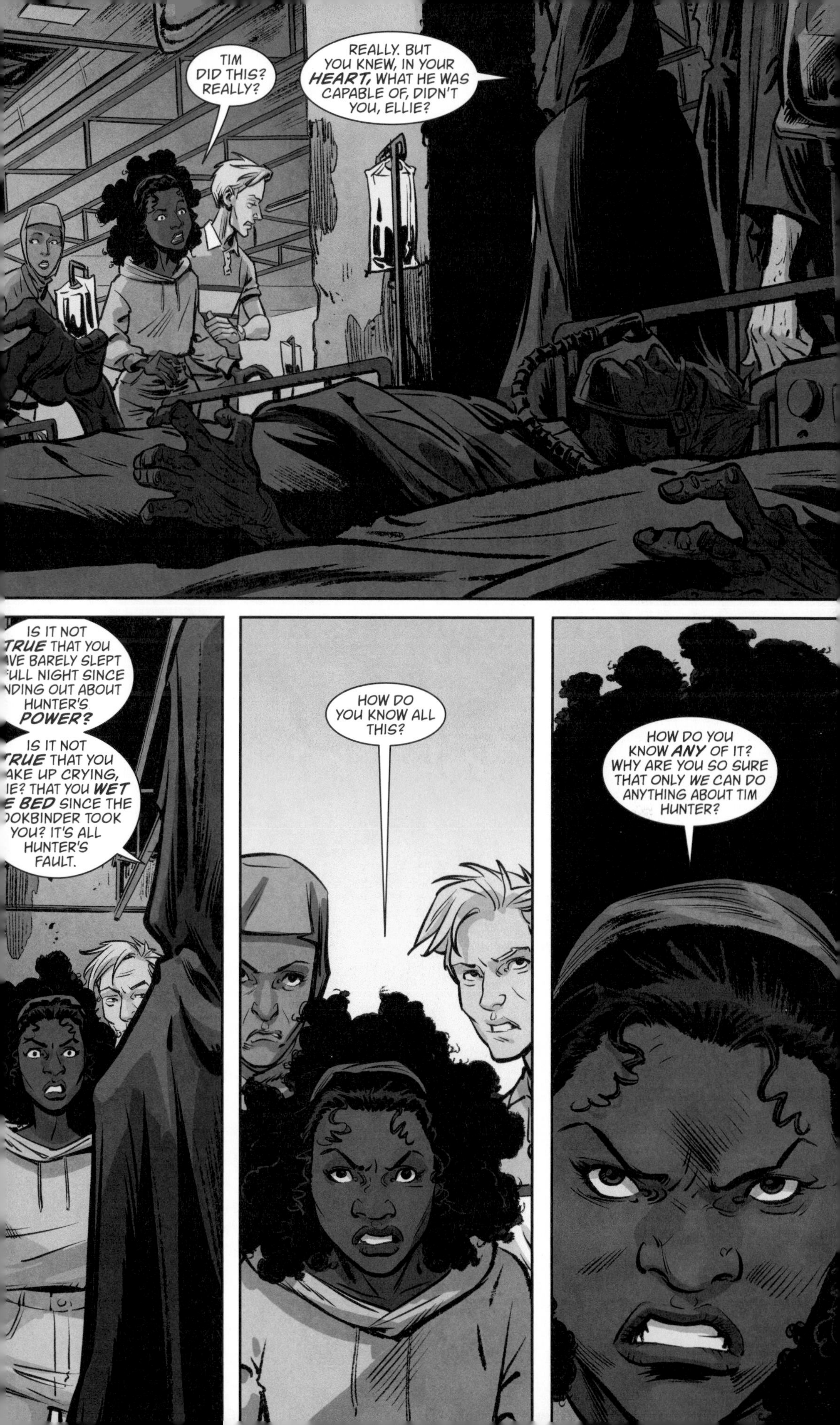
TIM DID THIS? REALLY?
REALLY. BUT YOU KNEW, IN YOUR HEART, WHAT HE WAS CAPABLE OF, DIDN'T YOU, ELLIE?
IS IT NOT TRUE THAT YOU VE BARELY SLEPT ULL NIGHT SINCE NDING OUT ABOUT HUNTER'S POWER?
IS IT NOT TRUE THAT YOU AKE UP CRYING, IE? THAT YOU WET E BED SINCE THE OKBINDER TOOK YOU? IT'S ALL HUNTER'S FAULT.
HOW DO YOU KNOW ALL THIS?
HOW DO YOU KNOW ANY OF IT? WHY ARE YOU SO SURE THAT ONLY WE CAN DO ANYTHING ABOUT TIM HUNTER?

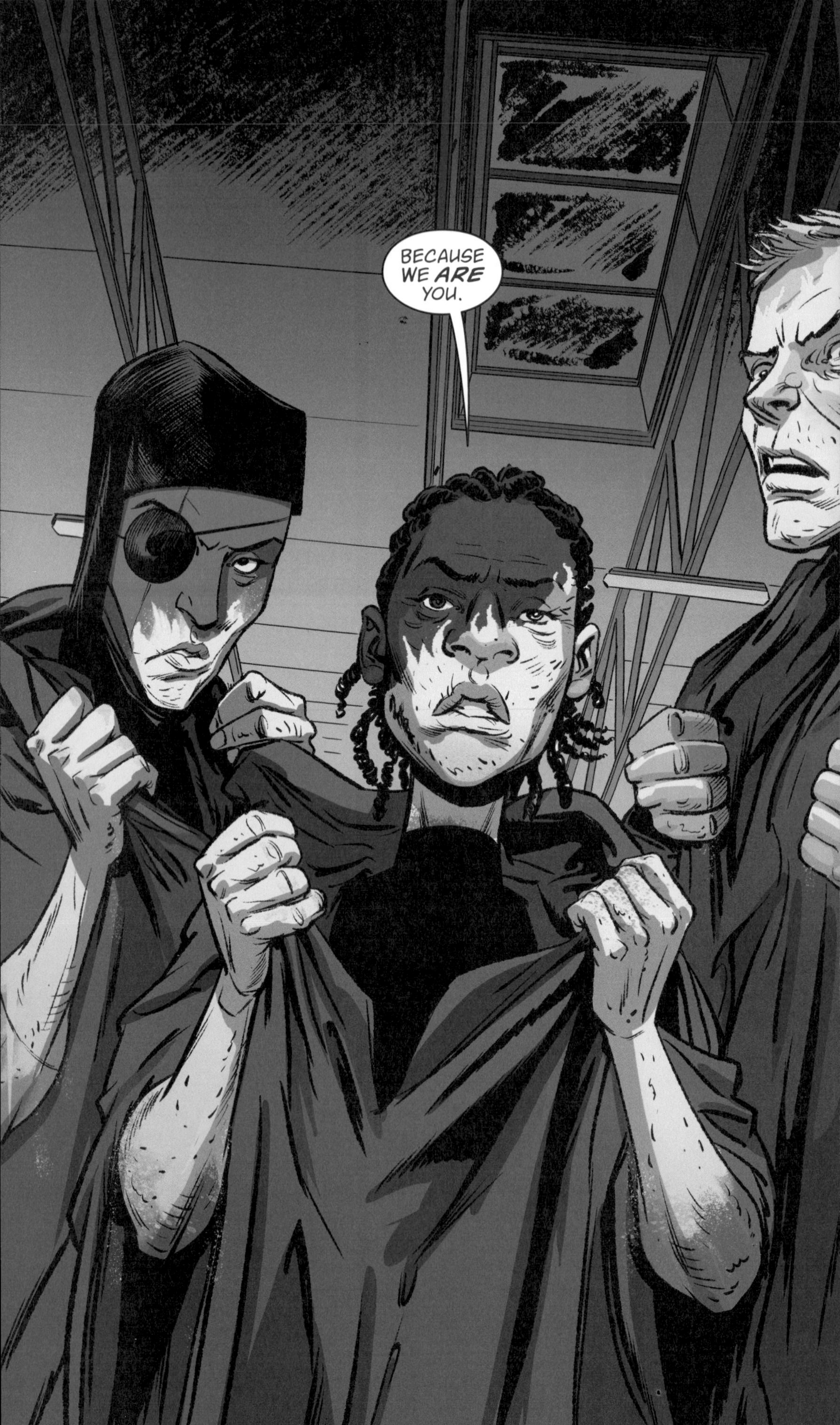
BECAUSE WE ARE YOU.

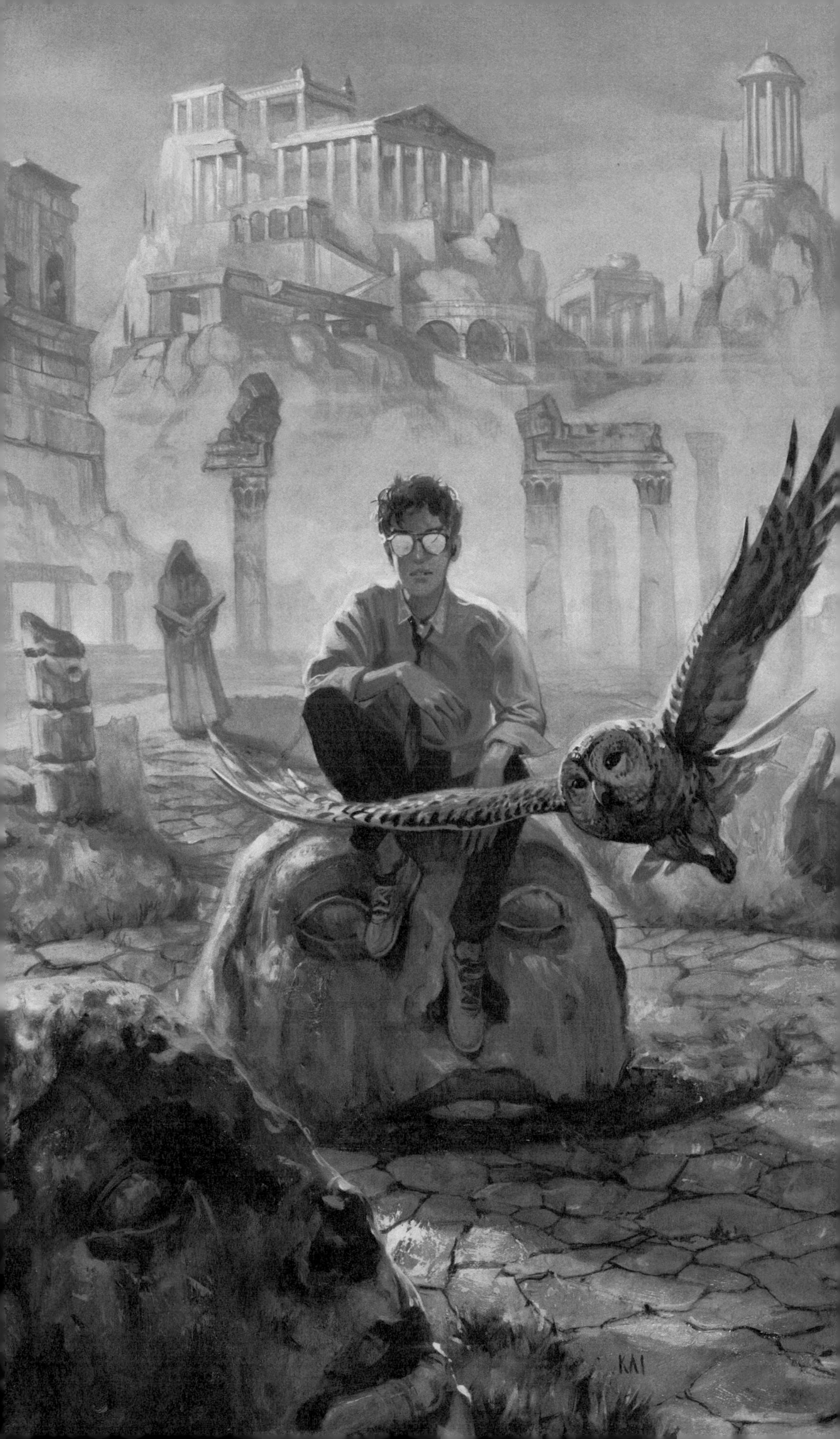
KAI

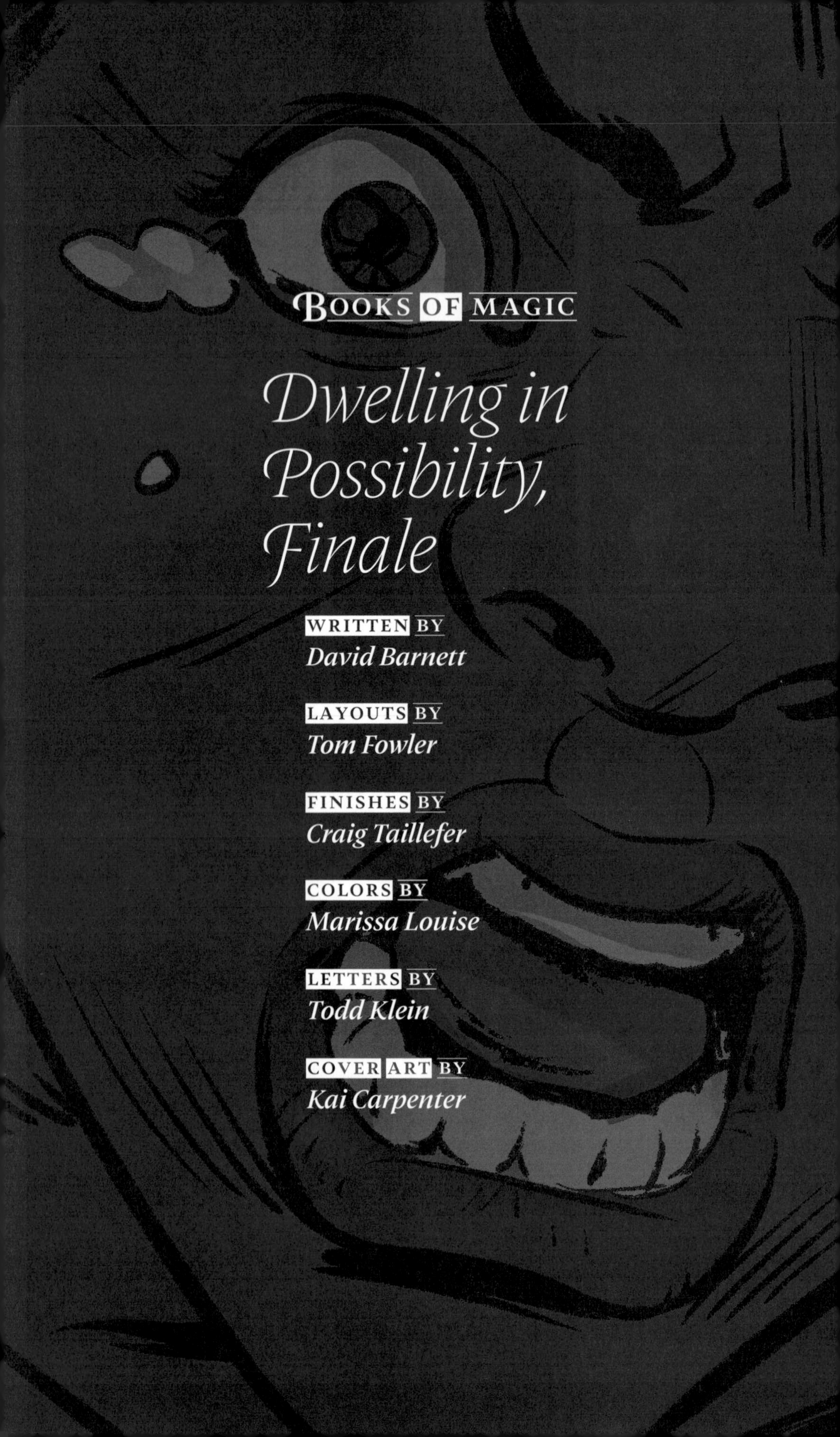

BOOKS OF MAGIC

Dwelling in Possibility, Finale

WRITTEN BY
David Barnett

LAYOUTS BY
Tom Fowler

FINISHES BY
Craig Taillefer

COLORS BY
Marissa Louise

LETTERS BY
Todd Klein

COVER ART BY
Kai Carpenter

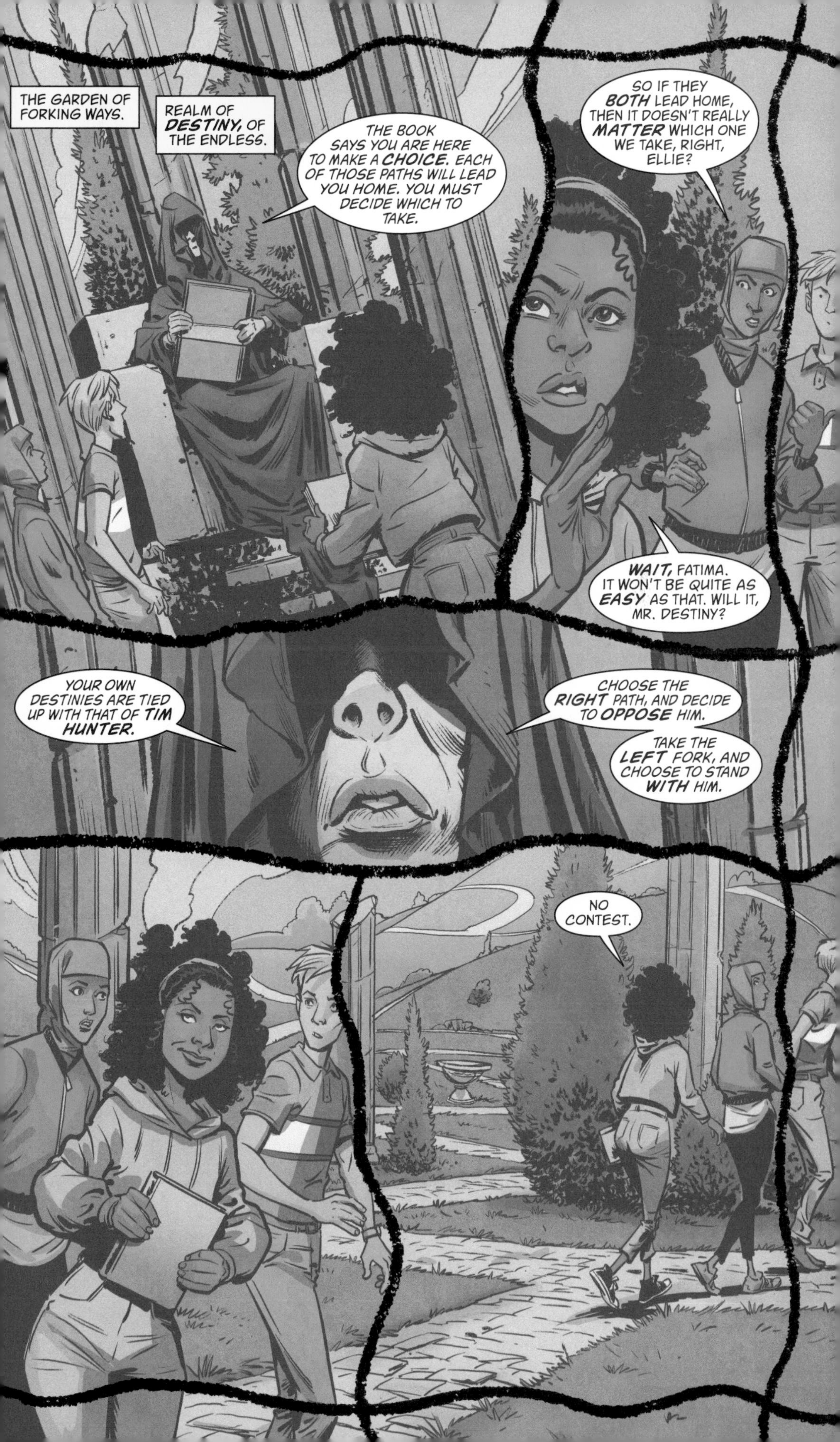
THE GARDEN OF FORKING WAYS.
REALM OF DESTINY, OF THE ENDLESS.
THE BOOK SAYS YOU ARE HERE TO MAKE A CHOICE. EACH OF THOSE PATHS WILL LEAD YOU HOME. YOU MUST DECIDE WHICH TO TAKE.
SO IF THEY BOTH LEAD HOME, THEN IT DOESN'T REALLY MATTER WHICH ONE WE TAKE, RIGHT, ELLIE?
WAIT, FATIMA. IT WON'T BE QUITE AS EASY AS THAT. WILL IT, MR. DESTINY?
YOUR OWN DESTINIES ARE TIED UP WITH THAT OF TIM HUNTER.
CHOOSE THE RIGHT PATH, AND DECIDE TO OPPOSE HIM.
TAKE THE LEFT FORK, AND CHOOSE TO STAND WITH HIM.
NO CONTEST.

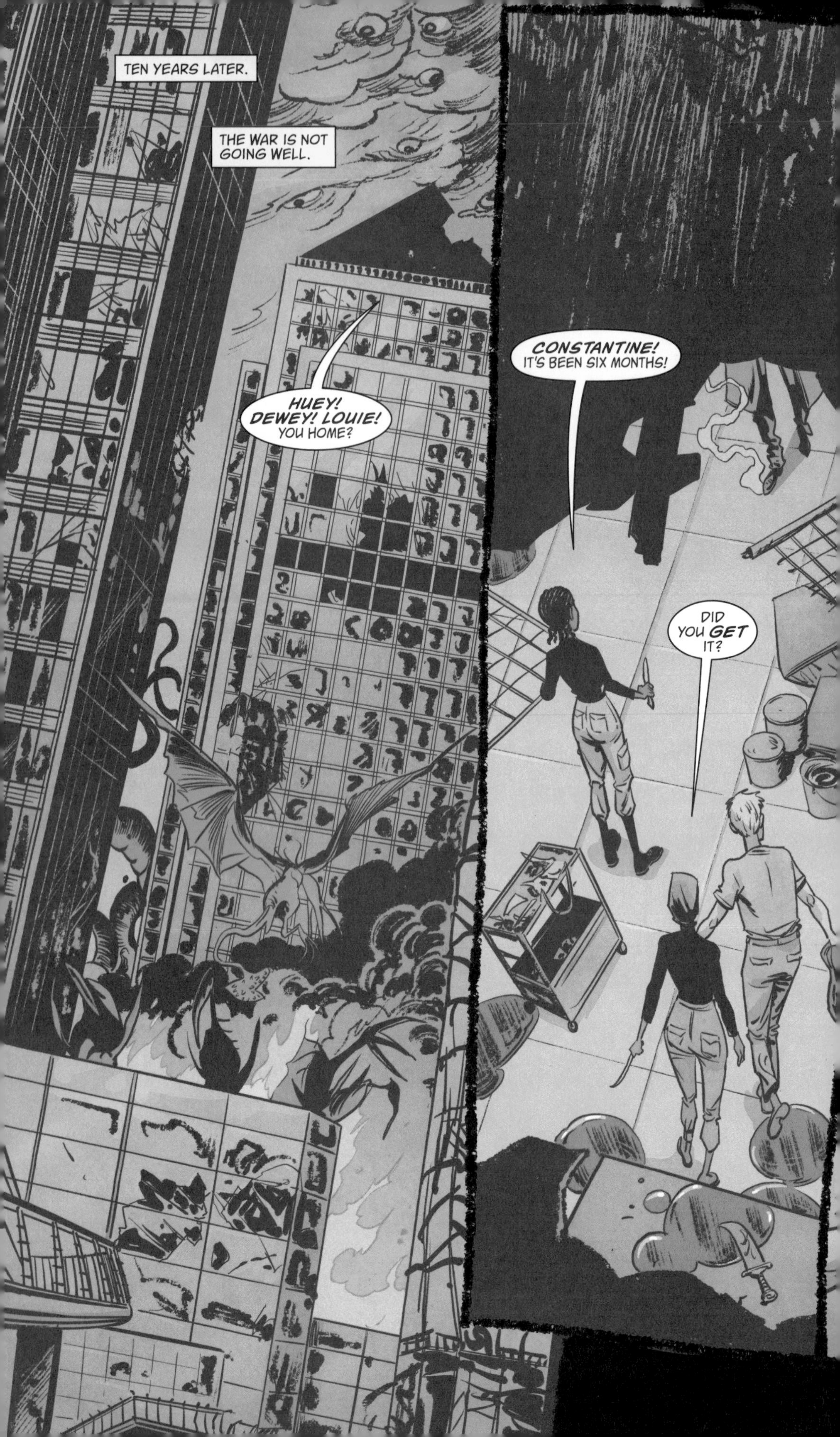
TEN YEARS LATER.
THE WAR IS NOT GOING WELL.
HUEY! DEWEY! LOUIE! YOU HOME?
CONSTANTINE! IT'S BEEN SIX MONTHS!
DID YOU GET IT?

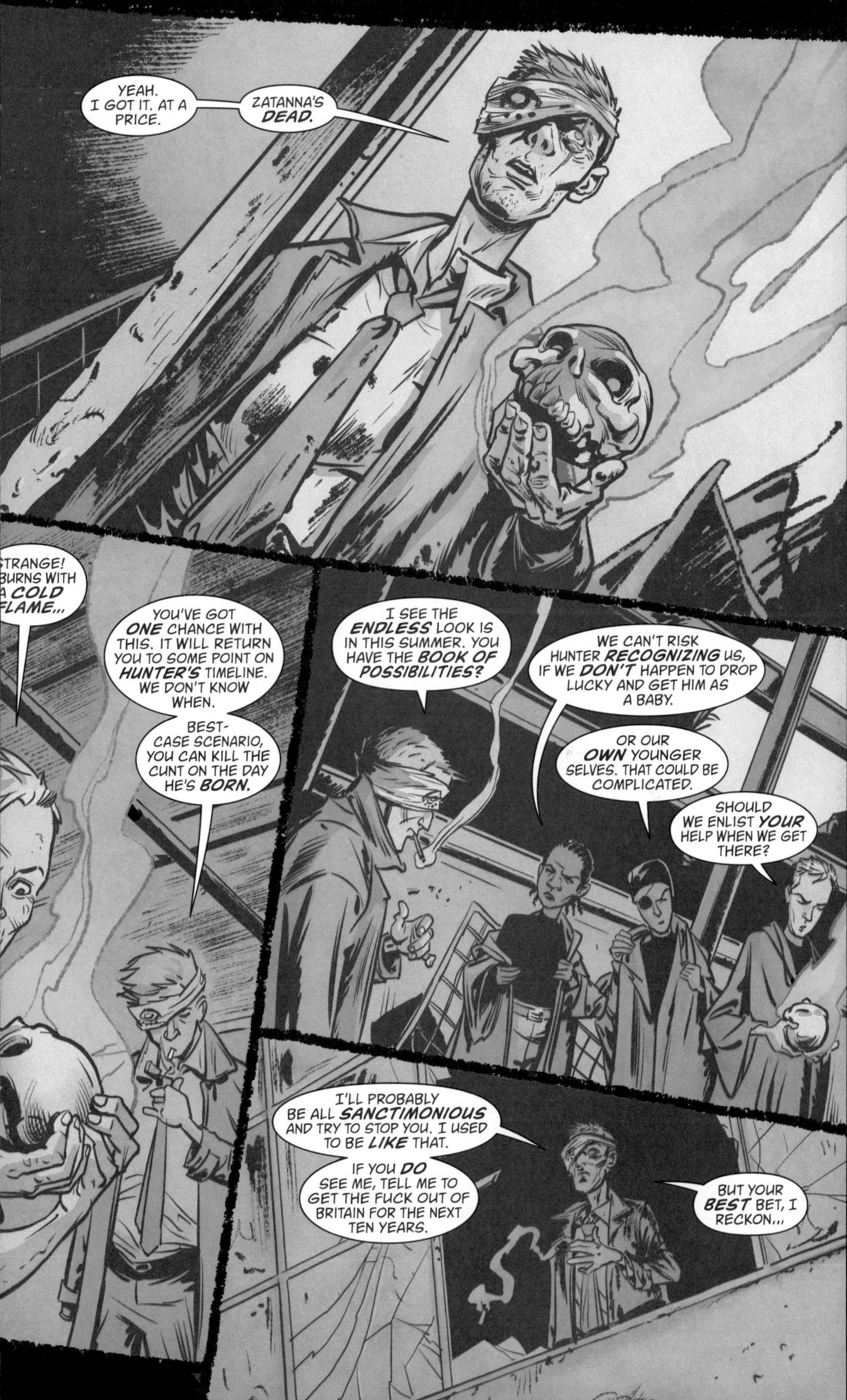
YEAH. I GOT IT. AT A PRICE.
ZATANNA'S DEAD.
STRANGE! BURNS WITH A COLD FLAME...
YOU'VE GOT ONE CHANCE WITH THIS. IT WILL RETURN YOU TO SOME POINT ON HUNTER'S TIMELINE. WE DON'T KNOW WHEN.
BEST-CASE SCENARIO, YOU CAN KILL THE CUNT ON THE DAY HE'S BORN.
I SEE THE ENDLESS LOOK IS IN THIS SUMMER. YOU HAVE THE BOOK OF POSSIBILITIES?
WE CAN'T RISK HUNTER RECOGNIZING US, IF WE DON'T HAPPEN TO DROP LUCKY AND GET HIM AS A BABY.
OR OUR OWN YOUNGER SELVES. THAT COULD BE COMPLICATED.
SHOULD WE ENLIST YOUR HELP WHEN WE GET THERE?
I'LL PROBABLY BE ALL SANCTIMONIOUS AND TRY TO STOP YOU. I USED TO BE LIKE THAT.
IF YOU DO SEE ME, TELL ME TO GET THE FUCK OUT OF BRITAIN FOR THE NEXT TEN YEARS.
BUT YOUR BEST BET, I RECKON...

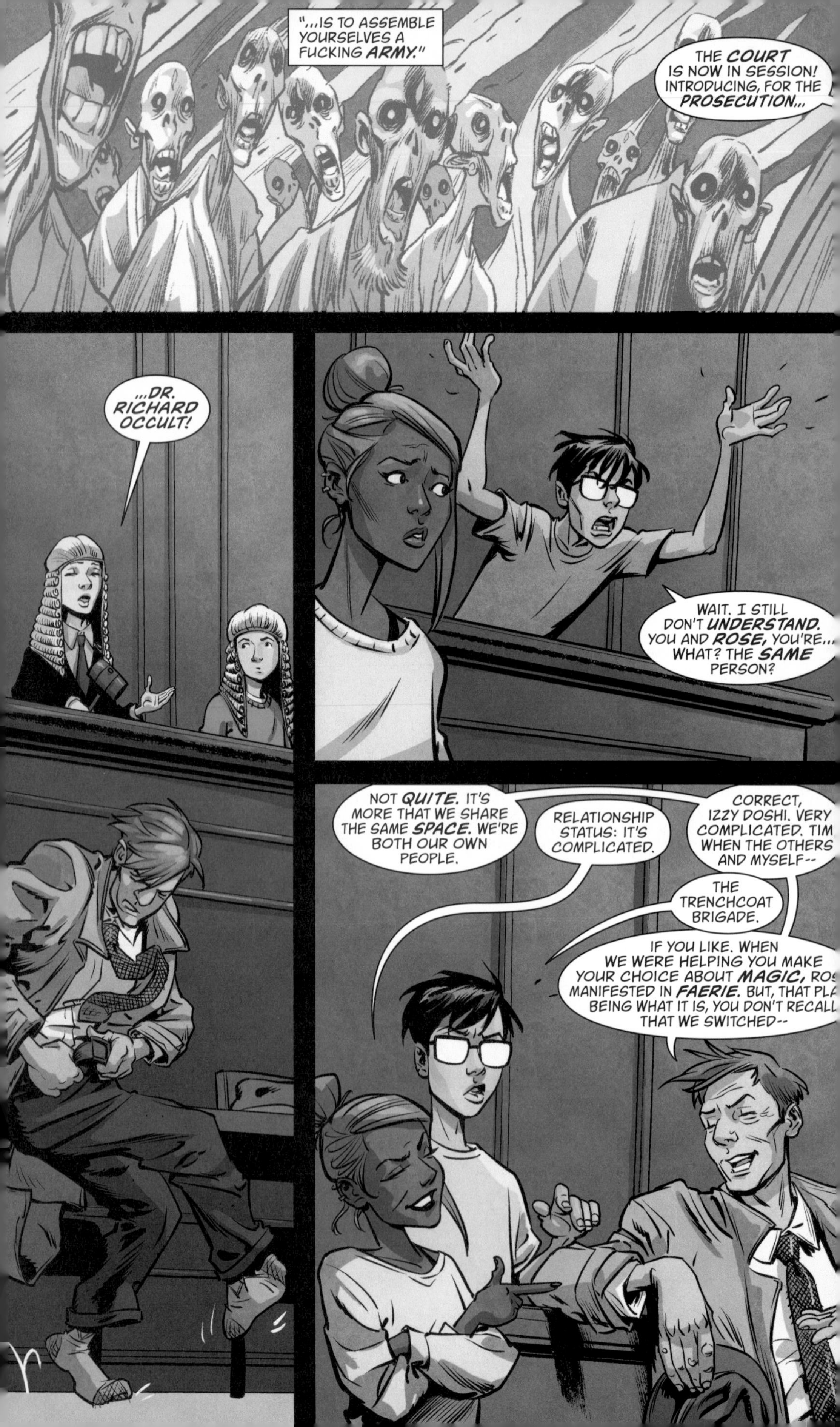

"...IS TO ASSEMBLE YOURSELVES A FUCKING ARMY."
THE COURT IS NOW IN SESSION! INTRODUCING, FOR THE PROSECUTION...
...DR. RICHARD OCCULT!
WAIT. I STILL DON'T UNDERSTAND. YOU AND ROSE, YOU'RE... WHAT? THE SAME PERSON?
NOT QUITE. IT'S MORE THAT WE SHARE THE SAME SPACE. WE'RE BOTH OUR OWN PEOPLE.
RELATIONSHIP STATUS: IT'S COMPLICATED.
CORRECT, IZZY DOSHI. VERY COMPLICATED. TIM WHEN THE OTHERS AND MYSELF--
THE TRENCHCOAT BRIGADE.
IF YOU LIKE. WHEN WE WERE HELPING YOU MAKE YOUR CHOICE ABOUT MAGIC, ROS MANIFESTED IN FAERIE. BUT, THAT PLA BEING WHAT IT IS, YOU DON'T RECALL THAT WE SWITCHED--

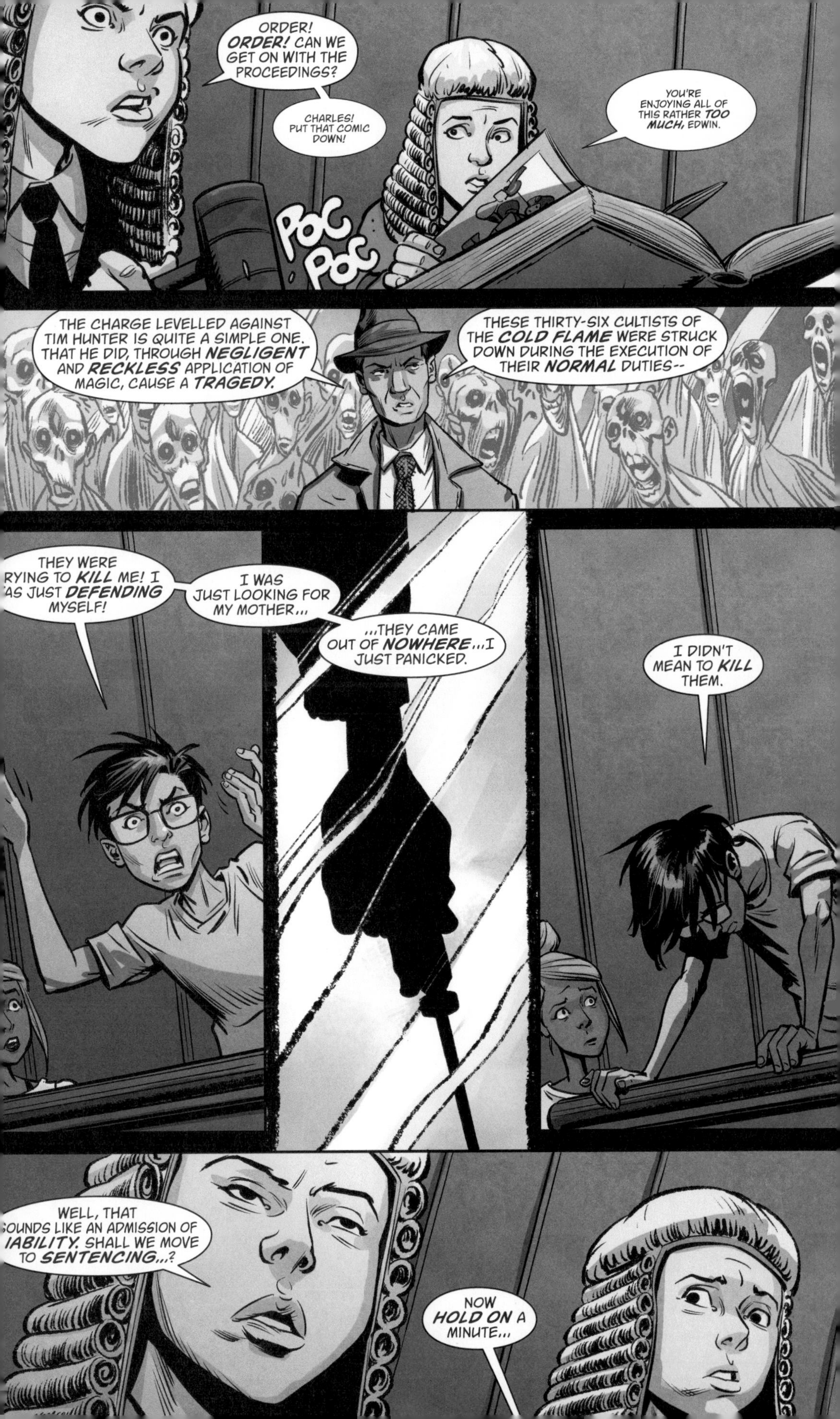
ORDER! ORDER! CAN WE GET ON WITH THE PROCEEDINGS?
CHARLES! PUT THAT COMIC DOWN!
YOU'RE ENJOYING ALL OF THIS RATHER TOO MUCH, EDWIN.
POC POC
THE CHARGE LEVELLED AGAINST TIM HUNTER IS QUITE A SIMPLE ONE. THAT HE DID, THROUGH NEGLIGENT AND RECKLESS APPLICATION OF MAGIC, CAUSE A TRAGEDY.
THESE THIRTY-SIX CULTISTS OF THE COLD FLAME WERE STRUCK DOWN DURING THE EXECUTION OF THEIR NORMAL DUTIES--
THEY WERE RYING TO KILL ME! I AS JUST DEFENDING MYSELF!
I WAS JUST LOOKING FOR MY MOTHER...
...THEY CAME OUT OF NOWHERE...I JUST PANICKED.
I DIDN'T MEAN TO KILL THEM.
WELL, THAT OUNDS LIKE AN ADMISSION OF IABILITY. SHALL WE MOVE TO SENTENCING...?
NOW HOLD ON A MINUTE...

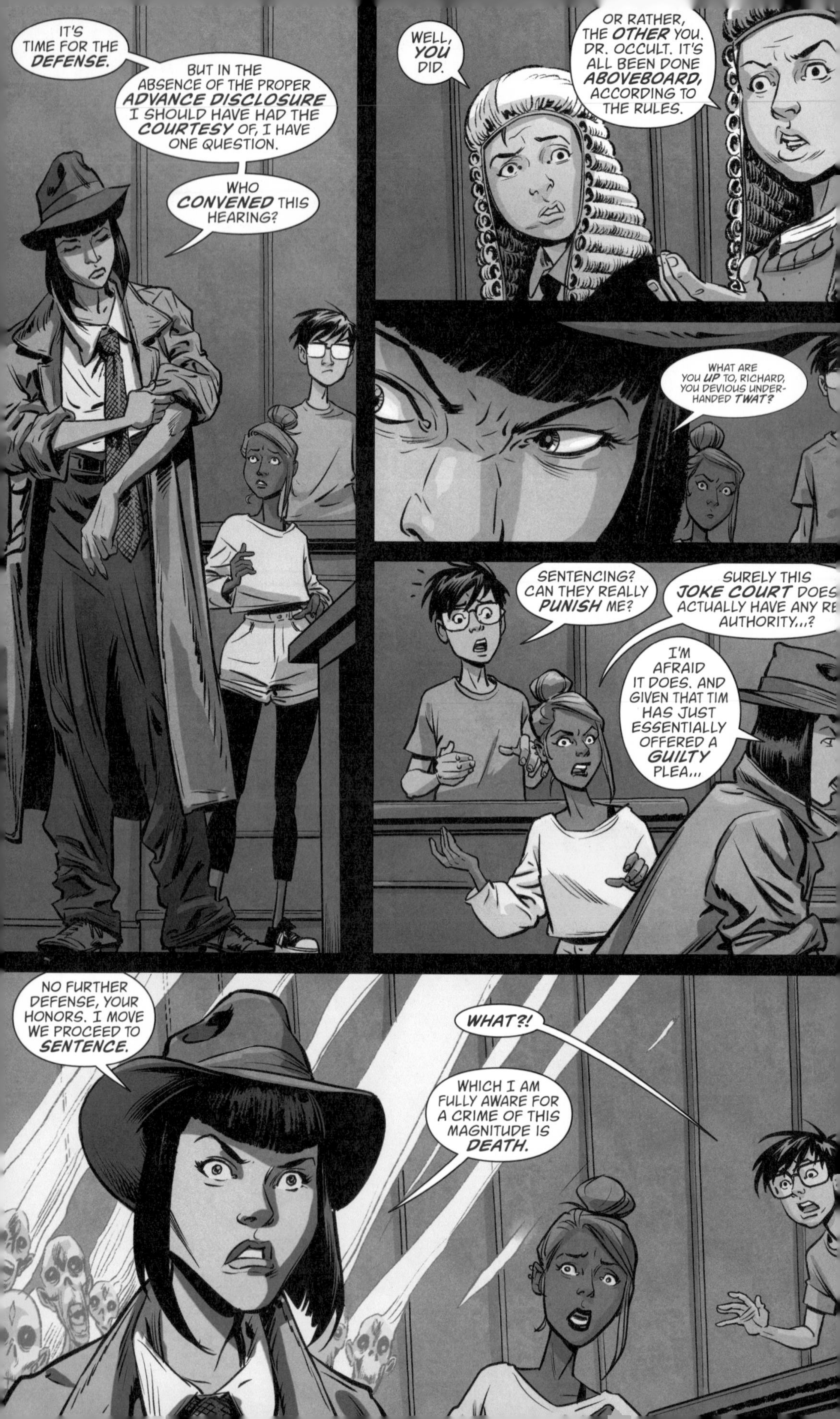

IT'S TIME FOR THE DEFENSE.
BUT IN THE ABSENCE OF THE PROPER ADVANCE DISCLOSURE I SHOULD HAVE HAD THE COURTESY OF, I HAVE ONE QUESTION.
WHO CONVENED THIS HEARING?
WELL, YOU DID.
OR RATHER, THE OTHER YOU. DR. OCCULT. IT'S ALL BEEN DONE ABOVEBOARD, ACCORDING TO THE RULES.
WHAT ARE YOU UP TO, RICHARD, YOU DEVIOUS UNDER-HANDED TWAT?
SENTENCING? CAN THEY REALLY PUNISH ME?
SURELY THIS JOKE COURT DOES ACTUALLY HAVE ANY RE AUTHORITY...?
I'M AFRAID IT DOES. AND GIVEN THAT TIM HAS JUST ESSENTIALLY OFFERED A GUILTY PLEA...
NO FURTHER DEFENSE, YOUR HONORS. I MOVE WE PROCEED TO SENTENCE.
WHAT?!
WHICH I AM FULLY AWARE FOR A CRIME OF THIS MAGNITUDE IS DEATH.

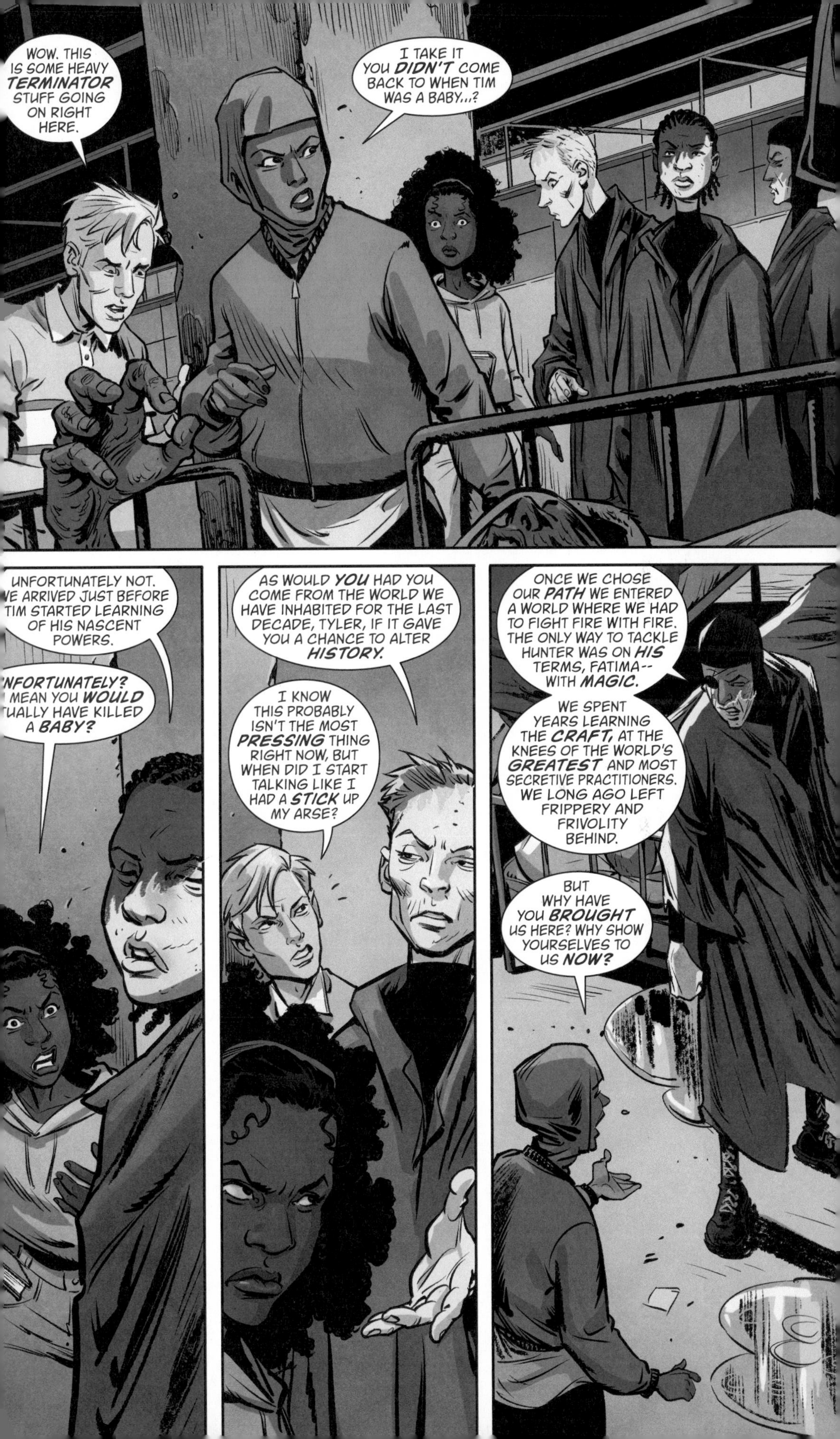
WOW. THIS IS SOME HEAVY TERMINATOR STUFF GOING ON RIGHT HERE.
I TAKE IT YOU DIDN'T COME BACK TO WHEN TIM WAS A BABY...?
UNFORTUNATELY NOT. WE ARRIVED JUST BEFORE TIM STARTED LEARNING OF HIS NASCENT POWERS.
NFORTUNATELY? MEAN YOU WOULD UALLY HAVE KILLED A BABY?
AS WOULD YOU HAD YOU COME FROM THE WORLD WE HAVE INHABITED FOR THE LAST DECADE, TYLER, IF IT GAVE YOU A CHANCE TO ALTER HISTORY.
I KNOW THIS PROBABLY ISN'T THE MOST PRESSING THING RIGHT NOW, BUT WHEN DID I START TALKING LIKE I HAD A STICK UP MY ARSE?
ONCE WE CHOSE OUR PATH WE ENTERED A WORLD WHERE WE HAD TO FIGHT FIRE WITH FIRE. THE ONLY WAY TO TACKLE HUNTER WAS ON HIS TERMS, FATIMA-- WITH MAGIC.
WE SPENT YEARS LEARNING THE CRAFT, AT THE KNEES OF THE WORLD'S GREATEST AND MOST SECRETIVE PRACTITIONERS. WE LONG AGO LEFT FRIPPERY AND FRIVOLITY BEHIND.
BUT WHY HAVE YOU BROUGHT US HERE? WHY SHOW YOURSELVES TO US NOW?

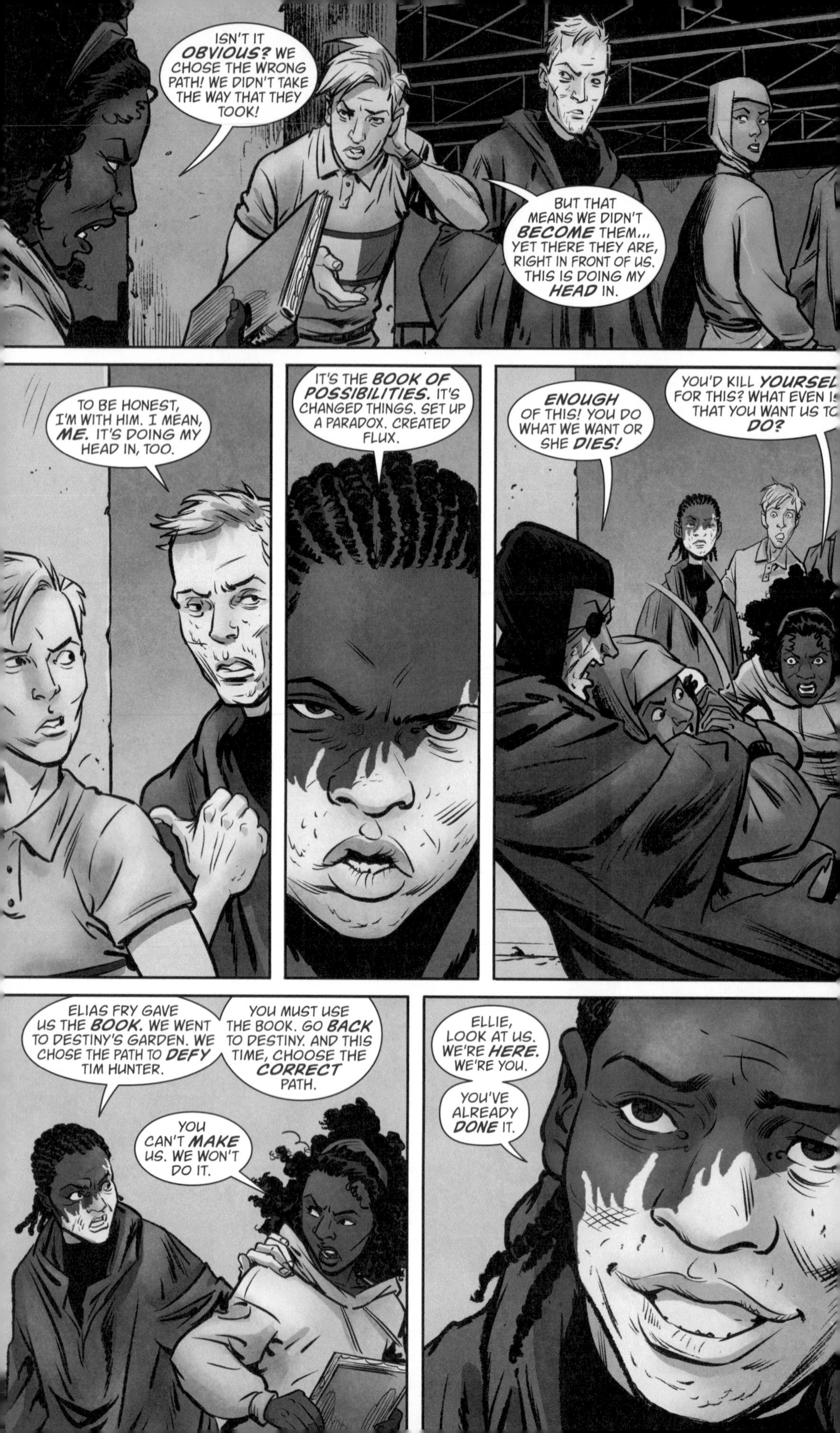
ISN'T IT OBVIOUS? WE CHOSE THE WRONG PATH! WE DIDN'T TAKE THE WAY THAT THEY TOOK!
BUT THAT MEANS WE DIDN'T BECOME THEM... YET THERE THEY ARE, RIGHT IN FRONT OF US. THIS IS DOING MY HEAD IN.
TO BE HONEST, I'M WITH HIM. I MEAN, ME. IT'S DOING MY HEAD IN, TOO.
IT'S THE BOOK OF POSSIBILITIES. IT'S CHANGED THINGS. SET UP A PARADOX. CREATED FLUX.
ENOUGH OF THIS! YOU DO WHAT WE WANT OR SHE DIES!
YOU'D KILL YOURSEL FOR THIS? WHAT EVEN IS THAT YOU WANT US TO DO?
ELIAS FRY GAVE US THE BOOK. WE WENT TO DESTINY'S GARDEN. WE CHOSE THE PATH TO DEFY TIM HUNTER.
YOU MUST USE THE BOOK. GO BACK TO DESTINY. AND THIS TIME, CHOOSE THE CORRECT PATH.
YOU CAN'T MAKE US. WE WON'T DO IT.
ELLIE, LOOK AT US. WE'RE HERE. WE'RE YOU.
YOU'VE ALREADY DONE IT.

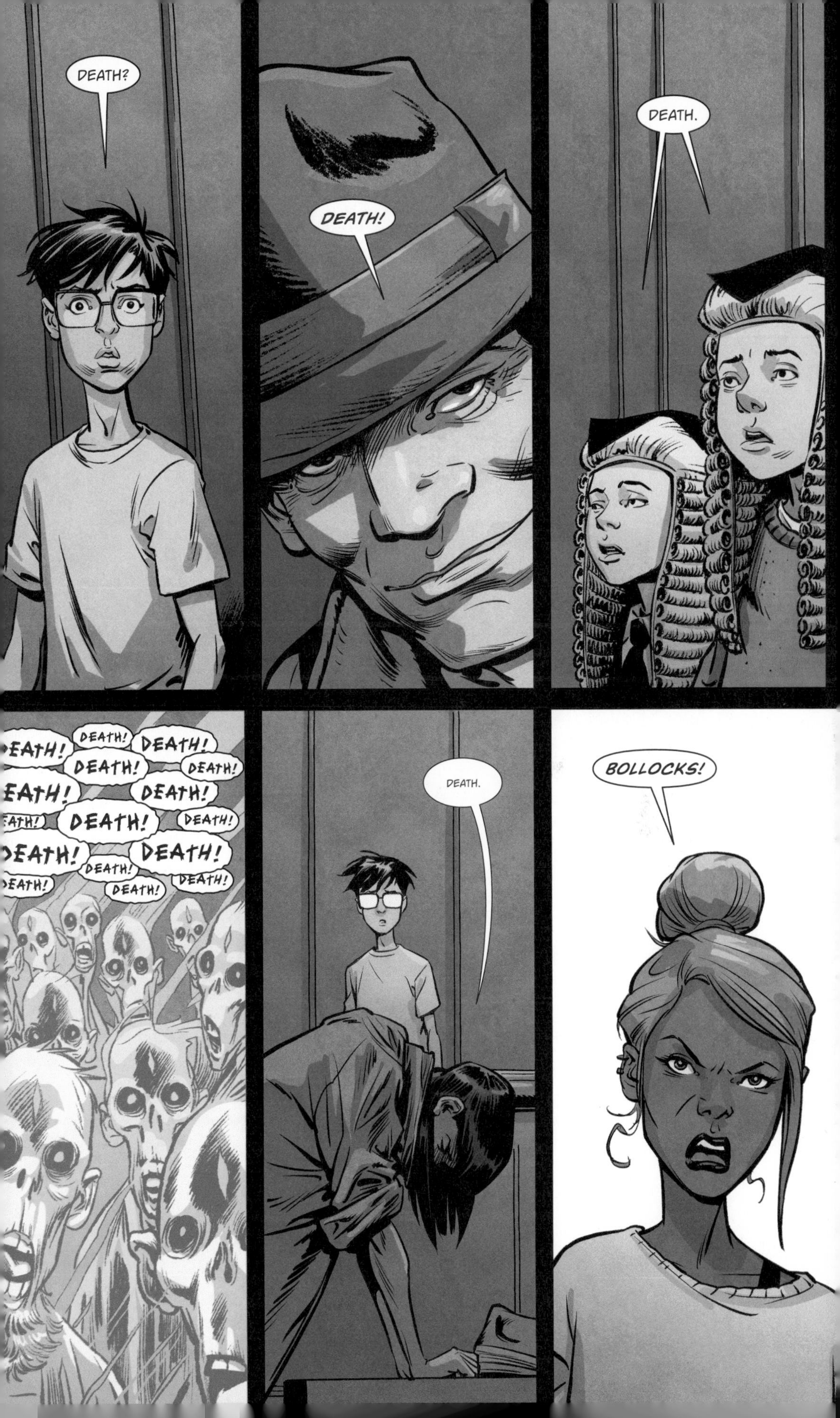

DEATH?
DEATH!
DEATH.
DEATH! DEATH! DEATH! DEATH! DEATH! DEATH! DEATH! DEATH! DEATH! DEATH! DEATH! DEATH! DEATH! DEATH!
DEATH.
BOLLOCKS!

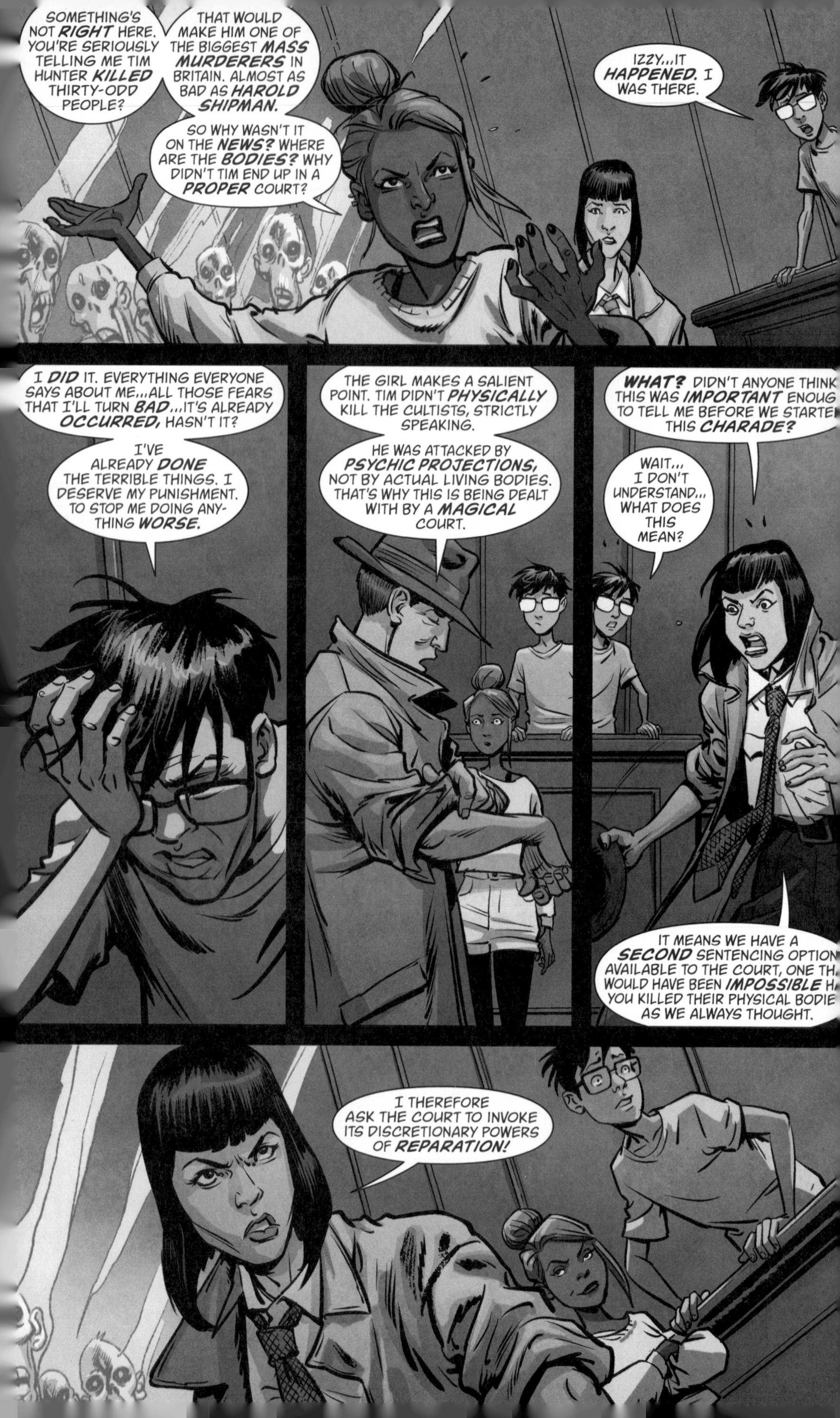

SOMETHING'S NOT RIGHT HERE. YOU'RE SERIOUSLY TELLING ME TIM HUNTER KILLED THIRTY-ODD PEOPLE?
THAT WOULD MAKE HIM ONE OF THE BIGGEST MASS MURDERERS IN BRITAIN. ALMOST AS BAD AS HAROLD SHIPMAN.
SO WHY WASN'T IT ON THE NEWS? WHERE ARE THE BODIES? WHY DIDN'T TIM END UP IN A PROPER COURT?
IZZY...IT HAPPENED. I WAS THERE.
I DID IT. EVERYTHING EVERYONE SAYS ABOUT ME...ALL THOSE FEARS THAT I'LL TURN BAD...IT'S ALREADY OCCURRED, HASN'T IT?
I'VE ALREADY DONE THE TERRIBLE THINGS. I DESERVE MY PUNISHMENT. TO STOP ME DOING ANYTHING WORSE.
THE GIRL MAKES A SALIENT POINT. TIM DIDN'T PHYSICALLY KILL THE CULTISTS, STRICTLY SPEAKING.
HE WAS ATTACKED BY PSYCHIC PROJECTIONS, NOT BY ACTUAL LIVING BODIES. THAT'S WHY THIS IS BEING DEALT WITH BY A MAGICAL COURT.
WHAT? DIDN'T ANYONE THINK THIS WAS IMPORTANT ENOUG TO TELL ME BEFORE WE STARTE THIS CHARADE?
WAIT... I DON'T UNDERSTAND... WHAT DOES THIS MEAN?
IT MEANS WE HAVE A SECOND SENTENCING OPTIO AVAILABLE TO THE COURT, ONE TH WOULD HAVE BEEN IMPOSSIBLE H YOU KILLED THEIR PHYSICAL BODIE AS WE ALWAYS THOUGHT.
I THEREFORE ASK THE COURT TO INVOKE ITS DISCRETIONARY POWERS OF REPARATION!

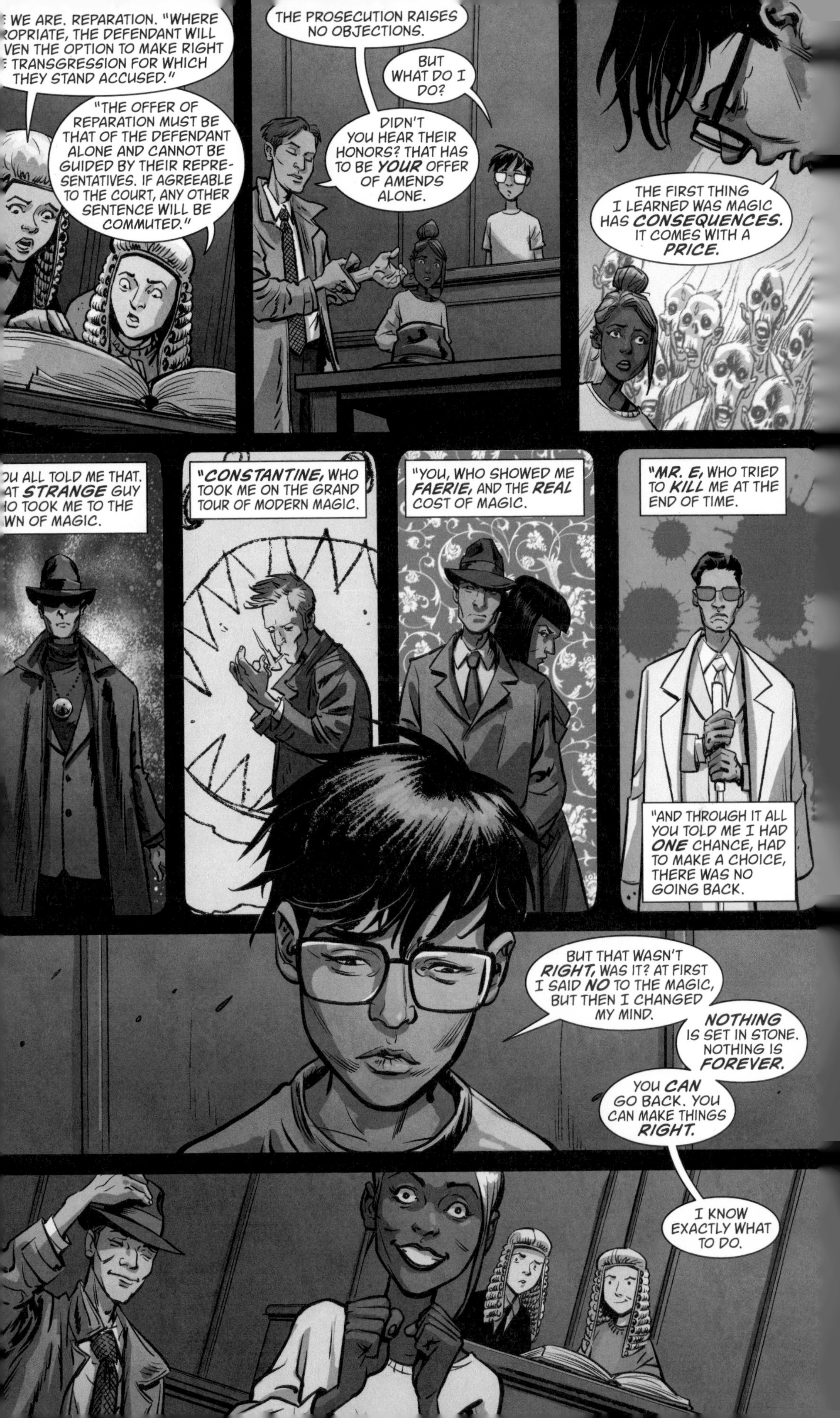

E WE ARE. REPARATION. "WHERE
ROPRIATE, THE DEFENDANT WILL
VEN THE OPTION TO MAKE RIGHT
E TRANSGRESSION FOR WHICH
THEY STAND ACCUSED."
"THE OFFER OF REPARATION MUST BE THAT OF THE DEFENDANT ALONE AND CANNOT BE GUIDED BY THEIR REPRESENTATIVES. IF AGREEABLE TO THE COURT, ANY OTHER SENTENCE WILL BE COMMUTED."
THE PROSECUTION RAISES NO OBJECTIONS.
BUT WHAT DO I DO?
DIDN'T YOU HEAR THEIR HONORS? THAT HAS TO BE YOUR OFFER OF AMENDS ALONE.
THE FIRST THING I LEARNED WAS MAGIC HAS CONSEQUENCES. IT COMES WITH A PRICE.
OU ALL TOLD ME THAT.
AT STRANGE GUY
HO TOOK ME TO THE
WN OF MAGIC.
"CONSTANTINE, WHO TOOK ME ON THE GRAND TOUR OF MODERN MAGIC.
"YOU, WHO SHOWED ME FAERIE, AND THE REAL COST OF MAGIC.
"MR. E, WHO TRIED TO KILL ME AT THE END OF TIME.
"AND THROUGH IT ALL YOU TOLD ME I HAD ONE CHANCE, HAD TO MAKE A CHOICE, THERE WAS NO GOING BACK.
BUT THAT WASN'T RIGHT, WAS IT? AT FIRST I SAID NO TO THE MAGIC, BUT THEN I CHANGED MY MIND.
NOTHING IS SET IN STONE. NOTHING IS FOREVER.
YOU CAN GO BACK. YOU CAN MAKE THINGS RIGHT.
I KNOW EXACTLY WHAT TO DO.

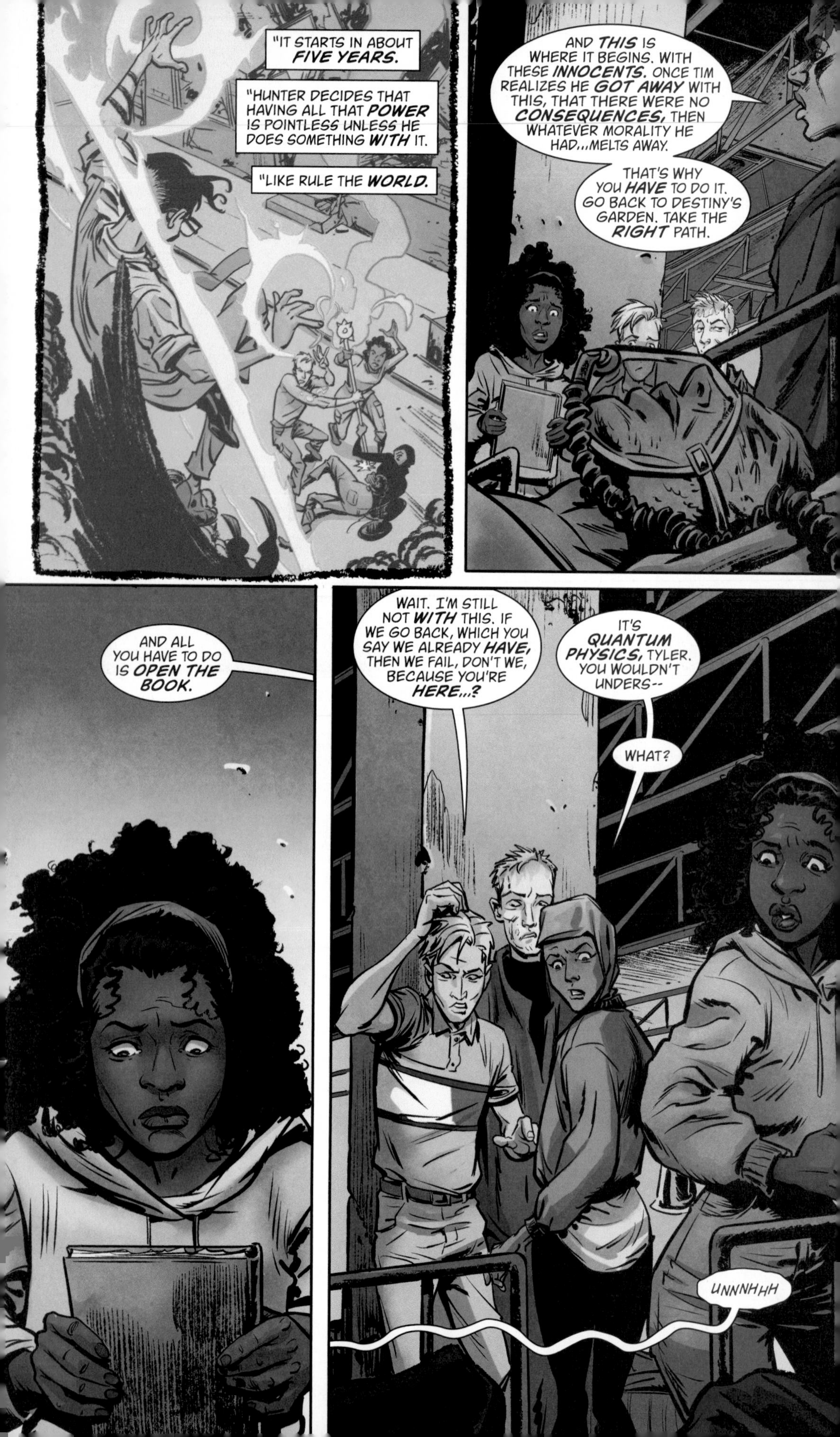
"IT STARTS IN ABOUT FIVE YEARS.
"HUNTER DECIDES THAT HAVING ALL THAT POWER IS POINTLESS UNLESS HE DOES SOMETHING WITH IT.
"LIKE RULE THE WORLD.
AND THIS IS WHERE IT BEGINS. WITH THESE INNOCENTS. ONCE TIM REALIZES HE GOT AWAY WITH THIS, THAT THERE WERE NO CONSEQUENCES, THEN WHATEVER MORALITY HE HAD...MELTS AWAY.
THAT'S WHY YOU HAVE TO DO IT. GO BACK TO DESTINY'S GARDEN. TAKE THE RIGHT PATH.
AND ALL YOU HAVE TO DO IS OPEN THE BOOK.
WAIT. I'M STILL NOT WITH THIS. IF WE GO BACK, WHICH YOU SAY WE ALREADY HAVE, THEN WE FAIL, DON'T WE, BECAUSE YOU'RE HERE...?
IT'S QUANTUM PHYSICS, TYLER. YOU WOULDN'T UNDERS--
WHAT?
UNNNHHH

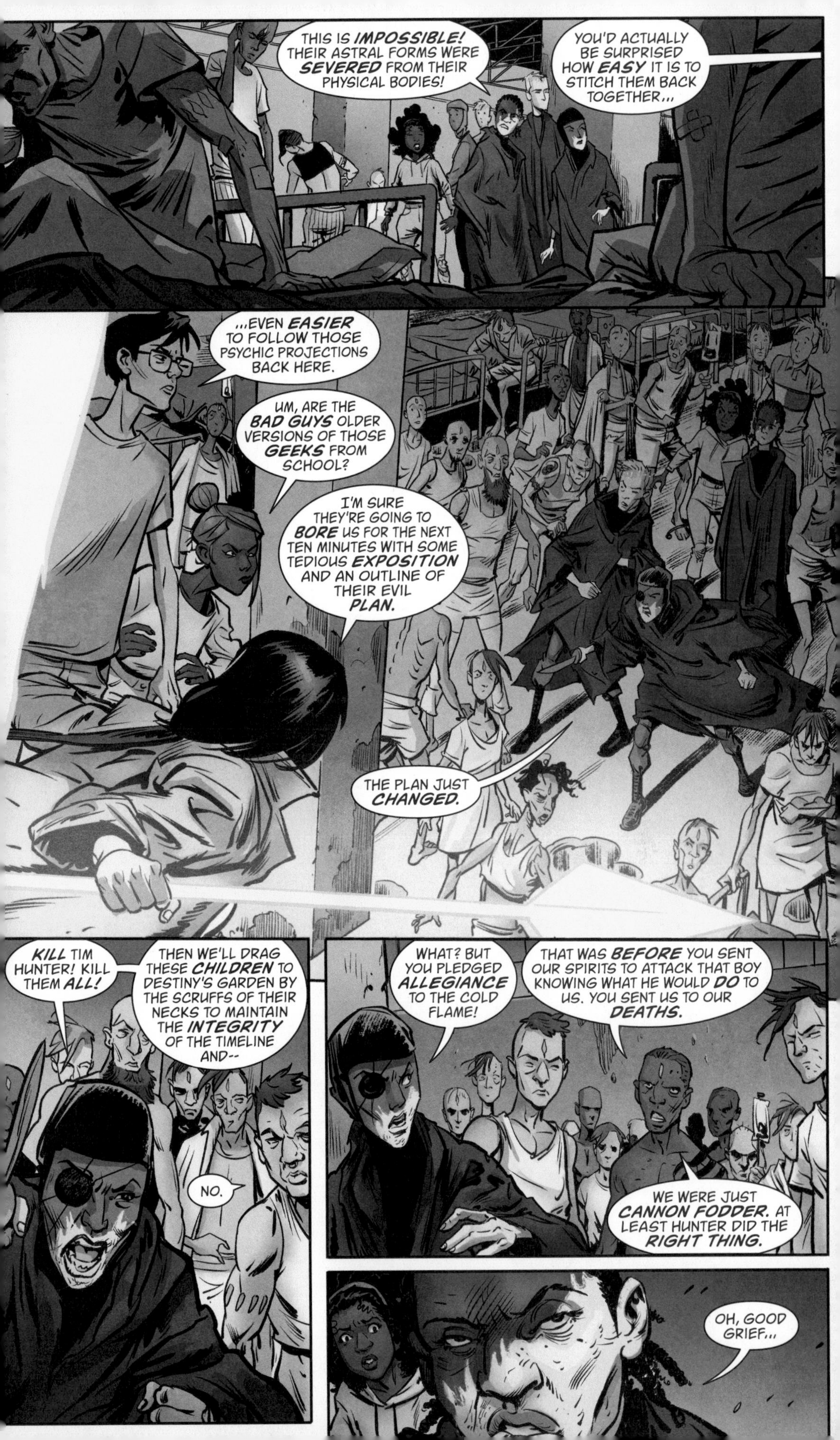
THIS IS IMPOSSIBLE! THEIR ASTRAL FORMS WERE SEVERED FROM THEIR PHYSICAL BODIES!
YOU'D ACTUALLY BE SURPRISED HOW EASY IT IS TO STITCH THEM BACK TOGETHER...
...EVEN EASIER TO FOLLOW THOSE PSYCHIC PROJECTIONS BACK HERE.
UM, ARE THE BAD GUYS OLDER VERSIONS OF THOSE GEEKS FROM SCHOOL?
I'M SURE THEY'RE GOING TO BORE US FOR THE NEXT TEN MINUTES WITH SOME TEDIOUS EXPOSITION AND AN OUTLINE OF THEIR EVIL PLAN.
THE PLAN JUST CHANGED.
KILL TIM HUNTER! KILL THEM ALL!
THEN WE'LL DRAG THESE CHILDREN TO DESTINY'S GARDEN BY THE SCRUFFS OF THEIR NECKS TO MAINTAIN THE INTEGRITY OF THE TIMELINE AND--
NO.
WHAT? BUT YOU PLEDGED ALLEGIANCE TO THE COLD FLAME!
THAT WAS BEFORE YOU SENT OUR SPIRITS TO ATTACK THAT BOY KNOWING WHAT HE WOULD DO TO US. YOU SENT US TO OUR DEATHS.
WE WERE JUST CANNON FODDER. AT LEAST HUNTER DID THE RIGHT THING.
OH, GOOD GRIEF...

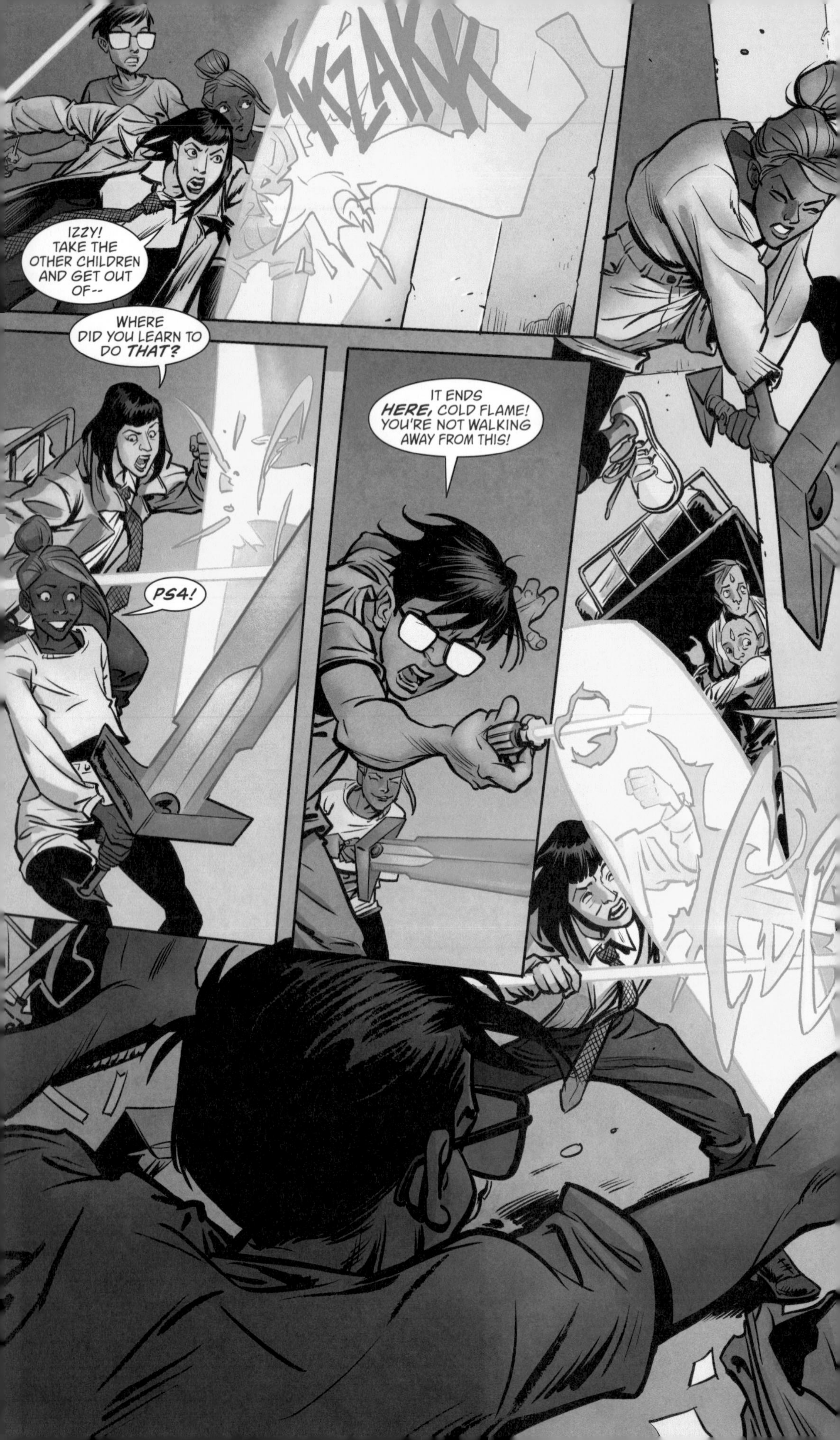
KKZAKK
IZZY! TAKE THE OTHER CHILDREN AND GET OUT OF--
WHERE DID YOU LEARN TO DO *THAT?*
PS4!
IT ENDS *HERE,* COLD FLAME! YOU'RE NOT WALKING AWAY FROM THIS!

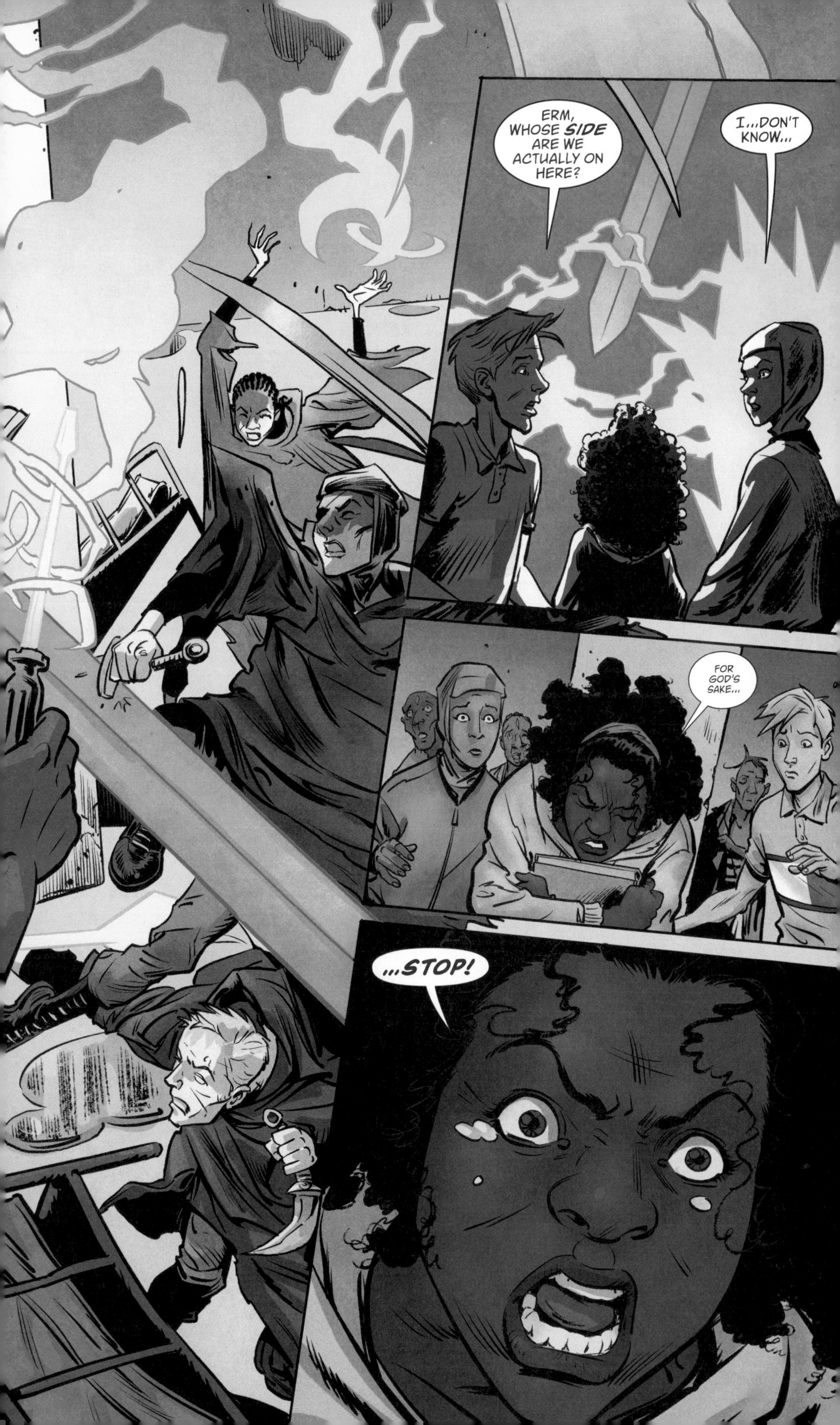
ERM, WHOSE SIDE ARE WE ACTUALLY ON HERE?
I...DON'T KNOW...
FOR GOD'S SAKE...
...STOP!

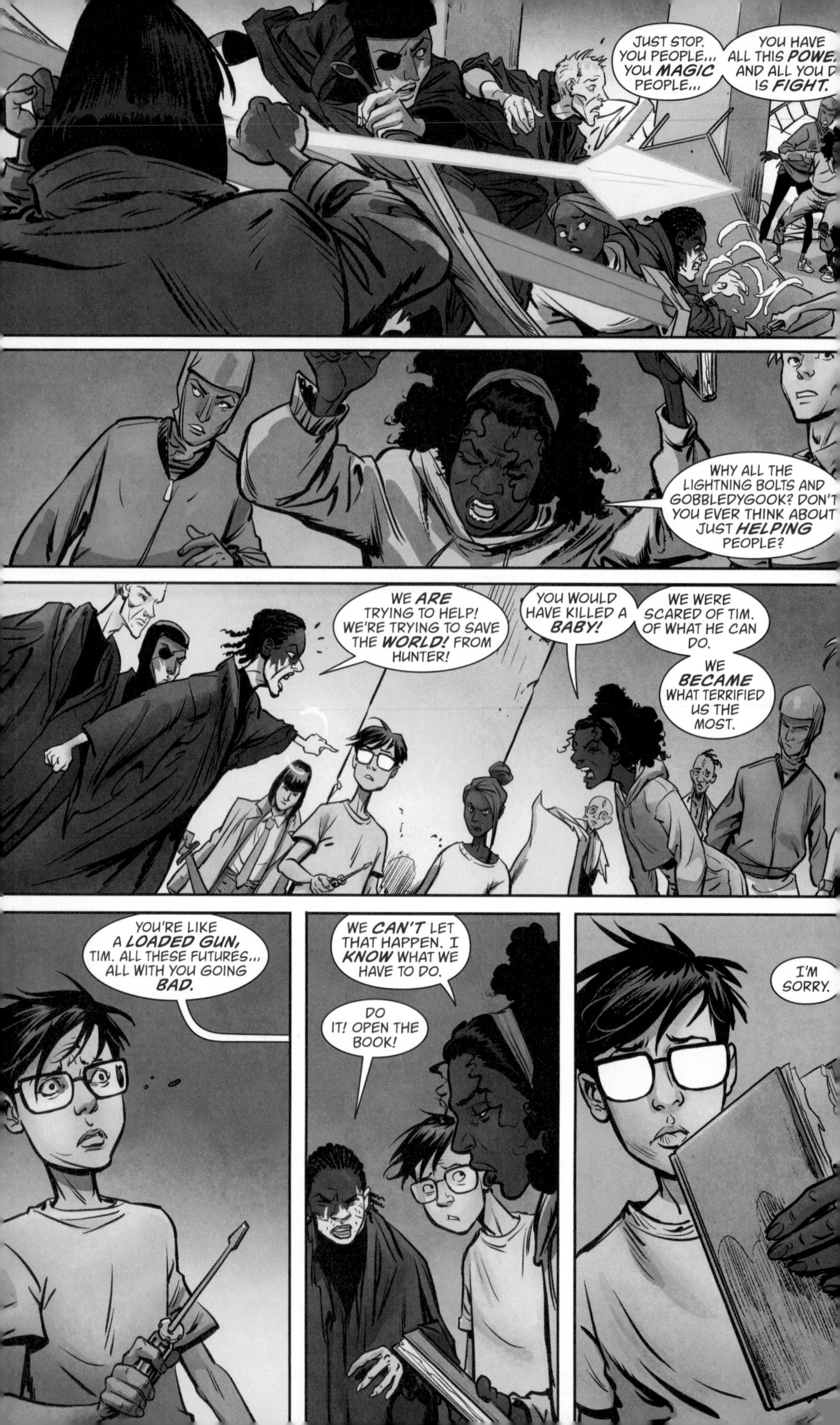

JUST STOP. YOU PEOPLE... YOU MAGIC PEOPLE...
YOU HAVE ALL THIS POWE AND ALL YOU D IS FIGHT.
WHY ALL THE LIGHTNING BOLTS AND GOBBLEDYGOOK? DON'T YOU EVER THINK ABOUT JUST HELPING PEOPLE?
WE ARE TRYING TO HELP! WE'RE TRYING TO SAVE THE WORLD! FROM HUNTER!
YOU WOULD HAVE KILLED A BABY!
WE WERE SCARED OF TIM. OF WHAT HE CAN DO.
WE BECAME WHAT TERRIFIED US THE MOST.
YOU'RE LIKE A LOADED GUN, TIM. ALL THESE FUTURES... ALL WITH YOU GOING BAD.
WE CAN'T LET THAT HAPPEN. I KNOW WHAT WE HAVE TO DO.
DO IT! OPEN THE BOOK!
I'M SORRY.

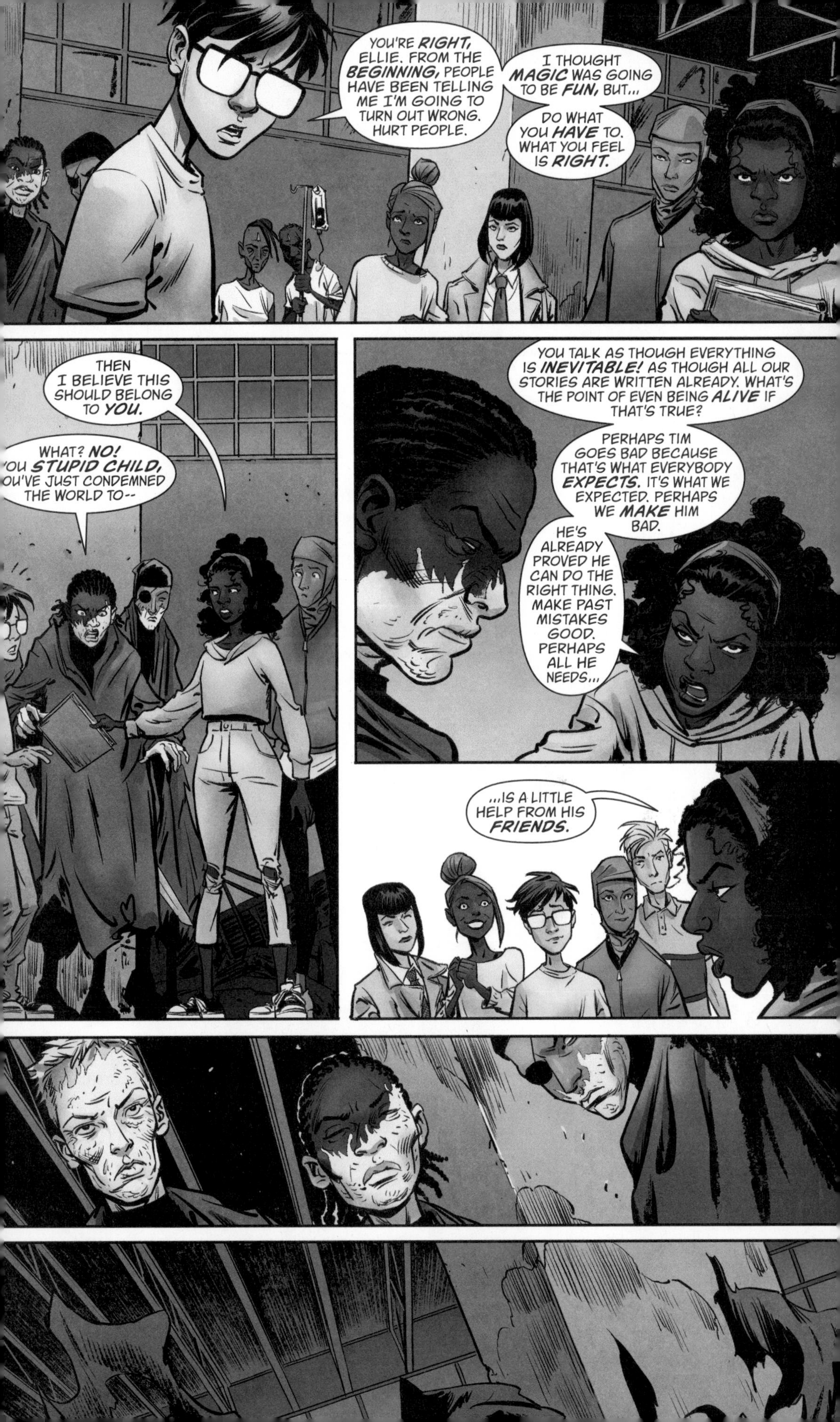

YOU'RE RIGHT, ELLIE. FROM THE BEGINNING, PEOPLE HAVE BEEN TELLING ME I'M GOING TO TURN OUT WRONG. HURT PEOPLE.
I THOUGHT MAGIC WAS GOING TO BE FUN, BUT...
DO WHAT YOU HAVE TO. WHAT YOU FEEL IS RIGHT.
THEN I BELIEVE THIS SHOULD BELONG TO YOU.
WHAT? NO! YOU STUPID CHILD, YOU'VE JUST CONDEMNED THE WORLD TO--
YOU TALK AS THOUGH EVERYTHING IS INEVITABLE! AS THOUGH ALL OUR STORIES ARE WRITTEN ALREADY. WHAT'S THE POINT OF EVEN BEING ALIVE IF THAT'S TRUE?
PERHAPS TIM GOES BAD BECAUSE THAT'S WHAT EVERYBODY EXPECTS. IT'S WHAT WE EXPECTED. PERHAPS WE MAKE HIM BAD.
HE'S ALREADY PROVED HE CAN DO THE RIGHT THING. MAKE PAST MISTAKES GOOD. PERHAPS ALL HE NEEDS...
...IS A LITTLE HELP FROM HIS FRIENDS.

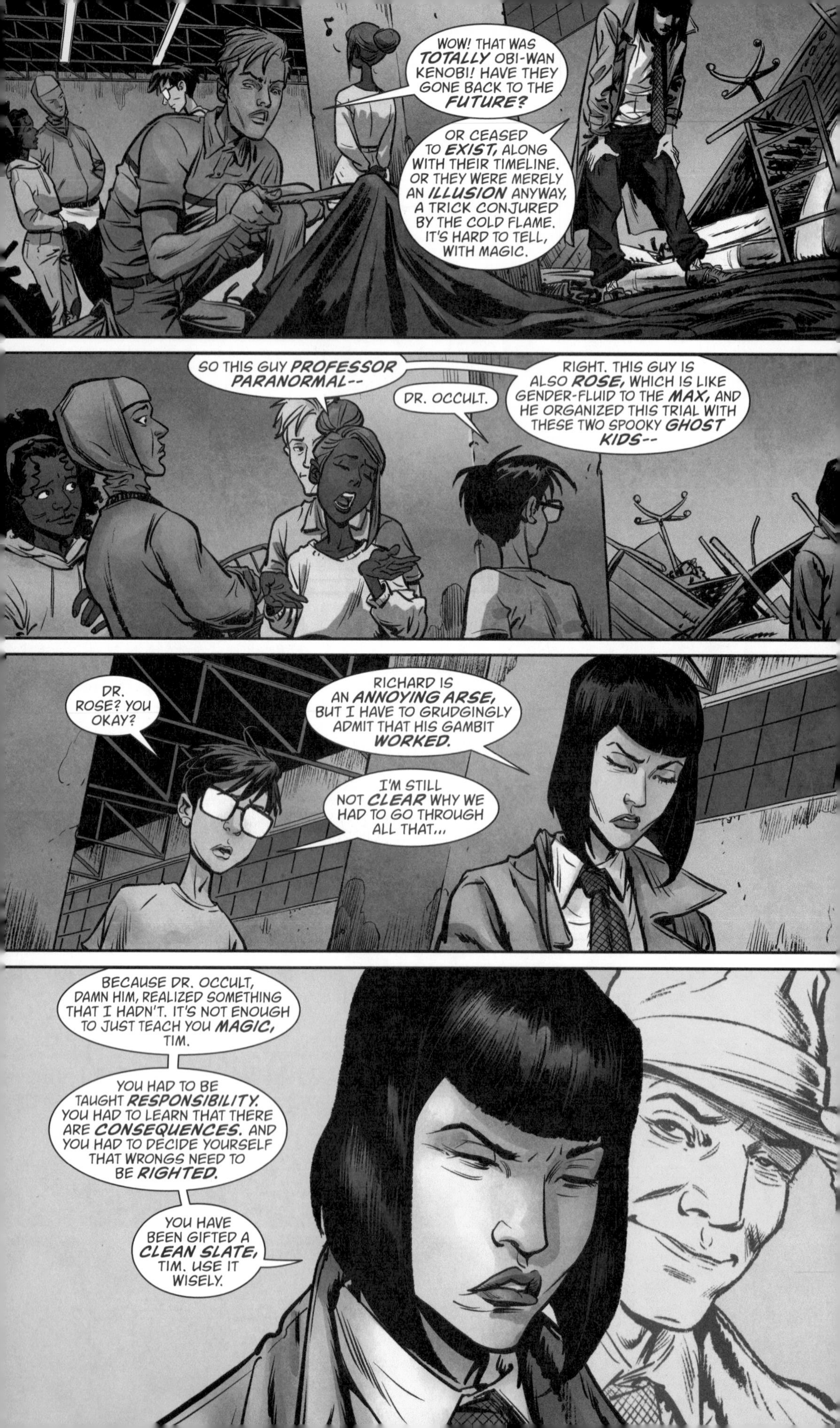

WOW! THAT WAS TOTALLY OBI-WAN KENOBI! HAVE THEY GONE BACK TO THE FUTURE?
OR CEASED TO EXIST, ALONG WITH THEIR TIMELINE. OR THEY WERE MERELY AN ILLUSION ANYWAY, A TRICK CONJURED BY THE COLD FLAME. IT'S HARD TO TELL, WITH MAGIC.
SO THIS GUY PROFESSOR PARANORMAL--
DR. OCCULT.
RIGHT. THIS GUY IS ALSO ROSE, WHICH IS LIKE GENDER-FLUID TO THE MAX, AND HE ORGANIZED THIS TRIAL WITH THESE TWO SPOOKY GHOST KIDS--
DR. ROSE? YOU OKAY?
RICHARD IS AN ANNOYING ARSE, BUT I HAVE TO GRUDGINGLY ADMIT THAT HIS GAMBIT WORKED.
I'M STILL NOT CLEAR WHY WE HAD TO GO THROUGH ALL THAT...
BECAUSE DR. OCCULT, DAMN HIM, REALIZED SOMETHING THAT I HADN'T. IT'S NOT ENOUGH TO JUST TEACH YOU MAGIC, TIM.
YOU HAD TO BE TAUGHT RESPONSIBILITY. YOU HAD TO LEARN THAT THERE ARE CONSEQUENCES. AND YOU HAD TO DECIDE YOURSELF THAT WRONGS NEED TO BE RIGHTED.
YOU HAVE BEEN GIFTED A CLEAN SLATE, TIM. USE IT WISELY.

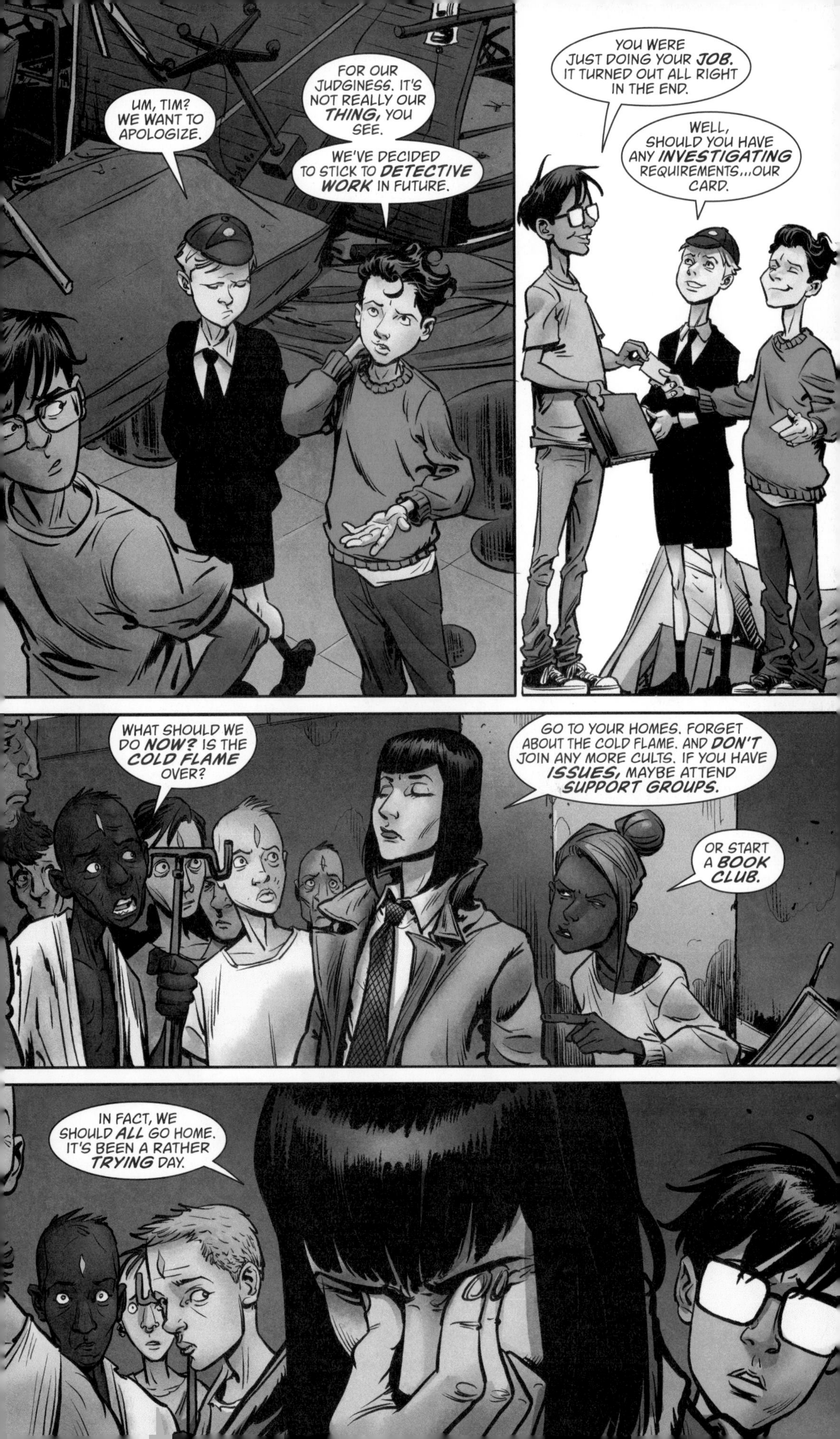
UM, TIM? WE WANT TO APOLOGIZE.
FOR OUR JUDGINESS. IT'S NOT REALLY OUR THING, YOU SEE.
WE'VE DECIDED TO STICK TO DETECTIVE WORK IN FUTURE.
YOU WERE JUST DOING YOUR JOB. IT TURNED OUT ALL RIGHT IN THE END.
WELL, SHOULD YOU HAVE ANY INVESTIGATING REQUIREMENTS...OUR CARD.
WHAT SHOULD WE DO NOW? IS THE COLD FLAME OVER?
GO TO YOUR HOMES. FORGET ABOUT THE COLD FLAME. AND DON'T JOIN ANY MORE CULTS. IF YOU HAVE ISSUES, MAYBE ATTEND SUPPORT GROUPS.
OR START A BOOK CLUB.
IN FACT, WE SHOULD ALL GO HOME. IT'S BEEN A RATHER TRYING DAY.

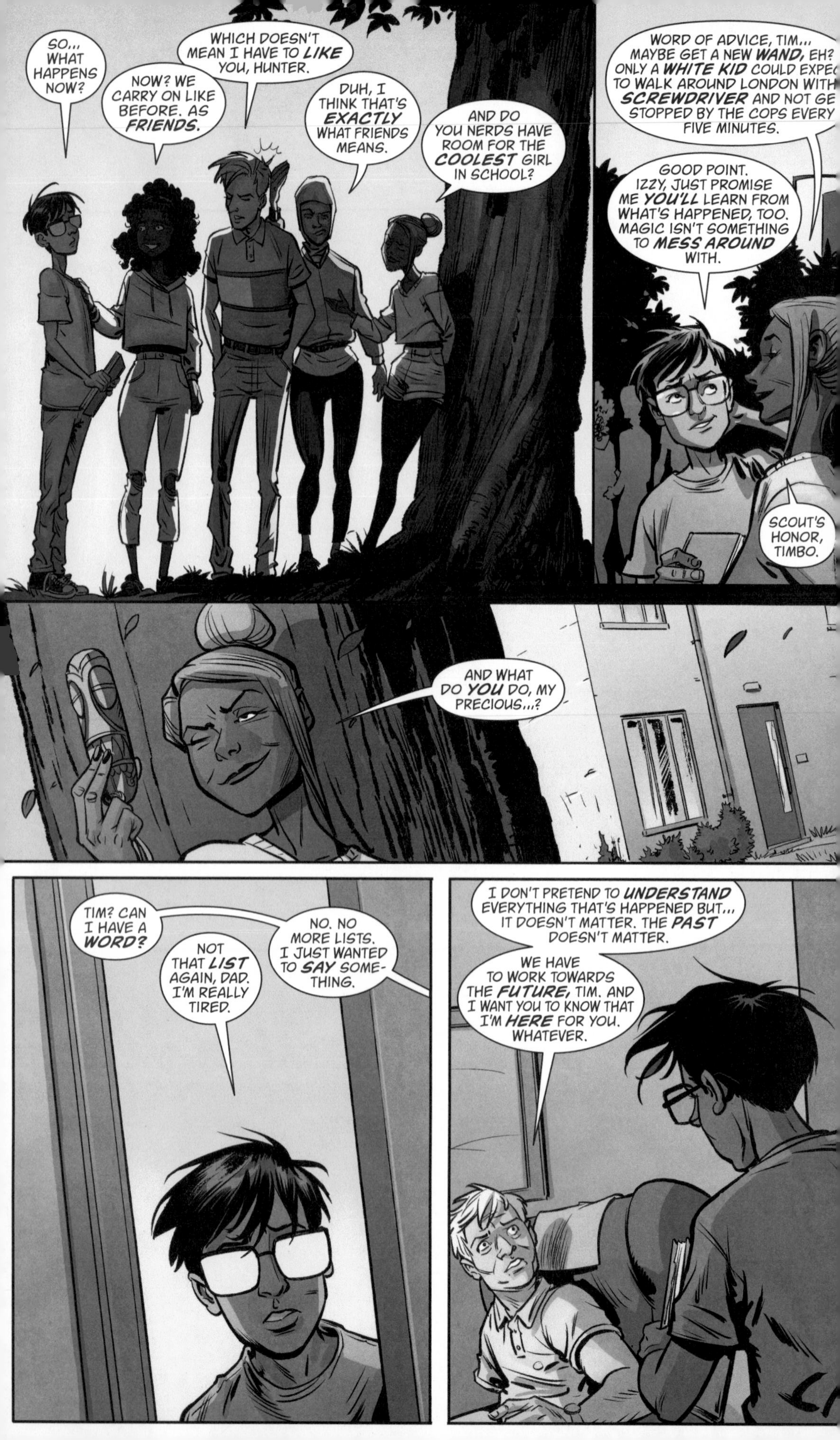
SO... WHAT HAPPENS NOW?
NOW? WE CARRY ON LIKE BEFORE. AS FRIENDS.
WHICH DOESN'T MEAN I HAVE TO LIKE YOU, HUNTER.
DUH, I THINK THAT'S EXACTLY WHAT FRIENDS MEANS.
AND DO YOU NERDS HAVE ROOM FOR THE COOLEST GIRL IN SCHOOL?
WORD OF ADVICE, TIM... MAYBE GET A NEW WAND, EH? ONLY A WHITE KID COULD EXPEC TO WALK AROUND LONDON WITH SCREWDRIVER AND NOT GE STOPPED BY THE COPS EVERY FIVE MINUTES.
GOOD POINT. IZZY, JUST PROMISE ME YOU'LL LEARN FROM WHAT'S HAPPENED, TOO. MAGIC ISN'T SOMETHING TO MESS AROUND WITH.
SCOUT'S HONOR, TIMBO.
AND WHAT DO YOU DO, MY PRECIOUS...?
TIM? CAN I HAVE A WORD?
NOT THAT LIST AGAIN, DAD. I'M REALLY TIRED.
NO. NO MORE LISTS. I JUST WANTED TO SAY SOME-THING.
I DON'T PRETEND TO UNDERSTAND EVERYTHING THAT'S HAPPENED BUT... IT DOESN'T MATTER. THE PAST DOESN'T MATTER.
WE HAVE TO WORK TOWARDS THE FUTURE, TIM. AND I WANT YOU TO KNOW THAT I'M HERE FOR YOU. WHATEVER.

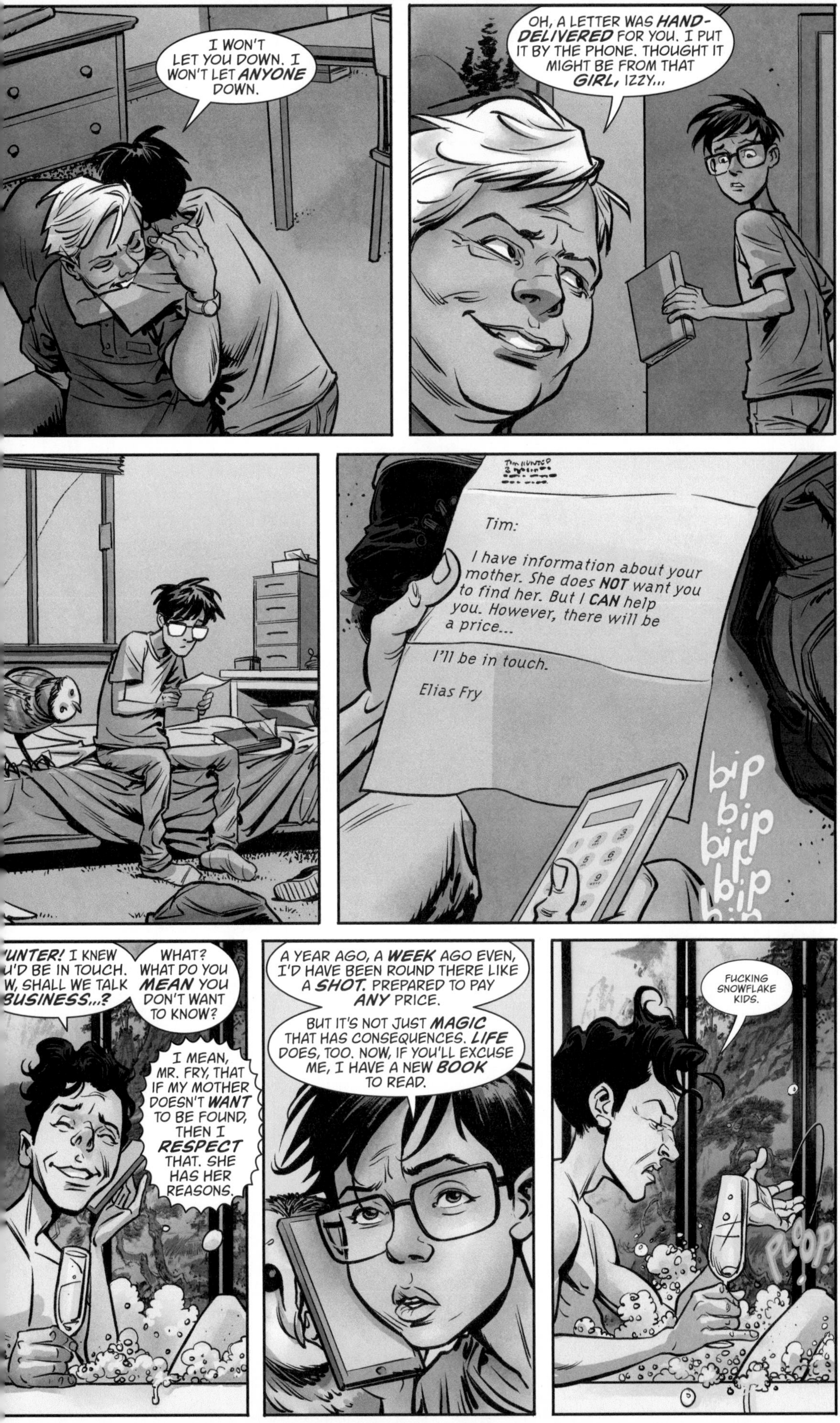
I WON'T LET YOU DOWN. I WON'T LET ANYONE DOWN.
OH, A LETTER WAS HAND-DELIVERED FOR YOU. I PUT IT BY THE PHONE. THOUGHT IT MIGHT BE FROM THAT GIRL, IZZY...
Tim:
I have information about your mother. She does NOT want you to find her. But I CAN help you. However, there will be a price...
I'll be in touch.
Elias Fry
bip bip bip bip
UNTER! I KNEW U'D BE IN TOUCH. W, SHALL WE TALK BUSINESS...?
WHAT? WHAT DO YOU MEAN YOU DON'T WANT TO KNOW?
I MEAN, MR. FRY, THAT IF MY MOTHER DOESN'T WANT TO BE FOUND, THEN I RESPECT THAT. SHE HAS HER REASONS.
A YEAR AGO, A WEEK AGO EVEN, I'D HAVE BEEN ROUND THERE LIKE A SHOT. PREPARED TO PAY ANY PRICE.
BUT IT'S NOT JUST MAGIC THAT HAS CONSEQUENCES. LIFE DOES, TOO. NOW, IF YOU'LL EXCUSE ME, I HAVE A NEW BOOK TO READ.
FUCKING SNOWFLAKE KIDS.
PLOOP!

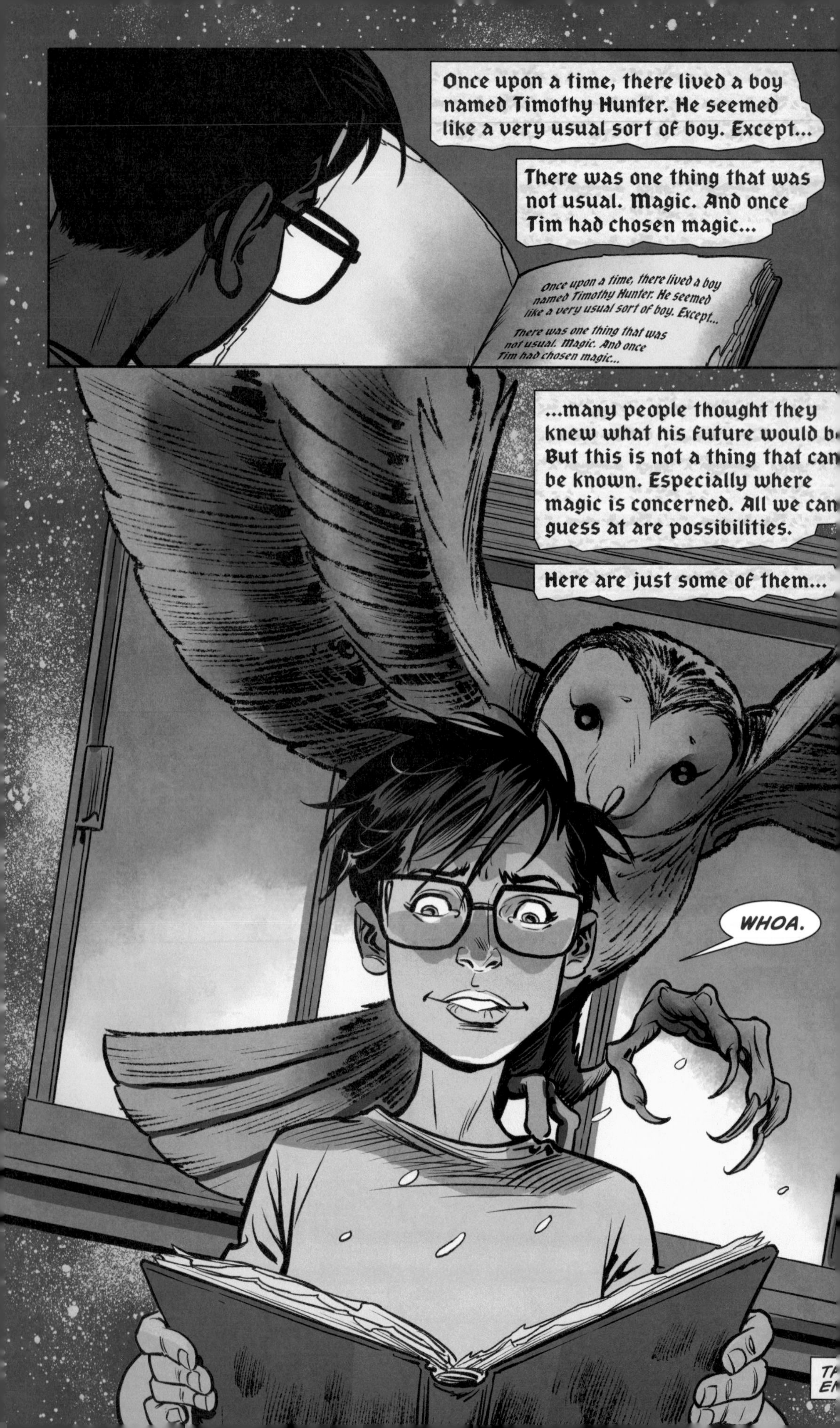
Once upon a time, there lived a boy named Timothy Hunter. He seemed like a very usual sort of boy. Except...
There was one thing that was not usual. Magic. And once Tim had chosen magic...
Once upon a time, there lived a boy named Timothy Hunter. He seemed like a very usual sort of boy. Except...
There was one thing that was not usual. Magic. And once Tim had chosen magic...
...many people thought they knew what his future would b But this is not a thing that can be known. Especially where magic is concerned. All we can guess at are possibilities.
Here are just some of them...
WHOA.

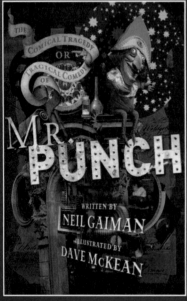

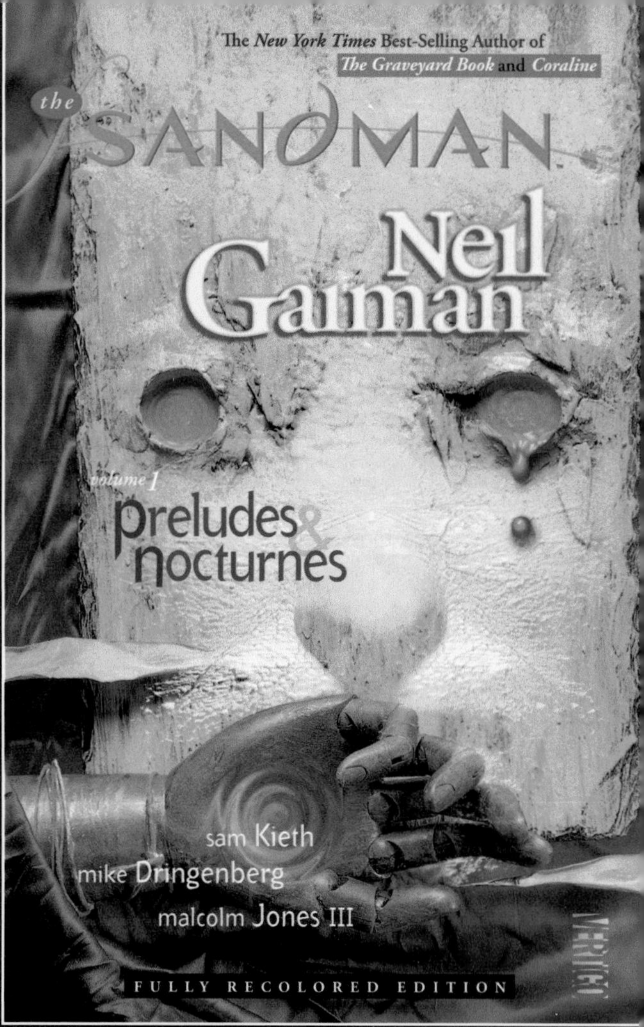
The New York Times Best-Selling Author of
The Graveyard Book and Coraline
the SANDMAN
Neil Gaiman
volume 1
preludes & nocturnes
sam Kieth
mike Dringenberg
malcolm Jones III
VERTIGO
FULLY RECOLORED EDITION

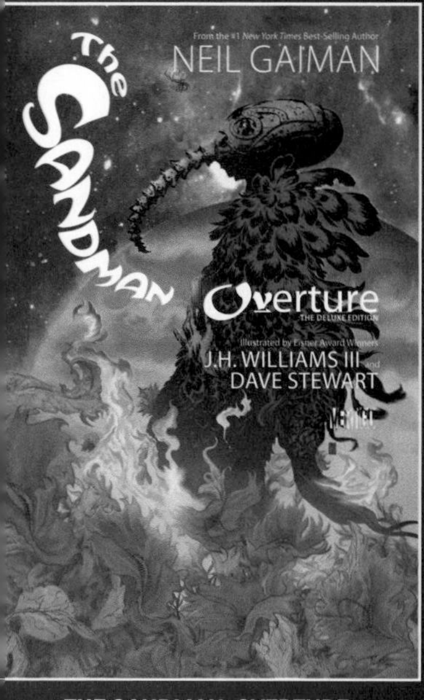
From the #1 New York Times Best-Selling Author
NEIL GAIMAN
The SANDMAN
Overture
THE DELUXE EDITION
Illustrated by Eisner Award Winners
J.H. WILLIAMS III and
DAVE STEWART

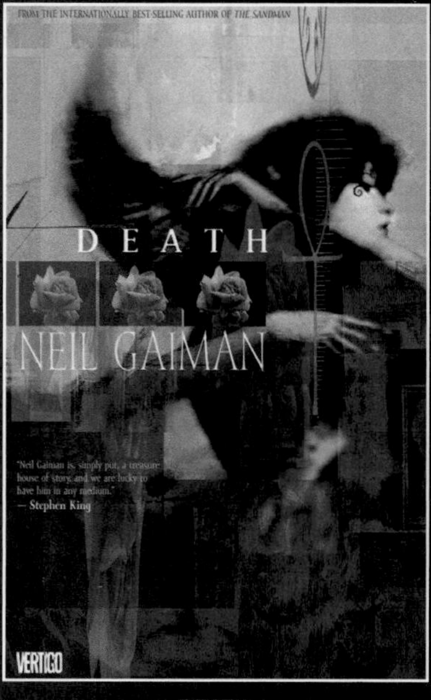
FROM THE INTERNATIONALLY BEST-SELLING AUTHOR OF THE SANDMAN
DEATH
NEIL GAIMAN
"Neil Gaiman is, simply put, a treasure-house of story, and we are lucky to have him in any medium."
— Stephen King
VERTIGO

VERTIGO

"Marvelous storytelling."
– PUBLISHERS WEEKLY

"Jamie Delano introduced John Constantine's solo title with breathless pace and little mercy."
– PASTE MAGAZINE

JOHN CONSTANTINE
HELLBLAZER
ORIGINAL SINS
VERTIGO
Jamie Delano John Ridgway
Alfredo Alcala Rick Veitch Tom Mandrake

JAMIE DELANO

JOHN CONSTANTINE

HELLBLAZER

VOL. 1: ORIGINAL SINS

JOHN CONSTANTINE
HELLBLAZER
THE DEVIL YOU KNOW
VERTIGO
Jamie Delano David Lloyd Richard Piers Rayner
Mark Buckingham Bryan Talbot

JOHN CONSTANTINE HELLBLAZER VOL. 2: THE DEVIL YOU KNOW

JOHN CONSTANTINE
HELLBLAZER
THE FEAR MACHINE
VERTIGO
Jamie Delano Mark Buckingham
Richard Piers Rayner Mike Hoffman Alfredo Alcala

JOHN CONSTANTINE HELLBLAZER VOL. 3: THE FEAR MACHINE

READ THE ENTIRE SERIE

JOHN CONSTANTINE HELLBLAZER VOL. 4: THE FAMILY MAN

JOHN CONSTANTINE HELLBLAZER VOL. 5: DANGEROUS HABITS

JOHN CONSTANTINE HELLBLAZER VOL. 6: BLOODLINES

JOHN CONSTANTINE HELLBLAZER VOL. 7: TAINTED LOVE

JOHN CONSTANTINE HELLBLAZER VOL. 8: RAKE AT THE GATES OF HEL

JOHN CONSTANTINE HELLBLAZER VOL. 9: CRITICAL MASS

And more!

VERTIGO

Get more VERTIGO graphic novels wherever comics and books are s

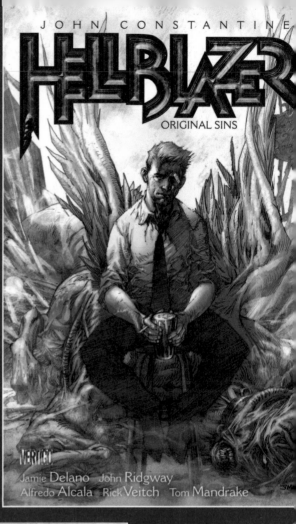

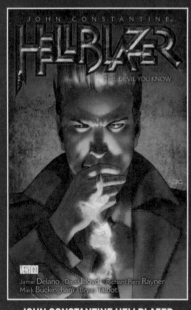

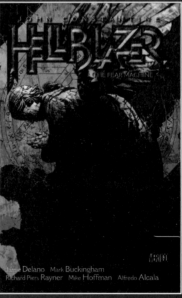

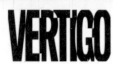